Mark Ellingsen, Ph.D. from Yale, is associate professor at the Institute for Ecumenical Research, Strasbourg, France. He is the author of *Doctrine and the Word* and several scholarly articles.

The Evangelical Movement

Growth, Impact, Controversy, Dialog

MARK ELLINGSEN

A study for the Institute of Ecumenical Research
(Strasbourg)

AUGSBURG Publishing House • Minneapolis

THE EVANGELICAL MOVEMENT
Growth, Impact, Controversy, Dialog

Scripture quotations unless otherwise noted are from the Revised Standard Version of the Bible, copyright 1946, 1952, and 1971 by the Division of Christian Education of the National Council of Churches.

Library of Congress Cataloging-in-Publication Data

Ellingsen, Mark, 1949–
THE EVANGELICAL MOVEMENT.

Bibliography: p.
Includes index.
1. Evangelicalism.   I. Title.
BR1640.E45   1988   270.8'2   88-6283
ISBN 0-8066-2312-8

The paper used in this publication meets the minimum requirements of American National Standard for Information Sciences—Permanence of Paper for Printed Materials, ANSI Z329.48-1984.   (∞)™

Manufactured in the U.S.A.   APH 10-2105

1   2   3   4   5   6   7   8   9   0   1   2   3   4   5   6   7   8   9

To my parents,
Emil Ellingsen
Edna Nilssen Ellingsen

Whose mutual love and respect
for each other's distinct theological commitments
first taught me and still serve as my model
for Conservative Evangelical–mainline dialogue.

CONTENTS

PART III: CHARACTERISTIC EVANGELICAL THEMES: THE
QUEST FOR ORTHODOXY IN MODERN DRESS

PART IV: DIALOGUE WITH A MAINLINE CHURCH HERITAGE:
BIBLICALLY BASED THEOLOGY FOR BORN-AGAIN
CHRISTIANS

CONCLUSION: EVANGELICAL–MAINLINE DIALOGUE:
A PRELUDE TO REVIVAL? ....

Acknowledgments

This volume owes its original inspiration to the Staff and the Board of Trustees of the Institute for Ecumenical Research, Strasbourg, France (associated with the Lutheran World Federation). I was asked by them to undertake a study of the Evangelical movement in order to help world Lutheranism clarify its relationship to the movement. This book represents one of the products of the study. Thus it is fitting, as I prepare to leave these good colleagues in order to take on new responsibilities, that I publicly acknowledge my indebtedness to them— not least of all to my former colleague, the Rt. Rev. Per Lønning and Ingunn, his wife, for all the personal kindnesses they shared with the entire Ellingsen family during our time in Strasbourg.

I owe significant debts to the world Lutheran community in general, for I have received official support for my work from the 1984 Lutheran World Federation Assembly, held in Budapest. The Assembly encouraged the Strasbourg Institute's study of the Evangelical movement and asked that the contacts established be cultivated and used as a means of assessing the viability of initiating an international bilateral dialogue between Lutherans and Evangelicals.

Thus, although the study and the book are largely the result of my own work, it is quite evident that they represent a cooperative effort. In addition to general institutional support, many individuals can be mentioned and thanked for being my partners in this endeavor. Members of the staff of Augsburg Publishing House have been among the most important. No less am I indebted to Carl Braaten who so kindly worked through an earlier version of the manuscript and provided helpful observations. I am similarly indebted to several colleagues from

9

the Conservative Evangelical side, especially Jerry L. Sandidge, David Hubbard, Carl Henry, and Don Dayton for the time they spent reading the manuscript, their insightful comments, and their many other kindnesses to me. For a volume that aims to stimulate dialogue between mainline churches and the Evangelical movement, it is especially gratifying to have the collaboration of so many who are associated with the Evangelical movement.

In fact, the number of Evangelical collaborators is so numerous that I cannot possibly mention here all those deserving mention. I hope that these friends will note my thanks to them in the form of notes throughout the text. They include a spectrum from the International Council on Biblical Inerrancy, on one side, to Don Dayton and like-minded Holiness tradition theologians on the other, not to mention such persons elsewhere and in between, like the late Francis Schaeffer, certain faculty members of Fuller Seminary, Wheaton College, and Gordon-Conwell Seminary, David Hubbard, Jerry L. Sandidge, Pat Robertson, Carl Henry, Bill Bright, Ralph Bohlmann, Gerhard Maier, Helmut Burkhardt and other members of the Arbeitskreis für evangelikale Theologie, Peter Beyerhaus, Hans-Lutz Poetsch, a variety of patient and kind Evangelical church presidents, and many, many others.

It is also significant to note that the leaders of virtually every Evangelically oriented church and organization mentioned in the book were directly involved in the writing and editing process of what appears in the book about their institutions. To be sure, I must still bear the ultimate responsibility for the way the book represents the Evangelical movement and for my suggestions concerning possible ecumenical rapprochement. But it is altogether fitting that a book like this, which aims to stimulate Evangelical–mainline church dialogue; should be in part the product of such a dialogue. Many thanks to all my new Evangelical friends are certainly in order.

Last, but certainly not least, my immediate family once again has made profound contributions. Our son Pat pushed me for clarity I could never have achieved without him, as he insisted that his father explain what he was writing about to him in a way that even a precocious five-year-old could understand. My wife Betsey's contribution was at least of equal importance, for she not only assumed the role of my chief editor and conversation partner but also did the bulk of the typing.

These two persons are my primary collaborators in this project. Yet we have all agreed that this book will be dedicated to two other important people in my life, whose direct contributions to my scholarship came at its earlier stages when the results of their collaboration wound up on my professors' desks. Of course, these two other persons helped with this book in various ways, not least by tracking down addresses and phone numbers for numerous contacts in the Evangelical community. But their real contribution is much more formative. For I had the privilege of growing up in the home of Emil and Edna Ellingsen, in a home where many a dinner conversation and discussion after Sunday worship involved a dialogue between a mainline Lutheran who believed that Darwin's insights must be somehow appropriated by the Church and a more or less Conservative Evangelical Pietist who insisted that the Bible really was *absolutely* correct. The faith commitments and love they have shared with me, with my "new" family, and with each other in the midst of their very real theological disagreements serve for me as a kind of idealized model of what a mainline church–Conservative Evangelical dialogue might be like. And so this book is for them.

Abbreviations

In all cases where a numeral or letter follows the abbreviation, the numeral refers to the corresponding article, section, etc., of the designated text.

With the exception of LCMS, when reference is made in the text to the theological positions of the churches and organizations listed below, reference to the document associated with that particular church or organization is assumed. Likewise, when reference is made in the text to the theological positions of the Internationale Konferenz Bekennender Gemeinschaften, the Evangelical Alliance [of Great Britain], the Church of England Evangelical Council, the Association Evangéliques d'Eglises Baptistes de Langue Française, the Albrecht-Bengel-Haus, the Lausanne Committee for World Evangelization, the Evangelical Congregational Church, the National Association of Free Will Baptists, and Wheaton '83, reference to the particular document associated with each of these organizations in Chap. 6, n. 11, Chap. 8, n. 51, Chap. 9, n. 8, Chap. 11, n. 1, Chap. 13, n. 74, Chap. 15, n. 24, or Chap. 16, n. 20 is assumed.

The name preceding abbreviations with an asterisk (*) designates that particular author's article appearing in the cited volume.

ACC	American Council of Christian Churches.
AD	Assembléias de Deus. When the reference also includes an Arabic number, the abbreviation refers to the church's *Fundamental Doctrines* (n.d.).
AEAM	Association of Evangelicals of Africa and Madagascar. When the reference also includes an Arabic number, reference to the Association's *Statement of Faith* (n.d.) is assumed.

AG   Assemblies of God. When the reference also includes an Arabic number, reference to the Assemblies' *Statement of Fundamental Truths* (1981) is assumed.

Apology   *Apology of the Augsburg Confession* (1531), in *The Book of Concord* (1580).

AUCECB   All-Union Council of Evangelical Christians-Baptists. When the abbreviation is followed by a Roman numeral, the reference is to the Union's *Confession of Faith* (1913).

BA*   Nathan O. Hatch and Mark Noll, eds., *The Bible in America* (New York: Oxford University Press, 1982).

BB   Harold Lindsell, *The Battle for the Bible* (14th printing, Grand Rapids: Zondervan, 1981).

BBF   Baptist Bible Fellowship. When followed by a Roman numeral, the reference is to the Fellowship's *Articles of Faith* (Springfield, Mo.: Roark Printing, n.d.).

BC   John Stott, *Basic Christianity*, 2nd ed. (Downers Grove, Ill.: InterVarsity, 1971).

BC (Ashland)   The Brethren Church (Ashland, Ohio). When followed by an Arabic number, reference to the church's *The Message of the Brethren Ministry* (Ashland, Ohio, n.d.), is assumed.

BEM   *Baptism, Eucharist and Ministry,* Faith and Order Paper No. 111 (Geneva: World Council of Churches, 1982) (= the Lima text).

BFC   Mark A. Noll, *Between Faith and Criticism: Evangelicals, Scholarship, and the Bible in America* (San Francisco: Harper & Row, 1986).

BGC   Baptist General Conference. When an Arabic number is included, the reference is to the Conference's *An Affirmation of Our Faith* (1951).

BH   Gerald Sheppard, "Biblical Hermeneutics: The Academic Language of Evangelical Identity," *Union Seminary Quarterly Review* 32 (1977): 81-94.

BHG   Peter Beyerhaus, *Bibel ohne Heiligen Geist?* (Bad Liebenzell, FRG: Verlag der Liebenzeller Mission, 1970).

Brief Statement or *BS*   *Brief Statement of the Doctrinal Position of the Missouri Synod* (St. Louis: Concordia, 1932).

BWA   Richard Quebedeaux, *By What Authority* (San Francisco: Harper & Row, 1982).

CA   *The Augsburg Confession* (1530), in *The Book of Concord* (1580).

CBA	Christian Booksellers Association.
CBAA	Conservative Baptist Association of America. When the abbreviation is employed in correlation with CBAA's doctrinal viewpoints, the reference is to the Association's *Constitution and Historical Summary* (Wheaton, Ill., 1984).
CBN	The Christian Broadcasting Network.
CC	Campus Crusade. Unless another statement issued by CC is cited explicitly, when a reference to the organization includes an Arabic number, the reference to its *Statement of Faith of Campus Crusade for Christ* (n.d.) is assumed.
CCB	Congregação Cristã do Brasil. When abbreviation is employed in correlation with CCB's doctrinal viewpoints, the reference is to the church's *Articles of Faith* (1946).
CCCC	Conservative Congregational Christian Conference. When it includes an Arabic number the abbreviation refers to the Conference's *Statement of Faith* (1978).
CEPRC	World Evangelical Fellowship, *A Contemporary Evangelical Perspective on Roman Catholicism* (Wheaton, Ill.: WEF, 1986).
CG	Church of God (Cleveland, Tenn.). When it includes an Arabic number, reference to the CG's *Declaration of Faith* (n.d.) is assumed.
Chicago Statement	International Council on Biblical Inerrancy, *The Chicago Statement on Biblical Inerrancy* (1978).
CM	Francis A. Schaeffer, *A Christian Manifesto* (Westchester, Ill.: Crossway Books, 1981).
CMA	The Christian and Missionary Alliance. When followed by an Arabic number, the reference is to the Alliance's *Manual of the Christian and Missionary Alliance 1983 Edition* (Nyack, N.Y., 1983). The numeral refers to the corresponding article of the Statement of Faith in that document.
CN	Church of the Nazarene. When followed by a Roman numeral, the reference is to the church's Articles of Faith in the *Constitution and Special Rules* (Kansas City, Mo.: Nazarene Pub. House, n.d.). The numeral refers to the corresponding article of that statement. Where other portions of the entire Constitution are cited the reference to CN is followed by a designation of the relevant section of the Constitution.

COGIC	Church of God in Christ. When followed by a page number, the reference is to the church's *Official Manual* (Memphis, Tenn.: COGIC Publishing House, 1973).
CR	Robert E. Webber, *Common Roots: A Call to Evangelical Maturity* (Grand Rapids, Mich.: Zondervan, 1978).
CRC	Christian Reformed Church in North America. When followed by a page number, the reference is to the church's *The Nature and Extent of Biblical Authority* (Grand Rapids, Mich., n.d.).
CT	*Christianity Today.*
CTA*	*Christian Thought and Action* (Carol Stream, Ill.: Christianity Today, 1985).
CVB	Brevard Childs, "Childs versus Barr," review of *Holy Scripture: Canon, Authority, Criticism,* by James Barr, in *Interpretation* 38 (1984): 66-70.
DEA	Deutsche Evangelische Allianz, *Basis* (1972).
DEH	Donald W. Dayton, *Discovering an Evangelical Heritage* (New York: Harper & Row, 1976).
DF	Cornelius Van Til, *The Defense of the Faith* (Philadelphia: Presbyterian and Reformed, 1955).
E*	David F. Wells and John D. Woodbridge, eds., *The Evangelicals: What They Believe, Who They Are, Where They Are Changing* (Nashville: Abingdon, 1975).
EC	Walter J. Hollenweger, *Enthusiastisches Christentum* (Wuppertal, FRG: Theologischer Verlag Rolf Brockhaus; Zurich: Zwingli Verlag, 1969).
ECC	The Evangelical Covenant Church. When followed by a page number, the reference is to the church's *Covenant Affirmations* (Chicago: Covenant Press, 1976).
Eclipse	Hans W. Frei, *Eclipse of Biblical Narrative* (New Haven, Conn., Yale University Press, 1974).
EFC	The Evangelical Free Church of America. When followed by an Arabic number, the reference is to the church's *Doctrinal Position* (1950).
EhkM	Gerhard Maier, *Das Ende der historish-kritischen Method* (Wuppertal: Verlag Rolf Brockhaus, 1974) (Eng. trans., *The End of the Historical-Critical Method* [St. Louis: Concordia, 1977]).
EKD	Evangelische Kirche in Deutschland.
EMA*	George Marsden, ed., *Evangelicalism and Modern America* (Grand Rapids: Eerdmans, 1984).

EMF   Union des Associations Cultuelles Evangéliques des
                 Eglises Méthodistes de France. When the abbreviation
                 relates to EMF's doctrinal positions, the reference is
                 to the Union's *La Déclaration de Foi* (1940).

EmK   Evangelisch-methodistische Kirche.

EPA   Evangelical Press Association. When accompanied by a
                 lowercase letter, reference is to the Association's *Doctrinal Statement* (n.d.).

ER   Donald Bloesch, *The Evangelical Renaissance* (London:
                 Hodder and Stoughton, 1974).

ERCD   *Evangelical–Roman Catholic Dialogue on Mission*
                 (1977–1984).

EREI   Union Nationale des Eglises Réformées Indépendantes
                 de France. When the abbreviation relates to EREI's
                 doctrinal positions and has no explicit mention of some
                 other text, the reference is to the Union's *Déclaration
                 de Foi* (1872).

ESA   Evangelicals for Social Action.

*ETA**   Leonard Sweet, ed., *The Evangelical Tradition in America* (Macon, Ga.: Mercer University Press, 1984).

EUB   The Evangelical United Brethren Church.

Evidences   Archibald Alexander, *Evidences of the Authenticity, Inspiration and Canonical Authority of the Holy Scriptures* (1826; reprinted. Philadelphia: Presbyterian
                 Board of Publication, 1836).

FAC   George M. Marsden, *Fundamentalism and American
                 Culture* (Oxford and New York: Oxford University
                 Press, 1980).

Falwell   Jerry Falwell, with Ed Dobson and Ed Hindson, editors,
                 The Fundamentalist Phenomenon (Garden City, N.Y.:
                 Doubleday, 1981).

FC   *Formula of Concord* (1577), in *The Book of Concord*
                 (1580).

FCC   Federal Council of Churches (in the United States).

FEC   Donald Bloesch, *The Future of Evangelical Christianity*
                 (Garden City, N.Y.: Doubleday, 1983).

FEEBF   Fédération des Eglises Evangéliques Baptistes de France.
                 When followed only by a Roman numeral, the reference is to the section entitled, "Doctrine," in the Federation's *Confession of Faith of the Federation of
                 French Baptist Churches* (n.d.). The numeral refers

to the corresponding article of that section of the document. When the abbreviation is followed by a noun placed within quotation marks, that noun and the number that follows designate the corresponding section and article of the document.

FMC

The Free Methodist Church of North America. When it includes an Arabic number, the reference is to the denomination's Articles of Religion, in its *The Book of Discipline 1979* (Winona Lake, Ind.: The Free Methodist Publishing House, 1980). Where other portions of *The Book of Discipline* are cited, the reference to FMC is followed by reference to the pertinent section, page, or paragraph of the book.

Fuller

Fuller Theological Seminary, *Statement of Faith* (1979).

GARB

General Association of Regular Baptist Churches. When followed by a Roman numeral, the reference is to the Association's *Constitution and Articles of Faith* (Schaumburg, Ill., 1980). The numeral refers to the corresponding article in the Articles of Faith.

GK

Martin Luther, *The Large Catechism* (1538), in *The Book of Concord* (1580).

GRA

Carl Henry, *God, Revelation and Authority*, 6 vols. (Waco: Word, 1976–1983).

GPD

F. Ernest Stoeffler, *German Pietism during the Eighteenth Century* (Leiden: E. J. Brill, 1973).

GS

The Lutheran Church–Missouri Synod, *Gospel and Scripture* (St. Louis: Concordia, 1972).

HAC*

D. A. Carson and John D. Woodbridge, eds., *Hermeneutics, Authority and Canon* (Leicester: Inter-Varsity, 1986).

HCB

Bruce Shelley, *A History of Conservative Baptists*, 3rd ed. (Wheaton, Ill.: Conservative Baptist Press, 1981).

ICBI

International Council on Biblical Inerrancy.

ICFG

International Church of the Foursquare Gospel. When followed by a Roman numeral, the reference is to the church's *Declaration of Faith* (Los Angeles, n.d.).

ICFG, *CS*

International Church of the Foursquare Gospel, *Creedal Statements* (n.d.).

Identity

Hans W. Frei, *The Identity of Jesus Christ* (Philadelphia: Fortress, 1975).

IFCA	Independent Fundamental Churches of America. When followed by an Arabic number, the reference is to the IFCA's "Articles of Biblical Faith," in the *Constitution and By-Laws of the Independent Fundamental Churches of America* (1979). The numeral refers to the corresponding article in the statement. Where other portions of the Constitution are cited, the reference to IFCA is followed by designation of the appropriate article and section.
IM	The Church Association for Inner Mission.
Inspiration	The Lutheran Church–Missouri Synod, *The Inspiration of Scripture* (1962).
Institutes	John Calvin, *Institutes of the Christian Religion* (1559).
IVCF	Inter-Varsity Christian Fellowship. When followed by an Arabic number, the reference is to IVCF's *Doctrinal Basis* (n.d.).
R. Johnston	Robert K. Johnston, *Evangelicals at an Impasse* (Atlanta: John Knox, 1979).
*JTTW**	Vinay Samuel and Chris Sudgen, eds., *Jesus in the Two Thirds World* (Bangalore: Partnership in Mission—Asia, 1983).
KD	Karl Barth, *Die kirchliche Dogmatik,* 4 vols. (Zurich: Zollikon, 1932–1967) (Eng. trans., *Church Dogmatics* [Edinburgh: T. & T. Clark, 1935–1969]).
LCED	Lutheran–Conservative/Evangelical Dialogue (USA), "Declaration," in *The Covenant Quarterly* 41 (1983): 7.
LCMS	The Lutheran Church–Missouri Synod.
LCUSA	Lutheran Council in the U.S.A.
*LEH**	J. D. Douglas, ed., *Let the Earth Hear His Voice* (Minneapolis: World Wide Publications, 1975).
LM	Liebenzeller Mission. When it includes an Arabic number, the abbreviation refers to LM's *Glaubensgrundsätze* (n.d.).
LW	Luther's Works, American Edition, ed. Jaroslav Pelikan and Helmut Lehmann, 55 vols. (St. Louis: Concordia, and Philadelphia: Fortress, 1955–1986).
MBC	Mennonite Brethren Churches. When followed by a Roman numeral, the reference is to The General Conference's *Confession of Faith,* 4th printing (Hillsboro, Kan.: Mennonite Brethren Publishing House, 1980).

MHB	W. Stanley Mooneyham, "Ministering to the Hunger Belt," unpublished but distributed interview (n.d.)
MM	Moral Majority.
NAE	National Association of Evangelicals (USA). When followed by an Arabic number, the reference is to the NAE *Statement of Faith* (1942).
NBC	Northern Baptist Convention.
NC	Richard Quebedeaux, *The New Charismatics* (Garden City, N.Y.: Doubleday, 1976).
NCC	National Council of the Churches of Christ in the United States of America.
NFBC	National Fellowship of Brethren Churches ("Grace Brethren").
NTC	Brevard S. Childs, *The New Testament as Canon: An Introduction* (Philadelphia: Fortress, 1985).
OF	Ernest R. Sandeen, *The Origins of Fundamentalism* (Philadelphia: Fortress, 1968).
OMF	Overseas Missionary Fellowship. When followed by an Arabic number, the abbreviation refers to the OMF doctrinal position listed in *Understanding OMF* (n.d.), p. 1.
OPC	The Orthodox Presbyterian Church.
OTS	Brevard S. Childs, *Introduction to the Old Testament as Scripture* (Philadelphia: Fortress, 1979).
OTT	Brevard S. Childs, *Old Testament Theology in a Canonical Context* (Philadelphia: Fortress, 1986).
PAC	The Pentecostal Assemblies of Canada. When followed by a Roman numeral, the reference is to the Assemblies' *Statement of Fundamental and Essential Truths* (1980). The numeral refers to the corresponding article of the statement (the accompanying Arabic numeral refers to a particular section of the designated article).
PB	Plymouth Brethren.
PCA	Presbyterian Church in America.
PD	Philip Jacob Spener, *Pia Desideria*, trans. and ed. Theodore G. Tappert (Philadelphia: Fortress, 1977).
PHC	The International Pentecostal Holiness Church. When followed by an Arabic number, the reference is to the PHC's Articles of Faith, in *The Pentecostal Holiness Church Manual 1981* (Franklin Springs, Ga.: Advocate Press, n.d.).

PJ	John Howard Yoder, *The Politics of Jesus*, reprint (Grand Rapids: Eerdmans, 1983).
PSIPC	*Prophetic Studies of the International Prophetic Conference* (New York: Revell, 1886).
PT	Mark A. Noll, ed., *The Princeton Theology 1812–1921* (Grand Rapids: Baker, 1983).
RCAH	Ronald J. Sider, "Rich Christians in an Age of Hunger," *Evangelical Review of Theology* 4 (1980): 70-83.
RC-P,I	*Final Report of the Dialogue between the Secretariat for Promoting Christian Unity of the Roman Catholic Church and Leaders of Some Pentecostal Churches and Participants in the Charismatic Movement within Protestant and Anglican Churches* (1976).
RC-P,II	*Final Report of the Dialogue between the Secretariat for Promoting Christian Unity of the Roman Catholic Church and Some Classical Pentecostals* (1977–1982).
REP	F. Ernest Stoeffler, *The Rise of Evangelical Pietism* (Leiden: E. J. Brill, 1971).
RHAP	Sydney E. Ahlstrom, *A Religious History of the American People* (New Haven, Conn.: Yale University Press, 1972).
RPC	Reformed Presbyterian Church of North America. When followed by the number of a chapter, the reference is to the church's *Westminster Confession and the Testimony of the Reformed Presbyterian Church in North America* (1980).
RPC,ES	Reformed Presbyterian Church, Evangelical Synod.
SA	*The Smalcald Articles* (1537), in *The Book of Concord* (1580).
SBC	Southern Baptist Convention. When followed by a Roman numeral, the reference is to the SBC's *The Baptist Faith and Message* (1963).
SBE	James Leo Garrett, E. Glenn Hinson, and James E. Tull, *Are Southern Baptists "Evangelicals"?* (Macon, Ga.: Mercer University Press, 1983).
SELKD	Selbständige Evangelisch-Lutherische Kirche.
SER	Francis Schaeffer, *Escape from Reason* (Downers Grove, Ill.: InterVarsity, 1968).
SM	Santalmisjonen.
TCU	Bernard Leeming, ed., *Towards Christian Unity* (London: G. Chapman, 1968).
TIN	Hans W. Frei, "Theology and the Interpretation of Narrative," lecture presented at Haverford College, 1982.

*TWB**	Gerhard Maier and Gerhard Rost, eds., *Taufe-Wiedergeburt-Bekehrung in evangelistischer Perspektive* (Lahr-Dinglingen: St. Johannis-Druckerei C. Schweickhardt, 1980).
*UB**	Robert K. Johnston, ed., *The Use of the Bible in Theology: Evangelical Options* (Atlanta: John Knox, 1985).
UFM	UFM International. When followed by an Arabic number, the abbreviation refers to UFM's *Doctrinal Statement* (n.d.).
USSR Dis. Bapt.	*Fundamental Principles of Evangelical [Dissident] Christians and Baptists [in USSR]* (n.d.). References in the text to the Dissidents' views, accompanied by Arabic numbers, are to *Statutes of the Union of Churches of Evangelical Christians-Baptists (Dissidents)* (1965).
*VSE**	David E. Harrell Jr., ed., *Varieties of Southern Evangelicalism* (Macon, Ga.: Mercer University Press, 1981).
WA	*D. Martin Luthers Werke,* Kritische Gesamtausgabe (Weimarer Ausgabe), 56 vols. (Weimar: Hermann Böhlaus Nachfolger, 1833ff.).
WADB	*D. Martin Luthers Werke: Deutsche Bibel,* Kritische Gesamtausgabe (Weimar: Hermann Böhlaus Nachfolger, 1906–1961).
WATR	*D. Martin Luthers Werke: Tischreden,* Kritische Gesamtausgabe (Weimar: Hermann Böhlaus Nachfolger, 1912–1921).
WC	The Wesleyan Church. When followed by a Roman numeral, the reference is to the Articles of Religion, in *The Discipline of the Wesleyan Church 1984* (Marion, Ind.: Wesleyan Publishing House, 1984). The numeral refers to the corresponding article in the statement. Where other portions of the entire *Discipline* are cited, the reference to WC is followed by the designation of the appropriate section of the *Discipline*.
WCC	World Council of Churches.
WE	Richard Quebedeaux, *The Worldly Evangelicals* (San Francisco: Harper & Row, 1978).
WEF	World Evangelical Fellowship. When the abbreviation is used in correlation with the WEF's doctrinal positions

and without explicit citation of some other text issued by WEF, the reference is to the Fellowship's *Statement of Faith* (1951).

WV   World Vision International.

Introduction

The new mainline Protestant whipping-boy?

"Good morning friends! So glad you could join us! Let me introduce you around. . . ." The greetings are warm and apparently genuine. When the service begins, the singing is boisterous; the enthusiasm of the congregation is even stirring. Of course the service is usually not quite the same as you are accustomed to in your own mainline church. The prayers are a bit longer, and some parts of the familiar liturgy (worship) have likely been omitted. But the preaching is solid, perhaps inspiring. It is often couched a bit more in the language of traditional doctrines than you normally hear (or preach yourself). It may even be too critical for your own tastes, stepping on some of your "sacred cows." Yet the preacher clearly knows his Bible, and the dynamic presentation of the sermon is attention-grabbing, powerful.

With the last hymn the intensity of the experience heightens . . .; then come the farewell greetings or the social hour. "They sure are a friendly group," you mention afterwards to your companion. Friendly they are! Several leaders of the congregation show you around, introducing you to everyone and especially to the pastor. Plenty of time is spent asking you about yourself and your companion. There seems to be a genuine interest, a desire to include you in all the conversations.

After a while the topic changes to Christianity, the church, and your own congregation, if you have one. The enthusiasm and commitment of your hosts for the church's work is quite evident. Even if they are not professionals, they seem able to talk about their faith in an articulate manner. The biblical concepts and stories roll easily and naturally off their lips, sometimes spiced with criticism of certain "liberal" church organizations you have supported (or suspected). Indeed, if you stay for the postworship discussion or find yourself at some other time in a discussion group of conservative Christians, it is quite likely that you will be impressed with the intellectual level of such a discussion. (The mainline church groups in which you have participated don't seem to be quite as conceptual, or perhaps as substantive as this group.)

23

Then it is time to depart. Likely you and your companion take the initiative, for indications are that your hosts are enjoying themselves too much to bring things to a premature halt. (Their sense of fellowship seems quite genuine.) With your departure comes the flurry of handshakes, the thank-yous for joining them, and the inevitable suggestion that you come again. It is evangelism in action!

"Why can't our church be like those Evangelicals!" you say to your companion as you leave. "It makes you wonder." Indeed it makes persons affiliated with mainline denominations wonder when they come into contact with conservative Christians exhibiting such warmth, commitment, obvious financial generosity, and biblical knowledge. It can be a threatening experience to mainline Christians. It may lead them to question their own Christian commitment and biblical fidelity.

The impressions I have been describing represent an amalgamation of experiences and reactions mainline Christians may typically have when they associate with Evangelicals. Of course, several conservative Christians would hasten to remind mainliners and themselves that too few Evangelical communities are as alive and dynamic as I have suggested.[1] However, Evangelical Christians need to recognize how mainline Christians, when they are honest with themselves, perceive Evangelicals. Encounter with conservative Christianity can be a threatening experience for non-Evangelicals, calling their commitment and their belief-structure into question.

If one were only to consider these interpersonal, existential dynamics, the problem of the relationship between the Evangelical movement and mainline Christianity (those churches belonging to the World Council of Churches or other organizations of the ecumenical establishment) would be important enough. But an examination of relevant data suggests at least five other difficult challenges posed by the present character of Evangelical–mainline church relationships. It is well to consider these issues in some detail, as their exposition may lead readers themselves to arrive at a rather startling conclusion concerning ecumenical priorities—one which most laypeople and parish pastors already sense at a "gut level": the relationship between Evangelicals and the mainline churches may be *the* question for ministry and Christian unity in the next decades!

Certainly, statistical evidence seems to intensify the feelings of threat posed by the Evangelical movement. Although in the two years immediately preceding publication there have been some exceptions, the general trend in the preceding two decades has been that, while mainline churches in North America are declining in membership and in the number of foreign missionaries, Evangelical churches and parachurch organizations have increased numerically in these areas. Most dramatic has been the membership growth of 25.2% by the Church of the Nazarene and 165.2% by the Assemblies of God in the period 1975–1985, while most American mainline churches were losing members. Of the nine religious bodies that experienced the most growth in 1985, six were aligned with the Evangelical movement, and only one unambiguously belonged to the mainline.[2] In the number of overseas missionaries, the mainline churches of North America registered a drop of 31% between 1958 and 1971, as well as a corresponding drop of almost 50% between 1968 and 1976. While in 1953 mainline American missionaries outnumbered Evangelical missionaries, at least as recently as 1982 Evangelicals outnumbered American Protestants in mission fields ten to one, and American Roman Catholics by about three to one.[3]

These observations are also relevant to the European scene. There are indications that independent Evangelical churches are growing steadily, in contrast to membership declines in the state or folk churches, and that traditional European mission societies are declining in their number of overseas missionaries.[4] Such data suggest that Evangelicals must be believing and doing something right, and seem to call into question the theology and practice of mainline churches.

Moreover, one must ask whether the established churches have lost touch with the Evangelical faith-orientation of their members. A 1976 Gallup Poll, based on in-person interviews with more than 1500 American adults in more than 300 localities, raises this question. The poll discovered that almost one out of every five Americans (18%), almost one out of every two Protestants, holds faith commitments which are compatible with Evangelical beliefs (having had a born-again experience, holding a literal interpretation of the Bible, trying to witness their faith to others).[5] It was on the basis of this data and its relation to Jimmy Carter's election to the American presidency that Gallup and *Newsweek* magazine dubbed 1976 "the year of the Evangelical." It clearly marked the beginnings of renewed interest in and attention to the Evangelical phenomenon.

Other recent opinion surveys have confirmed these results with regard to the influence and numerical strength of Evangelicals in North American Christianity. A 1980 study of American clergy of all denominations conducted by the Gallup organization indicated that more than half (53%) identify themselves as evangelicals. The proportion of younger clergy (under age 30) who identify themselves in this way is even higher.[6]

Given these statistics it is inevitable that a significant number of Evangelicals must be members of the mainline churches, not just of conservative denominations. Additional opinion surveys seem to bear this out. Thus, for example, in a massive 1970 study of Lutherans from The American Lutheran Church, the Lutheran Church in America, and The Lutheran Church–Missouri Synod, 44% of those surveyed identified their position as conservative. An additional 14% were found to be Fundamentalist.[7] Knowledgeable social scientists also conclude on the basis of additional opinion surveys that in addition to the Lutheran churches just noted and Evangelically oriented bodies like the Southern Baptist Convention and the Church of God (Anderson, Indiana), substantial proportions of the congregations of the American Baptist Churches, the Reformed Church in America, and the United Presbyterian Church (now Presbyterian Church [USA]) are basically Conservative Evangelical in orientation.[8] Few denominations, it seems, are without a significant Evangelical minority—or perhaps a majority. Religion analysts as diverse as the founder of the Moral Majority, Jerry Falwell, and the British Old Testament scholar and critic of Fundamentalism, James Barr, concur.[9]

Falwell's comment that members of more liberal churches are much more conservative than their leaders touches on a crucial issue in mainline–Evangelical relationships. It raises the question of whether the established churches are in fact losing touch with their grass-roots membership, which is to a great extent Evangelically oriented. At least in North America and in parts of western Europe one need not visit many congregations before discovering some degree of dissatisfaction on the part of local congregations with national church bureaucracies.

Of course such dissatisfaction or at least inattention to the national church is to be expected from churches in North America. The de facto predominance of congregational polity in the continent's denominations leads to a built-in suspicion of larger multi-congregational organizations. The breakdown of confidence in larger institutions in favor of local regionalism, a characteristic of all Western society since the 1960s, is also no doubt a factor causing suspicion of national church organizations.

Additionally one would expect a certain degree of suspicion about national church structure to emanate from Evangelical believers, at least as a kind of vestigal reaction implanted in the Evangelical psyche from the days of the Fundamentalist–Modernist controversy at the beginning of our century. Given the fact that old grudges and suspicions never really go away in the Church, but tend to take on a tradition of their own even when the reason for such suspicions is no longer understood, it is easy to appreciate why today's spiritual heirs of the Fundamentalists who remain in the established churches would continue to reflect the suspicions of their fathers.

Today the rationale for such Evangelical suspicions of the mainline churches to which they belong is even more understandable. Several analysts have noted that in the 1950s (or since the 1960s in Western Europe) the national church bureaucracies began to be staffed by a new kind of leader, the managerial-professional elite. Just as most large corporate organizations in the West have come to be managed by experts, the Church, though with a few notable exceptions, has also largely been given over to the expert managers.[10]

While church leaders of the preceding generation, prior to the mid-1960s, had generally been influenced by a theological position (neoorthodoxy) which allowed them to remain in dialogue with the conservatives, the new managerial leadership tends to bypass the traditional categories of neoorthodox thought in favor of social action or management techniques. In either case the new leadership models pay less attention to the conservative grass roots, either because prophetic ministry on behalf of social action warrants it or because management techniques are concerned only with the "experts" on the boards, committees, task forces, etc. (Think how the "representative" boards of most mainline churches are comprised of persons working in one of the classic professions, the "experts.")

As a result of this leadership style and its language of social action and management, often without much reference to traditional theological categories, most leaders of the mainline churches are increasingly perceived by conservatives and nonprofessionals in their churches as a new "elite," not in touch with their constituencies. The very nature of this style does tend to isolate its leaders in such a way that decision-making processes do not include nonexperts. Thus, conservative voices not speaking the language of the experts are also excluded. These dynamics are important factors in accounting for the internal tensions not far from the surface in many mainline churches. In their own way, then, these churches, despite the supposed openness of liberalism, can be just as narrow and unwilling to listen as the worst caricature of their conservative counterparts.[11]

These tensions are further exacerbated by the fact that many theologians of these churches also are speaking a language (and teaching it to the next generation of clergy) which is not precisely in accord with the familiar themes of conservative Orthodox theology (particularly with regard to an understanding of the nature of Scripture as inerrant). Even in those instances where such theologians are still speaking the mediating language of neoorthodox theology or some similar alternative, some professors may still perceive themselves as part of the "elite" establishment and may need to function as such in order to maintain their credibility with the bureaucracy. At any rate, they and those remaining church bureaucrats with similar theological orientation are not likely to open avenues of dialogue with conservative Evangelicals. Rather, conservatives are likely to be regarded as adversaries (and unsophisticated ones at that). It is one more dimension of the estrangement from their churches that Evangelicals in mainline churches may feel. Given the vast numbers of Evangelicals in these churches, their sense of estrangement raises the disquieting possibility to mainline church leaders that their churches are losing touch with the membership.

The issues at stake in this estrangement and its consequences are not just related to questions of leadership style and sociological distinctions between the church leadership and the grass roots. Theological differences are important, if not the crucial factors. Conservative, Evangelically oriented members of the mainline churches simply cannot understand the theological rationale of the leadership for its programs. The leadership's rationale is stated in language so sufficiently distinct from the orthodox categories of most (Conservative Evangelical) believers that the reaction of conservatives is inevitably to assume that the leaders (including the theologians) must be talking about something other than Christian faith (secular humanism?), or at least are representing an orientation distinct from their church's theological (confessional) heritage.[12] Likewise, the language of the Evangelical grass roots and its articulate spokespersons is so distinct from the leadership's normal theological rhetoric that the leadership suspects its church's Evangelicals of departing from the correct teachings of the church. The emergence of the contemporary charismatic movement among the Evangelical groups in many of these churches further heightens the leadership's suspicions.

In addition to the tensions within denominations which are stimulated by the confrontation between Conservative Evangelical and mainline theology, this confrontation also has a bearing on tensions between denominations belonging to the same Confessional family. Mainline denominations from virtually every Confessional family—Lutherans, Reformed-Presbyterian, Methodists, Baptists—have conservative sister churches holding theological positions so closely aligned with the Evangelical movement or Fundamentalism that these churches refuse to have fellowship with the mainline church, for the latter is perceived as too "liberal."

Some distressing and startling implications for Christian unity follow from these strained ecclesiastical relationships. It was certainly startling for me to learn recently from the arch-Fundamentalist and defender of orthodox Presbyterianism, Carl McIntire, that he can more easily share the Lord's Supper with orthodox Lutherans than he can with members of the new Presbyterian Church (USA).[13] In like manner there is something odd, even poignant, about the fact that the new Evangelical Lutheran Church in America engages in altar fellowship and interim sharing of the Eucharist with The Episcopal Church, while not having its own ministry recognized by the theologically conservative Lutheran Church–Missouri Synod or by the Wisconsin Evangelical Lutheran Synod. Lutherans in fellowship with Anglicans but not with fellow Lutherans! A similar situation exists in West Germany, where the Missouri Synod-related Free Lutheran Church as well as Lutherans of the larger state-related churches who belong to the largely Evangelically oriented Confessing Movement [Bekenntnisbewegung] have a special relationship with German Evangelicals in a way they do not with mainline Lutheran churches. These strained relationships between churches of the same Confessional tradition seem to reflect to some extent the tensions between contemporary mainline and Evangelical theology.[14]

These are heady days for Evangelicals. Their marked growth and the significant influence they have had upon recent American elections for federal offices have transformed this once castigated minority into a powerful religious and political force, at least in America. A number of successful church-related programs, like the Church Growth movement and Bill Gothard's Basic Youth Conflicts Seminar, were initiated by Evangelicals and have begun to make a significant impact on mainline churches. Also, media attention and the upward social mobility of many Evangelicals have to some extent made it socially acceptable to be an Evangelical or a charismatic, perhaps for the first time since the Fundamentalist-Modernist controversy early in this century. Since the presidency of Jimmy Carter, it has become fashionable to be a born-again Evangelical Christian.

A number of Evangelicals and other conservative Christian writers are sensing that the tide of the times is going their way.[15] This new-found confidence has manifested itself in several ways, in each case intensifying the already existing mainline-Evangelical tensions. The most readily apparent manifestation of this new confidence is evident in the formation of several Evangelical special-interest groups within mainline denominations. The purpose of these groups has been to provide a stronger voice for Evangelicals, a kind of Evangelical lobby within their denominations.

Thus in the recently formed Presbyterian Church (USA), Evangelically oriented members have organized themselves and formed the Presbyterians United for Biblical Concerns, The Covenant Fellowship of Presbyterians, and The Presbyterian Lay Committee. The pressures these groups have brought to bear on the leadership of the two predecessor bodies that have formed the new church led to a decision to appoint Evangelicals to the Joint Committee on Union, which constructed the structural plans and organizations for the new church, and subsequently to the new church's General Assembly Council. Likewise, Evangelically oriented groups were organized in the three constituting bodies which merged to form the new Evangelical Lutheran Church in America. These organizations also sought to influence the process leading to the formation of the new church body. In some cases they are promoting tension with the new denomination, even promoting secession from the new church. Nor is the emergence of such groups within mainline churches characteristic only in North America. Similar Evangelical organizations have also been formed in the Evangelical Lutheran Church of Württemberg in southwestern Germany, and the church can do little without keeping the constituencies of these Evangelical-pietist organizations in mind. The significant impact groups like these are having on the mainline churches and the questions they pose for many of their members would have been unthinkable at mid-century, at least in North America.

The new-found Evangelical confidence and visibility manifests itself and creates tensions not just within the mainline churches. Of course, Evangelicals and Fundamentalists outside the mainline have never exhibited any reticence about criticizing the liberal tendencies of both the mainline churches and the ecumenical movement. Yet the increased popularity of conservative Christianity has provided it with a more visible platform from which to make these criticisms. Among the more prominent critics have been the arch American anticommunist Fundamentalist, Carl McIntire; Jerry Falwell; the influential German Evangelical and foreign mission expert, Peter Beyerhaus; and, on at least one occasion, even Billy Graham.[16]

Not surprisingly, the increased visibility of these criticisms, coming from what is now perceived as an influential segment of the Christian community, has produced a certain backlash from the mainline ecumenical establishment. Throughout most of the decades since the peak of the Fundamentalist–Modernist controversy in the 1920s, mainline theological scholarship largely ignored the religious dimension of Fundamentalism and Evangelicalism. When these movements were studied they were regarded as reactionary expressions of a larger rural vs. urban conflict, with both identified as representatives of the anti-intellectual rural mentality.[17] (The popular view of Fundamentalists and Evangelicals as closed-minded, right-wing, and dogmatic has no doubt been encouraged by this standard characterization.)

More recently, however, the growth and emerging influence of Evangelicalism have led some mainline theologians to examine the movement in terms of its theological viewpoints. Yet, at this point in time, most of the mainline theologians who have undertaken studies of the Evangelical movement have done so to criticize it.[18] Insofar as Evangelicals continue to experience the academic community and the media as prejudiced against their beliefs, little has really changed.[19]

In fact, one might conclude that there is a modification in mainline attitudes towards Evangelicals. The difference is that with the growth and influence of the Evangelical movement it can no longer be ignored by the mainline churches. Its growth and influence now call these churches' doctrine and practice into question. Their response has been to take the Evangelical challenge seriously. Some denominational literature is now addressing this challenge. The mainline churches' concern with the Evangelical challenge is no doubt what has stimulated some of their theologians to address the issue. It would be unthinkable, for example, that the Lutheran church's ecumenical institute should have been authorized to undertake a study of the Evangelical movement had this not been a burning issue in world Lutheranism.

Yet, for all this increased attention to the Evangelical challenge, an examination of some of the literature thus far produced leads to the impression that what is under way is a kind of backlash against Evangelicalism.[20] In a sense, what is happening is that mainline Protestants are finding it necessary to establish their identity over against Evangelicals like the way they once (prior to the recent breakthroughs in ecumenical dialogues) defined themselves over against Roman Catholicism. To put it bluntly, at every level of church life, from the bureaucracy to liberal laity, Evangelicals have become the favorite mainline Protestant whipping-boy!

There is some indication that Evangelicals have sensed a mainline backlash.[21] It makes itself felt insofar as they believe that many of their spiritual kin are not associating themselves directly with the Evangelical movement, because to do so would damage their intellectual or social respectability.[22] In fact, one Evangelical goes so far as to suggest that current theological emphases of the mainline churches, such as the current Lutheran emphasis on baptismal regeneration, represents a deliberate attempt to counter the Evangelical concern with the need for personal decision.[23]

The last intriguing suggestion raises a very crucial issue in Conservative Evangelical–mainline church relationships. It raises the ecumenical question. Are Evangelicals theologically divided from the mainline church traditions? Or is it rather the case that a deep-seated agreement exists between the mainline churches and Conservative Evangelicals, even those outside the mainline traditions, but that this agreement has been overlooked because each side has been overemphasizing certain dimensions of its heritage to the exclusion of themes which converge with the other side?

These questions are especially pressing in light of the present ecumenical scene. The significant ecumenical agreements which have been achieved in recent decades among the mainline churches are hollow if it is at the cost of estrangement from the body of Evangelical Christianity. The ecumenical challenge is posed even more sharply by the official repudiation of the organized ecumenical movement by Evangelicalism.[24] (The ecumenical movement is seen by Evangelicals as the embodiment of the worst trends to be found in the mainline bodies which constitute it.)[25] This tension has been heightened still further in recent years by the conflict between Evangelicals and "liberation theology" (a theological approach developed in the Third World which, often aided by Marxist analysis, stresses the role of the gospel in liberating the oppressed from social injustice). This is a most significant development in view of the profound impact liberation thought has had on the mainline churches.[26]

Of course it is true that some signals of a lessening of tension between the Evangelical and the ecumenical movements have emerged in recent years. One thinks of the participation of a group of Evangelicals in the WCC Vancouver Assembly of 1983, the positive reaction of these Evangelicals to the event, and subsequent WCC follow-ups with Evangelicals. Even before that, a few church bodies in Europe and in North America (notably the United Church of Christ) sought to create structured opportunities for conversation between their leadership and various Conservative Evangelicals. Nevertheless, there are more than enough indications that the old tensions and suspicions of organized ecumenics remain.[27]

A number of important issues at stake in the present tensions between mainline Christianity and the Evangelical movement have been delineated. First, the internal harmony of mainline churches, the laity's confidence in these churches, is at stake in improving Evangelical–mainline relationships. In the course of dealing with this matter a number of other insights might be gained, specifically about the nature of the Confessional heritages of the mainline churches: What is it about these traditions which allows for the development of both Evangelical and mainline theological approaches within them?

In addition to these matters, intraconfessional tensions between sister denominations are also related to Evangelical–mainline church differences. This opens the question of intra-Protestant relationships: What is it about the Evangelical movement and the Protestant traditions to which Evangelicals belong that allows some Evangelicals to have closer fellowship with Evangelicals from other denominations than with non-Evangelical members of their own Confessional tradition?

This issue points to a third, the explicitly ecumenical concern of whether mainline churches must remain theologically divided from the characteristically Evangelical denominations. This ecumenical concern relates directly to two additional issues raised by present Evangelical–mainline tensions. We already have noted the fourth concern, that Evangelical–mainline tensions manifest themselves in tensions between the Evangelical and ecumenical movements. The negative consequences of this state of affairs for church unity are quite obvious.

Finally, the tension between Evangelicalism and the mainline includes the Evangelical movement's anti-Catholic tendencies.[28] Inasmuch as the Evangelical movement claims to be the guardian of the Protestant heritage, its anti-Catholic propensities raise the question of whether, despite all the recent ecumenical breakthroughs, there is something inherently and incorrigibly anti-Catholic in the Protestant heritage. Or is such anti-Catholicism the result of an Evangelical distortion of the Protestant heritage? Although we shall see that the answer lies somewhere in between these alternatives, they are questions which must be raised in any ecumenical dialogue with the Evangelical movement.

In view of all these significant implications of Evangelical–mainline relationships, given the predominance of an Evangelically oriented piety in most of the mainline churches, and in light of the tensions in American Christianity between Conservative Evangelicals and more liberal Christians, which a 1986 Gallup Poll has revealed, it is apparent that sympathetic theological clarification of the relationship between Evangelicals and mainline churches may be *the* question for ministry and Christian unity in the remainder of the century.

The conclusion of this book is that this is not necessarily an insoluble problem. Although the warrants for such a positive conclusion vary between one mainline church and another, and the question of differences between the characteristic Conservative Evangelical and mainline views of Scripture are particularly problematic, the succeeding analysis at least will provide some warrants for concluding that, on the whole, doctrinal differences do not appear unequivocally to divide the Evangelical movement from the mainline churches. Convergence is particularly noteworthy in cases where mainline churches are addressing concerns similar to the characteristic Evangelical preoccupation with sanctification and spiritual renewal. Even on the difficult question about the nature of Scripture, new models developing in the mainline, narrative and canonical approaches to biblical interpretation, will be shown to be worthy of further consideration in the endeavor to find ways to bridge the Evangelical–mainline gap.

Of course, all the problems will not be solved by this book. I intend my observations merely as suggestions for new models of facilitating the all-important Evangelical–mainline church dialogue. But even with these limited aims the task is a complex one.

The book in outline and context

The complex character of the challenge posed by an Evangelical–mainline church dialogue necessitates a kind of second introduction to the problem, one specifically aimed at experts in the field. It is necessary to make clear that this endeavor to identify areas of mainline–Evangelical rapprochement has some precedents. Also the method employed in this particular endeavor to discern rapprochement requires some elaboration. We begin with a brief survey of previous endeavors to foster dialogue.

Although, as we have noted, in recent years some representatives of the mainline churches have begun to pay attention to the Evangelical movement, to date only two efforts by mainline theologians to build bridges between the mainline and Evangelicals have appeared. One of these books aimed to overcome the tensions by proposing pastoral strategies and structures.[29] It was a helpful endeavor. From the Evangelical side, specifically from its left wing, Donald Bloesch has claimed that the difference between the mainline and Evangelicals is commonly thought to be sociological, not theological. If this were correct, then the development of efficient structures for managing conflict and strategies for changing perceptions certainly would be sufficient to resolve mainline–Evangelical tensions.[30]

Although it is correct to assert that there may exist a distinct Evangelical–Fundamentalist subculture, it is not at all clear that the challenges can be resolved only at that level. My own supposition, contrary to what Bloesch characterizes as the common view, is that theological differences do exist between Evangelicals and the mainline churches, at least with regard to their view of Scripture and the proper method of its interpretation. (There may well be no difference over matters of biblical interpretation between the mainline and such representatives of the Evangelical left as Bloesch. Yet what may apply to this one segment of the Evangelical movement is by no means directly applicable to its more conservative members.)

In fact, most Evangelicals do believe that theological differences divide them from the mainline. This supposition is quite evident in what are perhaps the two most theologically sensitive single-volume endeavors to stimulate Evangelical–mainline church dialogue. For in one of the books, written by an Evangelical, Richard Coleman, five general families of theological questions about which Conservative Evangelicals and "liberals" disagree were outlined. Likewise the other book, written by a mainline author, Alan Sell, sought to provide a theological analysis of issues at stake in the clash between Evangelicals and liberals. (His analysis of the history of the emergence of modern liberal theology represents a helpful complement to this book.)

Unfortunately, neither author sufficiently considered the impact of mediating positions like neoorthodoxy and other more recent theological movements rooted in the historic Confessional statements of the mainline churches. As a result, their analyses are not really analyses of the dialogue between Evangelicals and the mainline churches (which are influenced not just by liberalism but also by these mediating positions). This methodological decision to focus only on a particular theological stream in the mainline churches, or to interpret all mainline theology according to liberal paradigms, precludes a direct contribution of these books to the ecumenical, ecclesiological question concerning whether theological differences between Evangelicals and the mainline must exclude or might still permit church fellowship among dissenting partners. Coincidentally, both Coleman and Sell failed to provide readers with a conceptual framework which carefully demonstrates the conceptual compatibility of the dissenting theological emphases of Evangelicals and liberals. Nevertheless, these efforts are relevant. They underline a core commitment of the contemporary Evangelical-Fundamentalist renaissance—the belief that the Evangelical movement makes a distinct theological contribution which, contra Bloesch's characterization of the common view, cannot merely be explained away in terms of sociological factors.[31]

It is apparent, then, not just from the work of Coleman and Sell, but also on the basis of the characteristic Conservative Evangelical self-identity that if mainline Christians are to approach Evangelicals on their own terms, relationships with the mainline can only be established on a theological-biblical basis. Additionally, we have noted that the crucial factor in Evangelical–mainline interdenominational conflicts, in the loss of credibility of the mainline churches' bureaucracies, has been theological. Each side is communicating what appears to the other as a different faith-perspective. The real problem area dividing Evangelicals from the mainline is theology. Sociology and leadership style may be factors in heightening tension, but they are not ultimately its cause.

The evidence seems to indicate that, if we are genuinely concerned to mediate the present tensions between the mainline churches and the Evangelical movement, the proper procedure is through theological dialogue between the partners. In view of the important issues we have noted which are bound up with the present state of mainline church–Evangelical relationships, there is much at stake in such a dialogue.

Bilateral dialogue results

The theological dialogue between the Evangelical movement and several mainline churches has already been initiated in several bilateral dialogues with something like official church sanction. In the United States, a semiofficial dialogue between Lutherans and Evangelical theologians was held between 1979 and 1981. In Finland, a dialogue between Lutherans and Pentecostals had just commenced as this book was being edited. (The involvement of the Pentecostal tradition in such a bilateral dialogue is relevant to our concern with the Evangelical movement, for, as we shall show subsequently, although Pentecostals are often criticized by the Evangelicals, in some regions they are considered and consider themselves to be Evangelical.)[32] At the world level, two more or less official dialogues between theologians of the Roman Catholic church and various Pentecostal churches were held between 1971 and 1982, and a new round of these dialogues was initiated in 1985. Also a more or less official international Roman Catholic–Evangelical dialogue on mission was begun in 1977 and completed in 1984. The results of these dialogues were at once meager, yet promising.[33] (Since they were not completed prior to the final stage of editing of this book, no account of the latest round of the Roman Catholic–Pentecostal dialogues nor of the Finnish Lutheran–Pentecostal dialogue can be provided, though unconfirmed reports concerning the latter suggest that the parties have achieved agreement on the affirmation that justification is by faith alone.)

The Roman Catholic–Evangelical dialogue was able to speak of "initial if incomplete unity" between these traditions with regard to basic creedal affirmations.[34] Consensus was also identified insofar as areas of ministry in which all Christians bear a common witness were noted (7[2]).

Interesting doctrinal convergences identified by the dialogue included the idea that the Church is the fruit of the gospel and that through the Church the gospel is put to work (5[2, 4]). Both sides agreed that mission could not be understood nor fulfill its aims in converting the sinner apart from the work of the Holy Spirit (4[1]), and that mission entails certain sociopolitical involvements (2[3]). Among other areas of consensus agreement was also noted on the divine inspiration, perhaps even on the inerrancy of Scripture in some sense (1[1]). Likewise the necessity of the relationship between Baptism and conversion was affirmed by both parties (4[2]). However the partners could not reach agreement on the nature and outcome of Christ's saving work (3[3-5]), the role of the Marian dogma (appendix), and the role of the Church in mediating salvation (3[3]). The report even reflects some hesitation that Roman Catholics and Evangelicals really are committed to the same gospel (7[2/g]).

Similarly the American Lutheran–Evangelical dialogue could not agree on a common definition of the term *evangelical*. Yet agreement was reached that Scripture is the sole standard of doctrine, that fidelity to the ecumenical creeds is an article of faith, that there is a legitimate place for spiritual discipline in the Church, and, most significantly, that salvation is by grace alone though faith alone. (Those who have assumed that all Evangelicals are prone to legalism are certainly challenged by the results of this dialogue.) Further issues noted requiring clarification include common definitions of Baptism and the Lord's Supper as well as the office of discipline in the Church. Perhaps the most important question, a common definition of biblical authority and proper interpretive procedure, remains open.[35]

The Roman Catholic–Pentecostal dialogue shows similarly mixed results. There was agreement that although the discernment of spirits is necessary, charismatic manifestations should not be excluded.[36] In this discernment of authentic spiritual experience the community in exercising "the common wisdom of a group of believers, walking and living in the Spirit," exercises a crucial function. This is how discipline is exercised. To this statement the Catholics added that such discernment is exercised by the whole Church, of which its leaders receive a special charism for this purpose (I, 40-41; cf. II, 14-17). Likewise Pentecostals recognized a role for the Christian community in the interpretation of Scripture by maintaining that the authoritative interpreter is "the right interpretation under the illumination of the Holy Spirit leading to consensus" (II, 52). Despite an express indication in the second dialogue report of Pentecostal reticence about the infallibility of the Church's teaching ministry, such statements seem to open the way to maximizing the doctrine of the priesthood of all believers without forfeiting the Church's infallible teaching authority (cf. II, 53-57). (This construal of the Church's infallibility, akin to certain Eastern Orthodox and Roman Catholic notions, will subsequently receive further attention.) At any rate, this is a promising approach to the problem Evangelicals and Pentecostals might have with the question of the Church's teaching authority and the priestly hierarchy.

Other promising affirmations in the dialogue's two reports emerge when both sides acknowledge agreement "on the basic elements of the Christian faith" like the Trinity, the incarnation, and the inspiration of Scripture (II, 29, 49). It was also significant that, although there was disagreement on the role of tradition in the interpretation of Scripture, each church acknowledged that it has a history, some of which the

Catholics conceded may be questionable (I, 28-30; cf. II, 57, 30). It is also quite interesting that the Pentecostals concede that they recognize "the development in [their] own history toward some liturgy," a measure of structure in worship. Catholics also make a significant point in insisting along with Pentecostals on the faith of the recipient if the sacraments are to be rightly received (I, 32-33, 22). Yet, a few of the Pentecostals disagree among themselves and with Catholics on the question of rebaptism of those baptized as infants (I, 26-27). Related to this debate was a disagreement over whether there was a further imparting of the Spirit in the baptism of the Spirit, or merely a release of what was already given (I, 18). Nevertheless, a significant consensus statement, one which correlates with the Lutheran–Evangelical dialogue, emerges, namely, the primacy of grace, that grace "precedes and makes possible human receiving" (I, 23, 18).

Several open or unresolved questions remain in this dialogue, and the new round of the dialogue is taking up at least one of them. Among the issues already identified as deserving future consideration include differences between the partners on the sacraments, the nature of the Church, the personal moment of faith, the relationship between faith and Christian experience, the role of Tradition in the interpretation of Scripture (with special reference to aspects of the Marian dogma in the Roman Church), the proper attitude toward the Church's healing ministry, and the office and calling of the ordained (I, 45; II, 12-27, 30, 33-47, 51-93).[37] Yet despite these unresolved issues, the cumulative consensus in these dialogues regarding the primacy of grace in the process/event of salvation (justification by grace through faith) is a helpful starting point in developing a mainline church–Evangelical dialogue. Indeed, it is perhaps the sufficient rationale for pursuing the conversation with the Evangelical movement even though the first rounds of bilateral dialogues have revealed many difficult questions which are not easily answered.

Problems for the dialogue

If the problems for a mainline church–Evangelical dialogue were not raised sufficiently by the bilateral dialogues thus far completed, the nature of the contemporary Evangelical movement itself poses formidable difficulties for dialogue. Indeed, I find these difficulties so imposing that I would have preferred to deal with them on the first pages in order to make it clear to readers that I am not naive with regard to the problems of principle which are posed for a dialogue with the Evangelical movement.

The first of these problems is occasioned by the present state of flux within the Evangelical movement. It is ironic that at a time when the Evangelical movement is achieving perhaps its most profound impact (at least most profound since the high tide of its spiritual forebearer, Fundamentalism), there are some diverse and important voices inside the movement who are saying that the Conservative Evangelical consensus is breaking down. Indeed, given the fact that the movement has only nonbinding regional and no unified international structures one must be willing to entertain the possibility that it is not really fair to speak of *an* Evangelical movement.[38] The term may refer in the final analysis merely to an intellectual abstraction.

These considerations necessarily raise questions about the validity of any endeavor to engage the mainline churches, the ecumenical establishment, into a dialogue with the Evangelical movement. Indeed, if these considerations are accurate, the possibility must be conceded that in the foreseeable future there will exist no traces of a distinct Evangelical movement with which to carry on dialogue any longer.

My second trepidation about this sort of dialogue between the ecumenical establishment and the Evangelical movement is occasioned by the concern that perhaps a book like this, which treats the Evangelical movement as a separate entity, will unwittingly undercut Evangelical intentions and polarize the two segments. After all, a fundamental commitment of the Evangelical movement since the time of its inception has been to avoid separating from the churches, but to infiltrate them.[39] Thus this book may present the wrong format for dealing with Conservative Evangelical concerns. Perhaps it would be preferable, as some on the Evangelical left have suggested, to deal with these concerns bilaterally within the constituent traditions which make up Evangelicalism (e.g., to engage Lutheran Evangelicals in a dialogue with other Lutherans, Reformed Evangelicals in a dialogue with other segments of the Reformed/Presbyterian tradition, perhaps Methodists with the Holiness churches, etc.).[40]

Yet a third factor related to the nature of the Evangelical movement poses problems for a dialogue. The movement's character, its rich diversity, makes it virtually impossible to treat it adequately, least of all for someone like myself who stands outside the movement. Thus it is likely that much which is important has no doubt been omitted unwittingly or treated at second hand. As a result, whatever claims are made in this book with respect to the Evangelical–mainline dialogue must always be assessed critically in light of those segments of the Evangelical movement which may not have received their due attention.

Despite all these problems, some justification does exist for engaging Evangelicals in dialogue with the historic churches belonging to the ecumenical establishment, in the manner that I have done. A polarity between these segments of the Christian world does exist, and some precedent also exists, at least in the mind of the general public, for dealing with the tensions associated with this polarity by grouping together all "Evangelicals" on one side and all the "mainline churches" on the other.

If present ecclesiastical factors and perceptions of the general public seem to mandate as an ecumenical reality that we think in terms of an Evangelical movement over against something like a mainline church, ecumenical establishment, the problems we have noted with these categories serve as important reminders that one can only deal with the categories by reference to the specific members which comprise them. This entails appreciating the diversity which exists inside both the Evangelical movement and the mainline establishment, so that one is not too facile in making generalizations. Although not all Evangelicals would agree, the lessons taught by the problems we have identified for a mainline–Evangelical dialogue may suggest that the ecumenism of the future will best be carried out by means of a multiplicity of bilateral dialogues which involve only specific members from each of the larger groups, who encounter each other one or two at a time. In fact, as much as possible this emphasis and other lessons learned from the problems for ecumenical dialogue associated with the nature of the Evangelical movement reflect to some extent in the model for the dialogue employed in this book.

A model for the dialogue

Given the obviously complex character of an Evangelical–mainline dialogue, and in view of the vast number of churches involved, a comprehensive dialogue between every mainline church and the literally thousands of churches and organizations affiliated with the Evangelical movement is not possible. Thus, though not to the exclusion of the larger dialogue, special attention will be given in this book to the relationship between Lutherans and Evangelicals. This decision requires some backing. It has been made with the supposition that Lutheranism is both a sufficiently typical representative of mainline Christianity, yet also atypical enough to warrant focusing upon it.

Of course, at one level the decision to focus the dialogue on Lutheranism is a consequence of my own Lutheran background and the nature of the task my institution has asked me to undertake. However, these are by no means the only factors in the decision. Recently voices from within the borders of the Evangelical community have called for such a constructive Lutheran examination of and reaction to the Evangelical movement.[41] Such a concentration also seems warranted insofar as Lutherans, having already engaged in at least one official bilateral dialogue with Evangelicals, are further along the way than most other mainline churches in clarifying their relationship with the Evangelical community. These points notwithstanding, it is the representative, yet atypical character of Lutheranism that offers strongest support for this focus.

Concerning its atypicality, subsequent chapters will show that Lutheranism differs from all other churches in regard to its systematic-programmatic focus on the doctrine of justification by grace through faith. Other churches, including Conservative Evangelical churches, attend to this theme, but none with the single-minded emphasis of Lutherans. For this reason, the other mainline churches share more in common with the Evangelical movement's concern with sanctification and regeneration (being "born again") than does Lutheranism.

We might expect that, because Lutherans and Conservative Evangelicals do not share a common overriding concern, there would be less likelihood of finding areas of convergence between them than between Evangelicals and the other mainline churches. Thus, special attention to the dialogue between the Evangelical movement and the Lutheran heritage seems warranted precisely due to its potentially problematic character.

There are other reasons for concentrating more on problems of Lutheran–Evangelical doctrinal convergence than on a doctrinal convergence between the Evangelical movement and most other Protestant churches. For, as we shall see, the Evangelical movement is largely constituted by the theological heritage of the Reformed, Anglican, Baptist, Methodist, and Mennonite traditions. (Except in a few European nations, it is generally not the case that the Lutheran tradition has had a direct influence on the Evangelical movement.) Thus it is quite evident at the outset—as subsequent exposition of the theology of the Evangelical movement will further demonstrate—that detailed attention to the theological positions of these other Protestant churches is not necessary for purposes of the dialogue with Evangelicals as is the case for the Lutheran and Roman Catholic churches. The acceptability to Evangelicals of the classical doctrinal positions of these other Protestant churches will become readily apparent from the analysis of characteristic Conservative Evangelical theological themes and the recognition that Evangelicals holding these themes usually do so in the name of their commitment to these churches' historic positions. In fact, most Evangelicals belong to churches which explicitly identify with the historic theological/Confessional traditions of the mainline churches. (Thus their disagreement with these churches would only be over the question of whether these churches have been sufficiently faithful to their own heritage.) But since, with the exception of Conservative Evangelicals in Germany, this situation seldom pertains to Conservative Evangelical relationships with Lutheranism and rarely happens with respect to Roman Catholic theological commitments, giving special attention to the Lutheran heritage as a mainline church dialogue partner with the Evangelical movement seems further justified.

In another way, establishing the convergence between the Lutheran heritage and the Evangelical movement on at least some theological issues can also serve as a test case in establishing the possible convergence between the movement and other mainline partners. Theological convergence between Lutheranism and other churches (most prominently the Roman Catholic church) has been identified in recent years in various bilateral dialogues; thus, any convergence that can be established between the Evangelical movement and Lutheran churches could imply that the theological positions of Lutheranism's dialogue partners (including the Roman Catholic church) might also be acceptable to Evangelicals.[42] In this sense, and also in view of the fact that Lutheran churches encounter some of the same challenges and controversies posed by relationships with Evangelicals which concern most other mainline Protestant churches, it is precisely modern Lutheranism's typicality in relation to other mainline churches which suggests that this book's focus on Lutheran–Conservative Evangelical relationships has broader significance for the mainline Evangelical dialogue in general.

It should be evident, then, that the pertinence of this book for the broader question of mainline–Evangelical relationships need not be compromised by the special attention given the Lutheran theological tradition as the Evangelical movement's dialogue partner. The special focus is simply intended to render the dialogue data more manageable. Lutheranism has been given extra attention principally as a test-case, to help stimulate readers to dialogue with Evangelicals from the perspective of their own tradition. In order to facilitate this broader dialogue, Lutheranism will not be treated in isolation from other mainline traditions. The characteristic doctrinal standards of Methodism, Roman Catholicism, Presbyterianism, and the like, also will be considered in the discussion wherever feasible.

These last remarks make it appropriate to close this introduction with words on the book's actual structure. There are four parts.

The discerning reader will note that thus far no definition of *Evangelicalism* or of *the Evangelical movement* has been provided. There are methodological reasons for this, and they will subsequently be clarified.

At any rate, before initiating the dialogue it will first be necessary to introduce Lutherans and Evangelicals to each other. In the opening chapters I try to introduce mainliners to the Evangelical movement, as well as to begin to clarify what the movement is. Thus the book's first part is devoted to "roots"—a brief survey of the history of the Evangelical movement. In the second part, we shall become acquainted with some of the leading organizations of the movement. Because Evangelicalism is such a diverse, multifaceted movement, the only way to get some handles on it is to examine the movement on a case-by-case basis and then proceed to draw warranted generalizations.

These initial sections prepare us for the theological dialogue, which begins in Part III. In that part, an attempt to provide a theological profile of the Evangelical movement in its treatment of certain core themes is offered. At first glance, informed Evangelicals may be skeptical about this kind of effort, believing that Evangelicalism is such a diverse phenomenon that it defies unified theological description. Thus my efforts have been very modest. Part III does not claim to offer a description of *the* theology of the Evangelical movement. It merely aims to sketch the outer bounds of what are acceptable Conservative Evangelical theological alternatives.

In Part IV the actual dialogue is put in motion as the characteristic theological themes of the Lutheran and other mainline traditions are presented. In the course of this section comparisons will be offered between the various mainline church treatments of a doctrine and the characteristic Evangelical approach. The comparisons suggest that the all-important relationship between the Evangelical movement and the mainline is not so much problematic as it is an exciting ecumenical prospect.

Part I

A BRIEF HISTORY
OF THE EVANGELICAL
MOVEMENT

Chapter 1

Who Are the Evangelicals?
Methodological Considerations

A detailed treatment of the history of the Evangelical movement is neither necessary nor possible within the confines of this book. Not only is the movement's rich heritage simply too diverse, but also historical scholarship on the Evangelical movement has in recent years reached profound levels in terms of quantity and quality.[1]

The task of sketching the history of the Evangelical movement is further complicated by the problem of where to begin. Some would trace its roots back to the Reformation, to the identification of the earliest Protestant churches as "evangelical." Others might refer to the derivation of the term *evangelical* from the New Testament Greek word *euangelion*, meaning "gospel" or "good news," so that the history of the Evangelical movement must begin with Jesus or at least include the entire history of the Protestant tradition.[2]

The problem of how to identify or define the Evangelical movement is occasioned by a number of factors, not only by the rich history of the term *evangelical* and the widespread, often indiscriminate use of the term of late in the secular media. It is a particularly poignant problem for English-language Protestants, who have largely been deprived of their historic right to designate themselves as Evangelical, as the term has come to be exclusively attributed to a distinct subculture of theologically conservative Protestants. (The problem is somewhat less acute in German-speaking lands as a new word, *evangelikal*, has been coined in order to distinguish members of the Evangelical movement from the historic Protestant community in general [*evangelische*].) In this book, however, I shall follow ordinary modern English and use the term *evangelical* to refer only to Christians who actually identify with the Conservative Evangelical movement.

Since so many parties want to use the term *evangelical*, the normal procedure has been to ascribe it to all theological conservatives without remainder (even to those who do not wish to identify with the Evangelical movement) and then to define the term by attributing certain theological commitments to such persons. A remarkable continuity exists among these various attempts to characterize the Evangelical movement. From critics to adherents, analysts of the Evangelical movement have commonly identified certain characteristics which they attribute to the movement. These include the Evangelicals' purported belief in the full authority of Scripture (perhaps its inerrancy), the necessity of personal faith and the individual's conversion, as well as strong commitments to the importance of evangelism.[3] With these characteristics in hand, then, one might presume to determine and judge who is and who is not an "Evangelical."

The widespread acceptance of this manner of identifying Evangelicalism suggests why the Christian community and most secular observers are so befuddled in determining what the Evangelical movement is. The rich diversity of the movement is likely to be overlooked.[4] In fact, on the basis of most of these criteria the definition of *Evangelical* is so broad that it could include almost any Christian. No wonder there is such marked confusion about who are the Evangelicals.

The method of analysis on which I have ultimately settled in trying to understand and explain the Evangelical movement is, of course, not free of presuppositions. Yet I have worked not with theological but with formal, more nearly "sociological" presuppositions.

One of my assumptions is that there are a number of Christians throughout the world who identify themselves as "Evangelicals," as part of the Evangelical movement. As such, these Christians sense themselves to have a special kind of fellowship with others who identify themselves as Evangelical—a fellowship more intimate than Evangelicals have with those in their own denomination who do not identify themselves as fellow Evangelicals. There is some evidence, specifically the existence of many national if not international Evangelical fellowships claiming to be part of *the* Evangelical movement, which suggests that my assumption is simply a descriptive fact.[5]

Nevertheless, my method for arriving at conclusions about the Evangelical movement has been that one must begin sociologically, only with a consideration of those persons and organizations *explicitly identifying themselves* as Evangelical. In this way, on a more case-by-case basis one can better appreciate the diversity within the Evangelical movement. Only on this basis have I proceeded to ask the question which must be raised if dialogue with the Evangelical movement as such is to transpire: What provides a sense of coherence holding Evangelicals together? What are the outer bounds of their fellowship?

This method of analysis in turn allows us to pay some attention to those theologically conservative groups which many consider Evangelical but which do not identify themselves as part of the Evangelical movement. Because such groups share many of the theological convictions of Conservative Evangelicals, a dialogue between mainline-church traditions and Evangelicalism could have some pertinence for enhancing relations with them. Thus, the history and theological convictions of such groups as The Lutheran Church–Missouri Synod, the Southern Baptist Convention, and various Fundamentalists have been considered. Yet this data is not included in framing conclusions drawn about the nature of the Evangelical movement, but is regarded as distinct from what consensus we are able to identify within the movement. By proceeding in this way, more clarity may be obtained concerning the outer bounds of the Evangelical movement—what makes one an Evangelical and which theological positions or sociological factors fall outside the Evangelical ethos. Also by paying some attention to these other theologically conservative groups, this study may be of service in helping them clarify the nature of their relationship to Evangelicalism by assisting them to determine whether they are in fact "in" or "out" of the movement.

This methodological decision to draw conclusions about the Evangelical movement only after a consideration of the history and theological convictions of self-proclaimed Evangelicals have been analyzed indicates what is at stake in these initial chapters. Only by examining the historical roots of the Evangelical movement and its important organizations can we hope to identify the common features among its constituents which might explain what holds the movement together.

Our method also helps furnish an answer to the initial question asked at the outset of this chapter, the question of where to begin a sketch of the history of the Evangelical movement. Of course it must be conceded that different segments of the movement might direct us to start at different places. Yet insofar as one refers to an Evangelical movement, aware of itself as a worldwide *movement* in consequence of the work of several of its primary modern American institutional expressions, the obvious starting point for a presentation of historical origins of Evangelicalism is the Fundamentalist movement. For the organizations which really created or first incarnated the Evangelical movement as we know it today, organizations like the National Association of Evangelicals (and a number of its member denominations), the periodical *Christianity Today,* and even Billy Graham and his organization, have their roots in American Fundamentalism.

Chapter 2

Fundamentalist Origins: Prefundamentalist Influences

The history of the Fundamentalist movement deserves—and has been accorded by other authors—books in itself. Thus only the briefest sketch of the highlights of its development can be offered here.

Fundamentalism is an interdenominational, transconfessional movement that developed and flourished in the first decades of this century in American Protestantism, languished in the mid-decades, and has become in the last 10 years perhaps the fastest growing and most talked about religious phenomenon in the United States. The movement always has been a working coalition of various American religious streams, including revivalism, Pietism, dispensationalism, perhaps the Holiness and Pentecostal movements, and most profoundly the Reformed, even Puritan heritage of American Christianity (particularly as it was articulated with a Presbyterian flavor by the theologians of Princeton Seminary in the 19th and early 20th centuries). The coalition of these diverse streams was largely occasioned by a militant reaction against liberal theology in the churches and secularism in the broader culture. Fundamentalism is characterized by and so named with reference to its militant advocacy and insistence upon fidelity to the fundamentals of the faith, usually described in terms of the so-called five points which include (1) the inspiration and infallibility of the Bible; (2) the deity of Christ and his virgin birth; (3) the substitutionary atonement of Christ's death; (4) his literal resurrection; and (5) his second coming. In addition to these commitments, the movement has come to be marked by a separatist mentality, advocating religious separation from all persons and organizations not subscribing to the fundamentals.[1] It can also be shown that the movement is characterized by a theological emphasis on personal holiness—on sanctification or conversion (to personal holiness).

A number of widespread false impressions concerning Fundamentalism must be undercut if the movement is properly to be understood. First, it is necessary to recall its loose, amorphous character, its lack of central organization. In some ways the movement was a creation of the media, as the term *Fundamentalism* was first applied to conservatives upholding the "fundamentals of the faith" in 1920 by a national Baptist paper, the *Watchman-Examiner*.[2] The term was soon in widespread use, being applied to participants in the various prefundamentalist Bible and Prophetic Conferences at the turn of the century, to theological conservatives still within their denominations, and to those separatists who already had left them to form their own churches.

Given this amorphous character it is not surprising that, contrary to popular misconception, the "five points" of Fundamentalism do not represent a formal statement or creed of five articles to which all Fundamentalists formally subscribed. In fact, sometimes there were variations among Fundamentalists on the five points. Thus, contrary to popular misconception, they are not officially derived from the *Five-Point Deliverance* issued in 1910 by the General Assembly of the Presbyterian Church in the U.S.A. in response to perceived liberal trends in the thought of recent seminary graduates. They are not derived from the so-called *Niagara Creed,* drawn up in 1878 by a group later associated with the Niagara Conference, an influential Bible-study conference largely comprised of theologically conservative Presbyterians and Baptists who had been influenced by the new interest in prophecy and speculation about the end-times.[3]

Likewise, the five points were not derived from *The Fundamentals,* a series of well-known booklets comprised of various theological essays published between 1910 and 1915. In view of the renown of this series and the general ignorance about its contents, it deserves special attention. Distributed in mass (more than 3,000,000 booklets) to "every pastor, evangelist, minister, theological professor, theological student [etc.]. . . in the English speaking world," the purpose of *The Fundamentals* was to return American church and society to their old moorings. Although a group of the most distinguished conservative theologians was assembled to do the essays, they largely failed in their task. In its own day, the series had only minimal impact on American culture and religious life, including on certain segments of what would eventually become the Fundamentalist movement.[4]

Given the quality of the authors, it is not surprising that the product is quite good. People who think that all that is Fundamentalist must necessarily be anti-intellectual, simplistic, and polemical are in for a surprise when they read *The Fundamentals*. Although some articles are emotional or hostile in tone, the majority of them are irenic, calm, and well-balanced.[5]

Because of the quality of the authors and their product, it is not surprising that *The Fundamentals* have made a long-term imprint on the American religious psyche, even though their immediate impact was slight. By gathering together such eminent spokespersons for the theological conservatives' cause, the movement truly achieved an interdenominational, ecumenical character. By the same token, both the denominationally oriented conservatives and those from whom the first group was sometimes estranged, conservatives more oriented toward the Bible Conferences, were given a common point of reference by the series. Also after the First World War, when the Fundamentalist movement began to crystallize and the title *Fundamentalist* was coined in 1920, the series of booklets with the same title, though rarely read or studied, became a kind of symbolic rallying point or way of identifying the movement.

That the series could not be considered as *the* formal theological statement authoritative or valid for the entire Fundamentalist movement is quite apparent from a study of the literature and its balanced tone. Although the patrons and editors of the project were attracted to dispensationalism (a theological orientation which endeavors to distinguish within the biblical witness and the course of history a series of periods or dispensations in God's dealings with humanity, in which God introduces different tests and responsibilities in each period that do not apply to the other periods), with but few exceptions dispensationalism was not a central theme in the articles. Likewise, no support exclusive of other options was given to premillennialism (the prevailing Fundamentalist belief concerning the end-times, suggested by a compilation of texts like Revelation 20; 2 Tim. 3:1; 2 Thess. 2:1-8; and Mark 13:3ff., that the second coming of Christ will occur before his thousand-year reign when peace, justice, and plenty will prevail on earth [the millennium], so that the world will never come to peace and justice until Christ returns). Given the importance of these viewpoints for Fundamentalism and the relative lack of emphasis the booklets give to them it is little wonder that some Fundamentalists could not accept *The Fundamentals* as an adequate expression of their faith.[6]

There are other surprises for uninitiated readers of *The Fundamentals*. Insofar as they are symptomatic of the kind of theological convictions one can detect in Fundamentalism's theological heir, the Evangelical movement, they warrant our attention. Contrary to popular opinion, one can find a number of solid Reformation insights in the volumes. To be sure, one can identify some articles in which there is a stress on being "born again" (X, 31-33) or the believer is said to "cooperate" with the Spirit (VIII, 70). One also discerns language about the "power" given to the believer by the Holy Spirit (X, 31-32; IX, 72), terminology which clearly reflects an indebtedness to the Keswick Movement (a modified version of Holiness-Perfectionist teaching, both influential on Fundamentalism, which accepted the basic ideas and practice of the Holiness movement but generally preferred to speak of the Spirit's work in "empowering" the Christian for service rather than the total eradication of one's sin).[7] Yet these themes are more than balanced by numerous affirmations of the great Pauline and Lutheran theme of justification by faith *apart from works* (I, 124-125; II, 115-117; VI, 62-63; XI, 49-50). On one occasion a distinction, familiar to Lutherans, is made between the law (the condemning function of the word of God or its form as a command) and the gospel or grace (God's Word as promise or life-giving) (XI, 45ff.). On another occasion justification by faith is even identified as *the* truth of most of the New Testament witness (II, 106).

The pleasant surprises modern mainline church members can find in *The Fundamentals* even pertain to a few positions taken regarding the nature of Holy Scripture and the use of historical criticism (an approach for interpreting the Bible, largely developed by 19th-century German scholars, which presupposes that the Bible must be interpreted as a product of its times and must have its claims evaluated in light of present experience and standards of investigation). To be sure, one finds a number of articles in which the critical method is attacked (I, 88ff.; II, 48ff.; III, 99-100) and the inerrancy and historical accuracy of Scripture affirmed (I, 105; III, 12-14, 25; VIII, 75-85). Yet in at least one article an openness to the use of historical criticism is expressed (I, 106). Attempts are made to integrate evolutionary theory with the Genesis account of creation (IV, 101-102; VI, 94). But perhaps most striking is an article by the Scottish theologian James Orr (1844–1913), in which only the most limited affirmation of biblical infallibility is offered. Orr suggests only that the Bible is an "infallible guide in the way of life, and as to our duties. . ." (IX, 31). And he prefers not to consider questions of inerrancy (IX, 46).

That we should discover themes in early Fundamentalist literature which do not unequivocally affirm the absolute and detailed inerrancy of the Bible with regard to matters of science and history strikes a real blow to the normal stereotypes of the movement. It need not be too surprising in this case. Several scholars have suggested that the real issue which concerned Fundamentalism in its struggle against such manifestations of secularism like evolutionary theory and historical criticism was to assert the plenary, verbal inspiration of the Bible (that is, that every word of the Bible is of God). Only later in its development, in their view, has Fundamentalism placed special emphasis on biblical inerrancy.[8] The case seems to be made quite nicely by comparing two statements which had at least some formative influence on Fundamentalism. Thus the 1878 *Niagara Creed* (1) speaks only of the entire Bible being inspired "to the smallest word," while the subsequent 1910 Presbyterian *Five-Point Deliverance* (1) asserts the inerrancy of Scripture. This sort of openness within the Fundamentalist movement and its spiritual forefathers, even with regard to the nature of Scripture, is a most ecumenically promising feature for purposes of our dialogue with the broader Evangelical movement.

This appreciation of the relative theological openness, the quality of the theology of early Fundamentalism, affords us the occasion to correct one final false impression about the movement. It is common, even in some scholarly circles, to depict Fundamentalism as a manifestation in a religious guise of an agrarian, anti-intellectual class revolt, primarily based in the southern United States, against a growing urbanization and its influence.[9] In fact we have observed anything but an anti-intellectual, culturally deprived outlook in the movement's earliest leaders and their contributions.

It must be granted that today a kind of correlation exists between Fundamentalism and certain social classes, as most Fundamentalists tend to belong to the class of laborers.[10] Yet in its origins Fundamentalism was not a movement restricted to these classes, nor was it predominantly centered in the southern United States. Much of its earliest leadership came from the intelligentsia of metropolitan areas in the northeastern part of North America. The movement actually gained its support in the South only with the emergence of the antievolution movement and Fundamentalism's militant leadership against Darwinist teachings. At that time the Fundamentalist movement with its origins in the Northeast was able to stimulate and form alliances with the inherently conservative religious attitudes of Protestants in the southern United States, whose religious conservatism was and still is intimately related to southern religion's role in preserving the "southern way of life."[11]

This sort of coalition between Fundamentalism and indigenous southern religiosity is still pertinent to understanding the Evangelical movement today, at least in its North American expressions. For Evangelicalism, in drawing upon the coalition forged by its spiritual forefather, Fundamentalism, today draws much upon the American South religious subculture's tradition of the church's role as custodian of traditional social values. Many of its present leaders, such as Billy Graham, Oral Roberts, Jerry Falwell, and even Jimmy Carter have their roots in the southern United States, and surveys indicate that the greatest percentage of American Evangelicals reside in the southern United States.[12] In any case, it is evident that Fundamentalism was not originally a movement based in the South.

Nor can the case be made unambiguously that Fundamentalism was primarily a movement best understood sociologically—a social or class movement in religious guise. Some recent cutting edge scholarship has demonstrated that the Fundamentalist movement cannot be properly understood solely in terms of such sociological models of investigation. To be sure, these elements may have played a role in later stages of the formation of the Fundamentalist coalition. The movement and its spiritual heir, Conservative Evangelicalism, may today lend themselves to sociological demarcation, as to some extent each maintains itself as a kind of subculture. Yet increasingly some scholars have come to recognize that Fundamentalism is ultimately rooted in doctrinal, theological traditions and must be understood primarily on that basis, as a theological movement.[13] The following analysis should show the validity of this interpretive supposition.

Formative factors in the American context

We have already noted some of the persistent misconceptions about Fundamentalism as well as the diversity which characterized at least its early period. Now we need to consider how it was possible for these diverse streams and their yet more diverse theological forebears to coalesce—and what occasioned this coming together.

In some sense the answer to this question is easily given. The key factor which drew Fundamentalists together was a fierce opposition to modernist attempts at revising Christianity in order to bring it into line with new forms of modern thought. This is not to deny that there were other factors or that there exists an internal theological logic which holds together the various streams that comprise Fundamentalism (and the Evangelical movement). I am inclined to think that an emphasis on what might be called the regenerate life-style, including personal holiness, conversion, or sanctification, along with several other theological commitments, is the common trait for all the streams which comprise Conservative Evangelicalism in the broadest sense. In part, as we shall see subsequently, it is this trait which helps hold the Evangelical movement together.[14]

If it can be said that Fundamentalists were originally drawn together by opposition to a common enemy and a desire to reassert the fundamentals of the faith in face of apparent theological and social decay (secularism), much the same can be said about the original context or the prevailing factors in the formation of its constituent streams. To a great extent they also developed as theological responses to what was perceived as a society and Church in decay. This is even true of revivalism and the Holiness movement, although in some instances they were not so much reacting against Enlightenment secularism as against a perceived sense of spiritual and moral apathy in the church and society of their day. Thus, while these movements may exhibit certain tendencies towards innovation, as much as other constituent streams of Fundamentalism they embodied largely reactionary attempts to restore or maintain the "good old days"—"the old-time religion." In some sense, then, they all emerged from a similar context (shared a similar pastoral concern). A brief sketch of the social and religious situation in the United States just after the Civil War (1865) in tandem with the recognition of a few of the pertinent developments in the American situation through the beginning of this century as they bear on the emergence of Fundamentalism illuminate this point.

The Civil War and its aftermath were sobering experiences for the American nation and its Church. Prior to the war, the impact of the Protestant churches and their revival movements had been so great that one could rightly speak of an "evangelical civilization" in America at this time. However, with the Civil War this vision had been shattered. The common faith of Americans and their common Bible had not provided cultural consensus, as the American nation had been split.

American Protestantism was soon to face other challenges, more related to sociological considerations. They would ensure that in reality Protestantism was no longer "calling the shots" in American society. Perhaps the primary new factor was the marked social and economic revolution leading to new patterns of industrialization and urbanization, which followed the Civil War. Compounding this problem was a drastic shift in immigration patterns, which now included German Lutherans not inclined to follow the antebellum Protestant crusade for temperance and also Roman Catholics and Jews. The Protestant establishment, whose confidence had already been shaken by the war, could only experience these changes as crises which called into question its image and goal of America as a "Christian" (Protestant) nation. (To the degree that this period and its concerns were formative for Fundamentalism and so consequently for the Evangelical movement, we can perhaps attribute some of these movements' anti-Roman Catholicism to these circumstances.)

In addition to these changed circumstances, American Protestantism faced great theological challenges brought on by the belated and therefore unusually harsh confrontation with many revolutionary forms of modern thought. For it was only after the Civil War that American society became exposed to Darwinian evolutionary theory and methods of historical criticism. Churches were soon seriously to be divided over the problem of how properly to respond to these issues.[15]

The challenges posed by evolutionary theory and historical criticism were experienced as pertaining not just to the Christian faith. They called into question the prevailing intellectual underpinnings of American society at that time, the philosophy of Francis Bacon and of Scottish common sense realism (a philosophical movement developed in the 18th century in Scotland, very influential on the Founding Fathers of the United States and the institutions they created, which presupposed that human beings are capable of real knowledge and correct moral insight in virtue of universal common sense). As such, they seemed even to call into question the American Protestant vision of the American way of life and the worldview with which its understanding of faith had been connected.[16] Little wonder that such unsettling challenges would produce the kind of rage which came to fruition in Fundamentalism against the scholars who were introducing the new Enlightenment ideas and the liberal theologians who accommodated to them. (To some degree this dynamic may still be alive today, for it helps explain the passions which Darwinism and historical criticism can evoke in the United States, not just among Evangelicals.)

To be sure, despair over these changed academic and sociological circumstances and the new controversies they evoked was not the sole or even uniform reaction of American Protestanism in the half-century after the Civil War. The latter half of the 19th century was a period when American Christianity took up diverse crusades, including its push for temperance and its leadership in foreign missionary work. Yet, much of the earlier optimism of a large segment of American Protestantism and its reform impulses aimed at transforming the whole of society were squelched by these post–Civil War developments.

In an effort to mediate the new modes of evolutionary and historical-critical thinking, many of the major denominations of the North adopted a more liberal theological orientation. Although there is some debate about whether it may have more affinities to the older pre–Civil War American evangelicalism, the Social Gospel movement (a movement of the late 19th and early 20th centuries whose primary emphasis was on social reform of the unregulated industrial expansion of the day and the belief that such reform could establish the kingdom of God on earth, sometimes to the exclusion of concern with doctrine and faith affirmation) has been regarded by most observers, especially Fundamentalists, as a continuation of these liberal strands of thought. In response, in an effort to reassert the old-time religion and its associated antebellum cultural underpinnings, a conservative reaction to the new liberalism began to make itself apparent. The origins of the Fundamentalist movement and of Conservative Evangelicalism are embedded in these dynamics.

It has been said that Fundamentalism is a distinctively American phenomenon, that it is not at all indigenous to Europe or the rest of the world. In large part this is a function of the originating context of the Fundamentalist movement and its overriding concern to restore the "old-time religion" in face of the peculiar form of the American confrontation with the new Enlightenment modes of thinking; the crisis these modes posed to modern culture were not experienced as deeply in Europe and the rest of the world. (Granted, one could say that there was a kind of Fundamentalist movement in Canada, at least among some Holiness groups and Baptists. In fact, one Canadian Baptist, T. T. Shields [1873–1955], organized a Fundamentalist Baptist church in Canada [today its successors are both The Fellowship of Evangelical Baptist Churches in Canada and the Association of Regular Baptist Churches (Canada)] and played a major role himself in the movement's development in the United States.)

In the 19th century the European educational system, particularly in the area of theological education, was still superior to the American system. It was more in dialogue with its contemporary cultural context and was providing its students with developmentalist, nonstatic modes of thinking. Thus the development of evolutionary theory and historical criticism did not catch the European churches' clergy quite as unaware as was the case in North America.[17]

The European churches did experience some crisis at the time of their first encounter with the new modes of thought. One thinks of the Keswick Movement, the Plymouth Brethren, and the Anglican Evangelicals in Great Britain, of the revival of Lutheran Orthodox theology and neopietism in Germany, or of the revivals which led to the formation of Free Churches in Scandinavia, Germany, France, and in the Netherlands (preparing the way for its great 19th-century revival of Reformed theology). On the whole, however, a conservative reaction within the European churches to the new Enlightenment modes of thought was not as wrenching for church life as it was in North America, nor did it play as conspicuous and pervasive a role in the general society as was the case with Fundamentalism's impact on American society. (Most Protestant churches of the rest of the world were theologically conservative at the time. Thus they either never felt the need for a strong reaction against the liberal trends or else were located in a culture which had not been exposed to Enlightenment ideas.)[18]

There are several factors which may account for this milder reaction by theologically conservative Europeans. At least in England, the feeling of displacement by the new Enlightenment thought was not as pronounced as for their North American counterparts. In part this was due to the earlier British confrontation with the Enlightenment, so that as a result the rationalist, more static suppositions of common sense realism did not predominate in cultural life as they did in America. Consequently, British cultural suppositions were not radically threatened by the new ideas.

Moreover, the sense of displacement was not so sharply felt, because English civilization conceived of Christendom so broadly that Evangelicals in the Church of England always perceived themselves to be a minority, albeit a minority which had a clearly established place in the religious and cultural establishment. Thus to have their views called into question by new, more liberal theological alternatives and by new secular intellectual alternatives was not a radically novel experience. By contrast, American Evangelicals, who had been socially dominant, could only perceive these new alternatives as threatening. While most British Evangelicals had their place in the establishment already secured by British cultural conventions, the fluidity of American society entailed that widespread acceptance of the new critical mindset would banish conservatives from the religious and academic establishment.[19]

These factors account at least in part for why British theological conservatives were on the whole not as disruptive or demonstrative in their protest.

On the Continent there were other factors accounting for the conservatives' relatively milder reactions (in addition to the superior educational system which at least in the case of Germany had prepared many for the new ideas that challenged the older theological commitments). European church life was simply so structured that it tended to diminish the probability that the theological conservatives' reaction to the new modes of thought would be upsetting to the church and society in general. Thus the conservatives were sometimes separatists, starting small free churches (churches free from the government support or sponsorship that is characteristic of European state/folk churches), some of whose members emigrated to America in significant numbers. Or in some cases where classical Pietism (a Protestant movement emphasizing spiritual rebirth) had already dictated the main agenda of their churches, the impulses of modernism were not as severely felt. In other instances when the conservatives belonged to churches where Pietism found itself to be a minority position, little was radically new with regard to the influx of modernism; it was just a new enemy to fight. In both of these cases, theological conservatives (usually pietists) could stay in their church and work within it. Perhaps the structures of the folk church or state church system did not encourage the individual to take responsibility for the church, as in a Free Church system, and so the kind of reforming zeal one finds in Fundamentalism did not manifest itself on the European continent. (To be sure, some theologically conservative lobby groups were and have been created in order to work within the churches—groups like the Evangelical Alliance and various mission organizations.) All these factors, then, help account for the uniqueness of the Fundamentalist reaction and explain in part why the conservative reaction in Europe did not take the same strident and political form as it did in North America.

At any rate, the unpreparedness of American Christianity for the new modes of Enlightenment thought (especially evolutionary theory and historical criticism), a decline in certain Puritan moral standards, and changing social circumstances inspired a reaction by conservatives. The reaction eventually culminated in the Fundamentalist movement and its erection of a bulwark against modern challenges to faith and culture. The bulwark it typically employed took the form of a staunch affirmation of biblical inerrancy and a rejection of contemporary moral and intellectual developments for the sake of preserving the old-time religion and some "golden age of the past."

Given the fact that the people facing this crisis were members of a Victorian culture, shaped by common sense realism and so preoccupied with the need for order, it is quite understandable why Fundamentalists would seek to articulate a theological perspective that erected fortresses protecting them from the developmentalist, seemingly chaotic values and thought of the modernism encountering them. However, in so doing Fundamentalism became a movement whose identity was dictated primarily by polemical concerns, to affirm and defend the old-time religion over against apparent theological and social decay.

The Bible and Prophetic Conferences

For purposes of analysis, the various streams which constituted Fundamentalism may be grouped together in two major centers—Old School Presbyterianism led by Princeton Seminary, on the one hand, and the Bible and Prophetic Conference/revivalist group (which itself should perhaps be divided into two distinct centers with the argument that the revivalist heritage is itself uniquely distinct), on the other. At any rate, once we understand how revivalism and the Bible and Prophetic Conferences could converge into a coalition, and the indebtedness of the coalition to dispensational premillenialism, we can better understand how this center of Fundamentalism could incorporate Princeton theology.

Reaction by theological conservatives to the post–Civil War situation as we have described it was inevitable. Outside of academic environs, one of the earliest documented expressions of this reaction came in 1868 when a small group of mostly conservative Presbyterians and Baptists who were interested in millennialism convened a conference of Bible study in millennial prophecy. They continued to meet on an annual basis each summer at a resort until 1900. From 1883 until 1897 this group met for Bible conferences in Niagara Falls. They were the promulgators of the 14-point *Niagara Creed* (noted earlier).

This premillenialist perspective was quite significant for the subsequent development and impact of the Bible Conferences. As it turns out, it appears that some who were tied to the Niagara group but more influenced by dispensationalism were not entirely satisfied with the Niagara stance on questions of millennialism and prophecy. So in 1878 and again four more times until the First World War, persons associated

with the Niagara group and other eminent conservatives convened Prophetic Conferences. In comparison to the Niagara conclaves, these
conferences were much larger, and by comparison to earlier Niagara
meetings tended to place even more emphasis on premillennialism and
biblical inerrancy. They also reflected harsher criticism of the use of
historical-critical study of the Bible and other "liberal" viewpoints.

There are several significant points to be noted in connection with
the development of the Prophetic Conferences. They succeeded in providing the Niagara group with the opportunity to widen its influence,
to gain extensive regional if not national exposure for the group's views.
(One of the participants in the 1878 meeting was the wealthy and
influential founder of Wanamaker's Department Stores, John Wanamaker [1838–1922]). The distinct orientation of these meetings towards
dispensational premillennialism was quite significant; they aroused the
interest of many American conservatives of the day in this particular
theological orientation. In so doing, certain theological themes were
promulgated on which an alliance of various conservatives, namely,
biblical inerrantists, both those influenced by Princeton theology and
those by the revivalist traditions, could be built.[20]

To be sure, dispensationalism did have its adverse effect on the Bible
and Prophetic Conference movement. Its adherents associated with the
movement came to blows over whether the secret rapture (the trans-
migration of believers into Christ's heavenly presence to be with him
prior to his second coming, as suggested by Matt. 24:36-44; Luke
17:34-37; Gen. 5:24; 1 Thess. 4:15-17; 2 Kings 2:11) would remove
believers from the earth before or after the "premillennial tribulation"
of the end times. As a result of these controversies (a disagreement
that continues today in the Evangelical movement between adherents
of pretribulational premillennialism and posttribulational premillennialism [in one of its distinct versions]), the Niagara Conference was
never held again after 1901, and some of the prophecy conferences
before 1914 were canceled. Yet, in the final analysis the coalition of
American theological conservatives which became Fundamentalism
was well served by the dispensationalist orientation of the Prophecy
Conferences.

Dispensational premillennialism was not first introduced on the
North American continent by the Prophetic Conferences. It had begun
to make its impact in the United States in the 1860s, though it had
been taught there since the 1840s. The modern expression of dispensationalism, however, is not an indigenous North American movement
but an import from the British Isles.

Dispensationalism in its modern form emerged as a consequence of general speculations about the millennium which became somewhat common in the British Isles at the time of the French Revolution (around 1789) and its aftermath. Such speculation about the sequence of the end-times and the imminence of its coming had precedents in the earlier Puritan period in England and on the European Continent in German Pietism. Thus such prophetic, millennial speculations are found in the writings of a number of eminent Lutheran pietists, not least the father of Pietism, Philip Jacob Spener (1635–1705).[21]

Virtually all of these articulations of millennialism shared a common anti-Roman Catholicism and a missionary interest in the Jews.[22] (Certainly these characteristics carried over into the development of modern dispensationalism and as such continue to influence Fundamentalism and, to some extent, Evangelicalism.) All of these themes came to definitive expression in the Plymouth Brethren and its most influential theologian, John Nelson Darby (1800–1882).

Plymouth Brethren is the popular designation for a religious movement which originated in England and Ireland in the mid-1820s. Its emergence was conditioned by objections to what was perceived as the baleful effects of the church-state relationship in Great Britain, the dead formalism and ecclesiasticism of the church's life. In response, a number of Bible study meetings were held in Ireland and England. The groups came together in 1829 for the purpose of holding common services. They took the self-designation "Brethren" directly from the Scriptures, and received the designation "Plymouth" Brethren in consequence of the fact that their largest early "assembly" met in Plymouth, England.

A fundamental tenet of the movement was that in view of the decadence of ecclesiastical "systems" true Christians should withdraw from all established churches and worldly pretensions. These true believers should then carry on in the simplicity of a New Testament Christianity while awaiting Christ's secret return. At that time, it was maintained, Christ would rescue all true believers before the tribulation on earth which would precede Christ's establishing of a millennial kingdom. Thus the separatist tendencies of the Brethren were closely linked to speculations about the end-times and the millennium (a premillenialism maintaining that Christ will return before the establishment of an Israelite millennial kingdom, but that this will be preceded by a time of great tribulation including perhaps universal apostasy of the churches).[23]

The Brethren's prime theoretician, Darby, then proceeded to give systematic explication to these commitments. In so doing he developed modern dispensationalism. Obviously, the Brethren were operating with a periodization of time. They believed that the church's future, ultimately culminating in apostasy, differed radically from, and would be displaced by, Israel's future. For the future of Israel would culminate in a restoration of the Davidic monarchy with the coming of the millennium. In like manner the church had earlier displaced Israel, just as its Mosaic covenant had earlier displaced the Abrahamic covenant. The logical outcome, informed by a literal reading of certain Old Testament prophecies like Dan. 9:24ff., was that both history and Scripture must be distinguished into different eras or dispensations. And each dispensation must be sharply separated from each other in virtue of God's distinct way of dealing with humanity and God's distinct expectations in each period (see 2 Cor. 3:6-9). (The system also presupposed a literalistic reading of Scripture, as the prophecies of the Old Testament referring to Israel [Ezek. 37:15-28; Isa. 51:1-16] were thought to pertain literally not to the Church but to the Jews, to be fulfilled in the millennium.) At least in Darby's case, these dispensational premillennialist commitments also included the affirmation of the rapture.[24]

Darby's articulation of this dispensationalist system was not without precedent. The idea that God deals with humankind through successive covenants was first developed by the second great 16th-century Reformer of Zurich, Heinrich Bullinger (1504–1575). It is reflected to some extent in his *Second Helvetic Confession* (XIII, XX). The theme continued to be developed within the Reformed tradition in the Anglo-Saxon world. It came to full expression in the 1646 attempt to create a Presbyterian church order for the British Isles, *The Westminster Confession of Faith (VII)*. This Confession, which even makes one explicit reference to unique and distinct "dispensations," was heavily influenced by and subsequently further influenced Puritanism. Additionally, the theme of distinct dispensations also appears in the Dutch Reformed Pietism of Friedrich Lampe (1683–1729).[25]

Given its Reformed and Puritan roots, the impact of dispensational premillennialism on North America and the Fundamentalist movement is hardly surprising. There are other factors, however, which account for its impact. The United States was directly exposed to dispensationalist teaching by the great prophet, Darby himself. He traveled to North America to do missionary work on seven occasions from 1862 through 1877. Although he did not meet much success in encouraging his hearers to leave their denominations, he made many converts to dispensationalism.

In view of dispensationalism's Reformed roots, one of the best fields for propagating it was among conservative Presbyterian and Calvinist Baptist pastors. Some of the important converts included the organizers of the Bible and Prophetic Conferences, like A. J. Gordon (1836–1895, one of the founders of Gordon College which itself spawned Gordon-Conwell Seminary) and the Presbyterian pastor W. J. Erdman (1834–1923), as well as the great American proponent of dispensationalism and editor of the *Scofield Reference Bible*, Cyrus Scofield (1843–1921).

The timing was certainly fortuitous for the inbreaking of dispensational premillennialist ideas. As we have noted, following the Civil War, American Christianity and society in general had been going through a period of deep soul-searching. Prior to the war, American Christians were optimistic about the prospects of decisively "Christianizing" American culture so that the kingdom of God could truly be prepared by what was happening in American society. Thus, influenced by the great New England Congregationalist pastor Jonathan Edwards (1703–1758), the United States was dominated by a kind of postmillennialist ideal (the belief, traced to Psalm 110 and Isa. 11:6-10; 2:1-4, that the second coming of Christ will occur after the establishment of the millennium so that through missions and revivals, which would win the world to Christ and lead to general cultural progress, the millennium would be established and the world prepared for Christ to come again). (A third alternative, amillennialism, the idea as suggested by a certain kind of collective reading of Matt. 7:21-23; Luke 17:20-21; and Rom. 14:17 that there will be no millennial kingdom on earth, as the promises made to Israel are realized spiritually or refer to the state of blessedness in eternity, was also present in American Christianity at this time. Its primary constituency was among conservative Lutherans who rejected [and still reject] the millennium.[26] Yet at this time its influence on the American scene, like that of Lutheranism in general, was minimal.)

With the Civil War and the ensuing societal changes which we have noted, American Protestantism was no longer so confident that the kingdom of God could be achieved through America's social development in the historical process. Also, the growing impact of the new Enlightenment ideas and the accommodation made to them by theological liberals were most problematic to the conservatives. The rampant apostasy they experienced suggested to some that the last days

must be approaching. In such a context, dispensational premillennialism, specifically its premillennial commitments, seemed to be just
what the doctor ordered.

Premillennialism provided a more realistic framework for dealing
with millennial expectations. The failure to achieve the kingdom of
God in America need not be deemed a failure of God's promises, not
given the premillennialist scheme. Things had to get worse (the final
tribulation must precede) before they could get better (before Christ
would come again). Thus Christians could take heart that perhaps the
declining conditions of American society were simply what must be
in God's eternal plan.

The separatist tendencies of dispensationalism, the condemnation of
the existing churches, also served the early Fundamentalist cause well.
Like Fundamentalism it was concerned to criticize the existing churches
insofar as they had been co-opted by the new theological liberalism.
The full consequences of this separatist impulse would later influence
Fundamentalists as they withdrew from the denominations to begin
new churches after failing to influence reform.

Also dispensational premillennialism attracted the conservatives in
their struggle with the liberals because of its understanding and use of
Scripture. Under the influence of the new Enlightenment modes of
thought, theological liberals seemed unable to take biblical statements
at face value (as they were not apparently historically or scientifically
credible). But dispensationalism provided a new model which warranted and demanded a literal interpretation of the texts (albeit in relation to the historical scheme of distinct dispensations which provided
a degree of plausibility for such a literal reading). In so doing, it
classified the biblical texts in a "scientific" manner in accord with
principles that American theological conservatives would find ame-
nable, in accord with principles of the prevailing antebellum American
epistemology, common sense realism. In short, dispensationalism provided a model for shoring up places in the foundation of Christian faith
which seemed to be most in danger of erosion.[27]

For all these reasons it is little wonder that dispensational premillennialism made the kind of impact it did among American theological
conservatives and on the Prophetic Conferences. There is yet one other
commonality between these movements which may account in part for
dispensationalism's impact on Fundamentalism. It is interesting to note
that both dispensational premillennialism (as articulated by the Plymouth Brethren) as well as the Bible and Prophetic Conferences emerged

out of a similar polemical concern, to affirm the Christian faith in face of what they perceived to be a Church and society in decay. (One clearly sees this pessimistic and polemical assessment of their context by the early Fundamentalists in the Bible and Prophetic Conference reports.)[28] It is striking how so many of the theological traditions constituting Fundamentalism emerged in a similar social and ecclesiastical context and were aiming to address similar concerns. Perhaps in part it is the similar concerns and context which characterize their constituent traditions that holds Fundamentalism and the Evangelical movement together.

Dispensational premillennialism was at least the key distinguishing factor in drawing conservative Presbyterians and Calvinistic Baptists together in the Bible and Prophetic Conferences. (These conferences succeeded little in attracting Methodists or Lutherans, perhaps because of the obviously Reformed influence on dispensationalism. But the 1878 Prophetic Conference included an Episcopalian sponsor. Free Church involvement was embodied by the participation in the Second International Prophetic Conference of John Princell [1845–1915], one of the influential figures in the founding of The Evangelical Free Church of America. And two eminent Lutheran Pastors, Joseph Seiss [1823–1904] and G. N. H. Peters [1825–1909], who had written or were later to write books sympathetic to the conferences' themes, were in attendance at least at some of the conferences. Thus in view of the participation of these two widely read pastors one cannot say that Lutherans were completely uninvolved and unaffected by the Fundamentalist movement.) Dispensational premillennialism also helped provide opportunities for the Bible and Prophetic Conference group to broaden their conservative coalition to include the revivalist and at least to some extent the newly emerged Holiness traditions. This broadened coalition is nicely embodied in the foremost late 19th-century American evangelist, Dwight L. Moody (1837–1899), and to a greater extent in some of his chief lieutenants like Reuben Torrey (1865–1928) and A. J. Gordon.

Revivalism begins to join the coalition

As much as any historical factor, the American revivalist heritage's association with the dispensationalist-influenced Bible and Prophetic Conference group is indebted to the work of Moody and his associates in their organization of the influential Northfield Conferences, held annually from 1880 until 1902. (In the person of A. J. Gordon and his immediate circle this was especially evident, inasmuch as he was often in control of Moody's Northfield Conferences while also serving to arrange the earliest Prophetic Conferences.)[29] In this connection it is interesting to note that Moody's revivalism and the dispensational, premillennialist-influenced Prophetic Conferences shared similar underlying concerns. These conferences' statements, compared with Moody's own writing, indicate a mutual pessimism about the state of society and a mutual emphasis on the need to be born again and converted.[30]

To be sure, Moody was more concerned with promoting the teaching of holiness than he was with premillennialism. For he followed the trends in revivalism to emphasize holiness, a trend begun by the father of modern revivalism, Charles Gradison Finney (1792-1875). Yet it is less clear whether he actually brought about the inclusion of the Holiness movement in the emerging Fundamentalist coalition. (The Holiness movement is a religious movement begun in the 19th century largely among North American Methodists who, in face of the perceived decline in the church of the teachings of Methodist father John Wesley [1703–1791], sought to recapture his idea of perfection, the total "eradication" of sin or "entire sanctification," as the goal of Christian life [2 Cor. 7:1; 1 John 3:9; Jude 24]. According to usual Holiness thinking, redemption includes two stages: Justification as adoption and pardon, followed by a "second blessing," entire sanctification. [To be sure, it is acknowledged by Holiness proponents in varying degrees that even this state of "perfect love" is itself not an end in itself but requires maturity through subsequent growth in grace.]) The question of the possible involvement of the Holiness movement in the Fundamentalist coalition is a sensitive subject among scholars at the moment. Several who are related to the Holiness tradition are insisting that their tradition is not historically or properly rooted in Fundamentalism (or in the Evangelical coalition, for that matter).[31]

It must be conceded that the kind of Holiness teaching which Moody aligned with the Bible and Prophetic Conference groups was not precisely identical with its earliest and classical expressions emerging from the Methodist tradition. It was in fact a form of Holiness teaching which eliminated the typical Holiness belief that sin could be entirely eradicated.

Rather, Moody embraced the teachings of the Keswick movement, an originally British appropriation of Holiness themes which, interestingly enough, had its origins in connection with Moody revivals in

Great Britain in 1873 and 1875. At that time, several American evangelists influenced by Holiness teachings were participating in and came to lead a more or less indigenous revival for the promotion of holiness. Moody encouraged this development, and the American leaders wisely allowed the most influential British founders to avoid the language of perfectionism (no doubt because of the British participants' desire to avoid criticism of the new movement on grounds that it was overly indebted to American perfectionism). The new movement became institutionalized in larger conferences, settling permanently at the site of Keswick in 1875 (from which it derives its name). The movement became characterized by a doctrine which in practice had many of the same implications as classical Holiness teaching. However, although one can identify some significant references to the Holiness idea of a "baptism of the Holy Spirit" in some 19th-century Keswick meetings, the movement largely avoided the concept and its correlated ideas of perfection and a "second blessing." Rather, Keswick more typically called for "yielding to the Spirit," "fillings" with the Spirit to give "power for service." It was this latter sort of Holiness teaching which Moody ostensibly appropriated and in so doing brought into the emerging Fundamentalist movement.[32]

It must also be conceded that other differences seem to exist between Moody's appropriation of the Keswick insights and the original Holiness teachings. The latter had their origins in (1) Phoebe Palmer (1807–1874) and her famous "Tuesday Meetings for the Promotion of Holiness" held in her New York home, (2) in the emphasis on "entire sanctification" by Charles Finney and his colleagues at Oberlin College, and (3) in the secession in 1842–1843 of the Wesleyan Methodist Connection from the Methodist Episcopal Church, primarily over the issue of slavery, as well as the eventual formation of the Free Methodist Church in 1860, after its expulsion from the Methodist Episcopal Church. In addition to differences with Keswick over the use of the language of "perfection" and "entire sanctification," these persons and groups also seemed to differ from Moody's Keswick version of Holiness in that almost all of them assumed a socially active postmillennialism, in contrast to the premillennial perspective of Moody. In this way Keswick and dispensational premillennialism became allies. While premillennialism had implied the abandonment of an optimistic estimate of the power of the Holy Spirit to affect society, Keswick emphases allowed those influenced by premillennialism to speak of the Spirit's power in granting believers "victory" in their personal lives.

Thus the appropriation of Keswick teachings, especially when combined with the dispensationalist idea that the present dispensation of the Spirit differed radically from the Old Testament dispensation in which God worked through law (civil laws), reinforced the tendency to think of Christianity in terms of personal experience of the Spirit, not in terms of its impact on law and society.[33] As such, one can identify in this coalition some of the roots of Fundamentalism's eventual forfeiture of social concern.

Keswick and dispensational teachings could become ready allies for other reasons. Like dispensationalism Keswick was pessimistic about the state of the organized church and also shared the dispensationalist tendency to interpret the Bible literally.[34] This coalition of dispensationalism and Keswick Holiness was readily accepted in early Fundamentalist circles. The network of the coalition of Keswick Holiness, dispensationalist, and the Bible and Prophetic Conference teachings was pulled even tighter by the acceptance of Keswick by one of the leading organizers of these conferences, A. J. Gordon. The movement on the part of the theologically conservative forerunners of Fundamentalism to create their own Bible schools and institutes, the foremost among them being Moody Bible Institute, founded in 1886 in Chicago, was also heavily influenced by this dispensationalist-Keswick Holiness coalition.[35] These institutions have played and continue to play a vital role in providing cohesion to the unstructured Fundamentalist (and Evangelical) coalition. In this regard one cannot but note the profound role of the Holiness tradition in this coalition.

But the argument on the part of those Holiness scholars unwilling to identify their tradition with Fundamentalism (and Conservative Evangelicalism) is twofold: (1) The classical expressions of the Holiness movement, unlike Keswick, do maintain the possibility of the total eradication of sin and are not dispensationalist nor socially inactive premillennialist; and (2) the Holiness movement is believed not to conform to characteristic Evangelical/Fundamentalist views of Scripture. Additionally, it can be argued that the classical Holiness, perfectionist teaching predates the rise of Fundamentalism. Certainly this is true with respect to the earliest Holiness churches, most of which were formed prior to the emergence of Fundamentalism as an identifiable movement, and so do not embody its same spirit of polemics and pessimism, but rather the confidence of pre-Civil War American Christianity and its postmillennialist perspective. Also it can be argued that these churches did not play a prominent role in the movement once it began. In fact, there were tensions with it, insofar as the Wesleyan Holiness traditions clashed quite publicly at the turn of the century with teachers of Keswick Holiness.[36]

This issue of the degree to which the Holiness movement is properly part of Fundamentalism (and Conservative Evangelicalism) cannot be satisfactorily adjudicated at this time. Nevertheless, it can be pointed out that at a relatively early stage in their development some Holiness churches did support the Fundamentalist movement. And it must be conceded that today Holiness churches are identifying themselves with the Evangelical movement.[37] Nor can it be argued easily that this was an accidental co-option of the Holiness churches by Fundamentalism and the Evangelical movement. Despite important differences over specific theological issues, the logic of Holiness thought, even that inspired by its Methodist heritage in John Wesley (1703–1791), bears certain family resemblances to that of Fundamentalism. Thus, for example, Fundamentalism and classical Holiness theology both emerged out of a polemical context in which they criticized the theological and spiritual orientation of the churches of their day. In the case of the Holiness movement, the polemic was with American Methodism. And over against a theological heritage like that of Lutheranism, both the Holiness and Fundamentalist movements also emphasized conversion and therefore sanctification.[38]

In addition to these instances which demonstrate the sharing of common concerns, a somewhat common theological logic, the early Wesleyan Holiness movement appears to share something like Fundamentalism's dispensationalist heritage. Some have argued that the Holiness idea of entire sanctification as a "second blessing," as a "baptism of the Spirit," necessarily presupposes a dispensationalist scheme. This emphasis seemed to demand that a line be drawn between the new experience of the Spirit which, as a "second blessing," must come after Christ's work, and all that was given before the gift of the Spirit. Thus Charles G. Finney, one of the leading influences on the classical Wesleyan Holiness tradition, spoke of the experience of the Spirit as a "new dispensation."[39]

There can be little doubt that if the classical Holiness movement did not opt for dispensationalism it did encourage a clear distinction between the "era of the Spirit" and the "era of the law." In making this distinction it unwittingly prepared the way for widespread acceptance of a formal dispensationalist theology among the adherents of Holiness. It is little wonder, then, that even those arguing against the existence of a Holiness coalition with Fundamentalism concede that many Wesleyan Holiness pastors today continue to embrace dispensationalism. Despite their different emphases, or different ways of conceptualizing the same emphasis, could one consider that there is at least a family resemblance, a common set of concerns and a common theological logic between the Holiness traditions and Fundamentalism (or at least with today's Evangelical movement)?[40]

Nor can it be argued that the lines between the classical Wesleyan Holiness movement and its Keswick version were so sharply drawn that no Keswick-influenced Fundamentalists ever crossed the line into classic Wesleyan Holiness positions. In fact, Moody's chief colleague, Reuben Torrey, like other participants in early Keswick meetings, frequently broke with Keswick thinking and spoke like the Wesleyan Holiness movement of a "baptism with the Holy Spirit."[41] One can only assume that in so doing the Fundamentalism he represented was received with favor by all his Holiness hearers.

The lines between Fundamentalism and the classical Holiness churches are further blurred when one recognizes that a major Wesleyan Holiness church, The Wesleyan Church, is the result of a 1968 merger between The Wesleyan Methodist Church of America and The Pilgrim Holiness Church. The latter had antecedents in Holiness organizations explicitly maintaining a premillennial position, precisely the view of the early Bible and Prophetic Conferences.[42] Thus the Fundamentalist heritage seems to be represented *within* the history and heritage of The Wesleyan Church. If we bracket the question of whether the Holiness movement in its entirety belongs to the Fundamentalist movement, could one at least concede that Fundamentalism has been a conspicuous influence on the Holiness movement, and vice versa?

Perhaps a similar point could be made with regard to the Pentecostal movement (that branch of Christendom which first developed in its modern form in the United States at the turn of the century and is characterized by the practice of speaking ecstatically "in tongues" [glossolalia] as a kind of initial evidence of the "baptism of the Holy Spirit" subsequent to justification). From the outset, Pentecostals were not welcomed by the Fundamentalist movement as allies. Pentecostalism was deemed a heresy by many. This suspicion of the Pentecostal movement continues today in the Evangelical movement as even Billy Graham opposes the idea of a Spirit baptism after regeneration. Nevertheless, even Pentecostals themselves will concede that at least in North America the Pentecostal movement has had from the outset strong feelings of sympathy with Fundamentalism, so that the Fundamentalist influence has always been conspicuous on the Pentecostal movement.[43]

A coalition founded on polemics and holiness?

It is now evident how the influence of dispensational premillennialism as a tool in formulating a mutual polemic against theological modernism and perceived cultural decay was a key factor in bringing the various components of the Bible and Prophetic Conference/revivalist center of Fundamentalism into a coalition. But although this may have been a key factor in the coalition, it is also apparent that its distinguishing theological trait was not exclusively limited to such a polemically oriented dispensationalism. The contributing theological streams which formed this coalition also shared an emphasis or overriding concern with conversion and the regenerate life-style (sanctification or holiness). In addition, the constituent streams of Fundamentalism, like the Fundamentalist coalition in general, seem to have emerged from a similar polemical context. They were formulated as responses to perceived decay in Church and culture. Perhaps it is the common theological logic of the constituent strands of Fundamentalism, their similar formative context and overriding concern, which made their coalition possible despite their differences. Likewise, the different emphases these particular strands have given—either more to the concern for sanctification or more to the concern with polemics against modernism—may account for some of the tensions within the coalition. At any rate, as we turn to the other center of the Fundamentalist coalition, the Old School Presbyterians influenced by Princeton theology, we see that some of these factors pertain to Princeton theology's inclusion in this coalition.

Chapter 3

The Coalition Finds Its Intellectual Framework: Princeton Theology

Princeton theology designates a school of conservative Reformed Orthodox theology which was advocated by the major theologians of Princeton Seminary in the 19th and early 20th centuries. The term most typically refers to the theological positions of the Seminary's founder, Archibald Alexander (1772–1851), his student and successor, Charles Hodge (1797–1878), and Hodge's successor, B. B. Warfield (1851–1921). Sometimes Hodge's son, Archibald Alexander Hodge (1823–1886), and Warfield's successor, J. Gresham Machen (1881–1937), are also included. Although the seminary was inbred and aimed to educate only Presbyterians, the Princeton theologians had a significant impact on a number of American denominations through their non-Presbyterian students. One of these was Samuel Simon Schmucker (1799–1873), perhaps the first great ecumenist among American Lutherans.

The fundamental commitment of Princeton theology was to maintain American Presbyterian's fidelity to *The Westminster Confession of Faith*. This was a particularly timely concern for the "old school" Presbyterians whom Princeton represented. For it represented their opposition to the "new school" coalition of Presbyterians which was more inclined towards revivalism, even if these commitments implied certain latitude in interpreting the Presbyterian Confessional statements. Given these commitments, it is not surprising to find most of the characteristic themes of the Reformed tradition reflecting in the Princetonians, themes like an emphasis on the sovereignty of God, justification by faith, and the authority of Scripture.[1]

There is presently a good bit of debate on the question of the Princetonians' view of Scripture, the originality of their contribution, and the way in which their thought on the topic developed.[2] I shall not be able to adjudicate this debate for scholars, but will provide a brief survey pertinent to our purposes.

Perhaps the culmination of the Princeton efforts to articulate the nature of Scripture came to fruition in an 1881 article by A. A. Hodge and Warfield in which they claimed that all the statements of Scripture are inspired by God, absolutely infallible "in the original autograph." In this publication, Hodge and Warfield proceeded to emphasize again that the very words of Scripture are inspired ("verbal inspiration"), that all parts of Scripture are inspired ("plenary inspiration"), and that it will not be proven to err even with respect to history or science.[3] This statement of Biblical inerrancy subsequently became institutionalized by early 20th-century American Presbyterians in their 1910 *Five-Point Deliverance*. To the degree that this statement became a rallying point in the subsequent development of the Fundamentalist movement, and insofar as the Princetonians' articulation of biblical inerrancy provided a theoretical framework for articulating the basic suppositions of Fundamentalism's dispensationalist-influenced view and use of Scripture, the Princeton theologians' statement became a "fundamental confession of faith" for the Fundamentalist movement. In fact, it was primarily in respect to this issue of biblical inerrancy that Princeton theology had its impact on Fundamentalism.

The authoritative statement of Princeton theology on biblical inerrancy was quite logical, given its concern to articulate a "scientifically credible" version of Reformed Orthodoxy in an Enlightenment environment whose scientific/critical suppositions were calling into question the credibility of Christian faith. The project was to establish faith's credibility according to the ground rules of empirical science (ground rules imposed on the Princetonians by their reliance on Scottish common sense realism and its confidence in the reliability of sense perception) and in face of the newly discovered scientific "facts." Thus it was necessary for Hodge and Warfield to assert that the "facts" on which theology is based are presented with the same kind of unfailing accuracy as nature presents its facts to the scientist. Therefore Scripture as the "storehouse of facts" must be inerrant (not unlike the way nature functions for the scientist) with respect to all fields of inquiry.[4] The genius of the Princetonians' appeal to the inerrancy of only the original manuscripts is obvious. This move provided them with a way of discounting at least some of the discrepancies the biblical critic might discover.[5]

For all the logic of this authoritative Princeton statement, it has been deemed by some analysts to be a kind of clever innovation, a departure from both the views of earlier Princeton theologians and also from the Reformed, catholic tradition. If this were so, by accepting this articulation of the nature of Scripture, Fundamentalism would also be guilty of perpetuating a "modernist" form of Christianity.[6] It is not my intention to rebut this contention at this time, nor is it possible adequately to do so. Yet it can be noted that the Princetonians thought that their understanding of biblical inerrancy had been part of the church's historical faith. Insofar as *The Westminster Confession of Faith* (I.5,8), to which Warfield appealed as a precedent, does refer to the "perfection" and "infallibility" of the Scriptures, with reference to the inspiration of the original texts it is not necessarily the case that no precedent exists in the Reformed heritage for the Princetonian position.

Moreover, it has been shown by at least one scholar that the view of Scripture maintained by Warfield and A. A. Hodge in 1881 was essentially that of the entire Princeton tradition—and much of American theology generally at that time. Granted, there are some indications that a view of Scripture as fully inspired (plenary inspiration) in contrast to a theory of verbal inerrancy had an impact on some Anglo-Saxon evangelicals in the 18th and 19th centuries. But on the American scene affirmations of biblical inerrancy or infallibility are identifiable in at least two American Baptist Confessions of the early 19th century, *The New Hampshire Confession* (1833,i) and the *Terms of Union between the Elkhorn and South Kentucky, or Separate, Associations* (1801), as well as in publications by 19th-century American Reformed writers like David MacDill and American Congregationalists like Enoch Pond. Additionally it can be documented that as early as 1857 Charles Hodge was affirming the infallibility of Scripture as well as its verbal and plenary inspiration. During his lifetime he even conceded that only the autographs are infallible. And as early as 1826 Princeton theology's founder, Archibald Alexander, was speaking of Scripture's inerrancy and its verbal and plenary inspiration.[7]

The precedents for such affirmations could be traced back even further in the Reformed heritage, back to the Reformed Orthodox theologian Francis Turretin (1632–1687). It is hardly surprising to find the Princetonians' indebtedness to Turretin, for he had been very influential on Alexander, and his classic work, *Institutio Theologiae Elencticae*, was used as the principal text at Princeton from the time of the seminary's founding in 1812 until 1872.[8] As such, it is one more reminder that although the actual origin of the Fundamentalist and Evangelical movements has largely been a North American phenomenon, the movements have heavy debts to the European scene.

In view of the criticism we have noted, one must consider the issue of development within Princeton theology. It can be stated unequivocally that at least in one sense this tradition was always in the process of development, even as embodied in the person of Warfield himself. For early in his career Warfield followed the bulk of the Princeton tradition and sought to affirm the Bible's inerrancy by *induction* (determining Scripture's veracity by studying the correspondence between what it claims and natural phenomena which might confirm these claims). Yet several times subsequently he moved to a more *deductive* approach (verifying the Bible's inerrancy solely by the use of certain theological presuppositions or by a study of biblical texts in order to show that they teach inerrancy).[9]

Nor does one find such a development lacking in the other Princetonians. Thus both C. Hodge and Alexander generally employed the inductive approach (a fact that is hardly surprising in view of the confidence antebellum American Christians had in the compatibility of religion and science). Yet in some instances, particularly as certain scientists began to draw conclusions in conflict with the Bible, Hodge also seemed to move to the deductive approach.[10] Thus if the A. A. Hodge/Warfield statement on inerrancy is the fruit of adaptation to new cultural circumstances, this seemed to be occurring with earlier Princeton theologians, if not with Turretin and Reformed Orthodoxy.

This appreciation of the adaptability of Princeton theology, its relative openness, surfaces at a few other points. For example, it is quite common to indict the Princetonians for a kind of "rationalistic Biblicism" in which reason alone is deemed sufficient to authorize the truth of Christianity until no place is left for genuine spiritual experience and the work of the Holy Spirit. To be sure, one can identify occasions where particularly what Warfield wrote lends itself to such an interpretation. However, one can also find instances even in Warfield, just as in his predecessors, where the work of the Spirit and the experience of faith as the confirmation of Scripture's claims are affirmed.[11] This sensitivity to the impact of the Word on the believer's spiritual life, its reality-transforming impact, must be deemed also part of the heritage of Fundamentalism and the Evangelical movement, insofar as they are the heirs of Princeton theology.

In like manner one finds a surprising openness by the Princetonians at some points as they deal with challenges to the old-time religion posed by science or historical criticism. Despite his insistence on the verbal inerrancy of Scripture, Warfield rejected a mechanical theory of inspiration which would deny the biblical authors any freedom with regard to the vocabulary and style of what they wrote (a theory of divine dictation).[12]

With respect to apparent inconsistencies on the part of the biblical writers, Charles Hodge stated that "we are perfectly willing to let these difficulties remain."[13] With regard to interaction with theories of evolution and human origin, no less openness can be identified. Thus B. B. Warfield claims that scientific theories about the age of the human species have no theological significance, for the biblical genealogies were not intended to provide a definite chronological schema and do not accomplish this satisfactorily. Elsewhere he also indicated an openness to integrating the theory of evolution with the creation doctrine, a possibility his teacher Charles Hodge had raised as early as 1874.[14] This remarkable openness may also then be attributed to the legitimate heritage of Fundamentalism.

Princeton joins the coalition

Of course, it was not the theological openness of Princeton theology that attracted the "ecumenical attention" of the theological conservatives of postbellum America. Much more were they attracted to the Princetonian articulation of the authority, inspiration, and inerrancy of Scripture. On this issue, at least, Princeton theology was understood in the Bible and Prophetic Conference/revivalist circles to be articulating in the scholarly forum precisely what these conservatives, by their reliance on dispensationalism, were trying to affirm in face of modernism. In short, the insights of Princeton theology and its representatives at the turn of the century were drawn into the emerging Fundamentalist movement because the former provided an intellectual framework for elaborating the convictions of the dispensationalist-oriented Fundamentalists. With the Princetonians they shared common commitments to a literalistic interpretation of Scripture, biblical inerrancy, a pre-Enlightenment (Scottish common sense) philosophical orientation, and an opposition to all forms of theological liberalism or modernism. These common commitments were the basis of the coalition of these groups and account in large part for the notable influence and impact of Princeton theology on the Fundamentalist movement. With the entrance of Princeton theology into the emerging Fundamentalist coalition, the movement began to place special and explicit emphasis on the affirmation of biblical inerrancy.

To be sure, it was an uneasy coalition. The Princetonians were neither dispensationalist nor premillennialist in their orientation. At times their fervent commitment to the Presbyterian heritage and its insistence that we are saved by grace alone led them to criticize the "new school Presbyterian"/revivalist orientation of those associated with Fundamentalism. Also their intellectual, more cultured background led to a certain reticence on their part in identifying themselves totally with the movement. [15]

Despite this reticence, it is understandable, given the isolation they were experiencing in the academy, why certain Princetonians and other conservative theologians were open to the emerging movement. Thus the last great representative of Princeton theology, J. Gresham Machen, did participate in the Dwight Moody-inspired Winona Bible Conferences. He also engaged in correspondence with leading revivalists. Furthermore, inasmuch as Presbyterians, in at least one case former Princeton students, played a visible role in the Bible and Prophetic Conferences, the impact of Princeton theology on Fundamentalism is even more understandable.

An additional factor in its ecumenical influence must have been the thoroughgoing dominance of Princeton theology on the Presbyterian Church in the U.S.A. at the turn of the century. Conservatives within the denomination had successfully thwarted early attempts to introduce historical criticism into American Presbyterianism. *The Five-Point Deliverance* of 1910 and earlier declarations by the church's General Assembly virtually conferred an official status in the church to the positions of Princeton theology, particularly its view of biblical inerrancy. Given the social prominence of Presbyterianism at this time it is little wonder that these developments would also encourage theological conservatives in all denominations to rally around the "Princeton flag." The Princetonians' virtual dominance of their church's theological perspective could function as a rallying point to give even premillennialist conservatives hope that a fundamental orthodoxy like theirs could prevail in face of modernism.

That a coalition could be formed between the premillennialist Bible and Prophetic Conference/revivalist group and Princeton theology, despite their differences, is not simply a consequence of the historical and sociological factors which we have noted. As in the case of the coalition of other streams of the Fundamentalist movement, Princeton theology seems to have shared with them somewhat of a common theological logic. All emerged from a similar context and shared a similar overriding concern.

Thus, just as Fundamentalism and most of its other constituent streams appear to have emerged from polemical contexts in which the "old-time religion" was thought to be under attack by a secularizing culture and the church's perversion of the gospel in response to these cultural trends, so Princeton theology was originally framed in such circumstances. The polemic which shaped Princeton theology was not just confined to the early 20th-century confrontation with theological modernism. The founder of Princeton theology, Archibald Alexander, originally articulated his views in order to combat the growing influence of Deism (the idea that God can be known on purely rational grounds, correlated with the belief that although God created the world and its natural laws the deity takes no further part in its functioning). This polemical orientation has even more venerable roots in the Princetonians' forerunners. The principal theological text which they employed, Turretin's dogmatics, also was shaped by a polemical dialogue, specifically in response to challenges to 17th-century Reformed Orthodoxy issued by Counter-Reformation Roman Catholicism, the Anabaptists, and the new philosophies of Descartes and Hobbes. In fact, Turretin's Roman Catholic polemic also reflected quite markedly in his theological heirs at Princeton.[16] Such anti-Roman Catholicism was also typical of the other segments of the emerging Fundamentalist movement.

But it was not just a common polemical front or common enemies which united Princeton theology with the other constituent streams of Fundamentalism. Insofar as Princeton theology promulgated the Reformed tradition's emphasis on sanctification, its overriding concern correlated with the overriding concern about personal holiness, conversion, and sanctification which characterized the other constituent streams. (One need only examine the Prefatory Address at the beginning of the *Institutes of the Christian Religion,* the main dogmatic work of the founder of the Reformed tradition, John Calvin [1509–1564], in order to note how the earliest expressions of Reformed theology and its emphases were shaped by the concern to show that the Reformed faith does not lead to a laxity in ethics and the Christian life.[17] Of course elsewhere in the *Institutes* [III/XI.1] Calvin does designate justification as the "main hinge" on which Christianity turns. One wonders if this emphasis on the doctrine of justification, an emphasis not typical of other constituent streams of the Evangelical movement, could help explain why, despite the Presbyterian-Reformed overall preoccupation with sanctification, this tradition is still perceived by some Evangelicals, notably those of the Holiness movement, as not quite fitting the Evangelical coalition.)

This common theological logic shared by Princeton theology and the dispensationalist-influenced segments of the Fundamentalist movement is also suggested with respect to the earliest Princeton theologian's preoccupation with fulfilled prophecy as an evidence for Christian truth.[18] One might speculate whether this interest in prophecy did not help create a climate wherein even non-Presbyterian conservatives associated with the Prophetic Conferences and dispensationalism could more readily embrace Princeton theology.

With the inclusion of Princeton theology, the Fundamentalist coalition, though not a discernible movement until after the First World War, was virtually formed. To the extent that the modern Evangelical movement largely did emerge out of Fundamentalist roots, an understanding of the dynamics of the Fundamentalist movement supplies us with some clues regarding what holds the Evangelical movement together.

At least we have gained some insights about what holds Fundamentalism together. We have observed the role dispensational premillennialism played as the key factor in helping to bring together the various components of the movement. Yet this is not the whole story. To be sure, dispensationalism and a common enemy, modernist attempts to reconcile Christianity to new forms of Enlightenment thought, originally occasioned the coalition of Fundamentalism's various components. Yet the fact that certain concerns associated with these components made themselves felt in the Fundamentalist coalition—concerns like evangelism and social reform, which seemed to conflict with Dispensationalist commitments—indicates that the influence of dispensationalism on the Fundamentalist movement never totally controlled it or accounted for its sense of unity.[19] Instead, one can discern other factors which seem to hold the movement together.

In the course of our analysis we have noted several times a common theological logic, a common overriding concern, in the various components of the movement. This is not just the common affirmation of biblical inerrancy (usually as articulated by the Princetonians) on the part of the contributing streams of Fundamentalism. These components also seem held together by a common preoccupation with what we might identify as the regenerate life-style, or sanctification. Could this overriding concern coupled with the polemic against theological modernism and liberalism be the central trait of Fundamentalism, what ultimately holds together its components and those of its spiritual heir, the Evangelical movement?

Chapter 4

The Rise, Fall, and Revitalization of Fundamentalism

It was not until after World War I that Fundamentalism took shape as a discernible movement, building upon its earlier manifestations. In addition to the Bible and Prophetic Conferences and the theologically conservative network associated with revivalists like Moody, among others, *The Fundamentals* was published prior to the end of the war.

Despite its largely irenic tone, *The Fundamentals* also reflected at a number of points the polemic against liberal theological attempts to reconcile Christianity to modern thought (I, 91ff.; III, 98ff.; IV, 73ff.; VIII, 15ff.) and the despair over cultural decay (see Chap. 2, n. 6) which characterized the developing Fundamentalist movement in general. (One also can identify a quite harsh polemic against Roman Catholicism at points [XI, 100ff.].) But the general concern of Fundamentalists with the regenerate life-style (the need to be born again) and with evangelism is apparent in parts of the series (X, 32-33; XII). Although, as we have noted, *The Fundamentals* did not have an immediate impact and cannot be credited as the principal catalyst of the Fundamentalist movement, after the war the series did function as a kind of rallying point or way of identifying the movement.

Another important prewar publishing event was the publication of the *Scofield Reference Bible* in 1909 by C. I. Scofield. This dispensationalist-oriented commentary was and is widely accepted and employed by Fundamentalists. The widespread use of this "authoritative commentary" helped and still serves to unify Fundamentalism.

Although North American churches were largely untouched in this period by controversies between liberals and the theological conservatives, several exceptions could be observed. Granted, there were a few prewar tremors in the Presbyterian Church in the U.S.A. Yet, because Princeton theology and the old school Presbyterians were largely in control of the denomination at this time, the controversies did not split the church.

On the other hand, we already have noted how the emergence of the Holiness movement split the Methodist church and led to the formation of several independent denominations even before the Civil War. Also before the First World War the Pentecostal movement emerged and divided certain Holiness churches to which many of the earliest Pentecostals belonged. Although they did not play leading roles in the Fundamentalist movement, these churches clearly were sympathetic to the movement.[1]

Likewise, several other American churches later sympathetic to Fundamentalism emerged prior to World War I as a result of schisms within established denominations. Thus The Reformed Episcopal Church emerged out of the Protestant Episcopal Church in the second half of the 19th century in a controversy pertaining to the Low Church, more characteristically Protestant orientation of the dissenting party. The Southern Baptist Convention endured a small schism early in the 20th century as a result of the Landmark movement. In 1924 a number of these Landmarkists eventually came to form a Fundamentalist-related church, the American Baptist Association. (Landmarkism is a kind of "High Church" Baptist theological perspective. It holds that there has been a direct succession of Baptist churches since the time of Christ. This line of succession is said to include such nonconformist, even heretical groups like the Donatists [4th-century heretics who held that the church must be pure and that moral pollution of clergy invalidated the sacraments]. Other groups in this line include the Waldensians [12th-century reformers who stressed moral purity] and the 16th-century Anabaptist reformers. The Baptist church is then regarded as the only true Church, distinguished by "Old Landmarks" like the insistence that only a local Baptist congregation can properly authorize the administration of the sacraments/ordinances.)[2] Most of the Baptist separatists as well as the Episcopalian separatists have identified themselves with Fundamentalism.

Such a pre–World War I division took place among the Disciples of Christ, just as another rift ensued within the same church during the 1920s. The earlier schism was largely over the conservatives' insistence that only that which the Bible explicitly authorizes may be practiced by the Church. Thus the conservatives formed a loose conglomeration of congregations called the Churches of Christ (Noninstrumental). Given their presuppositions, they rejected and still largely reject reliance on missionary organizations and the use of musical instruments in worship. Although they generally shared the Fundamentalists' views on inerrancy, they were so immured within their own suppositions that they never became engaged in the Fundamentalist crusade. It was the later group of seceders who found themselves in sympathy with the Fundamentalists.

Prior to the war, there was little need for the theological conservatives to leave their denominations. With a few exceptions, already noted, they were largely in control of these denominations. To a great extent the war signaled a change in their leadership position both in the churches and in the broader American society. It also marked a change in their demeanor. Before the war the theological conservatives had largely been moderate in their critique of changes in American culture and liberalism in their churches. *The Fundamentals* perhaps typify this tone of moderation. But after 1920 theological conservative efforts were largely comprised and led by Fundamentalists engaged in a holy warfare to drive modernism out of Church and culture.

The events during and after World War I seemed to facilitate this dynamic in several ways. The war tended to sharpen interest in the premillennialist perspective of the early Fundamentalists. It seemed to call into question all hope of progress by European and American culture. In so doing, the last underpinnings of credibility for the old postmillennial view were undermined. The war was more likely understood as a sign of the coming End.

This premillennialist perspective was further strengthened in the minds of American theological conservatives by the markedly waning influence they were having on both the American church and society after the war. The theological liberals were becoming more influential in the churches. In the broader society the old American Protestant establishment, which had begun to deteriorate after the Civil War, was finally coming to an end. Intellectual and sociological patterns of deterioration begun after that war continued or were magnified. Thus the pattern of immigration begun after the Civil War, which brought many new citizens to America who because of their ethnic background would not likely affiliate with the major denominations, called the dominance of the Protestant establishment into question in some areas. Furthermore, Christianity was losing its hold on the country's intellectual and literary leadership. It was also apparently losing its capacity to shape

American opinion. The decline of legal enforcement ensuring strict observance of the Sabbath indicated this. And although the churches had had some impact on the Prohibition amendment, the failure to enforce and maintain this legislation functioned as evidence of the churches' loss of authority. Urban values rather than Christian values seemed to be dictating the American agenda. All this seemed a further indication to conservatives that the premillennialist orientation must be correct. Everywhere there were signs of the End.[3]

World War I prepared American theological conservatives for Fundamentalism also in another way. It taught them to become interested in politics. Of course, the crusade for Prohibition in the United States already had sensitized a number of American churches to the dynamics of political engagement. But the war forced the conservatives more thoroughly into political engagement. For it became necessary for them to take a position regarding the war's validity. This politicization of the conservatives opened them to taking a more active role in preserving American culture after the war ended. As such, their crusade on behalf of the old-time religion took on the character of a battle to save America (for Western civilization). In this respect the conservatives without recognizing it were breaking with their premillennialist perspectives, perhaps subliminally drawing upon the earlier postmillennialist belief that the Church should play a role in transforming and maintaining society. Contemporary Fundamentalists like Jerry Falwell who are endeavoring to exercise an influence on American politics are simply following in this heritage.

At any rate, the conservatives found an issue for which to crusade in the theory of evolution. It became a symbol for them of all that was going wrong with America. And now with their newly regained political sensibilities, the conservatives were ready to associate themselves with political endeavors to purge American society of this decadent mode of thought. (It is interesting to note that sometimes Darwinism was seen by the conservatives as the philosophy which epitomized prewar German culture, so that their antievolution stance and their polemic against German forms of liberal theology must be seen in relation to the anti-German sentiment in America during the war.) In their effort to purge American society of evolutionary theory, the Fundamentalist movement as it is popularly known was constituted and became a national movement. The active involvement in the antievolutionary cause of the American politician and three-time candidate for the presidency of the United States, William Jennings Bryan (1860–

1925), gave the entire conservative/Fundamentalist cause a new prominence. This new exposure broadened the base of the conservative's support in the southern United States, so that while the conservative, premillennialist movement had been to that time only a concern in the North, by 1920 it attracted national interest, and had ample attention in the media.

It is true that the secular media were principally interested in the antievolutionist position of the Fundamentalists and not so much in the broad range of their doctrinal concerns. But many members of the emerging movement seemed to recognize that by giving heightened attention to the problem of evolutionary theory, as it did, it could appeal to a broader constituency. In that way its overall concern to call back the churches and American society to the old-time religion would receive a wider hearing.[4] No doubt this dynamic accounts in part for the deep impression the Fundamentalist movement as a whole made on American society in the 1920s and afterwards.

We have already noted that in 1920 the media finally gave the conservative cause its name, Fundamentalism. By this time the movement also had its own national organizations. Thus in 1919 a prominent conservative Baptist pastor, William B. Riley (1861–1947), along with other prominent conservatives like R. A. Torrey, organized the World's Christian Fundamentals Association. Though premillennialist in its orientation, the organization differed from earlier Bible conferences in conveying a sense of urgency about counterattacking the negative trends in the American church and society. The association, like the emerging Fundamentalist movement in general, also became increasingly preoccupied with antievolution legislation and in so doing helped further increase the movement's visibility.

Other Fundamentalist-related organizations emerged in the next decade, including the Anti-Evolution League of America in 1924, the National Federation of Fundamentalists of the Northern Baptists (Fundamentalist Fellowship) in 1920 (a group inside the Northern Baptist Convention), and the more militant Baptist Bible Union in 1923. The latter included Fundamentalist Baptists from a variety of North American Baptist churches both in the United States and Canada including eminent Baptist Fundamentalists like Riley, T. T. Shields, and Frank Norris.

The struggle for the churches

The Fundamentalist movement was by this time enjoying wide national interest and substantial popularity within American society. Yet it did not encompass all American theological conservatives. It did not affect the Methodist church in the North or the Protestant Episcopal Church too dramatically. Perhaps this was a function of the fact that these churches were too little oriented toward strict doctrinal definitions for the Fundamentalists within these churches to have much impact. In the churches of the southern United States (Presbyterian, Methodist, and Baptist) there was approval of the Fundamentalists, and their theological orientation no doubt had its impact on these churches. But the conservatives were sufficiently in control of these churches so as to make a disturbance of church life by Fundamentalists unnecessary. (The only exceptions may be in The Methodist Episcopal Church, South, from which the well-known Fundamentalist Bob Jones Sr. [1883–1968] withdrew, and in the Southern Baptist Convention as its Texas Convention expelled one of the primary leaders of Fundamentalism, J. Frank Norris [1877–1952], as a result of his sustained criticism of its capitulation to modernism.)

The same situation pertained to the newly emerged Holiness and Pentecostal churches (though, as we have noted, a factor in the failure of Pentecostals fully to participate in the Fundamentalist coalition had to do with the fact that Fundamentalists never quite trusted them). In a similar manner, a number of churches with a strong ethnic identification, including Black churches, several churches rooted in Pietism, like The Evangelical Covenant Church or those Swedish Baptists who were later to form the Baptist General Conference, ethnic churches of the Reformed tradition like the Christian Reformed Church in North America, or the Mennonite and Lutheran churches were not directly involved in leadership roles in the movement and did not have their fellowships disrupted by it. But there is some debate, at least with respect to the ethnic pietist, Lutheran, and to some extent even Mennonite churches about the degree to which these churches may have been influenced by the Fundamentalist movement.[5] (At least the impact of dispensationalism, polemics against Enlightenment thought, and the ministry of Dwight Moody on segments of ethnic Pietism is apparent in view of their influence on certain predecessor bodies of The Evangelical Free Church of America and to a lesser extent even on segments of The Evangelical Covenant Church. And it cannot be denied that some Lutherans in the Midwest welcomed and supported the Fundamentalist influence with regard to the affirmation of biblical inerrancy. But in this case it is also undeniable that affirmations of the Bible's infallibility, if not its inerrancy, can be identified in the Lutheran heritage, even in American Lutheranism, prior to the full emergence of Fundamentalism.)[6]

Nevertheless, the real impact the Fundamentalist movement exerted on denominational life was restricted to two, perhaps three churches—the Northern Baptist Convention, the Presbyterian Church in the U.S.A., and perhaps the Disciples of Christ. With respect to the Disciples, a second schism developed in their ranks in the mid-1920s as a group of churches which came to call themselves the Christian Churches or Churches of Christ ("Centrist") began to distance themselves from the denomination. This group is quite distinct from the early seceders, the Noninstrumental group. The influx of liberal theology among the Disciples was clearly an issue. It is true that the tensions between the conservatives and the liberals had been evident since the first decade of the century. Although many of the conservatives did not formally separate until 1968, it was in the 1920s that they finally disrupted existing patterns of fellowship, organizing their own theological schools and foreign missions organization.

Some hesitancy among these churches' leaders exists today concerning the actual impact the Fundamentalist movement had on their separation from the Disciples. It is true that a major issue in the break was the openness of some liberal Disciples to baptism without immersion. The conservatives' reaction was symptomatic of the overriding concern to preserving strict observance of what they considered to be Disciples traditions. In this respect they differed from Fundamentalism. Yet the timing of their schism correlated with their polemic with liberalism clearly indicate Fundamentalist influence.[7]

In the case of the Presbyterians and the Northern Baptist Convention, prominent leaders of the Fundamentalist movement were involved in efforts to "rescue" their churches from liberalism. Thus in these instances one can speak unambiguously of a Fundamentalist effort to drive the liberals from their denominations.

In both cases mission work was a crucial factor in the controversies. This is hardly surprising, given the theological heritage of Fundamentalism's constituent streams. The conservatives tended to be strong in foreign mission work and to feel as though it were their domain.

The conservatives in the Northern Baptist Convention first tried to stop the drift towards liberalism in the Convention by aiming to have it approve a faith statement which would affirm the "fundamentals of the faith." Such a statement was approved by the Fundamentalist Fellowship. But even though they seemed on the verge of victory as the conservative coalition appeared to have a plurality of the Convention votes, confusion arose among the conservatives about strategy to use at the Northern Baptists' 1921 and 1922 Conventions. In the latter year an attempt to have the Convention adopt a traditional American Baptist creed which affirmed biblical inerrancy, the *New Hampshire Confession,* was defeated as a result of a parliamentary maneuver by the liberals. (It is interesting to note that the Baptist Fundamentalists appealed to this Calvinistic-influenced Confession and subsequently in 1933 expressed fidelity to another Calvinist Baptist statement, the *Second London Confession* [approved in 1689]. This seems to suggest the heavy Reformed influence on all segments of the Fundamentalist movement.) In consequence of the costly failure to agree on a strategy which could have united the conservative coalition and given it victory, the coalition broke apart. So the next year the most militant Fundamentalists organized the Baptist Bible Union as an alternative to the more moderate Fundamentalist Fellowship.

Never again would the fragmented conservatives have such a chance to control the denomination. They did make some effort to do so by challenging the policy of the Foreign Mission Board of the Northern Baptist Convention in 1925. But the Fundamentalists' attempt to propose a doctrinal test for missionaries also failed. All attempts in subsequent years to end the liberal hegemony were futile. Hopes for Fundamentalist victory were totally dashed when in 1932 the more militant Northern Baptist Convention members of what remained of the Baptist Bible Union withdrew from the Convention and formed the General Association of Regular Baptist Churches. In 1943 the moderate Fundamentalist Fellowship, frustrated in its attempts to reform their church's Foreign Mission Society, created its own independent foreign mission society. The Convention's failure to recognize this new society as a legitimate organization led the Fundamentalists completely to withdraw, and in 1947 they organized the Conservative Baptist Association of America.

The Fundamentalists' failure to take control of the Northern Baptists was paralleled by their defeat in the Presbyterian Church in the U.S.A. At the beginning of the 1920s the Fundamentalists, led by Princeton theology, were firmly in control of the denomination. The tide began moving in the other direction. This began first in 1921 when it was reported in some Fundamentalist circles that liberalism was rife among the church's missionaries. Controversy was further heightened the next year partly as a result of the published sermon of the great liberal Baptist preacher, Harry Emerson Fosdick (1878–1969), entitled "Shall the Fundamentalists Win?" In it he opposed Fundamentalism on grounds of its millennialism and exclusivism, and in response he pleaded for tolerance.[8] Since Fosdick, though a Baptist, had been preaching in a Presbyterian church in New York, the Presbyterian Fundamentalists resolved "to get him." Liberalism seemed to be spreading in their church. In this effort they had the encouragement of the great Princeton theologian, J. Gresham Machen. For, in his 1923 book, *Christianity and Liberalism,* which has become a kind of "Bible" to American Fundamentalists, Machen called for the expulsion of liberals from the churches.[9]

Thus, in 1923, the General Assembly of the Presbyterian Church in the U.S.A. reaffirmed the *Five-Point Deliverance* of 1910, setting the stage for the condemnation of Fosdick, who could not subscribe to the Five Points. This was the high tide of Fundamentalist control. The next year matters changed.

Early in 1924, more than 1200 ministers, reacting against the perceived lack of Fundamentalist tolerance and its hegemony, signed the *Auburn Affirmation.* It maintained that the Five Points were mere "theories" which could not be imposed on Presbyterians according to the church's existing constitution. The tide was swinging back to the moderates. Thus at that year's General Assembly it is true that Fosdick was invited to join the Presbyterian church, with the implicit understanding that he would soon be tried for heresy. However, it was significant that the Fundamentalists had not been able to secure his removal on strictly theological grounds by appeal to the Five Points. (Subsequently, Fosdick resigned from First Presbyterian Church and eventually became the pastor of the stunning Riverside Church in New York, built by John D. Rockefeller.)

The following year the moderates won another major victory. The General Assembly pushed aside Fundamentalist attempts to apply strict doctrinal standards. They did so at that time by appointing a special commission to investigate the issues raised by the *Auburn Affirmation.* In the succeeding years the General Assembly virtually ratified the Affirmation. It decided that the Assembly could not authoritatively define the "essentials" of the church's faith. In this way the *Five-Point Deliverance* of 1910 was effectively rejected. Contrary to Machen's plea, liberals would not be driven from the church on grounds of their failure to subscribe to Princeton's view of orthodoxy.

Having lost these important skirmishes, the Presbyterian Fundamentalists began losing leadership positions in the church. It was their turn to be on the defensive. Machen was elected to a prestigious professorship at Princeton. But the 1926 General Assembly delayed this appointment and in so doing initiated a process which by 1929 would reorganize the seminary's government. The aim was to ensure a broader representation of theological positions on the Princeton faculty. With this plan the hegemony of Princeton theology at the seminary would be a thing of the past! Enraged by the strategy, Machen and a number of his like-minded colleagues withdrew and founded their own institution as a last bastion of Princeton theology. This school, Westminster Theological Seminary located in Philadelphia, remains today a bastion of Evangelical, if not Fundamentalist, theological education.

Though in bitter retreat, the Fundamentalists tried one last stand. The church's Board of Foreign Missions was the last crusade. In 1933 Machen failed to find support in the General Assembly for inhibiting the spread of liberalism among the church's foreign missionaries. As a result, he and his colleagues organized their own Independent Board for Presbyterian Foreign Missions. Members of this organization would be expected to subscribe to the Five Points. The following year the General Assembly moved to squelch the new organization by banning the participation of Presbyterian officeholders in it. Machen refused, and so in 1936 he was suspended from the church's ministry. Then he along with other eminent Presbyterian Fundamentalists like Carl McIntire (b. 1906) organized the Presbyterian Church of America (today called The Orthodox Presbyterian Church). Unfortunately, the new church was soon wracked by the secession of a group which under the leadership of McIntire formed the Bible Presbyterian Church.

What caused these humiliating Fundamentalist defeats? How could a movement which enjoyed so much popular support in the 1920s fail so miserably in its effort to exert or maintain dominance in the very churches where it had its strongest base of support? In a way, the events we have considered were simply consequences of the broader loss of support Fundamentalism endured in 1925 in consequence of the famous Scopes Trial.

The Scopes Trial and its aftermath

The Scopes Trial placed the Fundamentalist movement's prestige on the line, because the movement had invested so much support in the crusade against the theory of evolution. Efforts by Fundamentalist-related organizations to legislate against teaching evolution in the schools succeeded in several states. In 1923 Oklahoma became the first state to forbid the teaching of evolution. Other southern states followed, including Tennessee in 1925. The stage was set for the first test of the legislation that year in Dayton, Tennessee.

Almost immediately after the legislation was signed, a young high school biology teacher, John T. Scopes, was indicted for teaching evolution in violation of the law. By this time the antievolution movement had obtained so much publicity and marshaled so many resources that a backlash was emerging. The American Civil Liberties Union (ACLU) led this backlash and announced that it would finance a test case to challenge the constitutionality of the Tennessee law. There is some evidence to suggest that Scopes volunteered to undertake this challenge. The most famous American criminal lawyer of the time, and an opponent of organized religion, Clarence Darrow (1857–1938), volunteered his services to help the defense. William Jennings Bryan, who had been heavily involved in the antievolution movement and was personally associated with Fundamentalism, volunteered to assist the prosecution.

The outcome of the trial (Scopes was found guilty, but the verdict was later reversed on a technicality) was not nearly as important to American society as what the media made of the event. And the trial was indeed a "media event." In view of the great interest and fears which had been aroused by the antievolutionists, it is not surprising that Dayton was besieged by more than 100 reporters to cover the "Monkey Trial." By their account, the high point of the trial came when Darrow cross-examined Bryan, who was testifying as an expert witness. Bryan and his Fundamentalist views were made to look very bad, quite naive and uncultured, by the ruthless questioning of Darrow. It was as if Bryan were incapable of answering standard village-atheist challenges to the Bible's authority. (Also of interest is that the arch-Fundamentalist Bryan reflected an openness to interpreting the seven days of creation as geological ages.[10] He died in Dayton, a broken man, not long after the trial ended.)

The press portrayed the trial, this exchange, and the quite obviously pro-Fundamentalist stance of the Dayton population in such a way that not only Bryan but also those associated with him were made to appear to readers as mindless bigots, opposed to all that was intellectually respectable, and largely rural or "southern" in their mentality.[11] In short, many of the false stereotypes of Fundamentalism, stereotypes which we have already challenged in this analysis, have their original source in press coverage of the Scopes Trial.

The brutal press coverage of the trial spelled the end of Fundamentalism's popular support, at least in the centers of American power and influence. Indeed, given their new media image, it is little wonder that the Fundamentalists were unable to take control of their denominations. They were no longer perceived as representing an identifiable Protestant consensus. Moderates in their churches or in society, who might have otherwise shared the Fundamentalist critique of theological liberalism and certain modern sociopolitical developments in American society, would not wish any longer to be associated with Fundamentalists who seemed to represent anti-intellectualism and strictly rural interests. Certainly this image was somewhat reinforced by the sectarian, nonintellectual, uncultured atmosphere associated with the crusades of Billy Sunday (1862–1935), the greatest American evangelist between the eras of Moody and Billy Graham. Nor was this helped by scandals involving two of Fundamentalism's most prominent leaders, Frank Norris and T. T. Shields.

With its image firmly fixed in the press and in the minds of most Americans (an image which has also been transmitted internationally), the press and academia soon lost interest in Fundamentalism—especially by the 1930s, after the burning-out of the antievolution crusade and the complete repudiation of the Fundamentalists by their mainline churches. Given its negative image, it is hardly surprising that the Fundamentalist movement was so neglected in these centers of power. Yet one must ask if another dynamic has been involved. Insofar as the academy and perhaps the media are intertwined with some of the values which Fundamentalism opposed, could their neglect of the movement, until just recently, be related to the establishment's repressing of challenges to the basic suppositions of post-Enlightenment industrial Western society?

After 1930, Fundamentalists largely began to retreat from the mainstream of American society. In a way, their new public image was self-fulfilling. No longer receiving support from the centers of power, the base of Fundamentalist support shifted to persons and regions, like the southern United States, which were removed from and suspicious of these centers. In virtue of the socioeconomic status of their new constituency and in virtue of their suspicions about some forms of modern culture, the media image of them as uncultured persons sponsoring educationally and theologically inferior institutions might in some cases have been appropriate.

Of course, all things considered, this retreat by Fundamentalists is understandable. Given the movement's new negative image and the hopelessness of its influencing the mainline churches, retreat into the ghetto seemed to be the only option. Thus Fundamentalists intensified their work in forming more of their own educational institutions (Bible Schools), mission organizations, and denominations. In addition to the precedents which already existed for forming their own institutions, such developments were also quite logical, in view of the separatist tendencies and the premillennialist perspective of the earlier Fundamentalism.

This orientation also tended to encourage political detachment on the part of the Fundamentalist movement, since Western society was thought to be on its way to destruction in any case. Political intervention on the part of Fundamentalists was likewise discouraged by their equation of such activity with the Social Gospel, which they perhaps unfairly equated with liberal theology. When political positions were taken, they were largely conservative. But this is no doubt a vestige of Fundamentalism's origins, as the reaction of an antebellum version of Christianity and American society against the inroads of theological liberalism and Enlightenment forms of thought. Given such an orientation, any political alternative presenting itself as liberal, as calling for change, quite naturally appeared to bury the antebellum values deeper in the past and so had to be opposed.[12]

The Fundamentalist retreat into a kind of ghetto and creation of its own subculture with its own institutions has rendered the movement a kind of "cognitive minority." That is, its members may perceive themselves to be a minority in relation to the broader culture. The imposition of certain behavioral norms, like strict, pleasure-denying life-style standards, has sometimes also served to heighten this minority syndrome and to strengthen the movement against cultural accommodation. This sense of being a cognitive minority most certainly also pertains to Fundamentalism's spiritual heir, the Evangelical movement. One senses this not just with respect to North American Evangelicals. It also pertains to Evangelicals who are not direct heirs of Fundamentalism, such as those in Europe (where many Evangelicals have a highly developed subculture in virtue of belonging to free churches or being part of a lobby inside state churches) and Evangelicals in the Southern Hemisphere (where for various reasons virtually all Protestants are a distinct minority in relation to the wider culture).

The Fundamentalist Renaissance

The development of such a subculture during the years of retreat since 1925 has not been without positive effect for the Fundamentalist movement. The subculture with its unique values and institutions helped Fundamentalists preserve their beliefs and their vision during the following decades of great flux and relativizing of values. They were especially well-prepared by this mentality and their premillennialist worldview to cope with America's great economic depression in the 1930s and the Second World War in the next decade.[13]

However, as we have already noted, dispensational premillennialist commitments did not so dominate the Fundamentalist movement as to negate commitments of its other constituent streams. Thus, even in this period of withdrawal, Fundamentalism was not devoid of a concern with revivalism and evangelism. In fact, the years prior to World War II were a period of numerical growth. The growth came both in terms of converts and in virtue of a broadening or strengthening of the Fundamentalist coalition. Thus, during the period before World War II, pietist churches with a strong ethnic background, Holiness and Pentecostal churches, some Mennonite churches, as well as segments of mainline churches in the southern United States came more and more under Fundamentalist influence. Fundamentalist growth in this period was also related to the beginnings the movement made in the use of the media for evangelism. Among the most notable examples were the "Old-Fashioned Revival Hour" of Charles Fuller (1887–1968) and a CBS network Christian broadcast hosted by Donald Grey Barnhouse (1895–1960). Fundamentalism was anything but dead, as its critics asserted in this period. The movement even experienced growth in respect to its parachurch agencies, including its schools.[14]

Another Fundamentalist commitment of long standing, which was not completely forfeited even after 1925, was the old Puritan concern with preserving the foundations of American society. Thus, the Fundamentalists' nationalistic attitudes were maintained, even intensified, during and after World War II. This manifested itself in the 1950s in the strident anticommunism of Billy James Hargis (b. 1925) and the American Council of Christian Churches led by Carl McIntire. Of course, some precedents existed in earlier Fundamentalism for this reaction. Just after World War I Fundamentalists participated with all the churches in leading a large-scale anticommunist American reaction (the "Red Scare" of 1919). The ardent anticommunism of much modern Evangelicalism in many parts of the world seems to carry on this heritage.

The growth and new ventures of the Fundamentalist movement after the mid-1920s had the unwitting effect of opening it to wider cultural influences, despite its avowed separatism. These factors, plus the upward social mobility of some Fundamentalists which led to a certain discontent with the "sectarianism" of their heritage and permitted a few to receive their theological education in prestigious academic settings, set the stage for the emergence of the Evangelical movement during World War II.

Although the emergence of the Evangelical movement effectively removed many former Fundamentalists from Fundamentalism, the latter has continued to flourish since the Second World War. The 1950s and 1960s were times of great numerical growth both for churches affiliated with the Evangelical movement and those of the Fundamentalist movement. In the 1970s and 1980s, the influence of Fundamentalism was even more profound, not least of all due to the political activities of the Moral Majority and its leader, Jerry Falwell.

In addition to denominational differences within the movement, Fundamentalism is today largely divided into two major segments. On one side there is "militant Fundamentalism." This group carries the commitment to separatism to an extreme. They insist not only that believers should avoid official fellowship with those not born again (see Matt. 18:15-17; 1 Cor. 5:9-13); they urge also second degree separation—avoiding fellowship even with believers who have "associated" or cooperated with unbelievers (see 2 Cor. 6:17; Neh. 13:1-3). This group is represented by institutions like Bob Jones University, the Southwide Baptist Fellowship, and Carl McIntire's International Council of Christian Churches. The second segment is a more "open Fundamentalism." This group does not demand shunning fellowship with believers who may have associated with unbelievers. To this group belong Jerry Falwell and several others associated with the Baptist Bible Fellowship. In fact, these two groups are somewhat split, and presently Falwell is under great suspicion by the militants for his purported "inclusivism" in his religious and political activities.[15]

There are some interesting parallels between the present success of the Fundamentalist movement and its prominence in the 1920s. In both situations a sense of cultural crisis prevailed. In the 1920s, the enemy was "modernism"; in the 1980s it was "secular humanism." Controversies over the theory of evolution occupied much of the attention of Fundamentalists in both periods. Similarly, in the early period Fundamentalism's success was largely related to the media exposure it gained by its entrance into the political arena in the struggle against evolution; in the 1980s, the media hype as a consequence of Fundamentalism's political involvements has provided the movement with much exposure and gained it some support.

In addition to a recognition of the influential role the media has played in solidifying the Fundamentalist (and perhaps the Evangelical) coalition, there is another lesson in this comparison of the two acts of the Fundamentalist success story. One wonders if a secret of Fundamentalism in these two decades has been that when the old-time religion is yoked with a concern to "Christianize" the structures of American society it seems to tap into some of the deepest—and for some the most attractive—roots of the American social psyche. In short, at those strategic points in history where the Fundamentalist movement and its spiritual heirs succeed, could it be because they have been the sole modern bearer of the American Puritan heritage? Fundamentalism now seems to be fulfilling these conditions.

Chapter 5

The Emergence of
the Evangelical Movement

Despite the organic interpenetration of the Evangelical movement and Fundamentalism, they are not identical. The Evangelical movement, as it is understood by most people in the 1980s, actually did not emerge until the 1940s. To be sure, it was and is a movement devoted to the Gospel *(evangelium)* as much as its Fundamentalist forebears. Also the original (and, to a large extent, present) North American leaders of the movement had their roots and education in one of the church traditions of Fundamentalism. But, as its title *Evangelical* connotes, it is a movement which intends a more constructive and less defensive separatist stance than the posture connoted by the term *Fundamentalist*. Evangelicals do not see themselves as defenders of the fundamentals of faith *over against* culture. Rather, in face of theological liberalism and cultural decay, they intend to maintain the fundamental gospel principles while engaging modern society in order to influence and transform it.

The separatist tendencies of Fundamentalism are largely repudiated by the Evangelical movement. The man usually given credit for organizing the movement, Harold Ockenga (1905–1985), proposed that the task of Evangelicals should be to "infiltrate rather than separate" from their churches.[1] Although in the broad sense the movement includes Fundamentalism and its organizations, it must be conceded that tensions between these two branches of Christianity are often quite apparent. Thus the eminent Conservative Evangelical Baptist theologian, Carl Henry, and Harold Ockenga have voiced criticism of Fundamentalism. These are not isolated instances. The critique of Evangelicals by Fundamentalists is equally harsh, as one observes in the official statements of some Fundamentalist organizations.[2]

Nor are these tensions peculiar to the North American scene. One observes this sort of mutual critique in Australia and in West Germany of Fundamentalists by Evangelicals. Some, for example, Jerry Falwell, a self-proclaimed Fundamentalist, are calling for an end to these tensions. And a few observers even have speculated about the possibilities of a coalition between the more "open" Fundamentalists and certain segments of the Evangelical movement.[3]

In any case, it is important to keep in mind the distinction between Evangelicals and Fundamentalists so that one not too quickly dismiss the Evangelical movement with unfair characterizations which only apply to Fundamentalism. Evangelicals are anything but simple, unsophisticated Biblicists. (We already have seen that such a charge is also not easily substantiated with respect to the heritage of Fundamentalism.) Consequently, we shall observe this distinction in this book. The focus will be upon the Evangelical movement as distinct from those persons or institutions claiming to be Fundamentalists. From this point on, as far as possible, our interest will focus on those persons or institutions explicitly identifying themselves with the Evangelical movement. Fundamentalists and their organizations will be considered alongside of Evangelicals, but always with some attention paid to their differences. Conclusions we draw about the Evangelical movement will be warranted solely on the basis of positions taken by self-proclaimed Evangelicals.

On the other hand, the commonalities between Evangelicalism and Fundamentalism—common concerns beyond the historical indebtedness of the Evangelical movement to the Fundamentalist heritage—cannot be overlooked. Both share a dogged desire to preserve the old-time religion in face of a somewhat hostile theological and cultural situation; in that regard both are reactionary movements. They also share common theological commitments. They differ principally with respect to attitudes concerning how best to present the fundamentals of the faith attractively to the world. This commitment on the part of the Evangelical movement to an attractive presentation of the fundamentals is perhaps nowhere more clearly seen than in the emergence of the movement and in its landmark event, the establishment of the National Association of Evangelicals in 1942.

Formation of the major Evangelical institutions

We already have noted the marked growth and upward social mobility of much of the Fundamentalist movement in the years between

1925 and the early 1940s. Late in this period, with the waning of the earlier cooperative agencies of Fundamentalism, a desire for new agencies of cooperation which might help stimulate a national revival began to emerge, particularly among some of the younger, better educated leaders of the movement.

One of the visionaries for such unity was a New England theological conservative, J. Elwin Wright (1896–1966). Sensing the need for a conservative coalition, already in 1929 he founded the New England Fellowship. This became his base of operations in the push toward a larger national coalition. Thus, from 1939 to 1941 Wright spent time touring the United States, romancing conservatives with the idea of a coalition. He was supported in this work of organization by Ockenga, who was a fellow member of the New England Fellowship.

At the same time, more militant Fundamentalists were trying to organize a national coalition of their own. The man at the forefront of these efforts was a committed separatist, Carl McIntire. In fact, since leaving the Presbyterian Church in the U.S.A. along with Machen and helping to form what is today The Orthodox Presbyterian Church, McIntire had seceded from the latter body and formed yet another church, the Bible Presbyterian Church. McIntire's interest in forming a national coalition was also inspired by his separatist orientation. He and his colleagues were quite concerned about the coalition of "liberal churches" embodied in the United States' Federal Council of Churches (FCC). Therefore in 1941 they formed the American Council of Christian Churches (ACC). Its primary stated purpose was to oppose the FCC.[4] Thus the ACC was clearly conceived as a separatist organization defining its purpose in negative terms.

At this stage, Wright's and Ockenga's nascent group faced a problem. If they did not join McIntire's group but proceeded to form their own organization, the old conservative, Fundamentalist coalition would be shattered. Yet the negativism of the ACC clearly conflicted with their own vision of the conservative cause. And so, in that same year they elected not to join forces with McIntire, on grounds that a new association of conservatives should be organized for positive purposes, not just for purposes of establishing a counterorganization to the FCC. In many ways this desire to present the old fundamentals of the faith in a positive, not merely defensive way was to set the agenda and rationale for the emergence of Evangelicalism out of its original Fundamentalist heritage. During the next year, a national conference of American theological conservatives from a broad constituency of Fundamentalism created the National Association of Evangelicals. A crucial decision made at this time was to invite Pentecostals to participate in the organization.[5] This represented a break with Fundamentalism, which never formally had included Pentecostals in its coalition. However, the NAE's inclusion of this segment of conservative Christianity was only possible because of the increasing influence Fundamentalism was having on these and the Holiness churches.

The decision to use the term *Evangelical* in the title of the new organization rather than *Fundamentalist* represented a deliberate step. Most observers give credit for the new designation to Harold Ockenga. At least he has claimed the credit for it himself. He designated the group of conservatives organizing around him as "New Evangelicals." This change in designation for the group indicated its perceived break from Fundamentalism in several ways. These included a concern that, in its period of retreat, Fundamentalism had been guilty of abdicating leadership in the area of social ethics, and also guilty of abdicating intellectual questions concerning science and history. This part of the Fundamentalist heritage must be disowned by the New Evangelicals, he urged. Ockenga's plea was that intellectual questions about Christianity should be dealt with in the framework of modern learning and that there should be liberty in minor areas. This commitment amounted to an affirmation of intellectual freedom in theological research and biblical studies, a commitment explicitly affirmed later by some of his colleagues. These commitments in turn had the practical consequences of a rejection by Ockenga and his colleagues of the most negative elements of Fundamentalist separatism in favor of a strategy of "infiltrating" the denominations and secular culture with the values and beliefs of the old-time religion.[6]

One consequence of this new Evangelical strategy of infiltration rather than separation was that the old Fundamentalist stridency was disowned. Thus one of the first great New Evangelical theologians, Edward John Carnell (1919–1967), urged that the movement should be marked by tolerance and forgiveness towards views which differ from one's own.[7] Another implication was that it guaranteed that the Evangelical movement would never become a well-defined movement whose outer boundaries could easily be delineated. Much like its forefather, Fundamentalism, it would be a somewhat loose, amorphous interdenominational movement, principally held together by common parachurch agencies and associated educational institutions. Also this strategy would inevitably open the new movement to ecumenical endeavors.

The intellectual openness, social concern, and irenic spirit of the new movement's program as sketched by Ockenga further alienated it from those retaining the Fundamentalist label. (There are intriguing personal dynamics in this rejection of Fundamentalism and Ockenga's and his colleagues' related rejection of uniting the emerging NAE with McIntire's version of Fundamentalism. Ockenga and McIntire previously had had a number of personal ties. They were part of the same class at Princeton Seminary, had left the seminary with their teacher Machen, and so were part of the first class at the newly formed Westminster Seminary. McIntire even claims that he was invited to serve as head usher at Ockenga's wedding.)[8] To be sure, the new Evangelical movement was quite explicit in its desire not to forfeit the fundamental theological commitments of Fundamentalism, even though the new movement's openness in the area of academic inquiry did lead many of its early representatives largely to reject characteristic Fundamentalist conceptions like dispensationalism and premillennialism. In fact, some have suggested that Fundamentalists and Evangelicals ultimately can be distinguished only on the basis of their respective positions on these issues, Fundamentalists embracing them and Evangelicals rejecting them as binding alternatives.

Despite differences on these issues, the new movement understood itself to be appropriating the best of the Fundamentalist heritage and, in turn, to be putting this in touch with the older, antebellum Protestant tradition of "American Evangelicalism." Given this commitment, it is hardly surprising that in the course of the next decades Ockenga's designation of the new movement as "New or Neo-Evangelical" was abbreviated simply to "Evangelical." This new designation connotes the self-understanding of many Evangelicals, that they represent a Christian heritage rooted in antebellum American Evangelical Protestantism, a heritage itself rooted in the Evangelical/Protestant traditions of the Reformation. Thus today we speak of this branch of conservative Christianity simply as the Evangelical movement.[9] The way in which this group of theological conservatives has so thoroughly succeeded in appropriating the title "Evangelical" for themselves, so that at least in North America it is only they and not the mainline Protestant churches who are regarded as "evangelical" in the mind of the public, indicates the profound impact of this new coalition. Is its success in this matter a function of its skillful handling of the media or a consequence of the possibility that it alone truly preserves the evangelical heritage of the Reformation?

In some respects the National Association of Evangelicals is what created the Evangelical Movement as we know it today. After the initial controversies about its formation, the NAE soon developed into a major symbol of the resurgence of the conservatives who found the new "Evangelical spirit" congenial. By 1947 it represented 30 denominations totaling 1,300,000 members, most of which had been influenced by, if not actually part of, the old Fundamentalist coalition. (This fact again indicates the degree to which the contemporary Evangelical movement is an heir to the Fundamentalist heritage.) The NAE spawned several Evangelical parachurch organs like the National Religious Broadcasters and the Evangelical Foreign Missionary Association. These organizations had the effect of providing the new Evangelicals with fresh confidence. While during the era of the Fundamentalist retreat they often had felt isolated from the broader American society and from each other, now they had tangible evidence that they were not so isolated and weak as they had supposed.

This new confidence manifested itself and received further encouragement in several other ways in the 1940s. Thus in 1947 the flagship educational institution of the new movement, Fuller Theological Seminary in Pasadena, California, was founded. The primary movers in its development were Ockenga and the famous radio evangelist Charles Fuller. Their intention was to establish an educational institution of the highest academic caliber for the new Evangelical movement. Largely through Fuller's funding, they succeeded in assembling a fine faculty of persons who would mature to become the first generation of important Evangelical scholars, namely, E. J. Carnell, Carl Henry (later the founding editor of the most important Evangelical periodical, *Christianity Today*, and probably today's most influential Evangelical theologian), and Harold Lindsell (Henry's successor at *Christianity Today*). Fuller remains perhaps the most influential and quality seminary in the Evangelical orbit. It has been influenced throughout its history by some of the more theologically liberal elements of the Evangelical movement.

Another high point in Evangelicalism's development in this period was the foundation and astonishing success of the parachurch organization, Youth for Christ. This organization influenced about 1,000,000 young people in the mid-1940s through its various youth rallies. Although the impact of the organization's still impressive ministry has not perhaps been as stunning in recent years, many of the young people whom it did influence grew to carry on its work through the founding of other Evangelical agencies. One of its young traveling evangelists went on to accomplish great things and in so doing provided the Evangelical movement with a degree of visibility and cohesion that is almost unthinkable without him. This former Youth for Christ evangelist is none other than Billy Graham.

From Billy Graham to the present

Billy Graham's career actually had its turning point in 1949 during a revival in Los Angeles. Several prominent personalities were converted during the crusade. Two of his contacts in this crusade were a Quaker couple whose son was a senator from California, Richard Nixon; later that year, Graham would meet him. With much media exposure to that event, Graham's career of extensive contacts with American politicians would be launched. But the turning point in the crusade, the event which is said to have "really made it happen" for the evangelist, was a purported decision by William Randolf Hearst, head of the Hearst newspaper syndicate, concerning coverage of the Los Angeles crusade. Based on his previous positive impressions of Graham, he is said to have instructed his staff to "puff Graham." Thus the crusade and Graham received nationwide media exposure. The evangelist's career was made![10] Through him and his identification with the new Evangelical movement, this segment of conservative Christianity received a new, more desirable image in the media and in popular consensus.

Billy Graham was also very instrumental in the founding of the other chief symbol (in addition to himself, the NAE, and Fuller Seminary) of today's "Evangelical establishment," the periodical *Christianity Today*. Begun in 1956 with Carl Henry as its first editor, the magazine's concept and initial support came from the Graham organization. The magazine has played quite an important role in binding together the emerging Evangelical coalition.

Despite his great and international impact, Billy Graham also unwittingly has been a further issue dividing the Evangelical movement and Fundamentalism. The problem largely has centered on his "inclusive" approach to evangelism (his strategy of inviting the participation of non-Fundamentalist Christians, even of liberals, in his crusades). Thus, after his famous 1957 New York City crusade in which this inclusive approach was programmatically employed, Fundamentalism rejected him. The issue at stake for the Fundamentalists was that by his inclusive approach Graham had rejected their commitment to separatism (to avoiding spiritual fellowship with those not born again).

This scenario suggests that the crucial, perhaps the only substantive issue dividing Evangelicals and Fundamentalists may be their different positions on the question of separatism. (To be sure, differences on this issue lead to differences between the movements with regard to matters of style, relative militancy, and ethos.) To the degree that this issue comes to noteworthy expression in the ministry of Billy Graham one could perhaps distinguish Fundamentalists from Evangelicals on the basis of what one thinks of Graham—Evangelicals support him; Fundamentalists largely reject him.[11] Indeed, it might not be totally inappropriate to identify the contemporary Evangelical movement in reference to the ministry of Billy Graham, to say that Evangelicals "are those who are connected with organizations founded by Billy Graham or which he serves as a trustee."[12] (In addition to his work in founding and serving as Chairman of the Board of *Christianity Today* as well as his own status as a central symbol for Evangelicals, he has full rights of a member of Fuller Seminary's Board of Trustees. As we shall note, a few of his international crusades also have stimulated the development of the Evangelical movement in some nations outside of North America.)

Thanks to Graham and the general religious revival of the 1950s, the Evangelical movement enjoyed growth and a new status in the first quarter-century after World War II. But in that period and perhaps even until the mid-1980s it was still largely identified by the media and in the minds of the general public with Fundamentalism. Thus it was hardly less the object of scorn than were its Fundamentalist brethren.

This continued identification of these two movements in the mind of the public is hardly surprising. In addition to sharing a common heritage and maintaining a conservative Christian subculture organized around organizations and persons which were formerly associated with Fundamentalism, the new Evangelical movement was also linked by a common theological logic which was more or less similar to what held the Fundamentalist coalition together. Recall that the Fundamentalist movement seems largely held together by its common polemical front against the inroads of secularism and theological modernism, as well as by the common emphasis on sanctification or the regenerate life-style. As the old Fundamentalist-founded organizations of Evangelicalism share these concerns, one finds a similar emphasis on being born again and on sanctification in the revivalism of Graham as well as in the faith statements of the NAE (4) and Fuller Seminary (7). Also, the role of polemics against perceived social decay and liberal theology—a factor which unites Evangelicals—is quite evident in some resolutions of the NAE.[13]

Some developments in the 1960s and 1970s helped further to enhance the image of Evangelicalism among the American public, to distance it from certain negative dimensions associated with Fundamentalism. Among these factors, which were also responsible for the increased international attention given the movement, were the continued positive image of Billy Graham and his contacts with influential politicians, the emergence of the Jesus People movement ("Jesus freaks"), as well as the prominence of various self-proclaimed Evangelicals like Charles Colson of Watergate infamy, Anita Bryant, and, of course, the new "Mr. Evangelical," Jimmy Carter. The image of the movement was also enhanced by the emergence of the charismatic movement (which, to the degree it has identified itself with the Evangelical movement, has provided Evangelicalism with a base in the mainline churches), favorable media coverage of several Evangelical evangelism (Key '73) and youth events, growth in religious broadcasting by various evangelicals, as well as the marked growth of Evangelical churches and parachurch agencies, which we already have noted. Also to be considered is the upward social mobility in this period of many Evangelicals. Many have risen out of the largely working-class cultural ghetto of Fundamentalism. They have joined the ranks of mainstream American society. They may be the opinion-maker's or the reporters' neighbors. Although its image has been somewhat scarred by several controversies in the late 1980s concerning certain prominent Evangelical media personalities, Evangelicalism has become respectable.

To some extent, this respectability may have been bought at a price—at least this is what some analysts are saying. Partly as a consequence of their accommodation to existing cultural standards as befitting the new place many Evangelicals hold in society, one can identify in recent years a certain openness with respect to life-style standards, politics, and theological orientation, even with regard to biblical inerrancy.[14] Among some Evangelicals, notably led by former *Christianity Today* editor Harold Lindsell, there has been a backlash against this openness. Thus, in his purported exposé of contemporary Evangelicalism, entitled *The Battle for the Bible* (Zondervan, 1976), Lindsell sent shockwaves throughout the whole Evangelical community, seriously called its unity into question, by listing a whole flock of notable Evangelicals who were said to have compromised the core Evangelical commitment to biblical inerrancy. His concern to check any further erosion of this commitment within the Evangelical movement found institutional expression, particularly in the United States, when a number of like-minded prominent Evangelicals organized the International Council on Biblical Inerrancy. Its work in highlighting the importance of safeguarding the doctrine of biblical inerrancy has helped ensure that the issues raised by Lindsell are still very much on the Evangelical agenda.

On the other hand, the apparent breakdown of consensus among Evangelicals at least since the mid-60s has also been counterbalanced in several ways. In the United States, largely as a result of their internal controversies, two theologically conservative mainline churches, the Southern Baptist Convention and The Lutheran Church–Missouri Synod, have been driven more and more into the Evangelical orbit. The same might be said about certain theological conservatives in the Black churches, as well as in some mainline denominations where Evangelical lobbies have been organized. Also outside North America this has been a period of growing awareness of an Evangelical consciousness and militancy on the part of theological conservatives. Through the work of Billy Graham and other parachurch organizations, previous international relationships between the North American Evangelical (Fundamentalist) community and these European and Third World conservatives have been strengthened. At least among North American Evangelicals, a sense of a worldwide Evangelical community has been in the process of formation.

Chapter 6

The Evangelical Movement Outside North America

The emergence of contemporary Evangelicalism in the rest of the world clearly has been indebted to the North American situation we have been describing. Yet the Evangelical movement in Europe and the Third World has not been so directly dependent on Fundamentalism as was the situation in the United States. Conservative Evangelicals in these nations had no indigenous Fundamentalism as a spiritual forebear. Nevertheless, the North American impact on these theological conservatives and the relative novelty of the Evangelical movement in their nations is readily apparent. Indeed, this fact is even apparent linguistically in German-speaking lands, where a new word, *evangelikal,* has been coined to refer to theological conservatives identifying with the Conservative Evangelical movement. (*Evangelisch* denotes "Protestant," more specifically "Lutheran.")

In a number of respects, the Evangelical movement is a post–World War II phenomenon in Europe and the Third World. In Germany the impetus for the eventual founding of several Evangelical parachurch organizations associated with what is called the *Bekenntnisbewegung* (confessing movement) developed largely in reaction to two distressing circumstances: (1) the emergence of new pluralistic social mores; and (2) the theological controversy generated by the work of German New Testament scholar Rudolf Bultmann and his program of "demythologization" (the idea that the gospel as presented in Scripture is framed by a mythological worldview and demands that we reconceptualize its deeper truth in terms of our modern worldview). One such organization, the Ludwig-Hofacker-Vereinigung, a German Evangelical lobby also related to Pietism, was explicitly organized on account of these two concerns.[1]

Nevertheless, the North American Evangelical influence is readily apparent in the German Evangelical community and elsewhere in Europe. Several students of the European community have noted the great impact of Billy Graham's 1960 Berlin crusade (and subsequent ones), his 1954 and 1955 crusades on the British Isles, and his Swiss crusades of the same era. They have suggested that to a great extent the Evangelical movement in these nations was given its impetus by these events. (It is true that Evangelicals were well organized about a century and one-half earlier than that in Great Britain and had a distinct, if not always indigenous theological tradition of their own. But Graham's work and that of the American Fundamentalist Donald Grey Barnhouse helped generate a period of mass conversions and also gained much publicity, albeit not all favorable, for British Evangelicals.) Billy Graham has had further impact on the Evangelical communities in these and in other nations through his sponsorship of the 1974 International Congress on World Evangelization held in Lausanne. He also participated in a visible way in the 1966 World Congress on Evangelism held in Berlin, a conference sponsored by *Christianity Today,* and chaired by its editor at that time, Carl Henry. These conferences are often regarded as having helpfully served further to organize the Evangelical movement in German-speaking lands. In fact, the Lausanne Congress inspired the formation of the Lausanne Committee for World Evangelization, an organization whose support by theological conservatives in several European nations, notably Scandinavia, led to their identification with the Evangelical movement.[2]

Not just in these ways has the international influence of the North American Evangelical community been felt. The burgeoning Evangelical publishing industry is making an international impact. Thus at least one important German Lutheran Evangelical, Gerhard Maier, notes the significant contribution translations of North American Evangelical literature have been making to the movement in his country. Likewise, American literature is having an impact on the Brazilian Evangelical community.[3]

The international influence of American Evangelicalism is apparent in that many of the international Evangelical evangelism organizations working outside North America, organizations like Campus Crusade for Christ, The Navigators, and Inter-Varsity Christian Fellowship, were either founded in the United States or are heavily dependent on American Evangelicalism for support. Also a number of churches in Asia, Africa, and Europe associated with the Evangelical movement were initiated by North American missionaries or are today heavily supported by North American Evangelical churches. Baptist churches in France and Eastern Europe as well as Pentecostal churches in continental Europe and in Brazil are examples of this kind of American influence on the international Evangelical community. There is even an indication of North American Evangelical-Fundamentalist influence on theological conservatives in Russia; one can document the influence of both Dwight Moody and dispensationalism on the USSR's All Union Council of Evangelical Christians-Baptists. Additionally, the influence of the charismatic movement on a number of mainline churches in Europe is largely the result of original contacts in Europe by American charismatics like Dennis Bennett and the Lutheran charismatic leader Larry Christenson.[4]

One would perhaps not be able to say that Evangelicals in Europe or the Third World have enjoyed the kind of impact on their societies or drawn the attention of the mainline churches in their countries that American Evangelicals have enjoyed in this period. For various reasons they are removed from the centers of power in their nations or their churches, either because the churches they control are small free churches with little social impact or because they belong to mainline churches whose leaders and theologians give them no more sympathetic hearing than their American counterparts receive. Thus these Evangelicals are at times recipients of the same kind of scorn North American Evangelicals and Fundamentalists still encounter. However, because in Western Europe the mainline churches exert so much social influence and in the East and Third World there is no chance for any Christians to exert strong influence, Evangelicals in these nations are perhaps less likely in the foreseeable future to gain the kind of respectability their North American counterparts enjoy. (Granted, Evangelicals in Russia and Pentecostals in Brazil certainly enjoy excellent reputations as workers in their countries as a consequence of the high moral standards which their Evangelical version of Christianity imposes on them.[5] Yet their nations' present political structures still do not make it possible for them to make an impact on their societies such as North American Evangelicals have.) Moreover, European and Third World Evangelicals are neither as well organized nor as conscious of their identity as Evangelicals as are their counterparts in the United States.

Of course, there are important exceptions to this pattern. In Latin America, Pentecostal churches, some of which are associated with the Evangelical movement, are experiencing phenomenal growth. Today there are large segments of Pentecostals throughout the Third World. In some Latin American nations, they comprise as much as 10% of the total population. Anglican Evangelicals nearly always have represented a significant lobby inside the Church of England. And in West Germany Evangelical lobbies, especially those associated with the Be-kenntnisbewegung, are forcing many mainline churches to increased sensitivity to the political and theological issues they raise.

Indeed, the German situation has been characterized by the formation of separate Evangelical organizations (such as Evangelical youth organizations) which parallel those of the mainline churches, a move that is creating much controversy within the German churches as some observers fear it is a first step towards a schism within these churches. And the German Evangelical Alliance even has undertaken lobbying efforts with the West German government on behalf of largely conservative Evangelical political aims. (We already have noted the particular impact of Evangelicals on the Evangelical Lutheran Church in Württemberg, a church whose heritage is deeply embedded and controlled by Pietism.) Thus in West Germany and in Scandinavia a significant number of conservative Lutherans, mainly those influenced by Pietism, identify themselves with the Evangelical movement. And such participation by North American Lutherans is virtually unknown, or at least very minimal.

International tensions

Despite these hopeful signs, there are clearly some internal problems in the international Evangelical movement. A few of them seem related to the predominance of North American Evangelicalism on the movement. Thus in a number of geographical regions not all or not even a majority of the theological conservatives identify themselves with the Evangelical movement.

In Eastern Europe, free churches, especially the Baptist churches, are quite theologically conservative. Some of their members even may consider themselves to be Evangelicals. Yet they largely decline to identify themselves with the movement. In large part, their theological conservatism is a function of the kind of precritical, pre-Enlightenment mode of thinking which still prevails in some of these churches—a conservatism not unlike American Evangelicalism prior to the Civil War. Not having fully confronted the challenges of the Enlightenment, they have no need to join a "post-Fundamentalist Evangelical movement" fighting the evils of modern thought and theological liberalism. The same dynamic may also pertain in many conservative churches in the Third World.[6]

Another problem raised for these churches as well as some in Western

Europe is that sometimes North American missionaries sent by Evangelical parachurch organizations do their work independently of these churches. This creates a dynamic whereby the conservative churches are pitted against "American Evangelicalism." In such a situation the indigenous conservatives are surely not about to identify themselves with such an "American" phenomenon as the Evangelical movement.

The perception of the Evangelical movement as a largely North American phenomenon tends to interfere with European theological conservatives' identifying with the movement, even when these conservatives are otherwise cooperating well with Evangelicals. Given the sociopolitical dynamics in these nations, which entail not allowing the United States to dictate the cultural agenda, it becomes essential to the credibility of theological conservatives that they in some way disassociate themselves from the North American overtones which the Evangelical movement carries with it. Thus they either must reject the label or, as a number of European Baptists do, go to some extremes to indigenize Evangelicalism.[7]

There are also problems of apparent theological substance, perceived as having been introduced by North American influence on Evangelicalism, which preclude a number of conservatives from identifying with the movement. Thus, several distinguished Latin American Evangelicals have blamed North American Evangelical missionaries for polarizing Protestant churches in their region. These missionaries are alleged to have done this by introducing issues pertinent only to the distinctively North America Fundamentalist-Modernist controversy.

The charge that Evangelicalism has exported North American cultural values into Third World Evangelical communities has been made by other Third World Evangelicals. Some, like René Padilla, are concerned that this form of Evangelicalism is faulty insofar as it has deprived Third World Evangelicals of a strong, dynamic social ethic. As we shall see, this debate concerning an adequate Evangelical social ethic is not simply carried on along regional lines within the Evangelical movement. It is a hotly debated issue in all segments of the movement, even among North American Evangelicals themselves.[8]

Links between the international Evangelical community and North American Evangelicalism (in this case Fundamentalism) leading to distasteful ethical and ecclesiological consequences are also evident in Ireland. Thus Ian Paisley, a principal Protestant agitator against Roman Catholics in Northern Ireland, was educated by American Fundamentalists and is recognized as a brother by them. It seems to have been precisely the influence of this kind of Fundamentalism with its separatist orientation which provided the impetus for the 1978 decision of the Presbyterian Church in Ireland to suspend its membership in the WCC.[9]

In Europe and perhaps elsewhere two other reasons are sometimes cited by theological conservatives when accounting for their failure to identify with the Evangelical movement. Church presidents or highly placed officials in quite theologically conservative churches like the Bund Evangelisch-Freikirchlicher Gemeinden in der DDR (East German Baptists), and the Evangelisch-methodistische Kirche (German, Swiss, and French Methodists) reject an unambiguous identification as Evangelicals on grounds of the movement's purported polemical and strident tone. Representatives of these churches as well as the Kirchliche Sammlung um Bibel und Bekenntnis (a West German conservative Lutheran lobby) and the Kyrklig Förnyelse (Swedish High-Church Movement) also reject identification with the Evangelical movement, partly on grounds of their discomfort with the idea of affirming a "Fundamentalist view of Scripture."[10] In these cases an implicit critique of North American influence on the Evangelical movement could be involved. At any rate, it is evident that a number of European theological conservatives who reject the title "Evangelical" for themselves are not quite clear about the distinction between Evangelicalism and Fundamentalism.

The data also show that the Evangelical community outside North America is generally more uncomfortable than their North American counterparts with a "Fundamentalist view of Scripture," perhaps not as inclined to make biblical inerrancy the cutting-edge issue for Evangelical identity. One sees this clearly in the Brazilian situation and elsewhere in the Third World. Several observers have agreed on this point, and it is reflected in a 1982 statement by Third World Evangelical theologians, *The Seoul Declaration* (3), which speaks only of the infallibility of God's Word, not the infallibility of Scripture. In Europe the same de-emphasis on biblical inerrancy is evident in the faith statements of several Evangelical organizations. The Internationale Konferenz Bekennender Gemeinschaften (International Conference of Confessing Communities), with its largely German origins, speaks only of the absolute authority of God's Word "as deposited in Scripture" (2a). The Evangelical Alliance in Great Britain, the Church of England Evangelical Council (6), and the Deutsche Evangelische Allianz in West Germany speak only of the inspiration of Scripture and affirm or at least imply its "entire trustworthiness." The Alliance Evangélique Française does affirm the infallibility of God's Word (and presumably

Scripture), but it only acknowledges the Bible's authority in matters of faith and life.[11]

Despite these obvious and prominent instances of a de-emphasis on biblical inerrancy, one finds a number of indications that many Evangelicals outside of North America do embrace the concept of inerrancy or at least insist upon remaining in dialogue with it. In Brazil at least two of the largest Pentecostal churches affirm the infallibility of Scripture. Such an affirmation appears in the Statement of Faith of the Association of Evangelicals of Africa and Madagascar (1) (albeit an infallibility in "matters of faith and conduct"), the Fédération Evangélique de France, and Det Norske Misjonsforbund (Mission Covenant Church of Norway), not to mention some important European Evangelical theologians.[12] It is true that some of these statements and individuals restrict the Bible's infallibility only to matters of faith and life. But at least one sees indications that Evangelicals from these continents are concerned to remain "in dialogue with" concepts like biblical infallibility or inerrancy. Even statements of the British Evangelical Alliance and the Deutsche Evangelische Allianz, in speaking of the "entire trustworthiness" of the Bible, appear to be in dialogue with a concept of the Bible's plenary inspiration (the very concept which the eminent Evangelical theologian Carl Henry seems to have identified as the cutting-edge issue of Evangelical identity).[13]

Thus it appears that there is only a de-emphasis of the concepts of biblical inerrancy/infallibility among Evangelicals outside North America, not an overall outright rejection of these concepts. Perhaps the difference in emphasis with North American Evangelicals is related to the different prevailing epistemologies on each continent. North America, dominated in the antebellum period by Scottish common sense realist philosophy, quite logically nurtured an Evangelical community which emphasized biblical inerrancy. As we noted, this sort of philosophical orientation with its stress on the reliability of perception logically entailed the idea that Scripture be inerrantly reliable. By contrast, the prevailing cultural influence on Conservative Evangelicalism in much of Europe and the Third World (through the work of missionaries) was classical Pietism, a movement which, as we shall note, was never particularly concerned to assert theories of biblical inspiration.[14]

At any rate, the differences between the North American Evangelical movement and Evangelicals in the rest of the world have not developed into an outright break. That all sides seem willing at least to remain in dialogue with the concept of biblical inerrancy/infallibility seems evident insofar as the two leading international Evangelical cooperative agencies, the World Evangelical Fellowship and the Lausanne Committee for World Evangelization (2), both affirm in some form the inerrancy/infallibility concepts in their statements of faith. Insofar as Evangelicals from all over the world belong to these organizations, can one not conclude that the Evangelical movement may at least be characterized by a dialogue with, if not an affirmation of biblical inerrancy?

One can identify other tensions within the international Evangelical movement, tensions not directly related to North American influences but rooted in the pre-Billy Graham heritage of the movement. Just as Pentecostals were integrated into the North American Evangelical movement only under extraordinary circumstances and were never really accepted by the Fundamentalist movement, so in other parts of the world, particularly in German-speaking lands, Pentecostals largely have not been embraced or welcomed in the Evangelical movement. This sentiment is rooted in the so-called *Berlin Declaration* (1[b]) of 1909, a statement issued by the theologically conservative Gemeinschaftsbewegung. The statement condemned the Pentecostal movement as the work of the nether world *(von unten)*, not a work of God. Today this attitude manifests itself in similar rejections of the charismatic movement by the Konferenz Bekennender Gemeinschaften. One finds a critique of speaking in tongues in the Fédération Evangélique de France's "Conditions of Admission." One can also identify tensions among Pentecostals and other Evangelicals in Russia and in Latin America (at least in Brazil).[15]

Yet the integration of Pentecostals and charismatics into the Evangelical movement is not exclusively limited to North America. In addition to the increased levels of cooperation between Evangelicals and Pentecostal churches in Brazil, Pentecostals are joined with Baptists and other Evangelically oriented theological conservatives in "free church" unions in both East Germany and the U.S.S.R. Also, the charismatic movement has had its impact in Europe not just in the mainline churches but also on the Evangelical movement. For example, charismatics cooperate and identify with the Evangelische Alliantie Nederland (Evangelical Alliance in the Netherlands) and Pentecostals likewise participate in the Swiss Evangelical Alliance.[16]

Another area of apparent tension in the Evangelical movement is that which exists between it and theologically conservative Lutherans who would otherwise seem to be of the same theological genre and ethos as Evangelicals. In North America one thinks of The Lutheran Church–Missouri Synod and like-minded churches such as the Wisconsin Evangelical Lutheran Synod which, though theologically conservative, avoid identification with the Evangelical movement. The same is also true of the LCMS-related churches like the Selbständige Evangelisch-Lutherische Kirche (Free Lutheran Church) in Germany. Some trepidation in identifying with the Evangelical movement also exists, as we have noted, among certain Lutheran participants in the Bekenntnisbewegung in Germany and among some theologically conservative Lutherans in Scandinavia. The factors in their discomfort with identifying themselves as part of the Evangelical movement will be elaborated at length subsequently. We may note here that their discomfort pertains to the lack of a distinct Lutheran theological profile in the Evangelical movement.[17]

Nevertheless, a number of missionary societies in Scandinavia, largely those indebted to the heritage of Pietism, do in fact identify with the Evangelical movement in virtue of their cooperation with the movement's Lausanne Committee for World Evangelization. Other Lutherans in Germany associated with certain organizations related to the Bekenntnisbewegung, especially those emerging from pietist roots (like the Ludwig-Hofacker-Vereinigung) and those of a transconfessional (Lutheran, Reformed, United) group called the Bekenntnisbewegung "kein anderes Evangelium" ("No Other Gospel"), identify themselves with the Evangelical movement. And even those theologically conservative German Lutheran groups like the Free Lutheran Church and the Kirchliche Sammlung um Bibel und Bekenntnis, which do not identify with the Evangelical movement, still continue to cooperate with it.[18]

A third additional area of tension within the Evangelical movement is the one between the Bekenntnisbewegung (Evangelicals with a more confessionally conscious, Protestant Orthodox theological orientation) and pietist Evangelicals in Germany. Some pietists tend to regard the Bekenntnisbewegung as not truly Evangelical, due to its polemical orientation and the undue confidence some of its members place in the conferral of grace by the sacraments.[19] This sort of controversy is also mounted from the side of Protestant Orthodoxy against Pietism and has North American manifestations.[20]

Despite these tensions, the various segments of the European and international Evangelical movement somehow hold together. We can begin to see how this is possible in Europe by examining the pre–Billy Graham influences on the Evangelical movement in Europe. And insofar as the religious situation on that continent shaped the Asian,

African, and American situations, such an examination provides further clues for understanding how the Evangelical movement holds together on these other continents.

European roots

In a certain sense, the Evangelical movement in Europe is rooted in pre-20th century, perhaps even pre-modern, European Christianity, not at all dependent on the American scene. No history of the Evangelical movement can ignore the founding of an international organization of Evangelicals in 1846, the Evangelical Alliance (the predecessor body of the present-day World Evangelical Fellowship). Original leaders in this movement were not Americans, but Scotch Presbyterians, English Evangelicals, and those from Germany and Switzerland. This organization itself inspired the emergence of several world mission organizations like the World Christian Student Association. In so doing, the Evangelical Alliance helped create a climate which made possible the establishment of various organizations which became predecessors of the World Council of Churches. The modern ecumenical movement would have been unthinkable apart from the contribution of these early European Evangelicals, a fact that is quite ironic, given present Evangelical critiques of the ecumenical movement.

Despite the diversity of its components (including Presbyterians, Church of England Evangelicals, pietists in the folk churches, and pietists belonging to free churches) the Evangelical Alliance was able to form a coalition. Understanding the dynamics of its formation is most helpful for understanding the nature of the modern Evangelical coalition in Europe. The basis of the original coalition was not unlike the factors which later made possible the Fundamentalist coalition in the United States and eventually the Evangelical movement. One of its prime objectives was stated to be "the defense of faith against movements challenging it." These included Enlightenment philosophical developments like Deism, modernist theology, and Roman Catholicism (not least as it was manifested in the Oxford Movement, a High Church, Catholicizing movement which was emerging at this time inside the Church of England). (It has even been suggested that antebellum American Evangelicals were finally attracted to the Alliance as a way of marshaling anti-Roman Catholic, nativist sentiments which were already emerging as a result of immigration patterns.)[21]

To be sure, the Alliance's collective reaction to these challenges was milder than the Fundamentalist reaction in North America. Nonetheless, it was a common polemic against common foes which brought the various segments of the Alliance together, just as the various components of Fundamentalism in North America were brought together by opposition to a common foe. And just as components of Fundamentalism and the North American Evangelical movement seem to share a common theological logic, a common overriding concern with regeneration and sanctification, so this appears to be the central emphasis of many of the segments which constituted the old Evangelical Alliance (the Evangelical coalition in Europe).[22]

This thesis tends to be borne out almost immediately when one recognizes that some of the prime movers in the formation of the Alliance were members of the Free Church of Scotland. As we have noted in relation to Princeton theology, a conservative Presbyterian stance like that which this church embodied seems to imply an emphasis on sanctification articulated in polemical circumstances, much like that of the theology of John Calvin. In fact the lines to Princeton theology can be drawn even tighter. A text by the principal mover of the Alliance, Thomas Chalmers (1780–1847) of the Scottish church, was used by early Princeton theologians as a refutation against Deism.[23] This kind of theological orientation on the part of this Scottish component of the Evangelical Alliance indicates how it shared the Alliance's polemical orientation against modern forms of thought.

This Presbyterian/Reformed heritage was shared by two other components of the original Evangelical Alliance—the Congregationalists in Great Britain and the Evangelicals of the Church of England. The Congregationalists had their roots in the old Puritan heritage. Puritanism itself was a 16th- to early 17th-century reform movement in the Church of England. In response to the political and ecclesiastical upheavals of its day, it sought to "purify" the church from Roman Catholic accretions and moral laxity. The Puritan movement was both historically and theologically indebted to the Reformed tradition and its emphasis on the covenant. This indebtedness was reflected also in its emphasis on sanctification and conversion, a logical consequence of its concern to deal with anxieties which might emerge as a result of the strong doctrine of predestination which one finds in Calvin.[24]

In addition to this Reformed heritage, one may refer to the influence of the Radical Reformation (as reflected in some of its separatist tendencies) and the mutual influence of Pietism on Puritanism. This point will receive more attention subsequently.[25] Suffice it to say here that, by the time of the formation of the Evangelical Alliance, Puritanism itself was no longer a major force in European Christianity. It had lost almost all its influence when the British monarchy was restored in 1660, following the period of the Puritan commonwealth. A few of these Puritans' spiritual heirs had seceded from the Church of England and not emigrated. As Congregationalists they brought this heritage, somewhat diluted, into the Evangelical Alliance.

A similar heritage was brought into the Alliance by Evangelicals of the Church of England. This group advocated and still advocates the kind of Calvinism, albeit in a more moderate form, which was reflected in the Presbyterians and in the Congregationalist Puritans. Its origins are usually traced to the 18th century, perhaps as a kind of revival of smoldering Reformation theology and Puritan devotionalism. Unlike the later Puritans, the Anglican Evangelicals are no separatists, for they hold firmly to the rules of Anglican church order. But, like the Puritans, they have been preoccupied with holiness/sanctification.[26] Also, like the Puritans, they were reacting against the prevailing social dynamics of their day (in the case of Evangelicals against an Enlightenment rationalism). Like the Puritans they have historically been inclined to de-emphasize "High Church" liturgical sensibilities. However, though the Evangelicals do not regard the office of bishops as indispensable to the essence of the Church, they still regard it as preferable to other forms of polity.[27] After some periods of decline, the Anglican Evangelical community has enjoyed a period of rejuvenation in the post–World War II period not unlike its American counterparts. During this period perhaps its most influential leader has been John Stott.

Given their common Calvinist-Reformed theological orientation, it is easy to see how the Free Church of Scotland, Congregationalists in Great Britain, and Anglican Evangelicals could all form a coalition as part of the 19th-century Evangelical Alliance. Other members of that alliance (and so of today's alliance of Evangelicals in Europe) were largely shaped by the heritage of Pietism.

Classical Pietism, as it came to expression in its most notable early proponent, P. J. Spener, was clearly influenced both by the devotional writings of John Arndt (1555–1621) and the pietistic strand of Puritanism.[28] Thus, at this point those streams of the Evangelical Alliance's coalition influenced by Pietism converge with the Alliance's Puritan and Reformed constituents.

These various streams converge in another way insofar as Spener and other pietists maintained that the principal article of faith pertains to being "born again" (whose end, it is insisted, can only be personal holiness—sanctification).[29] Although one finds exceptions in the literature to this emphasis, the overriding concern with sanctification is evident in Pietism's preoccupation with the spiritual life. It also is reflected in the ethic of the law which characterized the movement, as well as its use of language connoting the believer's active cooperation with grace and its call to strive for perfection.[30]

A common theological logic shared by Pietism and the more Reformed Evangelical streams of the Evangelical Alliance is also evident in that, like these other streams, Pietism emerged from a situation of perceived chaos and moral decay in church and society (in this case, out of the chaos of the Thirty Years' War on the European continent). Also Pietism shared with these streams certain anti-Roman Catholic sentiments.[31]

However, it must be noted that it was not primarily conservatives influenced by classical Pietism who joined the Evangelical Alliance coalition. Those from Germany who took leading roles in the Alliance tended to be part of the neopietist heritage. Neopietism is that segment of the pietist tradition which emerged during the second part of the 18th century during a period when the German church was particularly confronted with the challenges of the Enlightenment. This challenge somewhat altered the character of Pietism. On the one hand, it began to react against these Enlightenment developments and, on the other hand, in some sense it accommodated to them, particularly to Romanticism. Intertwined with these developments in the following century was the emergence of the revival movement in Europe which further transformed the pietist heritage. Particularly noteworthy in this connection is the influence of Anglo-American revivalism on the development in Germany of the revivalistic Gemeinschaftsbewegung in the second half of the century.

Among the most perceptible modifications in Pietism as a result of the 18th-century developments was that pietists began to manifest a new openness to the world. Following the Enlightenment paradigm, they began to take seriously intellectual and aesthetic impulses from contemporary literature and art. Also they began to reflect the Enlightenment confidence in reason to the extent that they employed it to defend their religious perspective. This preoccupation with apologetics coupled with the sense of a common enemy led the neopietists to form a coalition with the old Protestant Orthodox theology (a partnership which would have been unthinkable for classic pietists and the pre-Enlightenment Orthodox who virtually regarded each other as combatants).[32]

By the time of the early 19th century, Lutheran Orthodox theology was itself in the midst of a revival or revivification, usually designated as neo-Lutheranism or Lutheran Renewal. Among the new movement's foremost proponents were Ernst Wilhelm Hengstenberg (1802–1869) and Wilhelm Löhe (1808–1872). Orthodoxy's rebirth made a coalition between it and neopietism a formidable force, particularly as the coalition became embodied in leaders like Friedrich August Tholuck (1799–1877). This coalition, largely comprised of Lutherans and members of United churches, along with some Free Churches (Baptists and Methodists), eventually formed the German branch of the Evangelical Alliance (Deutsche Evangelische Allianz). The Alliance and the coalition were strengthened further in the later part of the 19th century by the development of the Gemeinschaftsbewegung. To be sure, this Protestant Orthodox–pietist coalition is an uneasy one, as is evident in the tensions between today's Evangelical pietists and the Orthodox-oriented Bekenntnisbewegung. Nonetheless, it is a coalition which has not fallen apart and still remains a most significant one, perhaps the major source for the modern Evangelical movement in Europe.

At any rate, the neopietist coalition with Lutheran Orthodoxy transformed Pietism theologically. The coalition opened it to the polemical orientation, the concern with doctrine and biblicism which characterized Orthodox theology. In a way, this coalition and the new agenda it imposed on much of German Pietism was a kind of preparation for the emergence of the Evangelical movement in Europe. For the Evangelicalism of North America and its preoccupation with polemics likely would have been in conflict with classical Pietism with its irenic spirit and relative disinterest in theories about the Bible.[33] But neopietism's sensitivity to doctrinal controversy and Orthodox concerns about the nature of Scripture helps explain why, at least in Germany, a number of pietists associate with the Evangelical movement and are so deeply involved in polemics and concerned with questions about biblical infallibility. Can one not say, therefore, that, although the modern Evangelical movement may not validly express all the concerns of classical Pietism, it may be seen as legitimately compatible with neopietism, so that the movement does not in this sense distort the pietist heritage?

The coalition of Pietism and Orthodox theology in Germany which made possible the participation of both segments in the Evangelical Alliance and in the modern Evangelical movement had implications for the broadening of the Alliance in other parts of Europe. Pietism also had become indigenous in the Lutheran churches in Scandinavia.

In these nations the movement was confronted in the 19th century with a kind of rationalism and, at least in Norway and Denmark, by controversies over the use of historical criticism in the interpretation of the Bible. Thus the situation in Scandinavia at that time was not unlike the circumstances which gave rise to neopietism in Germany.[34]

At any rate, given the similarities between pietists in the Scandinavian and German situations, it is hardly surprising to find that theological conservatives in Sweden also established their own branch of the Evangelical Alliance. Therefore, largely through the incorporation of Pietism, Scandinavian conservatives (including today a number of Free Churches founded in the 19th-century revival movement) joined the Alliance coalition and more or less have aligned themselves with the Evangelical movement today.

The incorporation of Pietism into a coalition with Reformed and Lutheran Orthodox theology also opened the way for the involvement of Free Churches influenced by Pietism, like Methodists in Great Britain and the European continent. For Methodism, with its roots in the 18th-century revival in Great Britain led by John Wesley, sanctification (the doctrine of Christian perfection) was regarded as the central doctrine.[35] Consequently, Methodism logically belonged in the Evangelical Alliance's coalition of theological conservatives from other traditions who were preoccupied with sanctification (and a common polemic against Enlightenment thought-forms).

The same dynamic permitted a number of European Baptists to join the coalition. For the Baptist tradition also has been historically preoccupied with the nature and renewal of the Christian life.[36] First emerging in Great Britain at the turn of the 17th century, influenced by Anabaptists of the Radical Reformation (those 16th-century reformers who repudiated the Roman Catholic heritage most radically, denying the validity of infant baptism), Baptists have in a real sense brought the heritage of the Radical Reformation and its preoccupation with sanctification into the Evangelical coalition.[37]

By recognizing that this coalition of conservatives was already in place in Europe by the mid-19th century, we can understand better how the modern Evangelical movement in Europe emerged and what holds it together. (Insights concerning how the Evangelical coalition maintains itself elsewhere outside North America are also provided by an appreciation of how the European Evangelical Alliance was formed. For, insofar as Christianity in Asia, Africa, and Latin America is to some extent an import from Europe, it makes sense to expect that theological coalitions formed in the Old World would be exported to these new locations, that the spiritual heirs of theological conservatives who cooperated in Europe could be expected to cooperate elsewhere.) In a sense, with the formation of the Evangelical Alliance virtually all the components of the present Evangelical movement were in place in Europe (and so, in consequence of later missionary work consistent with this and the similar North American coalitions, it was already in place in the Third World).

To be sure, not all segments of the modern European Evangelical movement's coalition were in place with the formation of the Evangelical Alliance. For example, there was no national branch from the Netherlands formed at the time of the Alliance's founding. Yet a very influential 19th-century renaissance of Reformed theology in the Netherlands, principally under the leadership of Abraham Kuyper (1837–1920) and Herman Bavinck (1854–1921), has clearly generated a significant segment of the present Evangelical movement and made important contributions to it. In short, it as well as other Free Churches originating in the 19th-century European revival movement and certain Mennonites represent later additions to the European Evangelical coalition.

Nor was the coalition we have been describing merely restricted to the nations we have analyzed—Great Britain, Germany, and Scandinavia. The coalition of Presbyterian and Lutheran Orthodoxy with various pietists was evident at the time of the Alliance's founding in other European nations, such as France.

When one considers that this coalition of theological conservatives was firmly in place before the Fundamentalist coalition itself actually crystallized, one readily recognizes that Billy Graham and the North American Evangelical movement are not themselves responsible for building the present Evangelical coalition in Europe. Long before Graham and the development of the modern Evangelical movement, the European coalition of theological conservatives was already in place (and derivatively from Europe had been established de facto in the rest of the world). The basic contribution of Graham and the North American Evangelical movement to the movement in Europe is that they have broadened the existing coalition, given it new impetus, and provided the coalition (at least in Germany) with a new name—the Evangelical movement. One must conclude that the Evangelical movement outside the United States both is and is not an American phenomenon.

Chapter 7

The Evangelical Coalition:
Its Constituents and the Glue
That Holds Them Together

The question of the origins of the Evangelical movement remains a disputed point among scholars. Some trace its origins to Protestant Orthodox theology (particularly to the Reformed tradition), others to Pietism, still others to dispensationalism, Puritanism, American revivalism, or the "American way of life."[1] Our reflections have suggested that all these movements have played some role in shaping the Evangelical movement. The variety of influences on the movement helps account for its marked theological diversity.

I already have suggested that the coalition of the various streams which formed the Evangelical movement is not an accidental one. These streams have been brought together by common enemies—theological liberalism and a perception of cultural chaos resulting from the impact of thought-forms and behavioral patterns derived from the Enlightenment. But the contributing streams also seem to be held together by a common theological logic. Each one itself tended to emerge in circumstances in which it perceived that society required some means of ordering in the face of social decay. In response to this concern, all of these streams tended to emphasize conversion and the regenerate life-style (sanctification or holiness). Perhaps the differences among the streams relate to the relative importance each places on conversion and how this conversion is thought to manifest itself (e.g., how much emphasis is placed on perfection or glossolalia or whether more emphasis is instead placed on the disciplined practice of the Christian life and theological orthodoxy, as in the Reformed tradition. Many of the present tensions within the Evangelical movement might be understood in light of these factors.

In any case, the common preoccupation of these streams with personal regeneration and holiness speaks to a question we raised at the outset concerning inter-Protestant relationships. It explains how these different streams can coexist in the Evangelical movement, what it is about the constituent traditions of the Evangelical movement which allows some Evangelicals to have closer fellowship with Evangelicals of other denominations than with Evangelicals in their own denominations. Given the common concern of all these traditions with personal regeneration and sanctification, it is quite logical that an Evangelical could find brothers or sisters in other traditions sharing this concern, and draw closer to this kindred spirit than someone in one's own church not espousing or embodying the centrality of the regenerated, sanctified life. Is it the emphasis on sanctification of the various constituent traditions of the Evangelical movement which ultimately makes the movement's "transconfessional" character possible?

Clearly, one can demonstrate the origins of the Evangelical movement in Princeton theology. But through the Princetonians the movement is in turn rooted in 17th-century Reformed Orthodoxy. We already have observed how Princeton theology emerged with polemical aims in view, and that insofar as it embodied the Reformed theological heritage of Calvin it was preoccupied with the question of sanctification. In these orientations, as well as in its affirmation of the verbal inerrancy of Scripture, Princeton theology was very much in touch with its original Orthodox forefather, Francis Turretin, whose dogmatics was also shaped by polemical dialogue.[2] The "American" influence on the Evangelical movement is at this point deeply rooted in European theology.

It is quite likely that Princeton theology and the Fundamentalist movement exerted such an important influence on late 19th- and early 20th-century American religion because they drew upon themes which characterized the American Puritan ethos. For, as we have noted, the Puritan tradition was itself rooted in Reformed theology, quite preoccupied with conversion and tending to stress an ethic vigorously governed by the law. But this emphasis on sanctification also seems to have been related to a concern Puritans shared with the Fundamentalists, with Reformed Orthodoxy, and even with Calvin—the concern to establish order on what was perceived as a culture in chaos.

Certainly, Calvin and the Orthodox theologians of the next generation were proposing a theocratic vision for a society shaped by Christian commitments. This new society needed to be developed in order to take the place of decaying medieval culture. Likewise the Puritans transplanted in America were proposing a theocratic vision (as exemplified in their stress on "covenant") for a new culture which needed to be established in order to overcome the chaos of the wilderness which confronted them as they settled.[3] This concern to establish or reestablish an antebellum Christian/Evangelical culture in face of present chaotic circumstances was the motivating factor in the development of Fundamentalism. It never really forfeited this concern, even during its retreat after the Scopes Trial. The emergence of the Moral Majority as well as the "new Evangelicals" and their concern with social ethics seems to reflect this Puritan tradition of endeavoring to establish a "Christian culture." Could the ability of these movements to tap into the Puritan heritage at this point, coupled with a certain nostalgic yearning by Americans to return to the "good old days," help account for Evangelicalism's and Fundamentalism's present success in the United States?

Links between the Puritan heritage and the Evangelical movement may reflect even in the Evangelical and Fundamentalist preoccupation with biblical inerrancy/infallibility. The pre-Enlightenment, "commonsense" Puritan approach to Scripture should not be overlooked, as some critics of the characteristic Evangelical view of Scripture are prone to do. For the Puritans, not unlike today's Evangelicals, had a rigorous, almost legalistic approach to Scripture in the sense that they tended to regard it as a "book of laws." Coupled with this precisionistic biblicism, one could justifiably conclude that the Puritans affirmed the inerrancy of Scripture insofar as the New England Puritans adhered to *The Westminster Confession*. At any rate, influential Puritans like John Eliot (1604–1690) could speak of the "perfection of Scripture."[4] Although the point cannot be pursued in sufficient detail at this time, the question may be asked: Far from being a post-Enlightenment adaptation of the antebellum American Evangelical heritage, could the Evangelical/Fundamentalist concern with biblical inerrancy touch upon the roots of the American (Puritan) religious experience? When one gets into the grass roots parishes of even the North American mainline churches, the appeal of biblical infallibility or its absolute reliability to much of the "folk piety" would seem to warrant an affirmative answer to the question.

In a sense, then, one might say that the Evangelical movement has preserved the Puritan heritage better than any of the major mainline churches. This is undoubtedly true in regard to that branch of Puritanism which was shaped by revivalism. For Puritanism itself, through Jonathan Edwards' ministry in the Great Awakening (an important American revival dated from about 1734 until the 1760s) and through the Second Great Awakening (a later American revival movement early in the 19th century), is the source of American revivalism. (Noteworthy also is the important impact the first awakening had on American Baptists. In a sense, then, one may say that conservative Baptists associated with the Evangelical and Fundamentalist movements are guardians of the Puritan heritage.)[5]

At any rate, as we shall see, the revivalist emphases on the individual's conversion and the personality/charisma of the preacher are themes which are reflected quite markedly in the Evangelical movement. Perhaps another factor which accounts for the movement's great impact in the American South (in addition to the South's innate "cultural conservatism") is that Evangelicalism is the transdenominational expression of the revivalist traditions (both Baptist and Methodist) indigenous to this region. Certainly the revivalist heritage reflects Puritanism's emphasis on conversion.[6]

Yet although revivalism was part of the American establishment prior to the Civil War, was acceptable to the elite, and reflected a strong social consciousness (as was evident in Charles Gradison Finney's involvement in the abolitionist movement), a number of these commitments were dramatically altered in the antebellum period. As a result, the revivalist tradition in America came to modify the Puritan heritage in several ways. Most notably in the great evangelist and major league baseball player Billy Sunday and his predecessor, Dwight Moody, one can detect a stronger focus on the individual to the exclusion of social concerns, an anti-intellectualism (at least in the case of Sunday), and a heavier emphasis on human responsibility for salvation at the expense of the primacy of grace.[7]

In fact the last of these emphases was evident in the first of the modern revivalists, Finney. He tended to follow his theological forebear, Nathaniel Taylor, in insisting upon a necessary role for human agency in coming to salvation.[8] Clearly, suspicions that Lutherans and other mainline churches might have about the Evangelical movement's compromising justification by grace through faith are aroused by the movement's indebtedness to revivalism. This accounts for the suspicions such mainline churches have of all revivalists, including Billy Graham.

Given the fact that the revivalist tradition is only one factor which influenced the Evangelical movement, one must challenge the validity of a blanket condemnation of the movement on grounds that the Revivalist tradition compromises the primacy of grace. Nevertheless, one must recognize that tensions between revivalists and mainline churches were in evidence as early as the 19th century, and so it is worth pondering whether such tension set the stage for the Fundamentalist controversy.[9] At any rate the revivalist heritage has clearly contributed to the Evangelical movement—and not just in terms of their shared emphasis on being born again. The Evangelical preoccupation with biblical inerrancy/infallibility also is reflected in segments of the revivalist heritage, not least in Charles G. Finney.[10]

To the degree that a correlation between Puritanism and revivalism became the dynamic factor in pre-20th-century American life, one can also affirm that the "American way of life," as it came to be influenced by these religious movements, also has been a formative factor on Fundamentalism and the Evangelical movement. The individualism and egalitarianism of both the revivalist heritage and American society, the worldview of Scottish common sense realism as it is so intimately bound to a number of American institutions, as well as the correlation of American society and the kingdom of God (as the latter commitment was more or less advocated by Jonathan Edwards) have all found their way into the Evangelical movement.[11] (For example, the Southern Baptist Convention claims that democracy is the biblical ideal.)[12] To the extent that they are committed by their theological heritage to defending these values, Evangelicals are indeed influenced by the "American way of life." Indeed, not just in the United States, but also elsewhere like in Australia and increasingly in Third World countries like Brazil, the establishment's middle class is the core of the Evangelical movement.[13]

Radical reformation and Pietist legacies

In showing the Evangelical Movement's indebtedness to both revivalism and Puritanism, I also have indirectly suggested its origins in both the Radical Reformation and Pietism. Certainly, the latter two streams share with the other constituent streams a common emphasis on the sanctified life and on being born again. In a sense, both developed in response to the concern to provide in some way Christian structures in face of what was perceived as a chaotic situation in church and society.[14]

We have already noted the theological connections between Puritanism and the Radical Reformation, particularly with regard to their sharing a similar concern to purify the Christian community, to make it holy. To the extent that this is accurate, the influence of the Radical Reformation through Puritanism on the Evangelical movement becomes readily apparent. We can also observe the former's influence insofar as a number of Mennonite and Baptist churches, both rooted in the Radical Reformation, identify themselves with the Evangelical movement.

Additionally, we should remind ourselves of the interconnections between Pietism and Puritanism. We have already observed their mutual preoccupation with being born again and sanctification, as well as the historical influence of Puritanism on Pietism (through Spener).[15] Thus to the degree the Puritan heritage perpetuated the themes of Pietism as well as the Reformed tradition, the Evangelical movement in its dependence on the Puritan heritage is also enriched by the legacy of both Pietism and the Reformed tradition. In so doing, could the movement furnish a case study for illustrating the correlation between the Reformed and pietist traditions (the idea that the Reformed tradition should properly be deemed part of the left wing of the Reformation)?

The heritage of Pietism influences the Evangelical movement in other ways. But as we have seen the major influences on the Movement have tended to come from neopietism rather than classical Pietism. In that sense one may speak of a dual influence on Evangelicalism, both Orthodox and pietist, insofar as neopietism represented a kind of coalition of the two.

One sees the influence of a post-Enlightenment Pietism on the Evangelical movement in those Methodists who have affiliated with the movement. Likewise, the Free Church traditions, heavily ethnic churches in North America like The Evangelical Covenant Church or the Baptist General Conference emerged in the 19th century in consequence of revival movements reacting against some forms of modern rationalism. Of course, these churches share with the Evangelical coalition a preoccupation with being born again and the regenerate lifestyle (sanctification).[16]

Similarly a post-Enlightenment pietist influence is reflected in the Evangelical movement in churches and organizations growing out of the Holiness movement. We have already sketched the circumstances in which the Holiness movement emerged. The concern is to revivify the Wesleyan doctrine of perfectionism clearly reflected in the 19th-century ministry of Phoebe Palmer. In time, the growing interest in Holiness led to the foundation of the National Camp Meeting Association for the Promotion of Holiness, which exposed many from all denominations to this kind of revivalist ethos. Thus the Holiness revival was not just confined to the Methodist heritage; it was a transdenominational movement as is evident in its influence on Charles G. Finney. In Finney and his colleagues at Oberlin College, as well as for the Wesleyan Methodists, the Holiness theme was a mandate to work for social reform, most notably for abolition. But among the Holiness groups most influenced by the camp meeting ethos, a number of which eventually formed the Church of the Nazarene, the interest tended to be more on personal holiness.[17]

At any rate, the widespread proliferation of these currents eventually created a backlash in the mainline churches; particularly in the Methodist Episcopal Church there was the formation of other separate Holiness churches and missions organizations. The original nondenominational vision of the Holiness movement, the hope of a number of its early leaders that denominational differences might disappear, was forfeited. Nevertheless, the Holiness heritage clearly embodies the pietist heritage and the collective concern of the various components of the Evangelical coalition to emphasize sanctification.[18]

In the same manner, pietist traditions—in fact, the Holiness traditions and their overriding concern with sanctification—are reflected in yet another component of the Evangelical movement, the Pentecostal tradition and its spiritual heir, the charismatic movement.[19] It can be shown historically that the earliest Pentecostals were members of Holiness churches. Theologically their preoccupation with speaking in tongues (glossolalia) emerged as a result of a problem raised by a development in their Holiness heritage which influenced certain segments of the movement, namely, the equation of the experience of perfection ("the second blessing") with the biblical concept of a "baptism with the Holy Spirit" (Mark 1:8; Acts 1:5). This equation had not been made by all the first proponents of Holiness teaching though it was articulated by Phoebe Palmer.[20] And, once it was made, a quite obvious reaction was to long for a physical manifestation that would give assurance of this baptism. Glossolalia soon came to be seen as the answer to this longing, as the "initial evidence" of "baptism with the Spirit" (Acts 10:44-47).[21] In a sense, then, the Pentecostal movement is a kind of continuation or mutation of the concerns of the Holiness movement and therefore also of Pietism.

At this point it is important to distinguish the Pentecostal and charismatic movements, as members of each are sometimes prone to press their distinction. The Pentecostal movement refers to those groups of

Christians whose experience of speaking in tongues has largely been characterized by exclusiveness both in terms of its structures (as manifested by the creation of its own churches and organizations) and its values (as manifested in an ethical austerity). Generally, it is said to have been initiated on December 31, 1900, in Topeka, Kansas, at Bethel Bible College, under the leadership of a Holiness pastor, Charles Parham. Historians have shown that this was not the first instance of glossolalia in the modern world. For the 19th century, more than 30 such outbreaks of speaking in tongues can be documented. Whether these outbreaks were particularly predominant in the Black community is a hypothesis presently under debate among scholars.[22]

In any case, it was in the outbreak of tongues under the auspices of Parham that Pentecostalism began to gather a following which would eventually gain it national attention. It is perhaps proper to say that Pentecostalism began with this event because, although there had been earlier instances of speaking in tongues, it was first with Parham that a key commitment of Pentecostalism was articulated—the equation of speaking in tongues with baptism in the Holy Spirit.[23] A turning point in the movement's subsequent development was the Azusa Street Mission in Los Angeles under the leadership of a Black Holiness preacher, a student of Parham's, William Seymour. Beginning in 1906, the Pentecostal revival emanating from this ramshackle church building was heard round the world. The revival received international press coverage and included participants from all over the world. Many of the earliest prominent Pentecostal leaders were first converted in this mission. One of those who came under its influence was the "apostle of Pentecostalism in Europe," the first great Norwegian Pentecostal, who was largely responsible for the Pentecostal revival on the Continent, T. B. Barratt.

Not unlike Pietism and other strands of the Evangelical movement, Pentecostalism seemed to emerge in a period characterized by a pervasive sense of social and religious dislocation. In response to perceived liberalism in the churches as well as the rootlessness imposed by the immigrant tide and the industrial revolution, Holiness movement Christians were attracted to Pentecostalism because the ecstatic experiences it offered seemed to provide not just assurances of salvation but also assurance of Christianity's truth.[24] Given these factors, it is not surprising that the greatest impact of early Pentecostalism was on the poorer, lower class. This is the pattern for today's marked growth of Pentecostalism in Latin America.[25]

In addition to these characteristics, Pentecostalism has been marked by a worship style which is spontaneous and enthusiastic (religiously fervent, marked by almost no structural limits). Except for proponents more recently influenced by the charismatic movement, Pentecostalism also has been characterized by a strong sense of urgency because the end times are near.[26] These characteristics as well as the separatist tendencies and particular sociological composition of Pentecostalism are largely reversed in the charismatic movement.

The charismatic movement (neo-Pentecostalism) is a transdenominational movement of enthusiastic Christianity which emerged in the mainline churches only in 1960. It even has made significant inroads in Lutheranism and the Roman Catholic church. The first well-known episode occurred at St. Mark's Episcopal Church in Van Nuys, California, under the leadership of Dennis Bennett (though glossolalia may have been experienced in The Episcopal Church as early as 1956). A commitment was made at that time to avoid Pentecostal separatism, to keep the movement within the established churches.[27] In this sense, charismatics share the Evangelical movement's commitment to infiltrating these denominations.

Eventually this commitment led to efforts on the part of charismatics to break with the older Pentecostal theological formulations in favor of ways of articulating the Pentecostal experience in a manner consistent with the heritage of the mainline churches. This break with Pentecostal models has taken several other forms. Unlike their spiritual forefathers, charismatics also insist on order, encourage speaking in tongues only for private devotional purposes rather than in public worship, reject the strict life-style standards of Pentecostalism, and even assert in some cases that glossolalia is not necessarily a sign of baptism of the Holy Spirit. None of these commitments should be too surprising, in view of sociological factors. For, while the early Pentecostals largely belonged to dispossessed lower social classes, naturally in opposition to the establishment, charismatics were and are mostly middle-class types. Thus it is hardly surprising to learn that, although the charismatic renewal has had a significant impact on European churches, it has largely not had the impact Pentecostalism has had on the Third World.[28]

Even though the Pentecostal movement actually laid the groundwork for the charismatic renewal, especially through its sponsorship of the Full Gospel Business Men's Fellowship (an organization of establishment-type Pentecostals which included mainline Christians interested in the Pentecostal experience), in the early days of the charismatic movement, Pentecostals tended to distance themselves from the renewal. Yet, more recently, as cultural accommodation has led Pentecostal churches to look more and more like established denominations, some Pentecostals, particularly the Assemblies of God, have come to endorse the charismatic renewal. One prominent Pentecostal has even suggested that God has used Pentecostal churches to mediate Pentecostal teachings to the whole Church, a divine aim now being fulfilled in the charismatic renewal.[29] In fact, thanks largely to the trailblazing efforts of the modern pioneer of Pentecostal ecumenism, David du Plessis, such new openness even has manifested itself in the involvement of various Pentecostals in ecumenical endeavors such as the international Roman Catholic–Pentecostal dialogue. At any rate, it may be that tensions between Evangelicalism and its Pentecostal wings still remain, particularly in Europe. Yet, the theological and sociological commonalities Pentecostals and charismatics share with the other streams of the Evangelical movement have led increasingly to the full integration of Pentecostals and charismatics in many parts of the world into the Evangelical coalition.

If the heritage of Pietism and its concerns are reflected in Pentecostalism, thereby helping to account for why Pentecostals fit in and share a common theological logic with the rest of the Evangelical movement, Pietism (or at least a neopietism reflecting Protestant Orthodox doctrinal concerns) is also an influence on the movement insofar as it broadens the Evangelical coalition to include Lutherans. For in the relatively few instances where Lutherans do explicitly identify themselves with the Evangelical movement, it is generally only those Lutherans influenced by Pietism who make this identification. One sees this most clearly in the case of such Lutheran pietist organizations as the Church Association for Inner Mission in Denmark and other Lutheran parachurch agencies in Scandinavia and West Germany. Likewise, it is interesting that at least two of the more prominent German Evangelicals, Peter Beyerhaus and Gerhard Maier, are Lutherans who see themselves in the tradition of Pietism.[30] On the other hand, those theologically conservative Lutherans who reject identification with the Evangelical movement, most notably The Lutheran Church–Missouri Synod, historically have identified themselves with Lutheran Orthodox theology rather than with Pietism.

The legacy of dispensational premillennialism

The coalition of neopietism and Reformed Orthodox theology is suggested even in the last of the theological movements which formed the Evangelical coalition—dispensational premillennialism. We have already observed the precedents for dispensationalism in the Reformed heritage, most notably in *The Westminster Confession of Faith* (VII.5-6). (Such an appeal to distinct historical dispensations also is reflected at least at one point in the theology of John Wesley. Likewise, it is interesting for Lutherans to note that one of their authoritative Confessional documents, the *Formula of Concord* [SD VI. 22], also speaks of distinct "dispensations" in biblical history, a theme which this text as well as dispensationalists link to a distinction between law and gospel.)[31] But dispensationalism also likely bears the influence of Pietism. The chief architect of modern dispensationalism, John Nelson Darby, seems to have been in touch with the theological currents of French-Swiss Pietism. And at least one scholar also claims that George Müller (1805–1898), one of the founders of the Plymouth Brethren, was directly influenced by German Pietism.[32]

Links between dispensationalism and Pietism, as well as with Reformed Orthodoxy and Puritanism, can also be identified in terms of a common theological logic. As we have noted the dispensationalism of the Plymouth Brethren emerged in consequence of a concern to create a more vibrant church life in reaction to the lifeless spirituality of the established church in the 19th-century British Isles. Such a context and overriding concern is not unlike those characteristic of classical Pietism and Puritanism. The lines to Pietism can be drawn even tighter when we are reminded that Pietism even in its classical form was quite preoccupied with the kind of speculation about the end times and the millennium which also characterizes dispensationalism.[33]

The impact of dispensational premillennialism on Fundamentalism and the Evangelical movement has received much—perhaps too much—emphasis in recent analysis.[34] We have shown how theological conservatives in the antebellum religious and cultural context in the United States were quite well prepared by a pervasive sense of cultural pessimism and earlier millennial speculations rooted in Jonathan Edwards to embrace dispensationalism. Thus, dispensational premillennialism may be rightly identified as the chief distinguishing mark of Fundamentalism, the key factor which occasioned the organization of the Fundamentalist/Evangelical coalition. But as we have seen it is by no means the controlling interest of the Evangelical movement. For the movement is a product of many components, most notably a coalition of Pietism and Reformed Orthodoxy, particularly as this comes to expression in a kind of Puritanism tinged by American revivalism.

In that sense, the Evangelical movement both is and is not a peculiarly American or even Anglo-Saxon religious phenomenon (dare one say only as peculiarly American and exclusively Anglo-Saxon, as devoid of continental European influence, as is Puritanism itself).

The lessons of history

Perhaps the most important lesson taught by our historical overview of the Evangelical movement is the marked diversity of the streams which constitute it. Of course, we have noted certain common features in these streams. They have been united by a sense of common enemies. All emerged out of a context which perceived their culture to be in chaos or decay. In response all took a position which stressed regeneration and the sanctified life, always with a strong affirmation of the Bible's authority (in all cases except classic Pietism its infallibility).

It is helpful to identify these common characteristics of the streams which have influenced/constituted the Evangelical movement. Since all these streams are able to coexist within the Evangelical movement, an appreciation of their common characteristics shows great ecumenical promise regarding the convergence of these theological streams, as for example the possible convergence among the Reformed, pietist, and perhaps Radical Reformation traditions. More pertinent for our purposes, an appreciation of the common characteristics of these streams provides us with insights concerning the nature of the Evangelical movement. The diversity of the constituent streams of Evangelicalism helps us appreciate the rich diversity which characterizes the Evangelical movement.

Part II

INSTITUTIONS OF EVANGELICALISM

Our survey of the historical influences on the Evangelical movement has anticipated the identification of a number of the institutions and characteristics of the movement. Certainly the diversity of its various constituent streams is reflected in the diversity one finds among contemporary Evangelical institutions. In endeavoring to explain how these diverse institutions can work together as one movement, at least one commentator has compared the collective structure of the Evangelical movement to the feudal system of the Middle Ages: it can be seen as being comprised of "superficially friendly, somewhat competitive empires built up by evangelical leaders competing for the same audience, but all professing allegiance to the same King."[1]

Due to this diversity, our attempt to examine the structures of the Evangelical movement must take the form of a survey. I hasten to add that this survey is in no way a complete presentation of the important organizations of the movement. An attempt has been made simply to find at least one representative organization in each group. In some cases, organizations not formally identifying themselves with the Evangelical movement but which are normally thought to be Evangelical (often because they are really Fundamentalist) have been considered. Attention to them in comparison to avowedly Evangelical organizations should help us further to clarify the unique characteristics and commitments of the Evangelical movement.

Only the most distinctive theological commitments of these organizations are mentioned in the following brief descriptions. Unless otherwise noted, virtually all the organizations considered affirm the inerrancy of Scripture (as well as most of the rest of Fundamentalism's five points), define the Church principally in terms of believers, emphasize conversion, personal holiness, and sanctification, and show a strong concern for evangelism and mission work.

Chapter 8

Churches

There are relatively few churches which avowedly identify themselves as part of the Evangelical movement, and the greatest number of them are located in North America. Hence, most of the churches we consider will be from this continent.

The Reformed tradition

Churches of the Reformed tradition more or less associated with the Evangelical movement include the Conservative Congregational Christian Conference (CCCC), the Reformed Presbyterian Church of North America (RPC), the Presbyterian Church in America (PCA), The Orthodox Presbyterian Church (OPC), to some extent the Christian Reformed Church in North America (CRC), and, outside the United States, the Union Nationale des Eglises Réformées Evangéliques Indépendantes de France (Evangelical Reformed Church of France; EREI).[1]

The first of these, the Conservative Congregational Christian Conference, has its roots in the Old American Congregational heritage grounded in Puritanism. It was formed in 1948 as the result of a withdrawal of conservatives from the main body of Congregational churches (now part of the United Church of Christ). The CCCC has not preserved its Reformed heritage in a separatist way, but has allowed congregations with different theological heritages to affiliate with it. This diversity is reflected in its openness regarding the mode of baptism, its view of the status of sacramental elements, and its views on predestination. Although its leadership insists that this openness is a consequence of its Congregational heritage, some observers contend that such theological openness may also be a reflection of the influence the Evangelical left has had on it.[2] It is a small church, with a membership of more than 25,000.

The Reformed Presbyterian Church of North America (RPC) has its roots in 17th-century Scotland. Firmly committed to the concept of covenant and disappointed by efforts of reform in their home country, staunch Presbyterians refused to acknowledge the validity of any state not supporting a Reformed church. Thus, until the 20th century they refused to vote in American elections and are now only advocating the validity of a vote for candidates publicly committed to biblical principles (Chap. 23). In worship they observe the distinct practice of singing only Psalms and always without instrumental accompaniment (Chap. 21). They reject the teaching that one cannot be saved without baptism (Chap. 28). Given its unique theological perspective, it is not surprising that the RPC has remained small (more than 5000 members in its 71 congregations) and not been a major voice in the Evangelical movement.

The Presbyterian Church in America (PCA) is the product of a secession of conservatives from the Presbyterian Church in the United States (Southern Presbyterians). Organized in 1973, it absorbed the Reformed Presbyterian Church, Evangelical Synod (RPC,ES) in 1982. The latter was itself the product of a merger between dissidents of the RPC who were endeavoring to make the church more open to American culture and the majority of theologically conservative Presbyterians who had been affiliated with Carl McIntire in the former Bible Presbyterian Church but had been left by McIntire due to their failure to support his extreme separatism. (The great modern apologist for Evangelicalism, Francis Schaeffer [1912–1984], was a member of this group. In the interim, McIntire has organized a new, very small, Fundamentalist-oriented Bible Presbyterian Church.) The cycle of mergers and secessions has nearly come full circle, as the PCA has been in merger discussion with The Orthodox Presbyterian Church (the church which was the result of the original schism with the Presbyterian Church in the U.S.A. and from which McIntire and the dissidents who had formed the old RPC,ES subsequently withdrew). And although the OPC failed to obtain enough votes at its 1986 General Assembly to consummate the merger, efforts to bring it about continue. Thus, large segments of institutions associated with the original Fundamentalist Presbyterian schismatics of the 1930s may still be reunited under the PCA banner. These old standard-bearers for Fundamentalism are moving clearly in the direction of the Evangelical camp, for the PCA with its 150,000 members in approximately 800 churches is self-proclaimed Evangelical.[3]

The Christian Reformed Church in North America (CRC) has its roots in the 19th-century revival of Reformed Orthodox theology in the Netherlands. Thus it is a church which has been strongly influenced since its inception by the major proponent of that revival, Abraham Kuyper. In remaining loyal to its ethnic makeup and maintaining a close-knit fellowship (including its own network of parochial schools, among which are the well-known Calvin College and Seminary in Grand Rapids, Mich.), the CRC has many affinities to The Lutheran Church–Missouri Synod (LCMS). Like its Lutheran sister, it has not affiliated itself unambiguously with the Evangelical Movement and is not a member of the National Association of Evangelicals (NAE) (though Evangelicals like to claim it as their own). Some observers contend that this reticence about Evangelicalism is largely a function of an allegedly Arminian and subjectivist tone to the theology of the Evangelical movement. Others think that the CRC distances itself in part due to its sociopolitical ethical agenda and in part to its theological openness and the impact neoorthodox theology has had on it.[4] Yet this church on the Evangelical border does affirm biblical infallibility as a consequence of a basic presupposition that Scripture is inspired (pp. 13-14). It also adds in a manner more compatible with neoorthodoxy that the divine authority of Scripture is recognized only "when one has submitted himself to the one of whom Scripture speaks" (p. 23), and that neither scientific nor historical investigation can invalidate the purpose of Scripture (pp. 29-30, 55). These theological commitments, coupled with the CRC's long-standing social consciousness (evidenced in one of its related periodicals, *The Reformed Journal,* a highly respected periodical in Evangelical circles), place the CRC in a pivotal position as catalyst for mainline–Evangelical dialogue. A recent report indicated that this pivotal church has a membership of over 300,000 with a significant percentage of the membership in Canada.

The Evangéliques Indépendantes de France (EREI) is one of the best examples of a Reformed church in the Evangelical movement outside of North America. Organized in 1938 by a group of theological conservatives who were unwilling to affiliate with a proposed union of all French Protestants, the church is quite small (about 2000 full members, an additional 11,000 parishioners in 50 congregations). But it has a strong mission consciousness, and has begun a number of home mission sites assisted by North American support, particularly from the PCA. It has played an influential role in the founding and support of a seminary for French Evangelicals, the Faculté Libre de Théologie Réformée d'Aix-en-Provence. This institution also trains some students from other French Evangelical churches, including the Union des Eglises Evangéliques Libres de France (a small church founded in 1849 in a secession by conservatives from the French Reformed Church, but somewhat distanced from the Reformed heritage by the heavy influence on it from the 19th-century European Awakening [which resulted in the formation of Free Churches in Scandinavia]).[5]

As theologically conservative churches, it is hardly surprising that all these bodies except the CCCC affirm the authority of one or more of the historic Reformed Presbyterian Confessions of Faith. Thus they all exhibit a traditional Reformed theological orientation with its emphasis on sanctification and an affirmation of justification.[6] (The only departures from Reformed norms might be the CCCC's openness to diversity in its views on the sacraments and predestination and the RPC's worship practices. Other noteworthy teachings of these churches, which shatter our ordinary impressions of the Reformed tradition, include the RPC's position which is also held to some extent by the CRC that one need not be baptized in order to be saved, and perhaps the CRC's position that a "common grace," distinct from "saving grace," makes it possible even for the unregenerate to perform deeds of civil righteousness [acts which are good in the eyes of society].)[7] All of these churches affirm the infallibility of Scripture (though EREI speaks only unofficially of the Bible's infallibility—no doubt a manifestation of the ambivalence of theologically conservative Europeans towards the Evangelical movement).[8] Numerically, Reformed churches do not comprise the largest segment of the Evangelical movement, but their heritage remains among the most theologically influential.

Mainline pietist traditions

Churches associated with mainline pietist traditions which are themselves part of the Evangelical movement are quite difficult to identify. It is a common misconception that almost all Methodist churches in continental Europe are Conservative Evangelical in their orientation. No doubt this impression is based on the fact that most of the Free Churches (Methodist and Baptist) in Europe have a membership which exhibits a kind of Conservative Evangelical piety. However, the only Methodist church whose identification with the Evangelical movement I have been able to document is the Union des Associations Cultuelles Evangéliques des Eglises Méthodistes de France (EMF).

Methodism first came to France in 1791. The various Methodist societies which had been founded within the Reformed church finally formed themselves into a church in 1852. However, in 1939, when French Protestantism sought reunification, more than half of the Methodist congregations joined the union. The six which elected to remain Methodist formed the EMF.

The EMF maintains the usual Methodist doctrinal commitments, with an especially strong emphasis in its case on the necessity of sanctification (holiness and living the Christian life). Although it affirms Scripture's authority only in matters of faith and life, at least in some quasi-official statements the church affirms the verbal inspiration and inerrancy of Scripture.[9] Also the church perhaps emphasizes Holiness themes a bit more than some Methodist churches in that it regards sanctification as a "second blessing" and, although it permits infant baptism, believer's baptism has become the normal practice. But it does not teach "entire sanctification" in the way Holiness churches do.[10]

The EMF has 320 professing members (though almost three times that number participate in its parishes). It is not the only Methodist church with a theologically conservative orientation in France. But the other church, the Eglise Evangélique Méthodiste en Suisse et en France, in spite of its conservatism, is related to West Germany's Evangelisch-methodistische Kirche (EmK) (which is itself the German branch of a North American mainline body, The United Methodist Church). Despite commonalities, these churches differ from the EMF in that they have an episcopal structure. They differ from the EMF also in that they take a critical position in relation to the Evangelical movement (even though the EmK participates actively in the German Evangelical Alliance).[11]

Holiness churches

Holiness churches represent a significant segment of the Evangelical movement, at least in North America. Those associated with the movement include The Wesleyan Church (WC), The Free Methodist Church of North America (FMC), the Church of the Nazarene (CN), and The Christian and Missionary Alliance (CMA).[12]

One usually associates the Holiness movement with the revivalist camp meetings. The Church of the Nazarene has its origins in this camp meeting movement. Originally calling itself the Pentecostal

Church of the Nazarene, the word "Pentecostal" was dropped from the church's name in 1919 in response to concerns that the church was supporting the emerging Pentecostal movement. (The presence of this theme in the church and its continuing affirmation of the Pentecostal language of "baptism with the Holy Spirit," which it equates with entire sanctification [Art. X], suggest the role the Holiness movement may have played in setting the stage for the Pentecostal movement.)[13]

The CN affirms the usual Holiness teachings concerning entire sanctification subsequent to regeneration (with qualifications [see pp. 431-432 below], akin to those of The Wesleyan Church) (Art. X), justification as a judicial (forensic) work of God (Art. IX), divine healing (Art. XV), and a number of behavioral rubrics including the expectation of tithing and simple dress by believers (Gen. Rules) as well as strictures against attendance at movies, dancing, and alcohol consumption (Spec. Rules). The church also affirms the plenary inspiration of the Bible, that it "inerrantly reveals the will of God concerning us in all things necessary to our salvation. . ." (Art. IV).

The CN has been heavily affected by the Evangelical movement, even though its Holiness heritage kept it out of membership in the NAE until 1984. There have been reports about theological tensions among theologians of the church concerning whether there are grounds in the New Testament and the Wesleyan theological tradition for speaking of the doctrine of entire sanctification in relation to the Pentecostal concept of "baptism with the Spirit." But apparently the debate never had a significant impact on the CN's laity, and it is no longer considered a pressing matter by the church's administrative officers.[14] Tensions or no, one cannot but come away impressed from a contact with the CN. Like most Holiness and Pentecostal churches, it has an admirable historical record in ordaining women. It is one of the fastest growing churches in the United States, having tripled its membership in the four decades since 1940. By the mid-1980s its membership was about 500,000 (though its rate of growth has dropped slightly).

Free Methodist Church of North America (FMC) and The Wesleyan Church (WC) have roots related, though not identical, to those of the CN. Both had origins in 19th-century America in the Methodist Episcopal Church. The FMC was created after the expulsion of several New York State residents in a controversy related to the founders' position that the policy of pew rentals, which excluded seating for the poor, should be abolished. We previously noted the WC's roots in the abolitionist movement. Yet social crusades are not the sole factor in the evolution of these churches. The Holiness revival, with its concern for temperance, deeply affected both churches. And, as we have noted, one of the bodies which merged to form the WC in 1968, The Pilgrim Holiness Church, was primarily rooted in the kind of camp meeting circuit which was influenced by the Bible and Prophetic Conference ethos and its preoccupation with premillennialism.

Both the FMC and the WC affirm the usual Holiness teachings, as well as associated life-style standards (rejecting gambling, alcohol, and smoking), tithing, and the inerrancy of Scripture.[15] (Some have pointed out that the affirmation of biblical inerrancy was not part of the original Articles of Religion of these churches, and in the FMC efforts are under way by some to return to the original Articles. Yet it also cannot be denied that the earliest Holiness tradition was at least in some dialogue with the concept of the Bible's infallibility.[16] Some observers suggest that the present debate on this matter of biblical inerrancy may be a consequence of the influence on the churches of the Evangelical left, but is not a reflection of the views of their constituency.)[17] The alliance of these churches with the Evangelical movement seems to be assured by their views of Scripture, certain aspects of their early heritage, and by their membership in the NAE.

In the mid-1980s, the WC had almost 115,000 full and provisional members. But it has many others in attendance on a given Sunday, perhaps more than many 200,000. In North America it dwarfs the FMC with its 81,000 members (perhaps as many as 200,000 members worldwide). But the FMC is the leader of all denominations in the United States in per capita giving. This is perhaps typical of Holiness churches: five of the eight top American denominations in per capita giving are Holiness bodies. These churches are impressive in a number of ways!

Our final Holiness church, The Christian and Missionary Alliance, has a distinct orientation and heritage in relation to the other churches insofar as it was founded under Keswick influence, specifically by a 19th-century, Princeton-educated Presbyterian, A. B. Simpson (1844–1919). The CMA's Keswick orientation seems to be reflected in its view of entire sanctification (perfection), which it regards as God's will for the faithful. However, in emphasizing the process aspects of entire sanctification (in contrast to the Wesleyan Holiness view of entire sanctification, which places more emphasis on its character as an instantaneous event) the CMA seems implicitly to suggest, as Keswick did, that sin is never totally eradicated in this life. The Alliance's *Statement of Faith* on this topic even uses the Keswick language of "power for service" to describe the effects of entire sanctification (7). Other distinctive CMA commitments include the rite of anointing with oil in connection with prayer for the sick (8), baptism by immersion (Aux. Const., Art. IV), a stress on the Church's task in evangelism (9), a premillennial second coming of Christ (11), and an affirmation of the verbal inspiration and inerrancy of Scripture (4).

The Alliance has historically been open to Pentecostal experience, while not encouraging it. Its openness also is reflected in the fact that it promulgates fewer life-style standards than do other Holiness churches. Another feature of this body is its concern for mission outreach. This is a dimension of its self-identity, as Simpson's purpose in founding the Alliance was to bring the gospel to the urban poor. This commitment to missionary work still is strongly reflected in CMA, as it continues to operate more than 20 foreign mission districts and keeps foreign mission concerns at the top of its priorities. In the mid-1980s CMA had a membership of more than 200,000.

Pentecostal churches

Pentecostal churches, as we have noted, are more readily identified with the Evangelical movement in the United States than in any other part of the world. Among those associated with the movement are the Assemblies of God (AG), International Church of the Foursquare Gospel (ICFG), Church of God (Cleveland, Tennessee) (CG), the Church of God in Christ (COGIC), and in the so-called Third World, the Assembléias de Deus (Assemblies of God) (AD) in Brazil.[18] The identification with the Evangelical movement by these U.S. churches is not a recent development. Three of them, the AG, CG, and ICFG, were charter members of the National Association of Evangelicals and, at the time of writing, a significant percentage of NAE member denominations (a total of 11 church bodies) belong to the Pentecostal movement. We begin with the AG, as it is one of the two largest Pentecostal church bodies in the world, and perhaps the most influential.

The Assemblies of God was organized in 1914 by diverse groups of Pentecostals who had broken with those commitments of earliest Pentecostalism that bore the marks of the Holiness movement's influence. This original group had taught that speaking in tongues is a "third blessing," subsequent to sanctification (the "second blessing") which is itself subsequent to justification/regeneration. Newcomers to Pentecostalism, who were not part of the Holiness movement, posited by contrast a "finished work," "two-step" theory. That is to say, they insisted that sanctification (holiness) was not a second distinct work of grace but was given (initiated) in conversion/justification. Essentially, the founders of the AG embraced this view (9).[19]

In AG's early years its initial efforts to bring all Pentecostals together into one body were greeted with some hostility. It was soon faced with another controversy, the "Jesus only" or "Pentecostal Unitarian" question. Proponents of this position held that baptisms performed by the Apostles were only in Jesus' name (Acts 10:48; 19:5). Thus there was only one personality in the Godhead, Jesus Christ; "Father" and "Holy Spirit" were merely titles to designate different aspects of Christ's person. The AG responded to this position with a strong assertion of the doctrine of the Trinity (2). The result was a schism in 1916 leading to the formation of several new Unitarian groups, which included certain predecessor bodies of both the Pentecostal Assemblies of the World and the United Pentecostal Church International.[20]

In addition to AG's affirmation of the Trinity and the "two-step" theory, it also insists that speaking in tongues is the "initial evidence" of the baptism of the Holy Spirit (8), that justification is by faith (5), that baptism is an ordinance to be administered only to believers by immersion (6), that believers may expect divine healing (12), that tithing is to be encouraged (Bylaws, Art. VIII, §7), and that Christ's return will be premillennial, preceded by a rapture of the saints and including the salvation of national Israel (14). All these doctrines are affirmed in face of what is perceived by the AG as an alarming erosion of moral standards (Bylaws, Art. VIII, §6). Also affirmed is the verbal inspiration of Scripture, its infallibility as authoritative for faith and conduct (1). An even stronger statement affirming the inerrancy of Scripture was issued by the AG's Executive Presbytery in 1970. As in the case of Holiness churches, some questions have been raised concerning whether biblical infallibility was part of the AG's original heritage. It can be documented, though, that infallibility was being affirmed as early as 1916, before the high point of Fundamentalist influence.[21]

Observers even within the AG tend to agree that there has been a general cooling in the AG and other Pentecostal churches of the enthusiasm that characterized early stages of the movement. Perhaps due to their memberships' upward social mobility, these churches increasingly fit the pattern of mainline churches. This is evident even in worship, which is today more structured, less spontaneous. At least prior to the outbreak of the charismatic movement, glossolalia seems generally to have been decreasing among Pentecostal churches.[22]

Despite these trends and several controversies in the second half of the 1980s concerning the ethics of televangelist Jim Bakker and Jimmy Swaggart as well as of a few other prominent AG clergymen, the Assemblies' growth and its missionary consciousness have not been impeded. Since 1940 it has grown by more than five times its membership so that in the mid-1980s it had well over two million members. It also carries on an active foreign mission program. As a result, it is the mother church of several Pentecostal bodies, such as The Pentecostal Church of God of Puerto Rico and The Pentecostal Assemblies of Canada, which were originally established by and were once part of the AG. These churches also subscribe to the theological orientation and Evangelical commitments of the AG.

Although smaller in its membership (in the mid-1980s it numbered less than 170,000), the International Church of the Foursquare Gospel (ICFG) has a similar theological orientation, unwilling to embrace the classic Holiness model of "three distinct blessings" (conversion, *then* entire sanctification, *then* speaking in tongues) (VII). Founded by the well known and controversial American evangelist Aimee Semple McPherson (1890–1944), the ICFG is perhaps the most open of the classical Pentecostal churches. It does reflect Holiness teaching to the extent that a reference to "perfection" as a goal for which to strive is made in its *Declaration of Faith* (VIII). But this Holiness language is clearly a subordinate theme and seems interpreted to relation to the theme of "power" given the believer by the Spirit, a theme quite suggestive of the Keswick movement (VIII). This is hardly surprising, in view of the likely influence of Keswick, as mediated through Moody, on McPherson as well as the early leaders of AG.[23]

These factors have contributed to the openness of ICFG, an openness manifesting itself in its rejection of typical puritanical Pentecostal standards of behavior. And although its president, Rolf McPherson, claims that biblical inerrancy is the official ICFG position, the church's *Declaration of Faith* (I) does not explicitly affirm this doctrine. In fact, so thoroughgoing is the rejection of the Pentecostal subculture that the ethos of the church is much more like that of the charismatic movement, in many of its congregations a kind of upper middle class environment. However, despite the ambiguity of its *Declaration of Faith* on biblical inerrancy, the ICFG identifies itself with the Evangelical movement and is a member of the NAE. (It is understood by NAE officials that the ICFG and its other member churches implicitly affirm biblical infallibility in virtue of their membership in NAE.)[24] In North America, at least Pentecostals are readily accepted as part of the Evangelical movement, their distinct theological characteristics notwithstanding.

The Church of God (Cleveland, Tennessee) (CG) represents by contrast a quite distinct theological perspective, as it maintains the three-step Holiness model for interpreting the Pentecostal experience. This is hardly surprising in view of the fact that CG originally emerged from a Holiness revival in the southern United States late in the 19th century, becoming a Pentecostal church officially by 1908 after most of its influential members had received the Pentecostal experience. (In its early period Cleveland, Tennessee, became the center of the movement and is still the location of CG headquarters.)

CG's Holiness background is reflected in its affirmation of holiness as God's standard of living (7), sanctification as a "second blessing" (6), and baptism with the Holy Ghost as subsequent to sanctification (8). Other characteristic CG positions include a belief in divine healing (11), the washing of the saints' feet as an ordinance (12), and the premillennial second coming of Christ preceded by the rapture of the saints (13). The church also maintains a strict code of moral conduct which includes strictures against the use of alcohol and tobacco, an undue use of cosmetics, attendance at movies, short haircuts for women, and swimming with members of the opposite sex. It also maintained an unfortunate segregationist polity along racial lines until 1967, when the CG wisely voted to abolish it.[25]

Like the ICFG, CG also exhibits a certain openness in its view of Scripture, only affirming the Bible's verbal inspiration (1). Yet this position also has not impeded its identification with the Evangelical movement. Nor has it impeded CG growth. Indeed, after some controversy and scandal in its early days its growth has been phenomenal. By the mid-1980s it had a membership of almost half a million, and since 1940 its membership has grown more than sevenfold.

By no means is CG the only Holiness Pentecostal church. Two others are The International Pentecostal Holiness Church (10) and the Church of God in Christ (whose doctrinal position is virtually identical to that of CG). COGIC is especially interesting for our purposes as it is the largest American Black Pentecostal church. Thus it provides occasion for a digression in which we can examine the distinct character of Black Pentecostalism and to some extent the American Black Evangelical community in general.

The Church of God in Christ (COGIC) is actually the largest of all Pentecostal churches with a membership of more than 3.5 million. Its ethos reflects the attributes which make the Black Pentecostal community unique. In part due to segregation, Black and white Pentecostals went their separate ways after the early days of the Pentecostal movement. Thus the Blacks were not participants in or recipients of influence from Fundamentalism. This is evident in that COGIC and perhaps other predominantly Black Pentecostal churches do not seem to embody in the same degree as their white counterparts the theological vestiges of Fundamentalism. One sees this in a lack of rigor concerning a strict inerrancy position and a relative openness concerning life-style, emotional expression, and social action. The first of these features seems to be reflected in COGIC as it affirms the inerrancy of the Scriptures but only in respect to what God "intended to convey to us" (p. 40). In respect to all of these emphases, the Black Pentecostal churches perhaps have more in common with other Black churches than with their white Pentecostal counterparts.[26]

To some extent, the exclusion of American Black Pentecostals from white Pentecostal experience can be seen in the history of COGIC. The church was founded in 1895 largely by the eminent Black Pentecostal C. H. Mason (1866–1961), after he and some colleagues were dismissed by the Missionary Baptist Church because of their advocacy of Holiness teaching. Ten years later, Mason and his supporters traveled to Los Angeles to participate in W. J. Seymour's Azusa Street Revival. There they received the experience of tongues, and returned to their churches. Some divisiveness in the church ensued between the Pentecostals and those who rejected the experience, but by 1907 COGIC was a Pentecostal church.

There are several ironies in this account which typify the Black Pentecostal experience. Mason was a man of great influence, as the success of his church suggests. His influence extended to white Pentecostals in the southern United States, and he ordained a number of white men to the ministry who would later become the first pastors of the AG. For a Black man to play such a leadership role among whites

in the United States at the turn of the century was virtually unprece-
dented. And this Black man, Mason, had himself looked to a Black
community in Los Angeles to lead him into the Pentecostal experience.
Thus Blacks took the lead in the early stages of the Pentecostal movement. Whites came by the hundreds to participate and learn from the
Black community at Azusa Street. Mason also led many white believers
to the Pentecostal experience, as from 1907 to 1914 his church was
interracial. In both cases, the whites then left to form their own churches. From then on white and Black Pentecostals largely went their separate ways.

We have previously noted the egalitarian character of early Pentecostalism and its corresponding attractiveness to the poor and disen-
franchised. To the degree that the American Black Pentecostal community has not lost touch with such a social ethos and has not forfeited
Pentecostalism's original model of racial integration, does it better
maintain the inheritance of early Pentecostalism than do its white brothers and sisters? The white Pentecostal community, thanks to upward
social mobility, has to some extent lost touch with such a "precritical
ethos." It was precisely the white Pentecostals' encounter with the new
ethos of modernity and Enlightenment criticism that also brought them
to some extent under the influence of Fundamentalism and, later, of
the Evangelical movement. Perhaps it is the Black Pentecostal community's failure to enter so thoroughly into this new post-Enlightenment
ethos that has kept it relatively more independent of Fundamentalist
concerns and spirit.

Some of the same points might be applicable to the American Black
Evangelical community in general. The discerning reader will have
noticed how little has been said about the Black church in the discussion
of the history of the Evangelical movement in Part I, above. The main
reason for this is that Blacks played a small role in this development.
Even today one cannot say that there exists a large constituency of
self-proclaimed Evangelicals in the American Black community. This
is not to say that no one in the Black community holds views akin to
those of Evangelicalism; on the contrary, it seems that the overwhelming number of American Black Christians do. It is simply the case that
the term "Evangelical" has little historical relevance to Blacks. Theological conservatives among them would be much more prone to employ the term "Bible-believing." Only in recent decades have some
openly identified themselves as Evangelical.

In fact, parallels between the belief structure of many Blacks and
that of conservative Evangelicalism are hardly surprising in light of

the common heritage they share. In a real sense, the American Black church emerged from antebellum American Evangelicalism and its revivalist heritage. One is tempted to make comparisons between the American Black Evangelical community and those of Eastern Europe and some parts of the Third World. All of them may represent a kind of precritical Evangelicalism, one which has not yet needed to confront the challenges posed by Enlightenment modes of thought. This may account in part for their relative lack of explicit identification with and participation in the Evangelical movement, for it represents an attempt to be "Bible-believing" in face of the challenges of Enlightenment thought. These dynamics also help account for the relative lack of impact Black Evangelicals have had on the Black church. Their lack of impact is also related to an earlier stage in the movement when some leaders became so caught up in the middle-class ethos of the Evangelicalism/Fundamentalism in which they had been trained that they lost touch with the emotional, egalitarian, precritical ethos of the Black church. At least one Black observer believes that, of Black Evangelicals, only Black Pentecostals did not go through this unfortunate process.[27]

At any rate, the Evangelical movement in the Black community is still very much in the process of organizing itself. The formation of the National Black Evangelical Association in 1963 was a step in that direction. To the degree that Black Evangelicalism succeeds, it may serve to mediate the Black church's "antebellum Evangelicalism" to an Evangelical movement seeking to preserve and embody that same heritage. Perhaps Black Pentecostals are already to some extent succeeding in this task. Yet the distance between them and the broader Evangelical community has been noted.[28] This distance may be evident in the fact that COGIC did not by the mid-1980s hold NAE membership.

In view of the fantastic growth of the Pentecostal movement in Latin America, at least one representative must be noted. For our purposes, the Assembléias de Deus (AD) in Brazil is perhaps most helpful to consider.

The AD is the largest Pentecostal—and the largest Protestant—church in Brazil (a nation where Pentecostals comprise 70% of the Protestant population). In the mid-1980s it reportedly had more than three million members. The AD was begun in 1910 by Swedish-American missionaries who had been heavily influenced by an early leader of the Assemblies of God (in the United States), W. H. Durham (the earliest proponent of the "two-step," finished work theory). In the first three decades or more, growth was slow. Like all Brazilian Protestants, the early Pentecostals did encounter a certain degree of Roman Catholic persecution. However, in the period prior to World War II, contacts were also made with missionaries from the Assemblies of God. The church's network of support was thereby established. Since 1949 it has enjoyed phenomenal growth.

The success of the AD and other Pentecostal churches in Brazil is quite understandable, given the international history of Pentecostalism as a movement which initially attracts the lower social classes. (In view of the movement's egalitarian spirit and its implicit challenge to the structures of power, as well as the opportunity it provides for all members to make spiritually significant contributions to Church life through speaking in tongues, Pentecostalism's success among segments of the population far removed from power is quite understandable.) The success of Pentecostalism in Brazil among the lower classes may also be related to the "humanizing process" which participation in the church and its rigorous ethical discipline has had on its members. As a result, the reputation of its members has risen to the point that they are among the most desirable employees in Brazil. No doubt as a consequence of this dynamic, much of the membership is enjoying upward social mobility, and a portion of it now belongs to the middle class. Also, some of the former persecution of the church by the largely Roman Catholic Brazilian establishment is abating. The AD has achieved government recognition, though it is still a political impossibility for high officials to associate with it.[29]

The AD and other Pentecostal churches in Brazil have succeeded well in becoming indigenous churches. Nevertheless, the AD still depends on missionaries from the United States Assemblies of God and from two Scandinavian Pentecostal mission agencies. The connection with the AG has largely influenced the AD's theological orientation, which is hardly surprising, given the relatively low level of theological training of its leadership. It is quite natural that it would look elsewhere for help in theological reflection. Thus, at least for its own internal purposes, the AD employs the United States Assemblies of God's *Statement of Fundamental Truths*. This means that the Brazilian church also affirms the "two-step" theory concerning the relationship of justification, sanctification, and baptism of the Spirit. (There are indications, however, that the AD employs the AG's old version of its Statement, in which reference was made to "entire sanctification" as the will of God [9]. The AG deleted this phrase in 1961. Whether the Brazilian church's continued affirmation of it is indicative of a theological break with its sister church remains an open question for this observer.)

Like its North American sister, the AD affirms the infallibility of Scripture (1). Such an affirmation is not atypical among theologically conservative churches in Brazil. However, as we have previously suggested, it seems that in the Latin American Evangelical community, at least in Brazil, such an affirmation may not carry the weight it does among North Americans. As in Europe, the affirmation of biblical inerrancy does not appear to be the cutting edge of Evangelical identity. But it is worth noting that at least some conservative churches in Brazil, as in the rest of the world, seem to remain in dialogue with the concept.[30]

The AD calls for the practice of a fairly strict life-style, especially with respect to alcohol consumption. Its extensive social ministry programs have clearly helped its evangelism outreach to the lower classes. Although such social ministry outreach may not be typical of the North American and European Evangelical communities, there seems to be a greater social conscience among Evangelicals in Brazil, if not throughout the Third World. Yet at least in Brazil this does not imply that Pentecostals or Evangelicals are joining forces with liberation theology. The social involvement of these conservatives usually does not take the form of political activity, as in Chile, but is more restricted to individual ethical involvements.

A final issue concerning the AD is the degree to which it is properly identified as part of the Evangelical movement. There may not be quite the strong consciousness of a distinct Evangelical identity in Brazil as there is in North America. However, this consciousness is growing as the Evangelical movement has been infiltrating into various Protestant churches. Among Lutherans in Brazil it is causing some internal controversy. Moreover, the Pentecostal tradition is generally regarded much as it is in Germany, as quite inimical to Evangelicalism. However, largely under the influence of AG, the AD has been tending more and more in the direction of Evangelicals.

To be sure, one still finds tensions between Brazilian Evangelicals and their Pentecostal counterparts. AD is surely not in the center of the Evangelical movement as it exists in Brazil. Probably that honor belongs to Baptist churches in Brazil like the Convençao Batista Brasileira (Brazilian Baptist Convention), which is heavily supported by the Southern Baptist Convention and other theologically conservative

Baptist churches. But the AD grows closer and closer to identification with the Evangelical movement. It is surely the most "Evangelical" Pentecostal church in Brazil; one of the other large Pentecostal churches, Igreja Evangélica Pentecostal "O Brasil para Cristo" (Evangelical Pentecostal Church "Brazil for Christ") has joined the World Council of Churches. And another, Congregação Cristã do Brasil (CCB) is far to the right of even the AD. Observers agree that CCB is the most sectarian of the churches in Brazil and least open to cooperation with Evangelicals or even with other Pentecostals. However, this does not seem to be a function of a unique doctrinal orientation.[31] That the AD, with its close working relationship to North American Pentecostalism, should be the Brazilian Pentecostal church most oriented to the Evangelical movement may be indicative of the important role North American influence plays in crystallizing a sense of Conservative Evangelical identity in the rest of the world.

Restorationist churches

Restorationist churches associated with the Evangelical movement must largely be limited to the so-called Churches of Christ ("Centrist") which first began to separate themselves from the Disciples of Christ in the 1920s. However, because these churches have no centralized organ but are strictly congregational organizations, one cannot easily determine the degree to which they are properly considered part of the Evangelical movement. Nevertheless, based on contacts with leaders of these churches, it appears that many of the "Centrists" do identify themselves as Evangelicals. A number of these local churches belong to the U.S. National Association of Evangelicals. On the other hand, the earlier secessionist group, the Churches of Christ (Noninstrumental), so called because they forbid the use of musical instruments in worship, has been unwilling to have intercourse with any other churches.[32] Thus it would not consider itself part of the Evangelical coalition.

The historical background on the schisms involving both groups has already been provided. The "Centrist" separation from the Disciples of Christ was perhaps more gradual, as many conservative congregations remained in the Disciples' Yearbook without supporting the organization. Only in 1968 during a restructuring of the Disciples of Christ did they formally secede. The two conservative groups differ among themselves not just with regard to the manner in which they separated from the Disciples' organization or with regard to the "Centrists'" openness to the use of musical instruments in worship. The latter is merely a symptom of their basic difference over the use of Scripture. "Noninstrumental" people take the silence of Scripture on any given topic as prohibitive of Christian activities concerning that matter. The "Centrists" regard such silence as permissive of activities concerning these matters.

Because the strictly congregational polity occasions so much diversity, it is difficult to characterize in a definitive way the "Centrists'" theological commitments. Indeed, the polity of these churches is almost a miniature carbon copy of what gives the Evangelical movement its cohesion. The Centrist churches are held together not by an ecclesiastical structure but largely by common educational institutions like Cincinnati Christian Seminary and by publications like the *Christian Standard*. At any rate, the Centrists are committed to characteristic Disciples' teachings like the weekly celebration of the Lord's Supper, Baptism by immersion, the rejection of all human creeds, and the refusal to distinguish between clergy and laypeople. On the question of biblical authority most Centrists, though not all, insist on the infallibility of the Bible. In this respect they continue the polemic against the liberal theology of the Disciples of Christ, which in large part originally generated their schism.

This view of biblical authority may also suggest a certain indebtedness of the churches to the Fundamentalist heritage. Such indebtedness is suggested by the presence of certain dispensationalist themes in the churches' thinking, an insistence on a strict distinction between the old covenant and the new covenant. However, the most prominent leaders of these churches insist that they are not advocating dispensationalism.

In recent years more cooperation with the "Noninstrumental" churches has been evident in some areas. But differences, both theological and sociological, remain. The Noninstrumental churches are more strongly concentrated in the southern United States, while Centrist churches are more thoroughly urbanized. Although statistics on these churches are difficult to verify, the Centrists probably number 2300 congregations with 125,000 members. They support an active foreign missions program.

Dispensationalist churches

Dispensationalist churches (those heavily influenced by dispensationalism) are only on the border between the Evangelical movement and outright Fundamentalism (cf. our earlier distinction between Fundamentalists and Evangelicals on the basis of their position on dispensationalism). Two of the best examples of these churches are the Plymouth Brethren (PB) and the Independent Fundamental Churches of America (IFCA).

Details concerning the polemical origin and general theological orientation of the Plymouth Brethren have been given. Because of the Brethren Movement's avowed congregationalism, with no formal ties among local assemblies, data about the movement is difficult to obtain. In the United States there are perhaps just over 1000 assemblies with almost 100,000 communicants. The Brethren have been divided into several groups, the major subdivisions of which are: (1) the "Open" Brethren, who believe that any believer who is personally sound of faith may be welcomed to the Lord's Table; and (2) the "Exclusive" Brethren, who follow the separatist inclinations of John Darby and reject fellowship with anyone who belongs to a church body harboring questionable teachings; this group is subdivided into smaller, mutually exclusive fellowships.

The Brethren continue to assert the inerrancy of Scripture, are largely dispensationalist, refuse to distinguish clergy and laity, and avoid creedal formulations. Their worship is very unstructured, though in most assemblies women are still not permitted to speak during worship (on the basis of 1 Cor. 14:34-35).[33] However a certain degree of cultural accommodation has evidenced itself among the Brethren. Thus, while the traditional style of the Brethren was often to meet in homes, some of the "Open" Brethren have begun to use "Bible Chapels" which are like the church buildings of denominationally related congregations. Moreover, while the Brethren historically have rejected the idea of an ordained ministry and its leaders normally supported themselves by secular employment, today many assemblies support full-time "resident workers" who may be theologically educated and preach frequently. In addition, a certain decline in the impact of dispensationalism is evident among the Brethren, such that the teachings of J. N. Darby only have minimal influence among the Brethren in Britain today.

Some Brethren suggest that the movement is facing a crisis of identity, that some of its constituency may be drifting into denominational churches.[34] It is true that a number of individual Brethren have played significant roles in various organizations of the Evangelical movement. Yet the separatist orientation and strict congregationalism of the Brethren have continued to distance them institutionally from the broader Evangelical coalition.

The Independent Fundamental Churches of America is an association of independent churches, pastors not denominationally affiliated, and related organizations. It is the continuing body of nondenominational Fundamentalist churches begun at the peak of the Fundamentalist controversy. The organization has grown markedly since 1940. In the mid-1980s it was comprised of more than 700 churches with over 100,000 members, perhaps as many as an additional 300 congregations with IFCA pastors, plus 35 additional organizations. A number of successful independent Bible churches in North America belong to the IFCA.

Congregational autonomy is guaranteed by the IFCA. It does have a doctrinal statement to which all members must subscribe. As a self-proclaimed Fundamentalist organization it is not surprising that all of Fundamentalism's five points (1, 2, 3, 15), as well as dispensational premillennialism (13, 15), the personality of the devil (14), and separatism (9, 12) are affirmed. There are indications that a number of original leaders of the organization were drawn from Congregational or Presbyterian backgrounds.[35] These commitments are reflected in the IFCA's affirmation of salvation by grace (6) and the eternal security of believers (7). Fundamentalist commitments are also evident in its denunciation of neo-Evangelicalism, the charismatic/Pentecostal movement, and the ecumenical movement.[36]

In recent years at least one militant Fundamentalist has raised questions about the IFCA's ability to maintain a truly Fundamentalist position over against the Evangelical movement.[37] However, at least in the mid-1980s, it was by no means certain that the IFCA was in the process of finding its identity within the Evangelical movement. It is apparently not removed from Evangelicalism on the basis of doctrinal disagreements. The dividing issues seem to be the IFCA positions on dispensationalism and separatism.

The heritage of the Radical Reformation

Churches rooted in the heritage of the Radical Reformation that belong to the Evangelical movement include both theologically conservative Baptist and Mennonite churches. Given their distinct denominational heritage, these two groups must be treated separately.

The Mennonite tradition has its roots in the Anabaptist movement of the Radical Reformation. A group of Anabaptists who had largely been dispersed by severe persecution was organized by Menno Simons

(1496–1561), whose leadership was so influential that his followers bear his name. Simons stressed pacifism as well as a strict communal discipline and separation of the church from the state.[38]

The 17,000 member NAE-member Mennonite Brethren Churches, USA (MBC) is a good example of this tradition. MBC has its origins in a 19th-century revival within the Mennonite community in Russia, a community which had its roots in Prussia and, before that, perhaps in the Netherlands. The revival seems to have been somewhat influenced by German Lutheran pietists, Moravian Pietism, and German Baptists. (It is interesting to note that this Mennonite revival coincides with the development of the Baptist church in Russia.) Like the pietist movement, it represented a reaction against the laxity of the spiritual life of the (Mennonite) religious community and emphasized also the life of discipleship (sanctification).[39]

The revival led to the new church in 1860. Extensive immigration to the United States began in 1874, and the church organized on American soil five years later. As one might suspect, its membership did not play a leading role in the formation of the Fundamentalist movement, as it was then still functioning very much as an ethnic church. However, the influence of Fundamentalist Bible Schools on the leadership was substantial, and the MBC was eventually drawn into that movement and subsequently into the Evangelical movement.[40]

Characteristic theological commitments of the MBC include affirmations of salvation by grace (IV), the importance of church discipline (VI), the ordinance of washing the saints' feet (VI), the responsibility of evangelism (VII), believer's baptism by immersion (IX), the Lord's Supper and its elements understood as symbols (X), and the historic Mennonite peace position opposing military service by Christians (XV). Although the classical Mennonite insistence on the distinction between church and state is maintained, the MBC shows an openness to its members' paying taxes and witnessing against discrimination (XIV). Likewise affirmed is the rapture of the saints (XVI) and biblical infallibility (II). In connection with possible influences from Fundamentalism on the these points, it is also interesting to note that the MBC *Confession of Faith* (V) speaks of how by "yield[ing] to Christ" the believer is "empower[ed]. . .to gain victory." Such language would seem to suggest the influence of Fundamentalism and the Keswick movement on the MBC.[41]

Largely having won the battle for Americanization (the MBC congregations in the United States no longer use German in the worship setting), the Brethren increasingly have become integrated into the Evangelical movement. They are joined in NAE membership by at least one other Mennonite church with a similar Russian heritage, the Evangelical Mennonite Brethren Church.

Interestingly enough, a similar heritage is shared by the All-Union Council of Evangelical Christians–Baptists (AUCECB) in the U.S.S.R. Their unique relation to the Evangelical movement warrants a more lengthy exposition. Comprised of four quite theologically conservative groups—Baptists, the Union of Evangelical Christians, the Union of Christians of Evangelical Faith (Pentecostals), and the Mennonite Brethren—the AUCECB was established in 1944 largely as a result of government pressure.

The Baptists in Russia had their origins in the 19th century among German immigrants—Lutherans and some Mennonites—who previously had been influenced by Pietism. These groups were further influenced by the father of the Baptist church in Germany, Johann Gerhard Oncken. Baptists had indigenous origins also in a Russian sect itself first influenced by Pietism, the Molokans. Early Baptists quickly won converts among this group. We already have noted the circumstances of the emergence of the Mennonite Brethren and the impact the development of the Baptist community in Russia may have had on the Brethren's schism from the established Mennonite community.

The Evangelical Christians was first initiated by a group of Russian aristocrats in St. Petersburg. Their Bible studies and evangelistic meetings were heavily influenced by the Plymouth Brethren. The Union of Evangelical Christians, therefore, came to reflect a kind of openness in worship practices, particularly pertaining to baptism, and an anti-clericalism typical of the Brethren. Other English-speaking influences on the Evangelical Christians and the Baptists included the American evangelist Dwight Moody and the Keswick movement. Thus a concern with Holiness came to characterize both groups.

The third group in the Union, the Pentecostals, were initiated in 1921 by a former Russian Baptist who had been influenced by American Pentecostalism. Norwegian Pentecostalism also had an impact on them. Nevertheless, at this point also American Evangelical experience was influential on the Russians. The connections to the American experience are no less apparent with regard to the fourth group, the Mennonite Brethren (whose American heirs we have just discussed).

During the period until 1940 the first three of these groups suffered persecution at various times from both the Czar and the Communists.

However, they also grew rapidly. This growth was perhaps not surprising, because their high moral standards have helped them obtain a reputation as exemplary workers.[42] However, for this same reason these evangelical movements became even more of a threat to governmental authorities. This phenomenon explains in part the uneasy truce between Russian Evangelicals and the Soviet hierarchy today.

The union of these groups in 1944 (complemented by the addition of the Pentecostals the next year and later by the Mennonite Brethren) has had a certain instability from the outset. Of the Mennonites, only the Brethren joined. It was possible for them to affiliate, largely because these Mennonites had forfeited a number of the distinct Mennonite attributes such as absolute pacifism and refusal to take oaths.[43] Also, the Pentecostals joined only under duress, and were forced to renounce the practice of glossolalia in public gatherings.[44]

Given these circumstances, it is hardly surprising that not all Protestant conservatives have associated with the AUCECB. The problem posed by the failure of many Mennonites to affiliate has been exacerbated further by the fact that some Russian Pentecostals are "Pentecostal Unitarians." Pentecostals who have sought asylum in various foreign embassies in order to avoid government persecution were mainly those who did not affiliate with the AUCECB. It is their lack of affiliation which makes them suspect to Soviet authorities, for it is normally through affiliation with the Union that a Protestant congregation becomes "registered" and therefore officially recognized.[45]

With regard to the Union's doctrinal views, most of the usual Baptist positions are taken with regard to Church and sacraments (Arts. V, VII). It is insisted that we cannot save ourselves, yet a necessary role for believers' consent to the work of the Spirit is affirmed (Art. IV). No statement of biblical inerrancy is officially made, but, in a correspondence course prepared for leaders in the Union, verbal inspiration and inerrancy are affirmed, along with strict life-style standards pertaining to restrictions on smoking, drinking, movies, and dancing.[46] In any case, a relatively passive submission to government authority also is advocated (Art. IX).

This last point underlines another, perhaps the greatest area of instability with the Union. Controversy has been evident on issues related to the relationship between church and state, the Christian's activity in the social and political realm. Matters came to a head in the 1960s when the All-Union Council, likely under pressure from Khrushchev, tried to enforce restrictions on the attendance of children in worship and insisted that the church's chief officers should be approved by the government. In response, dissidents formed in 1965 the Union [Council] of Churches of Evangelical Christians-Baptists (sometimes called Dissident Baptists). This new union basically maintains the same faith stance as the AUCECB, with the same emphasis on sanctification and a Church comprised of believers. Differences emerge on the clearer insistence of the Dissidents on the separation of church and state (33). This has implications for the Christian's involvement in social and political activities, as only the Dissidents and some unregistered Pentecostals carry on charitable activities, a practice the AUCECB has avoided in accord with government regulations.[47] The Dissidents' position also includes some implicit challenges to the U.S.S.R.'s system of registration for churches (33, 43). In taking these positions, the Dissidents have refused fellowship with the AUCECB. They are suspicious that the All-Union Council has so heavily cooperated with the government that it has become a kind of Soviet puppet.

The Union (Council) of Dissident Baptists has commanded much international attention for the persecution (much of it invited) to which some of its segments have been subjected. It is as if the Dissidents were actively seeking persecution, developing a doctrine of the necessity of a suffering Church. The Dissidents peaked in 1966 when their numbers reached about 155,000. More recently their membership seems to have declined, perhaps to a low of 100,000, though a recent report claimed that their numbers had swelled to a membership of between one and two million. In any case, they seem to represent an attractive countercultural alternative for many youth in the U.S.S.R. A good percentage of their membership is young.

Although the establishment AUCECB has been hurt by these developments, it has enjoyed a period of less harassment from the government. (Dissidents may have absorbed some of the pressure it would otherwise have experienced.) In the early 1980s the Union had a membership of roughly half a million, the largest Baptist church in Europe, with the possible exception of the Dissidents. This last point concerning AUCECB membership suggests another bone of contention between the Dissidents and the All-Union Council: the Dissidents do not include Pentecostals in their membership.

The question of the degree to which both factions of Soviet Evangelicalism are properly deemed part of the Evangelical Movement is raised by the fact that the AUCECB holds membership in the WCC. This ecumenical commitment is reflected in the AUCECB's recent appeal to restore harmony with the Dissidents. By contrast, the Union (Council) of Dissident Baptists is highly critical of all ecumenical involvement. Such a critical view of the ecumenical movement and the WCC is typical of much Russian Evangelicalism. At least one observer believes that this is a consequence of the influence of radio broadcasts and literature from Evangelicals in the West.[48]

Certainly no examination of Evangelicalism in the U.S.S.R. can overlook the role of Evangelical mission societies like Underground Evangelism, Christian Missions to the Communist World, Inc. (founded by Richard Wurmbrand), and the Slavic Gospel Association. These organizations have been involved in broadcasting religious programs into the U.S.S.R., as well as distributing religious literature—often Bibles—and some economic aid to Soviet Evangelicals. The work of these missions has been somewhat controversial, as at times it involves illegal activities like Bible smuggling. Clearly, these efforts seem to have been effective in making more literature available to Soviet Evangelicals. But much controversy has been raised about the degree to which such illegal means are justified and the degree to which their financial contributions have created an unhealthy dependency on the part of Soviet Evangelicals. In addition, the work of these North American and Western Evangelicals seems to have nurtured an increased factionalism within the Soviet Evangelical community (as witnessed by the growing negativism among Soviet Evangelicals towards the ecumenical movement).[49]

One can ask whether in effect what has transpired is that the issues and identity of the Conservative Evangelical movement have been artificially imposed on Soviet Evangelicals. Certainly the worldwide, largely Western Evangelical movement would wish to claim the Soviet Evangelicals as part of their movement, despite the Soviets' occasional reticence in affirming biblical inerrancy. It is clear that the Soviet Evangelicals constitute a Bible-centered movement, a movement committed to the restoration of a "primitive Christianity" by self-conscious appropriation of the Anabaptist heritage. Yet perhaps because they are largely a lower-class group without a well-educated leadership, their use of the Bible exhibits a kind of precritical naiveté which is suggestive of pre-Enlightenment, antebellum Evangelicalism—the kind we noted in the Third World. Neither Soviet Evangelicals nor other Baptists in Eastern Europe nor many Evangelicals in the Third World would normally classify themselves as part of an international Evangelical movement, at least not unless Western Evangelicals nurtured such an identity among them. This raises the question of whether the modern Evangelical movement is in reality so much a post-Enlightenment phenomenon that a precritical Evangelicalism like that in Russia, not truly exposed to modernism, does not really quite fit into the modern Evangelical movement as we know it.[50]

Elsewhere in Europe, particularly in Eastern Europe, one finds other theologically conservative Baptist churches which, like the Russian Baptists, seem to stand on the borders of the Evangelical movement. A possible exception might be the Bund Evangelisch-Freikirchlicher Gemeinden in der DDR (a federation that includes East German Baptists, a very ecstatic group of Pentecostals called the Elim Fellowship, and Christians of the Brethren tradition who were influenced by J. N. Darby and his dispensationalism). Although a number of my European colleagues claim that this federation is properly understood as part of the Evangelical movement, its official view of Scripture is actually quite in harmony with more liberal, neoorthodox theology, and some leaders of the East German federation explicitly distinguish their church from the Evangelical movement.[51]

In France, the situation with Baptists is a bit different. The Fédération des Eglises Evangéliques Baptistes de France is a conservative church which affirms the infallibility of Scripture, at least in a qualified way (II), and, perhaps through the support it receives from the Southern Baptist Convention (USA), seems to align itself with the Evangelical movement in France. The other Baptist church in France, the Association Evangéligue d'Eglises Baptistes de Langue Française (I.2), holds a similar view of the nature of Scripture. But its early separatist history has led it to avoid all contact with French churches, even those related to the Evangelical movement.

Finally, we may mention conservative American Baptist churches that have roots in the Radical Reformation. Among these are the Baptist Bible Fellowship (BBF), the General Association of Regular Baptist Churches (GARB), the Conservative Baptist Association of America (CBAA), and the Baptist General Conference (BGC).[52] Of these, the first two more properly belong to the Fundamentalist movement.

The BBF is one of the largest of the theologically conservative Baptist organizations—if not the largest. In the mid-1980s it had more than 2500 churches in membership. (No figures on total membership of the churches are available, as the BBF does not in principle exclude its churches from membership in other Baptist bodies.)

The Fellowship has its origins in a 1950 secession from the World Baptist Missionary Fellowship (led by Fundamentalist, J. Frank Norris and today called the World Baptist Fellowship). The secession came over a controversy concerning the leadership of Norris. The seceders have still basically accepted the doctrinal statement of Norris's group. Thus the BBF affirms the five points of Fundamentalism, including the inerrancy of Scripture (I, VI, VII, XVII). Also affirmed are the personality of the devil (IV), justification through faith apart from works (XI, X), the requirement that one be born again in order to be saved (IX), the belief that the saints will persevere in faith to the end (XV), as well as the commands to tithe (XX) and to engage in the work of missions (XIX, XIII). As a self-consciously Fundamentalist church body which practices separatism, it is perhaps not surprising to find that it condemns both the Evangelical movement and any attempt to reconcile the creation account and the theory of evolution (V).[53]

Given its commitments, it is not surprising to learn that the BBF has an extensive foreign missions program working in 67 countries with more than 650 missionaries. It also has some large Baptist congregations inside the Fellowship, including Jerry Falwell's Thomas Road Baptist Church in Lynchburg, Virginia, and his Liberty Baptist College located in the same city. (Falwell is also associated with another, smaller Fundamentalist Baptist church body, the Liberty Baptist Fellowship comprised largely of churches founded by his school's graduates.)

We previously noted the origins of the General Association of Regular Baptist Churches (GARB) during the Fundamentalist-Modernist Controversy. Self-consciously intending to embrace the Calvinist Baptist perspective of some historic Baptist Confessions like the *Second London Confession* (1689) and the *New Hampshire Confession* (1833), GARB affirms virtually every one of the doctrinal positions held by the BBF. Additionally, GARB affirms a premillennialism that involves the rapture and the salvation of Israel as a nation (XIX, XVIII).

Fundamentalists generally praise the GARB's orthodoxy. But the emergence in the Association of certain sympathies with the Evangelical movement has been a source of some concern.[54] Nevertheless, GARB is still very active in an extensive foreign missions program. Its missionary corps numbers over 2000! Its total membership in the mid-1980s was almost 240,000 in more than 1500 congregations.

The Conservative Baptist Association of America (CBAA) has a somewhat parallel history as an organization formed as the result of a secession of the old Fundamentalist Fellowship from the Northern Baptist Convention. With a more irenic spirit than the group which had formed GARB (the Fundamentalist Fellowship was strongly committed to avoiding schism if possible and so had not joined the Baptist Bible Union and had not seceded at the time of the formation of GARB), the members of the Old Fundamentalist Fellowship were not able to merge with that group when they finally seceded from the NBC in 1947, though the possibility was explored. The possibility of merger was also discussed with the Baptist General Conference (an organization of Swedish Baptists in the United States which, in 1944, had severed its association with the Northern Baptist–related American Baptist Foreign Mission Association and became independent). This merger was also not carried out. It failed to be realized, not because of doctrinal differences between the groups (as the fellowships which were both eventually created employ virtually parallel Declarations of Faith), but because the strongly ethnic character of the BGC ultimately precluded merger. As a result, both groups created independent churches which identified themselves with the emerging Evangelical movement.

The CBAA affirms Fundamentalism's five points, including an insistence on the inerrancy of Scripture and the supreme authority "in all matters of which they speak." The usual Baptist views on the Church and the sacraments/ordinances are also affirmed, as well as salvation by grace and the importance of regeneration. In addition, passing affirmations are made in its present Constitution of a kind of Fundamentalist separatism and premillennialism. Yet it should be noted that such affirmations were not included in the earliest CBAA doctrinal statement.

A price was paid by the CBAA for its original openness on these latter commitments. Thus, avowed Fundamentalists in the Association gradually separated from it and by 1968 formed the Fundamentalist Baptist Fellowship. An earlier, smaller secession preceded it. Ongoing controversies between the more rigorously conservative CBAA membership and its seminary leadership, largely committed to the Evangelical movement, have also been a part of the CBAA's history, though it is reported that such controversies largely have ceased to exist.[55]

These controversies do not necessarily mean that the grass roots membership of the CBAA has become a part of the Evangelical movement. Its leaders in its national offices prefer to identify the CBAA theologically with Fundamentalism rather than with the Evangelical movement. But several of its leaders report that many of the Association's members would identify themselves as Evangelicals, at least with reference to their style of ministry and openness to cooperate with non-Fundamentalists.[56] It has continued a steady growth in its support of the foreign and home missions societies associated with it. And in the mid-1980s the Association had more than 1000 congregations with about 240,000 members in its fellowship. Partly due to its polity and perhaps also due to the Fundamentalist identity of some of its leaders, it is not presently a member denomination of the NAE. Interestingly enough, however, the group with which it almost merged and with which it largely shares common theological beliefs, the Baptist General Conference, is a member denomination of the NAE.[57]

The Free Church tradition

Churches with origins in the European Free Church tradition that belong to the Evangelical movement include The Brethren Church (Ashland, Ohio) (BC), to some extent the National Fellowship of Brethren Churches ("Grace Brethren") (NFBC), and, most definitely, The Evangelical Covenant Church (ECC), as well as The Evangelical Free Church of America (EFC).[58] The first of these, the BC (Ashland) is an NAE member church of more than 14,000 members with roots in an 18th-century revival of sectarian Pietism in Germany. When transplanted to America, the parent church continued to perpetuate many of its early, European traditions of plain dress and simplicity of worship. However, in 1882 it was rocked by a schism involving the excommunication of a "liberal" pastor who with his colleagues formed the BC. At stake in the schism was the implementation of "denominationalism in the church" (creating Sunday schools, opting for professionally trained and salaried ministry, etc.).

The Ashland Brethren affirm at least in a qualified way biblical infallibility and the perfection of revelation (2), justification by personal faith (3/5), and the Christian's obligation to avoid all swearing and carnal strife (3/8). In addition to believer's baptism, the Lord's Supper is celebrated as a complete meal. Also the anointing of the sick with oil and the washing of the saints' feet is advocated (3/9).

The Brethren Church was itself marred by schism in 1939 by the secession of the "Grace Brethren," known today as the National Fellowship of Brethren Churches. The NFBC emerged as a reaction against the perceived theological liberalism in Ashland Brethren seminaries and in protest to the Ashland group's inadequate position on the issue of the eternal security of believers. The "Grace Brethren" took a more Calvinist position in holding that once persons are saved they remain saved ("eternally secure" in their salvation).[59] The warrant for this schism on grounds of the purported "liberalism" of the Ashland group seems increasingly valid in view of the secessionist NFBC Fundamentalist position vis-a-vis the growing influence of the Evangelical left on the Ashland Brethren. The new church, the NFBC, has grown to more than twice the size (over 40,000) of the Ashland Brethren.

The Evangelical Covenant Church (ECC) and The Evangelical Free Church of America (EFC) share a similar heritage in Scandinavian Pietism and ethos. Of the two, the ECC is among the most open of Evangelical churches; the EFC tends self-consciously to allow less latitude than the ECC.[60] The strong ethnic heritage of both churches has limited the impact of the Fundamentalist movement on them (though the EFC in particular and the ECC to a lesser extent were affected somewhat by the revivalism of Dwight Moody, by dispensational premillennialism, by Methodism, and by the temperance movement).

The ECC emerged in the United States from the Swedish Lutheran Church, the Augustana Synod (a predecessor body of the Evangelical Lutheran Church in America). Pietists in the Synod formed mission societies and continued at least until 1878 to adhere to the fundamental doctrinal formula of Lutheranism, *The Augsburg Confession*. At that time news reached North America that the Svenska Missionsförbundet (Swedish Mission Covenant Church) had been formed under the leadership of Paul Peter Waldenström (1838–1917). The parent church had been occasioned largely as a result of doctrinal controversies arising over the growing interdenominational pietist revival in Sweden. Some have even argued that the Covenant tradition's European origins also include certain non-Lutheran influences—not so much the Anglo-American millennialism which affected the Norwegian and Danish revivals and have in turn had their impact on the EFC, but rather the Reformed tradition with its emphasis on covenant and its implications for Christian community.[61] (However, the Swedish parent church today perhaps should not be considered as a church of the Evangelical Movement as it holds membership in the WCC.) In any case, when the news of the formation of the new Swedish church reached North America some of its American sympathizers with roots in the older Swedish

Lutheran mission societies were themselves led to break entirely with Lutheranism and in 1884 formed the Swedish Evangelical Free Church (a predecessor body of the EFC). Two other groups/synods of Swedish-American pietist sympathizers who were less influenced by premillennialism than their Free Church brethren likewise were influenced in the following year to form the Swedish Evangelical Mission Covenant of America. It was this predecessor body which in 1929 became the ECC.

Despite these complex dynamics, the dependence of the ECC on the Lutheran heritage is evident and self-conscious (p. 2). This heritage seems to be reflected in the importance it places on the priesthood of all believers and the doctrine of justification by faith alone (p. 7). In addition, the ECC explicitly acknowledges its debt to Pietism. This is reflected in the priority given by the ECC to the practice of the Christian life, in the emphasis on sanctification and regeneration, rather than on theological precision as a "Confessional church" like Lutheranism (pp. 8, 13).

The pietist emphasis on sanctification and the Christian life also is reflected in the ECC description of the Church as a "fellowship of believers" in which faith is a "requirement for membership" (pp. 16-17). In harmony with the non-creedal character of its church, no position is taken regarding the status of the elements in Baptism and the Lord's Supper. (Something like the Lutheran version of the real presence can legitimately be affirmed in the ECC since, in harmony with the Lutheran *Augsburg Confession* [XIII.1], a description of the sacraments as "visible signs of the invisible grace" is employed [p. 17]. Some members, though by no means all, reportedly hold such a view or some view of the real presence akin to that of Reformed theology.)[62] An openness to the validity of both infant and adult baptism is acknowledged (p. 17).

The pietist, noncreedal commitments are most profoundly apparent in the ECC's views on Scripture. The church simply claims that the Bible is "the Word of God and the only perfect rule for faith, doctrine, and conduct" (pp. 5, 23). The heritage of Pietism with its reticence to define a doctrine of inspiration is quite apparent (p. 11). Such a treatment of biblical inspiration permits the ECC to assume a very open theological stance, an openness which has made possible a distinct drift towards the Evangelical left. Limitations/restrictions on the affirmation of biblical inerrancy could easily be accommodated by the ECC *Covenant Affirmations*, and, in fact, believers who cannot accept biblical inerrancy are still welcome in the fellowship.

A price has already been paid by the ECC's theological openness. In 1945 the Evangelical Covenant Church of Canada, a church of approximately 1200 members that is affiliated with the ECC, was racked by a dispute over the church's purported failure satisfactorily to articulate a substitutionary doctrine of the atonement with sufficient stress on the penalty Christ paid in his death. Some of the seceders joined a predecessor body of the EFC, presumably because it held more satisfactory views on the subject.

On the positive side, the theological openness of the ECC has led it to cooperate with both the NAE and the ecumenical movement (for example, the National Council of Churches of the U.S.A.). But it is a member neither of the NAE nor the NCC and seems to refuse to characterize itself as either Fundamentalist or liberal. The church has continued to grow in recent years, endeavoring to "Americanize" and move beyond its original ethnic base. In the mid-1980s it had a membership of well over 80,000.

The ECC's status as a church in the middle, between Evangelical and mainline churches, coupled with its concern for the unity of the Church as well as its Lutheran origins make its role a potentially most important one in ongoing Lutheran–Evangelical dialogue. The same might be said of the theologically conservative Free Churches in Europe like Det Norske Misjonsforbund (the Mission Covenant Church in Norway) and of the ECC's North American counterpart, the EFC.

The EFC was shaped by the same Swedish pietist influences as the ECC. However, in addition to Swedes who belonged to the Swedish Evangelical Free Church, it is comprised of former domestic missionary societies of Norwegian and Danish pietists. These organizations merged in 1950 to form the EFC and have since been joined by the ECC Canadian dissidents. It is hardly surprising, then, that the EFC takes most of the same doctrinal positions as the ECC. Its self-conscious intention to allow less latitude than the ECC is evident in its affirmation of the inerrancy of Scripture—that it is authoritative for Christian life and faith (1). This statement is interpreted as not limiting the Bible's claims to inerrancy in the areas of history or science.[63] Also in distinction from the ECC, the EFC affirms a substitutionary/sacrificial view of the atonement (3) and regards Baptism and the Lord's Supper as "ordinances" (7). Thus it is more explicit in its construal of these rites as mere symbols. The ordinances are regarded as rites to be observed "during the present age" (7). This statement and the EFC's affirmation of premillennialism (11) reflect an openness to dispensationalism which has characterized the church at several points in its history.[64] The EFC aims to affirm Christian liberty in such a way as to avoid both license and legalism. Yet some congregations prohibit—and all frown upon—the use of alcohol and tobacco.[65]

In the mid-1980s, the EFC was continuing its process of "Americanization." Its membership at this time was almost 150,000. Much like the ECC, the EFC's Lutheran origins, its concern to affirm justification by faith (6) but to balance this with an emphasis on holy living, coupled with its stated commitment to ecumenics "in spirit" render it a potential bridge between the Evangelical movement and mainline Lutheran churches. Nevertheless, despite its many similarities with the ECC, it has remained separate from the latter because of differences between them concerning church polity, and also because of the more theologically conservative orientation of the EFC. Perhaps this conservatism is reflected in the EFC's overt identification with the Evangelical movement in virtue of its membership in the NAE (while the ECC is not a member denomination).

Lutherans

Among Lutherans associated with the Evangelical movement, many observers think of The Lutheran Church–Missouri Synod (LCMS). The LCMS was founded in 1847 by German Lutheran immigrants to the American Midwest. These immigrants had been profoundly influenced by the 19th-century revival of Lutheran Orthodox theology in Germany. The church today continues actively to promote this heritage.

As a church which has largely preserved its ethnic character, the LCMS has promoted parochial education and a distinct ethos in a manner very similar to what we found in the Christian Reformed Church. It adheres to all the doctrines of the Lutheran Confessional writings *(The Book of Concord) because,* it is said, they agree with Scripture.[66] These doctrines will largely be enunciated in the book's third section. Most interesting is the insistence of the LCMS that the Law may legitimately function as a guide for living the Christian life ("third use of the Law") and that the Scriptures are verbally inspired and inerrant *(Brief Statement,* 1). The latter affirmation is made both on the basis of what Scripture teaches about itself and also, in a manner like the Christian Reformed Church, by arguing that inerrancy is a consequence of the "presupposition" of faith in Christ.[67]

The LCMS was racked by a bitter controversy in the 1970s, largely over its view of Scripture and the use of historical criticism. The greater number of its theologians and church presidents along with more than 200 congregations formed the Association of Evangelical Lutheran Churches (a predecessor body of the newly formed Evangelical Lutheran Church in America). This departure of those church leaders who were influenced by mainline theology has strengthened the dominance of Protestant Orthodox theology in the Synod. The LCMS has survived the schism, reorganized its major seminary, and remains the second largest Lutheran church in the United States, with a membership of more than 2.5 million.

As a strongly ethnic church deeply embedded in the heritage of Lutheran Orthodoxy, the LCMS was not actively involved in, and claims not to have been influenced by, the Fundamentalist movement. In the same manner, although some of its leaders cooperate with segments of the Evangelical movement on issues like biblical inerrancy, and surveys conducted in the last decade suggest that its members' attitudes correspond to those of Evangelicals, the LCMS does not officially identify itself with the Evangelical movement and is not a member of the NAE. The reasons for its failure to identify with Evangelicalism will be dealt with in some detail later, as they are quite pertinent to this study. They seem to pertain to LCMS's hesitancy about the interdenominational, largely Reformed-pietist character of the Evangelical movement and to what LCMS leaders perceive as Evangelicalism's inadequate views on biblical inerrancy.[68]

A similar doctrinal orientation and relation to the Evangelical movement is evident in several theologically conservative Lutheran churches closely related to LCMS, for example, the Lutheran Church of Australia, the India Evangelical Lutheran Church, and the Selbständige Evangelisch-Lutherische Kirche (Free Lutheran Church) in West Germany. A number of other conservative Lutheran churches in the United States, like the Wisconsin Evangelical Lutheran Synod, similarly avoid identification with the Evangelical movement.[69] However, one can find numerous persons in Evangelical and charismatic lobby groups within various Lutheran churches who do identify explicitly with the Evangelical movement.

Thus, for example, Lutherans are highly visible and even predominate in the Bekenntnisbewegung (Confessing Movement) in the established churches of West Germany. As we have noted, this movement as a whole was largely occasioned by the negative reaction of German theological conservatives to the impact of Rudolf Bultmann's theology and continues to try to reassert the influence of traditional doctrinal positions of the Reformation churches (their "Confessions") on the present-day institutions of these churches. For various reasons, some related to the pietist roots of many of its members and the impact of Billy Graham and other American Evangelicals on them, the movement has largely identified itself as Evangelical *(Evangelikal)*. Much of its collective efforts are devoted to educating its constituency to the dangers posed by modern theology and new pluralistic social mores, to lobbying inside the churches in order to shake them loose from these influences, and to organizing alternative programs to those organized by liberal elements in their churches.

The largest blanket organization of the Bekenntnisbewegung, comprised of several Evangelical organizations, is the Konferenz Bekennender Gemeinschaften (Conference of Confessing Communities). Its notable leaders are Lutherans like Peter Beyerhaus. The organization includes in its membership two groups inside the Evangelical Lutheran Church in Württemberg which identify themselves as Evangelicals. These groups of Evangelicals, the Evangelische Sammlung in Württemberg and the Ludwig-Hofacker-Vereinigung, are composed of Lutherans. Likewise included in the larger Bekennenden Gemeinschaften is a transdenominational group of self-proclaimed Evangelicals from Reformed, Lutheran, and United churches, the Bekenntnisbewegung "kein anderes Evangelium" (No Other Gospel). Besides lobbying for theologically and politically conservative causes in their churches, these organizations also sponsor alternative church programs, the most noteworthy being their own alternative educational festivities to the large church festivals *(Kirchentage)* sponsored by the established German churches.

In addition to these Evangelical organizations which, if not exclusively comprised of Lutherans, include many Lutherans, the Bekennenden Gemeinschaften cooperates with at least two additional entirely Lutheran organizations. They include: (1) Selbständige Evangelisch-Lutherische Kirche; and (2) Kirchliche Sammlung um Bibel und Bekenntnis (Ecclesiastical Assembly around Bible and Confession) (an exclusively Lutheran Evangelical lobby working to effect the aims of the Bekenntnisbewegung inside the German Lutheran churches). Members of these and the other German Evangelical organizations, along with various Evangelicals from other nations, have formed the Internationale Konferenz Bekennender Gemeinschaften. Among the most

important non-German groups to have joined the international conference is the Kyrklig Samling kring Bibel och bekännelse (an umbrella
organization of various Swedish Evangelicals including the Kyrklig
Fornyelse [Church Renewal Movement], the High Church group in the
State Lutheran Church in Sweden, a group which has so thoroughly
objected to the ordination of women and other manifestations in the
Swedish Church of what it deems liberal theology that it has organized
a Free Synod [a self-governing group of churches with leaders in agreement with the conservatives' cause while still maintaining membership
within the State Church]).

It must be reiterated that the German and Swedish Lutheran organizations noted in the preceding paragraph seem explicitly to reject
identifying themselves as part of the Evangelical movement. (At least
the Swedish organizations and the Kirchliche Sammlung um Bibel und
Bekenntnis seem to be uncomfortable with the characteristic Evangelical insistence on the Bible's verbal inspiration and inerrancy.[70]
Nevertheless, the fact that these Lutheran organizations are able to
cooperate with segments of the Evangelical movement is also indicative
of the profound influence the Evangelical movement is having on the
Lutheran church.

In North America this influence is also quite apparent. Evangelical
lobbies have been formed within American Lutheranism in order to
work for purposes similar to those of the Bekenntnisbewegung. At least
prior to the formation of the Evangelical Lutheran Church in America,
among the most prominent and militant of these groups was the Fellowship of Evangelical Lutheran Laity and Pastors (which also included
charismatics in its membership). Likewise, the International Lutheran
Renewal Center, an exclusively charismatic lobby which seems willing
to be associated with the Evangelical movement, has been formed in
North American Lutheranism. One finds similar charismatic organizations elsewhere, like the Oasis movement in Norway.[71] In many
instances Lutherans are found on the borders of, if not within, the
Evangelical movement.

Other mainline churches

Most prominent among other mainline churches thought to be associated with the Evangelical movement is the Southern Baptist Convention (SBC). Largest of the United States Protestant churches (14.5

million members) and continuing to grow while other mainline churches register membership losses, theologically conservative in the orientation of its membership and with several prominent members of the
Evangelical movement (Billy Graham, Harold Lindsell, and even Jimmy Carter) belonging to it, the SBC would seem to qualify as a Conservative Evangelical church. In addition to these factors, the SBC,
while maintaining most of the traditional Baptist doctrinal positions
and emphasizing foreign missions (VI, VII, XI), with a distinct Calvinist influence with emphasis on the primacy of grace (IV, V), also
affirms the inerrancy of Scripture (I).[72] The general expectation that
Convention members abstain from alcohol as well as its rapid membership growth are also apparent indications of the family resemblance
between SBC and the Evangelical movement. In spite of these similarities, however, the SBC has never joined the NAE, and a number
of its theologians as well as some of its theologically conservative
members refuse—albeit for different reasons—to identify with the
Evangelical movement. In fact, in the 1970s and the 1980s the question
of the SBC's compatibility with the Evangelical movement, centered
on heated debates about the use of historical criticism and mainline
theology, helped occasion a major controversy within the SBC.[73]

Historically, the SBC's identification with the Evangelical movement
and the latter's spiritual forefather, Fundamentalism, is at best ambiguous. Its original constituency and present methods are drawn largely
from the southern United States; this stems from the circumstances of
the SBC's organization in 1845, when it and Baptists in the North went
their separate ways over issues that would lead to the Civil War. As a
result of this constituency, the Convention retained the theologically
conservative orientation typical of the South even in the postbellum
era. As a result, although there were some controversies in the Convention occasioned by Landmarkists and J. Frank Norris, the SBC,
like other churches in the South, was largely untouched by the Fundamentalist Controversy until the South became concerned about antievolution legislation; then it "hopped on the Fundamentalist band-
wagon." In 1926, the SBC went on record as opposing the theory of
evolution. And in 1925 it officially affirmed the inerrancy of Scripture.
But that these affirmations did not reflect deep-seated Fundamentalist
fervor and do not unambiguously entail SBC identification with the
Evangelical movement is suggested by the fact that almost until 1980
the theological and ecclesiastical leadership of the Convention was
largely in the hands of persons influenced by mainline theology.

In the early 1970s the tide began to swing the other way. In reaction to the moderates' hegemony, theological conservatives in the Convention, not all of whom identified with the Evangelical movement (in some cases because of the movement's "theological inclusiveness") organized their own lobby, the Baptist Faith and Message Fellowship. Particularly influenced by Harold Lindsell's attack on the drift toward liberalism within Evangelical circles, by the mid-1980s the SBC conservatives were to a great extent on the way to taking control of the major SBC institutions. At least one observer has suggested that this development may be more a sociological function, an attempt on the part of the conservatives to preserve the 19th-century southern ethos of the church. At any rate, the conservatives regularly have controlled the Presidency of the Convention, and thus also many appointments to various Boards of SBC-related institutions. Perhaps these conservatives are in the process of remaking the largest Protestant denomination in the United States into a church which, though its leaders may not unanimously identify with the Evangelical movement, at least reflects core Conservative Evangelical theological commitments.[74]

Evangelicals in other mainline churches are endeavoring to make a similar impact on their churches through the formation of Evangelical caucuses and/or lobbies. We have already noted a few within mainline Lutheran churches and in the Presbyterian Church (U.S.A.). Examples of such Evangelical lobbies in just two of the mainline denominations in which these groups have developed include the Good News Movement, an Evangelical lobby within The United Methodist Church, and the newly formed Episcopalians United for Revelation, Renewal, and Reformation among American Episcopalians. (It is noteworthy that the impetus for efforts by conservatives in The Episcopal Church to create a self-governing "church within the church" for those opposing ordination of women and other liberal trends largely has come from its High Church, Anglo-Catholic elements. But Evangelicals in the church have been included in a coalition aimed at encouraging these efforts.) Anglican Evangelicals even have their own organization inside the Church of England, the Church of England Evangelical Council, the Standing Committee of the Anglican Evangelical Assembly. It has been said that one-sixth of this church's priests are Evangelical.[75] The Evangelical movement is quite evidently making an internal impact on many mainline churches.

Chapter 9

Educational Institutions

As already noted, because of the diverse denominational heritages which constitute the Evangelical movement, it is not so much the churches that hold the movement together. Rather, its cohesion depends much more on parachurch agencies and common educational institutions. At least in North America, the most typical Evangelical institution is the Bible School (a postsecondary school usually providing a three-year course of study with a curriculum confined almost exclusively to the study of the Bible for the purpose of preparing church leaders and evangelists).

Of the great number of such schools, perhaps the most prestigious is Moody Bible Institute, located in Chicago. Even Fundamentalists still largely regard it as an orthodox institution. Its *Doctrinal Statement* affirms a number of Fundamentalist commitments including the rapture (V), the requirement that one must be born again (IV), and an understanding of Christ's death as a substitutionary sacrifice (III). Moreover, dress codes enforcing modesty in appearance are imposed on students.[1] We may note, however, that only the verbal inspiration of Scripture is affirmed, not its inerrancy (II). The Moody enterprise is involved in a number of projects, including Moody Press, a magazine with large circulation called the *Moody Monthly,* and its own radio broadcasting network.

The Evangelical movement's educational network also includes four-year colleges and universities as well as seminaries. Among colleges, perhaps the flagship institution is Wheaton College in Wheaton, Illinois. It was begun in 1848 by Wesleyan Methodists who later gave up control to Congregationalists. The heritage of the Holiness movement in Wheaton's origins was still reflected in the late 1980s in its code of conduct which includes prohibitions against alcohol and social dancing. The school's Evangelical orientation is reflected in its Confession of Faith, which affirms Biblical inerrancy.

Wheaton's reputation as a quality institution is well deserved. It has a faculty with advanced degrees from high-caliber institutions. Moreover, unlike some schools, academic standards really are enforced. However, for some Evangelicals and Fundamentalists the excellent education it provides has its dark side. The spirit of academic freedom and high standards of the school are reflected in the fact that a number of its faculty have been influenced by the Evangelical left. Campus life is not unlike other colleges related to mainline churches, as the conduct codes, particularly related to alcohol consumption, are by no means scrupulously followed.[2] Nevertheless, Wheaton's credibility and respect in the Evangelical movement remain high.

Wheaton is only one of a whole network of Evangelical colleges. Among the other well-known institutions are Gordon College in Wenham, Mass., founded by one of the foremost leaders of the Prophetic Conferences, A. J. Gordon; Oral Roberts University in Tulsa, Okla., founded by the well-known evangelist; Jerry Falwell's Liberty Baptist College in Lynchburg, Va.; denominationally related institutions like Seattle Pacific University, a school of The Free Methodist Church of North America; Houghton College, Houghton, N.Y., operated by The Wesleyan Church; and also the chief educational institution of the most militant Fundamentalists, Bob Jones University in Greenville, S.C.

A number of quality seminaries are associated with the Evangelical movement, for example: Gordon-Conwell Theological Seminary in South Hamilton, Mass., a nondenominational school influenced in this century by Princeton theology; Trinity Evangelical Divinity School in Deerfield, Ill., owned and operated by the Evangelical Free Church of America; and Dallas Theological Seminary, a nondenominational school which has been the leading propagator of dispensationalism. In addition, seminaries related to the Evangelical movement are found on virtually every continent.

The flagship of Evangelical institutions, however, is Fuller Theological Seminary in Pasadena, Calif. We have noted previously the origins of Fuller Seminary in the ministry of the radio evangelist Charles Fuller and its commitment to top-flight scholarship. That commitment is still reflected today in the first-rate faculty which continues to staff the school. Its high standards are reflected in the fact that many of the graduates have gone on to obtain doctorates from the most prestigious universities, and its Presbyterian students—at least in the 1970s—consistently attained the highest scores on standardized United Presbyterian preordination exams.[3]

Fuller's reputation is evidenced in the impressive size of its student body. In the mid-1980s it registered more than 2500 students in its degree programs (with almost as many Presbyterian students as the largest Presbyterian seminaries). Indeed, one who spends time on campus comes away sensing that the student ethos is very similar to what one finds on the campuses of other quality mainline ecumenical seminaries (except perhaps for the large concentration of charismatic/Pentecostal students). Chapel attendance is not compulsory, and there are no dress or behavior codes. But it is perhaps worth noting that, at least in the mid-1980s, Fuller's most popular course (recently reinstated with a new course title after temporary suspension for reevaluation and restructuring), the one that had by far the greatest enrollment at the seminary, was a class devoted to healing entitled, "Signs, Wonders and Church Growth."

Despite its stellar staff and solid reputation, Fuller has received its most intense attention from Evangelicals and mainline observers as a result of its controversial *Statement of Faith*. The crucial issue has been an alteration of the original statement which had claimed that the Bible was "free from all error in whole and in part." The present statement (3) maintains a position of "limited inerrancy" (the idea that the Bible is infallible only on matters of faith and conduct but not necessarily in its assertions pertaining to history and the cosmos).

This departure from the position of total inerrancy caused much internal controversy. Matters came to a head in 1976 with the attack by Harold Lindsell's book, *The Battle for the Bible*. In defense, Fuller's eminent and highly influential president, David Hubbard, has argued that the Bible's own emphasis is on "what the Holy Spirit is saying to the churches through the Biblical writers," not on matters of science, geography, or history.[4] Some of what he says has been interpreted to suggest what contemporary neoorthodox theology maintains about Scripture "becoming" the Word of God, being a witness to the Word but not the Word itself. Of course Hubbard rejects the idea that such a similarity exists. He and several of his colleagues insist that the Bible *is* the Word of God.[5] And the seminary's *Statement of Faith* (3) seems to reflect this same commitment to a kind of plenary inspiration, insofar as it states that "all the books of the Old and New Testaments, given by divine inspiration, are the written word of God. . . ." This affirmation of a kind of plenary inspiration (the idea that the whole Bible is Word of God), then, seems to be the crucial distinguishing factor between Fuller Seminary's version of Evangelicalism and mainline theology. Could this suggest that the affirmation of plenary inspiration is the cutting edge of Evangelical identity?

At least in terms of enrollment levels and financial support, Fuller has not been hurt by the controversy. But one can notice a certain weakening of the ties between Fuller and the NAE, a relationship which in the early years of the seminary was crucial to its identity. Also it is alleged that neoorthodox theology is taking hold in the classrooms. Indeed, in the mid-1980s, at least one of Fuller's faculty members was concerned to establish neoorthodoxy as the prevailing paradigm for Evangelical theology. But the predominance of such a viewpoint on campus is rejected by the administration, and my contacts lead me to agree that relatively few on the faculty explicitly or even consciously would endorse neoorthodoxy.[6] As to the question of what makes Fuller a uniquely Evangelical institution, the answer given by David Hubbard is instructive. He speaks of the school's Evangelical identity in terms of its contribution to helping the Evangelical movement rethink its identity.[7] That indeed may be Fuller Seminary's greatest contribution.

The last word concerning Fuller's character as an institution of the Evangelical movement may have come in a 1983 statement of its faculty and Board of Trustees, entitled *Mission beyond the Mission*. President Hubbard directed me to it. One notes the seminary's explicit identification with the movement. The statement proceeds to assert that the seminary does "not assume that evangelical purity demands an isolation from other Christians who do not share our particular [Conservative Evangelical] heritage." My first-hand contacts with the Fuller community indicate that these commitments are being lived out in the institution's life. In so doing, the school takes very seriously the question of Evangelical identity.

Outside the United States one of the interesting educational institutions aligned with the Evangelical Movement is the Albrecht-Bengel-Haus in Tübingen, West Germany. Founded in 1969 by the Gesprächs-kreis of the Württembergian Synod (today called the Lebendige Gemeinde) the Bengel-Haus is a study house and residence for Evangelical students who are studying at the world-famous University of Tübingen and its Faculty of Theology. The rationale in creating the center by this Evangelical lobby in the Lutheran Church in Württemberg was that it would act as corrective for students to the predominant liberal theology of the lecture hall.

At the Bengel-Haus, Evangelical students are provided with a supportive community in which they may work through some of the challenging and disturbing material they are learning in the classroom.

Noncredit courses from an Evangelical theological perspective are sometimes offered. These are seen as complementing the students' work in the university. Likewise the house offers opportunities for training in the practical aspects of pastoral ministry. Spiritual fellowship among members of the house is also important.

Like most Evangelical institutions, the Bengel-Haus has its own doctrinal and behavioral standards (7).[8] These standards are quite typical, but it is interesting to note that the Bengel-Haus only calls on its students to accept the divine authority of the whole of Scripture, not necessarily its inerrancy (2). The concept of the Bengel-Haus has drawn much attention among European Evangelicals; a few similar institutions are being established in conjunction with other European universities.

Among unofficial educational institutions which do not offer courses for credit, by far the most famous is L'Abri Fellowship in Huémoz, Switzerland. It was established by the well-known American Evangelical theologian, Francis Schaeffer, and his wife, Edith Schaeffer. The purpose of the center has been to provide an accepting atmosphere for students and other seekers to study Scripture and theology in a context of Christian fellowship and worship.

Located in a beautiful section of the Alps, all sorts of people, including atheists and liberals, are welcome to study. I have found the level of discussion in study groups and lectures there to compare favorably with Christian education events in mainline churches. Francis Schaeffer, however, was the real drawing card with his Sunday afternoon "Table Talks" with students and his Saturday night question-and-answer sessions. Schaeffer's renown as an apologist for Evangelicalism, his numerous publications, his gifts for relating in an engaging way Evangelical theological commitments to contemporary cultural trends—not to mention his and his wife's gracious cordiality—made L'Abri a place and an experience which has been formative on a large number of present Evangelical leaders and has left an imprint on the Evangelical psyche. L'Abri has been the object of pilgrimage for Evangelicals, a place "where the action is." A number of similar or sister institutions have been begun in various parts of the world by those associated with L'Abri. Only time will tell whether the rich heritage and renown of L'Abri Fellowship will survive Schaeffer's death. But recent contacts revealed that its ministries are continuing to thrive.

Chapter 10

Parachurch and Mission Agencies

It is not possible to discuss the foreign mission and evangelism work of the Evangelical movement (among the highest priorities for Evangelicals) apart from consideration of parachurch agencies related to it. Parachurch organizations are those organizations which operate alongside of and serve to extend the influence of the Church. However, such organizations are independent and have no official relationship to the churches. In a sense they have become a kind of "second home" for Evangelicals. Given the dominance of mainline theology in the established churches, the failure of Evangelicals/Fundamentalists to control these churches, and the inability of the smaller Evangelical churches to carry out alone certain aspects of ministry (like foreign missions), it is quite understandable that various coalitions of Evangelicals would be formed in order to allow them to carry on these aspects of ministry in their own way.

The parachurch agencies largely provide alternatives to the mainline churches' ministries in certain areas (and in so doing sometimes drain financial support from these churches insofar as the Evangelicals in them prefer to support the parachurch organizations rather than their own denominations). Since most mainline church leaders tend to be good "company persons" it is not surprising that many of these parachurch organizations have exacerbated existing tensions between mainline churches and the Evangelical movement. The same organizations thereby also serve to undergird and support the distinct subculture which one finds in the Evangelical movement. The various parachurch organizations can be classified in several groups according to the specific tasks they undertake.

Foreign mission organizations

No discussion of the foreign missions and evangelism work of the Evangelical movement can proceed without at least a little attention to the prevailing theories or approaches advocated in the movement. The first of these is the Church Growth movement.

Church Growth and its associated programs have become catchwords and institutional pillars of a number of North American mainline churches. Thus it may come as a surprise that the program has its roots in the Evangelical movement. It was formulated and articulated by Donald McGavran of Fuller Seminary's School of World Mission. This institution continues to be the center of the movement.

Although no adequate exposition of the Church Growth paradigm can be given here, we can note a few of its distinct characteristics. Its basic supposition is that the Church's main task is to grow in numbers. The discipline of Church Growth involves the study of what facilitates such growth. One of the chief findings and commitments of the movement's practitioners has been that churches grow best when they are indigenous people movements, not corporate institutions of largely Western culture into which individuals must be brought.[1]

The implications of these commitments for foreign mission work are quite apparent. It follows that missionary organizations must be servants of the indigenous churches, and the churches themselves must be indigenized.[2] Other fundamental commitments of the Church Growth school include a distinction between "discipling" (evangelism as such) and "perfecting" (nurturing congregational life); emphasis is placed on discipling. Thus, the focus of mission is on verbal proclamation and, though social outreach is not ignored, examination of the institutional dynamics involved in social change is virtually ignored by the Church Growth movement.[3]

The Church Growth movement may give nurturing and spiritual renewal a secondary focus, but it still indirectly affirms that growth in these areas is a necessary component of church growth. Thus the practitioners of its theories have engaged more recently in leadership training, a trend which is reflected in many of the mainline churches' appropriations of the theory.[4] The theories of the Church Growth movement are quite essential for understanding the foreign missions and evangelism work, not just that of the Evangelical movement but also that of the mainline churches.

The Evangelical movement has given rise to other original contributions in foreign mission thinking. Another good example is the Evangelism in Depth program. This somewhat controversial approach was developed by Evangelicals in Latin America and has also been influential in Africa. Its most unique tenet is that the total membership of the church must be mobilized in carrying out the work of evangelism. Obviously, in this model much stress is placed on mobilizing the laity, on developing indigenous leadership. The old model of professional evangelists is largely rejected.[5]

Yet a third evangelism program, this one more centered on domestic evangelism, has had a profound impact on the Evangelical movement. This is the Evangelism Explosion program of James Kennedy. Kennedy's program has made deep inroads both in the Evangelical movement and in mainline churches. Its basic supposition is that ministers who want their church to grow should recruit several people to learn and practice evangelism. At the end of the program the volunteers are to enlist more recruits. Emphasis is placed on very direct personal witnessing to prospective converts in their home. Sometimes the mode of this witnessing is so direct as to be controversial, relying on a question posed to prospective converts about their eternal fate.[6]

The Evangelical movement and mainline churches clearly overlap in their use of a number of theories of evangelism and overseas missions. The proximity is even more apparent when one recognizes that, like the mainline churches, Evangelicals are often open to contextualizing missionary work (even to the point of countenancing polygamy in contexts where the practice is normal) and urge conscious goal-setting in the missionary task.[7] This kind of open missionary/evangelism style among Evangelicals is in part what is causing further estrangement between Evangelicals and Fundamentalists. At any rate, the models we have been discussing provide a useful entrée to understanding the ethos and activities of the Evangelical movement's parachurch agencies.

The Overseas Missionary Fellowship (OMF) is one of the oldest and most venerable Evangelical mission societies. It has its origins in the China Inland Mission founded in 1865 by J. Hudson Taylor (1832–1905). Its origins in the Fundamentalist movement are evident not only by the fact that Taylor was heavily influenced by the Keswick movement, but also because its missionaries played a central role in agitating against liberals in mission fields during the Fundamentalist-Modernist controversy.[8]

For almost 100 years the society worked on mainland China—until the Communist takeover forced the evacuation of all missionaries. Its missionaries were redeployed in other sections of East Asia, and the organization took its new name. OMF has largely reorganized itself as an Evangelical rather than a Fundamentalist mission. It is under some fire from militant Fundamentalists as a result of its alleged use of the Evangelism-in-Depth method, an approach Fundamentalists condemn for its inclusiveness, its openness to cooperating even with liberal Christians.[9]

OMF does continue to affirm the five points of Fundamentalism including the inspiration of Scripture as the inerrant and infallible Word of God (2, 3, 8) and the necessity of being born again (4). Keswick commitments also seem reflected in the organization's claim that the Spirit "empowers" Christians to live a godly life (6). But an insistence that salvation is by faith, apart from works, is also maintained (5).

Among the tasks undertaken by OMF are the planting of new congregations, pioneer evangelism, campus ministries, religious publication, and radio ministry. Like mainline church missions, there is a growing awareness that it must work under the leadership of national churches. In the mid-1980s it was still a large society with a staff of more than 900 working in 10 East Asian nations.

The Liebenzeller Mission (LM) was founded in 1899 as the German branch of the China Inland Mission. Although the organization is composed of several national councils, our focus shall be on the German national council. In West Germany LM has played an important role in rallying conservative pietists to the cause of the Evangelical movement.[10] As such it is clearly on the side of the more militant Evangelicals.

Three years after the establishment of the mission, it moved its headquarters to Bad Liebenzell in South Germany, and around the time of World War II it became independent of the mother organization. Nevertheless, the LM retains much of the heritage of its parent, both in terms of the areas of work (East Asia and the Pacific Isles) and in affirming most of the same doctrinal commitments, including the affirmation of the Bible's inerrancy (1), salvation through faith (3), and reliance on the Keswick image of the empowering of the believer by the Spirit (3). Also affirmed by the German national council is a millennial kingdom and the restoration of Israel (5).

A worker in the organization has noted that some points of controversy seem to exist between the various national councils within LM over issues like the German council's views on the end times and its more restricted ethos (in North America, LM is more interdenominational in character). By contrast, the German national council, for example, publishes its own periodicals and operates its own seminary. The entire organization is still active, vibrant, and particularly a force to reckon with in the West German Evangelical community—a source of tension in the eyes of some mainline church leaders.

A host of other European foreign missions societies associated with the Evangelical movement could be noted. One of these is the Allianz-Mission-Barmen (which had a similar early relationship to the China Inland Mission). In Scandinavia a good example is the Santalmisjonen (SM) in Norway.

Like many Scandinavian mission societies, the SM is largely Lutheran but independent of the Lutheran State Church. Also, like many of its equivalents in other Scandinavian nations, it largely identifies itself with the Evangelical movement in virtue of its participation in the Lausanne Committee for World Evangelization.[11] (Full details on the latter cooperative organization will be given shortly.) To be sure, due to the strictly Lutheran composition of this and other Scandinavian missions, some hesitancy about outright identification with the movement exists. However, in the final analysis most still are willing to identify themselves in this way.

The SM itself was originated in 1867 on the mission field in India and was soon supported by Norwegians. Although not the largest of the Norwegian missionary societies, it carries on work in India and in Latin America. It subscribes to a conservative interpretation of the fundamental doctrines of Lutheranism.

A good example of a more conservative, perhaps Fundamentalist mission society is UFM INTERNATIONAL (formerly called "Unevangelized Fields Mission"). This interdenominational organization has its origins in London in 1931 when several missionaries left the Worldwide Evangelization Crusade, partly over doctrinal differences. In the mid-1980's the mission carries on work in more than 12 fields (including Europe). In addition to its work in establishing national churches, it also engages in education, medical work, and radio broadcasting.

Theologically, the Fundamentalist orientation of UFM is evident in its affirmation of the five points (no explicit reference is made to Christ's resurrection, though that is implied) (1, 3, 4, 8).[12] Also affirmed are the necessity of being born again (5), premillennialism, and the rapture (8). Additionally, though it is an interdenominational organization, baptism is administered only to believers and only by immersion

(7). Its Fundamentalism is also reflected in its policy of separation from the charismatic, Evangelical, and ecumenical movements.[13] UFM continues to flourish. In the mid-1980s it had more than 500 missionaries placed in 18 nations.

Another example of a Fundamentalist mission organization based in the United States is the New Tribes Mission. Other mission societies worthy of note, though they largely are not Fundamentalist but Evangelical in orientation, are the Eastern European mission societies, already noted, and the Wycliffe Bible Translators. The last of these is the largest of all agencies, translating the Bible into the language of indigenous peoples, as well as administering medical missions.

The rich diversity of parachurch missionary organizations sometimes leads to conflict and competition with the churches and with each other. But in the last decades Evangelicals have sought ways to stimulate cooperation among these organizations.[14] This desire has taken institutional expression in several ways, in organizations like the Lausanne Committee for World Evangelization, and the Evangelical Foreign Missions Association (affiliated with the National Association of Evangelicals).

Domestic missions organizations

Inter-Varsity Christian Fellowship (IVCF) is one of the largest Evangelical youth organizations that has a primary focus on college students. The organization was established in the United States in 1939, and in 1946 merged with the Student Foreign Missions Fellowship. Actually, IVCF has roots in the Universities and Colleges Christian Fellowship of England (formerly called Inter-Varsity Fellowship) in the 19th century. These sister organizations together with related campus organizations in other nations constitute the International Fellowship of Evangelical Students.

In the United States in the mid-1980s, IVCF was working on more than 800 campuses. Its chapters meet weekly for Bible study, prayer, and fellowship—and to encourage recruitment for overseas missions. IVCF also convenes triennial missionary conventions. The meetings in the 1970s were so well attended and received so much media coverage that they made a significant contribution to the improved image and heightened visibility of the Evangelical movement.

By comparison to other Evangelical campus organizations, IVCF has the reputation of being open and influenced by the Evangelical left. This is evident even in its social ethical orientation, for as early as 1948 it insisted on absolute racial integration. Likewise its openness is reflected in its style of evangelism, which is not particularly aggressive, and in its life-style expectations, which are less legalistic than other organizations.[15] Standard Evangelical doctrinal affirmations are made in the organization's *Doctrinal Basis*. But it speaks only of the inspiration and "entire trustworthiness" of the Bible, with no reference to biblical inerrancy (1). (The English sister organization of IVCF does speak of the Bible's infallibility.)[16] Because of this organizational openness there tends to be a great variety in regard to ethos and theological orientation among the different chapters on different campuses.

Campus Crusade for Christ International (CC) is by far the largest and perhaps most aggressive of the Evangelical parachurch youth organizations. Although its focus was and continues to be on evangelization of young adults on college campuses, CC has branched out to several specialized ministries to work with youth in high schools and has been international in its area of service. In recent years it has also taken on social justice issues through a variety of channels, including The Agape Movement (a kind of "Christian Peace Corps," where young people are recruited to serve in underdeveloped countries, not only to evangelize but also to offer vocational service with a view towards its possible social impact).

CC was founded in 1951 by a Presbyterian layman, Bill Bright, who is still its driving force. His initial work with students at UCLA has grown phenomenally until in the mid-1980s CC was working in a variety of ministries in more than 150 countries with a staff of about 16,000. Another dimension of the expanded outreach is CC's growing ministry to congregations, in which CC staff help train clergy to initiate church growth programs. This is an especially prominent dimension of its work outside North America. In North America CC and its work with congregations perhaps became most visible in 1975 with its "I Found It" campaign—"Here's Life, America!" Thousands were exposed to this campaign, and its emblematic automobile bumper sticker became a kind of code word.

The heart of the CC approach to evangelism is its method of "aggressive evangelism." At its center is the well-known and controversial Four Spiritual Laws developed by Bright: (1) God loves you; (2) man is sinful; (3) through Christ you can know God's love and plan for your life; and (4) we must individually receive Christ.[17] The method of aggressive evangelism is to present these laws to a potential convert who is then invited to "receive Christ."

Although the organization's *Statement of Faith* affirms that "the salvation of man is wholly a work of grace" (8), and Bill Bright himself has argued that "the number one heresy in the Christian world is legalism," a kind of legalism seems connoted by the idea of "spiritual *laws*" and that "*I* [actively] have found Christ." In response to this concern, European staff has modified the program, speaking of evangelism in terms of "knowing Christ" rather than four spiritual *laws*.[18]

CC has the reputation of being more conservative than other Evangelical youth organizations. This conservatism is reflected in Bright's political stance. The conservatism is also apparent in CC's *Standards for Staff*, which mandates certain standards of physical appearance (8). With regard to theological standards, the CC *Statement of Faith* goes well beyond Inter-Varsity fellowship and states that Scripture is "without error" (inerrant). Baptism and the Lord's Supper are referred to as "ordinances," not "sacraments" (13).

In the context of this organizational conservatism, some anomalies do exist, particularly in Europe. What is surprising is the apparent hesitancy of some members of the European staff to identify themselves with the Evangelical movement. From this it follows that while all staff members are committed to affirming the authority of Scripture and endeavor to believe as much of its testimony as they can, some do not appear to endorse the precise verbal formulations of the CC statement concerning biblical inerrancy. What holds the organization together, it is said, is not common beliefs but the practical questions of mission and the Christian life. (In this respect Campus Crusade–Europe seems to reflect its indebtedness to classical Pietism, a development that is hardly surprising in view of the fact that CC seems to have its greatest impact in Europe, at least in Germany, among a pietist constituency.)

If we ask how such diversity can be reconciled with Bill Bright's own views on inerrancy, it is perhaps helpful to recall that Bright is no separatist but himself maintains membership in a mainline Presbyterian church. This is reflected in CC's commitment to cooperating with all—even mainline—churches.[19]

Today CC is thriving not just in terms of its large staff but also in terms of its financial support base. This fact coupled with the openness it shows towards mainline churches make it potentially a most influential voice for enhancing mainline–Evangelical relationships.

A number of other influential Evangelical youth organizations could be noted: The Navigators, whose first though by no means exclusive constituency has been among military personnel; Young Life, which focuses on high school students; and the highly profiled Teen Challenge, an organization founded by Pentecostal Dave Wilkerson after the publication of his successful book, *The Cross and the Switchblade*. Teen Challenge works with teenage drug addicts.

On the European scene a good example of domestic missions akin to the work Campus Crusade carries on in Europe is evident in The Church Association for the Inner Mission in Denmark (IM). The IM has its roots in the Pietism of Danish Lutheranism; it works inside the Lutheran church but is independent of it. It seeks to bring about revival in the church by means of evangelism, and to that end sponsors prayer-houses for Christian meetings, employs about 115 home missionaries who attempt to do evangelism in Denmark, and administers its own independent youth work apart from and in addition to the church's organizations.

Like most of the Scandinavian foreign missions societies, IM clearly identifies itself with the Evangelical movement (albeit with some of the same hesitations as these other Scandinavian organizations). As is typical of other European Evangelicals, its staff is not particularly concerned about questions of biblical inerrancy. But its General Secretary does insist that the whole Bible must be considered the sole authority for religion and morality and that the historicity of the Genesis accounts should be affirmed.[20]

Social action organizations

Though the organization for Pat Robertson's 1988 presidential campaign may qualify as an entry under this heading, the Moral Majority (MM) is perhaps the first to come to mind as a Conservative Evangelical organization in this category. Not long before publication of this book, it had become part of a blanket organization, Liberty Federation, which had been created in order to extend MM's "lobbying and education work" to political issues not merely restricted to purely "moral" questions. Of course, since Jerry Falwell has resigned as president of both organizations (ostensibly to devote more time to his ministry in Lynchburg, Virginia), the future of these organizations could only be deemed uncertain as this analysis was written. Nevertheless, in view of MM's profound influence, it and its associated organization still deserve attention.

Given the influence of Falwell's leadership, MM and Liberty Federation are perhaps more correctly identified with Fundamentalism. The MM was founded in 1979 not so much by Falwell but through the organization and persuasion of an aspiring "new right" Evangelical politician, Robert Billings (later Ronald Reagan's political liaison to the religious community). Billings approached Falwell with the idea that the audience of Falwell's religious broadcasts had great political potential if it could be aligned with his own right-wing politics. Billings and Falwell succeeded in forging the coalition, the impact of which on the 1980 elections in the United States and subsequent politics is well known.

In terms of the organization's self-identity, Falwell has claimed that MM is a "nonpartisan political organization to promote morality in public life." The political positions it takes are well known. It stands for many of the values of "Reaganism"—the traditional family, strong national defense, as well as opposition to feminism (the Equal Rights Amendment), abortion, pornography, and the like.[21] It has been envisaged that one of the ways that the new organization, Liberty Federation, would broaden MM's scope would be by means of explicit advocacy of conservative causes in foreign policy.

Although the point was perhaps not always made so clearly, most recently MM has not conceived itself to be a religious organization. In fact Falwell even claims that MM is not based on theological considerations but welcomes the involvement of non-Fundamentalists, even theological liberals, Jews, and Roman Catholics. Thus it is presupposed that common moral convictions can be shared and ascertained by all these parties, regardless of religious commitments. In this sense MM and Liberty Federation are not so easily accused of seeking to subordinate the state to the Church. Falwell and his colleagues insist on the separation of church and state.[22]

These commitments have been reflected in MM's disinclination to support only candidates for political office who are "born again" Christians. Its aims are more specifically political—to lobby in Congress for its perceived political interests, to "educate" Americans to the important issues in government, to inform voters about voting records of their representatives, as well as to encourage and promote private schools.[23] Some have suggested that active support in the campaigns of certain candidates will be carried out even more openly and aggressively by Liberty Federation. Its leadership does insist that it will continue to avoid supporting candidates officially. But it rates the voting records of the various politicians on the basis of their conformity to MM standards, and these ratings are circulated widely.

If the future of MM can only be deemed as uncertain at the time of publication, the organization certainly will continue to be controversial. However, given the theological-ethical suppositions we have sketched, it does not seem quite fair to question the legitimacy of its attempts to influence the political sphere with its moral (and religious) commitments. Such interventions seem no less legitimate in principle than the political interventions of Christian leaders like Martin Luther King Jr. or Desmond Tutu on behalf of more liberal causes.

By no means are MM and Liberty Federation the only Conservative Evangelical/Fundamentalist sociopolitical organizations. Other such organizations with a similar conservative political orientation include the Roundtable (a religious lobby first put together in 1980 with television evangelist James Robison as its visible leader) and Christian Voice, Inc. (another conservative political lobby known for its "Congressional Report Card" on voting records of representatives).

A much different kind of organization, more characteristically Evangelical than Fundamentalist, perhaps more oriented to liberal than conservative political positions, is Evangelicals for Social Action (ESA). This organization was formed by a number of the leading American Evangelicals in late 1973 who met to formulate an important statement, the *Chicago Declaration of Evangelicals to Social Concern*. Since then ESA has become principally concerned with education of its members concerning social issues. Organized political action is not often taken, though it does encourage local action. Thus, the impact of this group has been far less than that of MM and largely limited to the academic centers of the Evangelical movement in North America. A more open theological orientation for the group may be reflected in the fact that its formal statements make no reference to biblical inerrancy. But the 1984 "ESA Statement" does affirm the characteristic Evangelical commitment to the centrality of evangelism in relation to social action (VI).

Perhaps the flagship organization for Evangelical social action is World Vision International (WV). Founded in 1950 to care for Korean War orphans, WV has grown to a social action ministry in more than 40 nations with an annual budget in the millions. Its programs include assistance to families, emergency relief, development aid, and leadership development. The primary emphasis is to promote indigenous self-development of undernourished, preindustrial societies. Consequently, these programs are chiefly carried out through indigenous local organizing committees.[24]

WV reflects the usual Evangelical concern with evangelism, the unwillingness to engage in social action in a vacuum without it. Thus it also combines its humanitarian work with evangelism and leadership training for local clergy and laity. In this connection it operates the Missions Advanced Research and Communications Center which provides research and planning aids to help groups formulate mission strategies to reach and understand previously "unreached tribes."

WV is usually linked with the left-wing of the Evangelical movement; it is committed to working through local, indigenous leadership and willing to conduct its ministries ecumenically without imposing agreement on a faith statement as a requirement for service. Despite this, WV has come under fire in some mainline church quarters for exporting Western values and politics to the Third World. But it is by no means clear that this charge can be substantiated, in view of WV's policy of relating to national governments in such a way that "it avoids intimate identification with any particular political party, economic system or the incumbent government. . . ."[25] One comes away from the controversy with the impression that WV's effectiveness and visibility as an Evangelical institution may be inspiring some of the backlash of mainline churches and mission agencies against a dynamic and vibrant Evangelical movement. The fact that WV has been so successful in soliciting funds from members of mainline churches (more than half of its budget reportedly comes from this constituency) should perhaps not be overlooked in trying to understand this backlash.

Organizations associated with the mass media

Few areas are more controversial in the relationship between the Evangelical movement and mainline churches than their competition for time on the airwaves. Radio and television broadcasting by Evangelicals and Fundamentalists is big news and big business. The controversy about Evangelicals' use of the media is related in part to allegations, at least in two cases confirmed, about the life-style and business practices of certain Evangelical media evangelists. But although no full analysis of the controversy raised by Evangelical use of the media can be provided here, and one can only speculate about how much damage the recent controversies have done to its influence, there are indications that the real reasons for controversy are more substantive than the personal habits of certain media evangelists.

In view of the impressive quantity and financing of Evangelical broadcasting, there should be little wonder that some conflict among Evangelicals and mainline churches concerning media broadcasting would emerge. An estimated $1 billion a year flows into organizations associated with religious broadcasting in North America. In the late 1980s more than 660 radio stations and 94 television stations were concentrating almost exclusively on religious broadcasting.

At least in North America the real heat in the controversy seems to be generated by the fact that Evangelical broadcasts have been knocking mainline church broadcasts off the air. The dynamic is one of simple capitalism. While into the 1970s the networks were still in the habit of donating free air time to mainline church broadcasts, Evangelical programs operated on a system of buying commercial time. Eventually the profit motive eroded the stations' commitment to free "public interest" time. The result has been that only the Evangelical broadcasts have been able to get on the air, for only they have been able to pay for them. The stations were thereby free to eliminate their donation of air time to the mainline broadcasts. By airing the Evangelical shows which were yielding a profit, the stations could still claim to be working in the "public interest" by offering some religious programming. Little wonder tensions between the mainline churches and Evangelicals are so evident on this matter of religious broadcasting.[26]

A typical mainline rejoinder to the phenomenal Evangelical success in broadcasting has been to question the actual impact of Evangelical broadcasting, whether it might in fact be detrimental to church attendance. Surveys indicate that such concerns are only partially justified. Although a more recent study by A. C. Nielsen Co. suggests that the estimates of earlier analyses may have been too low, the audience of Evangelical religious broadcasting in North America seems not to be as large or as universal as some media evangelists have claimed.

Thus, for example, Jerry Falwell is on record as claiming that 25 million people watched his program, "Old-Time Gospel Hour." But Arbitron, an independent audience measurement unit, estimated his audience that same year as about 1.5 million. Likewise it appears that a disproportionate number of Christian broadcasting viewers are women who are over 50, live in the southern or midwestern United States, and are more theologically conservative than a typical sample of Americans.

Perhaps the most significant finding emerges from research done in the early 1980s by several pollsters for the National Council of Churches in the United States. The poll found that with but a few exceptions viewers of religious broadcasting have not decreased their church attendance or their giving patterns to their local congregations![27] This new data, coupled with this book's findings concerning the compatibility of Conservative Evangelical theology and that of the mainline churches, should go a long way toward helping to undercut false stereotypes that mainline churches have of Evangelical religious broadcasting. But it is not about to put to rest the controversy over the issue of religious broadcasting. In fact, there are signs that such a controversy between Evangelicals and the mainline is heating up also in Europe, at least in West Germany.

Perhaps the largest and most influential media broadcasting parachurch organization is The Christian Broadcasting Network (CBN). Its founder and president, the first host of its flagship program, the "700 Club," is Marion G. "Pat" Robertson. A Pentecostal, one of the best educated and articulate televangelists, and a candidate for the United States presidency in 1988, Robertson founded the station almost from scratch in 1960. Since then the operation has truly grown into the status of a kind of network for religious broadcasting and "family programming."

From its humble beginnings, the CBN Cable Network has become the third largest cable network in the United States. In the mid-1980s it owned four television stations and one radio station. The "700 Club" is itself aired on almost 200 broadcast stations. Nor are Robertson's enterprises restricted only to media broadcasting. His staff operates a counseling service for viewers who call in. He has organized "Operation Blessing," a program of service to the poor and needy in which persons who phone in with material needs are matched up with church members willing to help. Another new program is "Operation Heads Up," through which reading will be taught to functional illiterates in urban ghettos. Also the Robertson organization has established CBN University, an institution which offers only graduate (masters) degrees especially in subjects like communication and public policy.[28]

Although he is a Pentecostal, Robertson does not professionally exhibit all of its characteristic commitments. He does not broadcast glossolalia. And despite his claim to affirm the inerrancy of Scripture, he does not deem the concept to be of "burning interest," and on one occasion even seems implicitly to have rejected it.[29]

Considering Robertson's impressive organization, it is somewhat surprising to find that CBN's "700 Club" has not always been the top religious program in terms of audience. For that matter, neither Jerry Falwell nor Oral Roberts (the well-known Pentecostal faith-healer evangelist who has established a large enterprise that includes Oral Roberts University) has been at the top of the ratings list. At least until recent revelations about his sexual misconduct, throughout the mid-1980s that honor seems to have belonged to Jimmy Swaggart, a Pentecostal who has offered a lively musical show of religious songs (although CBN claims that a recent survey by A. C. Nielsen Co. places the "700 Club" first in the ratings of religious programs, and Swaggart second).

Although he is not especially associated with media evangelism, we already have noted to what extent the career of Billy Graham is indebted to media hype. No study of the Evangelical movement can overlook him and his organization.

Very early in his ministry, Graham recognized the value of the media. After his rise to national prominence through his Los Angeles Crusade, he launched his "Hour of Decision" radio broadcasts. In 1950, in recognition of the need to put his ministry on a solid business basis, Graham founded the Billy Graham Evangelistic Association, Inc. In the mid-1980s this organization had a staff of more than 500. It serves to organize and plan the evangelist's crusades, publishes and distributes religious literature, including the organization's *Decision* magazine, provides counseling-by-mail to those who write Graham with problems, and organizes various conferences concerning evangelism, not least the important International Congress on World Evangelization held in 1974 in Lausanne.

Much has been written about the reasons for Billy Graham's success. It is not possible to elaborate on these factors here. One can note, in addition to his personal and administrative gifts, that the evangelist may have been helped by a down-to-earth theological orientation which emphasizes most of the key themes of antebellum American revivalism. Thus repentance and being born again are central themes in his preaching. But he also has affirmed salvation by faith, and (as we shall note later) he does affirm biblical infallibility in some way, although perhaps not as rigorously as some other Evangelicals.[30]

We have already noted the important role Billy Graham and his international impact have had in the coalescence of the modern Evangelical movement. His skills and the sophisticated techniques employed in his crusades have made important contributions to the more positive media image Evangelicals and conservative Christianity have received in the second half of the 20th century. Graham's ecumenical openness, his willingness to cooperate with all Christians in his crusades, may be making a subtle impact on the Evangelical movement in another way—perhaps opening it to ecumenical contacts outside the movement.

Previously we noted the important role certain periodicals play in giving the Evangelical movement cohesion. Of these, *Christianity Today (CT)* is by far the most important, at least in North America.

The founding of *CT* in 1956 with the help of Billy Graham has already been discussed. In the mid-1980s the biweekly had a circulation of about 180,000, larger than the most prestigious North American liberal religious journal, *The Christian Century*. The magazine's purpose has been to present the Evangelical approach to contemporary issues in church and society. Its original audience tended to be clergy and seminarians, though in the last decade it has become more lay oriented. In general, its editorial policy has been conservative, both with respect to politics and theology (with a strong commitment to biblical inerrancy, especially evident during the editorial term of Harold Lindsell). In the area of politics *CT* has largely reflected the Evangelical commitment to Christian social responsibility. But it has not typically advocated any specific action for dealing with the burning social issues of the day.[31]

We have observed that the *CT* enterprises are not just restricted to publication of the magazine. It has sponsored international conferences of Evangelicals and an institute for the study of the day's critical issues from an Evangelical perspective. Not surprisingly, certain critical voices have been raised about *CT* within the Evangelical community. But the magazine continues to exert an influence on the movement far beyond its circulation. It is one of Evangelicalism's pillars and still a prime image maker.

There are several other influential Evangelical periodicals which play an important role in holding together certain segments of the movement. In addition to the influential *The Reformed Journal* (a more left-wing, socially conscious periodical related to the Christian Reformed Church), the *Christian Standard* (the principal rallying point of the Evangelical Christian Restorationist Movement), *Moody Monthly Magazine* (a conservative family magazine associated with Moody Bible Institute), and *Eternity* (a more left-wing Evangelical monthly), *Sojourners* cannot be overlooked.

Founded in 1971 (formerly called the *Post-American*), *Sojourners*, a monthly magazine edited by Jim Wallis, is the "chic" religious publication of North America, read by the political left in both Evangelical and mainline communities. Theologically, *Sojourners* reflects the Evangelical left; it is largely staffed by Evangelicals who came to maturity in the turbulent years of the 1960s. Of particular interest is the fact that the periodical is published by members of a residential community located in the urban ghetto in Washington, D.C. The magazine reflects this community's political values and cultural life-style. Heavily influenced by John Howard Yoder, a Mennonite often associated with the Evangelical movement, both the community and its periodical reflect an emphasis on a communitarian life-style. In alternative communities like that of the Sojourners, the old political structures are thought to be challenged by the vision of these communities. Nor is this communitarian impulse deemed a retreat from social responsibility. The Sojourners community is actively involved in its present location in solidarity with the poor, by organizing food cooperatives and day school tutoring. *Sojourners* still reflects a critical perspective on American government and society (though never in such a way as to imply that political power can be the instrument for achieving the new order).[32] This sort of leftist, liberal orientation, even to the point of using Marxist categories of analysis akin to that of liberation theology, has made *Sojourners* a very controversial voice within the Evangelical movement.

The dependence of the Evangelical movement on common literature as a ground for its cohesion is reflected outside North America. For example, in West Germany IDEA, the information service of the Deutsche Evangelische Allianz (German Evangelical Alliance), plays an important role in linking the German-speaking Evangelical community particularly through its main publication, *Spektrum*.

In view of the large number of different Conservative Evangelical organizations involved in religious publishing, it is hardly surprising that the concern for Conservative Evangelical cohesion has led to the formation of several cooperative agencies in religious publishing. Among such organizations is the Christian Booksellers Association (CBA), which gives coherence to the far-flung activities of the various publishing houses associated with the Evangelical movement and its organizations.

Another significant agency of cooperation in religious publishing is the Evangelical Press Association (EPA). Created in the late 1940s for the twofold purpose of providing fellowship among journalists of Evangelical publications and to provide its members with practical assistance, EPA includes a large number of Conservative Evangelical periodicals, ranging from those with a few thousand subscribers to the giants of the genre like *Christianity Today* and *Moody Monthly Magazine*. Among its practical services, EPA offers a news service, an annual wrap-up of the year's top stories, representation on questions of U.S. postal services, and the sponsoring of regional seminars for editors, writers, and photographers. The diversity of EPA's membership is reflected in the theological diversity of its membership, though its *Doctrinal Statement*, to which all members must subscribe, affirms most of the usual Conservative Evangelical themes, including Fundamentalism's five points *(a-c)*, the necessity of the regeneration of the believer *(d)*, and the spiritual unity of believers *(g)*. The Bible is described as "the only infallible, authoritative Word of God" *(a)*.

The purpose of both of these agencies, to stimulate cooperation in the narrowly defined area of religious publications, typifies the Conservative Evangelical concern for cooperation in the broad spectrum of ministry. The next chapter provides several examples of such organizations.

Chapter 11

Evangelical Cooperative Agencies

Several of the organizations created by Evangelicals in order to hold the movement together and stimulate cooperation in a variety of areas have an international character. Among Fundamentalists the best known is the International Council of Christian Churches, an organization founded by Carl McIntire, which does not in fact represent a very significant constituency and has had relatively little international impact. The World Evangelical Fellowship (WEF) is its equivalent among Evangelicals.

WEF was created in 1951, largely under the influence of the National Association of Evangelicals in the United States and the Evangelical Alliance of Great Britain. It was envisaged as a kind of successor to the then moribund international Evangelical Alliance.

The WEF's function is to organize and stimulate the development of national Evangelical fellowships and serve as a catalyst and liaison for Evangelicals involved in missions, theological research and education, communications, and emergency relief. In its *Statement of Faith,* most of Fundamentalism's five points are affirmed, including the infallibility of the Scriptures, their authority "in all matters of faith and conduct," as well as salvation by faith apart from works whereby believers are "enabled to live a holy life." Membership in WEF is determined regionally, composed of various national Evangelical fellowships. But although its leadership has worked hard to overcome its image and has succeeded in making some significant structural changes in the organization, WEF has been perceived at least until recently as exhibiting a pronounced North American influence. This factor and the somewhat amorphous character of the Evangelical movement have entailed that WEF is an organization whose time has perhaps not yet fully come.

The other large international Evangelical cooperative agency is the Lausanne Committee for World Evangelization. As we have noted, it was founded in 1974 at the Lausanne Congress on World Evangelization, a large international gathering of Evangelicals convened by the Billy Graham organization. A continuation committee was created at that time in order to nurture and advance both the desire for more cooperation expressed at the Congress (7) as well as to uphold and advance the tenets of the important Covenant (theological statement) drafted by the Congress.[1]

The continuation committee has carried out its mandate by organizing meetings and preparing publications in areas like world evangelization strategy, intercession, communications, and theology. Working Groups have been created in each of these areas—some of the same areas in which WEF is working.

As much as any factor, the uniqueness of the Lausanne Committee in comparison to WEF may lie in the openness reflected in its Covenant, which articulates a call to Christian social responsibility (5), the missionary character of the Church (6), the reminder that evangelism summons the Church to visible unity (7), and the affirmation of Scripture's "entire truthfulness," that it is "the only written Word of God, without error in all *that it affirms*" (2). Although WEF and the Lausanne Committee differ somewhat regarding structural accountability and raison d'être, basic differences are not readily apparent. Both are working in similar areas, often with similar programs. It is still not clear how the turf is to be divided between them; efforts aimed at merger have been initiated, but have been without success thus far.

There are a great many national and regional Evangelical fellowships on every continent. Among the most important outside North America are the Evangelical Alliance (of Great Britain), the Deutsche Evangelische Allianz, and the Association of Evangelicals of Africa and Madagascar. We already have observed how the European organizations do not affirm the infallibility of Scripture with quite the vigor as their North American—or African—counterparts.[2] In fact, the German Alliance prefers, for "historical reasons," not officially to identify its name with the term "Evangelical" *(Evangelikal)* in the sense of the Evangelical movement (since, as part of the original 19th-century Evangelical Alliance, it predated the Evangelical movement).[3]

Perhaps the most influential of all such agencies is the National Association of Evangelicals (United States), the origins of which were mentioned in Part I. In the mid-1980s the NAE provided Evangelical identification for about 4 million Christians in more than 45 member denominations (among them, several Pentecostal denominations) and in congregations from about 40 other denominations. The organization has a number of publications. It promotes Evangelical cooperation through its Office of Public Affairs (an Evangelical political lobby in Washington, D.C.), its associated Evangelical Foreign Missions Association (promoting foreign missions cooperation and education), and the National Religious Broadcasters (promoting Evangelical cooperation in this area). In addition, the NAE promotes cooperation among Evangelicals in areas of armed forces chaplaincy, Christian education, world relief, and several other areas. At its annual conventions it takes action on (nonbinding) resolutions that often concern contemporary social or ethical questions. The positions taken are usually conservative. This matches the theological orientation of the NAE *Statement of Faith,* in which the five points are affirmed (3), along with the infallibility of Scripture (1) and the necessity of being born again (4). (Not all NAE member denominations affirm biblical infallibility in their official statements of faith.) These commitments are made in the context of repeated NAE resolutions which decry the decaying trends in modern society.[4]

Some critics claim that a spirit of déjà vu has come to pervade the NAE in the mid-1980s. It has never quite achieved the impact that was dreamed for it in its first years. The very conservative tone of those years associated it with Fundamentalism in the minds of so many that it has not been able to attract a large number of mainline denominations, although several of them, including the American Baptist Churches and the Reformed Church in America, have experienced internal pressure to join the NAE and forgo membership in the U.S.A.'s National Council of Churches.[5] Nevertheless, with the current unrest in the Evangelical movement, a certain tendency can be observed among American Evangelicals to ignore the NAE.[6] Yet the Evangelical renaissance of the 1970s has kindled a self-confidence and respectability in the organization, a sense of its significance which is increasingly obvious even to those outside the Evangelical subculture (as is evident from Reagan's efforts to woo its support).

Evangelical institutions: concluding reflections on Part II

Evangelical organizations exhibit certain common features, most of which are apparent in the NAE *Statement of Faith.* The great majority of the organizations, with a few notable exceptions, affirm the infallibility and/or inerrancy of Scripture, emphasize being born again and personal sanctification, coupled with a concern for evangelism and missions. In many cases these themes are asserted in face of suspicions about the liberalizing-decaying trends in contemporary society.[7] By preserving and appealing to this historic Christianity of the past, Evangelicals seem to think they can reverse these trends.

These common features suggest a possible way of answering the question, "What is the Evangelical movement, and what is an Evangelical?" The answer to this question is given more fully in Part III.

Part III

CHARACTERISTIC EVANGELICAL THEMES: THE QUEST FOR ORTHODOXY IN MODERN DRESS

Chapter 12

Introduction to Evangelical Theology

There are a number of difficulties entailed by any attempt to provide a theological profile of the contemporary Evangelical movement. The movement's diversity and the self-proclaimed unwillingness of some of its segments to be bound to Confessional or creedal formulations seem to militate against an effort to identify *the* Evangelical position.[1] (Of course, some churches associated with the Evangelical movement are self-consciously bound to Confessional statements. Some Evangelicals represent themselves as "Confessionalist Evangelicals" and deliberately seek to preserve theological continuity with the historic Confessional statements of the Reformation like the Lutheran *Augsburg Confession* or the Presbyterian *Westminster Confession*. And as the eminent Evangelical theologian Carl Henry has pointed out in arguing that a "Confessional consciousness" exists in the movement, virtually all Evangelical organizations, as we have seen, do formulate some kind of statement of faith to which all members of the organization are expected to adhere).[2] Nevertheless my aims are quite limited.

This chapter aims not to capture the essence of Conservative Evangelical theology but merely to identify the boundaries—acceptable theological alternatives—for Evangelicals. It represents an effort to discern what one Evangelical theologian has identified as the "touchstones" or "family traditions" of the Evangelical movement.[3] Given the diversity within Evangelicalism, it is not surprising that we shall discover a number of Evangelically credible alternatives on most theological topics, a kind of theological spectrum.[4]

I am concerned that my portrayal of Evangelical theology be based on truly representative material and not merely on the private opinion of a few avant-garde theologians who may not be in touch with the Evangelical grass roots. My description of an Evangelical theological profile, therefore, relies principally upon representative documents, upon statements issued by international conferences of Evangelicals, and upon statements of faith of various representative Evangelical organizations. Statements of Fundamentalist organizations and of those churches, like The Lutheran Church–Missouri Synod, which do not identify themselves as part of the Evangelical movement but which seem to share an Evangelically oriented theological commitment, or are generally regarded by observers as Evangelical organizations, have also been examined. The question is raised whether the theological positions of these groups confirm the theological profile of the Evangelical movement or whether they differ significantly with that profile.

The views of only the most eminent Evangelical theologians have been called upon to make significant contributions to this summary, and only when their writings have confirmed or significantly revised doctrinal positions advocated in the other, more "official" documents. Furthermore, as much as possible in defense of the movement's international character, conclusions about the theological commitments of the Evangelical movement have been drawn only when the position of given theologians or statements can be identified in an Evangelical statement originating from another part of the world. (In addition to these considerations it should also be noted that the contemporary Evangelical movement is heavily influenced by the French Evangelical Jacques Ellul, the English author C. S. Lewis, and a mainline German Lutheran, Helmut Thielicke.[5] Their influence on contemporary Evangelicals, particularly the influence of the latter two authors, suggests the openness of the movement to insights of non-Evangelicals, as long as they are found to be trustworthy.)

This decision to focus on the official statements of faith by Evangelicals and on the most representative, prominent Evangelical theologians as the basis for descriptions of Evangelical theology is a self-conscious methodological one aimed at correcting errors often made by mainline church observers of the Evangelical movement. Too often such observers make their judgments about Evangelical theology on the basis of the observer's personal acquaintance with particular Evangelicals or groups. But this approach represents a double standard. A Lutheran, for example, would not dream of characterizing Lutheran theological convictions on the basis of what parish pastors or radical Lutheran theologians said about their heritage. No wonder negative judgments about the quality of Evangelical theology often ensue! By focusing on the thought of the official faith statements of Evangelicals and their most prominent academic theologians we may well discover that Evangelical theology is at some points quite good theology indeed.

The theology of the Evangelical movement will be summarized in chapters devoted to seven different doctrinal issues. Finally, a summary of the main theological characteristics of Evangelical thought and an attempt to define the movement will be offered.

We may note briefly here our conclusions about the identifying characteristics of Evangelicalism. Our analysis basically confirms a description of Evangelicalism proposed by Sydney Ahlstrom.[6] The theological profile offered here follows Ahlstrom's proposal at most points, with just a few amendments. (Of course, it must be acknowledged that the Evangelical movement is so diverse that it defies description. If one asks a group of Evangelicals to define the movement, one will receive as many descriptions as there are persons asked. Some would even object to the possibility of discerning distinct Evangelical characteristics. Nevertheless, certain common concerns held by Evangelicals seem to emerge.) Based on what self-professing Evangelicals say they believe, the Evangelical movement seems characterized by: (1) a critical orientation towards Roman Catholicism and the ecumenical movement; (2) an insistence that theology be done in dialogue with a concept of the propositional inerrancy of Scripture, or at least its plenary inspiration; (3) the affirmation that the Bible has serious importance for Christian life; (4) The priority of the experiential dimensions of becoming and being a Christian (conversion and sanctification) over the sacraments, the ministry, and ecclesiastical structures; (5) an emphasis on evangelism and missionary work; (6) an understanding of Christian ethics in terms of law rather than situationally; and (7) a resistance to fellowship with persons or churches not sharing the above commitments, but an openness to fellowship with all who do, regardless of differences in doctrine on other matters.

Some diversity does exist on these points, and extreme viewpoints can be found on each of them. However, the reaction of the Evangelical establishment to these extremes further suggests that this profile describes the core of the Evangelical movement, the working theological presuppositions it must draw from its heritage. Since its view of Scripture is so much at the center of Evangelical theology, we begin our description at this crucial, controversial point.

Chapter 13

View of Scripture
and Theological Method

Although not all students of the Evangelical movement would agree, there is some evidence which indicates that the most crucial, if not the first affirmation typically made by Evangelicals is to establish their own position concerning the confession of the verbal and plenary inspiration of the Bible, of its infallibility and inerrancy (in the autographs [original manuscripts]).[1] On occasion, these affirmations are correlated with an insistence upon the apostolic authorship of the New Testament Scriptures.[2] Given the centrality of these commitments for the Evangelical movement, a definition of these terms is in order.

"Plenary inspiration" is the belief that Scripture is "fully" inspired by God. Thus *all* Scripture in all its parts is to be considered Word of God (cf. 2 Tim. 3:16). Given this commitment, no challenge can be issued to the status of any of the books of the Bible (not even James and Esther) as authoritative Word of God. Even those somewhat embarrassing, apparently culturally conditioned verses in Scripture regarding the status of women and slavery cannot be explained away as merely the reflections of their authors (see 1 Tim. 2:8-12; 1 Cor. 14:34-35; 1 Cor. 11:2-16; Eph. 6:5-8; Philemon 10-17; Titus 2:9; Exod. 21:1-11). Some biblical precedent exists for this sort of respect and veneration for the authority of even the most apparently obscure portions of Scripture (cf. John 10:34-35; Gal. 3:16).

Closely related to the concept of plenary inspiration is the doctrine of "verbal inspiration." This doctrine entails the belief that it is not just the thoughts of the biblical writers that are inspired, but the actual words written in the text. Inspiration is said to pertain to the biblical text and only secondarily to its authors.[3] This commitment is undergirded even further by some Evangelicals who insist that the revelation of God in historical events is in itself no more authoritative than the divine interpretation of these saving events as recorded in Scripture.[4]

In this way, the language of the Scriptures is indispensably connected to divine revelation in history. As such, one cannot distinguish the Word of God from the Scriptures by appealing to the inspired character of the biblical authors' experience or intention in order to criticize the language of the text (such an approach is frequently employed by modern theologians). Thus the Evangelical commitment to verbal inspiration necessitates its criticism of mainline theology at this point.[5] Again, appeal might be made to the same New Testament precedents for backing. One can observe several instances where New Testament authors or characters in the Gospel narratives indicate respect for the divine authority of Old Testament verbal formulations (see John 10:34-35; Rom. 4:23; Gal. 3:16).

Intimately connected to this understanding of the divine inspiration of Scripture is the affirmation of the Bible's inerrancy and infallibility. Inasmuch as the whole Bible is God's Word, it must be inerrant and infallible or else God would be a deceiver and a liar, which is not possible.[6] A representative gathering of prominent Evangelicals in Chicago in 1978 offered somewhat typical definitions of these terms. *Infallible* is defined as "the quality of neither misleading nor being misled. . . [so that] Scripture is a sure, safe, and reliable rule and guide in all matters." *Inerrant* is defined as "the quality of being free from all falsehood or mistake. . . [so that] Scripture is entirely true and trustworthy in all its assertions."[7]

Obviously, *inerrancy* is intended as the stronger term, connoting not just the trustworthiness of the Bible but also its absolute truthfulness and precision. The former term perhaps pertains more to the Bible's existential impact on readers.[8] Not all Evangelicals, however, are prepared to accept this distinction. At stake here is the concern of some to bypass the term *inerrancy* in favor of simply emphasizing Scripture's infallibility.

Such a preference for *infallibility* is sometimes employed to set limits or conditions on the Bible's authoritative claims. For if the Bible is not identified as inerrant, its infallibility more easily can be regarded as "limited" to certain spheres of knowledge.[9] As we previously noted, Pentecostals typically do not employ the term *inerrancy* with reference to Scriptures, which accounts in part for Evangelical suspicions about them. Nor does the term play as significant a role in areas outside of North America, partly due to the pre-Enlightenment culture of some of these areas and churches, partly due to Pietism, and in Germany in part because the equivalent German term *(Unfehlbarkeit)* allows for no distinction between inerrancy and infallibility.[10]

In any case, despite the reticence of a few Evangelicals, many analysts maintain, and this book will confirm, that the doctrine of biblical inerrancy (or at least an affirmation that the Bible is reliable and authoritative in all its parts) is the principal affirmation which provides the Evangelical movement with unity and a distinctive character.[11] Granted this Evangelical affirmation (and movement as a whole) is sometimes labeled a "modern" aberration; it is true that the way the accuracy of the Bible is stressed and the appeal to the autographs as the only truly inerrant Word are relatively new developments. Nonetheless, it cannot be denied that some historical precedents for this affirmation exist in the 17th-century *The Westminster Confession of Faith* (drawn up by early Scotch and English Presbyterians aimed to bring about the Puritan reformation in 17th-century England) and in certain Protestant Orthodox theologians of the same century, who even claimed authority for the infallible Scripture in nontheological areas like science.[12] The doctrine's present status in the Evangelical movement, however, is clearly indebted to the 1910 *Five-Point Deliverance* (1) of the Presbyterian Church in the U.S.A. and so to the impact of Princeton theology on the Fundamentalist movement.

Several misconceptions of this Evangelical synthesis of verbal inspiration, plenary inspiration, and biblical inerrancy have developed in mainline church circles. It is common to indict Evangelicals either for maintaining a "divine dictation theory," which denies the biblical authors their individual personalities and stylistic peculiarities, or for making the Bible rather than God the object of worship (bibliolotry).[13] However, these charges generally cannot be substantiated.

Conservative Lutheran churches like The Lutheran Church–Missouri Synod are quite concerned about the dangers of bibliolotry and respond by insisting upon a distinction between the gospel and Scripture. The gospel is prioritized over Scripture; its power does not derive from Scripture, for it is prior to Scripture. There are some suggestions that LCMS may suspect the Evangelical movement of improperly prioritizing the Bible over the gospel (a factor which may further account for its discomfort in identifying itself with the movement).[14]

In fact, many Evangelicals insist on an appropriate distinction between the Word and Scripture, self-consciously rejecting bibliolatry.[15]

Of itself, at least one Evangelical argues, the Bible cannot bring salvation, for this also requires faith which is worked by the Holy Spirit.[16] The Evangelical insistence that only the original manuscripts of the Bible are inerrant also serves to avoid undue veneration of Scripture.[17] It is true that some of the more conservative American Fundamentalist groups continue to insist wholeheartedly on fidelity to the King James Version of the Bible as the only valid English translation.[18] However, most Evangelicals are not prone to such veneration of available texts and translations. A few handle our available texts quite critically, arguing along the lines of the Princeton theologians that errors in these texts may be attributed to errors of scribes in copying the original inerrant manuscripts.[19] The eminent Evangelical theologian Carl Henry goes so far as to conclude that the Bible translations we possess today cannot be regarded as the Word of God in an unconditional sense.[20] This sort of qualified, limited identification of the Word and the Bible represents anything but the worship of the Bible!

Mainline stereotypes about the Evangelical movement and its view of Scripture are further challenged by the rejection of the theory of divine dictation by many Evangelicals. Although they assert that the words of Scripture themselves are divinely inspired and given, most refuse to maintain that inspiration is a mechanical activity which did not permit expression of the individuality of the biblical authors or their unique perspectives.[21] It is true that a few hints of this notion of divine dictation are suggested in the writings of Calvin and then in the Protestant Orthodox theology of the 17th century. Yet the notion has not been integrated into the Evangelical heritage, for it was rejected even prior to the Fundamentalist-Modernist controversy.[22] Evangelical approaches to biblical authority and interpretation are far more sophisticated than most mainline Christians appreciate. Most Evangelical theologians are anything but naive literalists. In addition to their subtle treatments of biblical authority, the commitment to interpreting all texts in accordance with their particular literary genre, so that the poetic and parabolic portions of Scripture not be taken literally, has gained widespread acceptance.[23]

Biblical inerrancy: contemporary significance and fundamental presuppositions

It must be admitted that the Evangelical insistence upon biblical inerrancy has functioned since the earliest days of the movement in the early Fundamentalist period as a tool for polemics against liberals.[24] However, the typical Evangelical affirmation of the Bible's plenary and verbal inerrancy and/or inspiration also makes an important contribution to the viability of the movement's Christian witness in the contemporary world. This view of Scripture is tenaciously held by Evangelicals today in order that they may receive certainty and security that God is addressing his people even in face of the complexities and pluralism of modern life.[25]

The emergence of a pervasive secular humanism in Western society with the breakdown of moral norms in favor of a self-consuming relativism and individualism in our contemporary situation are commonly noted by Evangelicals and other social critics. Some sense the impending collapse of Western civilization.[26] People are seeking for meaning and purpose in life. A firm foundation is necessary. Some social analysts like Dean Kelley have argued that the phenomenal growth of Evangelical churches is directly related to their ability to provide such a sure and firm meaning-structure for life. In part, as Francis Schaeffer has noted, the Evangelical view of Scripture with its claims to absolute authority and inerrancy provides this firm structure of meaning.[27]

While much mainline contemporary theology locates the foundation of Christian faith in some kind of religious experience, Evangelicals insist that Christian truth can be expressed in propositions and is accessible to all.[28] Even though this insistence on propositional revelation has always been implied by the Evangelical commitment to verbal inspiration, it has required special attention among Evangelicals since mid-century in consequence of polemics with neoorthodox theologians who largely regarded revelation as a noncognitive experience.[29]

At any rate the Evangelical argument on behalf of propositional revelation, on the objective universality of the propositional claims, is a helpful corrective to the subjective pluralism of modern society. The propositional character of the biblical revelation lifts one above one's cultural perspective. It allows Evangelicals to draw on the insights of biblical revelation without contaminating it with modern cultural attitudes, for the biblical propositions are accessible to all.[30] Consequently they can be understood regardless of one's cultural and social milieu, and so cannot be dominated by human experience.[31] It is this dimension of Evangelical thought that provides a certain cerebral character to Evangelical faith-expressions at a grass-roots level in a way sometimes lacking when mainliners informally gather to "share" their faith.

To be sure, there may be a danger that such an emphasis on the objective propositional Word can lead to an undue de-emphasis on the work of the Holy Spirit. This is a charge which some charismatics, Pentecostals, and mainline theologians might level.[32] However, as will be indicated, contemporary theology has too often been guilty of reducing the truth and meaning of Christian claims about God to the mere personal relevance of these claims for contemporary believers.[33] In so doing it unwittingly often supports the cultural relativism of today. It may well be that the Evangelical movement is pointing to some serious deficiencies in contemporary mainline theology, as many Evangelically oriented church members in mainline denominations sense.

In contrast to these deficiencies the Evangelical insistence on objective propositional revelation provides Evangelicals with a comprehensive worldview, a system which allows them to find security and to make sense of the world in face of the apparent chaos of contemporary pluralism. And it is a comforting world that has been proposed by the Evangelicals. A framework for understanding all there is to know about the world is offered by the inspired, inerrant Scripture.[34]

The vast majority of Evangelicals insist that the bulwark which Scripture provides is severely compromised if inerrancy is not affirmed. If the Bible is not inerrant, it is argued, we cannot rely with certainty on its teachings. No norm would be established for determining what is true and false.[35] If the Bible contained errors even in minor matters, it might be wrong about the major matters of faith. Thus, given the role inerrancy has played historically in the Evangelical movement and plays in the present context, it is not surprising that some Evangelicals like the former *Christianity Today* editor, Harold Lindsell, insist that inerrancy's abandonment inevitably leads to a denial of all faith commitments.[36] With the doctrines of verbal inerrancy and inspiration we stand at the historical and logical center of the Evangelical movement.

Several presuppositions underlie the prevailing Evangelical commitments regarding Scripture. Evangelicals generally maintain: (1) that Scripture is the Christian's principle for verifying his or her understanding of reality, because the Bible is divinely inspired and true; (2) there is only one system of truth, not many "contextual truths";[37] (3) the meaning of the biblical text is universally accessible. That is, the meaning of a·text is not contingent on an interpreter's perspective or point of view.

This third commitment clearly represents a break with much mainline theological reflection. Since the time of the 18th-century German philosopher Immanuel Kant, philosophers and educators have been inclined to think of reality in terms of distinct points of view. "You have your perspective; I have mine." Most Evangelicals, however, tend to reject this notion by insisting that objective meaning not influenced by one's perspective is possible to attain. No doubt this may be a reflection of Evangelical indebtedness both to the Puritan theological heritage, which held that "there is only one meaning for every place in Scripture," and to Scottish common sense realist philosophy.[38]

Scottish common sense realism has its origins in the 18th century, first developed by the Scotch thinker Thomas Reid (1710–1796); largely in reaction to the skepticism of the English philosopher David Hume, it offered an alternative to Kant's "perspectivalist" efforts to reestablish some degree of human certainty in face of Humean skepticism. As previously noted, through some of Reid's popularizers it exerted a profound influence on colonial and postrevolutionary American society. In part this resulted from its impact on Thomas Jefferson and, in the next century, on Princeton theology through University president, James McCosh.

The basic presupposition of this philosophy was that human beings are capable of real knowledge. Truth is much the same for everyone, everywhere. All human beings are seen to possess a certain prerational intuition for distinguishing right from wrong, truth from falsehood. Cultural differences do not alter this core of commonsense beliefs. Despite these differences, all people share a common humanity. As a result, people could assimilate data accurately without any interpretive distortion because their own perspective does not skew their perception. In short, one can trust one's common sense, and trust that it was sufficiently universal to allow for the possibility of agreement with others about mutually accessible data. Such confidence in empirical observation set the stage for American confidence in scientific progress and the 19th-century influence of Francis Bacon and his philosophy.

In terms of hermeneutics—Biblical interpretation—the consequence of this philosophical view was that one could assume the clarity of Scripture and the possibility that interpreters might come to agree on the "objective" descriptive meaning of a given text. Such assumptions may appear odd to our post-Kantian eyes.[39] However, one cannot overlook the profound impact common sense realism has had, at least in North American society. For this fact, along with the mutual insistence of Evangelicalism and Puritanism that the descriptive meaning of a text can be identified, must clearly be reckoned as factors contributing to the popularity and success of contemporary Evangelicalism. While the proclamation of many mainline churches frames the gospel in dialogue with post-Kantian perspectival philosophies which are alien to many North Americans, it is only in Evangelical proclamation that the grass roots hear a "commonsense gospel" which is presented in a way more nearly correlating with their commonsense understanding of reality. In short, Evangelical proclamation is down-to-earth, sharing common assumptions with its hearers, at least in North America.

There are liabilities inherent in this philosophical model. Given the supposition that clear conclusions are always available to one who exercises common sense, it is more difficult to tolerate diversity and differences of theological opinion. This relative intolerance, based on common sense philosophy, no doubt helps to account for the schismatic effects theological differences have had on the Evangelical movement.[40]

Evangelical diversity

The three presuppositions we have sketched should be noted carefully. Collectively, they represent the common framework from which diversity in the Evangelical movement emerges, as there is some diversity in the appropriation of each of these presuppositions. Evangelicals themselves insist that there is no one monolithic view of biblical authority.[41] In dealing with this diversity we will begin in inverse order, first noting diversity on the third presupposition, the universal accessibility of Scripture's meaning.

In regard to the supposition that each biblical text has a universally accessible objective meaning, it should be observed that some Evangelical theologians seem open to acknowledging a variety of possible perspectives on what constitutes the "center" of the Bible or else to suggesting that the Bible is only rightly understood by converted/redeemed exegetes. For some this commitment may be a consequence of the influence of neoorthodox theology (shaped by Kantian "perspectivalism") and Pietism. This is especially evident in the thought of some German Evangelicals.[42]

Other Evangelicals, who have been influenced by liberation theology (an approach to Christian faith developed in the Third World which stresses the gospel's role in liberating the oppressed), insist that a correlative relationship between Scripture and the concrete situation must be acknowledged. The call for contextualization of Evangelical theology is apparent today in a number of segments of the Evangelical community.[43] These commitments seem to undermine the possibility of objectively identifying Scripture's descriptive meaning since on these grounds the Bible would have different meanings in different contexts.

To be sure, although those who maintain such perspectivalist views remain in the minority among Evangelicals, the rightful place of cultural and personal perspectives in Christian theology remains an issue of disagreement for Evangelicals. Lest any imagine that this diversity represents a departure from the Evangelical heritage, it should also be acknowledged that the great Princeton theologian, Charles Hodge, was open to necessity of adapting the interpretation of Scripture to accommodate scientific discoveries.[44] Likewise Abraham Kuyper, the Dutch theologian who has had so much impact on America's Christian Reformed Church, claimed that only the redeemed could possibly reason from and understand Scripture.[45] In view of Kuyper's influence on this church, such perspectivalism would seem to be a legitimate Evangelical alternative. Thus, although the main direction of Evangelical thought is to affirm the possibility of ascertaining the objective, nonperspectival meaning of Scripture, not all segments of the movement agree.

Diversity is also apparent regarding the second Evangelical hermeneutical presupposition—the question of truth and how this truth may relate to other "truths." Evangelicals seek to defend the Christian truth and the authority of Scripture in a variety of ways. Their various approaches embody the different theological methods which are considered viable Evangelical alternatives. We may briefly characterize these alternatives in three general types, keeping in mind the fact that very few Evangelicals embody any of the types perfectly: (1) proofs for God's existence, sometimes based on inductive arguments for the historical truth of the biblical accounts; (2) the establishment of biblical inerrancy by appeal to the authority of Christ; and (3) presuppositionalist method.[46]

The first method takes two different forms. Some, like Norman Geisler (professor of theology at Dallas Seminary), employ a kind of proof for the existence of God akin to the cosmological argument of the 13th-century Roman Catholic theologian Thomas Aquinas. Others, like John Stott and B. B. Warfield, at least appeal to the concept of a natural revelation of God in order to establish the existence of a Supreme Being (see Rom. 1:20-21).[47]

A variation of this method has been developed by a Lutheran Church–Missouri Synod theologian, John Warwick Montgomery (and certain statements of his church could be interpreted in this way). He contends that it is possible to provide sufficient historical evidence for the deity of Christ and his resurrection, so that the truth claims made by Scripture may be verified.[48] At an early stage in B. B. Warfield's career, he seemed also to take such an approach, using historical and scientific investigations to verify Scripture as revelation (later, because of the inroads of modern science and historical criticism, he changed his approach). This was clearly in the tradition of Princeton theology initiated by Archibald Alexander.[49]

The second method, the endeavor to establish the inerrancy of Scripture on the basis of the authority of Christ and his appeal to the inerrancy of the Old Testament, is employed by a variety of Evangelicals, including John Gerstner of Pittsburgh Theological Seminary, John Stott, Edward John Carnell (former president of Fuller Seminary), and the influential African Evangelical, Gottfried Osei-Mensah. The Assemblies of God, a Pentecostal denomination, also appears to embrace this approach.[50] The basic argument is that whoever acknowledges the lordship and authority of Christ has no logical alternative but to acknowledge the complete trustworthiness and divine authority of Scripture, since that is what he seems to have taught (Matt. 5:17-19; Mark 12:35-37).

The third method, presuppositionalism, is perhaps the dominant approach in contemporary Evangelicalism. Among the practitioners of this approach are Carl Henry, Westminster Seminary professor Cornelius Van Til, and perhaps the founder of L'Abri Fellowship, Francis Schaeffer. On the European scene Gerhard Maier also seems to rely on something like an appeal to presuppositions in his hermeneutics (although it is by no means clear that he means what Henry does by "presuppositions"; more like Kuyper, Maier insists that Scripture is understood only by means of a "special hermeneutic" available only to faith). Among the churches in which something like presuppositionalism appears to be reflected are The Lutheran Church–Missouri Synod (GS, p. 15), The Orthodox Presbyterian Church, and the Christian Reformed Church (pp. 13-14, 23). (The use of this method by the latter church comes as no surprise, given its indebtedness to Abraham Kuyper and other Dutch theologians of the last century who employed it.) The method seems to have gained widespread support insofar as the representative gathering of theologians which formulated the widely accepted *Chicago Statement on Biblical Inerrancy* (XV, Exp.) appears to rely at least in part on this approach.[51]

The basic contention of this method is that arguments for Christian truth are valid only if employed in the context of an initial presupposition (or faith) that God/Christ exists and that he has infallibly revealed himself in Scripture. From this presupposition all other Christian claims follow. Thus some presuppositionalists, after establishing this basic presupposition, proceed to argue for the existence of God and the authority, historicity, and inerrancy of the biblical accounts.[52]

This perspective, its more Reformed practitioners maintain, is not a mere antirational fideism. Rather, Christianity is presented as the only rational interpretation of the universe. All perceptions of reality are said to require some presuppositional starting point. Belief in the God who reveals himself in Scripture is regarded as the most rational of presuppositions.[53]

A kind of presuppositionalism which would avoid making faith a necessary prerequisite for understanding the Bible literally could be particularly helpful to Evangelicals in our postcritical era. For insofar as it maintains that a given reality can be known only by those who share its presupposition, the method provides a conceptuality by which to maintain that the biblical presupposition cannot be disconfirmed by historical and scientific research.[54] This dimension of the method is most suggestive of other mainline theological alternatives, particularly those influenced by the language philosophy of Ludwig Wittgenstein and certain methods of narrative biblical interpretation. As such, presuppositionalism has warranted further consideration in the final chapters, where a comparison of Evangelical and mainline hermeneutical approaches is offered. At any rate, it is quite evident that a whole spectrum of Evangelically legitimate theological methods are present within the movement.

The inerrancy controversy

A third area of diversity on hermeneutical questions is related to the first of the three Evangelical presuppositions previously identified—the degree to which the Bible's inerrancy is affirmed. There is much diversity represented on this issue and, given the importance of the question for Evangelical self-identity, it is perhaps *the* crucial issue today for Evangelicals. A 1957 poll of conservative clergy in America, commissioned by *Christianity Today,* confirms that many hard questions are being raised in the movement about this doctrine. Only one-half of these Evangelically oriented clergy were sure that they accepted the concept of inerrancy. More recent opinion surveys indicate that about 40% of American Evangelical theologians as well as an even higher percentage of younger Evangelicals are raising similar questions about biblical inerrancy.[55]

The traditional Evangelical position, "detailed inerrancy," is probably rooted in the Fundamentalist heritage of the movement. This viewpoint would assert the historical and scientific accuracy of all the biblical accounts (including the Genesis creation account).[56] This conclusion is arrived at either *inductively* by a study of the phenomena reported on by Scripture in order to determine their veracity, or *deductively,* by studying the biblical texts to determine whether inerrancy is taught by Scripture, or by making this claim on the basis of prior presuppositions.

The inductive approach correlates with the first theological method we noted, specifically, the endeavor to prove the historical truths of the biblical accounts. It is the more readily accessible approach for those who would challenge absolute inerrancy. The deductive approach, by contrast, correlates with the other two Evangelical methodologies (including presuppositionalism) which we noted. It is more typically associated with efforts to defend detailed inerrancy.[57]

With both approaches, detailed inerrantists often find themselves committed to harmonizing apparent conflicts one finds in Scripture. Harold Lindsell is an especially prominent Evangelical who undertakes these efforts.[58] This commitment is often correlated, particularly in Fundamentalist segments of the Evangelical movement, with a rejection of the historical-critical method.

The role of historical criticism in contemporary Evangelical theology is in fact a very neuralgic theme, particularly for North American Evangelicals. Though there were exceptions in Europe, especially among Evangelicals in Great Britain, before the end of World War II there was little critical academic study of the Bible in Evangelical circles. Several factors no doubt contributed to this situation. The influence of dispensationalism on early Fundamentalism is certainly a factor, for the dispensationalist method is not particularly favorable to critical textual study. Also, the association of historical criticism with modernism led to Evangelical suspicions of the method.[59] Nor can the influence of common sense realism on Evangelicalism be overlooked. Given its presuppositions, Evangelicals came to believe that historical realities could be grasped intuitively without regard to the critical apparatus of human consciousness, the critical principles, on which the historical-critical method relies.

In fact, to this day most Evangelicals still reject the historical-critical method's principle of analogy.[60] This principle is the idea that no historical claim can be substantiated unless the historian has some analogy to the event in his or her own present experience. Obviously, a rigorous use of this principle would preclude the historicity of many of the biblical accounts, including the Resurrection, for most contemporary historians would know of no analogies to a bodily resurrection. Thus, for self-evident reasons Evangelicals have rejected this principle, in order to free them to make historical claims. In place of this principle it is not uncommon for some Evangelicals to substitute other presuppositions, like the presupposition of divine activity, which allow them to substantiate Scripture's claims.[61] Such a move is not without precedents; a proposal of this sort of "proper use" of historical criticism was offered by writers of *The Fundamentals* (I, 106; IX, 33ff.). One basic supposition is that the historicity of the biblical accounts may be assumed until these claims are disproved.[62]

Although these procedures are viable for Evangelicals within their own communities, Evangelical theology is nevertheless faced with critical challenges to the credibility of its claims from outside the movement. Much like certain mainline theologians, some Evangelicals deal with these challenges with genuine philosophical sophistication. The presuppositionalists are in an especially good position to deal with such challenges. They can argue that the empirical tools of science and history cannot ultimately judge Christian claims.

The historical-critical mentality has made its presence felt in the Evangelical community by forcing redefinitions of the concept of inerrancy. One way this has been manifested is in a kind of inductive Evangelical exegesis that concerns itself solely with the internal relationship of the various elements of the biblical content. By relying on the Reformation principle of analogy of Scripture, when correlated with the critical mentality, some Evangelicals have begun to use the Bible programmatically to criticize itself. This has been accomplished with particular efficiency by feminist Evangelicals like Nancy Hardesty, Letha Scanzoni, and Virginia Mollenkott as a means of reinterpreting biblical passages which imply a hierarchial-sexist ecclesiology (1 Cor. 11:2-16; 1 Cor. 14:34-35; 1 Tim. 2:8-12). These texts are seen as incidental, contextually bound statements in conflict with the theological center of the biblical witness. The outcome of such an inductive approach is perhaps best summarized by the Evangelical Clark Pinnock's conclusion: The Bible "*contains* errors but *teaches* none."[63]

The critical mindset and its conclusion that certain errors may exist in the biblical text has had its impact in all areas of the Evangelical movement, in the schools, the churches, even among proponents of total inerrancy. For example, historical-critical tools increasingly are being employed in the better Evangelical schools. Even staunch inerrantists like Carl Henry as well as many Fundamentalists will concede that "the Bible is not a textbook on science or on history." They do go on to insist that the Bible has a bearing on these issues.[64] However, an increasing number of contemporary Evangelicals are not prepared to assert the Bible's bearing on science and history.

One way in which this development manifests itself is evidenced in the controversy over the scientific veracity of the Genesis creation account. Although Evangelicals have to a great extent presented a united front to the media in their struggle to institute the teaching of creationism in North American public schools, there is diversity in the ranks on this matter. The diversity hinges on the question of the degree to which the insights of evolutionary theory can be integrated with the Genesis account.

Although the controversy over evolution is primarily a problem raised by American Evangelicals, it has now come to the fore in Great Britain, on the European continent, in Africa, and in Australia.[65] The more conservative creationists reject the idea that the biblical doctrine is compatible with a concept of creation which regards creation as a process of gradual change. Rather, this group, like Henry Morris and his Institute for Creation Research, insists upon the creation occurring in six 24-hour days. (It is interesting to note that this more militant strand of "creationism," at least as exemplified by its prime theoretician, Morris, bases its argument on a highly debatable theological assumption, that "God is not now creating anything. . . [that] His present work is not creation . . . ."[66] Since this supposition seems basic to these creationists' insistence that there can be no integration of creation and evolution [for creation was an event in the past], it would seem that a most fruitful debating point for those opposed to creationism might be to question the theological validity of assuming that God is no longer creating [Psalm 104].) Other eminent Evangelicals, like Francis Schaeffer and Carl Henry, indicate an openness to interpreting the six days of the Genesis account in terms of longer periods, even geological ages, in order that some integration of the biblical witness and scientific insights might be achieved.[67]

There is clearly an openness on the part of the latter group to allowing Christian theology to be informed by insights of critical and scientific research. In fact, one can find other distinct attempts to synthesize the creation account with evolutionary-geological insights. For although the media is inclined to focus its attention almost exclusively on the strict creationist view, this theistic evolutionist or the progressive creationist views tend to predominate in the faculties of most Evangelical schools.[68]

There is some historical precedent for these attempts at harmonization by Evangelicals. We previously noted that it is rooted in their Fundamentalist heritage. Thus Princeton theologian Charles Hodge, as early as 1874, was open to the possibility that others might be able to integrate the biblical account with evolutionary theory. B. B. Warfield explicitly credited Calvin with integrating a "doctrine of evolution" into his understanding of the creation doctrine. And William Jennings Bryan testified during the Scopes Trial that the six days of creation did not "necessarily mean a twenty-four hour day." Dispensationalists also made efforts to account for scientific data concerning the age and changed character of the earth. They argued that between Gen. 1:1 ("In the beginning God created. . .") and Gen. 1:2 ("And the earth was without form and void") the earth had undergone cataclysmic change as the result of divine judgment.[69] Evangelical history, then, tells the story of efforts to integrate theology with the modern critical spirit. However, the inroads made by the critical mentality have in effect forced the acknowledgment of the Bible's lack of scientific veracity, at least with regard to the creation accounts. The consequences of this are made more apparent by the development of theories of "limited inerrancy."

Limited inerrancy

Limited inerrancy is the idea that the Bible is infallible on matters of faith and conduct but not necessarily in all its assertions. Previously we noted that such a view characterizes the *Statement of Faith of Fuller Seminary* (3). (A certain reading of 2 Tim. 3:15-16 might be used to authorize such a position.) The debate among Evangelicals on this issue, at least in North America, was opened in the 1960s, in part by a book by Dewey Beegle entitled *The Inspiration of Scripture*. In it Beegle claimed that the Bible contained errors, even in areas related to the authors' intention. He went on to suggest that the inspiration of the Scriptures is not radically distinct from a mere heightening of human creativity.[70]

The book led to a debate on inerrancy which brought many of the issues related to the challenge of historical criticism to a head in the Evangelical community. In this connection it is interesting to note the process of further redefinition by detailed inerrantists in face of the critical onslaughts. Thus Carl Henry and *The Chicago Statement on Biblical Inerrancy* (Exp.) now claim that the Bible's inerrancy is not negated by the reporting of falsehoods. Indeed, it is acknowledged, Scripture may not report with precision every minute detail of the events which it relates or the Old Testament passages cited by The New Testament. Nonetheless, the claim is still made that the accounts recorded are inspired by God, true insofar as they are part of the express message or truth aimed for by their authors.[71]

A further affirmation of interest by Henry and the eminent theologians who drafted the *Chicago Statement* is their openness to dealing with pre-Newtonian statements about the world as indicative of the biblical authors' use of common idioms of the day. Insofar as the authors' use of these idioms occurs when they are not teaching ontology, the lack of scientific accuracy in such passages does not imply the errancy of Scripture. This openness to acknowledging Scripture's scientific inadequacies, to affirming the Bible's inerrancy only in relation to its own purpose, is no recent development in Evangelicalism. One finds precedents for this as early as the pre-Fundamentalist period in B. B. Warfield, as he claims that scientific theories about the age of the human species have no theological significance, for the biblical genealogies were not intended to provide a definite chronological scheme and *do not accomplish this satisfactorily.*[72] Virtually the same point was echoed by the influential series, *The Fundamentals* (IV, 100-101; cf. V, 44-45).

A remarkable openness to conceding the lack of scientific and historical veracity is acknowledged by modern inerrantists. These theologians and a number of others will even go so far as to acknowledge that culture-bound biblical statements, like those pertaining to the status of women, should not be applied to our present situation. This is not a new liberalism. Even these culture-bound passages are considered Word of God.[73] However, it is quite evident that there exists even among these Conservative Evangelicals an undeniable openness for allowing historical-critical judgments to determine appropriate proclamation.

The impact of the historical-critical method on even its most characteristic theologians is further confirmed by *The Chicago Statement on Biblical Inerrancy* (XIX) when this representative group states that one need not believe all Evangelical doctrines concerning Scripture (presumably including inerrancy) in order to be saved. Historical criticism's impact has not only opened the Evangelical movement to diversity, but also tends to mitigate the Fundamentalist separatist tendencies.

In view of its impact on the centrist and the right-wing theologians of the Evangelical movement, it is not surprising that historical criticism has had a radical impact on the development of the concept of limited inerrancy. Among Evangelicals holding to such a view of Scripture, disagreement has emerged over whether it is preferable to refer to the Bible as infallible or as inerrant.

As previously noted, a number of Evangelicals, including the influential president of Fuller Seminary, David Hubbard, have proposed that it is preferable to discard the term "inerrancy" and speak only of the Bible's "infallibility."[74] This perspective has had its impact on the faith statements of several Evangelical institutions, notably Fuller Seminary (3) and Inter-Varsity Christian Fellowship (1). A statement emerging from an international gathering of Evangelicals in 1974, *The Lausanne Covenant* (2), also notably avoided the language of inerrancy in favor of reference to the Bible's "truthfulness," its infallibility for faith and practice. Although it was probably not the intention of its framers, this use of the concept "truthfulness" rather than "inerrancy" (though the statement does say that the Bible is "without error" in all that it affirms) was employed by some left-wing Evangelicals as authorization for their views. Perhaps even more striking is the final report of the international Evangelical-Roman Catholic dialogue; the Evangelical participants, among whom were David Hubbard and Peter Beyerhaus, described Evangelical theological convictions with no reference even to Scripture's infallibility or its trustworthiness. The report (Int.[1]) speaks only of the Bible's "authority" and inspiration. Later in the report, however, all parties were willing to speak of Scripture's "inerrancy," insofar as what the biblical authors wrote is what God intended (1[1]).

In essence, the position of the limited inerrantists and those who opt only for speaking of the Bible's infallibility or its truthfulness is well summarized by the observation of Clark Pinnock cited earlier: The Bible "*contains* errors but *teaches* none."[75] Such a perspective has opened the way for left-wing Evangelicals and to some extent even for Pinnock himself to speak only of the Bible's inerrancy taken as a whole in regard to its spiritual intention for the building-up of faith. Consequently Scripture's truthfulness, even its character as revelation, in regard to certain details of geography, cosmology, and history is relegated to a matter of no import. One can even cite some precedent in the Fundamentalist period for this development within contemporary Evangelicalism, as an article by James Orr in *The Fundamentals* (IX, 46) proposes that the question of the Bible's inerrancy need not be considered.

This sort of limiting of verbal and plenary inspiration has taken other related forms in contemporary Evangelicalism. One proposal has been to regard the biblical authors as mere ambassadors of God, authorized to speak for God but not necessarily writing a word which directly coincides with his Word.[76] Others develop this tendency even further by endeavoring to undermine the propositional character of revelation, at least in one case by arguing that human language, including that of the Bible, is inadequate to portray God.[77] In fact, some Evangelicals have gone so far as explicitly to assert that the Gospel accounts, though true to their authors' intentions and without any deception of their readers, represent departures from the actuality of the events they report.[78] Such commitments bear genuine similarities to contemporary mainline neoorthodox theology.

Neoorthodoxy is a theological movement begun in the second decade of our century in reaction to the encroachments of liberalism on the Church. As initiated by the Swiss theologian Karl Barth, it was an endeavor to revive the traditional theological categories of Protestant Orthodoxy in a new way. The movement was heavily influenced by insights from existential philosophy, particularly Kierkegaard, and never entirely repudiated the Kantian perspectivalist manner of viewing reality. Although this movement took various forms, it has influenced the Evangelical movement perhaps first through the work of the Alsatian biblical scholar Oscar Cullmann, but more recently through the work of Karl Barth.[79]

Barth understood the Bible as the Word of God in a *functionalist* sense. That is to say, Scripture itself is not Word of God. It only *becomes* the Word of God when, enlivened by the Spirit, it brings its readers to faith. The Bible was regarded as making historical claims only in a "special" sense. Barth employed the concept of a "special salvation history" which is not accessible to ordinary critical history, can only be known from the perspective of faith, and so cannot be disconfirmed by historical research. In this way he was able to affirm the Bible's historical veracity without requiring a challenge of the presuppositions of historical criticism, as Evangelicals have done. Insofar as this procedure suggests two different, unrelated kinds of history—a conclusion Barth himself seems to reject—it conflicts with the second Evangelical hermeneutical presupposition noted earlier, namely, that there is only one system of truth, not many distinct truths.[80]

At any rate, the influence on the Evangelical movement of this kind of Barthian neoorthodoxy, particularly as it was mediated by the influence of Cullmann on the movement, is explicitly reflected in the thought of some left-wing Evangelicals. Thus the eminent American-born Latin American Evangelical theologian Orlando Costas took a position with Barth in advocating a functionalist view of Scripture, that Scripture becomes the Word of God.[81] He is not alone among Evangelicals in maintaining such a view. Other Evangelicals, including framers of *The Lausanne Covenant* (2), the Dutch Reformed theologian G. C. Berkouwer and even Billy Graham, are inclined to follow this lead and distinguish the Word from the Scriptures, a legitimate Evangelical claim in itself but one that easily lends itself to a Barthian interpretation.[82] (It should be noted that Graham elsewhere has affirmed the Bible's infallibility and, at least in a qualified sense, as a conviction or presupposition of faith, inerrancy.)[83] The Barthian step is in fact completely taken by Evangelicals like George Eldon Ladd and Donald Bloesch who seem to appeal to a special salvation-history intelligible as history only to faith, as a means of authenticating the historicity of the biblical accounts.[84] The inroads of neoorthodox theology on contemporary Evangelicalism are quite apparent.

Given the influence of Pietism on the Evangelical movement, some of these developments regarding the doctrine of inerrancy may be appropriate. As we have noted, Pietism was not particularly concerned to articulate theories of biblical authority.[85] Thus it is altogether appropriate that European Evangelicals influenced by Pietism, particularly those in Germany, have not tended to articulate the doctrine of biblical inerrancy with quite the vigor that their American counterparts have. These Evangelicals, notably Peter Beyerhaus and Gerhard Maier, as well as their associated organizations, the Internationale Konferenz Bekennender Gemeinschaften (2[a]), and the Albrecht-Bengel-Haus (2), are more inclined to refer with *The Lausanne Covenant* (2) and various European national evangelical alliances to the Bible's "truthfulness" (in its entirety) or its absolute authority, without reference to inerrancy. These theologians and a number of their European colleagues are self-proclaimed pietists who understand their involvement in the Evangelical movement as a consequence of their pietist heritage. Other

European Evangelicals, notably The Free Evangelical Theological Academy in Basel, Switzerland, and the Association Evangélique d'Eglises Baptistes de Langue Française (I.2), are quite insistent upon affirming the characteristically Evangelical concepts of inerrancy and infallibility.[86] And even those who seem to avoid a dialog with the concept of inerrancy affirm something like plenary inspiration insofar as they speak of the Bible's *entire truthfulness.*

The spirit of Pietism, with its tendency not to concern itself with too precise doctrinal formulations, is reflected also among American Evangelicals. One church heavily influenced by the pietist heritage, The Evangelical Covenant Church (pp. 5, 8, 11, 23), self-consciously affirms this heritage and, as we have noted, asserts in reference to Scripture simply that it is "the Word of God and the only perfect rule for faith, doctrine and conduct." A number of younger theologians of the Wesleyan/Holiness traditions have taken similar positions by appealing to the hesitancy of the founders of their churches to assert a Fundamentalist view of inerrancy. And in the case of some of the churches, for example, the Evangelical Congregational Church (104) and the Church of God (Cleveland, Tenn.) (1), which officially affirm only the divine inspiration of Scripture, this point seems substantiated.[87] Such viewpoints can easily accommodate views of "limited inerrancy" and consequent influences from neoorthodox theology. Could it be that its pietist (and Holiness) heritage has unwittingly prepared the contemporary Evangelical movement for the growing influence the concept of limited inerrancy and Barthian theology are presently having on it?

Other dimensions of the Evangelical heritage may have prepared the movement for the present impact made by neoorthodoxy. We have previously noted both dimensions. The influence on Evangelicalism of the great 19th- early 20th-century Dutch theologians like Abraham Kuyper, with their perspectival tendencies cannot be overlooked. Recall that Kuyper insisted that only the redeemed could rightly understand and reason from Scripture. Such a view easily converges with the Barthian insistence that the Scriptures are understood as Word of God only when faith is awakened.[88] The influence of Kuyper on the Christian Reformed Church, then, readily suggests why the Evangelical left and neoorthodoxy have made recent inroads into this Evangelical church.

Another segment of the Evangelical community which is also usually not as inclined to affirm total inerrancy is the Pentecostal community. This may be a reflection of the Pentecostal emphasis on personal experience; it may also be a factor in the suspicions some Evangelicals have of Pentecostalism. This reticence is reflected in most of the official statements of Pentecostal churches. Even Pat Robertson, perhaps today's most visible American Pentecostal, shares this orientation. He once suggested that Scripture is errant, for the canon was given through human agents and only Christ, who is filled with the Spirit, is the inerrant one. In recent correspondence, he did concede that biblical inerrancy is not of "burning interest" to him.[89]

Such statements are quite removed from the characteristic Evangelical position of detailed inerrancy and are much closer to mainline neoorthodox theology. The differences within Evangelical theology on this issue are quite pronounced.

Summary reflections

Given the fact that so many interpreters, including Mark Noll, Francis Schaeffer, and Harold Lindsell, regard the concept of biblical inerrancy or the sacredness of Scripture as the unifying principle of the Evangelical movement, the one that provides it with its most distinctive characteristics, the diversity of approaches we have observed on this issue raises important questions.[90] Of course it could be argued that this diversity is so generally accepted at the grass-roots level of the movement that it poses no problems. Some like Donald Bloesch, however, have claimed that outsiders are incorrect in identifying inerrancy as the distinctive characteristic of Evangelicalism.[91]

Even if we were to grant this point as a valid theological observation, the observation of the Pentecostal theologian, Gerald Sheppard, cannot be overlooked. He reminds us that inerrancy is for Evangelicals the language of social identification over against so-called non-Evangelical institutions. Even more liberal Evangelicals like Richard Quebedeaux will concede that the vast majority of Evangelicals believe in the detailed inerrancy of Scripture.[92] The fact that the statements of faith of virtually all Evangelical churches and organizations affirm biblical infallibility—if not inerrancy—seems to lend credence to this observation. Thus even on a purely sociological basis inerrancy seems to be acknowledged by many as *the* distinctive issue for the Evangelical movement, the affirmation which ultimately distinguishes it from mainline churches.

The case can be made in another way for identifying biblical inerrancy as the distinctive Evangelical issue. For with the possible exception of a few Evangelicals, particularly those outside North America, whose traditions are absolutely untouched by the influence of

Fundamentalism or Protestant Orthodoxy (and the Puritan heritage with its biblicist tendencies), even the most left-wing Evangelicals are formulating their proposals in dialogue with the concept of inerrancy/infallibility in order to indicate their Evangelical identity.[93] And, as we have just noted, even those Evangelicals outside North America who are not explicitly in dialogue with the concept do at least remain in dialogue with its suppositions to the extent that most of them endorse something like plenary inspiration. By contrast, such consideration of or dialogue with these concepts is no longer a mandatory issue to be addressed in the constructive proposals of mainline, ecumenical theology.

Even if biblical inerrancy or at least plenary inspiration is the central Evangelical affirmation only for sociological reasons, the diversity of approaches to inerrancy which we have observed does seem to challenge the unity of the Evangelical movement so severely as to raise questions about whether one can really identify Evangelicalism as a distinct group of Christians. Some prominent Evangelicals, like Francis Schaeffer, have suggested that Evangelical unity has been undermined, that there is no longer a distinct Evangelical movement held together by common theological convictions. This opinion, however, still represents a minority point of view; Carl Henry and other eminent Evangelicals continue to maintain that there is a basic theological consensus about Scripture amid the disagreements.[94]

To the degree that Henry and others are correct in identifying a core of basic Evangelical agreement, several intriguing questions emerge. Insofar as the distinct approaches to biblical inerrancy/infallibility do share some common consensus, and several of them are closely correlated with contemporary theological approaches of the mainline, are these similar mainline approaches acceptable in principle to Evangelicals? (The question of Barth's acceptability to Evangelicals has been and continues to be directly raised.)[95]

Certainly, the more radical Evangelicals and most of those espousing "limited inerrancy" would seem to be able to embrace neoorthodox Barthian approaches which influence many of the mainline churches. However, the more characteristically Evangelical position still seems to be the kind of "qualified detailed inerrancy" which we noted in *The Chicago Statement on Biblical Inerrancy* and in Carl Henry. If a dialog with Evangelicalism is to achieve some agreement between the Evangelical movement and the mainline churches, it is necessary to engage in dialogue with this detailed inerrancy position more seriously, and not bypass it in favor of dialogue only with the more readily reconcilable views of the Evangelical left.

The question of the nature of scriptural authority seems to be a major reason why some conservative Lutheran church bodies like The Lutheran Church–Missouri Synod hesitate to identify themselves with the Evangelical movement. We already have suggested some other factors, including the purported Evangelical lack of fidelity to the historic Confessional documents, its doctrinal inclusiveness. The characteristically Evangelical de-emphasis of the Sacraments is another.[96] But a major concern in the minds of some conservative Lutherans is that the characteristic Evangelical view of the Scripture is too much influenced by John Calvin. Evangelicals are thought to place too much stress on an intellectual understanding of Scripture, its propositions, and not enough stress on the transforming power of the gospel as mediated through, yet distinct from Scripture. In short, the Lutheran concern is that Evangelicals may not adequately communicate that through Scripture God reveals not only doctrines but God's Being.[97] This tension between conservative Lutheran churches and the Evangelical establishment will be dealt with in the final chapter.

Dispensationalism and eschatology

No discussion of Evangelical approaches to Scripture can omit attention to the method of dispensationalism, even though its influence on part of the Evangelical movement is waning. It retains its influence on several Evangelical churches, like the Independent Fundamental Churches of America (13), and in educational institutions like Dallas Theological Seminary, which are officially committed to dispensationalism. Some analysts have suggested that adherence to dispensationalism is one of the dividing lines between Evangelicals and Fundamentalists, Fundamentalists supporting the method and Evangelicals criticizing it. Nevertheless, dispensational themes relating to the millennium and an appreciation of distinct dispensations in the history of God's interaction with humanity continue to appear in the work of some important thinkers, like Carl Henry.[98]

This reference to the millennium raises questions about Evangelical teachings on the doctrine of last things (eschatology). A consideration of this topic in conjunction with dispensationalism is quite appropriate for, as we have noted, dispensationalism is in its origins always very much in dialogue with eschatological concerns and a belief in the millennium. On these questions, too, one observes a diversity of opinion within the Evangelical movement, though not such a diversity as to tolerate denial of Christ's literal, even imminent second coming.

In the second chapter we noted that disagreements among Evangelicals about the millennium and its mode of being established are rooted in the movement's pre-Fundamentalistic period. The distinct approaches, premillennialism, postmillennialism, and amillennialism, were described there. Another related issue of controversy was and continues to be whether believers will experience the rapture, and, if so, at what point it might happen in relation to the period of tribulation, which, according to the premillennialist scheme, precedes the millennium's advent.

Today, not only is more diversity on these matters tolerated in the Evangelical community, but also the relative importance of these questions has diminished, except among conservative Fundamentalists.[99] All the historic alternatives continue to have proponents,[100] and Evangelicals would never consider the rejection of a literal understanding of Christ's second coming.[101] On the whole, however, in recent years amillennialism, the denial of a literal earthly millennium, has tended to become the dominant view among educated Evangelicals and has begun to achieve more of a parity with premillennialism within the Evangelical movement as a whole.[102] (This development is one more indication of the self-conscious differentiation by Evangelicals from Fundamentalists since the Second World War.) However, new trends have been developing. For example, in this decade renewed interest in the almost totally abandoned view of postmillennialism, the idea that through the establishment of earthly peace and justice the second coming of Christ will be hastened, has received renewed attention especially from left-wing Evangelicals.[103] Likewise most of the major American TV Evangelists, including Jerry Falwell, Pat Robertson, and—at least prior to his original resignation of his duties due to a sex scandal—Jim Bakker, appear to embrace and propagate some form of millennialism. The Fundamentalist-dispensationalist expectation of an imminent second coming continues to perpetuate itself in a number of Evangelical churches and organizations.[104] Debate continues, even over the rapture, and even in academic circles, between dispensationalists and strict premillennialists like George Eldon Ladd, who denies the rapture.[105]

Mainline Christians—and Lutherans in particular—are apt to observe these ongoing controversies within the Evangelical movement with a certain degree of self-satisfaction. The Lutheran Confessional document *The Augsburg Confession* (XVII.5) rejects the concept of a millennium, insofar as it compromises the character of justification as free gift by suggesting that the godly will gain possession of worldly power before the resurrection of the dead (and presumably apart from Christ). From this perspective, the controversies which have ensued among Evangelicals can only be regarded as the consequence of their venture into religious speculation.

However, the waning importance of these issues within the contemporary Evangelical movement and the increased impact of amillennialism can only be regarded as a happy sign that disagreements on eschatology separating the mainline and the Evangelical communities are no longer quite so insurmountable. Mainline church views on the subject would seem to be acceptable to Evangelicals, since the viewpoint of these churches correlates with an amillennial perspective, a legitimate Evangelical alternative. Conversely, as amillennialism comes increasingly to influence the Evangelical movement, Lutheran strictures against the millennium will less and less apply to Evangelicalism. Presumably, even the affirmation of a millennialist view by Evangelicals need not divide them from Lutherans as long as this affirmation not unduly stress the obtaining of worldly power by believers and not imply a compromise of the doctrine of justification.[106]

The preceding reflections on the emerging consensus between the mainline and the Evangelicals and the awareness we have gained of the theological hermeneutical variety within the Evangelical movement which includes the appropriation of some forms of mainline neoorthodox theology should not be construed simply as an indication that Evangelicals are finally modernizing, gravitating towards mainline alternatives. There may be some truth in comparing the situation of today's left-wing limited inerrantist Evangelicals to the situation of younger American Lutherans a generation or two ago who broke out of Orthodox theological paradigms. However, it would be unfortunate were we to assess the contemporary Evangelical movement solely in this light. It would lead mainliners regrettably to overlook the important challenge that the Evangelical movement is posing to their churches regarding the inadequacies of mainline post-Kantian perspectival presuppositions for interpreting Scripture. The inherent subjectivism which Evangelicals identify in most mainline theological alternatives, in contrast to the Evangelical insistence on an objective and infallible standpoint, warrants attention.[107] It is to the detriment of the ministry of mainline churches that this challenge has not sufficiently been faced.

Chapter 14

Traditional Creedal Affirmations

The prevailing evaluation of the Evangelical movement as lacking a creedal or Confessional orientation has been observed, and the validity of this evaluation to some extent can be acknowledged. It is likely that this disinterest in Confessionalism reflects an antitraditionalism characteristic of the left-wing Reformation and the American ethos in which Evangelicals are rooted. Nevertheless, significant exceptions can be observed among Lutheran, Presbyterian-Reformed, Anglican, and the "Catholic [Ecumenical] Evangelicals." In addition, we have seen that the vast majority of Evangelical churches and formal groups, even those composed of a broad spectrum of Evangelicals, affirm the traditional Trinitarian and Christological formulations. Indeed, some Evangelicals like Carl Henry go so far as to praise a Confessional orientation and speak of the biblical summaries contained in Confessional documents as expressions of the "best human wisdom."[1]

On the whole, however, creative Evangelical theologizing on these doctrines is not much in evidence. There are notable exceptions; for example, Carl Henry proposes that the social relations of the Trinity might function as the chief warrant and model for Christian social outreach. And Church of the Nazarene historian Timothy Smith suggests a Trinitarian basis for explaining what holds the Evangelical movement together. For Smith, an appreciation of the unity and involvement of all three persons of the Trinity in the divine acts of redemption and sanctification helps explain why the various Evangelical constituencies, each emphasizing different aspects of the Christian faith, different aspects of God's work in the world, can manifest some degree of fellowship; when one emphasizes the Spirit's work it is not to the exclusion of Christ's work and vice versa.[2]

On the whole, however, the traditional Trinitarian and Christological doctrines play an important role in the various faith statements of

Evangelical communities only for purposes of defining orthodoxy. Not since the Fundamentalist–Modernist controversy have these doctrines played a vital role in theologizing or in the life of Evangelical churches. Given their Fundamentalist heritage, Evangelicals would be inclined to consider themselves "Christocentric" in their theological orientation.[3] After all, four of the points made in the Presbyterian Church in the U.S.A., *Five-Point Deliverance* of 1910 pertained to Christology. (This may in part account for why the relatively less Christocentric, more perfectionist-oriented, Spirit-illuminated Holiness and Pentecostal traditions do not always seem to fit perfectly in the Evangelical fold.) Yet in view of our present interest in the creedal doctrines, it must be noted that the real concern of the Presbyterian declaration and early Fundamentalism tended to focus more on Christ's work than his person. (Although the second point of the "five points of Fundamentalism" refers to "the deity of Christ," redactional criticism of the five points suggests that the real concern in this affirmation was to protect the integrity of the biblical account of the Virgin Birth.) In only one instance in a segment of the Evangelical community—the Pentecostal churches—have the actual ancient formulations of the creedal doctrines played a readily apparent role.

Pentecostalism, as we previously noted, has been marred by schisms related to the doctrine of the Trinity, schisms occasioned by the Unitarian Pentecostal movement. In order to distinguish themselves from the proponents of this Oneness/Unitarian Pentecostalism, most Pentecostal churches, the Assemblies of God (2) in particular, make strong and detailed affirmations of the Trinity, devoting to the doctrine attention which is atypical of the rest of the Evangelical community.

In addition to observing the unanimous affirmation of the ancient creedal doctrines within Evangelicalism, one can also observe commonalities in regard to the philosophical presuppositions employed by the movement in depicting these doctrines. Usually, Evangelicals rely on the categories of ancient Greek philosophy for this purpose. No less an expert on Evangelicalism than Carl Henry acknowledges the impact of Greek thought on Western systems like Evangelicalism.[4] This is reflected in the repeated use of traditional Protestant Orthodox concepts like "essence," "eternity," and "infinity."[5] This Greek conceptuality is reflected in the Evangelical portrayal of the doctrine of God also in other ways.

Thus, although there are exceptions such as the Christian Reformed theologian Nicholas Wolterstorff, Evangelicals are inclined to posit a somewhat static, undynamic picture of God (cf. Rom. 1:20).[6] There is an outright rejection on the part of most Evangelicals of a concept of God as changeable, of the being of God as affected by what God does. This viewpoint implies their suspicion of process theology and also reflects some discomfort with any view of creation as an ongoing phenomenon.[7]

To be sure, Evangelicals do not wish to deny the action of God in history. Some are willing to define God's being in terms of God's works.[8] However, even at these points the Greek philosophical perspective is reflected insofar as these prominent Evangelical theologians still depict God's being as always logically prior to God's work. God's works are not said to constitute God's being.[9] Such a Greek philosophical orientation not surprisingly leads to an emphasis on divine omnipotence and divine transcendence. Here the indebtedness of the Evangelical heritage to Reformed-Calvinist theology is apparent. Just as Calvin stressed the transcendence of God, so Evangelicals like Carl Henry typically are concerned to emphasize the transcendence of God, God's holiness, and also the Reformed notion that finite creaturely reality cannot contain the omnipotent God *(finitum non capax infiniti)*.[10] It follows for Evangelicals that God is not totally revealed in God's Word.

Carl Henry picks up this last point and develops it in a way which is germane to the concerns some mainliners and conservative Lutherans have about the Evangelical movement. He argues that Evangelicals cannot be accused of worshiping the Bible (bibliolotry), precisely because the Word of God is not exhausted by the Scriptures.[11] In response to all these concerns, the gospel has been distinguished (but not separated) from Scripture. Thus we must concede again that many mainline stereotypes are undercut once one considers what Evangelicals are actually saying.

Evangelicals and Lutherans seem to disagree on some of these points. But their disagreement appears to be a repetition of the old differences between Lutherans and the Reformed tradition. Lutheranism insists on affirming *finitum capax infiniti,* the idea that earthly reality can be the vehicle for the infinite God so that God's intention regarding the salvation of humanity is *totally* revealed in God's Word.[12] Yet the Lutheran and Reformed traditions have been coming to recognize, as they have in Europe in the *Leuenberg Concord* (esp. 21-23), that the differences between them are not church dividing. In fact something like the Lutheran insistence on the ability of the finite to bear the infinite seems

to be endorsed implicitly by Evangelical Presbyterian churches subscribing to *The Westminster Confession of Faith* (VIII.7), which exhibits an openness to attributing to Christ's finite nature what belongs
to his divine nature. In view of these considerations the emphases we
have observed in the Evangelical concept of God and the divine relation
to creaturely reality do not seem to be a necessary barrier to fellowship
with mainline churches.

Anthropology

To the extent that Greek philosophical categories also are reflected
in the Evangelical movement's characteristic treatment of the doctrine
of human nature, there are more serious challenges to discerning Evangelical theological agreement with the mainline churches. The dualist
view of reality in Greek philosophy, according to which human beings
were understood essentially as spirits living within bodies, tends to
manifest itself in Evangelical thought. Thus, although most members
of the Evangelical movement, from the Overseas Missionary Fellowship (4) to The Evangelical Free Church of America (5), affirm the
sinfulness of humanity, there exists a certain reticence among them to
assert humanity's absolute fallenness.[13] Like classical Greek thought,
Evangelicals insist that a central core of human nature (the soul) remains
in touch with its eternal origins, and that this spiritual core is not
ultimately affected by the events of individual and collective human
history. (There may also exist here an unwitting correlation between
Evangelical thought and the formative influence that the "American
way of life" has had on it; some Evangelicals seem to reflect the latter's
confidence in humanity's unlimited capacities.) It is not unusual for
Evangelicals to insist that even fallen humanity bears the image of God
(human reason).[14]

The rationale for insisting upon a maintaining of the image in fallen
humanity is to preserve even in sin the possibility of an ontological
link between God and humanity, the possibility of something like a
natural knowledge of God (the knowledge of God through God's activities in creation known apart from biblical revelation).[15] The concern
is that such a natural knowledge and ontological link would not be
possible, were the image of God (identified with human reason) destroyed.

Indeed, diversity exists within Evangelicalism on this question of
the natural knowledge of God ("general revelation" is the term generally preferred by Evangelicals). Thus, some Evangelicals like Norman Geisler claim to be able to formulate proofs for the existence of

God. This tradition is clearly in continuity with the Evangelical reliance on Scottish common sense philosophy, especially its idea that common sense could provide access to the existence of God. Presuppositionalists, like Carl Henry, Francis Schaeffer, and statements of the Christian Reformed Church (pp. 20-21, 18), are more inclined to insist that since the Fall, even by means of general revelation God cannot be known apart from faith, apart from Scriptural disclosure.[16] In short, the Scriptures must function as the glasses for Christians which they must wear in order for them to see God's presence in nature. Either of these alternatives, presumably, could be acceptable to mainline theologians.

The Evangelical reliance on Greek thought and the corresponding insistence that some relic of the image of God *(imago dei)* remains after the Fall does raise certain concerns. Some compromise of the total fallenness of the human race in sin is suggested. Something in human nature, the image of God or its relic, remains unfallen. If so, the character of salvation as unconditional gift, that it is completely the work of Christ *(sola Christi),* is compromised. For if some part of me, the image of God, is untainted by sin, then there is that in me for which Christ need not have died! The consequences of this unwitting denial of the *sola Christi* and the pervasive character of sin surface in a few statements of faith issued by Evangelical churches, particularly the Southern Baptist Convention (III) and the Association Evangélique d'Eglises Baptistes de Langue Française (I.3), which claim that the Fall has only "inclined us to sin." Several Evangelicals, including the influential turn-of-the-century Norwegian Pentecostal T. B. Barratt, the spiritual forefather of the movement in Europe, while affirming the Fall and its consequences without apparent qualification continue to insist on human free will.[17] To be sure, such compromises are not what most segments of Evangelicalism intend.[18] Yet their reliance on Greek philosophical concepts in developing their view of human persons inclines the logic of their theological reflection in the direction of these abuses. These tendencies may surface in the reticence of many contemporary Evangelical leaders, including—as we shall see—Bill Bright and Billy Graham, fully to depict the consequences of sin.[19]

Other potential difficulties follow from the Evangelical appropriation of classical Greek philosophy and its dualistic orientation. Many statements emerging from the Evangelical movement, from the time of the 1878 *Niagara Creed* (13) to a few of today's theological statements by Fundamentalists or Conservative Evangelicals like the philosopher

Gordon Clark, seem to opt for this kind of dualist view by depicting human beings in terms of a body-soul dualism.[20]

Modern scholarship, however, has questioned whether there is a biblical basis for such a dualism. It is not at all clear that the ancient Hebrews had a concept of "soul" or that the Hebrew term *nephesh* (breath, life) is rightly translated "soul" as the RSV occasionally does (cf. Ps. 6:3-4; Josh. 23:14; Lev. 17:11). It seems quite clear that the soul has no independent existence apart from the body, as Christians speak of a "resurrection of the body," not of an "immortal soul" (1 Cor. 15:35). This may be obscured, though, by the dualist tendencies embedded in the Evangelical movement.

The dualism can be extended even to imply a denial of the goodness of the entire cosmos by an overemphasis on the devil as the counterdeity to God, as the ruler of the world. The Evangelical movement, especially its Pentecostal segments, characteristically devotes much attention to the devil and his victimization of the creation. However, when the Fundamentalist church, the World Baptist Fellowship, claims in its *Doctrinal Statement* that Satan is the God of this world, one can only conclude that the creation has been forfeited to evil.[21]

These dualistic tendencies are particularly intensified in the Fundamentalist wing of the Evangelical movement. Coupled as they are by Fundamentalists with a strict, sometimes life-denying ethic guided by God's law and with the separatist tendencies of historic Fundamentalism, it is little wonder that Fundamentalists are often criticized, even by Evangelicals no less conservative than Francis Schaeffer, as dualistic "spiritualizers."[22] However, this is not the whole story, for many Evangelicals are sensitive to these potential abuses.

Thus, an international group of Evangelicals meeting during the International Congress on World Evangelization in Lausanne in 1974 drew up a statement recommended to the whole congress in which the group confessed Evangelicalism's tendency to fall prey to the sort of dualistic thought-forms that we have noted.[23] A number of Evangelicals, then, confirm our analysis, are aware of the dualist tendencies in their theological heritage, and clearly wish to remedy the situation. In addition to those who voiced concern at the Lausanne Congress, some Evangelicals like Francis Schaeffer and Carl Henry seem to be breaking with the Greek models. They insist instead on the integral connection of soul and body, that the soul is no more important to God than the human body, and that human beings are not essentially self-contained essences but have a necessary relationship with others and the physical world.[24] Contrary to the recent assessment of some mainline analysts, the gaps between the Evangelical movement and mainline theologians endeavoring to emphasize the wholistic, historical, antidualist biblical view of reality do not seem insurmountable.[25]

The differences between Evangelicalism and mainline churches regarding the influence of Greek philosophy on the Evangelical movement seem to be even less pronounced if one considers the historic Confessional documents of the Lutheran, Reformed-Presbyterian, and the Roman Catholic traditions. For they too employ Greek philosophical categories to portray human beings in terms of unchanging essences, as eternal souls with bodies.[26] It is not easy for mainliners from these churches to indict the Evangelical movement for devaluing the physical-bodily reality on account of the movement's reliance on Greek categories; the same charges would then have to be leveled against their own heritages. On the basis of these historic Confessional documents, Evangelical thinking about the doctrine of human nature and the appropriateness of Greek philosophy in making these points can only be deemed legitimate mainline options.

Granted, one might say that because Evangelicals have been less critical than recent mainline theology about the use of Greek philosophical insights, there exists in the Evangelical movement a tilt in the direction of an unbiblical dualism. Yet even this observation must be balanced not only with the realization that these matters are being rethought by prominent Evangelicals, but also by an awareness of the movement's increased involvement in social ethical questions (e.g., Pat Robertson, the Moral Majority, Evangelicals for Social Action). These developments represent anything but a dualistic, life-denying stance.

Chapter 15

The Work of Christ

Although there are exceptions, Evangelicals, at least those influenced by Reformed and Lutheran traditions, normally insist on a substitutionary (satisfaction) theory of the atonement in describing the work of Christ on behalf of humanity's redemption.[1] This commitment has its roots in the pre-Fundamentalist days of the movement, in the Presbyterian Church in the U.S.A.'s 1910 *Five-Point Deliverance* (3).[2] In fact, the commitment is even more venerable, reflecting the influence of 17th-century Protestant Orthodox theology on the Evangelical movement.[3] The term "satisfaction" was more typically employed by these theologians and the term predominated in Evangelical circles. However, in this century, probably in response to mainline critiques of this way of understanding the atonement, the term "substitutionary" has come into more widespread use to describe Christ's atoning work.[4] Whether the term represents an exact equivalent of the satisfaction theory or is a more general term intended to encompass both the satisfaction and another related approach (the governmental theory) is an open question.

The substitutionary or satisfaction theory of the atonement interprets Christ's death and resurrection principally in terms of a sacrifice. The sacrifice must be offered in order to placate God's wrath against sin (the just demands of the Law) (Eph. 5:2; cf. Heb. 2:17; 9:14; 10:12). An important dimension of this viewpoint is the understanding of God associated with it. Evangelicals insist that God is a God of justice whose wrath against sin cannot be minimized, as mainline liberals are sometimes prone to do.[5] To make their point, Evangelicals will often insist upon equating New Testament references to "the righteousness of God" (*dikaiosunē tou theou;* Rom. 3:21-22) with the "justice of God."[6]

Challenges have been raised to this way of understanding the atonement. The Swedish Lutheran Gustaf Aulén, in his classic book *Christus*

237

Victor, has been the predominant and most influential critical voice. The problem with the substitution-satisfaction view is that it can connote a kind of legalism which does not take the radical newness of the gospel seriously enough, for, according to this view, God's legal order is not overturned by Christ's work. The Law is still the basis for God's relationship with humanity. It is simply that Christ fulfills the Law's demands on our behalf.[7]

In addition to the question which may be raised about the exegetical accuracy of its equating "the righteousness of God" with "divine justice" (more likely, "the righteousness of God" refers only to God's fulfillment of God's promises, "the righteousness by which we are made righteous by him," as Luther claimed, and not to an attribute of justice, see Rom. 3:21,26; 15:8), the legal framework of the substitutionary view raises other problems. It could lead to a tendency to interpret the gospel in light of the demands of the Law, so that the unconditional character of salvation as free gift is compromised. To some extent Lutheran suspicions that Evangelicals have undercut the doctrine of justification by grace through faith are related to this concern.[8]

Nevertheless it must be acknowledged, despite its potential abuses, that the Evangelical substitutionary-satisfaction view appears to have a foundation in the New Testament (see Eph. 5:2; Heb. 10:12). Also this view is reflected in the Confessional documents of a number of mainline churches, including the Lutheran *Augsburg Confession* (III.3) and the *Smalcald Articles* (III/III.38).[9]

The other related treatment of the atonement which is typical of at least one segment of the Evangelical movement might be termed the governmental theory. This view is most notable in the thought of the earliest theologians of the Holiness movement, and something like it is suggested in the thought of the original leader of the Scandinavian Free Church movement, Paul Peter Waldenström.[10] The fundamental commitment of this theory is that it is not so much God himself who must be reconciled to humanity nor God's wrath which must be satisfied; rather, the fundamental problem is that the moral order has been violated by human sin. As with any governmental system, the moral law, when it has been violated, demands that justice receive its due recompense. Thus Christ's death may be understood primarily as the "substitutionary" payment due the moral law by those who have transgressed it (Gal. 3:13). His death, then, is not primarily for the purpose of satisfying God's wrath but aims at making sinful people acceptable to God. For as ruler of the moral order, God cannot suspend the punishment due the moral law if God would continue to preserve the moral order. Thus God cannot deem sinful people acceptable until they are so on grounds of the moral law. And this can only happen when the Law's demand for punishment has been met. This, then, is the purpose of Christ's atoning work: to make believers righteous in face of the moral law.

Adherents of the governmental theory self-consciously define it over against the satisfaction theory insofar as emphasis is placed on the contention that it is not God who requires reconciliation, but rather that reconciliation is a work which proceeds from God. Yet, despite this important difference between the two views, it must be noted that the governmental theory also does not in principle undercut a legal framework for interpreting the gospel. Moreover, this theory has not enjoyed a heavy impact on the Evangelical movement as a whole, but has been and remains a much less significant theological orientation in comparison to the satisfaction theory.

Despite the general predominance of the satisfaction theory, many Evangelicals do not totally repudiate other ways of describing the atonement. The Church of England Evangelical Council in its 1967 National Evangelical Anglican Congress (9) has formally assented to a variety of modes of interpreting the atonement (although the penal concept is identified as "the deepest"). The Evangelical Covenant Church (pp. 22-23), Carl Henry, Billy Graham, and other Evangelical theologians make the same point, showing an openness to the classic view of the atonement (Christ's atoning work depicted as his victory over the powers of evil), as long as it retains in some way the element of Christ's satisfaction of the punishments due to the sinner.[11] Also the appropriation of insights from liberation theology by some Evangelicals from the Third World entails describing Christ's work as liberator of the oppressed, which could be regarded either as a classic view or as a kind of moral influence theory (Jesus' activity influences believers to redemption).[12]

Concerns are raised by Evangelicals, though, about the predominance of the classic view in modern theology, insofar as the mainline version of this view tends to deny a personal devil and divorce the love of God from God's righteous love and wrath.[13] At any rate, the increased openness of Evangelicals to alternatives to the substitutionary-satisfaction view entails that differences with the mainline over the description of Christ's atoning work need not necessarily be a source of division with mainline churches. After all, even Evangelical communities insisting on the exclusivity of the substitution-satisfaction view do not let this commitment annul fellowship with other Evangelicals who are open to alternative views of the atonement.

Against universalism: what the atonement really accomplishes

Without exception, the Evangelical understanding of Christ's atoning work is closely linked with an insistence that his work does not create a situation of universal salvation (cf. Mark 16:16; 1 Cor. 15:2).[14] Even the idea of a "second chance," the belief that those who have died apart from faith may hear the Word after death in order that they might believe, is generally rejected.[15] The one Evangelical exception to this perspective is the controversial position of America's Christian Reformed Church (to some extent, also the position of the Church of the Nazarene [VI], The Wesleyan Church [IX], at least two Princeton theologians, and of the prominent Norwegian Evangelical, T. B. Barratt), which maintains that the children of believers are "likely" redeemed even prior to baptism (1 Cor. 7:14).[16]

The Evangelical commitment to denying any affirmation of universal salvation is rooted in the heritage of many Evangelical churches, at least those indebted to the Reformed tradition with its concepts of the "limited atonement" and double predestination whereby Christ's atoning work is regarded as accomplished only on behalf of the elect. Such a position is by no means universally acceptable to Evangelicals.[17] However, the Evangelical denial of universal salvation does seem tied in to the very logic of the movement's thought structure. Any tendency toward universalism must be resisted, because such views undermine the importance of personal faith and evangelism (two high priorities for the Evangelical movement).[18]

Universalism and its negative consequences have been identified by a large gathering of leading American Evangelicals convened at Wheaton College in 1966 (*Wheaton Declaration*, 29, 31) and several individual theologians as the hallmark of liberal mainline theology.[19] Mainline Christians must begin to ask themselves if the lack of growth in their churches and corresponding lethargy about missions could be related to a kind of universalism in much contemporary theology. It should at least be considered whether such a view has not fostered a certain permissiveness regarding Christian living. Some mainline theologians and analysts are asking these questions.[20]

The same point might be made with regard to the missionary task in mainline churches. To the degree the mainline ecumenical establishment inclines toward universalist tendencies and becomes less interested in numerical growth as a measure of missionary work, we should not wonder at the decreasing emphasis on evangelism and proclamation. If all might be saved, mission and evangelism must be defined in a new, more inclusive way with new priorities. Social action often plays this role for mainliners. As we shall see, no such prioritization is possible for Evangelicals, whose denial of universal salvation mandates prioritization of bringing others to Christ. Indeed, this range of questions related to evangelism is perhaps *the* principal issue for many Evangelicals in ecumenical discussions with the mainline ecumenical establishment.[21]

Evangelicals, in turn, typically combine the rejection of universal salvation with an insistence that salvation must be appropriated through personal decision. Redemption is "offered," repentance is "required."[22] No doubt these emphases are indebted to the Evangelical movement's revivalist and Arminian heritage. (Arminianism was originally a movement within the 17th-century Dutch Reformed Church, so named for its leader, James Arminius. He and his followers taught that God's election of human beings to salvation was on the basis of God's foreknowledge of a human person's perseverance in faith, that regeneration must precede salvation, and that grace brings a believer to perfection.) These emphases may also be due in part to the influence on Evangelicalism of the "American way of life" and its fascination with freedom.

Arminian influences are reflected at a few points in language which could be understood as semi-Pelagian synergism (the idea that one is not saved *totally* by grace but must contribute to one's salvation by fulfilling certain requirements). Thus the National Association of Evangelicals' (USA) *Statement of Faith* (5, 4) claims that we are "enabled to live a godly life," the *Confession of Faith* of the Association Evangélique d'Eglises Baptistes de Langue Française (I.3, 5) asserts that we determine our eternal destiny freely, and the French Baptist G. Millon argues that one is a disciple "by grace and free will." The Southern Baptist Convention (V) insists that the divine election of believers is consistent with free will. Synergism is evident in the Holiness churches. It is even evident in the strictest Presbyterian heritage of Evangelicalism, as it is represented by B. B. Warfield with his insistence, growing out of his "Orthodox rationalism," that the Holy Spirit does not produce faith but only actualizes as saving faith the knowledge which rational argumentation must first provide as the ground of faith.[23] Perhaps the best known instance of this sort of theological orientation is the Bill Bright Campus Crusade slogan: "I found it!" This famed slogan, which has been inscribed on many an automobile fender, suggests that we contribute to our salvation, insofar as *we* have found it.

All of the organizations and persons cited, including Bright's Campus Crusade, even a borderline Evangelical church like the National Association of Free Will Baptists (USA) (X), do insist on a necessary role for God's grace in bringing about salvation.[24] It is true, then, that many Evangelicals envisage a role for the human will in bringing about salvation. Yet such assertions are normally highly qualified by an appreciation of the primary function of grace in motivating this contributing act of the will. To the degree that the qualification is made successfully, one cannot easily criticize the Evangelical movement for a works-righteous compromise of justification or salvation by grace. To be sure, a kind of synergism appears at these points. Yet such a synergistic notion of a role for the human will motivated by grace in the attainment of salvation is a legitimate affirmation for several mainline traditions, primarily the Roman Catholic church, but even for Lutheranism (see Phil. 3:13-14).[25] Given the overriding Evangelical concern to emphasize regeneration and to stimulate efforts to lead the Christian life, these Evangelical affirmations of the important role of human responsibility in the process of salvation follow quite logically.

The appropriateness of the synergist theme for mainline churches will be elaborated in the next chapter. For the present it is helpful to note that even on these points the Evangelical movement reflects diversity. Alongside of the Arminian strand of thinking there exists a Reformed predestinarian strand.

One of the factors in the emergence of Arminianism was to repudiate the Reformed insistence on double predestination (the idea that God elects *some* to salvation *and* some to perdition). Thus in addition to the Arminian repudiation of this view a few churches associated with Evangelicalism affirm double predestination. Within this predestination stream exist several alternatives. The two best known to non-Evangelicals are supralapsarianism (the idea that God's electing decree is prior to the Fall) and infralapsarianism (the idea that God's plan to provide salvation for humankind, God's electing decree, was subsequent to the Fall). Both of these approaches have representatives within the Evangelical movement.[26]

Another approach, which Carl Henry regards as the dominant American Evangelical Baptist alternative, is Amyraldian (so named for the 17th-century Calvinist theologian, "Moïse Amyraut, who held that God *"provides* salvation for all but *applies* salvation [only] to some*").[27] There is significant ambiguity with this alternative regarding the difference between God's providing salvation and "applying it." But the logic of this position comes very close to the view held by some Evangelicals that the children of believers are "likely" redeemed and also to the characteristic (and paradoxical) Lutheran concept of single predestination (the idea that God elects only the redeemed and that the damnation of the lost is their own fault).[28] The primacy of grace is by no means overlooked in the Evangelical movement, and this concern is even formulated in a manner congenial to Lutherans.

On all these issues related to the work of Christ, election, and the like, the Evangelical movement once again reflects a marked diversity. Could the fact that so many different views can coexist in the movement imply its ecumenical openness?

Chapter 16

Justification
and the Christian Life

The concern that the Evangelical movement is insensitive to the Reformation emphasis that justification (salvation) is worked by God's grace through faith, and not the reward for what believers do, is alleviated in most cases by a study of official Evangelical statements of faith and the writings of some of the movement's most eminent theologians. One would certainly expect to find this theme among Evangelicals associated with the historic Reformation traditions. Evangelical churches like The Orthodox Presbyterian Church and organizations like Lutherans Alert National insist on fidelity to their traditions' historic Confessional documents, which teach justification by grace through faith. However, the commitment to this doctrine surfaces also in the literature of Evangelicals not belonging to Lutheran and Reformed churches. A few examples suffice. Thus the international group of Evangelicals at the Lausanne Congress asserted:

> Salvation is by God's grace on the sole ground of Christ's death and resurrection and is received by obedient faith.[1]

In like manner the doctrinal position of the Overseas Missionary Fellowship (5) states:

> We believe that salvation consists in the remission of sins. . . received by faith alone, apart from works.

Even Carl Henry, Evangelical Baptist that he is, writes: "Scripture insists on God's unqualified righteousness and connects salvation with grace alone."[2] In fact, Evangelicals in the American Lutheran–Evangelical Dialogue claimed to be in agreement with Lutheranism in affirming that "salvation is by grace alone, through faith alone." On at least one occasion this commitment has been echoed even by Billy Graham.[3]

Examples of this concern by Evangelicals to assert that salvation and justification are God's work could be cited at great length (Gal. 2:16; Rom. 3:24,28).[4] We have already observed this concern in the statements of those Evangelical churches and organizations affirming predestination.[5] Such a commitment is no new or recent development within the Evangelical movement. One discovers affirmations of salvation mediated by faith apart from human works stated in the pre-Fundamentalist era of the Niagara Conferences (6,7) and in *The Fundamentals* (II, 115-117; IX, 52-54, 56-58).

In a number of cases, members of the Evangelical movement develop this theme by drawing upon conceptuality which is characteristic of the Lutheran tradition. Thus one finds affirmations of the unconditional character of grace, criticisms of efforts to attain salvation by works of the law, and some suggestions that the redeemed Christian remains simultaneously both saint and sinner *(simul iustus et peccator)*. Even the classic Lutheran distinction between law and gospel (the insistence that the demand-portions of Scripture not be confused with the pronouncement of the gospel, that God gives salvation freely) is evident in the work of Carl Henry. It is likewise prominent in the dispensationalist theology influenced by the *Scofield Reference Bible.*[6]

In fact, the Lutheran commitment to the centrality of the doctrine of justification, that it must be the criterion for judging all other doctrines, is reflected at several points in the Evangelical movement. Thus, in one American Evangelical commentary, *The Zondervan Pictorial Encyclopedia of the Bible,* it is stated that "all other doctrines of the Scriptures serve the doctrine of justification by faith."[7] The Evangelical Covenant Church (p. 7), historically indebted as it is to Lutheranism, asserts that an "emphasis on salvation by grace alone through faith alone—apart from works of the law—has been particularly important." Such a commitment to the centrality of the justification doctrine is implicit in Bill Bright's comments, cited earlier, where he claims that "the number one heresy in the Christian world is legalism."[8] Also to be considered is an affirmation in the official 1981 manual of The International Pentecostal Holiness Church (p. 11) where the doctrine of justification by faith is identified as "the basic doctrinal foundation of evangelical churches." All of these affirmations have precedent in the Fundamentalist heritage of Evangelicalism, as an affirmation of justification by faith as *the* doctrine/truth of Christian faith appears in *The Fundamentals* (II, 106).

The parallels between the Evangelical movement and the Lutheran and other Reformation traditions at this point are striking. Nor can the critic of Evangelicalism easily deny the similarities by arguing that for Evangelicals the work of faith is what accomplishes salvation, not merely the vehicle for receiving it. It is true, as we have noted, that there are some Evangelicals influenced by Arminian synergism who assert a necessary role for human activity motivated by grace in the process of salvation. In fact the Evangelically oriented Fédération des Eglises Evangéliques Baptistes de France (V) almost explicitly states that it is the act of faith which saves.[9] However, the affirmation of predestination by other Evangelicals, their insistence that regeneration, conversion, and even faith are divine acts, clearly reflect the Reformation commitment to understanding faith merely as the means of receiving God's gracious gift.[10] Evangelical members of the American Lutheran–Evangelical Dialogue seem to be quite explicit about this. In so doing they were in harmony with their Fundamentalist heritage. A similar claim that faith is not a meritorious work but merely receives God's gift was explicitly made in *The Fundamentals* (II, 116-117).

Despite these intriguing similarities between Evangelicalism and the Reformation heritage, the doctrine of justification by grace through faith probably receives less emphasis in the Evangelical movement than it does in Lutheranism. A number of Evangelicals, even Lutheran Evangelicals like Gerhard Maier and official statements of The Lutheran Church–Missouri Synod, reject the concept of a "canon within the canon," the appeal to justification as a principle for criticizing other aspects of the biblical witness not in accord with the doctrine of justification. Other Evangelicals refuse to make such an appeal to the "canon within the canon."[11] Some of these same theologians, notably Carl Henry, actually make a special point to note that the central theme of Scripture is not justification but the moral judgment of God or the Lordship of Christ.[12] Also the heavy reliance of the Evangelical movement upon a substitutionary/satisfaction view of atonement characteristically links the justification doctrine with the theme of divine justice and the fulfillment of the law's demands.[13] These factors, plus the Arminian influence on many Evangelicals, represent important distinctions from the characteristically Lutheran treatment of the doctrines of justification and soteriology (how one is saved).

In fact the Arminian-synergist themes emerge in such a pronounced fashion in a certain peculiar form at times that the Evangelical movement appears to resemble more nearly the Roman Catholic tradition in some of its teachings. Thus, prayer and seeking God function for Billy Graham, Dallas Seminary's Norman Geisler, and Donald Bloesch as kinds of "preparation" for grace.[14] (The title of Graham's 1977 book, *How to Be Born Again*, suggests this theme, that believers must prepare themselves for grace.) Also a concept of repentance as a condition (preparation) for grace and salvation appears regularly in Evangelical literature, for example in representative documents like the 1973 *Chicago Declaration of Evangelicals to Social Concern* (5) and in church statements of faith like those by the Church of God (Cleveland, Tenn.) (4), The Southern Methodist Church (p. 15), the Baptist General Conference (6), the International Church of the Foursquare Gospel (VI), two different Evangelically related French Baptist churches, and several other churches. These Evangelical statements concerning a preparation for grace reflect the movement's indebtedness to classical Pietism, which also embraced this theme.[15]

The similarities to the Roman Catholic understanding of justification warrant further elaboration. The traditional Roman position has been that salvation is merited, grace is obtained, through a cooperative effort of grace and the human will which is first inspired by grace. The initial gift of preparatory grace makes it possible for believers to prepare themselves (which includes repentance) for further grace.[16] The correlation between this concept and the Evangelical approaches we have been describing is quite apparent, as these Evangelicals also envision a role for believers, inspired by grace, to prepare themselves "to receive Christ." The similarities between these traditions are undergirded further when one recognizes that just as justification must be an ongoing process in the Roman Catholic tradition—for it is not complete until sins are entirely remitted (until one is fully cleansed from sin)—so a few Evangelicals like Carl Henry seem unwittingly to imply that justification is an ongoing process (cf. 1 John 3:2).[17]

While this concept is not characteristic of the mainline Reformation traditions, we have previously argued that it is not necessarily Pelagian (compromising the divine initiative in bringing about salvation). In fact, it can be shown that this concept of the human role in contributing to the process of salvation through a "preparatory act" motivated by grace is a legitimate dimension of Pietism, as particularly reflected in the Methodist heritage in its First Annual Conference report. The concept is reflected also in the Reformed *Heidelberg Catechism* (Q.116) and sometimes, to the chagrin of Lutherans, in the Lutheran *Formula of Concord* (SD.II.90).

The structured Christian life

The correlations between the Evangelical movement and historic Pietism, the movement's dissimilarity with the characteristic themes of the Lutheran tradition, are even more apparent in regard to the treatment of the Christian life *(sanctification)* and how it might be nurtured. Evangelicalism, like Pietism and the other mainline Protestant churches, tends to denote more specifically than Lutherans normally do what is expected of Christians.[18]

Of course, there is a sense in which both Evangelicals and Lutherans affirm that Christians *want* to do good works, that works follow spontaneously from faith (Rom. 6:2, 17-18). This commitment to free Christian response is reflected especially in a 1966 meeting of Evangelicals which drafted the *Wheaton Declaration* (2), and in portions of statements issued by churches as diverse as The Evangelical Covenant Church (p. 15), The Evangelical Free Church of America, and the Southern Baptist Convention (XI).[19] Yet Evangelicals are much more prone than Lutherans to require good works as a sign of one's Christian orientation and to identify what these good works should be like.[20]

We observe this tendency even among Lutherans associated with the Evangelical movement. For example, the India Evangelical Lutheran Church, associated with The Lutheran Church–Missouri Synod, has developed an elaborate code of conduct. Likewise the Albrecht-Bengel House in Tübingen, Germany, largely administered by Lutherans, maintains a code of responsibilities. In encouraging good works in these ways, the Evangelical movement often calls upon believers to "imitate Christ" and function as Christian examples. In so doing, legal models for Christian ethics, a concept of the Bible as a "rule for discipline," are established.[21]

Although, as we have seen, there are exceptions, and some Evangelicals endeavor to assert the freedom of the Christian, the law-ethic we have noted is quite prominent in the Evangelical movement. It is most visible in the always apparent life-style standards drawn up by the vast majority of Evangelical parachurch agencies, schools, and churches. Members of these organizations and those coming to work for them are expected to subscribe to these standards and abide by them in their personal lives. The strictures in these statements include prohibitions against the use of alcohol, eating blood food, smoking, social dancing, attendance at movies, and work on the Sabbath. Tithing is often mandated as well as certain standards of personal appearance.[22]

There is a temptation here to indict the Evangelical movement for lapsing into a kind of legalism, a forfeiture of the gospel's freedom. It appears that some—but not all—conservative Lutherans refuse to align themselves with the Evangelical movement in part because of this kind of Christian ethic.[23] However, this does not seem to be a satisfactory reason to prevent fellowship with the Evangelical movement. We have already observed that at least one conservative Lutheran body, the India Evangelical Lutheran Church, has developed a code of conduct akin to Evangelical life-style standards. Yet this has not fractured its fellowship with other Lutherans. Why should a similar code drawn up by Evangelicals be a source of division from Lutherans?

In the final analysis, Lutherans and other mainline Christians must concede that precise definitions of how Christians should live are part of the history of their traditions (Matthew 5; Luke 6:17ff.; Gal. 6:1-10; James 2:14-26). In the Lutheran and Reformed traditions one is reminded of the concept of the "third use of the law" (the law as a guide for the Christian life).[24] Further clarification of this point and arguments that even these heavily structured standards of behavior that characterize the Evangelical movement need not divide Lutherans and Evangelicals will be offered in subsequent chapters. (The fact that at many Evangelical institutions these codes of conduct have been discontinued or are not strictly enforced may also be a factor in Lutheran reactions to the contemporary Evangelical movement.)[25]

At any rate, it is quite evident that Evangelicals believe that faith makes a difference—a visible difference—in the life of a Christian. Some Evangelicals go so far as to insist that living in a "Christian" manner will bring material rewards and spiritual healing (Mark 16:17-18; Acts 4:29-30; James 5:11,14-16). Robert Schuller exemplifies the belief that material success follows faith. A number of Pentecostal churches, individuals like Oral Roberts, and even some Evangelical churches outside the Pentecostal tradition maintain that the gift of healing is an integral part of the gospel. A number of these churches, as well as The Brethren Church (Ashland, Ohio) (3/9) continue the practice of anointing the sick with oil.[26]

It must be noted, in order to undercut false stereotypes, that such views regarding material success and divine healing as necessary consequences of the gospel are by no means embraced by all Evangelicals, as is exemplified by Carl Henry, who offers some pointed criticism of such.[27] It is a distortion for mainliners to attribute all that is religiously exotic to the Evangelical movement.

The central concern

What accounts for the difference in emphasis between Evangelicals and Lutherans regarding the question of the precise delineation of the shape of the Christian life and the question of the relation of this to the doctrine of justification? Five related factors will be noted, the last of which is perhaps the most pivotal.

First, it is possible that the rigorous strictures Evangelicals sometimes place on Christian living are a consequence of their characteristic life-denying dualist view of persons. However, inasmuch as Evangelicals seem to be increasingly more critical of this view of human persons, other factors in accounting for the typical Evangelical emphases seem more germane. (One might speculate about a possible correlation between the gradual distancing of Evangelicals from the Greek dualist perspective and the decline in strict enforcement of codes of conduct among Evangelicals.)

Second, the Evangelical emphasis on a precise delineation of an emphasis on the Christian life may be a reflection of its dependence on the Reformed theological heritage. This is evident specifically in the reliance of several Evangelical churches on the Reformed concept of "perseverance," the idea that believers can be assured of their election if they continue to practice the Christian life. Thus sanctification receives attention from Evangelicals as a way of providing assurance to individuals that they are elect (Phil. 1:6). Some Evangelicals, including the Independent Fundamental Churches of America (7) and perhaps Campus Crusade (9), go so far as to assert the eternal security of believers, that they can never fall away (see Ps. 37:28b).[28] However, a number of Evangelical communities reflecting Arminian influence reject this concept, for presumably it could function to undercut concern for Christian living.[29]

A third factor accounting for the Evangelical emphasis on encouraging and structuring the practice of the Christian life relates to the influence of the Holiness movement on Evangelicalism. This commitment is reflected in the emphasis of the Holiness churches on striving for perfection in this life (Phil. 3:12; 1 John 4:17). Yet also on this matter there exists diversity within the Evangelical movement. The predominant Holiness view, as we have previously noted, understands perfection as an instantaneous event, a "second blessing" subsequent to initial regeneration (justification) in which one can be delivered *totally* from all sin and truly love God and one's neighbor with all one's heart (see 2 Cor. 7:1). Today the adherents of this doctrine normally add the stipulation that subsequent maturity through growth in grace must follow this event.

This viewpoint, maintained by churches like The Wesleyan Church (XIV) and The Free Methodist Church of North America (XIII), has been modified by others, notably the Southern Baptist Convention (IV) and the Evangelical Congregational Church (111,131). These churches seem more closely to follow John Wesley's notion that perfection is to be realized gradually through the process of living the Christian life.[30] Other Evangelicals go even further and deny the concept of perfection outright, although never without a concern for the Christian's life-style.[31] At any rate the debate over the concepts of perfection and holiness clearly helps create a climate within the Evangelical movement for emphasizing sanctification and for encouraging attempts precisely to define the Christian life-style.

The fourth factor accounting for these Evangelical emphases relates to the way Evangelicals characteristically envisage the relationship between regeneration and/or justification and the actual practice of living the Christian life. Evangelicals typically do not correlate or directly relate justification to the Christian life (sanctification). In some cases the distinction is seen in terms of a difference in temporal sequence; justification/regeneration comes *before* sanctification (or at least precedes "entire sanctification").[32] (Lutherans associated with the Evangelical movement, like Swedish Bishop Bo Giertz, represent a significant departure from this tendency to separate justification from sanctification.)[33] This distinction between justification and sanctification clearly accounts for why Evangelicals so specifically delineate the content of the Christian life. If the doctrine of justification does not appear to have direct implication for Christian living, it must be supplemented by legal directives.

At any rate the Evangelical estrangement of justification from the Christian life, and its consequences for Christian ethics, no doubt has its roots in the heritage of 16th- and 17th-century Protestant Orthodoxy. In order that the doctrine of justification not appear to be dependent on the Christian's good works, Orthodox theologians made a distinction between justification and sanctification to the point of implying their estrangement at times.[34] However, the impact of John Wesley and the Holiness movement on Evangelicalism also cannot be overlooked.

Wesley himself maintained that sanctification *begins* in justification, a position picked up by his heirs in the Holiness movement. But the fact that he seemed to imply that perfection followed these events opened the way (legitimately or illegitimately) for the early proponents of the Holiness movement to distinguish—in fact, in some sense, to separate—justification (regeneration) from sanctification (holiness), usually in a chronological way. Holiness was then identified as a "second blessing."[35] However, with this commitment one can discern again theological diversity within Evangelicalism. This diversity is apparent not just in the dialogue between the characteristic Evangelical view and Evangelically oriented Lutherans on the proper relationship of justification and sanctification. It emerges most pointedly in the debate on the issue carried on in the Pentecostal wing of the Evangelical movement.

A number of Pentecostals, notably the Church of God (Cleveland, Tenn.) (6, 10) and the Church of God in Christ (pp. 57-58), accept the traditional Holiness view of sanctification as a "second blessing." Speaking in tongues then came to be identified as evidence of the actual baptism with the Holy Spirit, a "third blessing."[36] We already have noted how conflicts began to emerge when Pentecostals without a Wesleyan Holiness background joined the movement. They did not accept the idea of sanctification as a "second blessing," but instead held to the "finished-work [two-step] theory." This view entails that sanctification is not understood as a second distinct work of grace but as included or at least initiated in the experience of conversion (justification). Baptism with the Holy Spirit is then seen as subsequent to this initial union with Christ, with tongues understood as the witness to this Spirit baptism.

This "finished-work theory" is far more acceptable to noncharismatics, as it is claimed at least by some Pentecostals that because believers also are sanctified in conversion, failure to speak in tongues does not necessarily mean that they have not received salvation. This is basically the position of the Assemblies of God (5, 7-9) and The Pentecostal Assemblies of Canada (V, VI).[37] (An insistence on the simultaneity of justification and sanctification is suggested in literature from non-Pentecostal Evangelical communities, churches like the General Association of Regular Baptist Churches [XII] and the Mennonite Brethren Churches [V].)[38]

Later we shall note how this "finished work" viewpoint is of significant ecumenical interest. For the present it is sufficient to observe that the prevalent Evangelical position seems to entail a distinction between justification and sanctification to such an extent that justification has relatively little impact on the shape of the Christian life.

When the gospel does not shape the Christian life it must receive its form elsewhere, from the Commandments. This factor, then, helps account for the Evangelical movement's preoccupation with delineating in specific rubrics the precise shape of the Christian life.

This brings us to the final factor in trying to account for the Evangelical movement's emphasis on delineating the shape of the Christian life. Previously we noted a distinct Evangelical preoccupation with issues related to sanctification (the character of the Christian life) and a concomitant concern for how one comes to be sanctified, namely, a concern with regeneration (being "born again").

In several ways a number of Evangelicals confirm this characterization of the movement's overriding concerns. Donald Bloesch, Francis Schaeffer, and Carl Henry all note the centrality of regeneration and sanctification for the Evangelical movement.[39] The centrality of these concerns for Evangelicalism is also observed and confirmed in several official statements made by Evangelical organizations about themselves. Thus The Evangelical Covenant Church (pp. 8, 9, 13) identifies itself with Pietism and its emphases on sanctification; the necessity of the new birth is stressed. Likewise The Evangelical Free Church of America claims for itself that it places an "emphasis on holy living."[40]

Perhaps the most striking statement on the question of the Evangelical movement's overriding concern emerges from the 1966 *Wheaton Declaration* (20). It is stated that the core of the good news is: "You must be born again"! The centrality of regeneration is evidenced in a wide variety of Evangelical statements, most notably in the National Association of Evangelicals (USA) *Statement of Faith* (4), which emphasizes that there is no salvation apart from regeneration (John 3:3).[41]

This recognition of the centrality of the regeneration/conversion theme for Evangelicalism provides several insights about the Movement. First, although this theme clearly reflects Evangelicalism's dependence on the heritage of American revivalism, it is an incorrect caricature to assume that all Evangelical groups insist upon a dramatic, emotional born-again experience. A statement by The Evangelical Covenant Church (p. 13) makes this point explicitly.[42] (It is significant that such openness to accept as converted those who have no recollection of the precise moment of the new birth but have been converted through the process of Christian nurture, should be expressed by an Evangelical church with such close historic ties to Lutheranism. Such a characteristically Lutheran approach to the question of conversion is presumably considered a legitimate Evangelical viewpoint even among some non-Lutheran Evangelicals.)

The Evangelical emphasis on conversion and holy living (sanctification), its occasional reliance even on the Puritan work ethic, indicates its indebtedness to and perpetuation of the American Puritan heritage. For as we have previously noted, the Puritan spirit also included an overriding concern with conversion and holy living, which in turn led Puritans to advocate an ethic rigidly structured by the law.[43] In view of the continuing influence of the Puritan spirit on American society and in view of the role the Evangelical movement plays in perpetuating that spirit, one can more readily understand why Evangelicalism has experienced so much recent growth and impact on the American scene. The characteristic Evangelical emphases intuitively resonate to the American Puritan mind, and so the Evangelical formulation of the gospel is more likely to be received with empathy as it inspires confidence in what Americans already cherish.

This correspondence with the Puritan spirit also provides further insights regarding how the Evangelical movement can hold together its various theologically distinct components—historic Reformed Confessionalism, classic Pietism, Puritanism, the Holiness movement, and Pentecostalism. As we have noted in earlier chapters, all of these theological perspectives share the common Evangelical concern for renewal, regeneration, and the stimulation of regenerated Christian living. Each has marked out certain distinct standards for determining the nature of the regenerated life and for encouraging its practice (e.g., obedience to the law for Presbyterians; the work ethic for Puritanism; speaking in tongues for Pentecostals). Yet these distinct standards, reflected as they are in the various segments of contemporary Evangelicalism, do not fragment the movement.

Finally, our recognition of the centrality of regeneration/conversion for the Evangelical movement also helps account for the great emphasis Evangelicals place upon evangelism and missionary work as well as their propensity to delineate precisely the nature of the Christian lifestyle—to emphasize sanctification.[44] A concern for conversion quite logically leads one to seek the conversion of others (evangelism). Likewise a preoccupation with conversion raises the question of criteria for determining whether one is converted. The believer's life-style is obviously a most helpful landmark in determining the authenticity of his or her conversion. Thus the Evangelical preoccupation with questions of life-style, its propensities to place certain strictures on the behavior of Christians, quite logically serves the movement's concern with regeneration (being born again).

The nature of society and the Evangelical movement

The profile of Evangelical thought gains additional clarification when we recall the characteristic Evangelical pessimism about contemporary society. This also helps to account for the Evangelical emphases on conversion, sanctification, and consequent tendency to place certain rubrics on the life of the Christian.

We already have noted that Evangelicals typically regard Western society as on the brink of chaos, threatened by a pervasive secular humanism which is eroding moral norms in favor of an all-consuming drive for self-gratification at any cost. (Enlightenment thought is sometimes identified as the source of these abuses.)[45] Evangelical literature is virtually consistent in this sort of characterization of our present context. Such analysis is reflected even in official statements issued by churches and international gatherings of Evangelicals.[46]

In *Why Conservative Churches Are Growing* Dean Kelley virtually confirmed both the Evangelical movement's analysis of our contemporary situation as well as the Evangelical prescription for our ills. Kelley claims that the phenomenal growth of the Evangelical movement is the direct result of its demand for moral rectitude, commitment, self-sacrifice, and assent to traditional uncomplicated doctrine. Even if some segments of popular Evangelical literature suggest that contemporary Evangelicalism has been co-opted itself by a kind of narcissistic preoccupation with self-fulfillment, our analysis indicates that the Evangelicals have in fact emphasized precisely the themes which Kelley claims account for their success in face of contemporary narcissist society.

To the degree Evangelicals are correct in identifying our present societal upheavals, which are also perceived as threatening Christian faith, the best attempt to impose order on the chaos might seem to be to call for a return to the old, secure ways of life and their values. This concern to stimulate commitment and moral rectitude, to order one's life and one's society, represents the kind of emphasis on questions of sanctification which typifies Evangelical theology. Order and moral fidelity can best be implemented by proposing norms or laws by which one can be guided. (Appeal to an infallible source for these norms helps to undergird their authority and provides additional security in face of social chaos. At least one analyst has suggested that the Pentecostal/charismatic experience of glossolalia could be understood in a similar way, as an experience which undergirds the authority and truth of Christian faith in face of modern society's challenge to authority and truth.)[47] This is exactly what Evangelicals have done in their precise descriptions of appropriate Christian behavior and appeal to an inerrant Scripture. They have offered norms which help order the chaos and lack of authority modern people experience in society. Little wonder, then, that the Evangelical movement is enjoying such success. Given the social context it is addressing, its emphases make common sense!

One may question whether such common sense is a legalistic distortion of the gospel. No doubt it is such when systematically carried to its extreme and it no longer remains clear that all we do is accomplished by God's grace. Yet one finds precedents for such emphases in Paul and elsewhere in the New Testament, where norms and exhortations for Christians to live in a certain way are offered (Rom. 12:9-21; Gal. 6:1-10; 1 Peter 5:1-11; 1 John 2:1-16). The Reformed churches, the Puritan tradition, Pietism, and much of the Roman Catholic tradition maintained these theological emphases. Thus, given the influence the first three traditions have had on the Evangelical movement, it is not surprising that Evangelicalism should find that it has emphases common to them.

Like the Evangelical movement, all these theological traditions were concerned to provide some means of ordering the Christian life or society in face of what each perceived as cultural decay. The Reformed tradition, Pietism, Puritanism, and Roman Catholicism propose theologies of sanctification, emphasizing a concern for the shape and nature of the Christian life so that church and society may be ordered in a way that better conforms to Christian standards.

Thus, Roman Catholic scholastic theology as it developed in the Middle Ages tried to provide a theological rationale for the church's task of ordering chaotic and sometimes barbaric medieval society in accord with ecclesiastic standards and classical learning.[48] Calvin, in his development of the Reformed tradition, was concerned with similar challenges in ordering the new Reformation society emerging in Geneva. At the same time, he was concerned to answer charges that Reformation teaching undermined the Christian moral life (*Institutes*, Pref.).

In like manner, Puritanism emerged in a period of controversy in 16th-century England when the church structure of Anglicanism was just beginning to develop, and many questions about the shape of the new church and English society were being raised. The Puritan concern with holiness and purification did not restrict itself to individuals, but took the form of a concern for ordering civic society according to

Christian principles as illustrated in the American colonial period. Moreover, Pietism was a response to the decay it perceived in the church and society of its day, though it was less oriented towards ordering society as a whole and focused more on the life-style and spirituality of individual believers.[49] (In this sense one can rightly say that Pietism has an "individualistic" orientation. To the degree the Evangelical movement has appropriated the pietist heritage one may correctly refer to its individualistic orientation. This tendency, as we shall note, is somewhat reflected in Evangelicalism's orientation in the area of social ethics as well.)

Given the priorities Evangelicals are seeking to address, their emphases on regeneration/conversion, evangelism, and the Christian life, seem quite appropriate. In this respect they appear to share a common theological profile with a number of mainline Christian traditions. We have endeavored to show that in fostering these emphases Evangelical theology at its best is not necessarily Pelagian (compromising the primacy of God's grace).

This raises the question of whether Lutherans and other mainline Reformation churches might appropriately cultivate the characteristic Evangelical emphases—even draw upon Evangelical formulations of these themes—when they seek to engage in evangelism and deal with lackadaisical church life or the breakdown of moral values in society. In view of the pronounced success of contemporary Evangelicalism and in view of its already pronounced influence on the life of many mainline churches, the legitimate use of the movement's insights is a most pressing and practical question.

For the present it is sufficient to note that the characteristic Evangelical emphases seem to have a legitimate place in most of the Reformation traditions. When one considers references to the third use of the law (the Commandments used as a guide to Christian life) in the Lutheran *Formula of Concord* (SD. VI) and in Calvin's *Institutes* (II/VII.12), the endorsed homilies devoted to behavior directives in Anglicanism's *The Thirty-Nine Articles* (XXXV), and the behavioral strictures in the Methodist *General Rules,* it seems at least possible that these traditions might all be able to remain faithful to their heritage and still embrace, within certain limits, many Evangelical strategies for encouraging Christian commitment and regenerate life-style. The impact and success of the Evangelical movement implies the importance of determining whether Evangelical insights might have a legitimate role to play in these mainline churches. The stakes are high, not just for church unity but also for the sake of vibrant and effective contemporary proclamation.

Chapter 17

Church and Ministry

A follow-up statement on the work of a large international gathering of Evangelical leaders held in Wheaton, Illinois (United States), in 1983 summarized much of what must be said about the issues here. The author of this statement observed that the doctrine of the Church has not been a central theme for Evangelicals but usually has been subordinated to their overriding preoccupations with Scripture and sanctification. Indeed, Carl Henry goes so far as to state that, for Evangelicals, if the Church would crumble but the Bible survive, God's saving work could get along without it.[1] This tendency to de-emphasize the Church for the sake of the overriding Evangelical concern with nurturing the regenerate life-style is also evident in the movement's treatment of the ministry and the sacraments.

Nevertheless, the Evangelical preoccupation with sanctification and conversion in order to encourage the practice of a regenerate life-style does have several implications for the movement's characteristic understandings of the doctrines of the Church, the sacraments, and the ministry. Thus, the emphasis on the believer's response to the Word encourages a tendency among Evangelicals to describe the Church, in virtually all doctrinal statements which touch on the doctrine, in terms of believers (its members) or in terms of what they do (cf. Rom. 12:4; 1 Peter 2:9). It is typically defined as an association of (regenerate) believers. This is a commonly accepted emphasis, irrespective of the different forms of polity or church organization (episcopal, congregational, or presbyterian) one finds within the Evangelical movement.[2]

Unlike the Lutheran, Anglican, Roman Catholic, Methodist, and sometimes the Reformed traditions, Evangelicals generally exhibit little inclination to define the Church in terms of something "objective" (the external Word, the sacraments, the episcopacy) standing over against the individual believer's faith, or to refer to it in terms of the creedal formula as "one, holy, catholic, and apostolic."[3] With this forfeiture of the "objective" character of the Church, the Church's role in nurturing faith as a "mother" of the Christian life is largely neglected. (This reticence to think of the Church as something "more" than a collection of individual believers may also be an expression of anti-institutional sentiments associated with Evangelicalism. Such anti-institutionalism may be a consequence of the influence of premillennialism with its criticism of established churches, and it may be a result of a commitment to the sole authority of Scripture, which in the minds of some Evangelicals might be undermined if the Church as an institution were granted too much authority and autonomous existence.)[4] In fact, the overriding Evangelical concern with regeneration and the sanctified Christian life surfaces in some cases with an emphasis on discipline in the Church. Thus certain conditions, usually conversion and regeneration, are stipulated as necessary in order to become a church member.[5] This opens the way to a separatist mindset, the insistence on absolute separation from unbelievers in both worship and social settings, so typical of the Fundamentalist wing of Evangelicalism (see Rom. 16:17-18; 2 Cor. 6:14-18; Eph. 5:3-7).

By way of digression it should be noted that the rigorous Fundamentalist emphasis on separatism is perhaps the crucial issue at stake in dividing Fundamentalists from the prevailing Evangelical consensus. In our analysis we have been able to discern differences between Fundamentalists and Evangelicalism only on this and three other issues: Fundamentalists are suspicious of the ecumenical openness of many Evangelicals; in consequence of their separatist stance they tend to be more insistent on a dualistic, life-denying view of reality; and many Fundamentalists have a dispensational and millennial orientation that reflects a difference in emphasis from the declining role these themes are playing in the characteristic Evangelical profile.

Of course, Fundamentalists do not tolerate the idea of "limited inerrancy" as some Evangelicals do. However, we have seen that the official Evangelical profile on biblical inerrancy is certainly acceptable to hard-line Fundamentalists. Thus one can only conclude that differences between Fundamentalism and the Evangelical movement are differences in degree, not differences in kind. Given their profound areas of agreement, it does seem appropriate to consider Fundamentalism in relation to the Evangelical movement, as we have done. At any rate, among Evangelicals the separatist tendencies are most influential in Europe. The Evangelical call for a "believers' church," a church composed of regenerate members, coupled with the anti-institutional tendencies of Evangelicalism, often lead Evangelicals to form Free Churches, independent of government sponsorship.[6]

Recently some Evangelicals—notably an international group of Evangelicals meeting in Wheaton, Illinois in 1983 to discuss the nature and mission of the Church—have sought to reflect Evangelicalism's seriousness about mission work and evangelism in its view of the Church. Thus Wheaton '83 (II) and several other Evangelicals insist on referring to the Church in terms of its task of evangelization.[7] This same tendency to understand all doctrines in relation to the overriding Evangelical concerns is reflected at a number of points. We see this clearly in the characteristic Evangelical understandings of the office of the ordained ministry.

Ministry

Much like its spiritual forefather, classical Pietism, the Evangelical movement's principal concern for encouraging the practice of the Christian life leads it to emphasize in a radical way the concept of the priesthood of all believers.[8] The result is a characteristically "low" view of the ministry. That is to say, the distinction between clergy and lay is minimized (see 1 Cor. 12:14-31). With the possible exception of The Pentecostal Assemblies of Canada (VII.2), the ministry is not a Church-constituting office, making the Church the Church, as is the case in Roman Catholicism.[9] The ministry is usually defined in terms of its functions—usually preaching, but sometimes as a ministry of both Word and sacrament. These commitments can be found even among those Evangelicals, like the Anglican Evangelicals, who belong to episcopal church traditions.[10]

This understanding of the ordained ministry, coupled with the anti-intellectualism and some segments of Evangelicalism inherited from American revivalism, leads the movement to a de-emphasis on an educated clergy, particularly among certain Fundamentalists, or to no clergy at all, as in the case (at least theoretically) of the Plymouth Brethren. (It is interesting to note that Billy Graham is not a graduate of a theological seminary, and that the National Association of Free Will Baptists employs a number of theologically untrained clergy.)[11] If pastors are at all distinguished from the laity, it is on the basis of their higher level of spirituality, their function as spiritual examples to the Church.[12] This point of view is reflected not just in the official statements of Evangelical organizations; it is also embedded in Evangelical grass-roots attitudes. A recent survey of American Evangelicals reflects the high priority placed on having pastors embody their faith.[13]

This understanding of the ministry with its radical emphasis on the priesthood of all believers correlates with certain egalitarian tendencies of historic Fundamentalism and its associated movements. In part this egalitarian spirit has contributed to the success of revivalism and Pentecostalism among the lower classes. Given the Evangelical presuppositions, presumably *anyone* who is spiritually qualified may be ordained, even women. Thus, particularly in the Holiness and Pentecostal wing of Evangelicalism, women have historically played important roles. One thinks of Aimee Semple McPherson and her International Church of the Foursquare Gospel. This practice of female leadership continues today in the Pentecostal tradition as about one-third of the ordained women in the United States serve in Pentecostal churches. Thus, in addition to McPherson's Church of the Foursquare Gospel, the Assemblies of God also ordain women, as do the Midwest Congregational Christian Fellowship, the Church of the Nazarene, and the Church of God in Christ (p. 144).[14]

Despite their tendency to compromise the corporate character of the Church, to be antitraditionalist, interesting possibilities for Evangelical openness to the role of tradition in determining orthodox teaching are suggested by the characteristic Evangelical view of the ministry. For on the basis of its strong emphasis on the priesthood of all believers, the whole people of God—not just the clergy—are responsible for preserving orthodoxy. This commitment has had the salubrious effect among Evangelicals of helping to nurture a theologically sophisticated laity in comparison to the mainline lay profile.[15] Such an appreciation of the role of the whole people of God in clarifying and identifying doctrine is being encouraged by some Evangelicals, with theological-doctrinal—not just practical—aims in view. No less influential an Evangelical than Carl Henry has argued for the Church's teaching authority insofar as he concedes a role to the Church (and so to tradition) in distinguishing genuine from false versions of Scripture. The Church's role in clarifying or acknowledging the canonical books of Scripture has also been embraced by the noted American "High Church" Evangelical Robert Webber and by Clark Pinnock.[16] Likewise on the German scene the Konferenz Bekennender Gemeinschaften takes as its official position on principles of biblical interpretation that the permanence of a given understanding of Scripture depends on its being affirmed by the whole community of faith. And the Evangelical church historian Mark Noll has argued that the doctrinal commitments of the Evangelical community as a whole have considerable weight among American

Evangelical theologians in restraining any of them from hasty theoretical speculations.[17]

These ideas suggest the concept of the *consensus fidelium* ("consensus of the faithful") of Eastern Orthodoxy or the "ordinary magisterium" of Roman Catholicism. Both of these concepts maintain that when a consensus of the whole Church is achieved throughout history on a given doctrine, this establishes the doctrine's infallible authority.[18] (In the case of Roman Catholicism, consensus only of the Bishops is of interest.)

Of course, it is not the intention of the Evangelical community to embrace these Catholic views. The infallibility of the Church's teaching authority is a concept which is foreign to Evangelicals. In some instances they reject it explicitly. In fact, among some Fundamentalists their separatist tendencies lead them to identify the true Church and its pure doctrine with historic movements which actually broke with the established Church.[19] Among Evangelicals, however, the real problem with the idea of the infallibility of the Church's teaching authority is the fear that it may lead to placing this teaching authority on an equal footing with biblical revelation.[20] These fears seem to be groundless. An examination of the Second Vatican Council's decree *Dei Verbum* (8) clearly suggests that the Roman Catholic church now insists on the subordination of tradition to Scripture.

In addition, several Evangelical churches seem in fact unwittingly to function with presuppositions akin to Eastern Orthodox concepts of the Church's teaching authority. Thus the strong Confessional orientation of some churches associated with the Evangelical movement, for example, the Christian Reformed Church, The Orthodox Presbyterian Church, and the various Evangelically oriented Lutheran churches, reflect a confidence in the Church's teaching authority which is highly suggestive of the concept of the Church's infallibility in situations where the faithful have found doctrinal consensus over a long period of time.[21] Even "Landmark-Baptists" of the American Baptist Association, who have insisted in their *Doctrinal Statement* (12) upon a continuity of true Baptist teaching since biblical times, seem to draw on a concept of infallibility—the idea that ultimately the true Church cannot fall away from truth. Likewise Pentecostal members of the international Roman Catholic–Pentecostal dialogue (I, 40-41; cf. II, 16-17, 52) expressed a willingness to concede a role to the Church in discerning authentic spiritual experience, a role which would presuppose its legitimate teaching authority on matters of practice and doctrine. A similar point was made by Evangelical members in the Evangelical–Roman Catholic Dialogue (1[3/a,b]) concerning the Church's legitimate role in safeguarding against false interpretations of Scripture. Such a theme is found even in the early days of Fundamentalism, in *The Fundamentals* (I, 19; VIII, 6-7, 26), as an appeal is made to the history of the early Church as a warrant for exegetical conclusions about Scripture, specifically to warrant the doctrine of the Virgin Birth and the historical accuracy of the Old Testament accounts.[22]

In fact, the broader Evangelical community seems to reflect unwittingly this willingness to embrace the Church's teaching authority. In Europe the Internationale Konferenz Bekennender Gemeinschaften (2[c]) acknowledges and encourages its members' fidelity to the historic Confessional statements of their churches.[23] *A Letter to the Churches* (I) drafted by the international Evangelical gathering, held in Wheaton, Ill., in 1983, also reflects the fidelity of the participants to the ancient creeds. Additionally, the affirmation of the creedal trinitarian and Christological formulas in most statements of faith of Evangelical organizations is a further indication of an unwitting openness to accept the Church's infallible teaching authority when its teaching stands the test of time and is "received" by the whole community of the faithful. Evangelicals presumably would not wish to concede the possibility that the creeds could be incorrect interpretations of Scripture! Interesting possibilities for Christian unity are implied by the Evangelical understanding of the office of the ministry in its relation to the priesthood of all believers and the implications of this relationship for the transmission of correct doctrine.

Sacraments/ordinances

Just as the logic of Evangelical thought typically discourages an emphasis on the doctrine of the Church or the authority of the ordained ministry, so also the sacraments are de-emphasized. Prominent Evangelicals like Francis Schaeffer and even the Lutheran Peter Beyerhaus are inclined to characterize Evangelical faith without any reference to the sacraments.[24] (Many of the statements of faith of Evangelical parachurch, cooperative, and educational organizations make no reference to the sacraments or any of the issues dealt with in this section.) In a few churches influenced by extreme versions of dispensationalism, notably the "Prison Epistles" Dispensationalist Groups, the sacraments are completely devalued and dismissed as rites belonging to a previous dispensation. (The Lord's Supper is regarded as Baal's supper which emerged from sun worship in Babylon.)[25]

The Evangelical movement's de-emphasis on the sacraments is no doubt in part a consequence of the denominational heritages that constitute the movement. One certainly sees a de-emphasis on the sacraments in the Baptist and Wesleyan traditions. The heritage of Fundamentalism also is antisacramental, as evidenced in the critique of Calvin's understanding of the Lord's Supper offered by the Princeton theologian Charles Hodge and also as reflected in at least one article in a later volume of *The Fundamentals* (IX, 6). In view of the impact of the "American way of life" on Evangelicalism, it is hardly surprising to observe how these factors were also intertwined in the priority of preaching, a prioritization which typified pre-20th-century American Protestantism.[26]

Given this heritage, it is also not surprising to find the predominance of a "symbolic" understanding of the sacraments prevalent in the Evangelical movement. Many Evangelical churches even decline to refer to Baptism and the Lord's Supper as "sacraments," for this conveys the idea that the rites are "means of grace" in which Christ pledges his presence. Rather these rites are often referred to as "ordinances," for this term conveys merely the idea of the recipients' pledging themselves, giving testimony to their faith.[27] By participating in the rites, believers testify to the community around them that they are believers (1 Cor. 11:26). The rites are only an occasion to exercise faith, precisely because Christ is not present in the elements. They merely "symbolize" him, remind us of him, and in so doing exercise our faith through the act of remembrance.

The idea that the ordinances are occasions to give testimony to one's faith is nowhere more apparent than in the preference shown for adult, "believer's" baptism by many Evangelicals. Such a preference is shown not just by Baptists, though, to be sure, believer's baptism is unanimously prevalent in this segment of Evangelicalism. Believer's baptism is also adhered to by most Pentecostal churches, some Holiness and Mennonite churches, as well as churches of the Free Church and Fundamentalist heritage like The Brethren Church (Ashland, Ohio) (3/9), the Independent Fundamental Churches of America (4), and the Bund Freier evangelischer Gemeinden in Deutschland (the German Free Church).[28] In a number of these cases, most notably and explicitly in certain Pentecostal and Holiness churches, a distinction is made between water baptism and baptism in the Holy Spirit (see Luke 3:16; Acts 1:5; 11:16).[29] Precedents for these commitments are sought sometimes in the 16th-century radical reformers, like Michael Sattler (1490–

1527), a leader of those Anabaptists who formulated the 1527 *Schleit-heim Confession*, or even in Ulrich Zwingli (1484–1531), all of whom maintained an understanding of Baptism which is at least compatible with the viewpoint of these Evangelicals. In my view, however, the lines of inheritance from these reformers may not be so direct, for the influence of the English Baptist tradition on these churches cannot be overlooked.[30]

Of course, the involvement of other traditions in the Evangelical movement—the Reformed/Presbyterian, Lutheran, and, to some extent, Free Church traditions—does provide other alternatives regarding sacramentology. For these churches, to some degree, affirm Christ's real presence in the sacraments, baptismal regeneration, and at least an openness to infant baptism.[31] However, these affirmations are not prevalent among Evangelicals; in fact, some Evangelicals belonging to these churches de-emphasize them.[32] The logic of the Evangelical pattern of thought favors the symbolic view. This has been sensed by conservative Lutherans, notably The Lutheran Church–Missouri Synod and the Wisconsin Evangelical Lutheran Synod, and accounts in part for their reticence about being identified with Evangelicalism.[33] It is quite evident that the Evangelical movement's characteristic approach to the sacraments is a consequence of the movement's emphasis on regeneration and the practice of the Christian life (sanctification).

Given such concerns, it follows logically that a strong sacramental orientation would be rejected, for it could give the impression that grace can be conferred automatically apart from a life lived in commitment to Jesus Christ. If Christ were really present in the sacraments, and if baptism actually conferred regeneration, then one might have the impression that grace is received in the sacraments regardless of the believer's faith. In order to avoid these consequences and in order to provide occasion to exercise the faith of recipients, an understanding of the sacraments as "ordinances" by which one gives testimony to the faith is the preferable viewpoint, the best response to the overriding Evangelical concerns.

Given these presuppositions, it has been observed by some Evangelicals that the movement tends to prioritize preaching, for in preaching the hearer's active rational involvement is necessitated in a way that does not necessarily occur when one is receiving the sacraments. Correspondingly, even among Evangelicals who belong to liturgically oriented church traditions, liturgical sensibility tends to be de-emphasized in favor of "freer" worship forms, for the liturgy is often perceived as dry formal ritual.[34]

This reference to liturgical sensibility within the Evangelical movement suggests our attention to two unique liturgical contributions offered by some members of the movement. One relates to the introduction of additional ordinances, alongside of baptism and the Lord's
Supper. Thus, in addition to The Brethren Church's (Ashland, Ohio)
(3/9) and others' designation of anointing the sick with oil as an additional ordinance, a fourth unique rite is practiced by some Evangelical
churches—the practice of washing the saints' feet. This is still practiced
in several Evangelical churches, including the Church of God (Cleveland, Tenn.) (12), The Brethren Church (Ashland, Ohio) (3/9), National
Association of Free Will Baptists (XVIII), and the Mennonite Brethren
Churches (VI).[35] Inasmuch as the rite has biblical precedent, it seems
to offer a meaningful symbolism to remind participants of the need for
cleansing and to admonish them to serve one another (John 13:5-17;
1 Tim. 5:9-10).

A second rite distinctive to a segment of the Evangelical movement
also represents an intriguing possibility for mainline Christians. Both
The Brethren Church (Ashland, Ohio) (3/9) and the Brethren in Christ
Church occasionally celebrate the Lord's Supper in the context of a
complete meal.[36] This rite also has biblical precedent (see 1 Cor. 11:20-
22; Jude 12) and could function to correct an undue spiritualism which
sometimes accompanies the celebration of the Lord's Supper. Regardless of one's assessment of these particular rites, one cannot examine
the Evangelical movement's treatment of the sacraments without recognizing how its conception of them, of the Church, and of the ordained
ministry follows quite logically from the prior Evangelical commitment
to emphasizing regeneration and encouraging the practice of the Christian life. We can discern the same kind of symmetry between overriding
concern and doctrinal formulation in the mainline traditions.

Evangelical diversity: ecumenical openness?

The characteristic Evangelical positions on the Church, sacraments,
and the ministry also account at least in part for its characteristically
critical assessment of Roman Catholicism. Polemics with Roman Catholic views spice virtually all Evangelical literature, though they are
perhaps more pointed in the Fundamentalist wing of Evangelicalism.[37]
Roman Catholicism seems to represent precisely the opposite position
to the characteristic Evangelical viewpoint on these doctrines (it defines

the Church objectively, maintains a high view of the ministry, radically distinguishing clergy and lay, and has a sacramental orientation).[38]

These anti-Catholic sentiments are rooted in the Evangelical movement's pietist—if not its Puritan and Reformation—heritage.[39] One must ask whether the Evangelical de-emphasis on the doctrines considered in this chapter is what necessitates its anti-Catholicism, or whether the anti-Catholicism is the prior concern which in turn conditions the de-emphasis on the doctrines of the Church, ministry, and sacraments.

There can be no doubt that there are other factors which account for the Evangelical–Roman Catholic tensions. Although we have noted some eminent exceptions among Evangelicals—Robert Webber, Clark Pinnock, Robert Johnston—as well as some Confessionally oriented Evangelical churches and organizations, the Evangelical commitment to the sole authority of Scripture typically does not allow for a *conscious* appreciation of the Roman Catholic insistence that tradition function as an interpretive guide to understanding Scripture. The concept of the Church's infallible teaching authority is simply not acceptable to most Evangelicals. Even though, as we have seen, many in fact unwittingly presuppose this notion, the Roman Catholic understanding of the relationship of Scripture and tradition is yet another factor that stimulates anti-Catholic Evangelical sentiments.[40]

Nondoctrinal, sociological factors must also be considered in coming to terms with anti-Catholic Evangelical sentiments. Differences in ethnic origin between these groups cannot be discounted. Nor should the formative influence on Evangelicalism of late 19th-century American cultural attitudes, its strong anti-Catholic "nativism," be overlooked. Of course, since the middle of this century a growing sense and appreciation of cultural diversity in all Western nations have rendered these sociological factors in Evangelical–Roman Catholic relationships less of a barrier. And as indicated by their engagement in an international bilateral dialogue with the Roman Catholic church and a 1987 declaration of the U.S. National Association of Evangelicals which affirms common agreement between Evangelicals and Roman Catholics on many ethical questions, Evangelicalism's anti-Catholicism has not been as strident as it was previously.[41] Increasingly, the real crux of the matter dividing these traditions is their theological disagreements about the nature of the Church, the ministry, and the sacraments. Attention to these issues may be the most fruitful way of enhancing Evangelical–Roman Catholic relationships.

As already noted, the Evangelical movement can accommodate a great deal of theological diversity. Some of this diversity opens it to finding areas of agreement with mainline churches, including Roman Catholicism. There seem to be sufficient, hitherto unnoticed areas of convergence between Evangelicals and Roman Catholics—many of these occasioned by their common concern with ordering the Christian life—to raise the suspicion that Evangelical anti-Catholicism is occasioned as much as anything else by sociology and historically conditioned polemics. Those theological differences that exist, largely differences in emphasis, appear to be a function of the Evangelical appropriation of the individualistic tendencies of Pietism.

One can certainly discern some ecumenically promising diversity on the doctrines of Church, ministry, and sacraments among Evangelicals. With respect to the Church it is true that it is typically defined by Evangelicals in terms of its members, their spiritual quality, and what they do. However, one finds several statements by international Evangelical groups and by Evangelical churches in which the Church is defined as a creation of God through Word and sacrament (see Eph. 5:25-27). These statements are not confined to Evangelically oriented Reformed and Lutheran churches which have Confessional traditions that affirm God's role in creating the Church; they are made also by the Fédération des Eglises Evangéliques Baptistes de France (VIII), the Association Evangélique d'Eglises Baptistes de Langue Française (II.1), and the 1970 *Frankfurt Declaration* (27), a statement drafted by a large gathering of German Evangelicals.[42]

This strand of thought represents an affirmation of the "objective" character of the Church (that the Church is God's action and something more than a collection of individual Christians) in a way which is most congenial to the concept of the Church posited by mainline Lutherans, Anglicans, and Roman Catholics.[43] The diversity in all partners of this dialogue is evident as one can identify strands in the heritage of some mainline Reformation traditions, including Lutheranism, which seem open to describing the Church, as Evangelicals more typically do, in terms of its members and what they do.[44] The possibilities for discerning agreement among these traditions on these issues become even more intriguing as we begin to recognize the sense in which the various emphases Evangelicals, Lutherans, and Roman Catholics give to the concept of the Church are largely reflections of the overriding concerns each addresses. When these traditions address similar concerns one begins to find them agreeing, so that their differences are largely of emphasis, not of kind. After all, Evangelicals and the mainline Protestant churches do share common Reformation traditions.

The same sort of theological diversity which could open the Evangelical movement and mainline churches to each other's traditions is apparent in the Evangelical concept of the ordained ministry. We previously noted that the Evangelical movement characteristically understands ordained ministers as set apart from the laity on the basis of their distinct functions. Usually the crucial function denoted is preaching. However, in at least one case these functions are identified by Evangelicals as a ministry of preaching the Word and administering the ordinances (sacraments). This description approaches the definition of the ministry that characterizes several mainline Protestant traditions.[45]

In like manner, one can discern a high, even episcopal view of the ministry articulated in the Evangelical movement. There is a sense in which Evangelicals distinguish ordained ministers from the laity, and not just in terms of their distinct functions. Ministers are distinct also in terms of their persons, their deeper spirituality whereby they serve as examples to the Church. The historic tendency of Evangelicals to accord a particular authority to the personalities of their leaders, charismatic preachers, is a feature of the movement rooted in the formative influence of American Christianity on it.[46] This concept of ordained ministers as distinct from laity in terms of their person is clearly consistent with Roman Catholic understandings of ordination.[47]

As regards the actual Evangelical attitude towards an episcopacy (church government by bishops), in addition to the involvement of episcopally oriented Anglicans and Lutherans affiliated with the Evangelical movement, there are several churches associated with the movement, including the Free Lutheran Church (West Germany), The Free Methodist Church of North America (§285), and the Church of God in Christ (p. 4), which maintain the office of bishop. As we noted, The Pentecostal Assemblies of Canada (VII. 2) seem to go even further, claiming that the ordained ministry is a third ordinance alongside of baptism and the Lord's Supper. In this particular case it is almost as if the ministry were deemed a church-constituting office, not unlike the situation in the Roman Catholic tradition where the Church is not fully the Church without the clergy. Presumably, then, the Evangelical movement can tolerate the coexistence of a high view of ministry alongside the movement's emphasis on the priesthood of all believers.

The Roman Catholic understanding of the ministry presumably need not divide Evangelicals from Catholics any more than this issue need divide Lutherans and Roman Catholics. Progress made in Lutheran–Roman Catholic dialogue should be pertinent to Evangelical–Roman Catholic discussions.

Hopeful signs of the abatement of anti-Catholic sentiments are emerging in the Evangelical movement. Several prominent Evangelicals on both sides of the Atlantic have observed that Roman Catholics and Evangelicals share a common understanding of biblical inerrancy.[48] The implications of this emerging appreciation will be interesting to observe.

The Evangelical movement's treatment of the ordained ministry shows ecumenical promise in yet one other way, the willingness of some of its churches to ordain women. Actually, segments of the Pentecostal and Holiness movements have been "out front" of the mainline churches on this issue. The fact that the National Association of Evangelicals has among its membership both churches which do and do not ordain women indicates that the Evangelical movement is providing a model for all Christendom that this issue need not divide the Church.

Finally, we should consider the diversity present within the membership of the Evangelical movement and its implications for Christian unity. The involvement of Anglicans, Calvinistically oriented Presbyterians, and Lutherans in the Evangelical movement introduces this element of diversity regarding the sacraments. For although Evangelicals from these traditions could not usually be characterized as sacramentally oriented, these Evangelicals do maintain a commitment to Christ's real presence in the sacraments and the validity of infant baptism. This conflicts with the symbolic orientation of the prevailing Evangelical profile.

Evangelicalism has a way of incorporating this diversity within its own institutions. A good example is The Evangelical Covenant Church (p. 17), which is the child of both Lutheran and Free Church pietist strains. This church reflects both poles in its view of the sacraments. Thus among the membership one finds adherents of both infant and adult baptism, and both are officially sanctioned. No official position regarding the status of the sacramental elements is suggested.

Tensions arising from the diverse Evangelical viewpoints have been especially marked in recent years with the emergence of a group of influential Evangelical theologians, "Catholic [Ecumenical] Evangelicals," who have been urging Evangelicalism to recover the sacramental and liturgical heritage of the Catholic tradition. An influential meeting convened by this group in 1977 in Chicago issued a statement called "The Chicago Call: An Appeal to Evangelicals." The statement called upon the Evangelical movement to: (1) reclaim the whole Christian tradition; (2) maintain biblical fidelity; (3) define itself in terms of the creeds and a "Confessional consciousness"; (4) recognize that salvation is wholistic, including a concern for social justice; (5) practice "sacramental integrity"; (6) practice spirituality; (7) accept church authority; and—remarkably—(8) yearn for church unity.

In terms of the sacramental implications of this remarkable statement, "The Chicago Call" has both helped stimulate and thematize the new sacramental appreciation emerging within Evangelicalism. Thus, for example, one finds some important Evangelical Baptist theologians calling for a renewed appreciation of the sacramental character of baptism.[49] Pentecostal members of the international Roman Catholic–Pentecostal Dialogue (I, 32) observed that Pentecostals were moving toward the development of a liturgy. As early as 1967 the traditionally Low Church Evangelicals in the Church of England were supporting weekly celebration of the Eucharist. Among the intriguing factors which have been cited as influencing this new appreciation of the sacraments among Evangelicals of all denominational traditions is the pronounced impact of the Anglican author C. S. Lewis on the Evangelical movement, particularly in America.[50]

Nor can the Lutheran influence on the Evangelical movement be overlooked in this new appreciation of the sacraments. It is generally recognized that Evangelical churches with a Lutheran heritage like The Evangelical Covenant Church have a stronger liturgical sensitivity than other Evangelical churches.[51] Perhaps even more worthy of note are observations made by the 1970 *Frankfurt Declaration*, a statement heavily influenced by the strong German Evangelical Lutheran representation at the meeting which drafted the statement. The declaration (22) states that "the appropriation of salvation happens. . . through Baptism." In baptism, faith receives eternal life (Rom. 6:3-4).

Such statements seem to be consistent with a Lutheran understanding of baptism. They affirm the real effective presence of Christ in the sacraments, their ability (at least in the case of baptism) to effect regeneration.[52] However, these conceptions appear to conflict with the characteristic Evangelical views on the sacraments. One gains another interesting insight about how the Evangelical movement handles such theological diversity by attention to a 1971 formal response of the

National Association of Evangelicals (USA) to the *Frankfurt Declaration*. The NAE praises the declaration, which indicates its significance for the Evangelical community. The NAE response does proceed to take some exception to Frankfurt's position on the role of baptism in the salvational process. Yet the response then states that, because there is so much in the declaration to praise, the differences on the sacraments "are matters of longstanding disagreement that should not obscure our acceptance of the basic import of the Declaration."

What is clearly indicated here is that from the perspective of the Evangelical movement differences on the sacraments need not divide Christians who are otherwise in agreement about the "fundamentals of the faith." Thus a Lutheran or even Roman Catholic understanding of the sacraments could presumably be a legitimate Evangelical alternative (even for an Evangelical Baptist). The comment of the arch-Presbyterian Carl McIntire, noted earlier, regarding his openness to sharing the Lord's Supper with Evangelical Lutherans, further illustrates this point.[53] The question is whether the characteristic Evangelical views might be acceptable to Lutherans, Catholics, and other mainliners. This will be an important question in the future for the internal stability of the Evangelical movement, as the more sacramentally oriented "Catholic (Ecumenical) Evangelicals" come to clarify their relationship to and attitude towards church fellowship with the "Low Church" views of the Evangelical majority. As we have noted, this range of issues is a most crucial matter for conservative Lutheran churches like the Wisconsin Evangelical Lutheran Synod and The Lutheran Church–Missouri Synod in their relationship to the Evangelical movement.[54]

Although only suggestions can be offered at this point, it is helpful to reiterate the Evangelical movement's Reformed heritage. To the degree this heritage is reflected in Evangelicalism's characteristic view of the sacraments, Lutherans should keep in mind the agreements on this issue reached between Lutherans and Reformed theologians in ecumenical dialogues. The growing consensus in most churches is that differences on the sacraments between Lutheran and Reformed churches need not divide the churches when they are faithful to their historic positions.[55] Such insights would seem pertinent to at least some segments of the Evangelical movement. Thus, from the Lutheran side— both mainline and conservative Orthodox Lutherans—the sacraments need not in principle be an insurmountable barrier to fellowship with Evangelicals.

The diversity of Evangelical thought is at once frustrating for the student trying to understand the Evangelical movement, yet also a promising dimension for ecumenical dialogue.

Chapter 18

Social Ethics

The theological diversity we have observed within the Evangelical movement is reflected also in contemporary Evangelical approaches to social ethics. With some possible exceptions—American Black ("Bible believing") Evangelicals and some Evangelicals from the Third World, who have from their earliest origins been able to maintain a relationship between evangelism and social action, in addition to a few interventions in conservative politics against Communists and on behalf of prohibition or legislation prohibiting the teaching of evolution—the characteristic Fundamentalist position tended to be separatist, passively conservative, politically detached, and so not deeply concerned about seeking political power. Although this profile is changing, there is some evidence that this orientation still prevails at a grass-roots level in the Evangelical community. For example, at least until 1978, when the policy was amended in such a way as still to ensure close supervision of possible members, the Fundamentalist-related Southern Methodist Church, insisting that the Church's task was not philanthropy, continued officially to support racial segregation.[1]

No doubt these traditional reactionary attitudes were related to Fundamentalism's separatist tendencies, its retreat into a kind of cultural ghetto after the clash with liberalism. Its repudiation of the Social Gospel movement and of liberalism also discouraged conservative Christianity from bringing the gospel to bear on social issues. To do so could be perceived as endeavoring to do what the Social Gospel was doing. A possible additional factor in the retreat from social engagement was a sense of hopelessness which dispensational premillennialism instilled about the state of the world. Also the individualistic emphases associated with the pietist heritage and the corresponding widespread impact and use of common sense realist philosophy in such a way as to render it unable to account adequately for the self's ongoing relationship to institutions may have been contributing factors.[2] The reactionary politic of late 18th- and 19th-century neopietism may be an especially pertinent consideration for understanding the conservative politics of much of today's German Evangelical community.[3] Nor can the characteristic Evangelical prioritization of evangelism over social action be discounted as another contributing factor. Such an emphasis on evangelism necessarily follows from the emphasis Evangelicals place on conversion and regeneration.[4]

Although this lingering isolationism still persists, more recently Evangelicals have rediscovered their social responsibility and in several large representative gatherings of Evangelicals repented of their previous apathy in order to make new commitments.[5] Carl Henry's 1947 book, *The Uneasy Conscience of Modern Fundamentalism,* was a landmark in helping create this new social awareness.[6] Today the work of the largest Evangelical social ministry agency, World Vision International, and the creation of other divisions of social concern, self-help, and relief within the larger parachurch organizations—not to mention the increased awareness of Christian social responsibility reflected by American Evangelicals in recent opinion polls—further reflects this renewed Evangelical social concern.[7]

We previously suggested that this renewed sense of social responsibility represents a legitimate reappropriation of the Reformed and Puritan heritage of the Evangelical movement, and also a legitimate reappropriation of the social concern of conservative Christianity in 19th- and early 20th-century America. This renewed sense of social responsibility reflects the Evangelical heritage in other ways. On one hand, although some Evangelicals object, the renewed social awareness still tends to be individualistic in emphasis, more concerned with interpersonal compassion than in reforming social structures. Evangelical social agencies like World Vision International work with these suppositions.[8] (Appeal may be made here to Jesus' example of showing interpersonal compassion without seeking social reform [Mark 12:13-17; cf. Titus 2:9].)

A far more universally accepted supposition for Evangelical social action, but one which also links the movement to its heritage, is the priority of evangelism over social action. From Billy Graham to the most radical Evangelicals like John Alexander, former editor of the radical Evangelical periodical *The Other Side,* concern for structural change is always combined with, yet distinguished from, a concern with individual personal regeneration. In part, this commitment is tied to the Evangelical critique of the ecumenical movement, which is perceived as inverting these priorities.[9] Even on this point, however, some controversy is evident within Evangelicalism, as some social activists will not concede that all social action must relate *directly* to evangelism.[10]

At any rate, the characteristic Evangelical priority on evangelism and regeneration over social action may be a valuable lesson to mainline church leaders. To the degree that most Christians share an Evangelical faith-orientation, one can more readily increase trust levels for social ministry when it is clear that evangelism is not being overlooked. This seems to be a sound biblical insight as well (cf. Matt. 28:19-20; Mark 16:15), one so central to the Evangelical movement that it must be regarded as one of the pressing ecumenical questions for relationships to the ecumenical establishment.

The renewed Evangelical concern for social responsibility has moved in at least three politically conflicting directions—the militantly conservative Moral Majority position at one extreme; the radical Evangelicals for Social Action viewpoint at the other; and the moderates in between. We shall sketch the viewpoint of each of these groups.

Conservative social concern

The conservatively oriented political perspective probably represents the majority of Evangelicals. It has the greatest continuity with the political orientation of the Evangelical movement in its recent past. This group of Evangelicals and Fundamentalists is perhaps most visibly represented in the United States by Jerry Falwell's Moral Majority and in Europe by the Internationale Konferenz Bekennender Gemeinschaften and many other European Evangelicals. Radically anticommunist Fundamentalists like Carl McIntire and his International Council of Christian Churches, James Robison and his conservative group, the Roundtable, as well as the American Evangelical establishment embodied by *Christianity Today* and Billy Graham share this viewpoint. Of course, there are important differences among these groups. The anticommunist groups are more strident, less open to compromises necessitated by the political process than the other groups. Thus the arch-Fundamentalists associated with Bob Jones University have criticized Jerry Falwell and the Moral Majority for their political involvements. The concern is that such political activity inevitably compromises Fundamentalist commitments, for it forces Evangelicals to cooperate with those not born again. In addition, differences between these politically active conservatives and the American Evangelical establishment must be identified. The establishment differs from these other, largely Fundamentalist groups in that it is less inclined actually to enter into the political arena, to delineate specific action for bringing about structural change. It is more prone merely to provide informed reflection and principles for political action.[11]

Despite these differences, the groups and persons mentioned do share a similar political perspective on a number of issues. Generally speaking, these groups support legislation against abortion, pornography, homosexuality, and the propagation of secular humanism in the schools. They are suspicious of the feminist movement and the peace movement, oppose Communism and government welfare. (The anticommunism is often a consequence of their millennialist ideas, which tend to correlate the USSR with the final enemies of God.[12] It is also no doubt a consequence of the formative influence of the "American way of life" on Evangelicalism.) Correspondingly, these Evangelicals largely favor the Reagan economic policy of laissez-faire capitalism.[13] In Europe these commitments lead some Evangelicals to support European unity.[14] Although it may take a distinctly pro-American stance among American Evangelicals, on both sides of the Atlantic this segment of the Evangelical movement appears to reflect once again the formative influence of the "American way of life," insofar as it unconditionally supports democracy as the "biblical ideal."[15]

One should not be too quick to stereotype the political views of these conservative Evangelicals. They are not reactionary, seeking to undo what justice has been achieved under postwar liberal democracies. Thus both Jerry Falwell and *Christianity Today* are on record in support of racial justice and equal rights (although not necessarily the idea of busing for integration in the schools).[16] Some establishment Evangelicals, notably Billy Graham, have argued—in contrast to Francis Schaeffer, Falwell, and others—in favor of nuclear disarmament.[17]

The convergence between these conservatives and the positions of the new left in the 1960s is striking at two other points. These groups, notably the U.S. National Association of Evangelicals and some members of the Internationale Konferenz Bekennender Gemeinschaften, support renewed efforts to protect the environment.[18] Also, like the youth culture, the economic theory of the conservatives calls for restrictions on government control and advocates decentralization.[19]

Much has been written about the major impact this new religious conservatism has had on American political life. Conservative Evangelical political lobbies are forming also in Europe and are making an impact, not just on the political stands of their churches. An examination of the positions taken by these groups provides clues about their recent success. They reflect the general Evangelical-Fundamentalist commitment to preserving the heritage of some "golden age" of the past, specifically the golden age of Western democratic, presocialist liberalism. At a time like ours, when the future is so uncertain and people are nostalgic about simpler, happier days in the past when the system still worked, the Conservative Evangelical appeal to revivify the old institutions presents a most attractive alternative.

The moderates

Too often, mainline Christians are inclined to formulate their impressions of Evangelical social ethics solely on the basis of the positions of conservative groups like Moral Majority. The political diversity within the Evangelical movement is far richer. A group of moderates and reform-oriented Evangelicals assumes a somewhat different profile.

In identifying this middle-of-the-road group I have in mind specifically the Evangelical theologian Carl Henry, who was the modern trail-blazer in revitalizing social ethical concern among Evangelicals, and several like-minded Evangelicals including The Lutheran Church–Missouri Synod theologian John Warwick Montgomery. Of a like mind, though more critical and politically liberal, are U.S. Senator Mark Hatfield and the editorial policy of the Christian Reformed Church's influential periodical, *The Reformed Journal*. Basically, all these parties, both right and left, are united in that they do not uncritically accept Western capitalism, as the conservative groups do, yet maintain the commitment to work within the system for change.[20]

This centrist perspective by no means represents a unified position and should perhaps be divided into two groups, the moderate conservatives and the moderate liberals. Henry himself assumes a basically conservative perspective on economic equality, feminism, and government's role in achieving a loving society.[21] However, even some such conservatives take stands not typical of the conservative right. Thus, Henry himself supports the provision of sufficient economic sustenance for all and the Christian's responsibility to challenge unjust laws.[22] He has even voiced reservations about the political stance of the Moral Majority and other conservatively oriented Evangelicals.[23] Other similar centrist conservatives indicate a willingness to support the limited use of abortion in certain special circumstances.[24] Nor should we overlook the historic commitment to peace/pacifism on the part of several conservative Evangelical churches, like the Mennonite Brethren Churches, USA (XV) and the Brethren in Christ Church.[25] The Evangelical centrist position enables its adherents to speak to people across party lines.

On the left wing of the centrist perspective one finds Mark Hatfield and *The Reformed Journal* espousing positions akin to the post-New Deal liberal coalition. Unlike many Evangelicals, they insist upon the necessity of reforming societal institutions, not just individuals, if justice is to be achieved. These Evangelicals also support the right of all citizens of a society to share common goods. Hatfield's early criticism of the Vietnam War in the 1960s and his position on world hunger, as well as the centrist World Vision International's critique of standard Western democratic theories of economic development for underdeveloped nations also indicate a liberal political orientation.[26] (Interestingly enough the kind of development model for which World Vision opts bears profound affinities with those currently advocated by the World Council of Churches.) Nor should the position of some NAE spokesmen against school prayer be overlooked. However, in the final analysis these liberal centrists must be distinguished from the Evangelical left. They have more in common with the conservative centrists, insofar as they share a commitment to and confidence in the possibility of reform within the structures of the American system.[27]

Radical Evangelicals

The third distinct Evangelical social ethical profile, that of the Evangelical left, represents a far more radical perspective which is inclined to condemn and bypass the existing Western systems in order to accomplish its aims.[28] To the unsympathetic observer this wing of Evangelicalism appears to bear all the marks of the new left of the 1960s spiced with some aspects of "The Jesus movement" of that era. In fact, a number of this perspective's prominent leaders are children of that era. Among those associated with this perspective are John Alexander and the staff with whom he worked at *The Other Side,* the American-born Costa Rican Evangelical Orlando E. Costas, several influential American radical Evangelicals like John Howard Yoder, Lucille Sider Dayton, Clark Pinnock, Ron Sider, and Jim Wallis and his *Sojourners* magazine. In its early stages the movement was given impetus by the creation of the Evangelicals for Social Action group, which convened the 1973 meeting of American Evangelical theologians issuing the *Chicago Declaration of Evangelicals to Social Concern*. Although this group and the influential statement it drew up reflected the involvement of some centrist Evangelicals, the basic tone of the group was radical and it eventually moved in that direction.[29]

In terms of its concrete political positions, the Evangelical left is much in agreement with the new left. It tends to argue aggressively for international resource distribution, the simple life-style, disarmament, and feminism. The Vietnam War and its international economic ramifications have been crucial issues for these Evangelicals. They have been suspicious of ecological concerns for they seem to have no reference to the poor. This last point suggests the radicals' real agenda, that all issues must be subordinated to the overriding concern of poverty and the commitment to identify with the poor. What is intended by the radicals is a kind of revolution, a moral challenge to government authority.[30]

These commitments reflect the impact on this group of Evangelicals by Third World liberation theology. A number of Evangelicals in the Third World have come under its influence.[31] Indeed, American radical Evangelicals have been quite influenced by the Evangelical liberation theologian Orlando Costas.[32] Thus it is logical that the radicals employ Marxist modes of analysis to make many of their points; yet they do not embrace Marxism, nor do they usually support liberation theology's occasional advocacy of the use of violence in the course of liberation.[33]

On the contrary, radical Evangelicals embrace, perhaps more intensely than others, a commitment reflected in all the groups we have considered—that Christian social ethics must be rooted in the biblical witness and a regenerate life-style. Yet the radicals add another dimension to this commitment, an overwhelming focus on Christian community. They hold up the ideal of a community vision based on the biblical model as the only context in which human beings can become truly human, the only place where the regenerate life-style can be practiced.[34] This concept of an alternative community, a kind of extended family in which all goods are shared in common, suggests the new left ideal of the commune and points again to the affinities radical Evangelicals have to the children of the 60s.

In terms of the actual strategies for executing social aims, the radicals divide somewhat. Although all of them are suspicious of the political process, highly critical of the American system, some are still willing to look to the political arena as a way of accomplishing their aims. Unlike many conservative Evangelicals, the necessity of seeking to reform societal structures in order to achieve justice is advocated.[35] Still others, notably the Mennonite John Howard Yoder and the Sojourners Fellowship, which embodies in practice the ideal of the so-called "Anabaptist model," advocate at least temporary withdrawal from political involvement.[36] (The example of Christ, his willingness to become powerless in face of the governmental authority, may be cited as biblical precedent.)

The Anabaptist model developed by Yoder takes the 16th-century separatists of the Radical Reformation as its paradigm. As the early Anabaptists separated themselves into holy communities away from the "sinful world," so proponents of this view advocate withdrawal into communities of the faithful and the renunciation of all political power in favor of absolute pacifism.[37] The Anabaptist model's emphasis on pacifism is embraced by the historic peace churches, including Mennonite and Brethren churches which belong to the Evangelical movement. Certain Pentecostal churches like the Church of God in Christ advocate, or at some time in their history have advocated, pacifism. Most of these churches seem not to fit our typology of Evangelical social ethical options. They are a group unto themselves, to a certain extent. On the question of pacifism, none of them (with the possible exception of COGIC [pp. 129-131]) consistently shares the politico-ethical commitments of the radicals, but in some cases seem to maintain positions more consistent with conservatively oriented or moderate Evangelicals.[38]

The contemporary Anabaptist model clearly is not intended to be separatist. Its proponents, Yoder in particular, would have these faith communities function for a revolutionary purpose, to subvert the existing order. As such, the members of these faith communities, like the Sojourners Fellowship, go back into the world, specifically back into the local community in which they live in order to serve and in so doing witness to a countercultural Christian life-style. This alternative life-style is seen as offering a revolutionary challenge to government authority. For these communities can do far more to serve the poor than politics can ever achieve. Thus government's authority is undercut by this Christian challenge. The system is bypassed, not met on its own terms. From this countercultural perspective, free from the pragmatics of the political system and because of the moral authority Christians have gained in virtue of their life-style and community service, they may reenter the political sphere and make political contributions in certain appropriate circumstances.[39]

This Anabaptist model has served to create a good bit of controversy among even socially active Evangelicals. Critics have maintained that it ultimately leads to withdrawal from the world and presupposes a kind of "politics of perfectionism." The fallen character of our world is thought not to have been taken with sufficient seriousness.[40]

Needless to say, almost all the radical Evangelicals have received pointed criticism from the Evangelical establishment. Their radical views on politics made them objects of suspicion, no less than Evangelical moderates whose "liberal openness" made them suspicious to many in the Evangelical establishment.[41] Also problematic has been the radicals' appropriation of insights from liberation theology. The appropriation of modern theological alternatives by Evangelicals is never greeted by the Evangelical establishment except with suspicion. These suspicions of a sell-out to modernism are further heightened by the fact that many radical Evangelicals deny or at least dismiss the importance of affirming Scripture's detailed inerrancy.[42] As we have noted, many of the arguments by radical Evangelicals on behalf of feminism make their points by criticizing and challenging the authors of certain portions of Scripture. Additionally, the radicals' pointed criticisms of the Evangelical movement's record (or lack of it) on social issues, its bondage to the American status quo, further heighten tensions.[43]

There are indications that the negative reception radicals have received within segments of the Evangelical movement are not a matter of concern to them. Many prefer to be identified not as "Evangelicals" but as "radical Christians." And some like John Alexander will not consider themselves Evangelicals in any establishment sense. The links to Evangelicalism are seen more in terms of sharing common sociological bonds, common commitments to the centrality of evangelism and the authority of the Bible, than in sharing a common belief structure.[44]

In view of the Evangelical critiques of the radicals and their own propensity to associate themselves with the Evangelical movement, one may rightly raise cautions about the degree to which the views of the radicals may be said to represent legitimate Evangelical alternatives. Nevertheless, their intriguing and unique proposals merit attention. They provide one last reminder that the contemporary Evangelical movement can scarcely be accused of a lack of social concern.

Additionally the fact that the radicals generally are recognized as Evangelicals and perceive themselves as belonging to the movement—

not merely on a sociological basis (for they perceive themselves sharing certain Evangelical commitments)—serves to raise again an appreciation of the profound diversity the Evangelical movement can accommodate. The radicals clearly share with the Evangelical movement a commitment to the authority of the Bible and the importance of a regenerated life-style and evangelism. These common commitments suggest that we are close to the heart of the Evangelical theological profile.

Evangelical consensus

We have previously noted how the pronounced diversity within the Evangelical movement has led some of its leaders to raise questions about whether any discernible theological unity exists within it. A perhaps even more pointed question is whether the existence of the diversity we have noted within Evangelicalism calls into question basic suppositions about the inerrancy of Scripture and its objective meaning. If all Scripture is authoritative and accessible to all, why do Evangelicals disagree so markedly on what it says and its ethical implications?

In the previous chapters I have suggested, along with some Evangelicals, that the diversity within the movement need not necessarily call into question its basic assumptions about interpretation. This theological diversity is not only a reflection of distinct hermeneutical suppositions, but may also be a reflection of the different Confessional-denominational heritages that constitute the movement.[45]

Even amidst the diversity among Evangelicals on social ethics, one can identify a common Evangelical profile. Most Evangelical theological reflection on social ethics assumes a Christocentric or theocratic perspective. That is to say, the warrant provided for guiding social ethics is the gospel and its norms. One seeks good in society because Christ is said to be Lord of the political realm or because the Evangelical Christian is imitating Christ (see Matt. 28:18; Eph. 1:20-22). And for that reason one determines what is the good on the basis of how closely what is thought to be good conforms to the values associated with Christology or the gospel.

The references in Evangelical literature to such an orientation are innumerable. They emerge in the writings of Baptist, Presbyterian, Wesleyan, Plymouth Brethren, and Mennonite Evangelicals, as well as in statements by transdenominational Evangelical groups. It seems to be the basic contention of Senator Mark Hatfield and his "politics of love."[46] At times, correlated theocratic commitments (the idea that the Church should rule or influence the state) are pushed to the extreme, as is evident in Francis Schaeffer's suggestion that the values of Western civilization are essentially Christian values, or when some Evangelicals like the Reformed Presbyterian Church of North America (Chap. 23) urge that Christians only vote for spiritually devout political candidates, and those like the Christian Reconstructionists call for the reconstruction of society so that it might be based solely on the details of Old Testament law (with New Testament modifications). The efforts of Pat Robertson and Bill Bright in organizing American Evangelicals to participate in a political rally during the early 1980s have also been interpreted as a reflection of these commitments.[47]

This Christocentric-theocratic orientation is rooted in the earliest heritage of the Evangelical movement. It is reflected in the Reformed, Puritan, and, to some extent, the Radical Reformation heritage of the movement, as all these theological traditions maintained this sort of Christocentric ethic.[48] Additionally, the Fundamentalist heritage of Evangelicalism is unambiguously Christocentric. This is evident from the fact that four of the Presbyterian Church in the U.S.A.'s *Five-Point Deliverance* of 1910, the model for the well-known "five points of fundamentalism," pertain to Christology.

One must raise the question, however, whether the Evangelical movement's Christocentric framework for social ethics may conflict with one of the movement's most cherished commitments, the separation of church and state.[49] For on the Reformed-Puritan grounds just sketched, the best political values seem to be those informed by faith in Christ, by the gospel. In that case, despite objections by those standing in the heritage of the Radical Reformation, it should follow that Christians and the Church should rule in government, for they would be the most able politicians. (The call by some Evangelicals that Christians vote only for spiritually devout, regenerated candidates illustrates this. It is perhaps noteworthy that Jerry Falwell and the Moral Majority do not support this viewpoint.[50]

In order to avoid such a church-state confusion, it might be preferable for the Evangelical establishment to consider another more universally accessible basis for social ethics. The doctrine of creation is the obvious choice. Inasmuch as all humans are creatures and experience creation's beauty and its good orders (the laws or principles according to which it is structured), the rationale for seeking goodness and justice in society—because creation (the world) is itself good and just and reflects these principles in the Law which structures it—is a universally intelligible basis for ethics. Even if I am not a Christian, such a warrant for a specific political stance makes sense. Such a theological perspective does not necessarily separate the gospel from its possible political implications. Rather, the gospel motivates the Christian's ethical activity; however, in social questions the ultimate appeal is not so much to Christ and the gospel as it is to the structures and goodness of creation.

There are some indications that a few Evangelicals see the virtue of this argument. Two examples suffice, the first from the 1974 international gathering of Evangelicals in Lausanne (5):

> We affirm that God is both the Creator and the Judge of all men. We therefore should share his concern for justice and reconciliation throughout human society and for the liberation of men from every kind of oppression.

The Baptist theologian Carl Henry follows suit at several points, in one case condemning homosexuality because it conflicts with the "ethics of creation." Numerous other examples of such an appeal by Evangelicals to the doctrine of creation as a warrant for their social ethic could be noted.[51]

The attempt to ground one's ethical warrants in creation is not totally foreign to the heritage of the Evangelical movement. In addition to Lutherans associated with the movement, at least one member of its Reformed wing, the Christian Reformed Church, has historically employed appeals to God's ordinances in creation as a basis for its ethics. Such an appeal to creation as a basis for ethics is precisely what is proposed by the Lutheran two-kingdom ethic.[52] Thus it is here that Lutherans may be able to make a unique contribution to the Evangelical movement. The new radical Evangelical is clearly searching for the kind of inclusive ethical basis the Lutheran tradition offers, a framework which can exert an influence not just on fellow Evangelical Christians but on society as a whole.

Chapter 19

The Ecumenical Movement
and the Proclamation of the Gospel
in Contemporary Society

We have noted on several occasions that Evangelicals are quite pessimistic about the state of contemporary society. This negative assessment has been typical of the Evangelical movement since the Fundamentalist and dispensationalist eras. Thus, modern Evangelicals believe that Western civilization is in the process of breaking down, and that its moral norms have lost authority in favor of an all-pervasive relativism, moral permissiveness, and a self-consuming narcissistic preoccupation with self-gratification at all costs. The paradigms of modern psychology and secular humanism are seen as the order of the day. Many Evangelicals believe that the emergence of special-interest groups, single-issue politics, and new radicalism in Europe may be understood as a reaction to the disillusionment which has ensued from our modern relativism, psychologism, and selfism, whereby the individual's experience is the sole criterion. They fear that totalitarianism in some form may be the outcome of the present cultural dynamic.[1]

Some extraordinary similarities exist between this Evangelical profile and the analysis of contemporary Western society offered by prominent social analysts like Christopher Lasch, Robert Bellah, and Peter Berger. Although there are important differences between their analyses, they agree that the cultural norms of Western society, the common values which hold society together, are no longer functioning efficiently. People are not internalizing these cultural norms, like industriousness, the work ethic, whatever. In this regard these analysts seem to be in agreement with the characteristic Evangelical analysis. Lasch's argument that the deterioration of capitalist culture or its distortion by a new managerial elite has led to a turning inward, to a narcissist quest for self-gratification, has a striking correlation to the views of contemporary Evangelicals.[2]

I make this point regarding the apparent sociological credibility of how a significant number of Evangelicals understand our current social situation because, to a great extent, an appreciation of the Evangelical theological profile is related to the credibility of its diagnosis of the challenges of contemporary society. When one considers the data, one is struck by the cogency of the Evangelical diagnosis.

There seems to be a sense of anxiety today, at least in Western culture, if not in the East. The anxiety is largely rooted in a feeling that the old economic and political systems are deteriorating or at least not as efficient in dealing with present circumstances. As a result, they are not instilling confidence nor are they effective in inculcating traditional Western values like a sense of community, mutual fidelity, loyalty to work, family, and so on. This loss of confidence in the system and consequent diminution of common values has led people to turn inward, "to grab for all the gusto they can get." Yet there is unhappiness and emptiness in this narcissistic quest for self-gratification. People are seeking for meaning and values which are not to be found in humanitarian relativism or special interest self-fulfillment groups, no matter how efficiently their bureaucracies work. People are yearning for fixed objective values, something to which to dedicate their lives in order to give them meaning. Often, but not always, this takes the form of a call to return to the values of the "good old days," which at least in the West are thought to correlate with the values of pre-20th-century, precritical democratic free-market capitalist society and those of the "old-time religion."

The literature of the contemporary Evangelical movement seems to capture these social dynamics. At any rate, it would be difficult to account for the profound success of the contemporary Evangelical movement today were its theological emphases, related as closely as they are to Evangelicalism's analysis of the current social scene, related to an incorrect understanding of the contemporary scene. In short, contemporary Evangelicals appear to have their fingers on the heartbeat of Western cultural dynamics and to be offering a theological profile which is well-suited to proclaim the gospel in the midst of these dynamics.[3]

Evangelicals and ecumenism

It is in the context of this negative characterization of contemporary society, with its pervasive humanism, relativism, and quest for self-gratification, that one must understand the Evangelical movement's vocal criticisms of the organized ecumenical movement (and the World Council of Churches). Evangelical criticisms of organized ecumenism are apparent in virtually all segments of the movement. They are standard fare, although there is some variety with regard to openness to ecumenical activity.[4]

In part, the Evangelical critique of the ecumenical movement arises from the belief that many of the negative trends observed in society have taken a foothold in the church.[5] It is particularly in the organized ecumenical movement, Evangelicals believe, that one can identify the shotgun marriage of theology and humanism manifesting itself in a kind of theological pluralism which denies normative beliefs.[6] (In effect, the present patterns of mainline church leadership which we noted earlier are under attack.) "Ecumenism" functions as an Evangelical code word to describe all that is wrong with the contemporary church.[7] The ecumenical movement, and particularly the WCC, is accused of having compromised biblical authority and adopted a "sociopolitical understanding of the gospel." In effect what is attacked here is the growing influence of Third World liberation theology on the ecumenical movement.[8]

In some cases the Evangelical criticism is mounted on the grounds of the ecumenical movement's radical political views or its hierarchical tendencies.[9] Of course, Carl McIntire is quick to note that this is a mark of the communist influence on the WCC.[10] However, the main Evangelical point is that the ecumenical movement must be repudiated because it perverts the gospel. In the interest of achieving a unity among humankind, an organizational unity, fundamental doctrinal questions which divide the churches have been pushed aside. Particular criticism in this connection is directed against bilateral dialogue agreements between churches, like the *Leuenberg Concord* between Lutheran and Reformed churches in Europe, which have led them to closer fellowship. An important dimension of this critique is the suggestion that many of the agreements between churches in ecumenical dialogues have been achieved by reliance on the presuppositions of neoorthodox theology (as defined earlier). This method is said to permit the churches involved to overlook basic differences between them by speaking only of a "common witness" beneath theological differences.[11]

Evangelicals also perceive and criticize other presuppositions in the ecumenical movement. Some, like Peter Beyerhaus and Carl Henry, suspect that the WCC's concern for the unity of mankind as the presupposition for all its ecumenical work leads it to compromise the uniqueness of Christianity, as evidenced by mainline ecumenism's relative disinterest in evangelism or proselytism.[12] Another interesting criticism of the ecumenical movement is the comment by Carl Henry that organized ecumenism has perhaps overemphasized the doctrine of the Church.[13] Given the relatively low priority we have seen Evangelicals place on this doctrine and the correspondingly high priority it receives in many ecumenical bilateral dialogues and in the WCC, with its theological concern for the church-related issues of baptism, Eucharist, and ministry, one can only conclude that the ecumenical and Evangelical movements may unwittingly be talking past each other.

In any case, much of the real "heat" of controversy between Evangelicals and ecumenism emerges over the sensitive question of the WCC's political involvements, notably its Program to Combat Racism.[14] The impact of Third World liberation theology on the ecumenical movement is again quite apparent in these commitments. Thus there seems to be some validity to the observation of a few analysts that the sharpest ecumenical tension today is no longer one between Protestants and Roman Catholics but the one between the Evangelical movement and liberation theology.[15]

There are some signs that this tension can be overcome. The increasing political awareness and involvement of Evangelicals, the use of Marxist analyses and the influence of liberation theology on radical Evangelicals, are hopeful signs of growing convergence.[16] In fact, some centrist Evangelicals are even expressing an appreciation of Christian faith's responsibility for the "universal community" (unity of mankind).[17] Also the international meeting of Evangelicals in Wheaton, Illinois, in 1983 (II) called for alterations in the style of Evangelical mission agencies. Could this be an indication that Evangelicals are appropriating insights about missionary work from mainline ecumenism?

In the final analysis, however, the crucial issue in resolving tensions between the Evangelical movement and mainline ecumenism that is influenced by liberation theology will be the need for the ecumenical movement and its constituent members to indicate that evangelism, not the unity of humankind, is their first priority. (The proper "Evangelical" priority is generally accepted and practiced by most of the Third World churches. The main exception is perhaps in Latin America itself where it is not always so clear in some mainline churches that evangelism rather than human community is the priority.)[18] It must be made clear by ecumenists that the gospel has not been subordinated to the quest for the unity of humankind.

The WCC Faith and Order Commission has committed itself to this prioritization, particularly in connection with its work in following up the important consensus text, *Baptism, Eucharist and Ministry* (*BEM*, or the Lima document).[19] However, if these efforts are to have any impact on the Evangelical community four factors must be considered: (1) The anti-Catholic sentiments of Evangelicalism; (2) the Evangelical suspicion of a hermeneutic (theory of biblical interpretation) which makes meaning relative to one's perspective; (3) the suspicion of some Evangelicals about creedal formulations; and (4) the vision of ecumenics which Evangelicals practice.

We already have alluded to the first factor, the "Catholic" character of the WCC's concerns. *BEM* itself seems to reflect sympathy with a number of Roman Catholic commitments regarding the desirability of an episcopacy (M, 19ff.), real presence in the sacraments (E, 35ff.; B, 2ff.) and the like (especially M, 35ff.). However, we have observed tendencies within Evangelical theology which might allow Evangelicals to consider some of these themes as legitimate Evangelical alternatives. Given the low priority of the issues for Evangelicalism, one should not expect the movement to exhibit too much enthusiasm for *BEM*.[20]

In regard to the hermeneutical question, the Faith and Order Commission's present scheme suggests that creedal formulations are shaped by one's context. As such, the effort to stimulate ecumenical awareness and reception of *BEM* trades on a kind of "perspectivalism" (the Bible has different meanings in different contexts) which is not acceptable to most Evangelicals. Without some modifications in ecumenical methodology, as I suggest in a later chapter, one should expect Evangelical reactions to ecumenical consensus statements like *BEM* to be somewhat chilly.[21]

Next, the third factor, the general suspicion of some Evangelicals concerning the authority of creeds, must be considered. In its proper context, *BEM* is seen as a kind of commentary on the apostolic faith as expressed in the Nicene Creed. Yet this creedal orientation need not pose problems for all Evangelicals, certainly not for the so-called "Catholic [Ecumenical] Evangelicals" and for Lutheran, Anglican, or Reformed/Presbyterian Evangelicals. These segments of the Evangelical movement clearly envisage a role for the creeds, and so for a modern commentary on the Nicene Creed, like *BEM*. Indeed, one could ask whether the entire Evangelical community should not be open to this endeavor, whether it is not in fact really creed-oriented in view of the fact that virtually all of the movement's organizations formulate statements of faith.

The fourth factor is the vision of Christian unity held by Evangelicals. Evangelicals insist that organizational unity cannot become an end in itself.[22] In part this is because such unity might too easily be purchased at the cost of overlooking doctrinal disagreements. Another factor in their reticence about visible church unity may be that the congregational and independent parachurch agency structure of Evangelicalism does not easily accommodate itself to the concern with visible unity.[23] Besides, it is argued, Christians already have a spiritual unity. Such an orientation seems to confirm the anti-institutional inclinations of the Evangelical movement. It also suggests a certain devaluation of the physical in favor of a kind of "spiritualizing," a tendency which, as we previously noted, may be a function of Evangelicalism's continuing reliance on Greek philosophical presuppositions.[24]

It can be shown, however, that disinterest in organized institutional expressions of ecumenism is ruled out by Evangelical presuppositions. Evangelicals have been quite active in forming their own ecumenical organizations, like the National Association of Evangelicals and the Internationale Konferenz Bekennender Gemeinschaften. Moreover, parachurch organizations self-consciously reflect a similar dynamic, believing that the interaction of Christians from different denominations within an organization will help unite Evangelicals.[25]

All these organizations, as we have seen, exhibit a similar structure. A common statement of faith to which all members must subscribe is devised. However, at the same time, emphasis is placed on imposing only a minimum of structure on the members so that they might be permitted to maintain their particular denominational-Confessional commitments. In this regard one can observe a kind of "relativizing" of doctrine in the Evangelical movement in the sense that doctrinal diversity can be officially tolerated.

It is tempting to argue on this basis, as some have done, that the Evangelical movement has rendered doctrine and doctrinal differences unimportant. This case can be made with regard to certain Evangelical pietists who maintain the standard position of classical Pietism that not doctrinal agreement but mutual repentance and holiness best achieves unity.[26] Yet side by side the pietist heritage, one also encounters doctrinally oriented segments of Evangelicalism rooted in Protestant Orthodoxy and dispensationalism, groups ready to cause schism and to die over doctrinal differences. We also have observed a "Confessional consciousness" in important segments of the movement, a consciousness which has been expressed institutionally in the Vorläufige Grundordunung (First Principles) of the Internationale Konferenz Bekennender Gemeinschaften (2[c]), as it calls on members to bind themselves to their own Confessional traditions while striving to recognize the same apostolic heritage in the other Confessional traditions.

Thus it is not quite fair to conclude that doctrine is unimportant for all segments of the Evangelical movement, simply because it incorporates various denominational traditions. At the least, doctrine would seem to be no less important than it is for mainline churches incorporated in the ecumenical establishment.

In a certain sense, Evangelicals recognize that their transdenominational parachurch agencies might be functioning as "visible bonds" of unity.[27] This raises hopeful signs which invite ecumenical dialogue between mainline churches and the Evangelical movement. It indicates that a yen exists among Evangelicals for some kind of conspicuous visible unity. We have already observed this concern for unity reflected in the 1977 "Chicago Call," issued by a group of "Catholic [Ecumenical] Evangelicals," and in the "Open Letter" prepared by Evangelicals attending the WCC Vancouver Assembly. Other Evangelicals, including churches like The Evangelical Free Church of America and The Evangelical Covenant Church (p. 23), explicitly affirm these ecumenical commitments.[28] Moreover, the possibility of achieving closer relationships with all churches does not seem unrealizable even at the grass-roots level. An opinion poll of American Christians indicates that American Evangelicals' attitudes are in fundamental agreement with those of mainline Christians.[29]

Issues for rapprochement: reconciled diversity

The nature of the transdenominational, parachurch Evangelical organizations suggests a helpful model for initiating ecumenical dialogue with the Evangelical movement. First it is necessary to assure Evangelicals in such a dialogue that the aim is not merger into a "superchurch." The World Confessional Organizations' concept of "reconciled diversity" is the model which offers the most helpful resource for dialogue. For like the Evangelical models we have examined, it does not suggest that denominational-Confessional differences be canceled in a unified fellowship.

The basic supposition of the model of *reconciled diversity* is that Church unity can be achieved by reconciling differences between the churches, without leveling out these differences but allowing each church to be enriched by the others.[30] Of course some means of making visible the unity of the churches, in addition to common worship, is posited with this model. When their differences are reconciled, then some visible means by which the churches might make common decisions would be instituted.

In many respects the model sketched seems to have affinities to the structural dynamics which hold the Evangelical movement together. The differences between its constituents' traditions are not canceled; rather, they are envisioned as "reconciled" differences which do not preclude fellowship. The differences are "reconciled," insofar as different Evangelicals can share the common Evangelical theological suppositions or sign the common faith statement of a given Evangelical organization. This also seems to be the model for interdenominational relationships proposed by the Internationale Konferenz Bekennender Gemeinschaften (2[c]). It is also the model of virtually all the Evangelical parachurch agencies, and has been almost explicitly advocated by some Evangelicals.[31]

In dealing with all segments of the Evangelical movement, mainline Christians will best proceed by employing this "Evangelical" model of reconciled diversity. This means it is important for mainliners to assure Evangelicals that the aim of dialogue and cooperation with them is not to merge the churches. The point is simply to help Evangelicals recognize that the mainline churches in fact share basic faith commitments (fundamentals) with the Evangelical community. The process of dialogue is analogous to demonstrating that all participants subscribe to a common statement of faith (not unlike those of Evangelical organizations). Once this is established, one may envision the kind of cooperation and celebration of diversity among Evangelical and mainline Christians that goes on within parachurch Evangelical organizations. Our endeavor here and in Part IV is to help Evangelicals and mainliners to recognize that they might find that they actually share a common "fundamental" framework of faith. (Of course, such official ecclesial fellowship which might ensue from such a recognition need not preclude eventual organizational unity.)

Other agenda items

We may conclude these reflections on Evangelicalism and ecumenism with two parenthetical observations. First, the recognition that the Evangelical movement is established along lines of a kind of "reconciled diversity" model of unity suggests why Fundamentalists and conservative Lutheran churches like The Lutheran Church–Missouri Synod are unwilling to identify themselves with the movement. In this section it has been suggested that Evangelicals can accept characteristic Lutheran understandings as legitimate Evangelical alternatives. Thus the fundamental basis for LCMS reticence with regard to the movement seems to be its discomfort with Evangelicalism's ecumenical inclusiveness. After all, LCMS does reject the concept of reconciled diversity for failing to take doctrinal differences with sufficient seriousness.[32] Is this not the ultimate basis for conservative Lutherans' failure to identify with the Evangelical movement, their unwillingness to establish fellowship without *complete* doctrinal agreement in all particulars? The "precisionism" of the heritage of Orthodox theology which predominates in LCMS and like-minded churches will not concede the possibility—granted both by Evangelicals and ecumenists—that the same insight about the gospel can be conceptualized in diverse though complementary ways. Likewise the separatism of Fundamentalist churches seems to be the ultimate factor in their reticence to identify with an Evangelical movement committed to an inclusive reconciled diversity.

Despite the reticence of these churches to identify with the Evangelical movement, our analysis has shown how much conservative Lutheran churches and Fundamentalists have in common with the Evangelical movement. Thus, to the degree that these churches' theological positions represent legitimate Conservative Evangelical alternatives, as Evangelicals are wont to think, dialogue between mainline churches and Evangelicals could be pertinent to establishing agreement between conservative Lutheran churches, Fundamentalists, and the mainline.

Second, the growing openness of Evangelicals on ecumenism is reflected not just in Evangelicalism's relationship with other churches but also perhaps with regard to interfaith dialogue. Although efforts by some Evangelicals to proselytize Jews are challenged by the Jewish community and by some Christians, the Evangelical heritage of dispensational premillennialism has been generally open to enhancing Jewish–Christian relationships, and particularly supportive of the idea of a Jewish national state, if not the Zionist movement itself. This trend continues today among some nondispensationalist Evangelicals, including Jerry Falwell and Carl Henry. Such a viewpoint follows logically from the premillennialist and general Evangelical conviction that we are living in times of chaos. The return of the Jews to their homeland provides hope for Evangelical Christians that we are approaching the end times (Luke 24:9,24,28).[33] Paradoxically, then, there is genuine openness to Judaism even among dispensational Fundamentalists.

The reference to Evangelicalism's pessimistic characterization of contemporary culture serves as a reminder of the extent to which this characterization and its corresponding pessimism about the Church inform the Evangelical assessment of the ecumenical movement. The ecumenical movement is regarded as too closely aligned with the decaying mainline churches and their humanism in the guise of theology. Thus the ecumenical movement must be rejected as the ultimate distortion of the gospel. In most cases, the premillennialist heritage of the Evangelical movement is really never far removed from its views on ecumenism.[34]

Chapter 20

The Essence of Conservative Evangelicalism

We have referred to the relationship between the Evangelical movement's theological commitments and its negative, often polemical characterization of contemporary culture. Indeed, in some respects there is so much diversity in the movement that one is tempted to say that there is no *single* theological entity called the Evangelical movement, only a group of Christians united by their polemical attitudes toward common foes. The old Fundamentalist polemical, separatist mind-set is still very much in evidence in the work of even the most theologically sophisticated Evangelicals.[1]

Basically what we have found is a correlation between the Evangelical characterization of society as chaos and its commitment to impose order and morality on the chaos by emphasizing the regenerate life-style (sanctification) and the inerrant—or at least inspired and reliable—Scripture. Given the emphasis on these two commitments, the other characteristic doctrinal formulations of Evangelicalism follow. (Diversity in regard to these formulations never entirely bypasses the fundamental commitments.)

Let us reiterate the seven-point description of the characteristics of Conservative Evangelicalism which we noted earlier. Although there exists some diversity among Evangelicals with regard to how and to what degree they affirm each of these points, the Evangelical movement appears to be comprised of Protestants who (1) assume a characteristically critical viewpoint towards Roman Catholicism and the ecumenical movement; (2) insist on or at least remain in dialogue with the concepts of plenary inspiration, verbal inerrancy, and Scripture's propositional character;[2] (3) affirm the Bible's importance for Christian life; (4) prioritize the experiential dimensions of becoming and being a Christian (conversion and sanctification) over the sacraments, the ministry, and ecclesiastical structures; (5) emphasize evangelism and foreign missions; (6) understand Christian ethics in terms of law rather than situationally; and (7) resist official fellowship, in the sense of its implying formal institutional ties, with persons or churches not sharing the preceding commitments. One is tempted to add two additional points which often characterize Evangelical faith, namely, the expectation of Christ's imminent return, realistically interpreted, and a stress on the personal appropriation of the atonement (the denial of universal salvation), with the atonement understood in some way as a substitutionary sacrifice.[3] At any rate, the Reformed, pietist, and Anabaptist heritages of the Evangelical movement are clearly reflected in all of these, particularly in the emphasis on sanctification and structure in the Christian life.

The correlation between these commitments and the characteristic Evangelical assessment of contemporary society is quite apparent. Because society is perceived as in decay, some definite point of orientation, some absolutely certain way to make sense of the world and preserve the heritage of the past, is necessary. (This reactionary commitment to function as the caretaker of the riches of some past golden age is a fundamental motivating dynamic for Evangelicalism.)[4] Scripture provides this for Evangelicals. However, for most Evangelicals it does so only because it is inspired and inerrant. Thus Evangelicals must be Protestants who relate to the Bible as the inspired, inerrant Word of God.

Certainly, the controversy among Evangelicals over inerrancy, noted above, must be taken into account at this point. Some, like Francis Schaeffer, claim that the limited inerrantists have shattered Evangelicalism. Others would question our stress on inerrancy as the defining Evangelical characteristic. It may be that this critique is appropriate and, as at least one prominent member of the more theologically liberal Evangelical left has maintained, that the other characteristics which we have attributed to Evangelicalism no longer pertain to Evangelicals.[5] Yet to the extent that these critiques are accurate, all distinctiveness of the Evangelical movement seems forfeit. To be sure, this could be a real cause for ecumenical celebration. Henceforth the Evangelical movement would pose no special challenges to ecumenical conversation. The ecumenical agenda could simply proceed by way of dialogues among the mainline church traditions, with members of the dialogue team drawn from both those who do and those who do not constitute the Evangelical movement, with perhaps a special round of dialogues between these churches and those of the Holiness and Pentecostal traditions. If so, the appropriate agenda of this book, the ecumenical problematic, may properly come to an end.

Although the conclusion of the prominent Evangelical whose criticism I have cited may be appropriate when dealing with Evangelicals of the left, enough data has been adduced thus far to suggest that with respect to much of the Evangelical constituency matters may not be so simple. The characteristics I have identified still do seem to describe many segments of the Evangelical movement. Thus, for example, my observation has been that, with the possible exception of Evangelicals whose traditions are absolutely untouched by the influence of Fundamentalism or the traditions of Protestant Orthodoxy (including Puritanism), even among radical Evangelicals the inerrancy doctrine is never totally ignored; it is a kind of landmark for all discussion among Evangelicals, an affirmation which in most cases must at least be "interpreted" if one is to remain orthodox. And even where it is not an agenda item, as in the case of some Evangelicals outside of North America, at least something like plenary inspiration is affirmed. Consequently it still seems reasonable to maintain, as Harold Lindsell, Carl Henry, and even Gerald Sheppard suggest, that the doctrine of biblical inerrancy or at least an affirmation of the Bible's full, plenary authority (that all portions of Scripture *are* divine revelation) is the sociological, if not the theological focal point for the Evangelical movement, what holds it together, conditions (in tandem with the doctrine of sanctification/regeneration) its other positions, and so establishes the movement's uniqueness.[6]

The chaos Evangelicals perceive in society leads them to propose means of ordering their lives. Structures are necessary. Translated into theological terminology this means that "sanctification" (the Christian life) is an overriding Evangelical concern.[7] The importance of this theme for Evangelicalism also relates to the movement's emphases on conversion and renewal of life, for these emphases entail a concern for the character of the Christian life. In practice, all these emphases often manifest themselves among Evangelicals in a commitment to allowing Christian faith to be reflected in all parts of their lives. Thus the Bible becomes relevant to every aspect of life for Evangelicals.

The same concern to provide order or structure in the Christian life accounts for the law-oriented understanding of much Evangelical ethics. To receive such guidance from the law assures believers that their actions conform to the norms of the past, the good, old-fashioned values. Indeed, a situational ethic would simply be swamped by our contemporary cultural pluralism, so that it would be unable to discern right from wrong. Thus the Commandments must be relied upon as a guide to ethical decision making in order that Christians have some structure with which to deal with the confusion and chaos caused by contemporary pluralism. (The Christocentric character of the Evangelical movement, with Christ understood as Lord of all realms, may also be a factor in linking the law to Christian ethics and the gospel, as we observe here.)

The Evangelical emphasis on conversion and personal experience of the gospel involves three other characteristics of the movement. First, it leads to aggressive and dedicated efforts in evangelism and missionary work. This commitment is reflected not just in the faith statements of the movement. It appears to be reflected also in surveys concerning the belief structure of American Evangelicals.[8] (This commitment entails in turn a rejection of the concept of universal salvation, salvation apart from appropriation through personal faith.) Also the emphasis on personal experience typically leads Evangelicals to reject a strong sacramental orientation. Such an objective orientation is thought to misplace the focus of faith away from the individual's response.

Given this suspicion of all "objective" understandings of the Church and of grace, it follows quite logically that Evangelicals would define themselves over against churches which take these positions. Given the affinity of the Roman Catholic church to these views and its apparent compromise of *sola scriptura* (Scripture the sole authority) it is quite understandable that Evangelicals may typically be characterized as Protestants who usually assume a strongly critical stance over against Roman Catholicism. (To be sure, we have seen emerging variety within Evangelicalism on these issues, with increased openness to views of real presence in the sacraments, an episcopal view of ministry, and the authority of tradition. Such emerging Evangelical alternatives show promise for opening avenues for ecumenical dialogue with Evangelicals.)

Two final, related characteristics of Evangelicalism are its repudiation or criticism of the ecumenical movement and its related unwillingness to reestablish formal fellowship with Christians who are not in fundamental agreement with Evangelical principles. The separatist propensities inherited from Fundamentalism and from the Radical Reformation are not entirely absent in Evangelicalism. They present themselves at this point insofar as Evangelicals insist that the acceptance

of certain nonnegotiable beliefs and behavior patterns are preconditions
for fellowship.[9]

Here again, though, one observes a growing openness. But it is
evident how all these distinguishing characteristics of the movement
emerge in relation to the Evangelicals' characteristic assessment of
Western society as a society in decay, requiring the stability offered
by norms of the past. This assessment sets the agenda for the Evangelical preoccupation with questions of sanctification and the regenerate
life-style. However, in the final analysis, the principal commitment
which holds together these characteristic Evangelical themes is the
commitment to the (inerrant) full authority of Scripture (or at least the
commitment to remain in dialogue with these conceptions), which provides certainty and guidance in face of contemporary cultural decay
and pluralism. (This Conservative Evangelical agenda is in turn directly
exportable to the Southern hemisphere, where the prevailing concern
with "nation-building" also makes the Evangelical offer of safe, secure
norms, and so of some sense of social order, a most attractive one for
Christians.)

We have noted previously the affinities between the Evangelical
movement's characteristic depiction of our current cultural crisis and
the analysis of today's cultural narcissism offered by several contemporary social analysts. Much in these profiles seems to resonate in our
contemporary experience—the system not working, old values losing
authority, people seeking self-gratification at all costs, and everyone
going in a different direction and being confused about it.

The Evangelical movement's characteristic theological positions simply seem to reflect common sense in dealing with Western (perhaps
global) culture's challenges. They follow logically as necessary checks
against negative dimensions of cultural pluralism or chaos.[10] And we
cannot easily deny that the Evangelical positions are biblically based.
In the previous chapters we have, after all, identified a good bit of
biblical support for them.

Therefore, mainline churches must ask themselves whether they
could not accept and employ some characteristic Evangelical emphases
and techniques, both for evangelism and for nurturing Christian commitment in our contemporary narcissistic society. In the following chapters we shall indicate the validity of mainliners appropriating many of
these emphases.

Conversely, in the preceding chapters we have noted certain possible
theological abuses which could arise with the Evangelical movement

(Evangelicals themselves are not unaware of these possible abuses).[11] The tendency to compromise the primacy of grace by an undue concentration on Christian responsibility, so that salvation is contingent on what we do, and the use of dualist philosophical presuppositions which entails a compromise of historical physical reality are two possible abuses. An attempt will be made to show that the Evangelical movement can legitimately appropriate insights from Confessional Lutheranism and other traditions in order to avoid or correct these possible abuses. Evangelicals, Lutherans, and others in the mainline have much they can learn from each other.

Part IV

DIALOGUE WITH A MAINLINE CHURCH HERITAGE: BIBLICALLY BASED THEOLOGY FOR BORN-AGAIN CHRISTIANS

Chapter 21

The Proclamation
of the Gospel
in Contemporary Society

It is helpful to examine more closely some of the areas of agreement noted previously between various mainline church traditions and the Evangelical movement.[1] This will be accomplished by means of a summary of the characteristic theological views of mainline churches on the same doctrinal topics we examined in Part III, with special attention given to the Lutheran tradition as a point of reference. The basis for the analysis of Lutheranism is a conceptual study of the 16th-century Lutheran Confessional writings *(The Book of Concord)*, not the works of famous theologians like Luther himself. For only the Confessions represent the official Lutheran doctrinal standards. Consideration of the Confessional positions of other mainline churches ensures that the discussion between Lutheranism and the Evangelical movement may have broader relevance, but a detailed articulation of the positions of the other mainline Protestant churches is not necessary at this time. For as we have observed, many Evangelicals explicitly embrace the theological/doctrinal heritage of at least one of these other mainline churches (either the Presbyterian, Anglican, Methodist, Baptist, or Restorationist heritage). Thus the tensions between them and these churches are not so much a matter of differences over doctrine as it is a concern Evangelicals have that these churches have forfeited their heritage. Questions about the nature of Scripture and theological method, to be considered in a later chapter, are perhaps the most relevant issue for this particular dialogue. However, of doctrinal emphases in the case of the Roman Catholic and Lutheran heritages, there exists more ambiguity among some Evangelicals about a compatibility with their own doctrinal heritage. Thus a detailed comparison of Conservative Evangelical theological commitments and those particularly of the Lutheran church is still warranted.

It will not be possible to show that convergence exists between Lutheranism and other mainline traditions and all segments of the Evangelical movement on every issue. But to the degree it can be shown that the mainline churches converge with some segment of the Evangelical movement, then it can legitimately be claimed that on the issue at stake the mainline churches in question are positing legitimate "Evangelical" alternatives. In that sense one may speak of a convergence with the Evangelical movement as a whole, since when such a position is held by Evangelicals it does not fracture "Evangelical fellowship" with other segments of the movement.

Since special attention will be given to the dialogue between Lutheran and Evangelical theological commitments, we should reiterate that the Lutheran tradition with its emphasis on justification differs markedly from the Evangelical movement in regard to overriding theological concerns and orientation in addressing contemporary society. In some sense Lutheranism's overriding concerns are unique in Christendom, since the Reformed, Roman Catholic, and pietist traditions, like the Evangelical movement, tend to focus on issues related to sanctification.[2] This uniqueness of the Lutheran movement suggests why attention to Lutheran–Evangelical dialogue may be of broader general interest. If areas of convergence between Lutherans and Evangelicals can be ascertained, even though they have very different visions of the aim of ministry, the nature and degree of agreement between Evangelicals and other mainline churches that share with Evangelicals both a common vision of ministry and common doctrinal positions should be more readily apparent. For, unlike the Evangelical movement and virtually all the other mainline church traditions, the overriding issue for the Lutheran reformers was not decay in society and the need to provide order and structure for Christian life in the midst of chaos (even though the 16th century was not devoid of social crisis and upheaval).[3] For the reformers themselves one might say that the problem was too much structure in society and in the church's life: too much law!

The story of Luther's Reformation is well known and does not require detailed account at this point. Suffice it to say that the heavily structured existence of late medieval church life led Luther, the young Augustinian monk, to question whether these church laws, interpreted as the law of God, could be fulfilled. The result of encounter with God's law, Luther found, was either self-righteous pride (the belief that one can accomplish all the divine commands without God's involvement) or rebellion against God. In either case, the outcome is anxiety, humility, and a terror-stricken conscience (Rom. 5:20).[4]

Luther struggled with these experiences during his early days in the monastery. It was probably not until some time early in his teaching career as a professor at Wittenberg University that he found relief from his spiritual struggles. He came to recognize that the references to the "righteousness of God" in the Pauline epistles refer not to that "by which He is righteous in Himself but the righteousness by which we are made righteous by God."[5] For Luther this implied that God is not the stern judge but the giver of righteousness and salvation. The obvious consequence was a fuller realization that we are justified by grace through faith, saved by God's action, not by what we do.

Of itself this new insight did not immediately lead to schism with the medieval Roman church. The schism was occasioned by the indulgence controversy. Indulgences are certificates for the remission of temporal or purgatorial punishments still due Christians even after the guilt of their sin has been forgiven. The Roman church hierarchy, in which are found the successors of the apostles, is understood to be authorized to grant such forgiveness on Christ's authority (Matt. 16:19). During the late Middle Ages the practice of selling these indulgences developed. Some of the revenues came to be diverted to the Vatican as they were used to finance the rebuilding of St. Peter's in Rome. However, not so much this fact, but rather a concern for the effect of the selling of indulgences on the piety of the people in Wittenberg, led Luther to take action.

The marketing of indulgences for the deceased must be rejected, Luther concluded, because they compromised his new insight regarding the character of divine righteousness and the primacy of God's action in bringing salvation. The buying and selling of indulgences directed people away from the appreciation that God alone saves, but taught them instead to rely on their own works of satisfaction, the purchasing of indulgences.[6] With these thoughts in mind, Luther issued his famous 95 Theses on the entrance to the Castle Church in Wittenberg on October 31, 1517, inviting debate on issues related to indulgences. In effect, this constituted a challenge to the church's teaching authority, a challenge which attracted much attention and sympathy in Germany, not least from rulers in Luther's home in Saxony. In response to this perceived challenge, the new challenges Luther was raising to the church as a result of the continuing controversy (it had led him to discover other false Roman teachings), and in view of the turmoil these challenges seemed to be creating in its relationships with Germany, the Vatican finally excommunicated Luther.

Thus it was that Luther's efforts to seek reform in the Roman Catholic church of his day led to the beginning of a new church. Because he had the support of his ruler, a number of younger church leaders he had influenced, and the bulk of the common people caught up in the spirit of a new German sense of nationalism, the excommunication of Luther had no effect on his influence. But he and his followers could no longer be Roman Catholics. So although Luther preferred to avoid the name history has given his movement, the Lutheran church was born.

The Lutheran Reformation spread to various regions in Germany during the first decades of the movement. Efforts were made by the Holy Roman Empire to halt its spread by means of political and military pressure. It was largely during this period that most of the Lutheran Confessional documents were written. Finally, in the mid-16th-century and again in 1648 at the Peace of Westphalia, a territorial principle was established which guaranteed the legal rights and protection of Lutheran churches in those German regions where the prince of the region had become Lutheran. This regional principle very much affects and prevails in German Lutheranism today.

During the late stages of the Reformation the Lutheran movement came to Scandinavia and became the established state religion, supplanting Roman Catholicism. It has become a part of the American religion scene largely in consequence of emigration from Germany and Scandinavia. Today, although the Lutheran church is an international body and determined efforts are under way in North America to make it a more inclusive body, it remains very much an ethnic church.

Contrary to the impressions of some non-Lutherans, Lutheranism is by no means theologically homogeneous. Several distinct prevailing theological movements within Lutheranism may be identified. To some extent they have analogs in other historic Protestant churches and so deserve our attention.

In the period just after Luther's death Lutheran Orthodoxy emerged as a theological movement dedicated to codifying and systematizing the insights of Luther and other early reformers. This theological movement, particularly as it took shape in the Reformed tradition, has had a profound impact on Evangelicalism. In the 17th century, largely in reaction to the rationalizing propensities of Orthodoxy and the necessity of social reconstruction following the turmoil imposed on Europe by 30 years of Protestant-Catholic religious wars, Pietism developed within Lutheranism. Pietism had to contend with the liberalizing, often moralizing tendencies of Enlightenment theology.

In the 19th century came the self-conscious effort to return to the heritage of the Lutheran Confessions, the Lutheran renewal (also sometimes called neo-Lutheranism). This movement largely reappropriated the approach of Orthodoxy. In this respect it differs from a more recent, quite distinct theological movement which coincidentally is sometimes referred to by the same name, neo-Lutheranism. This more recent movement has been shaped and influenced by neoorthodox theology and claims to find precedent for its insights in Luther himself. (Needless to say, because of the influence of neoorthodox theology, the impact of neo-Lutheranism on mainline Lutheranism is a source of concern for many Evangelicals in their assessment of mainline Lutheran churches.) Today new movements are also in the process of developing.

In some way each of these movements continues to have an impact on various segments of Lutheranism. (Evangelically oriented Lutherans are usually those influenced by Pietism or by the Lutheran Renewal; those most inclined to identify with Evangelicalism embody some kind of coalition of the two movements [as is the case with another somewhat distinct Lutheran stream, neo-Pietism].) Despite their differences, these movements are united at least in their common commitment to emphasizing the centrality of the doctrine of justification by grace through faith. In fact, proponents of a given movement normally distinguish themselves from the other movements by contending that the others have compromised the doctrine of justification.

To the degree that other Protestant churches, notably the Reformed tradition, have developed analogs to these diverse Lutheran theological movements, most of the preceding comments might be applied to these other mainline churches. Only the last point, the central role of the doctrine of justification in determining what are the most authentic positions, applies solely to Lutheranism. But such an emphasis is the heart of the Lutheran heritage.

The centrality of justification for contemporary society

The history of the Lutheran tradition, from the time of the Reformation through the development of its various theological movements, clearly indicates that Luther's chief preoccupation, emerging from his spiritual struggles with the condemning law of God, has dictated and continues to dictate the principal agenda for Lutheranism. In fact, the Lutheran Confessional document *The Augsburg Confession* (XX.17) indicates that comforting the anxiety-ridden and despairing with an awareness that salvation and all dimensions of life are trustworthy because they have been given by God is *the* problem of ministry. The good news is not rightly encountered apart from the spiritual conflict of anxiety and the burden of the law. Given these commitments, it is quite easy to see why the doctrine of justification by grace through faith (rather than sanctification or regeneration) receives principal emphasis in the Lutheran tradition and is there designated as the chief article of faith.[7] For in this way it can be asserted that our salvation and all that we have is given by grace.

The Lutheran emphasis on justification, unique among other churches, seems to be related, then, to the unique understanding Lutherans have of the core problem of human existence. The crucial problem is not identified—as it is in most other traditions—as the need for structure and a regenerate life-style. Instead, the overriding concern is to offer comfort to those burdened with too much structure, who require release from such burdens.

This divergent analysis of the human condition's core problem raises the issue of whether the Lutheran or the Evangelical (and that of other like-minded traditions) analysis is the more accurate description of our present cultural situation. Since many of the basic theological commitments of these movements flow directly from their analysis of the human situation, it follows that the movement whose analysis of the human situation is most applicable to our present cultural situation might provide the best contemporary theological alternative.

Previously we noted the pertinence of the characteristic Evangelical characterization of the human condition for our present situation in several different social contexts. Evangelicals seem rightly to sense how the relative lack of efficiency of the old cultural-political systems in dealing with present demands has led to a loss of authority for the values associated with Western culture. They believe that, as a result of these dynamics, contemporary people are bereft of all points of orientation and have turned inward in search of their identity, to seek self-gratification and the good life at all costs. Thus people are yearning for structure and a point of orientation and meaning which Evangelical theology, with its emphasis on the regenerate life-style, commitment, an ethic structured by the law, and a sure and certain infallible source (the Bible), provides.[8] In this sense the Evangelical movement and its constituent traditions, like Pietism, Calvinism, and Wesleyanism, appear to propose *the* theology for our day.

A closer look at the narcissistic, "me first" dynamic of contemporary society indicates, however, that the Lutheran analysis of the human condition also captures certain dimensions of this dynamic. It is true that Western industrial and Eastern socialist societies' social structures generally are not functioning efficiently. Yet some of these systems, like our economic system, continue to exert a strong, almost binding influence on all segments of global society. This is coupled with feelings of anxiety and terror about oneself and the future, precisely because these systems are not working efficiently and seem out of control. Thus there is as much need to hear the Lutheran message of comfort, affirmation, and freedom from the bondage of the law and its temporal structures as there is need to hear the call to structure and regenerate life-style which typically emerges from the Evangelical community. In both traditions there are sufficient analogies between their overriding concern (as well as the central themes they stress) and our present cultural context to suggest that the insights of both can contribute to our present cultural situation.

It is helpful at this point to clarify one possible misconception about the Lutheran tradition. To say that Lutheran theology with its emphasis on the doctrine of justification is conditioned by certain contextual factors is a distortion if it leads one to conclude that the Lutheran tradition is only a product of and reaction to the concern for anxiety-ridden consciences. In fact, the Lutheran tradition has understood itself historically as a catholic movement, or a reform movement within the catholic church. That is to say, its emphasis on justification and its other characteristic modes of presenting the gospel are regarded not just as reactions to Luther's particular historical circumstances or as reactions to the problems posed by the anxiety-ridden conscience. Rather Lutherans propose their characteristic themes as portrayals of the faith of the catholic church throughout the ages.

This point is made explicit in a few passages in the Lutheran Confessional documents, specifically in *The Augsburg Confession* (XX.12; XXI.I) and the *Apology of the Augsburg Confession* (XXIV.67). To this extent Lutheranism's self-understanding stands in some contrast to the separatist, antitraditionalist propensities of the Evangelical movement. Luther, after all, had no intention of founding a new church, but was simply endeavoring to bring about reform within Roman Catholicism. Thus the Lutheran tradition must be understood as a movement which, since its inception and as reflected in its official Confessional documents (*The Augsburg Confession*, Pref. 2,10), has been committed to the ecumenical movement and the goal of Christian unity.

Traditional creedal affirmations

The affirmation of the ancient trinitarian and Christological doctrines by Lutheranism as well as by the other mainline churches reflects their catholic perspective. At first glance there is little that is unique about these traditions' treatment of these doctrines. The Trinity is simply described with little exposition, and what is said seems quite consistent with the Evangelical movement's characteristic use of Greek philosophical categories to depict these doctrines.[9]

In one respect, however, the Lutheran tradition tends to be innovative, although still catholic. It stresses the unity of the three persons of the Trinity and the unity of Christ's two natures. With regard to the Trinity, Luther insists that God cannot be known except in terms of all three persons, and yet God in himself is One.[10] Likewise in regard to the doctrine of Christ Lutheranism affirms the concept of *communicato idiomatum* (the communion of attributes). This is the idea that whatever can be affirmed of one of Christ's natures can be affirmed of the other.[11] Thus if we say God is omnipresent we must also say this of Christ's human nature.

Of course this way of stressing the unity of Christ's person, rooted in the theology of the 4th-century church fathers in Alexandria, is a catholic formulation which is reflected at least tangentially even in the mainline Presbyterian and Baptist heritages. But it has been especially important to Lutherans in developing their view of the Lord's Supper, in explaining how Christ could be bodily present in manifold celebrations of the sacrament in various times and places.[12] Also the concept of *communicatio idiomatum* implies that the finite (Jesus' body) can fully bear the infinite (*finitum capax infiniti*). Thus for Lutherans the will of God is *totally* revealed in Jesus Christ.[13]

To be sure, such an orientation appears to conflict with the viewpoint of a number of Evangelicals who insist that the finite cannot bear the infinite.[14] Also the *communicatio idiomatum* concept implies that God interacts with history in a radical way, that God's being is affected by what happens to the man Jesus. (If Jesus suffers and dies God must also suffer and die.)[15] This represents a break with an understanding of God as unchangeable, conceptualized in terms of static Greek philosophical categories, as is typical in much Evangelical theology.[16]

That differences seem to exist between Lutherans and many Evangelicals on these points is indisputable. However, as we previously noted, the characteristic Evangelical position on Christology and the Trinity reflects its agreement with and indebtedness to the Reformed tradition. Thus, inasmuch as Lutherans have come to recognize through ecumenical dialogues with the Reformed church that these positions, also held by Evangelicals, need not be a barrier to church unity with the Reformed tradition, so likewise it would seem to follow that the same differences should not divide Lutherans and Evangelicals.[17]

One final observation about the Lutheran treatment of the doctrine of Christ's two natures: The Lutheran Confessional document, the *Formula of Concord* (SD III.55-56), notes that the doctrine of the two natures must be affirmed if righteousness (justification) by faith is to be a reality. This point serves as a reminder that Lutherans formulate virtually all the classical doctrines in such a way that they bear a logical relatedness to the central Lutheran theme, justification by grace through faith, and the core concern to proclaim freedom and comfort to those burdened by the law. However, one must also bear in mind Lutheranism's ecumenical commitments. Its characteristic doctrinal formulations, related though they be to its core concern, are intended as representations of the catholic faith and therefore as appropriate to all churches.

One proof of a tradition's catholicity is its ability to speak the gospel in a variety of contexts to a variety of different concerns. (Such catholicity, richness of theological formulations, is clearly reflected in the Roman Catholic tradition, for example.) Thus one should expect to find in the Lutheran tradition as in the other mainline churches some doctrinal formulas which are conditioned by concerns other than comforting anxiety-ridden consciences. A number of themes in classic Lutheran theology, themes which gave rise to the development of Lutheran Pietism, address the question of order and the sanctified lifestyle in a way that converges with the theological themes of the Evangelical movement. These areas of agreement are particularly important for demonstrating to the Evangelical community and other churches that Lutheranism as well as Evangelicalism and other traditions can in fact nurture and portray a born-again (sanctified) existence. In fact, the Lutheran tradition's ability to address these issues is reflected even in its treatment of the doctrine of justification.

Chapter 22

Justification
and the Christian Life

Since the Lutheran Confessions designate justification as "the chief article of the entire Christian doctrine" it is appropriate to begin a discussion of Lutheranism and the theology of other mainline churches with this topic.[1] Unlike these other churches the Lutheran *Formula of Concord* and Luther himself suggest that justification by grace through faith should be the criterion for judging all other doctrines.[2]

Little wonder that this joyful doctrine should receive so much attention: it is good news to hear that we are justified, set right with God on the basis of what God has done, not contingent upon our performance of good works, our keeping of the law (Rom. 3:21ff.; Gal. 2;16). It is a message of affirmation, the unconditional affirmation of who one is, to know that "while we were [God's] enemies we were reconciled to God" (Rom. 5:10). To know that one is justified, accepted, and affirmed by God gives peace and confidence for facing both life and death (Rom. 5:1). But perhaps the crucial point is the recognition that all this comes without any effort or contribution on the believer's part. If justification and my salvation depended on me, I could never be certain that I had fulfilled all the requirements.

Given the overriding Lutheran concern to remove the burden of the law and its sense of demand from those oppressed and anguished by it, the Lutheran emphasis on justification follows quite logically. Also we must recall that with but one or two exceptions we did not find that Evangelicals, preoccupied as they are with other concerns related to regeneration and sanctification, give the doctrine of justification the central place it has in Lutheranism.[3] No doubt the difference in overriding concerns, the different conceptions of the core problem of the human situation, accounts for the different emphases Lutherans and Evangelicals accord the doctrine of justification (the same point can be made in accounting for Lutheranism's concentration on the doctrine and the failure to do so in other mainline churches).

Nevertheless, we must hasten to add that differences between Lutheranism and the Evangelical movement over the doctrine of justification seem to be differences of emphasis, not of kind. Contrary to popular mainline opinion, Evangelicals do not typically compromise the themes of *sola gratia* or *sola fide* (that we are saved by grace alone, faith alone) with a Pelagianism, implying that our good works contribute to salvation.[4] However, a crucial factor which also contributes to the differences between Lutherans and Evangelicals, and contributes to characteristic misunderstandings of Lutheranism, is the failure to recognize that Lutheranism treats the doctrine of justification in at least two distinct, though related ways.

The relationship between justification and sanctification

Two different ways of presenting the doctrine of justification by grace through faith can be identified in the Lutheran Confessions and in the heritage of other historic Protestant churches: (1) justification as purely forensic act[5] and (2) justification as union with (conformity to) Christ.[6] The latter concept implies that because in justification we receive all that Christ has and become as intimately united with him as a bride to her spouse, we become people who want to serve our neighbor just as Christ did (cf. Eph. 4:23-27; Rom. 6:1-11). The notion of the "blessed exchange" is at work here. Christ has taken all our sin and the consequences of death, and made it his own. Likewise we receive all he has—grace, life, and salvation. We are given a new identity and are made Christlike, much like what happens in the close bond of a marital relationship. Just as marriage partners who have spent a lifetime sharing with and loving each other come to take on some of the positive characteristics of their mate and spontaneously care and serve each other, so it is with the Christian who has been conformed to Christ through justification and baptism.

To be sure, the Christian does not always serve Christ with joy and spontaneity, just as no marriage is perfect. But as marriage partners need to renew their marriage by proclaiming their love for each other, so Christians crave God's proclamation of divine love for them through the doctrine of justification. This is why Lutheranism focuses so much on justification. Good works, regeneration, and sanctification do not require explicit attention any more than happily married couples require rigid rules to nurture their loving relationship.[7]

This accounts for why most Lutherans feel uneasy with the strict life-style standards of many Evangelical churches and organizations. To continue the Pauline analogy, to impose these standards on Christians feels a bit like having one's community or extended family tell me in quite specific terms how I must relate to my wife. Such standards are simply not necessary. In fact they interfere with the proclamation of God's justifying grace, just as they would interfere with one's relationship with a spouse.

This is not to say that those who maintain this understanding of justification forfeit a concern for living the Christian life (sanctification). The justified Christian is concerned to serve Christ as much as one who is in love is concerned to serve the lover. But the love, good works, come spontaneously in consequence of the relationship.

Often when Lutherans speak of the doctrine of justification they are not understood in this way by Evangelicals or other mainline churches, but are understood to regard justification as purely forensic. It is true that sometimes, in fact quite often, in popular piety this is the way Lutherans conceptualize the doctrine of justification.[8]

Forensic justification is best understood as a juridical metaphor. The guilty defendant is pronounced not guilty by the compassionate judge even though the defendant really had committed the crime. Thus the guilty party is regarded as not guilty (Rom. 4:5-8). Of course there is an element of this juridical metaphor in the concept of justification as conformity to Christ. Both concepts deem believers as totally *sinful* and *declared righteous* not on the basis of what they do. Because the self has continuity with itself (I am still the person I was 20 years ago), the justified sinner is still in some sense the person he or she was before, *totally* sinful. Thus there is an element of struggle in the Christian life, the struggle with evil, which is perhaps not as typical of the characteristic Evangelical emphases on sanctification, regeneration, and growth in grace. (Thus, though not without analogs in other traditions, Lutherans in particular speak of the justified Christian as *simul iustus et peccator,* totally righteous yet simultaneously totally sinful.)[9]

However, at some points the churches push this insight and the legal metaphor to their logical extreme. It is insisted that justification and sanctification must be logically distinguished, that justification does not include sanctification. Or, if the two are said to interpenetrate, it is not made clear conceptually how justification entails an actual holiness for believers, so that the holiness given in justification is more than merely a legal fiction. These are the characteristics of what I mean by a purely forensic view of justification.

There are good reasons for this viewpoint. It clarifies unambiguously that justification is contingent on no human activity, not even on the believer's response to grace. The problem with this conception is that it may imply that justification has no implications for the Christian life. This would obviously support the Evangelical concern that the mere proclamation of justification is not sufficient and must be supplemented by additional encouragement to lead the Christian life, sometimes by imposing life-style standards.

There is strong indication from Evangelical sources that the Evangelical movement largely understands justification in terms of the purely forensic understanding, with its distinction between justification and sanctification. For example, such a conception is implied (or at least the nature of the relationship between justification and sanctification is not clarified) in statements of The Evangelical Covenant Church (p. 13), the Southern Baptist Convention (IV), the National Association of Free Will Baptists (XII), all the churches associated with the Holiness movement, and Pentecostal churches which also maintain the "third blessing" theory.[10] (Pentecostal churches maintaining the two-step, "finished work" theory more closely approximate the concept of justification as conformity to Christ.) It even appears to be the dominant view in the theology of conservative Evangelically oriented Lutheran churches like The Lutheran Church–Missouri Synod, in its famous 1932 *Brief Statement* (17). Given the predominance of such an understanding of justification, a predominance which reflects its impact on Protestant Orthodoxy and Evangelicalism's indebtedness to Orthodoxy, it is little wonder that the Evangelical movement often appeals to the Commandments to provide a framework for Christian life.

It is obviously important for Evangelicals and other Christians in evaluating their reaction to Lutheranism's emphasis on justification to recall that justification need not be proclaimed as exclusively forensic. It may also be proclaimed as union with Christ, in which case justification includes the Evangelical concern for encouraging and stimulating Christian response. On these grounds the pronouncement of justification necessarily includes and encourages good works just as the marriage bond includes and encourages the life of love.

A renewed sense of this sort of understanding of the justification doctrine could make a helpful contribution to the Evangelical community, helping to guard against legalistic tendencies. Given this understanding, explicit description of the regenerate life and reliance on life-style standards for the sake of organizational and church discipline would not be as necessary. Rather the regenerate life-style can be nurtured simply through the proclamation of justification understood as union with Christ, through reminders of who the justified Christian is in virtue of his or her union with Christ (Rom. 6:2-5).

The applicability of this understanding of justification by grace through faith to the Evangelical movement and other mainline churches can easily be demonstrated. The concept of justification as union with Christ is affirmed by several Confessional traditions. It is evident in the Reformed *Second Helvetic Confession* (XV), the Methodist *EUB Confession of Faith* (IX), and the Roman Catholic Vatican II document *Lumen Gentium* (7). Also this conception is embraced by several Evangelically oriented Presbyterian churches subscribing to *The Westminster Confession* (XIII), by Evangelical churches and organizations as diverse as the Fédération des Eglises Evangéliques Baptistes de France (V), Pentecostal churches like the Assemblies of God (9, 5), which subscribe to the two-step, "finished-work" theory, and by the Wheaton '83 "Letter to the Churches" (I). It is also rooted in the movement's Fundamentalist heritage, as a reference is made to justification as union with Christ in *The Fundamentals* (II, 118-119; cf. VIII, 73; X, 30). This conception even has more ancient roots reflected in the literature of Evangelicalism's Puritan heritage, in the writings of the foremost theological influence on early American Puritanism, William Ames, and also in German Pietism with its notion of "mystical union of the believer with Christ."[11] A particularly clear and noteworthy contemporary instance of the concept's use by Evangelicals is evident in the *Confession of Faith* of the General Conference of Mennonite Brethren Churches (V). The statement reads:

> We believe that the Holy Spirit lives in every Christian and transforms him into the image of Christ. He empowers the believer to be an effective witness for Him.

Given the biblical basis and historical precedent in the Evangelical movement and other traditions for understanding justification as union with (conformity to) Christ, the Lutheran tradition can make an important contribution to the whole Church in sensitizing it to the proper and more extended use of this concept. Within Evangelicalism (as in all the churches) there is a particular need for this contribution, inasmuch as the biblical concept of union with Christ has been often misunderstood (Eph. 5:32; cf. Hos. 2:19-20).

Thus Evangelicals as diverse as Carl Henry and Donald Bloesch have sometimes spoken of union with Christ as something "on the way," presumably not given in justification. Or the concept is confused with the idea of the Christian's "imitation of Christ" (Eph. 5:1; 4:32).[12] In either case justification is necessarily correlated with human striving in order to achieve what God has not given fully in justification. The Evangelical commitment to the gospel of free grace can be seriously undercut if this tendency is not corrected.[13] It is evident that dialogue with the Lutheran tradition can be of service to the Evangelical community. Such a dialogue may help it correct certain legalistic abuses which can ensue as a result of misunderstanding the concept "conformity to Christ" or because of its emphasis on sanctification and the need to depict with specific rubrics the shape of the Christian life.

Third use of the law

Because the mainline Protestant churches have employed the notion of justification as "purely forensic," with no direct implications for Christian life, the problem of sanctification and the need to encourage the practice of a regenerate life-style by proposing definite rules must arise. In dealing with such matters these churches have a history of responding much like Evangelicals, by appealing to God's law as a guide for ordering the Christian life. This is called the "third use of the law." Its role in the Lutheran tradition is a further indication that Lutheranism is indeed sensitive to Evangelical concerns regarding the regenerate life-style and the need to see that it is nurtured and encouraged.

The Lutheran Confessions speak of three uses of the law (God's commandments).[14] The first use of the law is the restraining of evil, as secular government employs it. This is the basis for Lutheranism's social ethics. The second use of the law is the principal use, the law proclaimed to condemn sin in preparation for hearing the gospel. The third use of the law is that of a guide for the Christian life. This third use clearly seems related to the Evangelical reliance on an ethic shaped by the law, where behavioral expectations are spelled out quite specifically.

Something akin to the concept of the third use of the law appears in the Anglican tradition's *The Thirty-Nine Articles* (XXXV), the Roman Catholic Council of Trent's *Decree Concerning Justification* (XI, Can. 18), Methodism's *General Rules.* and John Calvin's *Institutes of*

the Christian Religion (II/VII.12-14), as he identifies it as the law's
"principal use." Nevertheless, the concept is a neuralgic theme in
contemporary Lutheranism, often dividing mainline Lutherans who
deny the concept from Evangelically oriented Lutherans who embrace
it.[15]

Many mainline Lutheran theologians have rejected the concept of a
distinct third use of the law.[16] The argument proceeds along several
lines. A third use of the law is rejected in deference to the claim of
the *Apology of the Augsburg Confession* (IV.204) that "the Law always
accuses," and to Luther's own insistence both on the radical differentiation between law and gospel as well as on the Christian's freedom
from the law.[17] (The distinction between the law [God's word of com-
mand] and the gospel [God's word of promise/justification] is central
to Lutheran theology in order that justification, the gospel, not be mixed
with works of the law. Although this distinction is a controversial matter
among Evangelicals, it is a crucial affirmation for some of them. Significantly enough, this suggests a similar concern among segments of
Evangelicalism that the doctrine of justification be purely presented,
not mixed with works of the law.)[18] Subsequent exposition shows that
this concern is valid only if the third use of the law is understood as
an extraneous demand on believers rather than a description of the life-
style to which they have been conformed.

A second rationale for rejection of the third use of the law is the
contention that the concept was developed at the end of the Reformation
by those who misunderstood Luther. After all, it is argued, Luther
himself never employed the term. Although this criticism cannot receive a full response, it can be argued that a reference to a third use
of the law does appear in a 1522 sermon of Luther. Granted, it has
been alleged that the Reformer has a different meaning in mind for the
term. But the authenticity of the text in which the term appears is
unchallengeable.[19] And a few examples elsewhere of Luther's comments on the subject offer more insight:

> We concede that good works and love must be taught; but this must be
> in its proper time and place, that is, when the question has to do with
> works, apart from this chief doctrine.[20]

> In due time we shall discuss the teaching that the Law and good works
> ought to be done.[21]

> Then what is the purpose of keeping it if it does not justify? The final
> cause of obedience to the Law by the righteous is not righteousness in

the sight of God, which is received by faith alone, but the peace of the world, gratitude toward God, and a good example by which others are invited to believe the Gospel.[22]

These statements, particularly the last one, indicate that in his practice Luther did see a place for teaching the law to the justified as a guide to Christian living. These references plus a little-noticed distinction which he posits between how the law is to be preached to the impious and how it is to be preached to the pious imply that something akin to the third use of the law has a legitimate place in the reformer's thought.[23]

Another factor in the rejection of a distinct third use of the law by a number of neo-Lutheran theologians relates to their dependence on a neoorthodox theory of interpretation. Recall that neoorthodox theology posited a *functionalist* view of Scripture. That is to say that Scripture itself is not the Word of God. It *becomes* the Word of God when it *functions* to render God present. So likewise for Lutherans subscribing to this hermeneutic it must follow that the difference between law and gospel cannot be determined on the basis of their distinct content but only on the basis of how they function. Whatever condemns is law; whatever gives life and justification is gospel. Thus one cannot talk about the law, some command portion of Scripture or proclamation which takes the grammatical form of a command, functioning as a guide to Christian life. If it succeeds in that function it gives life and so must be gospel.

Criticisms could be raised regarding the subjectivist implications of such an interpretation, its tendency to confuse law and gospel since their difference is rendered merely a matter of one's perspective on how they affect the believer. More basically one must question whether this interpretation should be permitted to override the commonsense wisdom of referring to New Testament exhortations as law (Gal. 6:1-10; Col. 3:12ff.; James 2:14-26).[24] Although there is precedent in the Lutheran heritage for distinguishing law from gospel solely on the basis of their distinct functions, one can also find precedent there for distinguishing law from gospel on the basis of their distinct content.[25] Thus it does not seem appropriate for mainline Lutherans to reject the third use of the law as an absolutely unpalatable Lutheran alternative, particularly in view of the traditional evidence at hand. At least in interests of Lutheran unity and its ecumenical implications, critics could refer to the concept as a legitimate but unnecessary formulation (unnecessary, insofar as good works are given in justification when justification is proclaimed in terms of union with Christ).

What precisely is this concept of a third use of the law? The Lutheran *Formula of Concord* (SD VI.18) provides an authoritative and clarifying insight. (It is interesting to note that the concept was formulated for a purpose analogous to its use by Evangelicals, to encourage the practice of Christian life in response to those who seemed unconcerned about it. Likewise, Lutheran Pietism, though it did not normally make explicit appeal to this concept, regularly employed a similar conception with its emphasis on the need for the Christian to imitate Christ.)[26] The authors of the *Formula* write in a manner more or less consistent with Calvin (*Institutes*, II/VII.12-14) but in such a way that perhaps a more precise distinction of the uses of the law is made: "Thus though they [believers] are never without Law, they are not under [*sub lege*] but in the Law [*in lege*], they live and walk in the Law of the Lord, and yet do nothing by the compulsion of the Law."

This distinction between being "in" the law and "under" the law is crucial for understanding and appreciating the concept of the third use of the law. It speaks to the concern that a third use of the law might compromise the insistence on the law's accusatory function in distinction from the gospel. Insofar as the law confronts us in our sin, insofar as we are "under" the law, it does indeed accuse and condemn. But because in justification we have been conformed to Christ, take on all that he has including his fulfillment of the law, we receive Christ-like identities which yearn to fulfill the law (cf. Rom. 10:4; 7:22). In that sense, believers as new creatures are "in" the law, not "under" it. Thus as they are new creatures, the law does not condemn them but describes who they are as persons conformed to Christ.

The distinction between law and gospel need not be compromised on these grounds. Only the gospel *gives* salvation; the law functions as a mere *description* of the kind of existence Christ has given the believer and his restored creation. (To deny at least this much continuity between law and gospel would imply denying that God's redemptive work and Christ aimed to restore creation and the law to their original status before the Fall.) It is quite evident that appeal to the concept of a third use of the law, understood in this way, need not necessarily overturn other core Lutheran commitments.

In short, the third use of the law is best understood as a kind of identity description of what the Christian already is and does in virtue of Christ's justifying work. It is a reminder to Christians of who they are, much like parents may encourage their children to great heights with loving reminders of their potentiality (see Romans 6). On these grounds an appeal to the law as a guide to Christian living, even strictures on certain behavior, as is typical of the Evangelical movement and a few other Confessional traditions, could presumably be integrated within Lutheran commitments. The only stipulation would need to be that such life-style standards be regarded exclusively as *descriptions* of the Christian life, not as demands on Christians.

From this perspective, when Evangelical life-style standards are represented clearly as attempts to describe to the baptized what the Christian life is like, all the mainline churches, including Lutheranism, could presumably appropriate selectively successful Evangelical evangelism and stewardship methods which use the law as a guide to Christian life. (The precise amendments necessary for mainliners to appropriate with theological integrity the Kennedy Evangelism Method and the Church Growth Models would require a book itself. Our remarks do provide some criteria for undertaking the task of appropriating these profoundly successful methods.)

In the same manner the view of some Evangelicals that the believer may attain perfection need not necessarily be church dividing if understood in the same context, as an attempt simply to describe what the baptized Christian life is like. The believer is totally righteous (perfect) yet still a sinner. To be sure, Reformed and Baptist Confessional statements implicitly reject the idea that a Christian might achieve perfection. And the Lutheran Confessional writings condemn a use of the term "perfection." Presumably, at least in the case of Lutheranism, the condemnation applies to those Anabaptists not using the concept with these qualifications, rather affirming the outright sinlessness of the believer.[27] However, even with this qualification, none of these traditions authorize the use of the concept of perfection. Nevertheless, its use by others would not seem to be church dividing or in violation of the heritage of these traditions. This is evidenced by the fact that perfection as a goal for which to strive is affirmed by several mainline churches, not just by Methodism but also by the Reformed *Heidelberg Catechism* (Q.115), the Baptist *Second London Confession* (XIII.3), and by the Roman Catholic church, at least in the Second Vatican Council (*Lumen Gentium* [39-40]). And it is also evidenced in the Lutheran tradition as the concept of perfection was employed by the Lutheran pietist Spener, and its use did not split the Lutheran church.[28] Thus one may ask why the use of the concept by Evangelicals should be problematic for church unity.

On questions of life-style standards, the concept of perfection, and the role of the law in guiding the Christian life, Lutheranism can offer an important contribution to Evangelicals. By insisting that the law and these related concepts never be used as a *demand* to conform to a given life-style, but only to condemn sin or to describe what Christian life is like, Lutheranism can help the Evangelical movement and other traditions to avoid the dangers of an encroaching legalism.

Human response as preparation and confirmation

We noted in Part III that Evangelicals, in order to underscore the importance of regeneration and a corresponding life-style, often employ the notion of repentance or some other act of the will inspired by grace as a kind of preparation for regeneration. On other occasions they regard the regenerate life-style as a kind of proof or confirmation of one's salvation (Phil. 1:6).[29] It will perhaps come as a surprise to some that these themes can also be identified in a number of mainline traditions, particularly when they address concerns related to the doctrine of sanctification, the Christian life.

With regard to the latter theme, works as a confirmation of faith and one's salvation, it is not surprising, given the influence of the Presbyterian/Reformed, Baptist, Anglican, and Methodist traditions on the Evangelical movement, to find this theme in these mainline traditions.[30] Yet both the Lutheran *Apology of the Augsburg Confession* (IV.275-276; XX.13-15) and the *Formula of Concord* (SD IV.33) affirm the notion that good works confirm one's salvation. The passage from the *Formula*, quoting the *Apology*, emerges from a dispute with those who wished to deny any need for concern about the character of Christian life, for good works were regarded by them as detrimental to salvation. The text reads:

> The Apology offers a fine example as to when and how, on the basis of the preceding, the exhortation to do good works can be instilled without darkening the doctrine of faith and justification. . . The Apology states in Art.XX: "Peter teaches why we should do good works, namely, that we confirm our calling, that is, that we do not fall from our calling by lapsing into sin. He says: 'Do good works so that you remain in your heavenly calling, lest you fall away. . . .'"

It is striking that when historic Lutheranism has been preoccupied with concerns akin to the overriding concern of the Evangelical movement and the Reformed tradition, specifically how to nurture and order the regenerate, sanctified life-style, it has drawn on conceptions more typical of these other traditions. One suspects that there may be a pattern in the history of Christian thought. When churches address similar concerns they tend to employ similar theological concepts.

As we now consider the Evangelical reliance on the concept of a preparation for grace (recall, for example, that Billy Graham's advice on "How to Be Born Again" implies that the believer makes some sort of preparation for conversion), it is helpful to note that this concept has a parallel in Roman Catholicism. Both Thomas Aquinas and the Council of Trent insist on a necessary role for the human will in preparation for grace. However, particularly in the case of St. Thomas, this is correlated with the insistence that "God saves man by faith without any preceding merits," that justification is by grace.[31]

Note again that there is no Pelagian compromise of the primacy of grace here. Perhaps more surprising is the suggestion of such a conception in the Reformed *Heidelberg Catechism* (Q.116) and in the Lutheran *Formula of Concord* (SD II.90). (Philip Melanchthon, Luther's principal colleague in Wittenberg, and the author of several of the Lutheran Confessional documents, including *The Augsburg Confession*, almost explicitly embraced the Roman Catholic scheme with his idea of the "three concurring causes of good action"—the Word preached, the Holy Spirit, and the human will.)[32] The text of the *Formula* reads:

> Toward this work [conversion] the will of the person who is to be converted does nothing, *but* only *lets God work* in him, until he is converted. Then he cooperates with the Holy Spirit in subsequent good work. . . [emphasis added].

The idea that the converted person "lets God work" on him or her in conversion clearly implies the element of human cooperation, motivated by grace in the process of salvation. There is certainly an intriguing family resemblance among this Lutheran Confessional statement, the Roman Catholic concept of a preparation for grace, and a similar insistence by Evangelicals on the role and importance of human response to grace. To the degree Lutherans accept the authority of the entire *Book of Concord* (many Lutheran churches influenced by neo-Lutheranism do not), Lutherans must begin to consider the possibility that these Roman Catholic and Evangelical themes might be regarded as legitimate Lutheran theological alternatives. In view of the appearance of the theme of preparation for grace in *The Heidelberg Catechism*, a similar set of questions is posed for the mainline Presbyterian/Reformed churches.

The agreement between the Evangelical movement and the Roman Catholic tradition regarding the Roman Catholic notion of a preparation for grace warrants attention. It is especially noteworthy in view of the number of analysts who observe that an emphasis on sanctification or holiness typifies not just the Evangelical movement but also the Roman Catholic tradition. In a way, not unlike the Evangelical heritage, the theologically formative medieval Roman Catholic theological tradition and the Council of Trent were developed at times when the surrounding culture was in a stage of flux. Thus order needed to be imposed on the culture in order that it could be maintained as a Christian culture, and this concern for order manifested itself in attention to the shape of the Christian life (sanctification).[33]

In view of their common concerns and common theological themes, at least on the issues of the role of the human will in the process of salvation and official positions on biblical inerrancy, one is tempted to regard these traditions as kindred spirits. To be sure, important differences between Evangelicals and Roman Catholics on the issues of Church, ministry, and sacraments remain. Yet an appreciation of what they do share in common suggests that the anti-Catholic sentiment in the Evangelical movement need not be regarded as a necessary consequence of its own theological profile or of Protestantism in general.

Likewise the likelihood that the Roman Catholic–Evangelical language of the human role in preparing oneself for grace may be a legitimate alternative for the Reformation churches represents interesting possibilities for Evangelical–mainline relationships. To the degree that Evangelicals are able to make clear, as Roman Catholics do, that the preparatory act of the will, repentance, is itself a work of grace, such an Evangelical theme must be regarded as a legitimate Christian, non-Pelagian alternative. At least, this theme need not be considered Pelagian when it is employed for the same purposes as the Reformers, Roman Catholics, and Evangelicals—namely, to emphasize sanctification and to encourage the practice of the Christian life.[34]

By the same token, the presence of this theme as well as the concept of perfection and good works as confirmation of one's salvation in Lutheranism, Roman Catholicism, Presbyterianism, and Methodism challenges certain Evangelical stereotypes of the mainline. It challenges Evangelicals to concede that a concern to emphasize the importance of practicing the regenerate life-style is very much a part of the mainline churches. Luther's claim in *The 95 Theses* (1), that "the entire life of believers [is] to be one of repentance," further confirms this observation with respect to Lutheranism.

Reflections

The Lutheran emphasis on the primacy of grace, the centrality of justification, may teach a helpful lesson to the whole church regarding the way the Evangelical/pietist emphasis on sanctification should properly be employed. The lesson seems to be that this emphasis on sanctification and its related theological concepts may be properly used in the life of the Church, even in Lutheran churches. Contemporary mainline Lutheranism has tended to reject a distinct third use of the law and thereby also the Evangelical concern with sanctification. The result has been that Lutherans and other mainline churches have communicated a message of permissiveness to the Evangelical movement and also closed off their own membership as much as possible to appropriating valid insights from Evangelicalism. The consequence has been polarization, not just between the Evangelical movement and the mainline. Sometimes the polarization has come within the mainline churches with Evangelically oriented mainliners choosing the Evangelical emphases on regeneration and their associated theological themes over the traditional and acceptable teachings of their own church. As a result, mainline church leadership has suffered further blows to its credibility.

In addition to opening all mainline churches up to the validity of Evangelical theological emphases, Lutheranism's own emphases offer another lesson to the Church catholic. This more profound lesson is the realization that the Evangelical emphases on regenerate life-style, sanctification, and their associated concepts are not ultimately necessary. At least they are not necessary in the Church's ministry if the theme of justification as conformity to Christ would be more properly presented. The Church may then be called to a realization that the proclamation of justification is itself sufficient, for it gives all that believers need, including the regenerate life-style.

Good works do indeed follow spontaneously from faith, given this understanding of justification. They follow spontaneously, just as love for others follows spontaneously when one is loved. Thus Lutherans teach the Church catholic that justification is the sufficient standard for all doctrines, including what it means to be born again. Evangelicals need to begin to appreciate that a concern about regeneration and being born again is reflected every time mainline Christians proclaim justification as conformity to Christ.

Chapter 23

Church and Ministry

A relationship between the doctrine of justification by grace through faith and the doctrines of the Church, ministry, and the sacraments of several mainline churches is readily apparent. With regard to the Church, the classic Lutheran definition is given in *The Augsburg Confession* (VII): "The church is the assembly of saints in which the Gospel is taught purely and the sacraments are administered rightly." Thus, the Church is defined not in terms of believers and what they do but rather in terms of God's action of Word and sacrament in creating the Church (Eph. 5:25-27). As such, the Church is not so much an institution as an "event" which happens whenever the Word is purely preached and the sacraments are rightly administered. The doctrine of justification is reflected in this view of the Church insofar as the emphasis is on the primacy of God's grace in creating the Church. As we have noted, something like this viewpoint is reflected, not just in Lutheranism, but also in Anglicanism (*The Thirty-Nine Articles*, XIX), Methodism (*Articles of Religion*, 13), as well as to some extent even in the Roman Catholic church's Second Vatican Council (*Lumen Gentium*, 1, 6, 64; *In Quibus Rerum Circumstantiis* [1972], II), and the Reformed tradition (*The Heidelberg Catechism*, Q.54).

In like manner, the characteristic Lutheran view of the ministry reflects the emphasis on the primacy of God's grace. Again *The Augsburg Confession* (V) provides the classic definition. Like the Church, the ministry is defined in terms of Word and sacraments—viz., not in terms of the person of the officeholder but in terms of God's actions, the Word (which is God's Word) and the sacraments (which God gives). This conception is also affirmed by the Reformed tradition in its *Second Helvetic Confession* (XVIII). And most prominently in Lutheranism— perhaps more only by implication in some other Protestant traditions— this conception of the ordained ministry is linked to a strong affirmation of the priesthood of all believers and a tendency at some points to minimize the distinction between clergy and laity.[1] At other points, the Lutheran tradition as well as virtually every other mainline Protestant church (to some extent, even the Baptist and Mennonite heritages) also posit a high, in some cases an episcopal, view of the ministry which emphasizes the clergy's distinction from the laity.[2]

Finally, insofar as the sacraments are conceived of as bearing Christ's real presence and thereby capable of effecting something objectively life-transforming for those who receive them, they also give testimony to the centrality of justification by grace through faith.[3] This is particularly evident in the Lutheran tradition. Although Lutheranism is a liturgically oriented church embodying many of the worship practices of Roman Catholicism, Lutherans do not embrace transubstantiation (the idea that the sacramental elements are no longer the earthly elements they appear to be, but have been transformed into Christ himself). Nor do they subscribe to consubstantiation (the idea that the sacramental elements and Christ's body combine to form a hybrid substance). Rather, Lutherans insist that the elements remain elements, yet at the same time miraculously Christ is "in, with, and under" the elements.[4]

Of course, such a conception poses some challenges for explanation. How can bread (or water) be both itself and the body of Christ (or the baptism of Christ) simultaneously? Perhaps the best response is an analogy. As love is really present in the physical embrace of a father for his son, yet the physical embrace has its own integrity and reality, so likewise Christ can be really present in the physical elements though they remain physical elements. Or to use the more familiar Lutheran analogy with reference to Christ: As Christ can be both God and man in one person, so the sacramental element can be both Christ's body and the element simultaneously.[5]

In any case, this concept of the real presence in the sacraments and the affirmation of infant baptism give testimony to the primacy of God's grace. This testimony is quite evident in the Lutheran tradition's insistence that the sacraments are worked by God. While the Reformed heritage largely maintains that Christ is not present to unbelievers, Lutherans hold that the sacraments are valid even apart from faith. This commitment seems to be reflected in the practice of infant baptism by Lutheranism and several other churches.[6] Given such suppositions, the sacraments offer testimony to the fact that God's action is not dependent on human response. This testimony is even more apparent in the insistence especially of Lutherans, Anglicans, and Roman Catholics that (although sin or its inclination is not entirely purged in the recipient) regeneration actually takes place in baptism (so that the sacrament is God's action on us) and is not a mere testimony that recipients give to their prior regeneration (see Rom. 6:2-4; Col. 2:11-15, 20; Titus 3:5).[7]

The Lutheran argument for infant baptism is interesting to observe. Because the biblical evidence for this practice is meager, limited only to a few references to the baptism of entire households (Acts 16:15, 33; 1 Cor. 1:16), Luther in *The Large Catechism* (IV.50-51) was led to argue for it on grounds of the predominance of the practice throughout the Church's history.[8] Thus, despite its commitment to *sola scriptura*, Lutheranism is willing to appeal to the (presumably infallible) teaching authority of the Church as determined by the reception of a given doctrine by the whole Church throughout the ages. By a similar appeal to the Church's consensus, the Lutheran *Formula of Concord* (SD Rule and Norm 11,8) establishes the authority of the Confessional writings. They are deemed authoritative in view of their widespread use.

The similarities between this sort of appeal to the trustworthiness of the Church's teaching authority as established through long-term consensus, the Eastern Orthodox concept of the *consensus fidelium*, and the Roman Catholic notion of the "ordinary magisterium" (infallible teaching established by the consensus of the bishops throughout the Church's history) are quite apparent.[9] (In *The Thirty-Nine Articles*, XX, the Anglican tradition also affirms a role for the Church in offering authoritative interpretations of the Christian faith.) We have noted previously that despite its staunch commitment to the sole authority of the Bible most segments of the Evangelical movement function with de facto appeals to the authority of the Church's teaching tradition, at least insofar as they accept the "infallible" character of the creeds and embrace certain historic Confessional documents.[10]

Avenues for rapprochement from the Evangelical side

One can find an openness on the part of the Evangelical community to accept the Lutheran, often characteristically Protestant, viewpoint on the doctrines of Church, ministry, and sacraments as a legitimate Evangelical alternative. Thus, one can seem to identify magisterial Reformationlike affirmations of God's role in creating the Church, in its "objective" character as something more than individual believers, not just in Reformed/Presbyterian churches associated with the move-ment, but also in *The Frankfurt Declaration on the Fundamental Crisis of Mission* (27), in doctrinal statements by two Evangelically related French Baptist churches, and in the *Statement of Faith* of Fuller Theo-logical Seminary (8).[11] And although a number of Evangelical churches insist on certain conditions for membership such as regeneration or the like, none goes so far as to insist that all members of its church are without sin, a position which would otherwise violate the Lutheran *Formula of Concord* (Ep. XIII.9; SD XII.14) and to some extent even conflict with the Baptist tradition as it manifests itself in a *Short Con-fession of Faith* (22).[12]

In like manner the Lutheran affirmation of the real presence and its liturgical orientation are acceptable as Evangelical alternatives. This is obvious not just from the participation of Lutherans, Anglicans, and Calvinistically oriented Presbyterians in the Evangelical movement. The *Frankfurt Declaration on the Fundamental Crisis of Mission* (22) implicitly affirms a real presence of Christ in the sacrament. Given the international character of the group drafting this statement, the ac-ceptance of this more or less Lutheran orientation is all the more im-pressive.

Also noteworthy in this connection is the impact of "Catholic (Ec-umenical) Evangelicals" on the Evangelical movement. Their call for renewed liturgical sensitivity and appreciation of the sacraments is reflected in the increased openness towards these matters we have noted among certain Evangelical Baptists and Pentecostals. It is quite evident that although the Evangelical establishment is in disagreement with the real presence view of the sacraments it will not allow this to be a source of alienation from fellow Evangelicals.[13]

Having found Christ in their fellow Evangelicals who have been baptized as infants, the question could be reasonably posed to Evan-gelicals who insist on adult baptism why their churches could not in turn recognize the legitimacy of the practice of *infant* baptism in the churches in which their fellow Evangelicals have been nurtured. (Given the relative unimportance Evangelicals place on the Church in com-parison to the individual's faith, why should not on Evangelical grounds the de facto recognition of the validity of a brother's or sister's infant baptism entail formal ecclesial recognition of churches practicing infant baptism?) Were the logic of this point carried out, it would negate any specter of condemnation of Evangelicals by the Lutheran and Reformed Confessions in connection with the condemnation of Anabaptist bap-tismal practice by the *Formula of Concord* (Ep. XII.23; SD XII.11-12,31) and *The Second Helvetic Confession* (XX). At any rate, the problem of mainline church–Evangelical rapprochement is at this point no more complex than the challenge facing magisterial Reformation and Roman Catholic churches in seeking to overcome church-division with any of the churches presently rejecting infant baptism.[14]

With the doctrine of the ministry there exists much more outright agreement between the mainline churches and the Evangelical movement. Like the Lutheran tradition the Evangelical movement tends to define the ministry in terms of its functions, sometimes as a ministry of Word and sacraments. As Lutheranism, in particular, emphasizes the priesthood of all believers and sometimes speaks as if the authority for the office of the ministry were derived from the universal priesthood, so such a view is quite evident among Evangelicals.[15]

It is also true that as one can find a "high" view of the office of ministry in Lutheranism and other mainline churches, an emphasis on the pastor's authority over against the Church, one can also identify a "high" view in the Evangelical movement. This is reflected not just in the presence of several episcopally oriented churches within the Evangelical movement, but also in the distancing between clergy and laity in the movement's characteristic elevation of clergy over the laity, insofar as clergy are understood to possess higher levels of spirituality and are to function as spiritual examples to their congregations.[16] Also the tendency towards strong unilateral pastoral leadership in many Evangelical congregations should not be overlooked as indicating the presence of this high view of ministry within the movement. This and the other Evangelical positions on the doctrines of Church and ministry are quite relevant to the problem of Evangelical–Roman Catholic relationships. In view of the tensions presently existing between these traditions, special attention to promising issues for dialogue is warranted.

Roman Catholics and Evangelicals in dialogue

Previously we have noted that, despite the Evangelical movement's anti-Catholic propensities, the two traditions are kindred spirits, at least in issues related to the doctrine of salvation. Both share a common commitment to something like the centrality of sanctification, to the quest for holiness and the regenerate life-style. Both often employ similar conceptuality in depicting the process of salvation.[17]

As regards the doctrine of the ministry, the Evangelical openness to a "high" view, and its willingness to endorse an episcopal ministry of bishops suggest that the Evangelical movement could *in principle* accept the Roman Catholic ministry as a valid ministry, as long as the office of bishop were not regarded as a constitutive element of the essence of the Church. (The major problem would be papal and episcopal authority, as it would be for most mainline Protestant churches.) Likewise from the Roman Catholic side difficulties with Evangelical ministry must emerge regarding its ordination of women, married clergy, and lack of apostolic succession among its bishops. Yet these are problems which pertain to Roman Catholic relationships with virtually every Protestant community, and a few Evangelical churches would support Rome's position on women's ordination. Thus the Evangelical movement does not appear to pose a special problem to Roman Catholic ecumenical endeavors, at least not in these areas.

Differences on the doctrine of the Church could be a special problem. The Roman Catholic concept of the Church as "sacrament," as enunciated by Vatican II in its *Dogmatic Constitution on the Church (Lumen Gentium)* (1), could suggest that the Church is a mediator of salvation. Assigning this function to the Church is a theme Evangelicals, with their tendency to place more emphasis on the "individual's piety," would surely reject. The issue is particularly problematic if, as some seem to imply, the sacramentality of the Church implies for Rome that the Church must on its own *independent initiative* mediate salvation.[18]

If this be the intention of the Vatican II statement, a problem is posed for relationships between Roman Catholics and all Protestant churches. However, at least at one point in Vatican II (*Lumen Gentium*, 64) the Church is designated as a mother begetting new life for Christians through Word and sacrament, a position that certainly seems acceptable to Lutherans (see the *Large Catechism*, II.42), who also see the Church as a mother nurturing the Christian life, as well as to Evangelicals of the Reformed traditions and to any others who insist that outside the Church there is no salvation. Moreover, a kind of official agreement that the Roman Catholic insistence on the Church's role as an instrument of salvation does not compromise justification *sola Christi* has been achieved by Roman Catholics and Anglicans in their international dialogue, in which case Roman Catholic ecclesiology need not be deemed illegitimate on Evangelical grounds.[19] After all, the Church functions in practice as an instrument of grace for many Evangelicals insofar as most Evangelical communities pay a great deal of attention to community fellowship and its role in Christian nurture.

Certainly, an emerging appreciation of the Roman Catholic tradition has been surfacing among contemporary Evangelicals. No doubt this is in part a consequence of the "Catholic [Ecumenical] Evangelicals" like Robert Webber and Donald Bloesch, who have sought to call the Evangelical movement back to its Catholic roots in regard to a higher appreciation of the sacraments, the historic liturgy, Church authority, the creeds, and Christian unity.[20]

No less prominent Evangelicals than Carl Henry and Robert Johnston recently have praised Roman Catholicism for its courageous affirmation of authority and biblical infallibility.[21] Also some Evangelicals like Donald Bloesch suggest the desirability of the Evangelical movement's reappropriation of the cult of saints in order to enhance devotional life. Already some American Evangelicals hesitant about the women's movement have appealed to the Virgin Mary as a model for Christian women.[22] Indications in the literature of Vatican II (*Sacrosanctum Concilium* 104, 111; *Lumen Gentium* 51, 60, 62) suggest that this is precisely the sense in which Mary and the other saints function in the Roman Catholic tradition. They mediate grace only in the Evangelical sense, as examples or models inspiring faith, not as departed souls who must complete Christ's work for him.

If not the doctrine of the saints, the sacraments appear at first glance to be a barrier to Evangelical–Roman Catholic relationships. But even this issue perhaps need not be an insurmountable barrier. For example, the Roman Catholic position on transubstantiation no longer need be regarded as problematic. Through ecumenical dialogues contemporary Roman Catholic theologians have begun to interpret this concept purely as an affirmation of Christ's real presence in the sacrament, not as an explanation of *how* he is present. Such an interpretation means that the status of the sacramental elements after consecration need no longer be a significant question. Thus Roman Catholics have come to regard themselves as in fundamental agreement with Lutheran and Anglican understandings of the sacraments.[23]

We already have noted that Evangelicals do not regard the emphasis on the real presence in other traditions as a barrier to fellowship with them. Thus the Roman Catholic treatment of the real presence presumably need not be a barrier to fellowship for Evangelicals. (It is tempting to suggest that this Evangelical openness to belief in the real presence in the sacraments is a function of the relative unimportance the movement assigns to the sacraments. However, it seems more likely that this openness may be a function of the emerging sacramental awareness stimulated by "Catholic [Ecumenical] Evangelicals" and a general sense of sacramental appreciation presently affecting Methodism and the Reformed churches.)[24]

In like manner Roman Catholics have been reinterpreting the idea of *ex opere operato* (the sacraments work by working, sometimes interpreted in a mechanistic way as overriding the importance of faith). In the context of some recent ecumenical dialogues, contemporary Roman Catholics have interpreted this concept to mean simply that one receives grace in the sacraments regardless of the recipient's faith, yet this grace is effective only when it is received in faith.[25] This viewpoint is almost in full agreement with the claim of the Lutheran *Large Catechism* (IV.52,53,55,36) that the sacrament is "valid" apart from faith but does one good only if he or she has faith. It was also found to be agreeable to a number of the Pentecostals participating in the international Roman Catholic–Pentecostal Dialogue (I, 33). Although some Evangelicals in the World Evangelical Fellowship who supported the recent WEF statement on Roman Catholicism would disagree (CEPRC, VIII), this seems consistent with the Evangelical commitment to emphasizing Christian response, yet in such a way that the objective character of divine grace is unambiguously affirmed.

Evangelicals who reject the concepts of the real presence or baptismal regeneration on grounds that such conceptions undercut the importance of faith and a concern for Christian nurture need to recognize that such concerns are not overlooked by traditions with a high view of the sacraments. In fact, with regard to baptismal regeneration we should reiterate that many Evangelicals in a 1971 statement of the National Association of Evangelicals (USA) asserted that such a doctrine need not divide Christians.

Even the Roman Catholic notion of the Mass as sacrifice does not seem necessarily to be a barrier to fellowship. Roman Catholics today may follow Thomas Aquinas and the Council of Trent in interpreting this concept of propitiatory sacrifice. Neither was inclined to regard the Mass as a propitiatory sacrifice in the sense that the Mass is a work which completes what is lacking in Christ's death on the cross (as Protestants thought Catholics were teaching at the time of the Reformation). Rather, the Mass is seen as a sacrifice only in the sense that the one true sacrifice, Christ, is present in it, and the work of redemption is carried on in us. It might be deemed a sacrifice also insofar as in the sacrament the sacrifice of praise is offered, and through it is given redemptive grace that drives recipients back into the world to serve God, to sacrifice themselves.[26]

The idea that the Lord's Supper may be deemed a sacrifice in the sense that in the sacrament *Christ* sacrifices *us,* makes recipients self-sacrificing people, was affirmed by Luther in his *Treatise on the New*

Testament (WA 6, 369, 3; LW 35, 99). There seems to be precedent for the use of this conception not just among Lutherans, but even among Evangelicals (cf. Rom. 12:1). Thus, when the Fuller Seminary *Statement of Faith* (9) speaks of the Church's summons "to *offer* acceptable worship," this is most suggestive of the concept of a eucharistic sacrifice, a sacrifice of praise in response to God's grace.[27] There are good indications that many of the traditional Roman Catholic themes, which seem to divide it from Protestantism, could, to the surprise of many, be deemed appropriate Evangelical alternatives.

Of course, it would be a mistake to conclude that all barriers between Evangelicals and Roman Catholics have been removed. The questions of the validity of Evangelical ministry (since Evangelicals do not maintain apostolic succession) and the number of sacraments remain. Both of these issues relate in part to the role tradition validly plays in the Church. The discussion in a subsequent chapter will deal with this question; for the present it is helpful to note that there may be some opening in the Evangelical heritage to deal with the problem of the number of sacraments.

Recall that several Evangelical churches, notably the Church of God (Cleveland, Tenn.) (15), The Brethren Church (Ashland, Ohio) (3/9), and the Mennonite Brethren Churches (VI), continue the practice of washing the saints' feet as a kind of third "ordinance" alongside of baptism and the Lord's Supper. The addition of this other biblically based rite seems in principle to open up the Evangelical movement to consider the arguments for additional sacraments. Thus if the addition of one ordinance does not lead the Evangelical establishment to break fellowship with the churches which practice foot washing, why should the additional five sacraments of Roman Catholicism be any more problematic? Additionally, the fact that at least two Evangelical churches, The Brethren Church (Ashland, Ohio) (3/9) and The Christian and Missionary Alliance (8) continue to practice anointing the sick is quite significant, as the analogies to the Roman Catholic sacrament of extreme unction are quite apparent.[28] The words of the Lutheran *Apology of the Augsburg Confession* (XIII.17) seem particularly applicable: "No intelligent person will quibble about the number of Sacraments. . . ."

To be sure, no concrete agreements have been established in these reflections. The purpose has merely been to point to directions Evangelicals and Roman Catholics might pursue in helping to overcome anti-Catholic sentiment within the Evangelical movement. As a matter of theological principle, relationships between these traditions should be no more difficult than Roman Catholic relationships with most mainline Protestant churches.

In this connection the Evangelical–Roman Catholic vision of the principal task of ministry, to nurture sanctification and structure the Christian life, is an important commonality. It manifests itself in their use of common themes to depict the process of salvation. Of course, the concern to provide structure for the Christian life was more oriented for the medieval Catholic church towards structuring society as a whole. The Evangelical movement, by contrast, influenced by Pietism as well as the American and Anabaptist paradigm of church-state separation, was more directed towards the individual and his or her spiritual development or towards the base community which was small enough to structure itself locally or through the personal authority of its leaders. This difference seems to manifest itself in the treatment of the doctrines of Church, sacraments, ministry and Church hierarchy, as well as in the attitude towards liturgy. Thus, Roman Catholicism tends to reflect a more communal, hierarchical, objective orientation in its treatment of these doctrines, while the Evangelical movement has a much more individualistic, subjectivist view of the Church and sacraments, and a noticeably less hierarchical view of the ordained ministry. Roman Catholicism defines the Church not as a group of individual believers but in terms of the apostolic office of ministry and the objective community-building sacraments, so that the Church in that sense mediates grace. Likewise its view of the sacraments does not regard the efficacy of these rites as contingent on the individual's faith. By contrast, these emphases are typically inverted by most Evangelicals.

Could the influence of Pietism's individualistic tendencies or the Radical Reformation's neglect of the broader society in favor of local base communities be the ultimate, crucial factor dividing these traditions? The heritage of the Reformation's Roman Catholic polemics and the difference in ethnic and sociological backgrounds are certainly also factors accounting for Evangelicalism's characteristic anti-Catholic stance. Yet these are not theologically related factors and should not ultimately justify Roman Catholic–Evangelical tensions. To the degree the divisions between Evangelicalism and Roman Catholicism are theologically related, it is quite evident that the cause is not some deep-rooted anti-Catholic element in the Protestant heritage but more likely Evangelicalism's indebtedness both to pietist (and American) individualism and the Anabaptist preoccupation with base communities.

Mainline Protestant recognition of Evangelicalism?

Thus far we have largely investigated only the possibility of Evangelicals' recognizing the characteristic theological emphases of Lutheranism and other mainline churches as possible legitimate Evangelical alternatives. Now we need to examine to what extent characteristic Evangelical treatments of the Church, ministry, and sacraments might be deemed legitimate mainline Protestant theological alternatives. Since this is not so much of a problem with respect to those mainline churches whose theological traditions constitute the Evangelical movement, the question of a possible Lutheran recognition of characteristic Conservative Evangelical themes warrants special consideration. In part, such a discussion involves a consideration of the issues at stake in the broad relationship between Lutheranism and churches of the left wing of the Reformation. Thus we cannot expect to resolve all the problems raised for a Lutheran ecumenical perspective by these churches. We can only point out some promising avenues for further investigation.

We have already noted the similarities between Lutheranism in particular and the Evangelical movement regarding their understanding of the ministry as an office distinct from the priesthood of all believers on the basis of its distinct functions. Not just Protestants but even Roman Catholics at Vatican II (*Lumen Gentium* 33) have recognized with Lutherans and Evangelicals that the ordained ministry must always stand in relationship to the priesthood of all believers.

In this connection it is interesting to note that the Evangelical insight regarding the role of the pastor as an example for other Christians, the differentiation of pastor and laity on the basis of the former's deeper spirituality, has precedent in Luther's own writings, even in the *Small Catechism* (IX.2). It is evident that Lutherans and Evangelicals and several other mainline traditions have a number of valid models for ministry at their disposal—the pastor as part of the universal priesthood (one of the guys or gals), as spiritual example, as authority figure. Given the diverse demands placed on the pastor today, this variety of models by which to inform one's ministry can make an important contribution to pastors in carrying out their day-to-day tasks. The dialogue between Lutherans and Evangelicals contributes to each in sensitizing the partners to this sort of legitimate biblical diversity which can help inform the actual practice of ministry.

Additionally, the characteristic Evangelical way of defining the Church in terms of believers and what they do has some precedents for being considered a legitimate mainline church alternative, even a legitimate Lutheran and Presbyterian alternative. We have observed that such a viewpoint is acceptable to the Lutheran heritage as long as such an emphasis on the Church's membership does not entail a claim that the membership is without sin. However, it is especially noteworthy that this understanding of the Church depicted principally in terms of believers is compatible with a certain reading of the Lutheran *Apology of the Augsburg Confession* (VIII.10), in an article which addresses a concern analogous to a formative Evangelical preoccupation, a defense of the Church's faith from the ungodly who would seek to undermine it, specifically by identifying the Church with a political institution. Likewise, Luther himself in his 1539 treatise *On the Councils and the Church* (WA 50, 643/LW 41:166), while addressing the characteristic Evangelical concern with sanctification, also spoke of the Church's marks in terms of the sanctified life-style of its members.

In addition, it is noteworthy that the Evangelical tendency to define the Church in terms of believers is especially evident in those mainline traditions that tend to constitute the Evangelical movement. It appears in the Baptist heritage, exemplified by the *Second London Confession* (XXVI), in the Mennonite heritage as exemplified by *The Dordrecht Confession* (VIII), in a Confessional statement related to the Methodist heritage, *The [EUB] Confession of Faith* (V), and, significantly enough, perhaps even in two Reformed Confessions, *The Westminster Confession of Faith* (XXV.1-2) and *The Second Helvetic Confession* (XVII). It seems that characteristic Evangelical themes become legitimate mainline alternatives particularly when the mainline traditions concern themselves with matters related to formative Evangelical concerns.

This same pattern in Christian theology, the use of the same theological concept by different churches for similar purposes, is even suggested with regard to Evangelicalism's characteristic understanding of the sacraments as mere symbols. We have noted previously how closely this Evangelical view of the sacrament relates to the movement's overriding concern with sanctification.[29] Thus it is interesting to note that on at least three occasions, when Luther was speaking of the Lord's Supper in relation to what are the characteristic Evangelical concerns, the proper Christian response to the Lord's Supper, or in response to the "rationalist modernism" of the day, he explicitly avoided the concept of the real presence. In fact, once he even referred to the Sacrament as a "symbol" (*symbola*).[30] It is also intriguing that in the treatises where he is concerned to describe the effects of the sacrament, such as his 1519 treatise, *On the Blessed Sacrament of the Body of Christ and the Brotherhoods,* while not denying but even affirming Christ's real presence in the sacraments, he is noticeably reticent about it. One can identify similar precedents in certain elements of the Roman Catholic heritage, notably in Augustine.[31]

One should not push these observations too far, to such an extreme as to suggest that Luther denied the real presence of Christ. What is suggested here is a certain sensitivity on the part of the Lutheran and Catholic traditions to recognize that, when the concern addressed is sanctification or a skeptical rationalism, it is better not to emphasize the real presence in the sacrament. In that sense these traditions can appreciate and better understand the failure of the Evangelical movement and related pietist traditions to affirm Christ's presence in the sacraments and their life-transforming, grace-bearing character. At least Lutherans seem to share with them a reticence to make such an affirmation when addressing the overriding Evangelical preoccupation with sanctification. Whether this insight might lead to the conclusion that a concept of the sacraments as "symbols" need not be a church-dividing issue for Lutherans, insofar as Lutherans and related traditions could legitimately de-emphasize the doctrine of the real presence and the concept of baptismal regeneration in some circumstances, is worth further consideration. It is certainly one of the crucial issues which confronts the more sacramentally oriented churches in their relationship with all churches of the left wing of the Reformation (Protestant churches not associated with the Lutheran, Reformed, or Anglican traditions).

Also worth consideration is the possibility that the concept of the real presence might in fact stimulate a concern for sanctification. Certainly, the idea of Christ's real presence in the sacraments, the belief that they serve to regenerate recipients, fits well with the concept of justification as union with Christ. To receive the Lord's Supper is to receive Christ through one's mouth, to receive him so that he becomes part of me (or, more properly, I become a part of his body) as much as the food that I ate for breakfast is now part of me. Yet this is precisely the kind of intimate union I have with Christ in virtue of the proclamation of justification. Receiving Christ in the sacrament nurtures that intimate union I have with him through baptism and faith. Yet I receive Christ in this intimate way only if he is *really present* in the sacrament. Otherwise I receive him only "spiritually."

We have noted that the concept of justification as union with Christ does not forfeit the concern for sanctification and the Christian life.

In fact, a concern for sanctification and good works is given in the proclamation of justification as union with Christ, for in receiving Christ believers become people who like Christ *want* to serve their neighbor. Thus, given the intimate relationship between this concept of justification as union with Christ and the affirmation of his real presence in the sacraments, it must follow that the doctrine of the real presence also communicates an explicit concern for nurturing sanctification. To say that Christ is really present in the sacraments and that the recipient has been regenerated in baptism does not at all minimize the Evangelical concern for structuring and nurturing a regenerate lifestyle. For to receive Christ's real presence in the sacraments and to be regenerated by them is to become intimately united to him who transforms recipients into regenerate people who, like Christ, serve the neighbor (see Rom. 6:1-11). This is what the Magisterial Reformation traditions have meant in identifying baptism as the content of the Christian life.[32]

Dialogue with traditions that emphasize the real presence, like Lutheranism and Roman Catholicism, may have the salubrious effect on Evangelicalism which the group of "Catholic Evangelicals" envisions. It may help the Evangelical community to appreciate the role a real presence understanding of the sacraments can play in nurturing the regenerate life-style, while helping the Church to safeguard the primacy of grace by reminding it that God acts and becomes present regardless of human response.

Once again we have been reminded how, at least for the Lutheran tradition, the commitment to the centrality of justification by grace through faith shapes its treatment of the doctrines associated with the Third Article of the creed, as profoundly as the Evangelical emphasis on sanctification influences its typical treatment of these issues. We can observe the way in which the overriding concerns of these movements shape their other characteristic doctrinal formulations when we compare how each deals with the atonement.

Chapter 24

The Work of Christ

At least since the time Swedish Lutheran theologian Gustaf Aulén wrote his classic book on the atonement, *Christus Victor,* mainline theology has tended to regard with suspicion alternative theories to the "classic view of the atonement." Aulén heartily criticized the "satisfaction theory of the atonement," which, as we have noted, predominates in the Evangelical movement. He insisted that this theory has had its impact on the modern church through the development of 17th-century Protestant Orthodoxy and so was not an authentic development of the Lutheran or patristic heritage. Luther and his colleagues were regarded as relying on the "classic view." Certainly, there are a number of texts in Luther and the Lutheran Confessions, not to mention even at selected points in the Reformed and Baptist traditions, which reflect this orientation.[1]

According to the classic view of the atonement Christ's atoning work is God's victory over the devil and the forces of evil (see Col. 2:13-15; and various references to Jesus' casting out demons). Even biblical references to the wrath of God (Rom. 1:18; 1 Thess. 2:16) and the law (Gal. 3:13) are interpreted in this scheme. They too are conceived of as God's enemies over which Christ triumphs.

This understanding of the atonement seems well suited to deal with the Lutheran Reformers' overriding preoccupation with comforting the terror-stricken and anxious conscience which is bound to the law. It is precisely with a concern for justification or freedom in view that images compatible with the classic view appear in texts from non-Lutheran mainline traditions like the Presbyterian *Westminster Confession* (XX.1), the Baptist *Propositions and Conclusions concerning True Christian Religion* (1612-1614, 33-34, 84), and the Roman Catholic Council of Trent (*Decree concerning Justification,* chap. III). In comparison with the satisfaction/substitutionary theory of the atonement, the classic view seems better able to portray God as a God of love. For, evil in the world and wrath are not what God wants. In the person of God's Son, God is contending against these forces.

By contrast, the satisfaction theory has a logically stronger emphasis on divine wrath. According to this view, God is a God of justice who has been offended and whose wrath must be placated by atonement offering. Such a theory and its implied picture of God seem better able to serve the overriding Evangelical concern to stimulate Christian responsibility. The emphasis on the wrath of God may serve as a threat to awaken the slothful. By contrast, the classic view, which presupposes a God whose sole intention is to overcome evil and wrath, is a more desirable and comforting affirmation by which Lutherans may better address the anxiety-ridden. Once again the logical interrelatedness between characteristic Lutheran and Evangelical doctrinal formulations and their overriding theological concerns is apparent.

We have noted a number of times that the concern to comfort those burdened by the law is not the sole Lutheran agenda. Thus the satisfaction theory appears in the theology of the earliest proponents of Lutheranism, particularly when Luther and the Lutheran Confessions are preoccupied, like Evangelicals, with the issue of sanctification. It tends to predominate also in the historic documents of the mainline churches which share with Evangelicals an overriding concern with sanctification.[2] By the same token, however, we have noted that Evangelicals will appeal to language which suggests a classic view, particularly when they move away from their normal preoccupation with the individual's regenerate life-style.[3] Thus, in view of the fact that virtually all the churches have certain precedents in their theological traditions for employing each other's characteristic view of the atonement and tend to employ a given theory for the same function as it is employed by the others, the doctrine of the atonement does not seem to be a necessary source of division (although Evangelicals might insist that mainliners not deny the wrath of God and a personal devil).[4]

For whom the atonement?

The Evangelical concern that the love of God not be so emphasized as to overshadow divine wrath relates to its vehement denials of universal salvation.[5] Although it is not a concern for Fundamentalist Presbyterians with their commitment to double predestination, those Evangelicals who would wish to affirm some universal implications for

Christ's atoning work might profit from the Lutheran concept of single predestination.

The Lutheran *Formula of Concord* (SD XI.5, 78) explains this concept. Single predestination is the idea that God's election only pertains to God's chosen children. Those who do not come to faith are not deprived of salvation because God did not desire their salvation. They have only themselves to blame.

Of course, a certain logical contradiction seems to be implied by such a view. If God elects, does God not by implication condemn those who are not chosen? The only way to render the view intelligible seems to be to argue that the gospel is for everyone, that all are elect. Yet some have rejected this election by willful disobedience and hard-heartedness. Could such an interpretation of the Lutheran concept of single predestination stem the universalistic tendencies of much modern theology, while functioning as a helpful corrective to a Pelagian over-emphasis on personal decision which Evangelicals inherit from their revivalist heritage?

In response to Evangelical concerns, this Lutheran conception would provide sufficient motivation for undertaking evangelism and missionary activity. In a global society like ours, where many already have heard the gospel, the task of evangelism is necessary, on Lutheran grounds, in order to help overcome the resistance of those who have rejected the Word previously. With regard to unreached peoples the motivation for evangelism provided by this view is that Christians aim to share the good news with others that they are already in Christ.

Enough Evangelical core commitments seem preserved by this view to suggest that it might function as a legitimate Evangelical alternative. It seems consistent with the Amyraldian Evangelical perspective with its notion that God provides salvation to all (elects all?) but only applies salvation to some. It is almost a precise equivalent of those Evangelicals holding that all children of believers are likely saved, and its more recently held correlate that all are elect except those who reject God. Even if the Lutheran proposal were regarded as universalistic, at least in the view of Harold Lindsell it need not destroy fellowship, as he grants that the belief in universalism does not necessarily preclude saving faith.[6]

The question of the objects of the atonement raises two other issues, both of which were previously noted. First, we consider the eschatological question. We should reiterate the rejection of the concept of a millennium by the Lutheran *Augsburg Confession* (XVII.5). We noted earlier that this viewpoint could be an acceptable Evangelical alternative as it more or less correlates with an amillennialist viewpoint. Conversely, the Lutheran strictures against millennialism seem to apply less and less to the Evangelical movement, given the increased dominance of amillennialism in the movement. However, the question still remains whether all Evangelical churches like The Evangelical Free Church of America (11), the Independent Fundamental Churches of America (15), The Mission Covenant Church of Norway, and numerous others, which hold to a belief in the millennium, are necessarily precluded from church fellowship with Lutheranism because of their views.[7]

On this point one should examine carefully the precise nature of the concern of *The Augsburg Confession*. A principal issue at stake seems to be the fear that the particular form of millennialism under attack insisted on the seizure of worldly power by believers. Since this dimension does not seem as explicitly evident in the teaching of the Evangelical churches we have noted, perhaps one could make the case that *The Augsburg Confession's* strictures need not necessarily apply to them.

A second issue for Lutheran–Evangelical relationships raised by the atonement relates to the question of the nature of the human persons to be redeemed. We already have noted that Evangelicals characteristically employ Greek philosophical concepts in describing their view of human persons. The concern raised by the use of these concepts is that it might lead to a life-denying, unbiblical dualism and compromise of the total fallenness of human beings.

However, we have seen that the Lutheran Confessions, the Presbyterian church, and the Roman Catholic tradition reflect this sort of reliance on Greek anthropological assumptions insofar as it leads to the positing of a body-soul dualism or of human beings as static essences.[8] Thus, criticisms of dualistic tendencies in Evangelicalism cannot be pressed too hard by mainline Christians, lest the same critique be pertinent to their own church as well.

In the last decades a new theological conception of human persons, one influenced by the Swiss theologian Karl Barth, has come to play a dominant role in the mainline churches.[9] This view picks up on contemporary biblical insights regarding the likelihood that the Old Testament has no concept of human soul. Thus the distinction between body and soul is rejected if such a distinction implies that they are entities which can exist separately from each other.

Also rejected is the idea that human persons are static individual essences. Rather, the relational character of human being is affirmed. Human persons are said to be necessarily related to each other and to their environment in such a way that priority is given to understanding a person's being as largely determined by his or her intended interactions with others. "We are what we do or have done to us!"

This conception can make a helpful contribution to Lutherans and Evangelicals in several ways. In addition to underscoring the social character of human beings, helping to account for why Christians need the Church and why the gospel inevitably has social implications, this conception provides more adequate tools for describing humanity's total fallenness. Because human nature is historically conditioned, not a static essence, it is possible to claim with the Lutheran Confessions that the image of God is not an unalterable quality of that essence, but original righteousness (the fear of God).[10] On such grounds it is easier to conceive of how humanity's historically manifested sin can be said to infect human nature itself, to destroy the image of God and not just damage it. Such a point is not so easily made with the conceptuality of Greek philosophy with its idea of a static spiritual human substance ultimately unaffected by its historical interactions. Moreover, on such grounds the image of God conceived of as an essential quality of that substance cannot be regarded as having been destroyed by sin. Otherwise sinners would be less than human, having lost in sin an essential quality (the image of God) of what makes them human. Thus in order to avoid these unhappy implications associated with the Greek view of persons, a number of Evangelicals, as we have seen, insist that sinners still bear the image of God. In that sense they unwittingly concede that human nature is not totally fallen.[11]

Inasmuch as the insistence that salvation is totally Christ's work is at stake here (the Evangelical view just sketched implies that there is some uncorrupted element in human nature for which Christ need not have died), this appears to be the one issue related to Christ's atoning work which could divide mainline Protestant churches and the Evangelical movement. However, there are indications at least from the Evangelicals' 1974 International Congress on World Evangelization (Lausanne) that, with respect to the question of an adequate view of human persons, Evangelicals are trying to find a better way.[12] Apart from this issue no ostensible barriers to church unity seem to exist between mainline Reformation churches and Evangelicals on issues related to the atoning work of Christ.

Chapter 25

Social Ethics

Differences with the Evangelical movement over theological suppositions for social ethics do not pose much of a problem for most mainline churches, as the movement largely shares these churches' Christocentric or theocratic orientation. But Lutheranism assumes a very different orientation. Thus it particularly warrants special consideration.[1]

The "two-kingdom" ethic is the fundamental basis for all Lutheran social ethics. This view takes seriously the Pauline injunction in Romans 13, which suggests that the state has its own integrity apart from the Church. The two kingdoms, the kingdom of the law to which the state belongs and the kingdom of gospel, cannot be confused. However, this is not to say that these realms do not overlap. The Christian lives in both realms, and God rules in both. God is understood to have established civil government as part of the created order. The state's purpose, then, is to help safeguard the creation by restraining evil in human society.

The two-kingdom ethic has had a rather checkered career, particularly in this century with its use by certain German Lutherans to authorize noninterference in Hitler's government policies. Part of the problem was the tendency of some Lutherans to identify the existing Nazi government with the order of creation, which could not be overturned. In reality, this is not the point of the two-kingdom ethic. It simply maintains that the *concept* of government, but not any particular government, is built into the created order. Thus *The Augsburg Confession* (XVI.7) goes so far as to endorse defiance of a particular government when it causes citizens to sin. Contrary to the way in which it has functioned in Lutheran history, the two-kingdom ethic is a potentially radical social ethic.

Because for Lutherans civil government is part of the created order, its governing principles must be the law, inasmuch as the creation itself is structured by the law (the Ten Commandments). Thus the task of the Christian, and of all human beings, is to ensure that government is in fact ruled by the principles of the Second Table (final six) of the Ten Commandments. That is to say, social ethical responsibility entails that citizens work to see that justice is served. The Christian can work side by side with the non-Christian in carrying out these responsibilities inasmuch as, since they are both creatures who experience the law by which creation is structured, both have access to a common criterion (the law, justice) for political decision making.[2]

Contrary to the way in which it is often misunderstood, the two-kingdom ethic's commitment to avoiding a bifurcation of the two kingdoms does not preclude a role for the gospel in inspiring Christian social ethical involvement, just as the gospel plays a role in inspiring any ethical decision Christians might make.[3] It is simply a matter of recognizing that, unlike the characteristic Reformed social ethic, the gospel is not to be employed by Christians as the criterion for social ethics. Its proper function is to motivate the ethic, not to structure it. For were the gospel to play such a role, were it injected into the dynamics of government by legislating its norms as though they were law, the gospel would be confused with the law. The end result could only be that the doctrine of justification through faith apart from works of the law would be compromised.[4] Once again we note how the Lutheran commitment to the centrality of the doctrine of justification and its defense reflects on other Lutheran positions.

The Lutheran model for social ethics might make several contributions to the Evangelical movement. We have already observed some interest within the Evangelical community in grounding social ethics in the doctrine of creation and the law by which creation is structured.[5] This is precisely what the Lutheran two-kingdom ethic proposes. Thus, in addition to its theological contribution in safeguarding the doctrine of justification, the Lutheran model would better allow Evangelicals to preserve their commitment to the separation of church and state.[6] For on these grounds the gospel only motivates, provides intentionality for political involvement; it can never function to structure or dictate political decisions. (Such a perspective has definite implications for the debate over prayer in American public schools. In light of the two-kingdom ethic, Evangelicals can better understand the rationale for mainline Lutheran opposition to school prayers.) Also the distinction of the social ethical realm from the realm of the gospel presumably frees Christians to employ non-Christian, even Marxist insights for their decision making in social ethics, as long as these insights do not conflict with an appreciation of the goodness of creation and its orders.

This last point could be especially significant for helping to overcome present tensions between the Evangelical movement and liberation theology, with its reliance on Marxist insights. (We already have noted the growing impact of insights from liberation theology on the radical Evangelicals.)[7] However, with the use of the Lutheran two-kingdom ethic much of the stigma of employing Marxist insights could be removed by arguing that the use of Marxism belongs to the realm of social ethics or the law and so does not corrupt the gospel. Implicit in this suggestion is that Evangelicals and mainline churches might best come to terms with the challenges of liberation theology without falling prey to some of its liberal reductionist tendencies by locating its insights in the realm of social ethics (the kingdom on the left) not the realm of the gospel (the kingdom on the right).[8] In short, the suggestion is that we employ insights from Third World theologians in constructing a liberation *ethic*, not a liberation *theology*.

To be sure, some questions may arise in the Conservative Evangelical community regarding the political consequences of the preceding proposal. Could it, even so, be considered a legitimate Evangelical theological alternative? A crucial issue in an Evangelical evaluation of this proposal and all other social ethical considerations is the question of priorities. Is the Church's first priority to preach the gospel or social ethics?[9] As already noted, mainline churches and the organized ecumenical movement would do well to give priority to the Evangelical emphasis of evangelism, especially in view of the large number of Evangelically oriented members in their churches. Although I know of no direct reference in the Lutheran Confessions to this matter, a commitment to the priority of proclamation as the Church's task, though never apart from a passion for seeking justice in society, seems to be common sense and is implied by the Lutheran description of the Church as "the assembly of all believers among whom the Gospel is preached. . ." (*The Augsburg Confession*, VII.1). Making this commitment to evangelism more apparent in the mainline churches, as the WCC Nairobi Assembly hinted, could be the crucial factor in enabling rapprochement with Evangelicals.[10]

A final consideration related to how social ethics may affect Lutheran–Evangelical relationships pertains to the recognition that most Evangelicals continue to appeal not to creation and the law as a warrant for social ethics, but to the nature of Christ and the gospel.[11] Does this constitute a church-dividing issue for Lutheranism? In most cases these Evangelicals simply are reflecting the Christocentric heritage of the Confessional traditions which make up the movement. With that insight in mind it is well to consider that a number of Lutheran churches which have achieved ecumenical agreement with the Reformed tradition do not regard as church-dividing the difference between their own model for social ethics and the Reformed insistence that the doctrine of Christ and the gospel are principal warrants for social ethics.[12] What does not divide the Lutheran and Reformed traditions need not divide Lutherans from the Evangelical movement.

In the final analysis, then, Lutherans and Evangelicals seem to be in a position to recognize each other's approach to social ethics. The topic need not divide these traditions. In fact the Lutheran two-kingdom ethic, with its appeal to the doctrine of creation and the law as a warrant for social ethics, offers promising possibilities to Evangelical theology.

Chapter 26

A Theology
for the Born Again

In the course of our discussion it has become evident that the theological heritages of a number of mainline churches share the Evangelical preoccupation with sanctification and the "born-again" lifestyle. Consequently, there are no theological reasons that would prevent these churches from nurturing the sort of warm Christian ethos and spiritual life which I described in the beginning of the book by way of a visit to a Conservative Evangelical parish. The characteristics of that ethos, drawn from a collage of encounters with the Evangelical movement, are perceived by most mainliners as all too lacking in their own churches. But to the degree that the Christian faith is more enthusiastically expressed and more intimately intertwined in the lives of members of the Evangelical movement, our analysis has shown that this cannot be attributed to a theological concern with sanctification and the Christian life among Evangelicals which is absent in the mainline church traditions. Even in the Lutheran tradition which, due to its emphasis on the doctrine of justification, seems to be the most likely candidate of the mainline for overlooking sanctification and the nurturing of a born-again life-style, a concern for these issues is by no means lacking. The ability of the Lutheran theological heritage to account for these characteristic Evangelical preoccupations has broader significance for Conservative Evangelical–mainline church relationships insofar as Lutheranism's manner of conceptualizing the doctrine of justification is endorsed by other mainline church traditions. Thus once again the relationship between the Lutheran and the Conservative Evangelical heritages warrants our attention.

Clearly, then, the Lutheran commitment to the centrality of justification by grace through faith has all sorts of implications for the shape and quality of the Christian life. The concept of justification as conformity to Christ necessarily entails a regenerate life-style. As we have seen, to be conformed to Christ in justification and baptism means that Christians have been given a new identity. They are regenerated or born again, people who are dead to sin and have risen with Christ (Romans 6). As such, they cannot be themselves without living for Christ and their neighbor (for, in virtue of the mystical union and the sacraments, the whole body of Christ is now in their blood, part of who they are). Good works necessarily follow from justification understood in this way. They follow in the same sense that loving actions towards one's spouse necessarily follow as a consequence of the union which comes about in a loving marriage. To proclaim the doctrine of justification in this way is to reflect a passionate concern with regeneration and sanctification.

If this were not sufficient indication of Lutheranism's sensitivity to the implications of spiritual rebirth for the Christian life-style, the Lutheran Confessions' reference to a third use of the law as a guide to Christian life undergirds this point further. No one who properly understands the Lutheran heritage can indict Lutheranism for encouraging sloth in the Christian life.

It may well be that the regenerate life-style does not receive quite as much attention in Lutheranism as in the Evangelical movement and related traditions influenced by Pietism and the Reformed tradition. In this regard the Evangelical movement can teach Lutheranism to reconsider the importance of this issue, particularly in view of our present cultural upheavals. Likewise a dialogue with the Evangelical movement calls the other mainline churches to reappropriate their historic commitments to the centrality of sanctification or the transformation of human life by grace.

However, as we have seen, neither an emphasis on the centrality of justification, as in Lutheranism, nor an emphasis on sacramental and liturgical life, as in the Roman Catholic, Anglican, and Lutheran traditions, necessarily ignores the necessity of being born again (in baptism) and its implications for the Christian life-style. Thus all parties can be assured that those nurtured by these traditions need not question their "Evangelical" character. As much as Conservative Evangelicals, those nurtured by traditions which stress the primacy of God's action or baptismal regeneration may be assured that they are "born again" Christians, and that, precisely because their theology offers comfort and confidence to believers, it is capable of nurturing a level of Christian commitment which recent Evangelical growth cannot call into question. In short, the most important conclusion to be drawn from the data about recent Evangelical growth and a mainline slump is that the problem is not with the various mainline theological heritages. The problem has been that the heritage of each of these churches in all its fullness and depth has not had sufficient impact on their actual practice.

It seems to follow, then, that Evangelicals and mainline Christians like Lutherans can celebrate the biblical character of each other's traditions and the life-style each nurtures. We have noted already that most mainline churches more nearly share a common theological perspective with Evangelicals than Lutherans do, inasmuch as these churches share the Evangelical movement's overriding theological concerns with sanctification. (This is also no doubt related to the fact that more Evangelicals are rooted in these traditions than in Lutheranism.) Thus, the prevailing themes of Evangelicalism need not necessarily lead to a Pelagian compromise of grace, any more than these non-Lutheran mainline churches necessarily maintain an unwitting Pelagianism. Furthermore, the Evangelical reluctance to make the doctrine of justification function as the criterion for judging all doctrines—a strong emphasis in the Lutheran tradition—need present no more problems for Evangelical–Lutheran convergence than it does for Lutheran fellowship with other mainline churches that do not affirm justification as the ultimate criterion of doctrine. Contrary to a few strident Lutheran voices, expressed even in certain bilateral dialogues, the problem seems not to be church-dividing, if, indeed, as this study has shown, characteristic Evangelical doctrinal formulations are not Pelagian.

Of course, some doctrinal barriers to convergence between a few mainline churches and Evangelicals may exist from the Lutheran, Roman Catholic, and Anglican side on issues like the sacraments, ministry, and perhaps even the Church's role in "mediating" salvation. However, we have observed a richness in the doctrinal heritages of the Evangelical movement and various mainline churches which suggests the possibility of appropriating each other's characteristic treatment of these doctrines, at least when each tradition shares the characteristic preoccupation (be it justification or sanctification) of the other. In addition, it should be noted that these problem areas are essentially the same issues which more liturgically oriented churches face in dialogue with mainline Baptist, Mennonite, Restorationist (Disciples of Christ), and Union churches. Thus, with the possible exception of the emphasis in the Pentecostal and Holiness segments of Evangelicalism with regard to their distinctive views on baptism with the Holy Spirit and (in the case of Pentecostalism) on the phenomenon of glossolalia, dialogue with the Evangelical movement presents no more special challenges regarding classical doctrines to Lutheran, Roman Catholic, Anglican, and Reformed churches than they encounter in dialogue with these other mainline churches.[1]

This observation may help account for the amorphous character of the movement. To the degree that ecumenical dialogue with Evangelicalism is no more than ecumenical dialogue with the movement's constituent traditions (mainline traditions which influenced it), it may be granted that the movement has no autonomous status. Yet this hardly need be lamented by Evangelicals. To the degree that mainline traditions constituting the movement reflect concerns identical with self-proclaimed Evangelicals, could one conclude that the Evangelicals' strategy of infiltrating the mainline churches is succeeding? Important consequences for the practice of local ecumenism follow from this.

Generally speaking, mainline churches, even those which have not yet reconciled their differences, extend a kind of de facto respect to each other. They do not interfere with each other's ministry; they do not seek to convert each other's members, and they support and celebrate each other's triumphs. This may be one of the triumphs of the modern ecumenical movement. Unfortunately, this has not usually been the case with regard to the relationships between Evangelicalism and the ecumenical establishment. But now, mainline churches and Evangelical communities, insofar as their remaining doctrinal differences resemble the differences mainline churches have with each other, may be able to celebrate the successes God gives each. There is no need for one to feel threatened by the other. (To be sure, the separatist heritage of Evangelicalism and questions which may remain about the biblical fidelity of mainline churches pose some special problems. However, a number of centrist and left-wing Evangelicals have already embraced this kind of open, accepting attitude towards mainline churches.)

Even more, insofar as mainline churches and the Evangelical movement often share common or mutually recognized theological perspectives on certain doctrines, the cooperation between these Christian bodies can be intensified. Because of the numerous points of agreement which have been shown, it should be possible for both mainline churches and Evangelicals legitimately to employ procedures for stimulating ministry, which have proved successful in the other's tradition and still remain faithful to their own traditions.

For example, mainline churches have much to learn from Evangelicals regarding use of the media, maintaining high educational standards in their colleges and seminaries (the academic requirements which are actually enforced, at least in some American Lutheran, if not in other mainline church, institutions do not always compare favorably with schools like Wheaton and Fuller), and successful evangelism techniques. Of course, insights from Evangelicalism about these issues have been borrowed for some time on an ad hoc basis. One thinks of the numerous Lutherans employing James Kennedy's "Evangelism Explosion" Program and the numerous mainline denominational programs relying on The Church Growth Movement devised by Fuller Seminary. Yet this adaptation of Evangelical methods typically has either been done without much fanfare or, where the adaptation has been explicit, it is met with criticism. The discussion to this juncture, however, suggests that at many points such mainline adaptations of Evangelical insights have theological warrant. Thus a more deliberate and public effort on the part of mainline church leaders to establish contact with qualified and theologically legitimate resources within the Evangelical movement would certainly be in order.

In addition to the important contribution the Lutheran emphasis on justification by grace through faith can make to the Evangelical movement, mainline churches also offer a sense of history and tradition to Evangelicals, often manifesting itself in a sense of Confessional fidelity and liturgical sensitivity. Evangelical Christians certainly have known all along about the validity of the historic Confessional traditions. At least they have acknowledged de facto the biblical character and born-again nurturing resources implicit in Lutheranism and other mainline traditions insofar as Evangelicals in these churches have been included as part of the Evangelical movement.

The last point underscores again the observation that the crucial question for the Evangelical movement, what holds it together, is not doctrinal formulations regarding the process of salvation, the sacraments, or the like. With the possible exception of a certain insistence upon affirming a few "fundamentals" of the faith—the Trinity, Christ's two natures, a literalistic belief in a real, nonsymbolic atonement which does not bring universal salvation, and in some cases an insistence upon adult baptism—almost any traditional doctrinal formulation is Evangelically acceptable (though perhaps not for the Fundamentalist wing of the movement). This suggests again that the basic issue for the Evangelical movement is the view of Scripture one holds, especially whether biblical inerrancy or at least plenary inspiration is affirmed in some way.[2]

Ultimately this is the question that overrides all other doctrinal issues for Evangelicals. In ecumenical conversations that include Evangelicals this issue must be on the agenda. Of course, Evangelicals also bring to these dialogues the concern to call the mainline churches actually to embody in their practice their historic Confessional beliefs (to practice what they preach). However, this concern or suspicion that the mainline churches' actual embodiment of their theological heritage is less than all it should be is often related to the Evangelicals' suspicion that these churches have compromised their faith by reliance on an inadequate biblical hermeneutic. Thus it follows that the Evangelical preoccupation with the question of biblical authority (inerrancy) is what gives the movement its uniqueness. Even when there is doctrinal agreement, as between members of the same Confessional tradition, if agreement cannot be found on the nature of biblical authority, Evangelicals will break fellowship. In fact, they are willing to concede the possibility of fellowship to brothers and sisters with whom they disagree on other doctrines—provided these parties maintain an appropriately Evangelical view of Scripture. This is *the* issue for Evangelicals in determining ecumenical relationships and church fellowship—more central than even one's theological/Confessional standpoint.

Thus it is necessary to examine the question of whether the theology of the mainline churches is sufficiently "biblical." It has been argued and shown in this section that Lutheranism and other mainline churches can portray and nurture a "born-again" life-style. But this in turn raises the question of why the mainline church ethos is not generally perceived as reflecting as lively a sense of spirituality, stewardship, commitment, and community as observers generally attribute to the Evangelical movement. Evangelicals are likely to ask if this may relate to a failure of the mainline churches to appropriate their theological heritage due to their inadequate hermeneutic and view of Scripture. Yet even if Evangelicals do perceive in the mainline churches a lively spiritual ethos as well as a theology which suitably addresses the concern for spiritual regeneration, that would not be sufficient for church fellowship (except perhaps for Evangelicals strongly influenced by Pietism); a mainline church's doctrine of biblical authority must be an appropriate Evangelical alternative.[3]

Biblical authority and hermeneutics are clearly the issues at stake in intra-Confessional (intra-Lutheran) and intradenominational tensions, inasmuch as in these instances there exists almost complete doctrinal agreement on other issues. Of course in intra-Lutheran discussions the third use of the law, the validity of associated emphases derived from Lutheran Pietism, an insistence on a satisfaction theory of the atonement, or the use of Greek philosophical conceptuality sometimes divide conservative Lutherans from mainliners.[4] Indeed, Evangelicals also may pose questions about the degree to which mainline churches actually appropriate their theological heritages in their day-to-day functioning. However, in the final analysis, the view of Scripture, the position on biblical inerrancy, divides. When we come to this question of biblical inerrancy and authority, we stand not just at the center of Evangelical-mainline church relationships, but also at the heart of intra-Confessional and intrachurch tensions.

Chapter 27

Scripture and
Theological Method

The preceding chapters on areas of doctrinal convergence between mainline churches and Evangelicals have their own integrity and stand on their own. The reflections that follow, by contrast, have a tentative nature and should be regarded as an invitation to further reflection.

We shall proceed on two fronts. First we shall examine the validity of the Evangelical movement's critique of mainline contemporary theological method. Then we shall examine the possibility that certain recently developed mainline theological methods, specifically a particular kind of narrative and canonical hermeneutic might be considered a legitimate Evangelical alternative while still retaining its "credibility" as an option for mainline theologians.

Contemporary mainline theology in Evangelical perspective

Since the 1960s, with the onslaught of the "God is dead" theology, contemporary mainline theology has been in turmoil. The old neoorthodox consensus which had dominated in most mainline circles since just after the First World War began to come apart. Although neoorthodox theology continues to have its monolithic impact on a handful of mainline American and European denominations (Lutheran ones included), the old consensus which permitted this theological perspective to dominate the thought of every mainline church has been shattered. No new alternative (although the "contextual theology" of modern ecumenism is influential) has really taken neoorthodoxy's place in terms of having an impact on the day-to-day life of the church.

The neoorthodox consensus was possible because of the particular style of theology which neoorthodoxy embodied. Recall that neoorthodoxy, as exemplified by two great modern Swiss theologians, Karl

Barth and Emil Brunner, and in America by the Niebuhr brothers, was an attempt to restate the Orthodox doctrinal positions in a new way. The new way meant taking account of developments in historical criticism and post-Enlightenment philosophy (particularly the work of the Danish forerunner of existentialism, Søren Kierkegaard, and of the great German critical philosopher of the 18th century, Immanuel Kant). At any rate, neoorthodoxy in its earliest stages represented a kind of consensus of the middle, an alternative which could presumably speak to both liberals and conservatives.

Throughout much of the middle third of this century neoorthodoxy played this role effectively in mainline churches. It was even the language of church leaders. It was what the theology students learned in seminary in a day before the anti-intellectualist rebellion of the 1960s made theology seem totally irrelevant to many. But in this earlier period it was the theology brought by the brightest and best of the seminary graduates into the more prestigious pulpits. Today, with the breakdown of neoorthodoxy and no theology really taking its place, for "theology is not relevant enough," the new mainline church leadership style of management and social action has filled the void. Yet the conservatives feel bypassed and left out, largely bereft of the neoorthodox mediator to proclaim the traditional orthodox dogmas to them. Indeed, some observers have suggested that it was the breakdown of the neoorthodox consensus that stimulated the recent Evangelical renaissance, at least the resurgence of Evangelicalism within the mainline churches.[1]

The demise of neoorthodoxy came as no surprise to Evangelicals. There was and continues to be strong criticism against it and its principal proponents. Basically the concern is that it fundamentally fails in its role as mediator between Orthodoxy and modernity, finally coming down on the side of modernity at the expense of the gospel.[2]

The history of the neoorthodox movement seems to warrant some of these critiques. Soon after Barth launched the movement with his famous book *The Epistle to the Romans,* more liberal directions appeared within the movement, eventually to Barth's chagrin. This was exemplified especially in the work of Rudolf Bultmann and his program of "demythologizing" the Bible so that it might be "translated" into the categories of modern existentialist philosophy.[3] Further liberalizing trends have appeared in the thought of second- and third-generation heirs of neoorthodoxy. Thus one of the children of the movement, University of Chicago theologian Langdon Gilkey, calls for a theological perspective where Christian doctrine is understood as "relative statements of Christian truth for their time, statements that reflect their own cultural situation and needs."[4] No doubt, Bultmann could have agreed—but certainly not Barth or the conservative Christian oriented towards traditional doctrinal formulations.

That such developments are legitimate appropriations of neoorthodoxy has been suggested even by the God-is-dead theologian Thomas Altizer, who confesses his indebtedness to Barth.[5] The neoorthodox synthesis of orthodoxy and modernism seems to have come down sufficiently on the side of modernism to open the way to all kinds of more liberal theological trends like the "new hermeneutic," theology of hope, liberation theology, and the "theology by management" of much mainline contemporary church leadership. All share a commitment to regarding contemporary experience or needs as one of the sources for theology. In that sense one may speak of a consensus in contemporary theology, a consensus whose impact is largely to compromise the relevance of traditional formulations of theological concepts.

Contemporary Evangelicals generally have arrived at a common account and assessment of the current theological situation and why neoorthodoxy has borne the fruits that it has. A survey of the writings of some of the important mainline theologians of the post–World War I era does not seem totally to negate their assessment. A detailed confirmation of this Evangelical assessment cannot be given here. However, a few examples of evidence of its accuracy can be noted.

A fundamental Evangelical criticism of contemporary mainline theology is its indictment of the latter for grounding its claims in human experience rather than objective and propositional revelation. This tendency is clearly evident in the theology of Bultmann, who claims that all theological statements are really statements about anthropology. It is also reflected in the German-American theologian Paul Tillich and his view of Christian symbols as "expressions of the New Being" as first experienced by the biblical authors.[6]

We can observe this forfeiture of objective revelation in several of today's prominent theologians. Jürgen Moltmann, one of the prime proponents of the theology of hope, insists that the historic elements of revelation are only known as such when these accounts are read in light of certain attitudinal suppositions about the future. Liberation theologian Rubem Alves makes this point in an even more radical way when he claims that the language of the community of faith is purely functional, for the purpose of creating new possibilities for life, and, as such, is an expression of human imagination.[7]

The list of such compromises of objective revelation in favor of grounding revelation in human experience could be elongated. The compromise is evident even in revisionist theologians who are self-consciously trying to break with what they perceive in the theological tradition of Tillich and Friedrich Schleiermacher as a compromising of the gospel's critical function in regard to the authority of contemporary human experience. Despite these intentions, they still tend to regard religious language as merely "thematizing" authentic human experience.[8]

Even Barth, for all his intentions to affirm divine transcendence, did not entirely escape from this tendency. Thus during much of his career he insisted that the Word of God is not objectively or universally accessible in the biblical text but is only known when it renders the experience of Christ's presence to believers through faith. This insistence on a necessary role for the believer's present experience if the Word of God is to be intelligible was further underscored by Barth's claim that the true criterion for determining the Bible's meaning is not the text itself but the author's intention or relationship to the content of the biblical revelation, and that present interpreters are to reexperience what the biblical authors experienced. No place is left for a Word of God over against human experience. (Granted, in his primary dogmatic work, *Die Kirchliche Dogmatik* [English: *Church Dogmatics*] Barth did argue that the presence of the Word of God mediated through the biblical text is "not the *experience* of it but its *actual presence*." However, the fact is that Barth often maintained that the Word of God, as the criterion for assessing when the Word really is present in proclamation, is not accessible to all who read Scripture or hear the Church's preaching. Thus on these occasions the only criterion he has for determining if the Word is present seems to be human experience—whether or not one has experienced the Word. On such grounds it still is not really possible to speak of God's Word over against human experience, since all meaningful judgments about the Word's reality are contingent on first having experienced it.)[9]

Evangelicals point out a number of consequences of these suppositions of contemporary mainline theology. Virtually all the theologians we have noted posit a distinction between the Word of God and Scripture, so that what they understand as the Word of God becomes a principle that can be used to criticize those portions of Scripture which seem to conflict with the theologian's perspective. In virtually all cases (except perhaps the revisionist theologians and other theologians influenced by the 20th-century German philosopher Hans-Georg Gadamer), the biblical authors' intention or experience is the criterion for determining this critical principle.[10] Another consequence of these suppositions is that a functionalist understanding of Scripture must be posited. The Bible is not regarded as Word of God in itself; it *becomes* the Word when it renders Christ present through faith.[11]

Certainly this sort of critical distinction between the gospel and Scripture has had a marked impact on mainline theology. The majority of mainline Lutheran theologians still reflects its influence. Some have argued that this approach and its consequences for the criticism of Scripture by the gospel is one of the earmarks of Lutheranism.[12] Although not all Lutherans agree that such a critical hermeneutic is part of the Lutheran heritage, it must be conceded that Luther himself employed something akin to it at times. To cite but one example, Luther, in his 1535 *Lectures on Galatians* (WA 40[1], 458,13ff./LW 26, 294-295), claims that even if the sophists cited hundreds of biblical passages in support of the righteousness of works he would "rather have the honor of believing in Christ alone than of being persuaded by all the passages they could produce." It was apparently on this basis that he could suggest the removal of the book of James from the canon.[13] From these suppositions follow the purely functionalist distinction between law and gospel, the idea that their distinction can be determined only on the basis of the impact a given Word of proclamation or Scripture has on the hearer. On such grounds one cannot determine if such a Word is law or gospel on the basis of its grammatical form.[14]

That these commitments do not fully characterize the Lutheran theological heritage will subsequently be clarified. They are not the only legitimate Lutheran alternatives. However, given their precedent in the Lutheran tradition and their utility for contemporary apologetics, the rationale for these commitments is readily apparent.

This kind of critical hermeneutic that employs the gospel to rule out the authority of certain embarrassing biblical texts can be a helpful tool for theologians in encountering the challenges raised by historical criticism and the modern scientific worldview. Some mainliners like Bultmann and Tillich also addressed these challenges by appealing to the "mythical" or "symbolic" character of biblical language, so that the Bible is not understood to be making historical and scientific claims and therefore cannot be discredited by historical investigation. Others regard the biblical accounts as a special "salvation history" which cannot be verified by means of historical and scientific investigations but is only understood as history when assessed in light of faith.[15] Such an approach seems to give the theologian the best of all possible worlds, an ability to affirm the Bible's historicity while maintaining the intellectual credibility of these claims. (In a different format, these endeavors are still today undertaken by a number of theologians, including representatives of the so-called theology of hope, who maintain that all historical judgments require a certain interpretive perspective. Faith is deemed as one of these valid interpretive perspectives.)[16]

Nevertheless, Evangelicals find a number of problems with these related approaches. The principal difficulty they identify emerges from their critical distinction between Word and Scripture. As a result, Evangelicals argue, it is difficult for the mainliners to explain what the Word is, inasmuch as the Word's content has been distinguished from Scripture. In like manner the same concern is raised about the mainliners' distinction of salvation history from ordinary history. The suspicion is that they have effectively divorced God from history and the world.[17]

The distinction of the Word from the objectively concrete (both Scripture and ordinary history) necessitates that the Word of God cannot be received directly and objectively; it cannot stand over against human experience as objective history or an objective text. For given the mainliners' presuppositions, the Bible becomes the Word of God only when we experience it through faith. God is known and Scripture is intelligible as history only on the basis of the subjective noncognitive decision of faith.[18]

The influence of the important 18th-century German philosopher, Immanuel Kant, and the inherent subjectivism of his thought are very apparent in all these theological tendencies. For Kant, nothing can be apprehended in itself; all objects are only known phenomenally on the basis of the experience and constitutive contribution of the knower. Several Evangelicals correctly identify this orientation as one of the central though problematic presuppositions of mainline theology.[19] It is necessary to insist that the Word is only intelligible in relation to faith when one's basic epistemological presupposition is that nothing can be known apart from one's subjective experience of the object.

The basic presuppositions of mainline theology as sketched by Evangelicals also reflect in the ecumenical movement. They are clearly evident in organized ecumenism's prevailing model of theological method, the so-called "contextual theology"—the idea that the meaning of the Word of God is altered in different cultural contexts. It is regrettable that the ecumenical movement has to a large extent adopted this presupposition uncritically.[20] The use of this method seems to confirm Evangelical suspicions of the movement. For if the Word cannot be conceived of apart from its correlation with human experience, if all our conceptions of God are imperfect and context-bound, there seems to be no way in which it can be asserted that the Word is more than human experience.[21]

Not just "contextual theology," but virtually all the mainline theological alternatives considered here are privy to this critique. Insofar as they, like the contextual approach, maintain the necessary relationship between the meaning of the Word of God or the historicity of its claims and human experience, no place is given for an objective Word of God standing over against or independent of human experience. The 19th-century German philosopher, Ludwig Feuerbach, who claimed that religion is nothing more than human experience, seems lurking in the background of these mainline theological approaches.[22]

Because biblical inerrancy and the universal accessibility of Scripture's meaning have been denied, Evangelicals argue, fallible human experience has become the foundation for all reality, including Christian faith. The result is a forfeiture of divine transcendence, threatening the existence of God by rendering faith a mere psychological projection.[23] This dynamic ultimately leads to a further reinforcement of the narcissistic mentality of contemporary culture.[24] For if the transcendence of God cannot be affirmed in face of anthropocentric views of reality like those of Feuerbach, the solipsistic mentality that all reality is a projection of the self and its needs remains unchallenged. Thus the predominant alternatives of mainline theology and their prevailing perspectival, subjectivist presuppositions unwittingly reinforce the narcissistic, self-seeking mind-set of present Western society. And insofar as contemporary narcissistic society embodies a kind of Feuerbachian reduction of all reality to human experience, theological perspectives like those of the mainline which fall prey to the Feuerbachian critique are also likely to present a God which is regarded by narcissistic society as nothing more than a human projection.

In view of these dynamics, the emergence of secular attitudes and the devaluation of theology in the structures and among the leadership of mainline churches are simply logical outcomes of the unwitting reduction of Christian faith to human experience which plagues much mainline theology. This secularizing tendency seems to manifest itself in another way. The prevailing currents in mainline theology are not fully "biblical" in the sense that they have unwittingly denied the Evangelicals' beloved principle of "Scripture alone." For these currents, the authority for Christian faith is not Scripture alone but Scripture and some external criterion like the interpreter's experience.[25] By contrast, it is precisely the Evangelicals' insistence that Scripture's authority is independent of our experience, that it provides us with universally accessible cognitive revelation, which allows them to assert the objective and transcendent character of God's Word.[26] The Word in Scripture (and its propositional claims) stands over against our experience, as a transcendent "other" which judges human experience.

With its generally staunch insistence on biblical inerrancy and the possibility of discerning the objective meaning of a text, not conditioned by an interpreter's subjective experience, the Evangelical movement serves an important warning to mainline Christian theology. Unfortunately, it is a warning that to date has largely gone unheeded in mainline circles, save for a few mainline theologians who have sought to take Feuerbach's critique of religion seriously.

Given the rising tide of secularism and the destructive features associated with contemporary narcissistic pluralism, the Church and the world are seeking some firm foundation, some secure point of orientation. Evangelicals call the Church's attention to the apparent shortcomings of the prevailing mainline "experience correlated" theologies for providing this. The question now to be considered is whether the only alternative is the doctrine of plenary inspiration and its characteristic Evangelical trappings.

Towards a mainline, evangelically credible alternative

For the mainline churches, the problem with the characteristic Evangelical positions is not so much the mainliners' lack of faith as the intellectual credibility of the Evangelical positions. Mainliners have generally been characterized by Evangelicals as unwilling to assert biblical authority while maintaining an appreciation of the Bible's errancy.[27]

The typical Evangelical solution for dealing with scientific-historical challenges to biblical inerrancy, either by assuming the historicity of the biblical accounts until disproved by critics or by an outright rejection of the operating presuppositions entailed by historical research, does not seem appropriate to mainline theologians.[28] The problem is that these Evangelicals seem to have overlooked the thoroughgoing way in which the presuppositions of historical research have filtered down to the mentality of ordinary people. (This critique applies to those mainline theologians and more recently to those theologically sophisticated Evangelicals who seek to redefine the principles of historical research in order to establish the validity of appealing to faith as a means of establishing the Bible's historicity.)[29]

It is usually conceded that historical research proceeds in its task with three principles: (1) the principle of criticism, which entails that all judgments about the past are only probabilities and must be put into question; (2) the principle of correlation, the presupposition that links must exist between a purported historical event and some antecedents or causes and consequences; and (3) the principle of analogy, according to which no account may be deemed historical unless it has some analog in the present experience of the historian.[30] The last two principles entail conclusions which attempts to establish the Bible's historical accuracy seem unable to overcome. For on these grounds Jesus' resurrection must be ruled out as an "historical" event, since it has no analog in present experience. (When is the last time you saw someone rise from the dead?) Likewise the miracle accounts cannot be regarded as having historical credibility for they have no analogs and by definition cannot be explained in terms of consequences and causes. When the principles of historical criticism are employed, the Bible's historicity and inerrancy are seriously called into question.

Nor can one easily dismiss these consequences by arguing that we are dealing here with intellectual abstractions divorced from reality. In fact ordinary people almost instinctively employ the critical historian's three principles. For example, suppose we see my young son Pat holding a lit cigarette in his hand and confront him with a reprimand. At that point he explains that he was not smoking but merely holding the cigarette for a friend. How are we likely to respond?

No doubt we would begin with skepticism (principle of criticism). Then we would proceed to inquire about the causes for his holding the cigarette, and what he expected to do (principle of correlation). Finally our judgment would be related to how many boys we have seen holding cigarettes without smoking, and what Pat's past record in telling the truth has been (principle of analogy).

This fictitious account and our commonsense reaction to it makes it quite evident that in assessing the historicity of ordinary events we instinctively rely upon the three principles of critical historiography. Therefore the proclamation of the gospel, if it is to be valid and compelling in our society, must be in dialogue with these principles. The failure of the characteristic Evangelical alternatives to take them into account (as they continue to assert the historicity of the miracles even though the critical principles rule this out) suggests why mainliners will not endorse these Evangelical viewpoints.

The credibility of the gospel in relation to our ordinary mode of experiencing the world is at stake. If this is not observed, as sometimes happens among Evangelicals, the Bible's historicity and inerrancy may be affirmed at the cost of denying one's ordinary manner of perceiving reality. As a result, the gap between the accounts reported in Scripture and ordinary modes of experiencing reality may become so great as to render the biblical accounts irrelevant to our daily lives. (Thus the concern for the gospel's intellectual credibility is also a concern for its ability to function relevantly in the daily lives of Christians.)

This provides the rationale for the search for alternatives to the characteristic Evangelical treatment of biblical inerrancy. The problem is how to find a credible alternative which takes into account the valid criticisms of the subjectivist tendencies of the main currents in contemporary mainline theology. We are trying to discern an approach to Scripture which is oriented to the mainline concerns regarding an intellectually credible understanding of the gospel that is at the same time an alternative acceptable to Evangelicals.

It is true, as we have noted, that some Evangelicals have been so sufficiently persuaded by the problems posed for detailed inerrancy by historical criticism that they have embraced in a qualified sense the neoorthodox distinction between Word of God and Scripture, its concept of a special salvation-history distinct from ordinary history, and its insistence that the Bible can only be understood by those with faith.[31] This would seem to suggest that many of the mainline neoorthodox theological alternatives inspired by Barth could be deemed legitimate Evangelical alternatives.

Were the dialogue between mainline churches and the Evangelical movement limited solely to the Evangelical left and to those mainline churches still thoroughly saturated by the influence of Barthian neoorthodoxy, establishing a convergence between the mainline and the Evangelical movement would not be difficult. However, given the relative dearth of neoorthodox influence on the leadership of mainline churches and given the fact that the Evangelical left is likely a small minority in the Evangelical community as a whole, no agreement between these traditions will be very convincing or effective unless it finds acceptance among the more conservative Evangelical establishment with its affirmation of detailed inerrancy.[32] Also in view of the risks associated with neoorthodoxy, the possibility of its lapsing into an experiential subjectivism, at least for purposes of dialogue, mainliners and Evangelicals would be wise to seek a common approach to biblical interpretation in other models. We shall examine the potential resources of a particular kind of mainline narrative/canonical hermeneutics for bridging the Evangelical–mainline gap. In addition to the role this hermeneutical model may play in bridging the gap between mainline theology and the more conservative Evangelical establishment, narrative/canonical hermeneutics may be of interest to helping those Evangelicals who are discontent with the old models of biblical inerrancy, so that they not repeat the mistakes some mainline theologians, heirs of neoorthodoxy, have made in the past generation.

Narrative and canonical methods of biblical interpretation are currently at the forefront of contemporary mainline theological discussion. One suspects that this is so because these approaches seem to embody in a more scholarly, sophisticated form the suppositions employed by most ordinary believers when they read the Bible. Nevertheless, it is important to emphasize that these hermeneutical methods are accepted almost universally as legitimate models for theology within the mainline, ecumenical establishment. Some theologians may find them unacceptable, but never to the point of deeming them as having no academic credibility, as quasi-Fundamentalist.

The endeavor which follows, then, does not aim to show that these narrative and canonical approaches are really Evangelical theological options in disguise, not properly products of mainline theology. The aim is simply to show the degree to which these approaches can logically accommodate Evangelical concerns. The significance is that to the degree such convergence between the logic of narrative/canonical hermeneutics and Conservative Evangelical views of Scripture can be shown, Evangelicals who would disdain Fundamentalist separatism would logically need to be open to regarding the options of mainline theology with which they disagree as not warranting schism. Narrative theologians, after all, do not allow their disagreements with other mainline theological alternatives to sever church fellowship. Therefore, to the degree Evangelicals find narrative theological alternatives acceptable, and these narrative theologians remain in church fellowship with those holding other mainline theological views, Evangelicals would seem obliged not to allow their differences with other mainline alternatives to lead to a break of fellowship.

A complication for such a dialogue between Evangelicals and narrative or canonical hermeneutics is that the concepts of narrative and canonical hermeneutics are defined so broadly at present that a variety of distinct theological alternatives often are classified under these rubrics. In the analysis which follows I am not arguing that all narrative or canonical approaches could be compatible with Conservative Evangelical suppositions. I shall describe only a particular kind of narrative approach, which, though it may not represent precisely the position of any well-known contemporary theologian, reflects the basic suppositions of an influential family of such approaches.[33]

The principal presupposition of the particular narrative and canonical approaches I have in mind is that Scripture is to be interpreted as a piece of literature, rather than as a sourcebook for the history of the early church. Of course, this approach does not rule out the insights of historical-critical research. On the contrary, it welcomes them insofar as they may inform the exegete of literary patterns and nuances of the meanings of words and phrases in a text. Generally speaking, techniques of literary analysis rather than historical criticism are deemed more appropriate for discerning Scripture's literal meaning. For the text as given final canonical form—and not some reconstructed "original" version of the text—is deemed authoritative. Neoorthodox attempts to identify the biblical author's intention and then to use this as a critical principle against Scripture are ruled out. For on grounds of the narrative hermeneutic the meaning of a text is determined by understanding its peculiar shape and literary function, not by speculating about its origin. The similarities are striking between these commitments and the characteristic Evangelical insistence, as expressed most notably by the International Council on Biblical Inerrancy, that the canonical text, not precanonical sources, is ultimately authoritative.[34]

The presuppositions of this kind of narrative/canonical approach also are helpful in responding to the challenges posed by historical criticism. If Scripture is considered as a piece of literature, properly analyzed by literary analytic techniques, it would seem to have its own integrity apart from the question of whether it actually refers to historical realities. At least historical criticism should not be able to disconfirm the biblical text's meaningfulness any more than it could serve to compromise the value of some great piece of literature like *Macbeth*. The proponent of narrative theology is thereby able to maintain the mainline-modernist commitment to a dialogue with critical historiography and its three principles without undermining the authority of the biblical text as it stands. Even proponents of these approaches like Brevard Childs, who has bluntly stated his reservations to colleagues who might proceed to deny the relevance of the Bible's historical referentiality, still concede that the Bible's referentiality is of a "theological order" which need not necessarily conform to modern historical categories.[35]

This idea that the Bible involves its own "language game" and is not vunerable to the vagaries of historical research, because the historical factuality of the biblical accounts has been relegated to a second-order status, is quite consistent with the approach of a number of Conservative Evangelical theologians, such as Carl Henry, the eminent charismatic Larry Christenson, and a whole host of Evangelicals who employ the method of presuppositionalism, including even some authors of *The Fundamentals*. Various modern proponents of the Dutch Reformed heritage of Abraham Kuyper, insofar as they reject the idea that faith need be founded on judgments about its truth in the court of certain secular "foundational" principles, seem to take a position which, if it is not outright Barthianism, might be compatible with the narrative hermeneutic concept of distinct language-games.[36] Additionally, it is helpful to note in response to those who would argue that a kind of neoorthodox critical hermeneutic is an earmark of the Reformation heritage that this sort of bracketing of historical questions in relation to the biblical accounts also has precedents in Luther. In a 1538 sermon on John 2:13-15, the reformer notes a discrepancy among the Gospel writers in regard to the time in Jesus' ministry when he cast the money-changers out of the Temple. Luther concludes that this problem is not essential. As a narrative theologian might, he suggests that we focus simply on the text and the articles of faith (WA 46, 726, 11ff./LW 22, 218). The family resemblances between this sort of narrative hermeneutic and certain typical Evangelical views of Scripture are suggested even more strikingly when one learns how narrative hermeneutics construes the kind of literature embodied in Scripture.

One consequence of narrative theology is that what its proponents claim about the nature of Scripture is based upon the Bible's literal content. A commonsense reading of the text, it is argued, shows quite clearly that at the center of Scripture are the accounts of Jesus, particularly his death and resurrection. The case for this conclusion seems indisputable. It is evident both from the standpoint of the centrality of the confession of Jesus for the early church and on the basis of literary analytic judgments about Scripture considered as a whole. (Such a description of a Christocentric center of the biblical witness is not inconsistent with the Lutheran insistence on justification as "the main doctrine of Christianity" [*Apology of the Augsburg Confession*, Art.IV.2; cf. *The Smalcald Articles*, II, Art.I.1].) A significant number of Evangelicals, among them the International Council on Biblical Inerrancy, John Stott, members of the Konferenz Bekennender Gemeinschaften in Germany, and even authors of *The Fundamentals*, agree.[37]

From this observation several hermeneutical implications follow. The centrality of Jesus and the account of his passion and resurrection, which constitutes who he is, are most evident in those portions of Scripture whose literary characteristics, according to some eminent literary critics, are somewhat akin to 19th-century English and French realistic novels. These texts are historylike narratives in the sense that the characters of the narrative are developed in their interactions with their environment. We know who the characters are by what they are doing. Often it is the reports of mundane daily existence rather than contrived, unrealistic situations that depict who the characters are. This attention to detail entails that unlike a myth the characters in such narratives are unsubstitutable. The Gospels and at least portions of the Pentateuch and the Old Testament histories appear to embody these features. One might concede to Evangelicals that these portions of Scripture as well as the remainder of the Bible are propositional, not in literary form but in the sense that history, novels, letters, and poetry *propose* something for consideration.

Given the fact that these narrative portions of Scripture occupy the focus of attention, and inasmuch as a summary of the Christian story from creation to the end times assumes the specific literary features of a realistic narrative, it is not unreasonable to regard the whole of Scripture in its canonical unity as a nonfictional narrative, to regard its nonnarrative portions like epistles, wisdom literature, and the like as commentaries on the overarching narrative of God's redeeming work through Christ. This awareness of the narrativelike character of the biblical content when considered in toto accounts for the designation of this approach as "narrative theology." Such an appreciation of Scripture's narrativelike character provides the kind of affirmation of the Bible's unity which Evangelicals normally seek to embrace.[38] It also entails certain hermeneutical commitments. These are quite suggestive of the view of Scripture that characterizes much of the Evangelical movement.

When one interprets a realistic narrative one reads it literally. The text means what it says. One does not seek for a deeper meaning hidden "under" or "in front of" the text. Thus for the particular kind of narrative hermeneutics I have been describing, at least in regard to those portions of Scripture of narrative genre, it should be possible, at least as an ideal for which to strive, to discern a single descriptive (normative) meaning for a text, not conditioned by the perspective or context of the interpreter. (The same claim is not made with respect to all portions of Scripture, such as the Psalms, where the poetic genre of the literature encourages and authorizes a multiplicity of valid inter-pretations. Nor is it claimed that it is possible to identify a single valid construal for harmonizing various portions of Scripture into a system-atic unity.) Such a commitment to the possibility of identifying a single fixed, descriptive meaning in a particular biblical text is a typical commitment of a large number of Evangelicals, especially those op-erating with the suppositions of Scottish common sense philosophy.[39]

These commitments represent a break with the prevailing Kantian presuppositions and their perspectivalism. Thus it is little wonder that the reader might find such commitments initially untenable. For as one commentator has noted, since Kant, "interpretation" has been under-stood to involve not mere "analysis of texts" but an analysis of the "process of understanding" texts.[40] On such grounds the interpreter has no immediate access to texts and so can never hope to identify *the* meaning of a text. But as we have seen, when such a supposition is left unchallenged, Feuerbach's critique of religion and its implications for reinforcing cultural narcissism seem vindicated. One can never speak of God's Word in itself over against human experience (for we can never know the meaning of that Word apart from what we add to it through our "creative interpretive intervention").

At any rate, given the monolithic, virtually unchallenged dominance of these Kantian assumptions, it is also little wonder that a number of mainline theologians employing narrative hermeneutics and a number of Evangelicals have rejected the possibility of identifying a single, descriptive meaning in narrativelike biblical texts. Among Evangelicals we have noted that an insistence on the necessary role of the interpreter's perspective, particularly faith, in determining one's understanding of Scripture is prevalent among those most influenced by German Pietism. Yet this perspectival orientation is reflected in the more left-wing Evan-gelicals, such as Orlando Costas and Anthony Thiselton.[41]

Many practitioners of the narrative approach who retain Kantian, perspectival assumptions could be mentioned. Among the more prom-inent are Paul Ricoeur, Gabriel Fackre, and a number of interpreters influenced by structuralism (a technique of interpretation which focuses especially on the peculiar systematic arrangement and patterns of lin-guistic signs). These interpreters also maintain that the meaning of the biblical accounts is related to the interpreter's reaction to them.[42]

In view of the orientation of these theologians it is important to keep in mind that the approaches I am discussing refer to specific kinds of narrative and canonical hermeneutics. In fact, though, even the main practitioners of the particular approaches I have been sketching make significant qualifications concerning the possibility of identifying the one, descriptive meaning of a text.

For example, Brevard Childs, the formulator of canonical exegesis, is somewhat ambiguous concerning this issue. On one hand, he has rejected Paul Ricoeur's idea that the meaning of a text is given anew in each new circumstance. He proceeds to argue that even unbelievers can understand Scripture descriptively (though they may not penetrate deeply into its theological significance).[43] In other places he speaks of Scripture as having a "determinative" and "plain meaning."[44] Yet on the other hand at least at one point Childs seems totally to reject the possibility of a single, fixed meaning to a text.[45] This ambiguity seems resolvable only by reference to Childs's idea that discerning the canonical shaping of a biblical text, though it may not yield its determinative meaning, does "chart boundaries" in which valid interpretation can take place.[46] In short, Childs seems to be opting for a certain descriptive, plain meaning in the biblical text which sets limits for interpretation but does not foreclose the possibility of the interpreter's contribution to the text's interpretation in a given context, particularly with regard to construing a unity among various texts. In principle we can all agree on the bare descriptive meaning of a text, but this does not foreclose the possibility of our appropriating it differently.

I take it that this was once also the position of another key narrative theologian, Hans Frei, as well as of a number of Evangelicals. For Frei explicitly and the International Council on Biblical Inerrancy implicitly have maintained that interpretation involves several stages. At the most basic stage, the sheer retelling of the biblical text, the literal meaning is descriptively ascertainable by all interpreters. But at the stage of applying the text, when it functions to render Christ present to readers so that they come to identify with the world that Scripture depicts and to acknowledge its truth, then a single descriptive meaning is no longer obtainable or desirable. That is because at this stage the text is meaningful by appropriation.[47] Thus, for example, though all might in principle agree on the descriptive meaning of the empty tomb account in Mark 16 and its relationship to the disciples' blindness throughout the Gospel, when this text is preached/appropriated it would take a variety of different sermonic forms. Yet the fact that some limits fixed by the biblical text to this diversity of legitimate appropriations are acknowledged entails that the Word of God and its meaning are portrayed as a reality transcending human experience. For on these grounds the Word itself furnishes some limits to its meaning and provides conceptions which are not contingent upon the interpreter's (human) experience of the Word. Also the descriptive or literal meaning of the text about which all may agree functions as a criterion by which to determine how the text legitimately can be appropriated, so that one is not free to make the text say whatever one wants to make it mean. In its openness to the possibility of attaining a single, descriptive meaning for some biblical texts, narrative theology, not unlike the characteristic Evangelical hermeneutic, offers a genuine alternative to the subjectivism of the prevailing streams of modern theology.

It may be that the differences are not so great at this point between the intentions of narrative theology and Evangelicalism, on one side, and the prevailing mainline streams, on the other. It is not so great a difference if the rejection by some mainline theologians of the possibility of discerning a text's descriptive meaning is fundamentally occasioned by the pastoral concern to allow for a variety of legitimate ways of appropriating or proclaiming a text. In that case all that is necessary to facilitate convergence would be for both sides to become more self-conscious and precise in positing a distinction between the meaning and appropriation of a text. One could then talk about certain texts reflecting a single descriptive meaning which might still be appropriated and proclaimed in a variety of ways. It may well be that some mainline theological alternatives are so committed to Kantian epistemological suppositions and the idea that meaning necessarily includes the knower's perspectival appropriation so as to render a distinction between the two untenable. But at least the possibility should be explored that both sides might be reconciled at this point, that they in fact share similar concerns in affirming that interpreters must be free to apply Scripture differently in different contexts.

Certainly in other ways the differences that narrative theology and Evangelicalism have with the prevailing streams of modern theology are not so dramatic. Both narrative theology and most Evangelicals will concede that some portions of Scripture, notably the Psalms and perhaps also the parables, are not to be read literally and so have no single determinative meaning.[48] Also the narrative and canonical approaches I have been describing are not precritical or pre-Kantian in the sense that they do not claim to be devoid of interpretive presuppositions. Indeed, the claims which can be made with these approaches concerning the possibility of interpreters' achieving agreement about a text's descriptive meaning presuppose that the interpreters share common interpretive presuppositions. However, the presuppositions which they employ aim to be "formal," not "material" presuppositions. That is, they purport not to affect the content of the biblical text.

The idea that it may be possible to identify a single, descriptive meaning in certain kinds of biblical texts finds support from a number of places. The continuing influence of Scottish common sense realism, with its supposition that people can agree on the "objective," descriptive meaning of interpreted objects by relying on their common sense, is still quite evident, at least in segments of society removed from university centers. Thus, at the grass roots, the kind of narrative hermeneutical approach I have been outlining would seem likely to meet with the kind of positive reaction that the theological suppositions of the Evangelical movement are enjoying.

Even in university centers the idea of the possibility of identifying the descriptive meaning of texts rather than reducing it to the interpreter's life-perspective is maintained in some schools of literary analysis, particularly in the thought of several older American new critics.[49] Nor can it be argued, as some Protestants heavily influenced by neo-orthodoxy might, that the narrative approach's quest for the single, descriptive meaning of certain texts represents a departure from the Reformation heritage. Martin Luther was adamant in insisting that one should not interpret Scripture according to one's own experience or context, but understand it on its own terms.[50] And, at least in the treatise *How Christians Should Regard Moses,* Luther claims that Scripture is Word of God regardless of how we experience or apply it:

> The Word in Scripture is of two kinds: the first does not pertain or apply to me, and the other kind does. And upon that word which does pertain to me I can boldly trust and rely, as upon a strong rock. But if it does not pertain to me, then I should stand still. The false prophets pitch in and say, "Dear people, this is the Word of God." This is true; we cannot deny it. But we are not the people to Whom He speaks, God has not given us the directive.   (WA 16, 385f., 26ff./LW 35, 170)

Alongside the kind of critical hermeneutic which we have previously observed in Luther, one on which he relied particularly when he polemicized against legalism, we find these other hermeneutical suppositions. Much like the kind of narrative hermeneutic I have been describing, when he employed this other, more typical hermeneutical approach, Luther regarded the meaning of the Bible as Word of God as not influenced by the interpreter's experience of it. One finds other instances of this commitment elsewhere in the premodern Lutheran heritage in the claim that the Word of God has its own power as Word of God regardless of its effects.[51]

To be sure, this commitment to the possibility of attaining the single, descriptive literal meaning of a biblical text entails difficulties in a number of ways. A great resource in seeking to accomplish this aim is the role the Church's tradition might play as a hermeneutical tool to rule out improper interpretations. One learns whether one has attained the goal of a text's descriptive meaning by seeing whether one can convince others of the validity of one's interpretation. This happens in community. The Church's tradition, how the church has historically understood a given biblical text or theme, may function as the interpreter's conversation partner. This kind of commitment is reflected in the work of both Frei and Childs. For Frei at least the literal sense of Scripture (its descriptive meaning) is said to be identical with the way that text has been used and experienced in the Church's history.[52]

Narrative and canonical approaches to theology may be most helpful in overcoming the Scripture/tradition dichotomy. *Sola Scriptura* is still affirmed, for the touchstone and norm for all Christian theology are still grounded in Scripture. But tradition functions to provide the basic Christian suppositions for a literal reading of the biblical text, to help interpreters identify Scripture's meaning, or at least rule out improper interpretations. Such an orientation not only converges with the Roman Catholic and Orthodox positions on the subjects; even the Lutheran tradition more or less reflects this kind of orientation, specifically in its *Formula of Concord* (SD Rule and Norm 7ff.).

Although the Evangelical movement is generally thought to favor a rigid separation of Scripture and tradition, the kind of orientation which we have seen exhibited in the narrative approach need not be inimical to all segments of the Evangelical movement. We have observed some Evangelical openness to the role of the universal priesthood in judging doctrine. Nor should one overlook claims to the Church's role in discerning truth from such widely diverse sources as *The Fundamentals*, Pentecostals on the Roman Catholic–Pentecostal Dialogue, and even the French Evangelical faculty, the Faculté Libre de Théologie Evangélique Vaux-sur-Seine. In fact, an appeal to tradition as in some sense the infallible rule of interpretation is consistent with Princeton theology's use of common sense realism and its notion that we can trust the testimony of many people which has endured over time.[53]

In any case, the narrative and canonical approaches we have examined are not necessarily incompatible with tolerable Evangelical options for the relationship between Scripture and tradition. By appeal to the tradition to rule out improper interpretations of Scripture, both the mainline narrative/canonical approaches and the more characteristic hermeneutics of the Evangelical movement are in principle better able to discern the descriptive meaning of the Word of God which can stand over against cultural relativism and subjectivism.

Other convergences

Two other areas of convergence between narrative/canonical hermeneutics and recognized legitimate hermeneutical alternatives within the Evangelical movement may be noted. First, to the extent Scripture is regarded as akin to a realistic novel, as the narrative approach maintains, all portions of the book must command the reader's attention if the whole book is rightly to be understood. Just as one cannot truly understand a novel if one skips certain chapters, so with Scripture. In that sense, the whole book must be deemed authoritative. No distinction between Word of God and biblical text is permitted if it leads one to bypass what the text actually says. Is this commitment not consistent with the Evangelical insistence on Scripture's plenary authority? (Could such an affirmation also not logically accommodate the concern to affirm plenary inspiration?) This idea that all Scripture is Word of God certainly is consistent with the Protestant heritage as well, as is demonstrated in Luther's statement that even those portions of Scripture which do not directly concern the hearer are God's Word.

The characteristics attributed to Scripture by narrative and canonical approaches indicate that these mainline alternatives place a high value on human language and its adequacy for communicating divine revelation. This commitment is especially evident when one considers the claim of Hans Frei that the written text *is* actually God's linguistic presence to God's people. A similar point is made by Childs as he claims, much as Evangelicals do, that history per se is not a medium of revelation but only functions as revelation in the final form of the biblical text (the words of Scripture) where normative history reaches its proper end as it is properly interpreted.[54] What else is this but an implicit affirmation of the verbal authority of Scripture? Could not a practitioner of such commitments logically affirm Scripture's verbal inspiration? Would not something like the latter claim be implicit in the prior affirmations of this hermeneutic?

Even this affirmation cannot be deemed by neoorthodox Lutheran and Reformed theologians as a complete distortion of the Reformation heritage. When he was not operating with a critical hermeneutic but with his more "narrativelike" hermeneutic, Luther himself could speak of the verbal inspiration of Scripture. He claims on one occasion that "Not only the words but also the expression that the Holy Spirit and Scripture employ is divine."[55] Similar affirmations were made by John Calvin.[56] The narrative and canonical approaches I have sketched seem in principle able to account for Evangelical concerns to affirm Scripture's plenary and verbal authority, and to do so in such a way that neither the heritage of the Reformation nor the Roman Catholic tradition need be distorted.[57]

The high valuation narrative hermeneutics confers on human language and its adequacy for communicating divine revelation is especially evident when one considers yet another characteristic attributed to the biblical narrative, what literary critic Erich Auerbach has called its "tyrannical authority." In the course of acknowledging the realistic narrativelike style of the biblical stories he asserts that the Bible's claim to truth is tyrannical in the sense that its claim to truth excludes all other claims. He then proceeds to state:

> The world of the Scripture stories is not satisfied with claiming to be an historically true reality—it insists that it is the only real world, is destined for autocracy. All other scenes, issues, and ordinances have no right to appear independently of it, and it is promised that all of them, the history of mankind, will be given their due place within its frame, will be subordinated to it. . . . Far from seeking, like Homer, merely to make us forget our reality for a few hours, it seeks to overcome our reality; we are to fit our own life into its world, feel ourselves to be elements in its structure of universal history.[58]

Auerbach describes an experience analogous to that which happens to readers of engaging realistic novels. On some occasions a text can become so captivating that one feels a personal loss when the book ends, as if one has bade farewell to friends made while reading. On occasion such texts can change one's whole orientation to life. (Some Gentile readers became ardent Zionist supporters after reading Leon Uris's novel *Exodus*.) For a narrative hermeneutic, this is how the Bible functions for Christians. The world it depicts becomes the world by which Christians orient themselves and their experiences. The principal biblical characters (Jesus and the Father) are made present by the text as Christians come to be identified with other biblical characters.

This sort of hermeneutic and its idea that the biblical world furnishes the Christian's framework for interpreting reality seems closely to resemble the worldview which typically is thought to characterize the ethos and spirituality of many Conservative Evangelical communities. Thus, those concerned that the prevailing mainline uses of Scripture impede the development of this sort of lively "Evangelical" spirituality may find a narrative hermeneutic to be an interesting resource for mainline Christians concerned about nurturing spirituality and evangelism in their churches.

These conceptions emerging from narrative hermeneutics offer other features which are quite congenial to Conservative Evangelical theology. The narrative idea that the biblical text functions like a realistic novel in overwhelming and transforming our reality suggests promising avenues for proclamation of the gospel. This dimension of the narrative approach is particularly promising to Evangelicals insofar as it affirms the importance of biblical language in shaping Christian response and suggests a way to move beyond a merely propositional view of Scripture. Thus it is in harmony with the commitments of many Evangelicals.

Of course, understanding Scripture can never be an end in itself. It cannot merely result in intellectual knowledge, a warning some have accused Conservative Evangelical theologians of failing to heed. But a narrative hermeneutic implies that an understanding of the biblical accounts can offer reality-transforming insights/experiences.

In the course of our discussion we have noted how theologically conservative Lutherans are sometimes hesitant to identify with the Evangelical movement, in part because of the latter's purported Reformed-propositional construal of Scripture. Their fear is that Evangelicals have placed so much stress on an intellectual understanding of the biblical propositions that they have overlooked the transforming power of the gospel, that they have missed God's self-revelation by concentrating merely on *teachings* about God in Scripture.[59] Insofar as the narrative hermeneutic we have sketched, with its idea that the Bible is tyrannically authoritative in picturing a world which defines the reality of believers, seems to account for this Lutheran concern as well as the intentions of conservative Lutheran preoccupation with verbal and plenary inspiration and like issues, could this hermeneutic ever be deemed a legitimate theological alternative by churches like The Lutheran Church–Missouri Synod and its sisters? In interests of Lutheran unity it is a question well worth asking.

Granted, some of the church-dividing tensions among Lutherans in Europe may be related to the ongoing family dispute between Lutheran Orthodoxy and Pietism. However, for the most part, divisions in the Lutheran community relate to the various churches' views of Scripture.

If conservatives like LCMS could deem narrative and canonical hermeneutics as practiced in the mainline churches legitimate approaches, they could presumably acknowledge the orthodoxy of some of the theology of these churches. In addition, our analysis has suggested that in Luther one finds a variety of approaches to Scripture, one consistent with the Orthodox and narrative approaches, the other a more critical approach which seems to converge with modern neoorthodox theological commitments. If both views can be shown to be rooted in Luther, and if he held these views together, why should these different views divide the Lutheran community today? At least insofar as it leads us to pose such a question the dialogue between mainline churches and the Evangelical movement has clear intra-Lutheran significance.

In fact, it is not altogether clear that theologically conservative Lutherans like The Lutheran Church–Missouri Synod and its sister churches represent a special case with regard to mainline–Conservative Evangelical dialogue. Their claim that their view of Scripture is markedly distinct from that of the Reformed-influenced, purportedly rationalistic and biblicistic Evangelical movement is by no means obvious.

In fairness first to the Reformed brothers and sisters, it must be noted that it is not clear that an emphasis on the existential, reality-transforming character of the Word is inimical to the Reformed tradition, as conservative Lutherans allege. Calvin seems to share this commitment. In his *Institutes* (I/II.2; I/VII.1; III/II.14), he stresses the knowledge of God, but by this concept he refers not merely to theoretical but to existential (reality-transforming) knowledge. For him, the Word of Scripture is a living Word. It is also hardly surprising to find this commitment to the effective power of the Word reflected in one of the leaders of the 19th-century Reformed revival in the Netherlands, Herman Bavinck. He insisted that Scripture is the Word of God *because of* its existential effects.[60]

To the degree that these Reformed thinkers have had an impact on the Evangelical movement, one must concede that the movement does reflect a concern with the existential impact of the Word. To be sure, one can identify occasions where a kind of "rationalistic biblicism" with no attention to spiritual experience is apparent. We already have noted instances of this in Princeton theology.[61] But we have also observed occasions among the Princetonians where the work of the Spirit and the experience of faith were seen as necessarily linked to and confirming the biblical Word.

One can find a whole host of examples of this tendency in the Evangelical movement. Evangelicals like Carl Henry, Don Dayton, and Gerald Sheppard, and, outside the United States, African Evangelicals like Kwame Bediako as well as West German conservatives of the Gnadauer Verband opt for a kind of "figural interpretation" of Scripture, insofar as they interpret the biblical accounts as present realities with power to shape and transform their hearers' lives.[62] Another significant segment of Evangelicalism, the American Black churches, have also quite typically employed a kind of narrative preaching style wherein the hearer's reality is defined and identified by the biblical accounts.[63] Indeed, the sort of vibrant spirituality and ethos which often is thought to characterize the Evangelical movement as a whole, the sense one has around Evangelicals that they consider themselves to be living in God's presence, seems to presuppose that Scripture functions for them not merely as a book of doctrine, but also as a living Word which provides a "world" for believers, a medium in which they move and can interpret reality.

In fact this sort of commitment to the living power of the Word to transform lives even could be related to the Evangelical movement's dependence on Scottish common sense realist philosophy. For a basic supposition of this philosophy is that memory makes possible immediate contact with the past, and this is mediated through words.[64] When these commitments are applied to theology they could permit one to affirm that the words of Scripture do not merely teach doctrine but render present the principal biblical characters, God and Christ, in an encounter which will presumably transform readers' lives. Something like this construal of Scripture is affirmed by narrative hermeneutics.

At any rate, concerns conservative Lutherans might raise about the attention Evangelicals give to the power of the Word to render God present and awaken faith seem well dealt with by a number of Evangelicals. Thus it is by no means clear that these conservative Lutherans can in fact distinguish themselves from the Evangelical movement on the basis of their view of Scripture. Likewise there appears to be a significant convergence at this point between Evangelicals and the kind of narrative and canonical hermeneutics I have been describing. Could it be that the Evangelical movement's appropriation and use of these mainline models could help it maintain its commitment to the reality-transforming character of the Word of God?

Despite this attractive feature and despite the narrative model's ability to affirm something like the verbal and plenary authority of Scripture, Evangelicals might at first experience certain hesitations about this theological model. The nagging question for most Evangelicals is whether, on narrative assumptions, Scripture is anything more than a piece of literature. Thus, for example, although the plenary and verbal authority of Scripture might in principle be allowed for by narrative theology it does not speak directly of the Bible's divine inspiration nor does it seem to make historical-scientific claims on behalf of the biblical accounts.

Further examination of the narrative approach, however, suggests that even these Orthodox concerns may receive adequate attention. In regard to the question of divine inspiration, Brevard Childs's narrative-related canonical approach makes an important point. According to narrative and canonical hermeneutics, the Bible is authoritative because the Christian community deems it authoritative; it is authoritative in virtue of the Church's use of it. Yet Childs proceeds to argue that although the Church has established the canon it has not done so by fiat. Rather in the canonical process Israel was simply receiving that which was already authoritative.[65] Although the language of divine inspiration is not explicitly used at this point a special (perhaps inspired) character to the biblical texts is clearly assumed. Additionally, insofar as narrative theology affirms the unity of Scripture, such suppositions would make it logically possible to regard Scripture as composed by a single author (who can only be God).

On the question of the relationship which narrative theology posits between the biblical accounts and historical reality, Evangelicals may also initially experience some reticence. The concern for Evangelicals would be that they seem to posit a "double truth" theory—the idea that the truth of Christianity is somehow a different kind of truth than that experienced in everyday life. There is an even more damning critique. By ignoring the question of truth, these approaches seem to relinquish the reality of the biblical referents like God, Christ, and grace.[66]

It must be noted, however, that these concerns reflect a modern post-Enlightenment theological mode of thinking. For among the new elements introduced into Christian theology by the 18th-century Enlightenment was a concern for the historical (empirical) verifiability of the Bible's claims as a test for truth. By contrast, prior to the Enlightenment the biblical text or the Church's authoritative tradition had been the criterion for truth, the measure of historical-scientific veracity. In some respects, insofar as they follow this sequence of grounding truth in Scripture and not making this truth depend on historical-empirical verifiability, narrative and canonical hermeneutics converge with pre-Enlightenment patterns of thought. But, as we have seen, Evangelicals also are aiming to present an antebellum, pre-Enlightenment version of Christian faith,[67] and so the critical questions they might pose at this point may be directed also to their own theological intentions.

At any rate, the question of the truth and historical reality of biblical accounts seems to be a concern of narrative and canonical theologians. Childs claims that the biblical text does refer at some points to God and the world.[68] The issue is directly addressed by Hans Frei as a consequence of his narrative hermeneutic's focus on the identity of Jesus Christ. The argument is that Jesus' identity is most manifest in the resurrection accounts, where he is truly identified as the promised one and Savior. As such, and insofar as the resurrection accounts do not possess the genre of myth but are historylike, they raise in a most pressing way the question of the historical probability of the biblical accounts in general. For it is here that Jesus is portrayed as most of all himself. His identity is literally depicted as that of the one who has risen and lives (John 11:25). Thus to *know* who Jesus is must entail *that* he is, that he lives! To say that he does not live is to speak of a "Jesus" other than the Jesus portrayed by the biblical accounts. But this construction of a Jesus other than the one portrayed in the biblical accounts is not possible for the Christian who accepts the authority of Scripture as the sole norm for assessing what we know and experience of Jesus. In short, the argument is that to be a Christian and to accept the authority of the biblical accounts logically entails a belief that Jesus has *in fact* risen; it is inconceivable to think of him as not risen. As such, resurrection faith is more nearly a belief in the inspired quality of the Bible than a theory that makes formal historical claims on behalf of the resurrection.[69] (At this point narrative theology seems explicitly to embrace the divine inspiration of Scripture.)

The concentration of this approach on the descriptive structure of the biblical accounts rather than their factual historicity is clearly a consequence of narrative theology's philosophical judgment about the nature of historical claims and the prevalence of the three principles of critical historiography on the modern mind. As we have noted, on such grounds no adequate warrants for asserting the historicity of the resurrection or of reports of miracles can be provided. However, Frei's narrative approach does take very seriously the factual implications of the resurrection accounts and belief in their divinely inspired authority. No meaningless, untestable claim to the resurrection's factuality is made; instead, it is conceded that historical evidence against the resurrection would be decisive in disconfirming Christian faith.[70] Presumably the "history" in which these factual implications of the resurrection are said to take place is the same sphere as that of "ordinary history."

This sort of treatment of the resurrection accounts is not foreign to the classical Protestant heritage. In his 1533 *Commentary on 1 Corinthians,* Luther likewise made no effort to defend the historical credibility of Jesus' resurrection. His argument for the resurrection is based solely on the Word and its logical implication that Christians cannot be Christians if they deny the resurrection (WA 36, 492-530/LW 28, 68-98).

Although it is only with respect to the resurrection accounts that such a narrative theology insists on the factual implications of the biblical witness, the truth and historicity of its other accounts is in no way called into question. The "tyrannical authority" of the Bible, to which we earlier alluded, is significant at this point.

Recall that for narrative theology the biblical accounts provide a world which overwhelms the reality of readers, becomes the worldview by which they orient themselves. Thus the question of the reality of this biblical world need not arise; it can be simply assumed. All this is a bit like being entranced by a realistic novel. One is no longer a spectator; the world depicted by the text is experienced as real. The depicted story renders reality in such a way that the question of the story's factual reference never occurs to captivated readers. For them the account simply *must* be real. On these narrative grounds, the question of the historical reality of the biblical narratives need not occur to believers. They have all the knowledge they need, for they are standing in the presence of God.[71]

The concern for the truth of Christian faith is reflected in this theological model, then, in the subjectivity (form of life) of believers, in the ability of the faith to help them make sense of the world. And this entails no mere relativism ("my truth is as good as yours"). Evidence adduced by those outside the Christian community which would unequivocally rule against the gospel's adequacy in making sense of the world could not decisively disprove the truth of Christian faith, but such evidence would count against its truth claims and tend to disconfirm them. Also the possibility of a rational comparison and conversation between Christian faith and other alternatives is by no means precluded by this narrative approach. It even allows that certain features of Christian faith could be persuasive to non-Christians.

Quite profound analogies exist between this narrative approach's treatment of the possible historical referentiality of the biblical accounts and the claims to the Bible's historical inerrancy made by Evangelicals, particularly those influenced by the method of presuppositionalism.

These Evangelicals, as we have noted, quite specifically deem the acceptance of the Bible's historicity and its inerrancy as second-order consequences of a basic presupposition that God has revealed himself in the biblical accounts. Thus the historical inerrancy of Scripture, the assumption that what Scripture reports is true, is not deemed the basic presupposition for exegesis but is regarded as a consequence of the basic presupposition.[72] This seems to be the kind of argument which could logically be employed by the sorts of narrative and canonical hermeneutics I have described for those inclined to deal more systematically with the question of the Bible's historical reliability or inerrancy.

Summary reflections

We have identified a remarkable number of possible convergences between Conservative Evangelical and narrative/canonical views concerning the nature of Scripture. These include a mutual commitment to the authority of the canonical text, to the possibility of discerning the single, fixed, descriptive meaning of a biblical text, and to certain convergences regarding the unity of Scripture, the sense in which one could speak of its verbal and plenary inspiration, as well as to the manner of how one might deal with the biblical accounts' factual implications and accuracy. One can identify even further points of convergence between these mainline approaches and those of the Evangelical movement, particularly the method of presuppositionalism.

Thus, for example, even the procedure of narrative theologians in maintaining that Scripture is a piece of literature which cannot thereby be discredited by historical-critical research is, as we have noted, consistent with contemporary Evangelical commitments. Nowhere is this convergence more apparent than in *The Chicago Statement on Biblical Inerrancy* (XIII) drafted by the International Council on Biblical Inerrancy. This distinguished group of Evangelicals stated that it is "not proper to evaluate Scripture according to standards. . . that are alien to its usage or purpose."

This kind of theological move, assigning the biblical accounts to their own unique "language game" so that these accounts cannot be discredited by other modes of investigation, is made by a wide variety of other Evangelicals. It is reflected among those Evangelicals like Carl Henry who claim that, because the biblical authors were not teaching ontology, the lack of scientific accuracy in their writing cannot imply the errancy of Scripture.[73] Likewise those numerous Evangelical churches and organizations which seem to claim that the Bible's inerrancy pertains only to its spiritual intention seem to converge with narrative hermeneutics on this point.[74] Such a distinction between religious and historical-scientific truth so that the Bible's claims to inerrancy are limited to the spiritual realm is even evident in the Fundamentalist period of Evangelicalism. Such a distinction marks at least one of the articles in *The Fundamentals* and in some of the literature of Princeton theology.[75]

This sort of treatment of the inerrancy of Scripture is quite consistent with narrative and canonical hermeneutics. To be sure, none of the proponents of these approaches with whom I am acquainted explicitly speaks of the inerrancy or infallibility of Scripture. However, insofar as the authority of the canonical text and even the appropriate factual implications of its accounts are accepted without criticism by these hermeneutical approaches, the canonical text appears to function infallibly for them in the Christian language game. Thus these approaches seem to treat the canonical text as inerrant in the sense that they regard Scripture as incapable of deceiving the Christian community or leading it away from the Gospel and truth. Ralph Bohlmann of The Lutheran Church–Missouri Synod has said that inerrancy is a necessary concept but the term itself "is perhaps expendable."[76] This may be the implicit position of narrative and canonical hermeneutics. Something like the concept of inerrancy could be implied, though the term itself is "expendable."

One can identify other remarkable convergences between the narrative approach and various hermeneutical views of the Evangelical movement. In protecting the integrity of the Bible's claims from historical and scientific criticism, the narrative approach relies on the notion of distinct "language games," a notion drawn from the philosophy of Ludwig Wittgenstein. Each language game has its own "presuppositions" which cannot be challenged by suppositions from other language games. The similarities to the Evangelical method of presuppositionalism are quite apparent. More striking is the fact that the prominent presuppositionalist Carl Henry has—like narrative theologians—actually invoked Wittgenstein's philosophical models as a way of making his point.[77]

Convergences between Evangelicals and the narrative approach are evident elsewhere. Hans Frei's argument for Jesus' resurrection, that Christian presuppositions make it logically necessary, even though historical proof is not possible, is reiterated by Henry in his own way.[78]

We have noted that narrative and canonical hermeneutics have certain affinities to pre-Enlightenment modes of exegesis. One of these affinities, particularly with Luther, renders these approaches most helpful in face of post-Enlightenment criticism of the patriarchal, premodern character of certain biblical values. When Luther employed a narrativelike hermeneutic, apparently deeming all Scripture Word of God, he would nonetheless concede that certain segments of Scripture are not Word of God *in this situation* (WA 16, 385f., 26ff./LW 35, 170).

Such an affirmation of the special appropriateness of some portions of Scripture in certain circumstances but not in others is affirmed by Brevard Childs.[79] This orientation allows the modern church to deal with problematic biblical texts like those concerning slavery (Exod. 21:1-11; Deut. 15:12-18; Philemon; 1 Cor. 7:20-24) and the role of women in the Church (1 Cor. 11:2-16; 14:34-35; 1 Tim. 2:8-15). On narrative grounds they still could be deemed as Word of God, applicable in certain historical periods, but not today insofar as there are no analogs between our present situation and concerns addressed by these texts. Thus it may come as a pleasant surprise to mainliners and Evangelicals alike to note that a number of prominent Evangelicals, including Carl Henry, the French Evangelical Henri Blocher, and even the International Council on Biblical Inerrancy in *The Chicago Statement on Biblical Hermeneutics* agree that not all Scripture is equally relevant to a given situation.[80] This approach represents a new (more traditional) kind of "contextual theology," one which does not allow the interpreter's context to affect the meaning of a text but rather to indicate which portions of Scripture are most appropriate in a given situation. Given the present ecumenical commitment to contextualizing theology, this "Evangelical" version is a most interesting possibility.

The number of convergences between characteristic Evangelical views of Scripture and at least what can be logically affirmed by proponents of narrative/canonical hermeneutics is remarkable. Given these affinities, it is hardly surprising to learn that some in the Evangelical community are coming to notice these similarities and even appropriating canonical hermeneutics for themselves. Among those who are in dialogue with, if not themselves employing the work of canonical hermeneutics are Carl Henry, Gerald Sheppard, Gabriel Fackre, and various faculty of The Free Methodist Church's Seattle Pacific University.[81] In the case of Henry and some other Evangelicals, the initial reactions have been somewhat critical, a kind of affirmation of the superiority of their own approaches over these mainline alternatives, particularly with respect to narrative theology's purported failure to relate the biblical accounts to the sphere of history and universal truth claims. Significantly enough, however, these critical voices have largely not dealt with the issue of the degree to which the logic of their own approaches converges with that of these mainline alternatives.[82] If they seriously take up the questions we are raising and recognize the appropriateness of the use of canonical hermeneutics by some of their Evangelical colleagues, the exciting possibility exists that certain techniques of mainline narrative and canonical hermeneutics might find more general acceptance in the Evangelical community. It would seem that Evangelicals could do this and still retain their long-standing theological commitments.

Despite all the convergences we have enumerated between Conservative Evangelical approaches to Scripture and what logically may be affirmed by these particular narrative/canonical approaches (see discussion on pp. 382ff.), one would still expect Evangelicals to regard these mainline approaches as less adequate than their own. The "inadequacies" pointed out by Henry, the failure of these approaches explicitly to affirm biblical inerrancy and the scientific-historical accuracy of the biblical accounts, would likely be identified. Previously I suggested that the lack of explicit affirmation of these themes by mainline theology is largely a function of a discomfort with denying, as Evangelicals have largely done, the validity or at least the influence on Western society of the historical-critical mind-set. If the validity and influence of this mind-set are conceded, unqualified affirmations of the Bible's inerrancy and historical accuracy are not logically possible. Thus the motives for the failure explicitly to affirm biblical inerrancy by mainline thinkers otherwise sympathetic to the authority of the canonical text are related to the concern for presenting the Christian faith in such a way that it remains in dialogue with the ordinary suppositions of daily life (the "commonsense" view of things).

The ultimate difference between certain narrative/canonical views of Scripture and those characteristic of the Evangelical movement, then, is a philosophical one—their disagreement over the desirability of an outright rejection of the historical-critical mind-set.[83] One may rightly ask those Evangelicals who might first respond negatively to narrative approaches if disagreement on such a question of philosophy or social psychology (whether the historical-critical mind-set has in fact had the impact on the social consciousness of modern society which some mainline theologians say it has) should keep Christians from sharing church fellowship with each other. If the answer to that question is no, then nothing would seem to preclude these particular narrative and canonical approaches from being deemed legitimate Evangelical alternatives.

We have noted that these approaches do not in principle rule out the historicity of the biblical accounts. At least in the case of the resurrection, the logic of the biblical accounts would require its historicity. Thus, the logic of these approaches would permit one to hold a position not unlike what is proposed by the eminent Evangelical Ron Sider. Sider claims that because certain biblical claims are psychologically impossible (the impact of the historical-critical mind-set on Western society makes belief in the miracles psychologically impossible for its citizens), such psychological difficulties should not be the ultimate criterion of truth concerning whether these claims are true.[84] And one need not ground Christian faith's validity in the adjudication of these claims. (I do not have to wait for the critical historian to tell me that I can be a Christian!) This is fundamentally the position of the kind of narrative hermeneutic described here.

The case can be made for this mainline theological model's being an appropriate Evangelical alternative in yet another way. At least one eminent Evangelical theologian, Carl Henry (and he is joined more or less by official statements of the Church of the Nazarene [2] and The International Pentecostal Holiness Church [5], as well as by a number of German Evangelicals), has maintained that an affirmation of Scripture's plenary inspiration is sufficient to guarantee one's standing as an Evangelical.[85] We have seen that something like this affirmation could be implied by the kind of narrative and canonical hermeneutics which I have described. Thus, at least on Henry's grounds, these mainline approaches could perhaps be legitimate Evangelical alternatives even though they do not explicitly affirm biblical inerrancy. At least there appears to be enough common ground between Evangelical theologians and mainline proponents of these kinds of narrative and canonical methods that these methods might be regarded as biblically oriented—even Evangelical—from the perspective of the Evangelical movement.[86]

The ecumenical implications of such a possibility would be potentially significant. For example, insofar as we and other Evangelical observers are correct in maintaining that the theological distinctiveness of the Evangelical movement is a function of its view of Scripture, to find an analogous approach to Scripture in mainline theology would be to call the uniqueness of the movement into question.[87] As such, dialogue with members of the Evangelical movement could be dealt with through the historic denominational traditions to which they belong. (As we have noted, special arrangements might need to be made in the case of Holiness and Pentecostal churches, perhaps by the mainline churches' initiating bilateral dialogues with them, as the Roman Catholic church has done with the Pentecostal tradition.)

In view of the fact that the Evangelical movement is largely indebted to Reformed and pietist treatments of most doctrines and, given the growing convergence evidenced in bilateral dialogues between these traditions and other churches, if the hermeneutical problem can be resolved in ways such as I have suggested, the Evangelical movement does not appear necessarily to pose insuperable ecumenical difficulties.[88] The dialogue with Evangelicals does implicitly raise pointed questions to the ecumenical movement with regard to the prevailing hermeneutical suppositions it has employed. In view of the convergences suggested in this chapter concerning narrative hermeneutics and Evangelicalism, and insofar as much multilateral and bilateral ecumenical discussion has relied upon the methodological suppositions of neoorthodoxy and the so-called "contextual theology," could the credibility of these dialogue results within the Evangelical movement be enhanced by ecumenists relying more on narrative hermeneutical suppositions in their work?[89]

To be sure, neoorthodox and "contextual" theological models prevailing in the mainline churches will not and should not evaporate. But as we previously observed, just as narrative theologians in the mainline are able to remain in dialogic, church fellowship with these more liberal alternatives, regarding their disagreements as philosophical ones (to some extent involving a preference for Wittgenstein's views of language to those implicit in Kant), so Evangelicals could also regard their disagreements with these more liberal mainline theological alternatives. Carl Henry has suggested that liberal theology's adherence to the philosophy of Kant could be regarded as the dividing line between it and Evangelical theology.[90] But if so, it may be rightly asked again whether differences over what is the more appropriate philosophical model for articulating the Christian faith should divide Christians. Should Evangelicals and mainliners who share common or at least complementary views on other doctrinal issues, who may otherwise belong to the same Confessional family, allow their merely philosophical disagreements to shatter church fellowship (as has happened within the Lutheran, Reformed, and most other Confessions)? This is no doubt the most crucial question raised in the dialogue with Evangelicals concerning Scripture and theological method.

Conclusion

Evangelical–Mainline Dialogue:
A Prelude to Revival?

The dynamics of cooperation

It seems to me that *the* ecumenical question in mainline church–
Evangelical relationships is the degree to which the Evangelical movement really has put aside its Fundamentalist heritage of separatism.
The barriers to cooperation and church fellowship with the mainline
are not insurmountable. Insofar as one could concede that many of the
commitments of narrative theology and to some extent of Karl Barth
are at least *compatible* with legitimate Evangelical theological options,
the question to Evangelicals is how they would relate to the mainline
theological alternatives which they do not deem Evangelical. Proponents of mainline theological alternatives, which are conceded by Evangelicals to function in principle as legitimate means of grace, continue
to remain in formal Christian fellowship with more liberal theological
alternatives.[1] Why then should Evangelicals not also be able to consider
these liberals with whom they disagree as Christians, and therefore
regard the liberals' churches as true churches? Significant ecumenical
breakthroughs could be possible to the degree that the Evangelical
movement could accept the logic of this question and not allow its
heritage of separatism to interfere. It would mark the beginning, if not
the culmination of a mainline church–Conservative Evangelical rapprochement.

To be sure, at the level of doctrinal formulation one could still speak
of a "basic difference" between the characteristic theological orientations of the Evangelical movement and those of Lutheranism. (For
reasons which are perhaps already apparent, no such basic theological
difference distinguishes the Evangelical movement from most other
mainline church traditions. For they largely share a common overriding

concern and to some extent a common theological heritage. As we shall note again subsequently, the differences between Evangelicals and the Roman Catholic tradition represent no more difficult ecumenical challenge than the problems which emerge in dialogue between Roman Catholicism and most segments of the Protestant tradition.) The basic difference between the Lutheran tradition and the Evangelical movement does not itself seem to mandate church division. Its further elaboration is desirable, as it provides a possible map for the ecumenical situation in general.

As we have said all along, the Lutheran theological heritage is distinctive in the catholic Church. Lutheran dogmatics are characterized by a heavy emphasis on the primacy of grace. We see this in the Lutheran *Formula of Concord* (SD IV.6) and its normative proposal that Lutherans use the doctrine of justification by grace through faith as criterion for all other doctrines. Moreover, because of this emphasis on the primacy of grace, on clear and sharp distinctions between the human and the divine (though without dividing the two), Lutheran theology is characteristically dialectical. That is, various polar opposites are presented in connection with most doctrinal themes, but the polarities are neither integrated nor unconditionally separated from each other. Thus, for example, we have seen that Lutherans insist on a radical distinction between law and gospel. In the doctrine of human persons they insist upon the simultaneity of the believer's *total* righteousness and *total* sinfulness. Likewise the dialectic is apparent in Lutheran social ethics, its notion of the two kingdoms and the insistence that they must not be confused nor intermingled.

The Lutheran emphasis on justification and the primacy of grace also manifests itself to some extent in an insistence on the real presence of Christ in the Eucharist and in baptismal regeneration. Similarly, this emphasis is reflected in Christian ethics, as Lutheranism is characteristically somewhat more reticent than other traditions to sketch in specific rubrics how Christians should behave (a third use of the law). Of course, given the overriding Lutheran preoccupation with the anxiety-laden and despairing, those caught up in the dynamic of self-justification, its emphasis on justification by grace through faith alone is quite logical and appropriate. If one is laid down with anxiety or endeavoring to save oneself, the appropriate Christian response is, respectively, a Word of comfort (that God has already delivered us from that which causes despair) to the despairing or a Word of condemnation (that God, not our efforts, can save us) to the self-righteous and proud.

On the other hand, members of the Evangelical movement do not characteristically emphasize the doctrine of justification as much as Lutherans do. (We have observed that this lack of emphasis does not connote a works-righteous Pelagianism. In fact, in some instances, particularly with respect to Lutherans aligned with the Evangelical movement, one can identify a heavy emphasis on the doctrine of justification.)[2] The more characteristic Evangelical emphasis is upon the regenerate life-style and the need for structure in the Christian life.

Indeed, although I have not been able to find any explicit admission by Evangelicals that this emphasis on sanctification is analogous to the Lutheran emphasis on justification, there are certain parallels.[3] Just as justification functions for Lutherans as the criterion for judging all other doctrines, so sanctification functions for Evangelicals as a kind of criterion for judging and influencing the shape of all other doctrines. (We have suggested that this emphasis on sanctification typifies many, if not most Confessional traditions, including Roman Catholicism.)[4] Thus, the Evangelical emphasis on the regenerate life-style and sanctification typically manifests itself in thought patterns which smooth out the dialectical elements of Lutheran thinking. Divine and human activity tend to be correlated more frequently.

This mode of thinking also manifests itself in the articulation of more explicit life-style expectations for Christians. So much emphasis is placed on believers' responsibility to exercise their faith that the sacraments or ordinances are more typically regarded as mere symbols which are efficacious to believers only when their faith is exercised. Likewise, this characteristic Evangelical emphasis manifests itself in the doctrine of the Church. For the Church is often conceived of as a voluntary community of true believers with certain membership requirements, not as a body created primarily by God regardless of the spiritual quality of its membership.

Given the context in which the Evangelical movement and most of its constituent traditions were generated, this sort of emphasis on the regenerate life-style, sanctification, and structure in the Christian life is also quite logical. Recall that the Evangelical movement is largely a product of perceived cultural chaos, a sense that traditional norms and values are withering away. This characterization of our cultural context continues to typify present Conservative Evangelical thinking. If one senses that culture is in chaos, the logical and appropriate response is to emphasize order, structure, and personal commitment— as Evangelicals have done. If society cannot be counted on to right itself, the individual must bear the responsibility for reforming society. Thus follows the Evangelical emphasis both on individual responsibility and on the character of the Christian life (sanctification).

In like manner, a sense that the old social norms are crumbling mandates that people need to find a firm structure of meaning for life. This need emerging from the context in which Evangelicals perceive themselves helps one better understand the internal theological logic of their preoccupation with an infallible/inerrant Bible. The infallibility of Scripture with its claims to absolute authority helps furnish the Evangelical movement with the sure and firm meaning-structure it seeks.

In short, then, the differences between Lutheranism and the Evangelical movement largely can be understood in terms of their distinct overriding concerns—justification in the case of Lutheranism, sanctification in the case of Evangelicals. In like manner, these different emphases can be understood in relation to the different originating contexts and perceptions of our current situation that characterize both movements. This summary of the basic difference between the Lutheran tradition and the Evangelical movement may also be pertinent to describing the basic difference between Lutheranism and the constituent traditions of the Evangelical movement, such as the Reformed, Baptist, and Methodist traditions.

Perhaps these observations also apply to Lutheran–Roman Catholic relationships, at least insofar as Roman Catholic soteriology (views concerning how one is saved) also reflects an emphasis on sanctification. In this sense, Evangelicalism and the Roman Catholic church are kindred spirits. Moreover, inasmuch as we have seen that the Evangelical movement's disagreements with Rome are no more pronounced than the problems the Catholic church faces with the movement's constituent traditions, much of the anti-Catholic sentiment in Evangelical circles seems unfounded, not a true expression of the Protestant heritage. Could Roman Catholicism's and Anglicanism's differences with the Evangelical movement and other kindred traditions over issues related to the Church, sacraments, and ministry be functions of a slightly different originating context—that these episcopal traditions' responses to perceived cultural chaos occurred in situations where the Church understood itself as called on to exercise (unlike in Geneva or among the Puritan and Evangelical fathers) an *international/national cultural hegemony,* so that more attention to order and so therefore to a Church hierarchy was warranted? That is a question for another day.

At any rate, the basic difference between the Lutheran tradition and the Evangelical movement concerning their respective doctrinal emphases and formative cultural contexts suggests again that the Evangelical movement may have the least in common with the Lutheran heritage. This is certainly true with regard to those traditions like the Reformed, pietist, and radical reformation traditions which have constituted the Evangelical movement. Because they share with it a similar overriding concern and more or less analogous originating contexts and evaluation of the cultural situation, the dialogue between mainline churches of these traditions and the Evangelical movement does not, as we have seen, pose the challenges it does for Lutheran–Conservative Evangelical relationships. The real problem for these mainline churches in relation to the Evangelical movement comes not typically with respect to differences on various doctrines, but on the sole issue of different views concerning the nature of the Bible (biblical infallibility).

We have suggested that the fundamental difference between the Lutheran heritage and the Evangelical movement need not be church-dividing. Because the Evangelical movement is a kind of spectrum embracing many traditions, it is not surprising that characteristic Lutheran themes (even the emphasis on the doctrine of justification and the concept of baptismal regeneration) are regarded at least by most Evangelicals as legitimate Evangelical theological positions. When they are embraced, as we have observed, it is not without regard for concerns similar to those that led Lutherans to propound them—a desire to combat all forms of legalism or works-righteousness.

In a similar manner, Lutheranism is a catholic tradition which, as such, can embrace a rich variety of theological orientations. Thus, characteristic Lutheran themes, as we have seen, are not devoid of a concern that believers be "born again." Likewise characteristic Conservative Evangelical themes appear explicitly in the Lutheran heritage at some points, both in relation to its Protestant Orthodox segments and especially in relation to its pietist streams. In the latter case Lutheranism has employed the characteristic Evangelical emphasis on sanctification and many of its associated theological themes (including in a few circumstances a certain disinclination explicitly to affirm the grace-bearing, real presence character of the sacrament) for many of the same purposes as Evangelicals have—in response to a sense of cultural chaos and its perceived negative consequences for individual morality and spirituality (the kind of context which originally generated Pietism).

Earlier we observed that it was something like this concern which generated the pietist or Orthodox heritages of the other mainline churches which have in turn directly influenced the Evangelical movement. Thus it seems to follow that if mainline Lutheranism and other mainline Protestant churches wish to underline the theological commonalities they share with the Evangelical movement in hopes of overcoming some of the present Evangelical–mainline church tensions, it may be important to revivify and give new intellectual credence to some of the Orthodox and pietist heritage of their traditions.[5] This is not to say that today's mainline Protestant churches at large would need to advocate these theological options, but only that these options could be recognized as legitimate alternatives of the heritage of these churches.

In making this suggestion I am not unaware of the modern critiques of these theological movements as purportedly having distorted the Reformation heritage.[6] Although this critique cannot receive a thorough refutation at this time, our discussion in Part IV has shown that most of the characteristic themes of Pietism and Orthodoxy can in fact be identified in the mainline Protestant heritage, and even in the Lutheran Confessional writings. It is quite apparent, then, that one of the salutary side-effects of dialogue between Evangelicals and the mainline churches is that each can call the other to reappropriate themes which are already part of each other's heritage.

It is at this point that the dynamics of possible cooperation between all parties become apparent. The emphasis on the doctrine of justification which characterizes the Lutheran tradition, particularly when it is conceptualized as conformity to Christ so that sanctification is included in justification, may help the whole Church catholic, and Evangelicals in particular, to get away from any tendency toward an undue preoccupation with sanctification. Of course, an overriding concern with sanctification is a valid catholic option—but not when it leads to works-righteousness, as Lutherans in particular remind the Church.

Evangelicals on their side call the Church, and especially Lutherans, to an emphasis on regeneration, sanctification, and evangelism, and to a piety rooted firmly in traditional biblical themes. Correlated with this is the strongly biblical and traditional theological orientation of the movement. To mainline churches, which since the 1950s have to some extent been bereft of leadership dynamics governed by traditional theological reflection, the Evangelical movement's passion for biblical, theological reflection and practice represents a promising model. Could a well-publicized dialogue with the movement help call these churches back to their roots, insofar as such a dialogue would force church leaders and the laity to reexamine the more traditional theological issues (with questions of "social relevance" put temporarily on the back burner)? In view of the areas of convergence we have noted between characteristic Evangelical views and those of narrative hermeneutics and even Barth, the prospects of success in such a dialogue would not seem to be impossible. At least we have shown that partners in such a dialogue would have important points in common.

One would think that a number of mainline theologians—not just narrative theologians, but any who would seek "to do theology in and for the Church's tradition"—would welcome the prospect of this sort of dialogue. Such theologians may not find conversations on traditional theological issues possible with the more liberal, university-centered style of theology. (Sometimes I have found it easier to strike up such a conversation with Evangelicals than with a group of mainliners.) At any rate, the coalition presently forged with this more liberal theological establishment by neoorthodox church theologians is not bringing about theological renewal in the mainline churches. (Perhaps this is because the methodological suppositions of the first group, its commitment to a correlation of Christian symbols with the secular conceptuality of the moment, unwittingly authorizes the leadership style of the church's managerial elite.) Establishing convergence or at least a coalition with the Evangelical movement and its theologians might be a better prospect for awakening theological interest in the mainline churches, particularly in view of the more or less Evangelical piety of many mainline church members. Mainliners oriented to traditional theology would be provided with more conversation partners (the Evangelicals) and so more support from Evangelically oriented laity in their own churches in challenging present church structures to be accountable to the tradition. Such a coalition might also capture the media's attention, making it all the more desirable.

It would also be desirable that such a coalition of mainliners and the Evangelical movement take institutional expression interdenominationally at a local level. The building of such a coalition might begin with contacts between mainline and Conservative Evangelical congregations, perhaps through parish visitations, evangelism or media workshops, joint worship, common Bible studies, and common service projects. (But mainliners at all levels must be certain that such common service or mutual activity not be perceived by Evangelicals as an end in itself, lest they confirm suspicions that they are really secular humanists in disguise. Mainliners should aim to use these occasions instead as opportunities to search for truth, to witness to their faith. For the relative importance a group of Christians places on evangelism is a crucial factor for Evangelicals in evaluating whether that group is truly a church.)

Risks and benefits

At all levels there are risks in the sort of cooperation I have outlined. Evangelicals risk assimilation into the mainline, the forfeiture of their distinct and characteristic subculture which has helped preserve their antebellum theological heritage. Mainliners risk rejection from the Evangelicals' subculture mentality and, in fact, should expect some initial difficulties in contacts due to social and sometimes even economic factors occasioned by the fact that a significant number of Evangelicals belong to a more rural, less well educated (or, in Europe, a more or less estranged) social class.

Also the more liturgical, sacramentally oriented catholic churches of mainline Protestantism could conceivably jeopardize their blossoming relationships with the Roman Catholic church. If commonalities with Protestantism's most anti-Catholic wing were made public, the Roman hierarchy might have good cause to rethink the convergence it thought it was finding with Lutherans, Anglicans, and others.

Yet the gains could outweigh the risks. For a deepened relationship between the Evangelical movement and the mainline churches might not be unlike the old revival coalitions. To be sure, its potential for Christian unity should not be overlooked. A deepened relationship with the Evangelical movement, the "most Protestant" of all brethren, could function to help traditions like Lutheranism and Anglicanism retain their important "middle ground" between Protestantism and Roman Catholicism. Yet this position could never serve to reconcile all sides of Christendom were it to lose its Protestant side in interests of more immediate Roman Catholic rapprochement.

But the real boon of an enhanced mainline church–Conservative Evangelical relationship is the hope of revival inside the churches. For we have been dreaming of nothing less than a revival of the original and perhaps most profound expression of the Reformation (the doctrine of justification related to a Catholic vision of the sacraments) within the Evangelical movement and a corresponding revival within the mainline churches of the Evangelical passion for theology, evangelism, and spirituality grounded in a biblical and traditional, if not creedal and Confessional orientation.

Notes

(See also the list of abbreviations, pp. 12-22.)

Introduction

1. Jerry Falwell, "Future-Word: An Agenda for the Eighties," in *The Fundamentalist Phenomenon*, ed. Falwell, Ed Dobson, and Ed Hindson (Garden City, N.Y.: Doubleday, 1981), p. 218; Carl F. H. Henry, *God Who Speaks and Shows: Fifteen Theses*, vol. IV: *God, Revelation and Authority*, 6 vols. (Waco, Tex.: Word, 1976–1983), 4:544.

2. These statistics are given in Richard G. Hutcheson Jr., *Mainline Churches and the Evangelicals: A Challenging Crisis?* (Atlanta: John Knox, 1981), pp. 113-114; Dean Kelley, *Why Conservative Churches Are Growing* (New York: Harper & Row, 1972); G. Gallup Jr., and D. Poling, *The Search for America's Faith* (Nashville: Abingdon, 1980), pp. 10ff.; Constant H. Jacquet Jr., ed., *Yearbook of American and Canadian Churches 1985* (Nashville: Abingdon, 1985), pp. 244-245. Similar statistics pertaining to Canada are provided in Charles A. Tipp, "The Religious Complexion of Canada," in *Yearbook of American and Canadian Churches 1974*, ed. Constant H. Jacquet Jr. (Nashville: Abingdon, 1974), pp. 254-257.

3. These statistics are available in Richard N. Ostling, "The New Missionary: Proclaiming Christ's Message in Daring and Disputed Ways," *Time*, December 27, 1982, pp. 42, 39-40; Kelley, *Conservative Churches*, p. 10; Edward Dayton, "Current Trends in North American Protestant Ministries Overseas," *Occasional Bulletin of Missionary Research* 1.2 (1977): 6.

4. Donald Bloesch, *The Evangelical Renaissance* (London: Hodder and Stoughton, 1974), p. 14; Prof. and Mrs. Peter Beyerhaus, private interview, Tübingen, West Germany, April 15, 1983.

5. "Half of U.S. Protestants Are 'Born Again' Christians," *The Gallup Poll* (September 26, 1976), pp. 1-7. It has been quite properly suggested that a distinction must be made between Evangelical beliefs and the Evangelical transdenominational community; see George Marsden, "The Evangelical Denomination," in *Evangelicalism and Modern America*, ed. Marsden (Grand Rapids: Eerdmans, 1984),

p. ix. Thus it cannot be assumed that one-half of American Protestants consciously identify with the Evangelical establishment.

6. Haddon Robinson, "A Profile on the American Clergyman," *Christianity Today,* May 23, 1980, pp. 27-29. The 1976 Gallup Poll results were confirmed in a subsequent 1979 poll; see "The Christianity Today–Gallup Poll: An Overview," *Christianity Today,* December 21, 1979, pp. 13ff.

7. Merton P. Strommen, Milo L. Brekke, Ralph C. Underwager, and Arthur L. Johnson, *A Study of Generations* (Minneapolis: Augsburg, 1972), pp. 107-108, 378-382.

8. David O. Moberg, "Fundamentalists and Evangelicals in Society," in *The Evangelicals: What They Believe, Who They Are, Where They Are Changing,* ed. David F. Wells and John D. Woodbridge (Nashville: Abingdon, 1975), pp. 168-169. Moberg's analysis is based on survey results of Douglas W. Johnson and George W. Cornell, *Punctured Preconceptions: What North American Christians Think about the Church* (New York: Friendship, 1972). For survey data suggesting a more or less Evangelical orientation in the membership of the Southern Baptist Convention, see David S. Schuller, Merton P. Strommen, and Milo L. Brekke, eds., *Ministry in America* (San Francisco: Harper & Row, 1980), pp. 277ff.

9. Falwell, "Future-Word," p. 217; James Barr, *Fundamentalism* (London: SCM, 1977), pp. 334-336.

10. For much of the preceding and following discussion concerning Evangelical suspicions of the mainline churches and the relationship of these suspicions to the style of leadership in the mainline churches I am indebted to Hutcheson, *Mainline Churches,* pp. 124ff., 40-43, 22-23. My analysis is also consistent with the observations of Peter Berger, "The Class Struggle in American Religion," *The Christian Century,* February 25, 1981, pp. 241-253.

11. Hutcheson, *Mainline Churches,* p. 136; Richard Quebedeaux, *The Worldly Evangelicals* (San Francisco: Harper & Row, 1978), p. 133.

12. Richard Quebedeaux, *WE,* pp. 132-133; Hutcheson, *Mainline Churches,* p. 38.

13. Carl McIntire, private interview, Frankfurt, West Germany, February 23, 1984.

14. Granted, a number of the theologically conservative churches estranged from their mainline sister churches do not identify themselves with the Evangelical movement. This is true in the case of The Lutheran Church–Missouri Synod (see Milton L. Rudnick, *Fundamentalism and the Missouri Synod* [St. Louis: Concordia, 1966]), the Free Lutheran Church in Germany (see Gerhard Rost, "Die Selbständige Evangelisch-Lutherische Kirche," in *Weg und Zeugnis,* ed. Rudolf Bäumer, Peter Beyerhaus, and Fritz Grünzweig, 2nd ed. [Bad Liebenzell: Verlag der Liebenzeller Mission, 1981], p. 89), and to some extent The Orthodox Presbyterian Church (as maintained by its Stated Clerk, John P. Galbraith, personal letter, February 2, 1984). Yet these and similar churches are considered Evangelical by a number of Evangelicals (see Quebedeaux, *WE,* p. 39) and, as we shall see, exhibit many characteristics of Evangelicalism.

15. Ron Sider, "What's in Store for '74? Evangelical Churches," *The Christian Century,* January 2, 1974, pp. 12-13; Falwell, "Future-Word," p. 187; Donald Bloesch, *The Future of Evangelical Christianity* (Garden City, N.Y.: Doubleday, 1983), p. 2.

16. Carl McIntire, *A Critique of the World Council of Churches by the International Council of Christian Churches* (published pamphlet, 1983), pp. 11, 16; Falwell, "Future-Word," p. 218; Peter Beyerhaus, "Christen zwischen Bekennender Kirche

und Weltkirche," in *Taufe-Wiedergeburt-Bekehrung in evangelistischer Perspektive*, ed. Gerhard Maier and Gerhard Rost (Lahr-Dinglingen: Verlag der St. Johannis-Druckerei C. Schweickhardt, 1980), p. 133; Billy Graham, *The Holy Spirit* (Waco, Tex.: Word, 1982), p. 152.

17. Timothy P. Weber, "The Two-Edged Sword: The Fundamentalist Use of the Bible," in *The Bible in America*, ed. Nathan O. Hatch and Mark A. Noll (New York: Oxford University Press, 1982), pp. 101-102; Robert Booth Fowler, *A New Engagement: Evangelical Political Thought, 1966-1976* (Grand Rapids, Mich.: Eerdmans, 1982), pp. 15ff.; Timothy L. Smith, "An Historical Perspective on Evangelicalism and Ecumenism," *Mid-Stream* 22 (July/October 1983): 308-309.

For examples of historians who regarded the movement in this way, see Stewart G. Cole, *The History of Fundamentalism* (New York: Richard R. Smith, 1931); Norman F. Furniss, *The Fundamentalist Controversy, 1918-1931* (New Haven, Conn.: Yale University Press, 1954); H. Richard Niebuhr, "Fundamentalism," *Encyclopedia of Social Sciences* (New York, 1937), 6:526-527.

18. Eric W. Gritsch, *Born Againism: Perspectives on a Movement* (Philadelphia: Fortress, 1982); Barr, *Fundamentalism*. The latest book by Barr on the subject, *Beyond Fundamentalism* (Philadelphia: Westminister, 1984), especially pp. vii-ix, though less controversial than the earlier publication, is not so much concerned to dialogue with the Evangelical movement or to discern commonalities with it as it is to propose to conservatives an acceptable mainline theological perspective. A discussion of mainline critiques of the Evangelical movement as offered by William Sloane Coffin and others is provided by Jeffrey K. Hadden and Charles E. Swann, *Prime Time Preachers* (Reading, Mass.: Addison-Wesley, 1981), pp. 151-153.

For references to two, more positive evaluations of the Evangelical movement by mainline scholars, see Alan P. F. Sell, *Theology in Turmoil* (Grand Rapids: Baker, 1986); Hutcheson, *Mainline Churches*.

19. Such Evangelical attitudes are reflected by Carl F. H. Henry, *God Who Stands and Stays: Part Two, GRA*, 6:389,195; cf. James Davison Hunter, *American Evangelicalism* (New Brunswick, N.J.: Rutgers University Press, 1983), p. 3.

20. In addition to the texts cited in n. 18, see LCUSA Division for Theological Studies, *The Born-Again Movement: A Response*, 1983 Meeting Agenda; WCC Vancouver Assembly Issue Group Report, *Struggling for Justice and Human Dignity* (1983), 6. Early in 1988 a statement on Fundamentalism was issued by the United States National Conference of Catholic Bishops. Though the document could not be obtained in time for analysis here, indications are that it is characterized by this kind of backlash against Conservative Evangelism.

21. Bloesch, *FEC*, p. 2; Peter Beyerhaus, "Okumene der drei monotheistischen Religionen? Bericht zur kirchlich-missionarischen Lage" (lecture delivered to the Theologische Konvent Bekennender Gemeinschaften, Frankfurt, West Germany, February 23, 1984); Henry, *GRA*, 6:101, laments that the Evangelical movement does not receive a fair hearing.

22. Bloesch, *FEC*, p. vii.

23. Ibid., p. 2.

24. In addition to texts cited in n. 16, most of which involve criticisms of the organized ecumenical movement, other references to the Evangelical repudiation of ecumenism are evident in Robert Dubarry, "Notre Place dans le Christianisme," in *Association Evangélique d'Eglises Baptistes de Langue Française 1921-1971* (published pamphlet, n.d.), p. 47; Assemblies of God, General Council Minutes,

1963, pp. 41-42; *The Southwide Baptist Fellowship 1966* (unpaginated pamphlet; Lauren, S.C.: The Southwide Baptist Fellowship, 1966); Letter, Bekenntnisbewegung "Kein anderes Evangelium" to Synode der Evangelischen Kirche in Deutschland, October 30, 1978, in *Weg und Zeugnis,* ed. Rudolf Bäumer, Peter Beyerhaus, and Fritz Grünzweig, 2nd ed. (Bad Liebenzell: Verlag der Liebenzeller Mission, 1981), pp. 263, 264; George Dollar, *A History of Fundamentalism in America* (Greenville, S.C.: Bob Jones University Press, 1973), p. 193; James DeForest Murch, *Cooperation without Compromise* (Grand Rapids, Mich.: Eerdmans, 1956), pp. 178ff.; Henry, *GRA,* 6:388-389; 4:57.

25. *The Berlin Declaration on Ecumenism* (1974), 2,4(c); Henry, *GRA,* 6:32; 4:17, 234.

26. For examples of criticisms of liberation theology by Evangelicals, see *The Berlin Declaration on Ecumenism,* II; C. Emilio Nunez, "Personal and Eternal Salvation and Redemption," in *Let the Earth Hear His Voice,* ed. J. D. Douglas (Minneapolis: World Wide, 1975), pp. 1061ff.; Gerhard Maier, *Das Ende der historisch-kritischen Methode* (Wuppertal Verlag Rolf Brockhaus, 1974), p. 77; Henry, *GRA,* 4:59-60, 555ff.; Bloesch, *FEC,* p. 102. The marked character of this tension between Evangelicalism and liberation theology has been noted in "Neue transkonfessionelle Bewegungen und die Kirchen—Stellungnahme des Strassburger Instituts," in *Neue transkonfessionelle Bewegungen,* ed. Günther Gassmann, Harding Meyer, and Gunnars J. Ansons (Frankfurt/Main: Verlag Otto Lembeck, 1976), pp. 16-17.

The influence of liberation theology on the ecumenical movement has been noted by Henry, *GRA,* 6:267; *The Berlin Declaration on Ecumenism,* 4ff. One need only examine recent WCC statements from the Nairobi Assembly, *Message: An Invitation to Prayer* (1975); *Structures of Injustice and Struggles for Liberation* (1975), and its 1979 Conference on Faith, Science and the Future, to confirm this observation.

27. The full text of the Evangelicals' "Open Letter" at Vancouver is available in *TSF Bulletin* 7 (September–October 1983), 18-19. Other indications of headway in overcoming Evangelical–ecumenical polarization are evident in the drafting by the National Council of Churches (USA) of a positive response to the Evangelicals' *Chicago Declaration of Evangelicals to Social Concern* (1973); see Quebedeaux, *WE,* pp. 135-136; H. Berkhof, "Berlin versus Geneva: Our Relationship with the 'Evangelicals,'" *Ecumenical Review* 28 (1976): 80-86. A good overview of events which are seen as contributing to improved Evangelical–WCC relationships is provided by Emilio Castro, "Ökumene und die Evangelikalen: Wo stehen Wir?" *Materialdienst* 11-15 (September 1985): 13ff. That tensions are still evident is noted by Castro and is apparent from the texts cited in nn. 25-26.

28. Bloesch, *FEC,* p. 31, confirms our characterizations, at least with respect to Fundamentalism. For a few references to Evangelicalism's anti-Catholicism, see *Die Bekennenden Gemeinschaften* (pamphlet, 1979), p. 4; Dubarry, "Notre Place dans le Christianisme," pp. 11-12; S. Bénétreau, "Qu'est-ce qu'une Eglise de Professants?" in *Les Eglises de Professants,* ed. S. Bénétreau and G. Millon (Paris: S. P. B., 1957), p. 29; "Interview mit Dr. Fritz Laubach," *Idea-Spektrum,* 5 December 1984; p. 2; Henry, *GRA,* 4:590; T. W. Medhurst, "Is Romanism Christianity?" in *The Fundamentals,* 12 vols. (Chicago: Testimony Publishing, 1910–1915), 11:100ff. A particularly significant example of the Evangelical movement's continued critical perspective on Roman Catholicism is evident in a 1986 resolution of the World Evangelical Fellowship General Assembly, entitled *A Contemporary Evangelical Perspective on Roman Catholicism.*

Cf. John P. Galbraith, *Why The Orthodox Presbyterian Church?* (Philadelphia: The Orthodox Presbyterian Church, n.d.), p. 39: "If Martin Luther . . . had done as some would do now in an equally hopeless situation, we would all be Roman Catholics today. *Thank God we are not!"* (emphasis added).

29. Hutcheson, *Mainline Churches,* pp. 131ff. See also Sell, *Theology in Turmoil.*
30. Bloesch, *FEC,* p. viii.
31. Richard J. Coleman, *Issues of Theological Conflict,* 2nd ed. (Grand Rapids, Mich.: Eerdmans, 1980), esp. pp. 5-7, 21-28, 36-38, 44-45, 49; Sell, *Theology in Turmoil.* For a similar characterization of the theological preoccupations of the Evangelical Renaissance, see T. Weber, "Two-Edged Sword," pp. 101-102.
32. For a representative sample of criticisms of the Pentecostal-charismatic movement, see Henry, *GRA,* 6:389; ibid., 4:252-253, 283-284, 499, 500; Graham, *The Holy Spirit,* p. 70; Peter Beyerhaus, "World Evangelization and the Kingdom of God," in *LEH,* p. 300. As we shall note, the status of Pentecostals and charismatics in relation to the Evangelical movement remains a much-debated point in several parts of the world. Yet, at least in North America (in virtue of the membership of a number of Pentecostal churches in the National Association of Evangelicals), they are usually identified with the movement and therefore will be dealt with as Evangelicals in this study. Cf. Peter Beyerhaus, "Lausanne zwischen Berlin und Genf," in *Reich Gottes oder Weltgemeinschaft?* ed. Walter Künneth and Peter Beyerhaus (Bad Liebenzell: Verlag der Liebenzeller Mission, 1975), pp. 307-308.
33. Perhaps one should also mention a dialogue in the German Democratic Republic in 1982 and 1983 between the Bund der Evangelischen Kirchen in der DDR (comprised mostly of Lutherans) and the Bund Evangelisch-Freikirchlicher Gemeinden (a predominantly Baptist group which is often regarded as Conservative Evangelical in orientation). A most significant conclusion in the dialogue report (3.1) was that because the Free Church communities are not seen to be in a continuity with the 16th-century Anabaptists condemned by the Lutheran *Augsburg Confession* (1530), see Articles V.4; XII.7; XVI.3; XVII.4, its condemnation of Anabaptists should not be understood to apply to the Evangelisch-Freikirchlicher Gemeinden. However, this dialogue will not receive as detailed attention as the others noted. For despite their image, the East German Baptists largely do not consider themselves to be part of the Evangelical movement (see above, pp. 110-111, 112, 161).
34. *Evangelical–Roman Catholic Dialogue on Mission* (1977–1984), 7 (1). (When the report is referred to in the text with accompanying Arabic numeral, the number is understood to refer to the corresponding article of the report.)
35. Lutheran–Conservative/Evangelical Dialogue (USA), *Declaration* (1981), in *The Covenant Quarterly* 41 (August 1983): 7.
36. *Final Report of the Dialogue between the Secretariat for Promoting Christian Unity of the Roman Catholic Church and Leaders of Some Pentecostal Churches and Participants in the Charismatic Movement within Protestant and Anglican Churches* (1976), 15, 17, 34, 38-41; *Final Report of the Dialogue between the Secretariat for Promoting Christian Unity of the Roman Catholic Church and Some Classical Pentecostals* (1977–1982), 8-11, 17. (When the reports are referred to in the text, Roman numerals designate the round of the dialogue [for example, II signifies the second round]. Arabic numbers refer to the articles of the report of the designated round.)
37. With regard to disagreements on the Marian dogma, it is perhaps significant to note that Roman Catholic participants in the dialogue do not insist that only those who hold this dogma can be saved (*RC-P,* II,69) and that Pentecostal participants

see a correlation between the Roman Catholic idea of Mary's assumption into heaven and their own belief in the rapture (ibid., 76).

38. Among those who have offered such warnings are Francis A. Schaeffer, private interview, Huémoz, Switzerland, November 12, 1983; "An interview with Donald Dayton," *Faith and Thought* 1 (Spring 1983): 24-34; T. Smith, "An Historical Perspective," pp. 311, 314. Some think that sociological factors like the upward social mobility of Evangelicals will lead to the breakdown of the movement; see Hunter, *American Evangelicalism*, pp. 131-132; Donald Dayton, "Evangelical Contradictions," *Sojourners*, April 1976, p. 26.

I shall use the term "Evangelical" to refer to the Conservative Evangelical movement. To be sure, other Protestants from mainline churches feel entitled to apply this term to themselves. But, for purposes of this book, my use of the term has allowed itself to be dictated by the common vocabulary of the day. I shall leave the controversy concerning the rights of other Protestants to apply the term to themselves for another day. In speaking of "Conservative Evangelicalism," I refer to all segments of the Evangelical movement; this sort of evangelicalism is "Conservative," in distinction from merely being faithful to the gospel (being evangelical) or as distinct from Protestantism/evangelicalism in general.

39. A programmatic articulation of this fundamental commitment was given by Harold Ockenga, "From Fundamentalism, through New Evangelicalism, to Evangelical-ism," in *Evangelical Roots,* ed. Kenneth Kantzer (New York: Thomas Nelson, 1978), pp. 35-48. Also see Edward John Carnell, *The Case for Orthodox Theology* (Philadelphia: Westminster, 1959), pp. 113-138. An expression of this kind of commitment by Evangelicals outside of North America is offered by the former President of the Deutsche Evangelische Allianz, P. Manfred Otto, "Auf der Suche nach der neutestamentlichen Gemeinde," *Evangelischer Allianzbrief,* September 1983, p. 1.

40. Prominent Evangelicals who suggest such an intraconfessional bilateral approach include G. W. Bromiley, private interview, Pasadena, Calif., March 14, 1985, and Jack B. Rogers, private interview, Pasadena, Calif., March 13, 1985.

41. Randall H. Balmer, "Fundamentalism redux," *The Reformed Journal* 33 (June, 1983): 28; cf. Mark A. Noll, "Children of the Reformation in a Brave New World: Why 'American Evangelicals' Differ from 'Lutheran Evangelicals,'" *Dialog* 24 (Summer 1985): 179-180.

42. Convergence statements between Lutherans and other churches at an international level can be obtained in Harding Meyer and Lukas Vischer, eds., *Growth in Agreement* (New York and Ramsey, N.J.: Paulist, 1984), pp. 167-275. Conver-gence statements from the Lutheran–Roman Catholic Dialogue in the United States are available in seven volumes from Augsburg Publishing House.

Chapter 1: Methodological Considerations

1. Among the most noteworthy texts which trace the history of the Evangelical move-ment or its predecessors are George M. Marsden, *Fundamentalism and American Culture* (Oxford/New York: Oxford University Press, 1980), Ernest R. Sandeen, *The Roots of Fundamentalism: British and American Millenarianism, 1800–1930* (Chicago: University of Chicago Press, 1970); Timothy L. Smith, *Revivalism and Social Reform in Mid-Nineteenth Century America* (Nashville: Abingdon, 1957); Donald W. Dayton, *Discovering an Evangelical Heritage* (New York: Harper & Row, 1976); Douglas W. Frank, *Less Than Conquerors* (Grand Rapids: Eerdmans, 1986). A more complete, if not entirely current list of such texts is provided by

Donald Tinder, "A Guide to Further Reading," in *E*, pp. 293-296. An important new book by George Marsden, *Reforming Fundamentalism* (Grand Rapids: Eerdmans, 1987), has now appeared. Unfortunately, it has not been possible to incorporate its insights. Also note the development of an Evangelical research institute—the Institute for the Study of American Evangelicals.

2. Quebedeaux, *WE*, pp. 6-7. John H. Gerstner, "The Theological Boundaries of Evangelical Faith," in *E*, pp. 22-24. A similar approach was taken by Ronald H. Nash, *Evangelicals in America: Who They Are, What They Believe* (Nashville: Abingdon, 1987), especially pp. 40-53; the book is the most recent popular introduction to the Evangelical movement.

3. Among those characterizing Evangelicalism more or less in this fashion are G. Gassmann, et al., eds., *Neue transkonfessionelle Bewegungen* (Frankfurt: Otto Lembeck, 1976), pp. 15-17; James Davison Hunter, *American Evangelicalism* (New Brunswick: Rutgers University Press, 1983), p. 47; Richard Quebedeaux, *The Young Evangelicals: Revolution in Orthodoxy* (New York: Harper & Row, 1974), pp. 3-4; Robert K. Johnston, *Evangelicals at an Impasse* (Atlanta: John Knox, 1979), p. 3; Marsden, in *EMA*, pp. ix-x; The Evangelical Covenant Church, *Covenant Affirmations* (Chicago: Covenant Press, 1976), p. 9; Gerhard Maier, private interview, Tübingen, April 27, 1983. Some interesting family resemblances exist between this profile and the 1846 *Doctrinal Basis* of the original Evangelical Alliance. A similar characterization was also offered by Evangelical participants in the *ERCD,* Int. (1), though they did not refer to biblical inerrancy. This is a significant point, given the nature of the dialogue group, and the point will receive further attention.

The influential character of this characterization of Evangelicalism receives further attestation inasmuch as the 1976 Gallup Poll which helped launch Evangelicals into cultural prominence employed these criteria in determining "Evangelical" responses.

For more nuanced attempts to define Evangelicalism, see Sydney Ahlstrom, "From Puritanism to Evangelicalism: A Critical Perspective," in *E*, pp. 270-271; Martin E. Marty, "The Revival of Evangelicalism and Southern Religion," in *Varieties of Southern Evangelicalism,* ed. David E. Harrell Jr. (Macon: Mercer University Press, 1981), pp. 9-10.

4. The marked diversity within the Evangelical movement has been acknowledged by at least two influential and sophisticated attempts to characterize it in terms of different subgroups. See Robert E. Webber, *Common Roots: A Call to Evangelical Maturity* (Grand Rapids: Zondervan, 1978), pp. 31-33, and Peter Beyerhaus, "Lausanne zwischen Berlin und Genf," in *Reich Gottes oder Weltgemeinschaft?* ed. Walter Künneth and Peter Beyerhaus (Bad Liebenzell: Verlag der Liebenzeller Mission, 1975), pp. 307-308.

5. Marsden, "The Evangelical Denomination," in *EMA*, pp. ix-xi, and Mark A. Noll, *Between Faith and Criticism: Evangelicals, Scholarship, and the Bible* (San Francisco: Harper & Row, 1986), pp. 3-5, employ something like my own analytic approach and confirm my assumption concerning the existence of an Evangelical movement as a more or less cohesive entity. They claim that the movement has a self-consciousness akin to that of a denomination. A similar point is made by a European Evangelical, J. I. Packer, "Relations with Roman Catholics: An Anglican Evangelical View," in *Towards Christian Unity,* ed. Bernard Leeming (London: Geoffrey Chapman, 1968), p. 37.

Chapter 2: Fundamentalist Origins

1. Jerry Falwell, with Ed Dobson and Ed Hindson, eds., *The Fundamentalist Phenomenon* (Garden City, N.Y.: Doubleday, 1981), p. 7. My own definition of

Fundamentalism is indebted to George Marsden, "Fundamentalism as an American Phenomenon: A Comparison with English Evangelicalism," *Church History* 44 (1977): 215, a definition heartily approved by Falwell, p. 3.

2. Curtis Lee Laws, "Convention Side Lights," *Watchman Examiner,* 1 July 1920, p. 834.

3. Ernest R. Sandeen, *The Origins of Fundamentalism* (Philadelphia: Fortress, 1968), p. 22.

4. This assessment as well as my later observations concerning the booklets' subsequent impact are indebted to Marsden, *FAC,* p. 119; Sydney E. Ahlstrom, *A Religious History of the American People* (4th printing; New Haven: Yale University Press, 1972), p. 816. The lack of a thoroughgoing impact of these booklets on Fundamentalism is attested to by their failure to gain an unqualified endorsement of a militant Fundamentalist like George Dollar, *A History of Fundamentalism in America* (Greenville, S.C.: Bob Jones University Press, 1973), p. 175.

The statement of the booklets' purpose is cited in *The Fundamentals,* 12 vols. (Chicago: Testimony Publishing House, 1910-1915), 1:3. (Subsequent references to the booklets in the text will cite volume with Roman numeral and appropriate page with Arabic numeral.)

5. For a similar assessment of the booklets' tone and quality, see Ahlstrom, *RHAP,* p. 816; Falwell, p. 80; cf. Noll, *BFC,* pp. 40-42.

6. This is the reason for their lukewarm assessment by Dollar, *A History,* p. 175. It is true that the Fundamentalist insistence on a premillennialism is undercut by an openness to a variety of views concerning the second coming; see Charles R. Erdman, "The Coming of Christ," in *The Fundamentals,* 11:98. On the other hand, one can identify in the booklets other articles, particularly those by Philip Mauro, where a pessimism about present culture is so strongly reflected that it can only imply a premillennialist perspective (see 8:100-102; 5:7ff., 24; 4:117-118).

There appears to be a debate among scholars on the absence of dispensationalism in the booklets. Marsden, *FAC,* p. 119, and Sandeen, *OF,* p. 20, stress its absence; Ahlstrom, *RHAP,* p. 816, is more inclined to speak of the theme's prominence. It is true that the theme does appear in a number of articles in the booklets, as for example in 4:46, 51, 52; 8:58; 9:83; 11:44ff. Nevertheless, I would maintain that when all the factors are considered the booklets are marked by a lack of emphasis on this theme.

7. Marsden, *FAC,* p. 119, notes this point. He offers a background on the Keswick movement (pp. 77-79). For samples of Keswick teaching, see Herbert F. Stevenson, ed., *Keswick's Triumphant Voice: Forty-Eight Addresses Delivered at the Keswick Convention, 1882–1962* (Grand Rapids, Mich.: Zondervan, 1963). For documents which indicate that some reference to Holiness themes like the "Baptism of the Holy Spirit" was present in the 19th-century Keswick movement, see *Account of the Union Meeting for the Promotion of Scriptural Holiness, Held at Oxford, August 29 to September 7, 1874* (London: S. W. Partridge, n.d.), reprinted in *The Higher Christian Life,* ed. Donald W. Dayton (New York: Garland Publishing, n.d.), 1: 102, 246, 253, 356, 371, 376; *Record of the Convention for the Promotion of Scriptural Holiness Held at Brighton, May 29 to June 7th, 1875* (Brighton and London: W. J. Smith and S. W. Partridge, 1875), reprinted in *The Higher Christian Life,* 29:383-387, 443, 460.

8. J. Ramsey Michaels and Roger Nicole, eds., *Inerrancy and Common Sense* (Grand Rapids, Mich.: Baker, 1980), pp. 49-70; Bloesch, *FEC,* pp. 24-25.

9. See the texts cited in n. 17 of the introduction.

10. Martin Marty, "Fundamentalism as a Social Phenomenon," in *EMA*, p. 58. One study suggests that even at the height of the Fundamentalist controversy those without established social lineage were more likely to have sided with the Fundamentalists; see Walter Ellis, "Social and Religious Factors in the Fundamentlist–Modernist Schisms among Baptists in North America, 1895–1914" (Ph.D. dissertation, University of Pittsburgh, 1974).

11. Marsden, *FAC*, p. 179; cf. Grant Wacker, "Uneasy in Zion: Evangelicals in Postmodern Society," in *EMA*, pp. 25ff. That the leadership of early Fundamentalism was drawn principally from the northern United States has been noticed by Dollar, *A History*, p. 48; Marsden, *FAC*, pp. 170, 202; Timothy L. Smith, "An Historical Perspective on Evangelism and Ecumenism," *Mid-Stream* 22 (July/October 1983): 309.

12. James D. Hunter, *American Evangelicalism* (New Brunswick: Rutgers University Press, 1983), pp. 51-53.

13. Marsden, *FAC*, pp. 4-5; Sandeen, *OF*, pp. 1ff.

14. This characterization of Fundamentalism's common emphasis seems to be shared by Marsden, *FAC*, pp. 231, 138, 4. Also recognizing the role that opposition to common enemies played in holding Fundamentalism together are Sandeen, *OF*, pp. 14, 24; Donald W. Dayton, "The Social and Political Conservatism of Modern American Evangelicalism: A Preliminary Search for Reasons," *Union Seminary Quarterly Review* 32 (Winter 1977): 74.

15. More or less similar characterizations of this period are offered by Ahlstrom, *RHAP*, pp. 681ff., 733, 735ff.; Robert T. Handy, *The Protestant Question for a Christian America 1830–1930* (Philadelphia: Fortress, 1967), pp. 3-14; Marsden, *FAC*, pp. 11-12, 86, 92-93. Enlightenment critical thought had reached North America in the early 19th century. But it was largely confined to the prestigious New England educational institutions and made little impact on the constructive religious thought of these faculties or on American culture in general.

16. For documentation of the impact of common sense realism on American cultural institutions, see Mark Ellingsen, "Common Sense Realism: The Cutting Edge of Evangelical Identity," *Dialog* 24 (Summer 1985): 197-205. Cf. Sydney Ahlstrom, "The Scottish Philosophy and American Theology," *Church History* 24 (1955): 257-272; Marsden, *FAC*, pp. 14-16, 214-216, 227. On the applicability of this range of issues to present Evangelical precritical views of history, see George Marsden, "Evangelicals, History, and Modernity," in *EMA*, pp. 98-99; Grant Wacker, The Demise of Biblical Civilization," in *BA*, p. 127.

17. For assessments of the superiority in this period of the European education system, see Jack B. Rogers and Donald K. McKim, *The Authority and Interpretation of the Bible* (San Francisco: Harper & Row, 1979), pp. 300-301; Marsden, *FAC*, pp. 222-226. The impact of Romanticism, an intellectual movement which fostered a suspicion of fixed definitions, also helped prepare the way for the European churches' more ready acceptance of Darwinism and the new scientific revolution which forsook the goal of finding fixed laws. While in America this challenge was more difficult to accept, because Romanticism had not at this time effectively challenged the American reliance on Baconian and commonsense intellectual traditions. See Marsden, *FAC*, pp. 226-227.

18. For a discussion of this dynamic as it occurred outside Western Europe and North America, specifically in this case in Australia, see David Parker, "The Evangelical Heritage of Australian Protestantism: Towards an Historical Perspective," *The Evangelical Quarterly* 57 (January 1985): 46.

19. See Marsden, *FAC*, pp. 222-226; Noll, *BFC*, pp. 85-88.

20. The impact of dispensationalist teaching on the Prophetic Conferences is evident in *Prophetic Studies of the International Prophetic Conference* (New York: Revell, 1886), Pref., p. 36; cf. Dollar, *A History,* pp. 43ff.; Marsden, *FAC,* p. 93. The growing influence of the premillennialist perspective among American theological conservatives of the period is evident in the case of the first president of Wheaton College, Jonathan Blanchard (1811–1892), who shifted from an optimistic view of the possibility of progress in American culture (postmillennialism) to an openness to premillennialism. His son Charles (1848–1926), Wheaton's second president, took the next step and embraced dispensational premillennialism; see Marsden, *FAC,* pp. 30-32.

21. Philip Jacob Spener, *Pia Desideria,* trans. and ed. Theodore G. Tappert, 4th printing (Philadelphia: Fortress, 1977), pp. 76-77; Friedrich Adolf Lampe, *Geheimnis des Gnadenbunds, dem grossen Gott zu Ehren* (1712–1719), 5:819f. Johann Albrecht Bengel is another well-known pietist who engaged in eschatological speculation; see F. Ernest Stoeffler, *German Pietism during the Eighteenth Century* (Leiden: E. J. Brill, 1973), pp. 96. The idea that millennial speculations in Great Britain were rooted in the earlier Puritan period is suggested by Eric Gritsch, *Born Againism* (Philadelphia: Fortress, 1982), p. 16.

22. Spener, *PD,* pp. 76-77, 125; Gritsch, *Born Againism,* pp. 16-17.

23. For an articulation of this separatism in response to a perceived sense of the Church's decadence, see John Nelson Darby, *Letters of J.N.D.,* 3 vols. (London: G. Morrish, 1866–1899), 2:228.

24. See John Nelson Darby, "The Hopes of the Church of God," *The Collected Writings of J. N. Darby,* 34 vols., ed. Wm. Kelly (London: Morrish, 1867–1900), 2:563. For full expositions of dispensationalism, see Marsden, *FAC,* pp. 52-54, 241-242. Cf. Gritsch, *Born Againism,* pp. 17-18; Daniel R. Fuller, *Gospel & Law: Contrast or Continuum?* (Grand Rapids, Mich.: Eerdmans, 1980), especially pp. 13-17.

25. Lampe, *Geheimnis,* 5:819f.

26. *The Augsburg Confession,* XVII.5. For Edwards' position, see Jonathan Edwards, *Union in Prayer,* in *The Works of President Edwards,* 4 vols. (New York, 1879), 3:450-451; Jonathan Edwards, *Thoughts on the Revival,* in *Works,* 3:316.

27. C. I. Scofield, ed., *The Scofield Reference Bible* (New York, 1917), p. iii. Cf. Marsden, *FAC,* p. 54.

28. A. J. Frost, "Condition of the Church and World at Christ's Second Advent; or Are the Church and the World to Grow Better or Worse until He Comes?" in *PSIPC,* pp. 173-176; Report on the comments of A. T. Pierson, in *PSIPC,* p. 36; and the *Niagara Creed* (1878), 14, provide an indication of the assessment of the Bible and Prophetic Conferences concerning the decaying situation of church and society. Cf. Darby, *Letters of J.N.D.,* 2:228; C. I. Scofield, *Rightly Dividing the Word of Truth* (New York, n.d. [1876]), pp. 12-16.

29. A. J. Gordon, *How Christ Came to Church: A Spiritual Autobiography* (Philadelphia: American Baptist Publication Society, 1895), cited by Sandeen, *OF,* pp. 11, 17; R. A. Torrey, *What the Bible Teaches* (New York: Fleming H. Revell, 1898). Moody's failure to embrace dispensationalism is argued by Marsden, *FAC,* pp. 37-38, and Sandeen, *OF,* p. 17.

30. Moody's cultural pessimism is well illustrated in D. L. Moody, "The Second Coming of Christ," in *The Best of D. L. Moody,* ed. Wilbur M. Smith (Chicago, 1971), pp. 193-195. His emphasis on conversion is maintained by Ahlstrom, *RHAP,* p. 745, and his preoccupation with sanctification/holiness through his reliance on Keswick teaching is reflected in D. L. Moody, *Secret Power: or, the*

Secret of Success in Christian Life and Christian Work (Chicago, 1881); cf. *Niagara Creed*, 8, 14.

31. Those insisting that the Holiness tradition is not properly part of Fundamentalism include D. Dayton, *DEH,* pp. 138-139; Paul M. Bassett, "The Fundamentalist Leavening of the Holiness Movement, 1914-1940," *Wesleyan Theological Journal* 13 (Spring 1978): 67, 76-77, 85; Larry Shelton, "John Wesley's Approach to Scripture in Historical Perspective," *Wesleyan Theological Journal* 16 (Spring 1981): 42-43, 38. References documenting the Holiness movement's soteriological scheme are amply provided in Chapter 8. The movement's preoccupation with Christian perfection, and so sanctification, as well as in some instances its sensitivity to the need for further growth in grace are more or less attested to by D. Dayton, *DEH,* pp. 138-139; *The Discipline of The Wesleyan Church 1984* (Marion, Ind.: Wesleyan Publishing House, 1984), pp. 16, 26; The Free Methodist Church of North America, *The Book of Discipline 1979* (Winona Lake, Ind.: The Free Methodist Publishing House, 1980), p. 363; Church of the Nazarene, *Church Constitution and Special Rules* (Kansas City, Mo.: Nazarene Publishing House, n.d.), Pre., 13.

   The preceding footnote provides documentation of Moody's preoccupation with the issue of holiness. Cf. Marsden, *FAC,* pp. 37-38. Concerning Finney's preoccupation with the theme of holiness, and even entire sanctification, see Charles G. Finney, *Lectures on Systematic Theology,* ed. J. H. Fairchild (New York, 1878), pp. 115-179, 204-281; Charles G. Finney, "Letters to Readers," *The Oberlin Evangelist* I, January 30, 1839.

32. Douglas W. Frank, *Less Than Conquerors* (Grand Rapids: Eerdmans, 1986), pp. 113ff.; Marsden, *FAC,* p. 34. Moody's Keswick orientation is documented in n. 30; Marsden, *FAC,* pp. 78-79. For pertinent references to the Keswick movement and its teachings, see n. 7.

33. For this observation I am indebted to Marsden, *FAC,* pp. 86-89, 100-101. The postmillennialism of the Holiness advocates is suggested in Finney, *Lectures on Systematic Theology,* pp. 214-218. For a discussion of this viewpoint in other Holiness figures, see D. Dayton, *DEH,* pp. 80-81, 126ff.

34. For references see Marsden, *FAC,* pp. 257-258.

35. Ibid., pp. 100, 128-129; Frank, *Conquerors,* p. 115. It should be noted, however, that Moody Bible Institute, *Doctrinal Statement,* IV, speaks only of the necessity of being born again and so does not reflect a direct dependence on the Holiness movement (except perhaps in its standards of conduct). But we have previously observed the impact of Keswick on Fundamentalism in *The Fundamentals* (see above, p. 52). Also note the Keswick impact on Gordon; see A. J. Gordon, *The Twofold Life: Or Christ's Work for Us and Christ's Work in Us,* 2nd ed. (New York, 1884), pp. 47, iv, 143. On his dispensationalism, see n. 29.

36. Marsden, *FAC,* pp. 94-95; Bassett, "Fundamentalist Leavening," pp. 77, 79.

37. Church of the Nazarene Seventh General Assembly, *Journal. . .,* 1928, pp. 49, 52, 58, 63; *The Discipline of The Wesleyan Church 1984,* p. 13; Donald W. Dayton, "Theological Roots of Pentecostalism," *Pneuma* 1 (Spring 1980): 18-19. Holiness churches considered in Chap. 8 belong to the National Association of Evangelicals.

38. On the Holiness emphasis on sanctification and also conversion, see relevant references in n. 31. That polemics were a primary influence in its originating context is evident in F. E. Hill, "The Holiness Movement and Its Opposition," *The Nazarene Messenger,* January 24, 1901, p. 4; cf. Arthur C. Piepkorn, *Profiles in Belief,* 4 vols. (New York: Harper and Row, 1977-1979), 3:3. For examples in

early Fundamentalism of this concern with sanctification and a polemical orientation against the churches of the day, see *Niagara Creed*, 8,14; *The Fundamentals*, 5:4; 9:4; 10:32-33. Also see relevant references in n. 28.

In response to those who would claim that the Holiness movement differs from Fundamentalism in that the latter is preoccupied with doctrine and not the "new life," it is well to keep in mind that the Reformed tradition, which so heavily influenced Fundamentalism, is primarily preoccupied with issues related to sanctification; see John Calvin, *Institutes of the Christian Religion* (1559), Pref., III/VI.5, III/XVI.1. This orientation is reflected even in Princeton theology, as Charles Hodge claimed that truth is not possible without holiness; see Charles Hodge, "The Theology of the Intellect and That of the Feelings," in *The Princeton Theology 1818–1921* ed. Mark A. Noll (Grand Rapids: Baker, 1983), p. 197. Cf. Marsden, *FAC*, pp. 136-138, for elaboration of the Princetonian concern to sanctify all realms of culture.

39. Charles G. Finney, *The Oberlin Evangelist* 1 (August 28, 1839): 147. In this respect he stands in the tradition of John Wesley, *A Plain Account of Christian Perfection* (1741), in *John Wesley*, ed. Albert C. Outler (New York: Oxford University Press, 1964), p. 262, who also employed the concept of "dispensation." On the logical interconnections between Holiness teaching and dispensationalism, see Marsden, *FAC*, pp. 87-88. Timothy L. Smith, "Righteousness and Hope: Christian Holiness and the Millennial Vision in America, 1800–1900," *American Quarterly* 31 (Spring 1979): 21-45, has argued that millennialism was the source of Holiness teaching.

40. Widespread acceptance of dispensationalism by adherents of Holiness teaching has been noted by H. Ray Dunning, "Biblical Interpretation and Wesleyan Theology," *Wesleyan Theological Journal* 9 (Spring 1974): 47. The role Holiness teaching played in preparing the way for the acceptance of dispensationalism is argued by Donald W. Dayton, "The Doctrine of the Baptism of the Holy Spirit: Its Emergence and Significance," *Wesleyan Theological Journal* 13 (Spring 1978): 124.

In connection with this issue of the relatedness of the Holiness movement to Fundamentalism, the impact of *the* formative philosophy of Fundamentalism, Scottish common sense realism, on the Holiness movement should not be overlooked; see Charles G. Finney, *Lectures on Revivals of Religion* (New York: Leavitt, Lord & Co., 1835), p. 29; Asa Mahan, *A Science of Moral Philosophy* (Oberlin, 1848), pp. 187, 183. Also the impact of Finney and revivalism on the Holiness movement should not be overlooked. The fact that large segments of the revivalist community became Fundamentalist helps explain the early Holiness identification with Fundamentalism.

The challenge raised by some that the Holiness movement in its earliest, pristine form did not share the view of Scripture which characterizes Fundamentalism is dealt with in subsequent chapters. Although the earliest Holiness leaders may not have affirmed explicitly the detailed inerrancy of Scripture, they did seem to remain "in dialogue with" the concept—seeking to affirm it in some sense. This is evident in one of the early leaders of the Nazarene movement; cf. A. M. Hills, *Fundamental Christian Theology*, 2 vols. (Pasadena, Cal.: C. J. Kinne, 1931), 1:134, 87. Also see H. Orton Wiley, *Christian Theology,* 3 vols. (Kansas City, Mo.: Nazarene Publishing House, 1940–1943), 1:170-172, 213-214.

41. See Marsden, *FAC*, pp. 79, 248-249. Also see n. 7 for pertinent references.
42. *The Discipline of The Wesleyan Church 1984*, p. 13; D. Dayton, in *Pneuma* 1:3, 1:8-19.

43. For such modern criticisms of the Pentecostal movement, including one offered by Graham, see Introduction, n. 32. For reference to early Fundamentalist critiques including the repudiation by the World's Christian Fundamentals Association, see William W. Menzies, *Anointed to Serve* (Springfield, Mo.: Gospel Publishing House, 1971), pp. 179-181, 72-73. Menzies, p. 24, documents the early Pentecostal support of Fundamentalism. Also see Stanley Frodsham, "Editorial," *The Pentecostal Evangel*, August 18, 1923.

Chapter 3: Princeton Theology

1. Charles Hodge, "Schaff's Protestantism," in *PT*, p. 158; Charles Hodge, "Inspiration," in *PT*, pp. 138ff.; Charles Hodge, "Bushnell on Christian Nurture," in *PT*, pp. 183-184; A. A. Hodge and B. B. Warfield, "Inspiration," in *PT*, pp. 226-227; B. B. Warfield, "Inspiration," in *PT*, pp. 286-287; B. B. Warfield, "Jonathan Edwards and the New England Theology," in *PT*, p. 316. The Princeton commitment to the theological positions of *The Westminster Confession* was evident at the outset in the original 1811 *Plan of the Seminary, PT*, p. 57. Cf. Marsden, *FAC*, p. 110.
2. A helpful summary of this debate, much of it touched off by the books of Sandeen (see Chap. 1, n. 2, and Chap. 2, n. 3) as well as the Rogers and McKim volume (see Chap. 2, n. 17) is offered by Mark A. Noll, "Introduction," *PT*, pp. 42-43.
3. A. A. Hodge and Warfield, "Inspiration," pp. 221ff.
4. The logic of the Princetonians' argument is traced by Rogers and McKim, *Authority and Interpretation*, pp. 308-309, as well as by George Marsden, "Everyone One's Own Interpreter? The Bible, Science, and Authority in Mid-Nineteenth-Century America," in *BA*, pp. 90-91. The idea of the Bible as a "store-house of facts" is articulated by Charles Hodge, *Systematic Theology*, 3 vols. (New York: Charles Scribner's Sons, 1872–1873), 1: 10. For the Princetonians' dependence on Scottish common sense realism, see ibid., 1:9; Archibald Alexander, handwritten manuscript for lecture entitled, "Nature and Evidence of Truth," in *PT*, p. 318.
5. B. B. Warfield, "The Inerrancy of the Original Autographs," in *PT*, p. 272.
6. See n. 2 for pertinent references. Especially note Sandeen, *OF*, p. 14.
7. Archibald Alexander, *Evidences of the Authenticity, Inspiration and Canonical Authority of the Holy Scriptures* (Philadelphia: Presbyterian Board of Publication, 1836), p. 230; letter, Charles Hodge to Marcus Dodds, cited in Rogers and McKim, *Authority and Interpretation*, pp. 288, 318; C. Hodge, "Inspiration," pp. 137, 139; David MacDill, *The Bible a Miracle; or the Word of God Its Own Witness* (Philadelphia: Wm. S. Rentoul, 1872), p. 501; Enoch Pond, "Lee on Inspiration," *Bibliotheca Sacra* 15 (1858): 47-48. The venerability of the Princeton view has been shown by Randall Balmer, "The Old Princeton Doctrine of Inspiration in the Context of Nineteenth Century Theology: A Reappraisal" (unpublished M.A. thesis; Trinity Evangelical Divinity School, 1981), and "The Princetonians and Scripture: A Reconsideration," *Westminster Theological Journal* 44 (1982): 352-365. A dissenting position, which opts for the prevalence of the model of plenary inspiration in this period, has been presented by Ian S. Rennie, "Mixed Metaphors, Misunderstood Models, and Puzzling Paradigms: A Contemporary Effort to Correct Some Current Misunderstandings regarding the Authority and Interpretation of the Bible: An Historical Response" (paper presented at "Interpreting an Authoritative Scripture" Conference, Toronto, June 22-26, 1981). Efforts to ground the Princeton view in historic Confessions of faith were made by A. A. Hodge

and B. B. Warfield, "Inspiration," p. 231; B. B. Warfield, "The Inerrancy of the Original Autographs," p. 274.

8. Francis Turretin, *Institutio Theologiae Elencticae* (1674), II:3-5, 7, 22, 24. Other precedents for the affirmation of detailed inerrancy by European Protestants prior to the Enlightenment are provided by John D. Woodbridge, "Some Misconceptions of the Impact of the 'Enlightenment' on the Doctrine of Scripture," in *Hermeneutics, Authority and Canon*, ed. D. A. Carson and John D. Woodbridge (Leicester: InterVarsity, 1986), pp. 241-270.

9. For an example of his use of an inductive approach, see B. B. Warfield, "The Idea of Systematic Theology," in *PT*, p. 248. For an example of his deductive approach, see B. B. Warfield, "The Present Problem of Inspiration," *Homiletic Review* 21 (May 1891): 416. It must be noted that Warfield is ambiguous on these matters for, most notably in his work with A. A. Hodge, "Inspiration," pp. 221-222, he employs a deductive approach but with certain inductive stipulations insofar as he insists that the historicity of the Bible should still be established. This ambiguity in Warfield has been noted by Colin Brown, *Miracles and the Critical Mind* (Grand Rapids, Mich.: Eerdmans, 1984), pp. 200-202, 284, 286.

10. Archibald Alexander, "Inaugural Address," in *PT*, pp. 75, 77-79; A. Alexander, *Evidences*, p. 89; C. Hodge, "Inspiration," p. 140; C. Hodge, *Systematic Theology*, 1:11. A deductive approach is suggested in Charles Hodge, "The Unity of Mankind," *Princeton Review* 31 (January 1859): 104-105, cited in Rogers and McKim, *Authority and Interpretation*, pp. 297, 319.

11. B. B. Warfield, "Inspiration," p. 288; C. Hodge, *Systematic Theology*, 1:16ff.; C. Hodge, "Finney's Lectures on Theology," in *PT*, p. 174. For an example of "rationalistic Biblicalism," see B. B. Warfield, *Selected Shorter Writings of Benjamin Warfield*, ed. John E. Meeter, 2 vols. (Nutley, N.J.: Presbyterian and Reformed Publishing, 1970–1973), 2:115.

12. B. B. Warfield, "The Divine and Human in the Bible," in *PT*, p. 276.

13. C. Hodge, "Inspiration," pp. 140-141.

14. B. B. Warfield, "The Antiquity and Unity of the Human Race," in *PT*, pp. 290-291; B. B. Warfield, "Calvin's Doctrine of Creation," in *PT*, pp. 297-298; Charles Hodge, *What Is Darwinism?* (New York: Scribner, Armstrong, and Co., 1874), p. 173.

15. Both the common features and the differences between these groups are summarized by Sandeen, *OF*, p. 14; Marsden, *FAC*, pp. 138, 103. Their common Scottish common sense philosophical orientation is documented in n. 4; Chap. 2, nn. 40, 27, 16. A good example of the Princetonians' critique on grounds of the early Fundamentalists' purported legalism is offered by C. Hodge, "Finney's Lectures on Theology," pp. 171-172.

16. For a reference to the Princetonian anti-Catholicism, see C. Hodge, "Schaff's Protestantism," p. 160. Their preoccupation with Deism is evident in the *Plan of the Seminary*, p. 57. For background on the polemical context of Turretin's work, see John W. Beardslee III, "Introduction," in *Reformed Dogmatics*, ed. and trans. John W. Beardslee III (New York: Oxford University Press, 1965), p. 10.

17. For a further indication of Princeton theology's concern with personal holiness, see Chap. 2, n. 38.

18. A. Alexander, "Inaugural Address," p. 78; Warfield, "The Idea of Systematic Theology," p. 248. It has been suggested by D. Dayton, *DEH*, pp. 132, 131, that Princeton's pessimistic views on human nature and society also help account for its ascendency in emerging Fundamentalism, for it incarnated the same pessimism as premillennialism. But challenges are raised by Ahlstrom, "The Scottish Phi-

losophy and American Theology," *Church History* 24 (1955): 269, and Marsden, *FAC*, pp. 136-138, concerning the degree to which Princetonians may have been in fact unduly optimistic in these areas.

19. This point made by Marsden, *FAC*, pp. 128, 231, in contrast to Sandeen, *OF*, p. 18. Cf. Marsden, *FAC*, pp. 210-211, on the Fundamentalists' continuing concern with reforming American society despite the influence of premillennialism.

Chapter 4: The Rise, Fall, and Revitalization of Fundamentalism

1. See Chap. 2, n. 43.

2. These distinct Landmark beliefs are sketched out in the American Baptist Association, *Doctrinal Statements* (n.d.), and in a booklet by I. K. Cross, *What Is the American Baptist Association?* (Texarkana: Bogard Press, 1984), p. 13. Valuable insights concerning the dynamics of the Noninstrumentalists' schism from the Disciples are offered by Ahlstrom, *RHAP*, pp. 822-823, and David E. Harrell Jr., "Seedbed of Sectarianism," in *VSE*, p. 49.

3. For this and the succeeding analysis of post–World War I developments and appropriate documentation I am indebted to Marsden, *FAC*, pp. 141-153.

4. References to the favorable hearing given by the secular and liberal religious press are provided in ibid., p. 175. For the preceding discussion of Fundamentalism's development I am also indebted to Marsden, *FAC*, pp. 169ff. Of particular interest in that discussion is the recognition that the issue of evolution was never a major one in church controversies, and that Fundamentalists were supported by many non-Fundamentalists in their antievolution campaign.

5. I have modified but more or less appropriated Marsden's characterization in *FAC*, pp. 291-292, 194-195, of Fundamentalism's relative impact or lack of impact on certain churches. He has been implicitly challenged by Bruce Shelley, *A History of Conservative Baptists*, 3rd ed. (Wheaton, Ill.: Conservative Baptist Press, 1981), p. 52, who claims that the Swedish Baptist General Conference was involved only tangentially in the Fundamentalist movement. Also, Marsden's claim that Fundamentalism was never a dominant force among Mennonites is indirectly disputed by J. B. Toews, "Mennonite Brethren Identity and Theological Diversity," in *Pilgrims and Strangers,* ed. Paul Toews (Fresno, Cal.: Center for Mennonite Brethren Studies, 1977), pp. 144ff., and Paul Toews, "Fundamentalist Conflict in Mennonite Colleges: A Response to Cultural Transitions?" *The Mennonite Quarterly Review* 57 (July 1983): 244ff. For the impact of dispensationalism, Fundamentalism, or at least anti-Modernism on all the Free Church groups except the Swedish Mission Covenant group, see Frederick Hale, *Trans-Atlantic Conservative Protestantism in the Evangelical Free and Mission Covenant Traditions* (New York: Arno, 1979), pp. 64, 90, 268, 283, 288, 303-306; Karl A. Olsson, *Into One Body . . . by the Cross,* vol. 1 (Chicago: Covenant Press, 1985), pp. 30-35, 41-42, 45, 76ff.

6. References to the situation of the Free Churches are given in the preceding footnote. Eric Gritsch, *Born Againism* (Philadelphia: Fortress, 1982), p. 40, and Todd Nichol, " 'Timely Warnings': Notes on Inerrancy and Inerrant," *Dialog* 24 (Winter 1985): 55-56, helpfully point to instances of American Lutheran support of Fundamentalism. But Milton Rudnick, *Fundamentalism and the Missouri Synod* (St. Louis: Concordia, 1966), and Gritsch, p. 40, have shown that the position of The Lutheran Church–Missouri Synod is not dependent on Fundamentalism but is rooted in Lutheran Orthodoxy. And it is not clear that Nichol, p. 59, can support his contention that other American Lutheran churches affirming the inerrancy of

Scripture reached their positions more in consequence of the influence of Fundamentalism than as a direct consequence of something like the presence of this conception in Lutheran Orthodoxy (John Baier, *Compendium Theologiae Positivae* [1685], 81; Abraham Calovius, *Systema Locorum Theologicorum*, 12 vols. [1655–1677], 1:551), in the pre-Fundamentalist period of American Lutheranism (*Referat af Forhandlingerene i Delegatmødet . . . i Willmar, Minnesota, . . .*" [Decorah, Iowa: Lutheran Publishing House, 1891], p. 49), and perhaps in the Lutheran Confessions (Preface to *The Book of Concord* [1580]), Martin Luther, *The Large Catechism* (1538), IV.57.

7. Not unlike Marsden, *FAC*, p. 178, who sees a mutual affinity between the schism and Fundamentalism, two theologians of the Churches of Christ, Joe Ellis, in a personal letter, June 19, 1985, and memo, Wayne Shaw to Sam Stone, June 20, 1985, concede the temporal connection to the Fundamentalist controversy. But neither would equate these churches with Fundamentalism.

8. Harry Emerson Fosdick, "Shall the Fundamentalists Win?" *Christian Work* 112 (June 10, 1922): 716-722 (also in *The Christian Century*, June 8, 1922).

9. J. Gresham Machen, *Christianity and Liberalism* (New York: Macmillan, 1923), pp. 8, 160.

10. Scopes Trial transcript, in Arthur Weinberg, ed., *Attorney for the Damned* (New York: Simon & Schuster, 1957), pp. 223-225.

11. The most devastating and influential critique of Fundamentalists during the trial was offered by H. L. Mencken, *Prejudices: Fifth Series* (New York, 1926), cited by Marsden, *FAC*, pp. 187-188, 281.

12. Discussions of this dynamic in Fundamentalism after the Scopes Trial, including the "Great Reversal" of its political-ethical commitments are offered by Marsden, *FAC*, pp. 85ff.; David Moberg, *The Great Reversal: Evangelism versus Social Concern* (Philadelphia: Lippincott, 1972); and George M. Marsden, "From Fundamentalism to Evangelicalism: A Historical Analysis," in *E*, pp. 127-128.

13. James Davison Hunter, *American Evangelicalism* (New Brunswick: Rutgers, 1983), p. 39; Joel A. Carpenter, "From Fundamentalism to the New Evangelical Coalition," in *EMA*, pp. 6-7.

14. Growth in this period is noted by Marsden, *FAC*, pp. 191-194; Carpenter, in *EMA*, pp. 4, 6, 10-14.

15. Falwell (see abbreviations), pp. 160-161. Separatist positions of these other institutions are documented in George Dollar, *A History of Fundamentalism in America* (Greenville, S.C.: Bob Jones University Press, 1973), pp. 242-243, 253, 281; *Constitution of the International Council of Christian Churches* (1954), III:1; *New Tribes Mission Separation Policy*, 1-2, in New Tribes Mission, *Manual* (Sanford, Fla., n.d.), p. 23.

Chapter 5: The Emergence of the Evangelical Movement

1. For references, see Introduction, n. 39.

2. Carl Henry, *GRA*, 4:289; Harold Ockenga, "From Fundamentalism, through New Evangelicalism, to Evangelicalism," in *Evangelical Roots*, ed. Kenneth Kantzer (New York: Thomas Nelson, 1978), p. 43; E. J. Carnell, *The Case for Orthodox Theology* (Philadelphia: Westminster, 1959), pp. 113ff.; cf. Independent Fundamental Churches of America, *Constitution and By-Laws of the Independent Fundamental Churches of America* (1979), Art. IV, sec. 2 (1); Art. IV, Sec. 2d; New Tribes Mission, *Doctrinal Statement* (n.d.), 10, in *Manual*, p. 7; UFM Interna-

tional, *Policies and Practice* (unpaginated brochure; Bala-Cynwyd, Pa., n.d.); George Dollar, *A History of Fundamentalism in America* (Greenville, S.C.: Bob Jones University Press, 1973), pp. 203ff.

3. Jerry Falwell, "Future-Word: An Agenda for the Eighties," in *The Fundamentalist Phenomenon,* ed. Jerry Falwell, with Ed Dobson and Ed Hindson (Garden City, N.Y.: Doubleday, 1981), pp. 222, 219. For speculations about the formation of a possible coalition, see Ronald H. Nash, *Evangelicals in America: Who They Are, What They Believe* (Nashville: Abingdon, 1987), pp. 74-75. Documentation of these tensions outside North America has been provided by David Parker, "The Evangelical Heritage of Australian Protestantism," *The Evangelical Quarterly* 57 (1985): 58, and by the chairman of the Kirchliche Sammlung um Bibel und Bekenntnis, Joachim Heubach, in a personal letter, February 8, 1985.

4. "Valiant for Truth," *Accent: Newsletter of the American Council of Christian Churches,* I, No. 6 (September-October, 1966): 1-5.

5. For references, see William W. Menzies, *Anointed to Serve* (Springfield, Mo.: Gospel Publishing House, 1971), pp. 185-188.

6. See Introduction, n. 39; Harold Ockenga, *Bulletin of Wheaton College* 37 (February 1960), as cited in Dollar, *A History,* p. 204.

7. Edward John Carnell, "The Glory of a Theological Seminary," Inaugural Address, May 17, 1955, p. 9. Cf. the statement by Carnell's successor as president of Fuller Seminary, David Hubbard, quoted in Falwell (see abbreviations), p. 153.

8. Carl McIntire, personal letter, March 27, 1984.

9. A good example of this self-understanding is evident in Bernard Ramm, *The Evangelical Heritage* (Waco, Tex.: Word, 1973), pp. 50ff.

10. See William Martin, "Billy Graham," in *VSE,* p. 82.

11. D. Tinder, in *E,* p. 295. Background on Graham's controversy with Fundamentalists is found in Falwell, pp. 129-131, 149-151.

12. Mark Noll, "Children of the Reformation in a Brave New World," *Dialog* 24 (1985): 176.

13. The polemical orientation of the NAE is noted by Bruce Shelley, *Evangelicalism in America* (Grand Rapids, Mich.: Eerdmans, 1967), p. 289. This pessimistic orientation concerning our cultural context is reflected in a number of NAE resolutions like *God's Word—Our Infallible Guide* (1977), p. 1, and *The Crisis in the Nation* (1968), p. 6. Martin, "Billy Graham," p. 75, is helpful in showing a similar orientation in Billy Graham. Graham's theological emphasis on being "born again" has been identified by J. Hadden and C. Swann, *Prime Time Preachers* (Reading, Mass.: Addison-Wesley, 1981), p. 21. See pp. 17, 19, for both Fuller and NAE statements.

14. See Donald Dayton, "Evangelical Contradictions," *Sojourners,* April 1976, p. 26.

Chapter 6: The Evangelical Movement Outside North America

1. Fritz Grünzweig, "Die Ludwig-Hofacker-Vereinigung," in *Weg und Zeugnis,* ed. Rudolf Bäumer, Peter Beyerhaus, and Fritz Grünzweig, 2nd ed. (Bad Liebenzell: Verlag der Liebenzeller Mission, 1981), pp. 80ff. The organization's early preoccupation with Bultmann is evident in a pamphlet it issued, *Es geht um die Bibel* (1951), in *Weg und Zeugnis,* p. 127. The influence of the polemic with Bultmann on German Evangelicalism as a whole has been noted by Joachim Heubach, private interview, Bückeburg, West Germany, September 6, 1985; Gerhard Sauter, "Einführung in die deutsche Ausgabe," in James Barr, *Fundamentalismus* (Munich: Chr. Kaiser, 1981), p. 12.

2. Lausanne's role in organizing Scandinavian theological conservatives was made clear to me by the general secretary of the Santalmisjonen in Norway, Gunnleik Seierstad, private interview during the Lutheran World Federation Assembly, Budapest, Hungary, July 28, 1984. The impact of Graham in awakening, if not stimulating, the Evangelical movement has been noted by P. Beyerhaus, interview, the general secretary of the German Evangelical Alliance, Peter Schneider, private interview, Strasbourg, France, May 17, 1985, and the Evangelisch-methodistische Kirche, *Unser Verhältnis zu den Evangelikalen* (Stuttgart: Christliches Verlagshaus, 1976), II, with regard to Germany; by H. Bolleter, "Wer sind die Evangelikalen?" lecture broadcast on Swiss radio, Btrg. I, with regard to Switzerland; and by Pete Lowman, *The Day of His Power* (Leicester, England: InterVarsity Press, 1983), pp. 94-95, and Randle Manwaring, *From Controversy to Co-Existence: Evangelicals in the Church of England 1914–1980* (Cambridge: Cambridge University Press, 1985), pp. 85-97, 112, with regard to Great Britain.
3. Maier, interview. Insights on the Latin American situation were offered by Gottfried Brakemeier, private interview, Strasbourg, France, March 8, 1984.
4. Richard Quebedeaux, *The New Charismatics* (Garden City, N.Y.: Doubleday, 1976), pp. 60, 63, 126; Walter Sawatsky, *Soviet Evangelicals since World War II* (Kitchener, Ont., and Scottdale, Pa.: Herald Press, 1981), pp. 340, 341, 34. The impact of North American Evangelicals on the Caribbean is noted by David Ho Sang and Roger Ringenberg, "Towards an Evangelical Caribbean Theology," *Evangelical Review of Theology* 7 (April 1983): 137, and on Eastern Europe it is noted by Keith Parker, personal letter, November 14, 1984.
5. Walter J. Hollenweger, *Enthusiastisches Christentum* (Wuppertal: Theologischer Verlag Rolf Brockhaus; Zurich: Zwingli Verlag, 1969), pp. 105, 307-308.
6. My understanding of the Eastern European situation is indebted to East German Baptist Seminary director, Klaus Fuhrmann, personal letters, January 29, 1985, April 15, 1985, and Keith Parker, letter, November 14, 1984. Sawatsky, *Soviet Evangelicals*, pp. 211, 448, 470-471, notes the precritical mentality of Soviet Evangelicals. R. Hutcheson, *Mainline Churches and the Evangelicals: A Challenging Crisis?* (Atlanta: John Knox, 1981), pp. 88-89, notes the relative disinterest of Third World Evangelicals in stimulating conflict between themselves and mainline churches. Also see the reference to Latin America in n. 8.
7. That this dynamic pertains in West Germany was made evident in my interview with Maier. It seems on the basis of discussion with a North American Evangelical working in France, Paul Cowan, private interview, Strasbourg, December 3, 1984, that resistance to "American Evangelicalism" also pertains to the French situation. A similar East German dynamic is suggested by Fuhrmann, April 15, 1985. Baptist efforts to "indigenize" Evangelicalism are reflected in remarks of Fuhrmann, January 29, 1985, and his colleague, Adolf Pohl, private interview, Neudietendorf, East Germany, April 18, 1985, who argue that the Baptist heritage in their nation is rooted not so much in the work of English Baptist missionaries (though it has roots there) but in the Reformation heritage of Ulrich Zwingli. (Also see *Bericht über die theologische Gespräche zwischen dem Bund Evangelisch-Freikirchlicher Gemeinden [BEFG] und dem Bund der Evangelischen Kirchen in der DDR [BEK]* [1982–1983] 1; Jörg Swoboda, "Die Verwerfungen der Confessio Augustana—eine historische Einschätzung," in *Wort und Tat* 67 [Bund Evangelisch-Freikirchlicher Gemeinden in der DDR, 1986], pp. 7-11.) On the problem in Latin America, see René Padilla, "Evangelism and the World," in *LEH*, pp. 125-126.
8. Chapter 18 describes the debate. The charge that American Evangelicals have imposed their own agenda on other Evangelical communities is made by *The Seoul*

Declaration toward an Evangelical Theology for the Third World (1982) 1: R. Padilla, *LEH*, pp. 136ff. On the role of American missionaries in polarizing Protestant churches in Latin America, see Samuel Escobar and Pedro Arana, Valdir Steuernagel, Rodrigo Zapata, "A Latin American Critique of Latin American Theology," *Evangelical Review of Theology* 7 (April 1983): 53-54. Also at this point must be considered the widespread rumor and debate that Evangelical organizations are being used by USA Intelligence for anticommunist purposes, see Gert Wendelborn, *Gottes Wort und die Gesellschaft* (Berlin: Union Verlag, 1979), p. 116; "Weltkirchenrat: Schwere Vorwürfe gegen evangelikale Werke," *Pressausgabe*, 64/84 (19 July 1984), p. 4.

9. Donald Gillies, *Revolt from the Church* (Belfast: Christian Journals Ltd., 1980), pp. 25, 79. On Paisley's Fundamentalist pedigree, see Falwell (see abbreviations), p. 151.

10. Fuhrmann, April 4, 1985; Karl Heinz Knöppel, personal letters, June 5, 1985, August 1, 1985; Evangelisch-methodistische Kirche, IV.5, I; VI; Joachim Heubach, personal letter, February 8, 1985; Erik Petren, personal letter, July 12, 1985. In all cases these leaders of their respective organizations see the distance of their organization from the Evangelical movement as related to the characteristic Evangelical views of Scripture.

11. References in the text to the doctrinal positions of the Alliance Evangélique Française designate its *Déclaration de Foi* (n.d.). The same system of documentation is used with regard to the Internationale Konferenz Bekennender Gemeinschaften, as mere citation of this organization or its doctrinal positions in the text and notes without citation of some other document presupposes reference to the *Vorlaufige Grundordnung der Internationalen Konferenz Bekennender Gemeinschaften* (n.d.) (and the accompanying letters or numbers refer to the corresponding article of the document). Likewise, citation of the Evangelical Alliance [of Great Britain] in the notes and mention in the text of its doctrinal positions presuppose reference to *The Evangelical Alliance Basis of Faith* (1846), just as a similar mention of the Church of England Evangelical Council, when followed by an Arabic number, refers to the corresponding article of its *Keele Congress Statement* (1967). Mention in the text of theological positions of the Deutsche Evangelische Allianz, without explicit citation of some other document, refers to its *Basis* (1972). References to the Brazilian situation were provided by Russell P. Shedd, personal letter, August 13, 1985; and Richard Sturz, memorandum, August 1985. A de-emphasis of inerrancy among African Evangelicals is suggested by the general secretary of the Association of Evangelicals of Africa and Madagascar [AEAM], Tokunboh Adeyemo, personal letter, May 22, 1985. For information about a corresponding de-emphasis in Europe I am indebted to those cited in the preceding note, Geoffrey W. Bromiley, interview, and Quebedeaux, *WE*, p. 87. See also J. I. Packer, *Fundamentalism and the Word of God* (London: Inter-Varsity, 1958), p. 95.

12. Maier, *EhkM*, p. 71; however, he regards the Bible's inerrancy primarily in terms of Scripture's fulfillment by God. A stricter sense of inerrancy is generally thought to be affirmed by Samuel Külling and his colleagues at the Freie Evangelische Akademie in Basel. Also see Association d'Eglises de Professants des Pays Francophones, *Base Doctrinale* (1972).

References to the AEAM followed by an Arabic number refer to its *Statement of Faith* (n.d.), and the numeral designates the pertinent article of the statement. Likewise, references to the theological position of the Fédération Evangélique de France without explicit mention of some other document refer to its *Base Doctrinale* (n.d.).

The position of Det Norske Misjonsforbund is reported officially in Heinz-Adolf Ritter, ed., *International Federation of Free Evangelical Churches* (Stockholm: Gummessons Boktryckeri, 1980), p. 30. The Brazilian churches cited are the Assembléias de Deus, *Fundamental Doctrines* (n.d.), 1; Congregação Cristã do Brasil, *Articles of Faith* (1946), 3. Two other French Evangelical organizations affirming inerrancy in some form are the Faculté Libre de Théologie Evangélique, Vaux-sur-Seine, "L'Ecriture Sainte," February 1970; Association Evangélique d'Eglises Baptistes de Langue Française, *Confession of Faith and Ecclesiastical Principles* (1979), I.2.

13. Henry, *GRA*, 4:179. It should also be noted that the Konferenz Bekennender Gemeinschaften, *Orientierungshilfe des Theologischen Konvents für die Schriftauslegung* (n.d.), 6, seems to insist on the historicity of the biblical accounts.

14. Good examples of this orientation are evident in Spener, *PD*, pp. 56-57, 67. Likewise one finds his claim in *Philipp Jacob Speners deutsche und lateinische theologische Bedenken* (1838, ed.), p. 333, that the Bible cannot be understood apart from the Spirit's work in the believer. The usual interpretation of Pietism is that it did not directly attend to the Lutheran Orthodox theories of biblical inspiration; see, for example, Theodore G. Tappert, "Introduction," in *PD*, p. 25. But that the Orthodox doctrine of biblical inerrancy was assumed seems evident in Johann Albrecht Bengel's claim in *Gnomon of the New Testament*, trans. Bandinel and Fausset (1860), 1:7, that the Bible is "unimpaired by defect." Perhaps those Evangelical pietists who have gone on to assert biblical inerrancy are remaining true to their heritage after all.

   For references to the predominance of Scottish common sense realism in American cultural institutions as well as in early Fundamentalism and its spiritual heirs, see Chap. 2, nn. 16, 27, 40; Chap. 3, n. 4; pp. 56, 211-212.

15. Key Yuasa, personal letter, July 29, 1985, a prominent Brazilian Evangelical, called my attention to these tensions in Brazil. I learned of tensions in Russia from W. Sawatsky, *Soviet Evangelicals*, pp. 285, 439. The reference in the text to the Fédération Evangélique de France pertains to *Conditions d'Admission et de Maintien Dans la F.E.F.* (n.d.), 4,3. Also see *Berlin Declaration on Ecumenism* (1974), 7.

   The original *Berlin Declaration* (1909) is discussed and cited in Hollenweger, *EC*, pp. 67, 201ff. It has been observed that the Gemeinschaftsbewegung is the supporting pillar of the Evangelical movement in Germany; see Erich Geldbach, "Evangelikalismus: Versuch einer historischen Typologie," in *Die Kirchen und ihre Konservativen*, ed. Reinhard Frieling (Göttingen: Vandenhoeck & Ruprecht, 1984), pp. 73-74.

   For examples of Fundamentalist rejections of the movement, see Falwell, pp. 71, 239; IFCA, 11a.

16. In his letter Yuasa notes this cooperation in Brazil; the eminent Dutch charismatic Willem C. van Dam, personal letter, May 29, 1985, refers to it in his country, and Theo Wettach, "Evangelikale heute" (lecture presented for the Board of the Evangelische Missionswerk in BRD and West Berlin, January 1985), p. 4, notes such cooperation in Switzerland.

17. Samuel Nafzger, quoted in Darrell Turner, "Ecumenical Institute Seeks to Define 'Evangelical,'" *Religious News Service*, March 12, 1985, p. 3, makes this point for LCMS; David Valleskey, "Evangelical Lutheranism and Today's Evangelicals and Fundamentalists," *Wisconsin Lutheran Quarterly* 80 (Summer 1983): 216, for the Wisconsin Synod; Gerhard Rost, "Die Selbständige Evangelish-Lutherische Kirche," in *Weg und Zeugnis*, ed. Rudolf Bäumer, Peter Beyerhaus, and Fritz

Grünzweig, 2nd ed. (Bad Liebenzell: Verlag der Liebenzeller Mission, 1981), p. 89, for the SELKD; Heubach, February 8, 1985, for his Bekenntnisbewegung organization; and Seierstad, interview, for Scandinavians.

18. Seierstad, interview; Poul Langagergaard, private interview during the Lutheran World Federation Assembly, Budapest, Hungary, August 3, 1984. All the German organizations mentioned identify themselves with the Evangelical movement insofar as they cooperate inside the Konferenz Bekennender Gemeinschaften.

19. Knöppel, June 5, 1985; Schneider, interview.

20. Francis A. Schaeffer, *A Christian Manifesto* (Westchester, Ill.: Crossway, 1981), pp. 18-19.

21. J. W. Ewing, *Goodly Fellowship* (London: Marshall, Morgan & Scott, 1946), pp. 85ff.; Gerstner, in *E*, p. 25, notes that the anti–Catholicism of the Alliance included anti–Anglo-Catholicism. This helps explain the attraction the Alliance had for Anglican Evangelicals. Ahlstrom, *RHAP*, p. 559, notes how nativist sentiments attracted American Evangelicals.

22. Nils Bloch-Hoell, *The Pentecostal Movement* (Oslo: Universitetsforlaget, 1964), p. 13. This emphasis is reflected in the seventh article of the Alliance's *Doctrinal Basis*.

23. Jack Rogers and Donald McKim, *The Authority and Interpretation of the Bible* (San Francisco: Harper & Row, 1979), p. 312, note A. Alexander's use of this text. See relevant texts in Chap. 2, n. 38 for the Reformed tradition's overriding concern. For a reference to Calvin's polemical concern to defend the existence of God from atheism (a similar concern as the Princetonians and the early Alliance leaders), see *Institutes*, I/III.2.

24. Puritan literature illustrating these commitments includes William Perkins, *Works of that Famous and Worthy Minister . . . Mr. William Perkins*, 3 vols. (1616 ed.), 1:255; Richard Baxter, *A Christian Directory*, in *The Practical Works of Richard Baxter*, 4 vols. (1847), 1: 8. Discussions by analysts which confirm my own characterization of Puritan origins and concerns are offered by F. Ernest Stoeffler, *The Rise of Evangelical Pietism* (Leiden: E. J. Brill, 1971), pp. 27-28, 31; Ahlstrom, in *E*, pp. 271-272; Ahlstrom, *RHAP*, pp. 91ff.; A. C. Piepkorn, *Profiles in Belief*, 4 vols. (New York: Harper & Row, 1977-1979), 2:366-368.

25. Piepkorn, *Profiles*, 2:364-365; Stoeffler, *REP*, pp. 27ff.

26. William Wilberforce, *Practical View of the Prevailing Religious System* (London, 1797), pp. 68, 69, 245; David Forrester, "Anglican Evangelicalism," *The Clergy Review* 60 (December 1975), especially pp. 778, 781. The Anglican Evangelicals' concern with sanctification and conversion still is reflected in the present, as is evident in their *Keele Statement*, 12-13.

27. Forrester, "Anglican Evangelicalism," pp. 782, 777; Packer, in *TCU*, pp. 55, 54; Manwaring, *From Controversy to Co-Existence*, p. 129. It should be noted that Anglican Evangelicalism is not monolithic but divides into different types, notably liberal and conservative; see Forrester, p. 785. The latter group probably has most in common with American Evangelicals.

28. Stoeffler, *REP*, p. 231, and Ahlstrom, *RHAP*, p. 237, show that Spener had read various Puritan books.

29. P. J. Spener, *Von der Wiedergeburt*, ed. Hans-Georg Feller (Stuttgart: J. F. Steinkopf, 1963), p. 13; Spener, *PD*, pp. 44-45, 64; Stoeffler, *GPD*, p. 16, finds a similar emphasis in August Hermann Francke. Offering a similar analysis of Pietism's emphasis are Martin Schmidt, "Pietismus," in *Religion in Geschichte und Gegenwart*, 3rd ed. (Tübingen: J.C.B. Mohr, 1957ff.), 3:370; Piepkorn, *Profiles*,

2:26. The correlation between the Reformed tradition and Pietism with their common emphasis on the Christian life has been noticed by Stoeffler, *GPD*, p. 218.

30. Spener, *PD*, p. 80; Friedrich Adolf Lampe, *Geheimnis des Gnadenbunds, dem grossen Gott zu Ehren*, 6 vols. (1712–1719), 1:416, 531. Stoeffler, *GPD*, p. 10, identifies in Francke the notion of cooperation with grace; cf. Bloesch, *ER*, p. 132. Burkhard Weber, "Der Artikel von der Wiedergeburt bei Philipp Jacob Spener," in *TWB*, p. 89, cites an exception in Spener where the centrality of the doctrine of justification is affirmed.

31. Spener, *PD*, pp. 39ff., 70, 77. Ahlstrom, *RHAP*, pp. 236-237, 91, provides background on the originating context for both movements, including Puritanism's anti-Catholicism.

32. The life of the foremost neopietist Johann Heinrich Jung-Stilling, as described by Stoeffler, *GPD*, pp. 255ff., is a good illustration of these commitments. The neopietist coalition with Orthodoxy and its originating context, including the impact of European revivalism are helpfully described in *GPD*, pp. 241-242, 265, and Gerhard Schäfer, "Württemberg und der Pietismus," in *Das evangelische Württemberg*, ed. Ulrich Fick (Stuttgart: J. F. Steinkopf, 1983), pp. 48ff. See also Dieter Lange, *Eine Bewegung bricht sich Bahn* (Giessen: Brunnen Verlag; Dillenburg: Gnadauer Verlag 1979).

33. See relevant texts in n. 14. The Orthodox, biblicist orientation of Tholuck and neopietism is noted by Sauter, "Einführung," p. 20.

34. August R. Suelflow and E. Clifford Nelson, "Following the Frontier 1840–1875," in *The Lutherans in North America*, ed. E. Clifford Nelson (Philadelphia: Fortress, 1975), pp. 163-164; F. Hale, *Trans-Atlantic Conservative Protestantism* (New York: Arno, 1979), pp. 64, 89-90.

35. John Wesley, "Letter to Robert Carr Brackenbury," (1790), in *Letters*, ed. John Telford, 8 vols. (London: Epworthy, 1931), 7:238; John Wesley, "The Principles of a Methodist Farther Explained," in *Works*, 14 vols. (Grand Rapids, Mich.: Zondervan, 1958–1959), 8:472. Piepkorn, *Profiles*, 2:535, shows that Methodism, like other Alliance partners, emerged in a period of religio-cultural turbulence.

36. *Second London Confession* (1689), Intro.; cf. *Lutheran–Baptist Dialogue* [USA]: *Three Common Statements* (1981), "Divine Initiative and Human Response," I.

37. *Ordnung der Gemein, wie ein Christ leben soll* (1527); *The Waterland Confession* (1580), Art. XXII. See Horst Weigelt, *Spiritualistische Tradition im Protestantismus: Das Schwenkfeldertum in Schlesian* (Berlin: DeGruyter, 1973), pp. 36ff.

Chapter 7: The Evangelical Coalition

1. The debates among scholars about the origins or proper starting point for analysis of the Evangelical movement are nicely summarized by Leonard I. Sweet, "The Evangelical Tradition in America," in *The Evangelical Tradition in America*, ed. L. Sweet (Macon, Ga. Mercer University Press, 1984), pp. 1ff.

2. See Chap. 3, n. 8. Note 16 of Chap. 3 gives references to the polemical context of both streams. Also see the relevant sections of Chap. 2, n. 38, for references to the Princetonian concern for sanctification, and pp. 73-77 for the Princetonians' views on biblical authority.

3. Ahlstrom, in *E*, p. 271; Bloesch, *ER*, p. 124; Marsden, *FAC*, p. 135. This theocratic orientation among Puritans is explicitly articulated by John Eliot, as quoted in H. Richard Niebuhr, *The Kingdom of God in America* (New York: Harper & Row, 1937), pp. 61, 203. See Chap. 6, n. 24, for references pertaining to other characteristics of Puritanism which I have described. Calvin's theocratic vision is

particularly apparent in the *Institutes*, IV/XX.2, 3, 9, though it must be conceded that at other points (II/VIII.1; III/XIX.15; IV/XI.3-5; IV/XX.1, 5) he did employ the categories of the two-kingdom ethic.

4. John Eliot, *The Christian Commonwealth: or, The Civil Policy of the Rising Kingdom of Jesus Christ*, in Massachusetts Historical Society, *Collections*, Series III, vol. 9 (Boston, 1846), p. 134. For the Puritans' precisionistic approach to Scripture, see Ahlstrom, *RHAP*, pp. 129, 131.

5. Ahlstrom, *RHAP*, pp. 292-293.

6. Ahlstrom, in *E*, p. 275. For more on the Puritan emphasis on conversion, see Chap. 6, n. 24; Alan Simpson, *Puritanism in Old and New England* (Chicago: University of Chicago Press, 1955), p. 2. For the convergence between the revivalist and Puritan heritage in other ways, see Marsden, *FAC*, p. 225.

7. A diminishing of social concern is evident in Dwight Moody, *Moody: His Words, Work, and Workers*, ed. J. H. Daniels (New York, 1877), pp. 431-432; cf. D. L. Moody, "The Second Coming of Christ," in *The Best of D. L. Moody*, ed. Wilbur M. Smith (Chicago, 1971), pp. 193-195. A reactionary nativism is apparent in Billy Sunday, *New Era Magazine*, September 1919, p. 522. Both Robert Booth Fowler, *A New Engagement: Evangelical Political Thought, 1966–1976* (Grand Rapids: Eerdmans, 1982), p. 102, and Marsden, in *FAC*, p. 135, describe Sunday's lack of social concern, but both acknowledge that he did reflect a certain concern for civic reform, albeit with a focus on the individual, which has characterized revivalism and Fundamentalism. Revivalism's individualistic tendencies have been noted by Marsden, in *E*, pp. 135-136, and its anti-intellectualism by Ahlstrom, in *E*, p. 277. Also see Billy Sunday, as quoted in Marsden, in *FAC*, p. 130. This anti-intellectualism and corresponding de-emphasis on a learned ministry, associated with later revivalism, help explain the growth of Baptist and Methodist churches in America and their dominance in Evangelicalism. For, while other churches did not have enough educated persons for leadership, these traditions, particularly the Baptists, which did not stress a learned ministry, could more readily engage in mission work; see Jeffrey K. Hadden and Charles Swann, *Prime Time Preachers* (Reading, Mass.: Addison-Wesley, 1981), pp. 69-70. Some historians have also claimed that the "great reversal" leading to the loss of Evangelical social concern is rooted totally in developments of later American revivalism. These arguments are discussed and documented in Marsden, *FAC*, pp. 85-86, 252. A critique of revivalism's compromise of the primacy of grace is offered by Gerstner, in *E*, p. 27. That Moody was guilty of such a compromise is evident in Dale Moody, *Sowing and Reaping* (Chicago, 1896), p. 83. This tendency is also apparent in the Keswick movement; see *Record of the Convention for the Promotion of Scriptural Holiness Held at Brighton* (Brighton and London: W. J. Smith and S. W. Partridge, 1875), pp. 441, 443-444.

For discussions of antebellum revivalism's identification with the American establishment, see Marsden, *FAC*, pp. 11, 55-56; Sweet, in *ETA*, pp. 26-27.

8. Charles G. Finney, *The Oberlin Evangelist* I (January 16, 1839), 18-19. His indebtedness to Taylor has been noted by the Princetonians; see Gerstner, in *E*, p. 21. For a discussion of Taylor's views, see Ahlstrom, *RHAP*, p. 420.

9. Hadden and Swann, *Prime Time Preachers*, p. 72. One thinks of the tension in American Presbyterianism between the "Old School" and the revivalist-oriented "New School."

10. Charles G. Finney, as quoted in G. F. Wright, *Charles G. Finney* (Boston, 1891), pp. 182-183.

11. Vernon Grounds, *Evangelicalism and Social Responsibility* (Scottdale, Pa.: Herald

Press, 1969), pp. 4-6; R. Johnston (see abbreviations), p. 105; Nathan O. Hatch, "Evangelicalism as a Democratic Movement," in *EMA*, pp. 72ff.; George Marsden, "Evangelicals, History, and Modernity," in *EMA*, p. 95. For the impact of revivalism and Puritanism on both Evangelicalism and American society, see Marsden, in *E*, pp. 134-135. The formative impact of Scottish common sense realism on both Evangelicalism and the American way of life also suggests the influence of the latter on the Evangelical movement.

On Edwards' postmillennialism, see Chap. 2, n. 26.

12. Southern Baptist Convention, *A Statement of Social Principles for Christian Social Concern and Christian Social Action*, as quoted in C. Brownlow Hastings, *Introducing Southern Baptists: Their Faith & Their Life* (New York: Paulist, 1981), p. 141.

13. James Davison Hunter, *American Evangelicalism* (New Brunswick: Rutgers University Press, 1983), pp. 47, 53ff., shows sociologically that American Evangelicalism is drawn from the middle class. Francis Schaeffer, *Escape from Reason* (Downers Grove, Ill.: InterVarsity, 1968), pp. 43-44, 93-94, was pleased to note an ideological connection between Evangelicalism and the middle class. For Evangelicalism's correlation with the middle class in Australia, see David Parker, "The Evangelical Heritage of Australian Protestantism," *The Evangelical Quarterly* 57 (1985): 60. For the emerging middle class status of Brazilian Pentecostals, see Hollenweger, *EC*, pp. 85-86. For historical examples of Fundamentalism's efforts to defend the values of the premodern American way of life, see Marsden, *FAC*, pp. 152-153; Richard V. Pierard, "The New Religious Right in American Politics," in *EMA*, pp. 162-163.

14. For references to the overriding concern and originating contexts of these traditions, see Chap. 6, nn. 29-31, 37. For the context from which the Radical Reformation was generated, a concern to restore the primitive church in face of social and ecclesiastical decay, see *The Schleitheim Confession* (1527); George H. Williams, *The Radical Reformation* (Philadelphia: Westminster, 1962), pp. xxvi, 857. My idea of the Evangelical movement's debt to the Radical Reformation and Pietism parallels the thesis of my predecessor, Carter Lindberg, *The Third Reformation?* (Macon, Ga.: Mercer University Press, 1983), esp. p. 320, concerning the origins of the charismatic movement. A recognition of such shared origins should hardly be surprising inasmuch as Pentecostals are part of the Evangelical movement.

15. See Chap. 2, n. 38; Chap. 6, nn. 28, 29.

16. ECC, pp. 8, 13; Baptist General Conference, *An Affirmation of Our Faith* (1951), 6. The BGC preoccupation with being born again is suggested by the fact that reference is made only to regeneration, not to justification, in its statement. An official pamphlet of the church, *What Is a Conference Baptist?* (Arlington Heights, Ill., n.d.), speaks only of conversion and not justification.

17. A similar distinction is offered by Donald W. Dayton, "Whither Evangelicalism? The Holiness Heritage between Calvinism and Wesleyanism" (lecture presented at the Sixth Oxford Institute Methodist Theological Studies Conference, n.d.), pp. 5-6.

18. See relevant references in Chap. 2, n. 31.

19. William Menzies, *Anointed to Serve* (Springfield, Mo.: Gospel Publishing House, 1971), pp. 57-58; Church of God (Cleveland, Tenn.), *Holiness Resolution* (1960). While insisting on the centrality of justification, numerous Lutheran charismatics claim to be preoccupied with sanctification and the quality of the Christian life; see Larry Christenson, ed., *Welcome, Holy Spirit: A Study of Charismatic Renewal in the Church* (Minneapolis: Augsburg, 1987), pp. 20-22, 81-84, 186, 228-230.

20. Phoebe Palmer, *Four Years in the Old World* (New York: Walter C. Palmer Jr., 1870), pp. 107, 76. See the argument for Pentecostalism's indebtedness to the Holiness movement in Donald W. Dayton, *Theological Roots of Pentecostalism* (Grand Rapids, Mich.: Francis Asbury, 1987).

21. Nils Bloch-Hoell, *The Pentecostal Movement* (Oslo: Universitetsforlaget, 1964), p. 12; Donald Dayton, "The Doctrine of the Baptism of the Holy Spirit," *Wesleyan Theological Journal* 13 (1978): 116, 122. For references to speaking in tongues as the "initial evidence," see The International Pentecostal Holiness Church, *Articles of Faith* (n.d.), in *The Pentecostal Holiness Church Manual 1981* (Franklin Springs, Ga.: Advocate Press, 1981), 11; Assemblies of God, *Statement of Fundamental Truths* (1969), 8.

22. Walter J. Hollenweger, personal letter, June 25, 1985. Early manifestations of glossolalia are described by Menzies, *Anointed*, pp. 28-33.

23. Menzies, *Anointed*, p. 39; D. Dayton, "Theological Roots of Pentecostalism," *Pneuma* 1 (1980): 20-21.

24. Quebedeaux, *NC*, pp. 4, 26-27; Bloch-Hoell, *Pentecostal Movement*, pp. 9, 12.

25. Quebedeaux, *NC*, pp. 27, 158-159; Bloch-Hoell, *Pentecostal Movement*, pp. 10-11, 172; Hollenweger, *EC*, pp. 85-86. It is interesting to note that it was to the lower classes that the Radical Reformation made its greatest appeal; see Stoeffler, *REP*, p. 110.

26. Jerry L. Sandidge, private interview, Strasbourg, France, May 14, 1985, claims that eschatology is a governing Pentecostal commitment; cf. Menzies, *Anointed*, p. 57. For reference to some weakening of these expectations, see Edith Blumhofer, "Divided Pentecostals: Bakker vs. Swaggart," *The Christian Century*, May 6, 1987, pp. 430-431. For Pentecostal worship practices, see Quebedeaux, *NC*, p. 30; Bloch-Hoell, *Pentecostal Movement*, p. 42.

27. Quebedeaux, *NC*, pp. 9, 54-56. This commitment manifests itself in efforts to articulate the Pentecostal experience in relation to the theology of the mainline churches; see Hollenweger, *EC*, pp. 245-246; Lindberg, *Third Reformation?* pp. 220-221.

28. Quebedeaux, *NC*, p. 5; Lindberg, *Third Reformation?* p. 217, for references to the distinct ethos of the charismatic movement, the openness of at least some like Arnold Bittlinger to recognizing that tongues does not necessarily correlate with the presence of the Spirit, see Lindberg, *Third Reformation?* pp. 233-234, 231.

29. H. Vinson Synan, as quoted in Donald W. Dayton, "The Holiness and Pentecostal Churches: Emerging from Cultural Isolation," *Where the Spirit Leads*, ed. Martin E. Marty (Atlanta: John Knox, 1980), p. 90. It is helpful to note early Pentecostalism's interdenominational character in both North America and Europe, see Bloch-Hoell, *Pentecostal Movement*, pp. 46ff., 69. For details concerning the initial rejection of the charismatic movement by Pentecostalism, see Menzies, *Anointed*, pp. 225-227; Quebedeaux, *NC*, pp. 173-174.

30. Peter Beyerhaus, interview; April 15, 1983; Gerhard Maier, interview, April 27, 1983.

31. C. I. Scofield, "The Grace of God," in *The Fundamentals*, 12 vols. (Chicago: Testimony Publishing, 1910–1915), 11:45ff. Marsden, *FAC*, pp. 87-88, notes the correlation this distinction made possible between the dispensationalists and the Holiness movement, as the latter also traded upon a kind of law-gospel distinction. On Wesley's appeal to distinct dispensations, see Chap. 2, n. 39.

32. Bloesch, *ER*, p. 104.

33. For references see Chap. 6, nn. 29-31; Chap. 2, nn. 21, 23.

34. The influence of Sandeen's thesis, *OF*, p. 3, on modern scholarship should not be discounted.

Part II: Institutions of Evangelicalism

1. Marsden, in *EMA*, p. xiv.

Chapter 8: Churches

1. When reference is made to theological positions of one of these churches, or their abbreviation appears in a note without explicit citation of some text, corresponding reference to the document of that church in the following list is assumed: CCCC, *Statement of Faith* (1978); RPC, *The Westminster Confession and The Testimony of the Reformed Presbyterian Church in North America* (1980); CRC, *The Nature and Extent of Biblical Authority* (Grand Rapids, Mich., n.d.); EREI, *Déclaration de Foi* (1872). In like manner, references to *The Westminster Confession of Faith* pertain to the RPC, PCA, OPC, and EREI, insofar as all subscribe to its theological orientation. (Among others, EREI also subscribes to the *Confession de la Rochelle* [1571] and the CRC to the *Belgic Confession* [1561], *The Heidelberg Catechism* [1563], and the *Canons of Dort* [1618–1619].) Whenever mention of these churches appears in the text with accompanying Arabic or Roman numeral, the number is understood to designate the corresponding statement, chapter, question, or page of the appropriate text.

2. My attention was called to this diversity by CCCC conference minister, Clifford R. Christensen, personal letters, December 26, 1984, and September 5, 1986. Quebedeaux, *WE*, p. 41, notes the influence of the Evangelical left and, while noting that most leaders in the CCCC reject a concept of "limited inerrancy," Christensen does reject the view that "inerrancy is the watershed of evangelicalism."

3. Information on mergers is from PCA Stated Clerk, Morton H. Smith, personal letters, June 25, l985, and August 27, 1986.

4. See Quebedeaux, *WE*, p. 41, for the latter diagnosis. The idea that Evangelicalism's Arminianism is the cause of the CRC's distance from the movement has been argued by Henry Zwaanstra, personal letter, July 16, 1986.

5. Information on the Union des Eglises Evangéliques Libres is from Claude Baty, "Les Origines des Eglises Libres de France," *Pour la Vérité*, May 1982, p. 1; Claude Baty, "L'Union de 1926 à 1951," *Pour la Vérité*, November 1982, p. 9. Information on EREI from Marie de Védrines, "Les Eglises Réformées Evangéliques Indépendantes," *Unité des Chrétiens*, July 1984, p. 20, and its general secretary, Anthony Lewin, personal letters, June 14, 1985, and July 21, 1986.

6. *The Westminster Confession*, 11, 13, 16ff.; *The Heidelberg Catechism*, 60-64, 86ff. (see n. 1).

7. Christensen; RPC, 21, 28. For the CRC's position on common grace, see Acta Synodi 1924, pp. 113-139, 141-150. Its position that children of believers are likely redeemed even if not baptized is a consequence of its subscription to the *Canons of the Synod of Dort*, I/17, which also make this affirmation.

8. CCCC, 1; *The Westminster Confession*, I; CRC, pp. 13, 14; EREI speaks only of the "sovereign authority of the Holy Scriptures in matters of faith and salvation." But Lewin (letter of 6/14/85) insists that his church regards the Bible as "totally inspired, the only rule of faith and life." This affirmation of plenary inspiration is seen as an affirmation of Scripture's infallibility.

9. EMF, *La Déclaration de Foi* (1940). Francis Guiton, "La Doctrine et l'Esprit du Méthodisme," *L'Evangéliste*, October-December 1956, p. 260. Scripture's verbal and plenary inspiration is affirmed in a more unofficial way by S. Samouélian, *Le Réveil Méthodiste* (Nimes, 1974), p. 41. On the conservative piety of Free Church membership, see Theo Wettach, "Evangelikale heute" (lecture, January 1985), p. 3.

10. Samouélian, *Le Réveil*, pp. 86, 82, 92. The assessment of EMF's position in relation to the Holiness movement was offered by its president, Francis Guiton (personal letter, September 19, 1985).

11. Guiton, September 19, 1985, Evangelisch-methodistische Kirche, *Unser Verhät nis zu den Evangelikalen* (Stuttgart: Christliches Verlagshaus, 1976), IV, V. Recently EmK leaders have issued pointed criticisms of the German Evangelical Alliance on account of its recent forays in church politics and government lobbying, see "Kein Kontakt mit der Basis," *KNA Ökumenischer Information* 10 (March 1986): 3.

12. Hereafter when reference is made to the theological positions of one of these churches, or their abbreviation appears in a note without explicit citation of some text, corresponding reference to that church's document in the following list of texts is assumed: WC, *The Discipline of The Wesleyan Church 1984;* FMC, *The Book of Discipline 1979;* CN, *Constitution & Special Rules;* CMA, *Manual of The Christian and Missionary Alliance 1983 Edition* (Nyack, N.Y., 1983). Hereafter whenever mention of these churches appears in the text with accompanying Arabic or Roman numeral, the number is understood to refer to the corresponding article of the Articles of Religion/Faith in the appropriate volume. Where other portions of the volume are cited, appropriate abbreviations usually will be employed in the text, e.g., Spec. Rules for Special Rules; Const. for Constitution.

13. D. Dayton, "The Doctrine of the Baptism of the Holy Spirit," *Wesleyan Theological Journal* 13 (1978): 122, 118ff. Donald W. Dayton, *Theological Roots of Pentecostalism* (Grand Rapids, Mich.: Francis Asbury, 1987), pp. 87ff. CN's history is sketched in D. Dayton, "Whither Evangelicalism?" (see Chap. 7, n. 17), pp. 5-6. One finds a reference to "baptism with the Holy Spirit" even in *WC*, XIV.

14. For a report on the tension, see Donald Dayton, "The Holiness and Pentecostal Churches," *The Christian Century*, August 15-22, 1979, p. 788. Information concerning its present status was supplied by CN's general secretary, B. Edgar Johnson, personal letter, August 19, 1986. Also note that in its Agreed Statement of Belief (2) in its *Constitution and Special Rules,* CN speaks only of the Scripture's plenary inspiration.

15. WC, X-XIV, Spec. Dir.; FMC, V,X-XIII; Christ. Conduct, 7-8; Temp. Econ., 4.

16. For the earliest statements on the subject, see FMC, p. 367; Lloyd H. Knox, "Toward a High View of the Scriptures," paper presented to the Wesleyan Theological Society, November 7, 1969, pp. 2-3. For reference to an early Holiness theologian in dialogue with these concepts, see the relevant references in Chap. 2, n. 40, especially the reference to A. M. Hills.

17. WC General Superintendent Robert W. McIntyre, personal letter, August 1, 1985, insists that the WC's statement on inerrancy reflects the constituency of most Holiness churches. Quebedeaux, *WE*, p. 156, deems leaders in the debate against inerrancy as part of the Evangelical left.

18. When reference is made hereafter to the theological positions of these churches, corresponding reference to the following documents is assumed: AG, *Statement of Fundamental Truths;* ICFG, *Declaration of Faith* (Los Angeles, n.d.); CG,

Declaration of Faith (n.d.); COGIC, *Official Manual* (Memphis, Tenn.: COGIC Publishing House, 1973); AD, *Fundamental Doctrines;* Congregação Cristã do Brasil, *Articles of Faith* (1946); The Pentecostal Assemblies of Canada, *Statement of Fundamental and Essential Truths* (1980); PHC, *Articles of Faith.* For references in text to these churches, use the same system of documentation as outlined in note 12. (Some references in the text to AG positions are cited from other sections of its *Constitution and Bylaws of The General Council of the Assemblies of God* [1981], and these sections will be designated in the text.)

19. William Menzies, *Anointed to Serve* (Springfield, Mo.: Gospel Publishing House, 1971), p. 75. W. H. Durham is usually considered the initiator of this theory. It should be noted that until 1961 the AG did maintain a reference to "entire sanctification" in its *Statement of Fundamental Truths,* see Menzies, *Anointed,* p. 318.

20. Menzies, *Anointed,* pp. 111ff., describes this Unitarian schism.

21. Gerald T. Sheppard, "Scripture in the Pentecostal Tradition: Part One," *Agora,* I, No. 4, 4-5, 16; idem, "Scripture in the Pentecostal Tradition: Part Two," *Agora,* II, No. 1, 14-19. But even Sheppard, *Agora,* I, No. 4, notes AG's 1916 affirmation of biblical infallibility. Quebedeaux, *NC,* p. 34, makes a similar point concerning the long-standing Pentecostal indebtedness to the Fundamentalist view of biblical infallibility. For the recent stronger AG statement, see *The Inerrancy of Scripture* (Springfield, Mo.: Gospel Publishing House, 1976).

22. Menzies, *Anointed,* pp. 344ff.; N. Bloch-Hoell, *The Pentecostal Movement* (Oslo: Universitetsforlaget, 1964), pp. 146, 227, 232; D. Dayton, "The Holiness and Pentecostal Churches," *Where the Spirit Leads,* ed. Martin E. Marty (Atlanta: John Knox, 1980), pp. 89-90.

23. Marsden, *FAC,* pp. 93-94.

24. This is the view of NAE Executive Director Billy Melvin, personal letter, June 17, 1985. On ICFG's openness, see Bloch-Hoell, *Pentecostal Movement,* pp. 63, 205-206. For additional information about the church I am indebted to Rolf McPherson, personal letters, August 28, 1986, and October 23, 1986.

25. A. C. Piepkorn, *Profiles in Belief,* 4 vols. (New York: Harper & Row, 1977–1979), 3:180.

26. D. Dayton, "The Holiness and Pentecostal Churches," p. 792.

27. William H. Bentley, "Bible Believers in the Black Community," in *E,* pp. 110-111.

28. D. Dayton, in *Where the Spirit Leads,* p. 89.

29. Hollenweger, *EC,* pp. 68, 85-86, 104-105. For additional analysis pertinent to Pentecostalism's success among the lower classes, see Chap. 7, n. 25.

30. Congregação Cristã do Brasil, 3. The analysis of the Brazilian situation is indebted to references in Chap. 6, n. 11.

31. CCB; Russell P. Shedd and Richard Sturz, personal correspondence, both in August 1985. The latter two observers as well as Key Yuasa, personal letter, July 29, 1985, and Gottfried Brakemeier, private interview, Strasbourg, March 8, 1984, have helped me to understand the AD's involvement in the Evangelical movement, the character of its social action involvements, as well as the Brazilian Evangelical movement in general. Hollenweger, *EC,* pp. 85-86, also provides information about the AD's social outreach programs. Information concerning its strict lifestyle standards is drawn from Harding Meyer, "Die Pfingstbewegung in Brasilien," *Sonderdruck aus dem Jahrbuch "Die evangelische Diaspora"* 39 (1969): 38.

32. On the Noninstrumentalists' schism and separatism, see relevant texts mentioned in Chap. 4, n. 2. I am deeply indebted to Sam Stone, editor of the *Christian Standard.* He put me in touch with the Deans of the "Centrists' " seminaries who

have provided me with information for this discussion. Two of these sources have been cited in Chap. 4, n. 7. The other was Delno W. Brown, personal letter, June 12, 1985. Also see Piepkorn, *Profiles,* 2:641-644.

33. Information about the PB was provided by Piepkorn, *Profiles,* vol. 2, especially p. 28; personal letters by one of the Brethren's trained theologians, Donald Tinder, and by Davis Duggins, an assistant editor of a chief Brethren periodical, *Interest.* A detailed history of the PB has been written by Harold H. Rowdon, *The Origins of the Brethren* (London: Pickering & Inglis, 1967).

34. James A. Stahr, "A Crisis of Identity," *Interest,* January 1985, p. 7. The entire issue of the magazine was a source for the preceding information concerning recent developments among the PB.

35. George Dollar, *A History of Fundamentalism in America* (Greenville, S.C.: Bob Jones University Press, 1973), p. 88. The preceding and all succeeding citations of IFCA positions are based on references to its *Constitution and By-Laws.* Unless otherwise designated by appropriate abbreviation, Arabic numbers in the text designate the corresponding article of the Constitution's Art. IV, Sec. 1, *Articles of Biblical Faith.*

36. IFCA, Art. IV, Sec. 2; IFCA, *Resolution on the Charismatic Movement* (1975).

37. Dollar, *A History,* pp. 192-193, 224-225.

38. *The Waterland Confession* (1580), Art. XXXVII; *The Dordrecht Confession* (1632), Art. XIV.

39. J. B. Toews, "The Significance of P. M. Friesen's History for Mennonite Brethren Self-Understanding," in *P. M. Friesen and His History,* ed. Abraham Friesen (Winnipeg: The Christian Press, 1979), pp. 158, 171; Cornelius J. Dyck, "1525 Revisited? A Comparison of Anabaptist and Mennonite Brethren Origins," in *Pilgrims and Strangers,* ed. Paul Toews (Fresno, Calif.: Center for Mennonite Brethren Studies, 1977), pp. 59-60, 82. For references to the context and principal emphasis of Pietism, see Chap. 6, nn. 29-31. On the possibility of Pietism's influence on the MBC, see John B. Toews, "The Russian Origin of Mennonite Brethren: Some Observations," in *Pilgrims and Strangers,* pp. 93-95, 91.

40. J. B. Toews, "Mennonite Brethren Identity and Theological Diversity," in *Pilgrims and Strangers,* pp. 144ff.

41. On Keswick teaching, see p. 53. The preceding and all succeeding citations of MBC positions are based on references to its *Confession of Faith* (4th printing; Hillsboro, Kan.: Mennonite Brethren Publishing House, 1980). Unless another MBC document is designated, subsequent references to the MBC accompanied by Roman numerals designate the corresponding article in the preceding document.
    Note the question of J. B. Toews, "Mennonite Brethren Identity," pp. 151ff., concerning whether the MBC concern with inerrancy represents a co-option by Fundamentalism.

42. Hollenweger, *EC,* pp. 307-308. The preceding background, particularly concerning English and American influences on the AUCECB is available in ibid., pp. 303-305; Walter Sawatsky, *Soviet Evangelicals since World War II* (Kitchener and Scottdale, Pa.: Herald, 1981), pp. 17, 35, 44-45, 82ff., 340-341.

43. W. Sawatsky, *Soviet Evangelicals,* p. 282. It is interesting to note in ibid., pp. 37, 13, 115ff., that Baptists in Russia formerly maintained a pacifist viewpoint, presumably as a result of Mennonite influence.

44. AUCECB, *The August Agreement* (1945), cited in Sawatsky, *Soviet Evangelicals,* pp. 477-478. cf. ibid., pp. 92-95.

45. Sawatsky, *Soviet Evangelicals,* pp. 284ff.

46. Ibid., pp. 344-346. The preceding and all succeeding citations of AUCECB positions are based on references to its *Confession of Faith* (1913). Articles in parenthesis in the text should be understood to designate the corresponding article of this document.

47. Sawatsky, *Soviet Evangelicals,* pp. 112-113, 177ff. The Dissidents have stressed holiness above all, even above unity (see ibid., p. 234). Preceding and succeeding references in the text to the Dissident Baptists' positions are based on the *Statutes of the Union of Churches of Evangelical Christians-Baptists (Dissidents)* (1965). Numbers in parenthesis at this point in the text designate the corresponding paragraph of that document.

48. Sawatsky, *Soviet Evangelicals,* pp. 369, 234, 245-246.

49. Ibid., pp. 394ff., esp. pp. 411-412. Also see *This Is Underground Evangelism* (12-page brochure; Camarillo, Calif.: Underground Evangelism, n.d.).

50. Sawatsky, *Soviet Evangelicals,* pp. 211, 338; Keith Parker, personal letter, November 14, 1984.

51. See Chap. 6, n. 6, and Bund Evangelisch-Freikirchlicher Gemeinden in der DDR, *Rechenschaft vom Glauben* (Berlin: Union Verlages, 1980), I.6, for references. Insights concerning the French situation are indebted to Keith Parker, personal letter, January 31, 1984. Subsequent French Baptist texts cited are *Confession of Faith of the Federation of French Baptist Churches* (n.d.); *Confession of Faith and Ecclesiastical Principles of the Evangelical Association of French-Speaking Baptist Churches* (1979). Hereafter, when these churches are cited in the text followed by a number in parenthesis, reference is to the text of that church cited here, in accord with the system of documentation outlined in nn. 12, 46, 47.

52. Hereafter, when reference is made to one of these churches' theological positions or their abbreviation appears in a note without explicit citation of some text, corresponding reference to the following documents is assumed: BBF, *Articles of Faith* (Springfield, Mo.: Roark Printing, n.d.); GARB, *Constitution and Articles of Faith* (Schaumburg, Ill., 1980); CBAA, *Constitution and Historical Summary* (Wheaton, Ill., 1984); BGC, *An Affirmation of our Faith.* Hereafter, whenever mention is made of these churches with accompanying Arabic or Roman numeral, the number is understood to designate the corresponding article of the appropriate document.

On BBF's policy of allowing members to affiliate with other groups, see Piepkorn, *Profiles,* 2:429; James O. Combs, "Other Movements Grew," in *Roots and Origins of Baptist Fundamentalism,* ed. James O. Combs (n.p.: John the Baptist Press, 1984), p. 87.

53. On BBF's separatism and Fundamentalism, see *Introducing Baptist Bible Fellowship Intl.* (brochure; Springfield, Mo., n.d.). On the condemnation of Evangelicalism, see Elmer Towns, "Independent Fundamental Baptists Looking toward 2000 A.D.," in *Roots and Origins,* pp. 129-130. On its history, see James O. Combs, "The Baptist Bible Fellowship Begins," in *Roots and Origins,* pp. 91ff.

54. Dollar, *A History,* pp. 52-53.

55. Quebedeaux, *WE,* pp. 91, 41. Shelley, *HCB,* pp. 85ff., describes some of the controversies concerning separatism and premillennialism. Assurances that such controversies have ceased to exist were offered by two CBAA seminary faculty members, Haddon Robinson, personal letter, September 2, 1986, and H. Crosby Englizian, personal letter, September 16, 1986.

56. H. Walter Fricke, personal letters, August 18, 1986, and September 2, 1986; Englizian, personal letter.

57. The BGC differs theologically from the CBAA only insofar as the former seems to hold a limited inerrancy position (1). For background on the earlier merger discussions with the BGC, see Shelley, *HCB*, pp. 52ff.

58. Hereafter, when reference is made to theological positions of one of these churches or their abbreviation appears in a note without explicit reference to some text, corresponding reference to the document of that church in the following list is assumed: BC (Ashland), *The Message of the Brethren Ministry* (Ashland, Ohio, n.d.); ECC, *Covenant Affirmations;* EFC, *Doctrinal Position* (1950). For references in the text to these churches with accompanying Arabic or Roman numeral, as in the case of all other churches, the number is understood to designate the corresponding article or page of the appropriate text.

59. See Piepkorn, *Profiles,* 2:484.

60. This characterization of the EFC is offered by its president, Thomas A. McDill, personal letter, May 13, 1985. The ECC's openness is noted by Quebedeaux, *WE,* pp. 41-42, and Harold Lindsell, *The Battle for the Bible,* 14th printing (Grand Rapids: Zondervan, 1981), pp. 125ff.

61. For a brief discussion of ECC's formation in the context of American Lutheranism, see Frederick Hale, *Trans-Atlantic Conservative Protestantism* (New York: Arno, 1979), especially pp. 188-201. The impact of Methodism, revivalism, etc. on it is noted by John Weborg, "Pietism: A Question of Meaning and Vocation," *The Covenant Quarterly* 41 (August 1983): 65. On the debate on the actual impact of Fundamentalism on these churches, see p. 86 above. For more information on the church's roots in Sweden, see Hans-Adolf Ritter, ed., *International Federation of Free Evangelical Churches* (Stockholm: Gummessons Boktryckeri, 1980), p. 33. The prominent pietist Carl Olof Rosenius was also instrumental in inspiring the formation of the Svenska Missionsförbundet. An argument for the Reformed influence on the ECC has been offered by its president, Paul E. Larsen, *The Mission of a Covenant* (Chicago: Covenant Press, 1985), p. 22.

62. Robert K. Johnston, personal letter, August 22, 1986. cf. Donald C. Frisk, *Covenant Affirmations: This We Believe* (Chicago: Covenant Press 1981), pp. 134-135, 139. But Paul E. Larsen, personal letter, October 22, 1986, discounts a Reformed influence on the ECC in its views on the real presence.

63. Thomas A. McDill, personal letter, November 9, 1983.

64. Piepkorn, *Profiles,* 2:508. But McDill, May 13, 1985, insists that few of the EFC's younger pastors, only some of its older ones, continue to affirm dispensationalism.

65. Piepkorn, *Profiles,* 2:508.

66. *Brief Statement of the Doctrinal Position of the Missouri Synod* (St. Louis: Concordia, 1932), 45, 47.

67. BS, 1; LCMS, *Gospel and Scripture* (St. Louis: Concordia, 1972), p. 15; LCMS, *The Inspiration of Scripture* (1962), pp. 16-17. Cf. CRC, pp. 13-14, 23. The LCMS position on a third use of the law is articulated in *GS,* pp. 8-9.

68. Samuel Nafzger, quoted in Darrel Turner, "Ecumenical Institute Seek to Define 'Evangelical,' " *Religious News Service,* March 12, 1985, p. 3; Samuel Nafzger, personal letter, April 2, 1984; Robert Preus, personal letter, February 20, 1984; Milton L. Rudnick, *Fundamentalism and the Missouri Synod* (St. Louis: Concordia: 1966). Similar reasons for rejecting identification with the Evangelical movement are offered by other conservative Lutherans like Erling T. Teigen, "Fundamentalism and Pietism: Threats to Lutheran Church Life," *The Lutheran Synod Quarterly* 21 (December 1981): 44-45, 49-50; D. Valleskey, "Evangelical

Lutheranism," *Wisconsin Lutheran Quarterly* 80 (1983): 204, 218. For the conservative orientation of LCMS membership, see J. D. Hunter, *American Evangelicalism* (New Brunswick: Rutgers University Press, 1983), p. 56.
69. See Chap. 6, n. 17.
70. See relevant references in Chap. 6, nn. 10, 17.
71. The self-proclaimed Evangelical orientation of the International Lutheran Renewal Center's director, Larry Christenson, personal letter, June 22, 1985, suggests its identification with the Evangelical movement. For details on it and a predecessor organization in Norway, the Agape Foundation, see Larry Christenson, ed., *Welcome, Holy Spirit* (Minneapolis: Augsburg, 1987), pp. 359-361.
72. Here and hereafter, unless another text is cited explicitly, Roman numerals appearing in conjunction with a reference to the SBC designate the corresponding article of SBC, *The Baptist Faith and Message* (1963). Quebedeaux, *WE*, pp. 37-38, notes the conservative orientation of the SBC membership, and recent surveys described in David S. Schuller, Merton P. Strommen, and Milo L. Brekke, eds., *Ministry in America* (San Francisco: Harper & Row, 1980), pp. 277ff., suggest the affinities between SBC and Evangelical member attitudes.
73. James Leo Garrett Jr., " 'Evangelicals' and Baptists: Is There a Difference?" in James Leo Garrett, E. Glenn Hinson, and James E. Tull, *Are Southern Baptists "Evangelicals"?* (Macon: Mercer University Press, 1983), pp. 111ff. Foy Dan Valentine, quoted in ibid., p. 119; E. Glenn Hinson, "Baptists and 'Evangelicals'—There Is a Difference," in *SBE*, pp. 166, 173, 182.

A good historical survey of the controversy has been provided by Richard N. Ostling, "Battling over the Bible," *Time*, June 24, 1985, pp. 41-42. The relative lack of impact of Fundamentalism on the SBC is noted by Garrett, pp. 96ff. On Lindsell's role, see James E. Tull, " 'Evangelicals' and Baptists: The Shape of the Question," in *SBE*, p. 25. The possibility that sociological dynamics may underlie the conflict has been suggested by Bill J. Leonard, "Southern Baptists: In Search of a Century," *The Christian Century*, July 17-24, 1985, pp. 683-684.
74. For information about the SBC's current conservative leadership's disinterest in identification with the Evangelical and Fundamentalist movements I am indebted to the Convention's former president, Adrian Rogers, personal letters, January 26, 1987, and March 3, 1987; press conference, Nashville, February 24, 1988.
75. For information concerning Evangelicals in the Church of England, see David Forrester, "Anglican Evangelicalism," *The Clergy Review* 60 (1975): 787, 784. Information about Evangelical involvement in The Episcopal Church's discussions was provided by one of the conservative Anglo-Catholic leaders, Clarence Pope, telephone interview, April 3, 1987. For a detailed discussion of many of the Evangelical lobbies in the mainline denominations, including those not referred to in the text, see Ronald H. Nash, ed., *Evangelical Renewal in the Mainline Churches* (Westchester, Ill.: Crossway, 1987).

Chapter 9: Educational Institutions

1. Moody Bible Institute, *1984–1985 Catalog* (Chicago, Ill.), p. 14. Roman numerals in text designate the corresponding article of the Institute's *Doctrinal Statement*. George Dollar, *A History of Fundamentalism* (Greenville: Bob Jones University Press, 1973), pp. 284-285, indicates Fundamentalist approval.
2. On the ethos of Wheaton and other schools, see Quebedeaux, *WE*, pp. 92-94; I have heard these assessments from numerous Evangelicals.
3. Quebedeaux, *WE*, p. 85.

4. David A. Hubbard, *What We Believe and Teach* (12-page pamphlet, reprint, 1981), pp. 6, 5.
5. Ibid., p. 5; David A. Hubbard, Colin Brown, and Paul Jewett, private interview, Pasadena, Calif., March 13, 1985. For a characteristic neoorthodox viewpoint, see Karl Barth, *Die kirchliche Dogmatik*, 4 vols. (Zurich: A. G. Zollikon, 1932–1967), I/2, pp. 512, 561-563, 588-589.
6. This assessment concerning neoorthodoxy's impact on campus has been offered by Gerald T. Sheppard, "Biblical Hermeneutics: The Academic Language of Evangelical Identity," *Union Seminary Quarterly Review* 32 (1977): 89-90; Ray Anderson, private interview, Berkeley, Calif., March 13, 1985. The assessment is rejected by David Hubbard, personal letter, August 4, 1986. For information about Fuller's progressive loosening of ties with the NAE I am indebted to one of its prominent faculty members, Jack Rogers, interview, Pasadena, Calif., March 13, 1985.
7. David Hubbard, interview.
8. Here and hereafter, numbers in the text following a description of the Albrecht-Bengel-Haus's theological orientation designate the corresponding article of its *Selbstverpflichtung der Glieder des Albrecht-Bengel-Hauses* (1972).

Chapter 10: Parachurch and Mission Agencies

1. Donald A. McGavran, "The Dimensions of World Evangelization," in *LEH*, pp. 94, 99-101, 105-106.
2. Ibid., p. 107; Donald A. McGavran, *The Bridges of God: A Study in the Strategy of Missions* (New York: Friendship Press, 1955), p. 136. Yet he insists in *LEH*, p. 98, that the missionary society must at times work independently or at creative cross-purposes with the immediate aims of the indigenous church.
3. This criticism is made by Rodger C. Bassham, *Mission Theology: 1948–1975* (Pasadena: Wm. Carey Library, 1979), p. 195. On the Church Growth emphasis on verbal proclamation, see McGavran, in *LEH*, p. 109. On the distinction between discipling and nurturing, see his *The Bridges of God*, pp. 13-16.
4. Bassham, *Mission Theology*, p. 193.
5. Orlando E. Costas, "In-Depth Evangelism in Latin America," in *LEH*, pp. 211ff. Bassham, *Mission Theology*, pp. 257ff., describes the program.
6. Quebedeaux, *WE*, pp. 61-62.
7. Lausanne Congress Group Report, *How to Evaluate Cultural Practices by Biblical Standards in Maintaining Cultural Identity in Africa Report* (1974), in *LEH*, p. 1236; Lausanne Congress Group Report, *In Depth Evangelization Programs Report* (1974), in *LEH*, p. 695. A full discussion of the emerging rapprochement between the missiological approaches of the ecumenical establishment and the Evangelical movement has been offered by Efiong S. Utuk, "From Wheaton to Lausanne: The Road to Modification of Contemporary Evangelical Mission Theology," *Africa Theological Journal* 15 (1986): 151-165; Bassham, *Mission Theology*, pp. 331-367; Emilio Castro, "Ökumene und die Evangelikalen: Wo stehen Wir," *Materialdienst* 11-15 (September 1985): 11-15.
8. Marsden, *FAC*, p. 97.
9. George Dollar, *A History of Fundamentalism* (Greenville: Bob Jones University Press, 1973), pp. 272-273, 287. OMF's Evangelical orientation is suggested in its pamphlet, *Understanding OMF* (n.d.), p. 23. Hereafter, numbers in the text following a description of OMF's theological position designate the corresponding article of its doctrinal position, listed in *Understanding OMF*, p. 1.

10. This observation is that of the ecumenical officer of the Lutheran Church in Württemberg, Walter Arnold, private interview, Stuttgart, May 29, 1985. For historical background concerning LM, see Burton Goddard, ed., *The Encyclopedia of Modern Christian Missions* (Camden, N.J.: Thomas Nelson & Sons, 1967), pp. 366-367. This text provides much of the historical background for the other mission societies I am considering.

    Here and hereafter, numbers in the text following a description of LM's theological position designate the corresponding article of the German national council's *Glaubensgrundsätze* (1979). (At the time of writing, each LM national council had its own Statement of Faith, though all are closely related.) In interest of confidentiality I am not revealing my source in LM concerning its internal controversy.

11. Gunnliek Seierstad, private interview, July 28, 1984, Kurt Åberg, private interview held during the Lutheran World Federation Assembly in Budapest, August 2, 1984. Some hesitancy was expressed by these representatives of two different Scandinavian societies concerning an unambiguous identification with the Evangelical movement. For more background on the Santalmisjonen, see Goddard, *Encyclopedia*, p. 572.

12. Information on UFM's Fundamentalist orientation and historical background is from its associate director, Charles E. Piepgrass, personal letter, May 10, 1985. Here and hereafter, unless another text is cited explicitly, numbers appearing in conjunction with a reference to UFM designate the corresponding article of its *Doctrinal Statement* (n.d.).

13. UFM, *Policies and Practice* (Unpaginated brochure, Bala-Gynwyd, Pa., n. d.).

14. Lausanne Congress Regional Summary Report, *A View of Latin America* (1974), in *LEH*, p. 1334. Another well-known cooperative mission agency is the Interdenominational Foreign Mission Association of North America.

15. IVCF, *Proposed Personal Policy Statement* (n.d.), p. 2, though never formally adopted (a circumstance which suggests IVCF reticence concerning the legislation of behavioral norms), calls for "freedom in personal styles of living." For a history of the organization, see Pete Lowman, *The Day of His Power* (Leicester: Inter-Varsity, 1983). Of particular interest in this connection is to observe the leadership role in the International Fellowship of the influential Norwegian Lutheran pietist, Ole Hallesby.

    The next reference and succeeding references in the text to the IVCF's theological positions are to its *Doctrinal Basis*, (n.d.), and the number in parenthesis refers to this document's corresponding article.

16. *Doctrinal Basis of the Inter-Varsity Fellowship* [Great Britain] (n.d.), c (now the basis of faith for Universities and Colleges Christian Fellowship).

17. *Have You Heard of the Four Spiritual Laws?* (pamphlet; San Bernadino, Cal.: CC, 1965). Quebedeaux, *WE*, pp. 55ff., gives a helpful introduction to the organization.

18. Kalevi Lehtinen, private interview, Müllheim, West Germany, March 23, 1984. As European Director of CC he was also helpful in providing information about the European programs. The quotation from Bright is cited from his personal letter, August 15, 1986.

    The preceding reference and, unless another text is cited explicitly, all succeeding references in the text to Campus Crusade accompanied by an Arabic number refer to the corresponding article of the *Statement of Faith of Campus Crusade for Christ* (n.d.). Subsequent references are also made to CC's *Standards for Staff* (n.d.).

19. Lehtinen, interview, provided these observations concerning how CC is able to maintain itself despite such theological diversity. Bright's openness on such points

is also noted by Richard Quebedeaux, *I Found It!* (London: Hodder and Stoughton, 1980), p. 185. Names of members of the European staff who were uncomfortable identifying with the Evangelical movement have been withheld to ensure confidentiality.

20. Poul Langagergaard; *Innere Mission in Dänemark* (published brochure, n.d.)
21. Jerry Falwell, "Future-Word," in *The Fundamentalist Phenomenon* (Garden City, N.Y.: Doubleday, 1981), pp. 188-190, 195ff.
22. Ibid., pp. 188-189, 191.
23. Ibid., pp. 193-194.
24. *World Vision International* (12-page brochure, n.d.); W. Stanley Mooneyham, "Ministering to the Hunger Belt" (unpublished but distributed interview, n.d.), p. 2.
25. *World Vision International*, p. 3. The director of the WCC Commission on World Mission and Evangelism, Eugene Stockwell, was unfortunately quoted as making this allegation (see "Weltkirchenrat: Schwere Vorwürfe gegen evangelikale Werke," *Pressausgabe*, 64/84 [July 19, 1984], p. 4). On relevant financial statistics, see Quebedeaux, *WE*, p. 111.
26. These dynamics are sketched by Jeffrey K. Hadden and Charles E. Swann, *Prime Time Preachers* (Reading, Mass.: Addison-Wesley, 1981), pp. 56-57; Richard N. Ostling, "Evangelical Publishing and Broadcasting," in *EMA*, pp. 50-51. Statistics in R. Hutcheson Jr., *Mainline Churches and the Evangelicals* (Atlanta: John Knox, 1981), p. 68.
27. For results, see Constant H. Jacquet Jr., ed., *Yearbook of American and Canadian Churches 1985* (Nashville: Abingdon, 1985), pp. 263-266; News from CBN, October 25, 1985. A typical criticism of the media evangelists has been offered by Martin Marty, as cited in Hadden and Swann, *Prime Time Preachers*, pp. 176-178.
28. Data in William B. Furlong, "'The 700 Club': On Screen and behind the Scenes," *The Saturday Evening Post*, November 1982, p. 2; Ostling, in *EMA*, pp. 52-53; Hutcheson, *Mainline Churches*, pp. 68-69; Erling Jorstad, *The Politics of Moralism* (Minneapolis: Augsburg, 1981), p. 36.
29. Pat Robertson, personal letters, July 15, 1985, and August 6, 1985. His apparent rejection of biblical inerrancy occurred on the 700 Club, Station WDCA, Channel 20, Washington, D.C., August 7, 1977. On his Pentecostalism, see Jorstad, *Politics*, p. 33.
30. The Graham theological profile is sketched by Hadden and Swann, *Prime Time Preachers*, p. 21. For his affirmation of both salvation by faith and biblical infallibility, see Billy Graham, "Why Lausanne?" in *LEH*, pp. 28-29, though even here his language seems to suggest that the Bible is not inerrant in itself but is made inerrant to us by the Spirit. Also see Billy Graham, *How to Be Born Again* (Waco, Tex.: Word, 1977), pp. 39-40, where he distinguishes Word and Scripture.
31. Robert Booth Fowler, *A New Engagement: Evangelical Political Thought, 1966–1976* (Grand Rapids: Eerdmans, 1982), pp. 23-37; R. Johnston (see abbreviations), pp. 84-87.
32. Jim Wallis, "The Move to Washington, D.C.," *Post-American* 4 (August-September, 1975): 4; Jim Wallis, *Agenda for Biblical People* (New York: Harper & Row, 1976), pp. 5, 114, 117. For a discussion of Yoder's impact on *Sojourners*, see Fowler, *A New Engagement*, p. 161. For a discussion of Yoder's views, see pp. 280-281.

Chapter 11: Evangelical Cooperative Agencies

1. Here and hereafter Arabic numerals appearing in the text in conjunction with a description of the Lausanne Committee's theological viewpoints refer to *The Lausanne Covenant* (1974), which was formulated by the International Congress on World Evangelization held in Lausanne. For additional information on the formation of the Lausanne committee and its tasks, see *Lausanne Committee for World Evangelization* (published brochure, n.d.).
2. AEAM, 1. For other references, see pp. 112-113.
3. Peter Schneider, private interview, May 17, 1985.
4. See Chap. 5, n. 13. For a more recent example, see NAE, *Save the Family* (1982), pp. 1-2.
5. This information is from the NAE's executive director, Billy Melvin, personal letter, November 10, 1986.
6. Jack B. Rogers, interview March 13, 1985; Joel A. Carpenter, "From Fundamentalism to the New Evangelical Coalition," in *EMA*, p. 14; Richard Pierard, "Ecumenism and the New Evangelicalism" (paper presented at American Academy of Religion meeting, Chicago, December 11, 1984), pp. 6-7.
7. For examples of this sense that society and the church are decaying, see, in addition to note 4, AG, *Statement on Abortion* (1971); *Berlin Declaration on Ecumenism*, 1; Albrecht-Bengel-Haus, 6; IFCA, Preamble; *Campus Crusade for Christ—Europe* (booklet; Müllheim, n.d.); Fédération Evangélique de France, *Devant la Marée Montante*, in *Annuaire Evangélique 1982*, ed. Gérard Dagon (Moulins-lès-Metz, n.d.), p. 456; Internationale Konferenz Bekennender Gemeinschaften, 1.

Chapter 12: Introduction to Evangelical Theology

1. For examples of hesitancy by Evangelicals to bind themselves to creedal or confessional formulations, see ECC, *Covenant Constitution* (1885), Preamble; SBC, Intro.; Churches of Christ ("Centrist") (as per Deino W. Brown, letter, June 12, 1985); BC (Ashland), 1; cf. Bloesch, *FEC*, p. 125. It is interesting to note the relative lack of an explicit criticism of creeds in the formal statements of Evangelical churches.
2. Carl F. H. Henry, private interview, Strasbourg, France, July 8, 1986. The idea of a "Confessionalist Evangelicalism" is proposed by Beyerhaus, "Lausanne zwischen Berlin und Genf," p. 308, and Bloesch, *FEC*, pp. 35ff. The Reformed and Lutheran churches described in the last chapter exemplify this orientation by subscription to the historic Confessional documents of their tradition. Others with a similar self-orientation include Internationale Konferenz Bekennender Gemeinschaften, 2(b); *The Chicago Call: An Appeal to Evangelicals* (1977).
3. John Weborg, "Pietism: A Question of Meaning and Vocation," *The Covenant Quarterly* 41 (1983): 69.
4. Francis A. Schaeffer, private interview, Huémoz, Switzerland, November 12, 1983; Timothy L. Smith, "An Historical Perspective on Evangelicalism and Ecumenism," *Mid-Stream* 22 (1983): 311; F. Burton Nelson, "An Evangelical Approach to Biblical Authority," *The Covenant Quarterly*, 41 (August 1983): 94.
5. R. Hutcheson Jr., *Mainline Churches and the Evangelicals* (Atlanta: John Knox, 1981), p. 34; R. Johnston, p. 126; Webber, *CR*, pp. 143ff.
6. Ahlstrom, in *E*, pp. 270-271.

Chapter 13: View of Scripture and Theological Method

1. The churches and organizations discussed in the second section provide ample documentation of this point, and the list of those affirming these commitments

could be expanded markedly. However, it should be noted that some of these organizations only speak of the Bible's "infallibility" or "trustworthiness." See, for example, NAE, 1; Internationale Konferenz Bekennender Gemeinschaften, 2(a); WEF, *Statement of Faith* (1951); 1VCF, 1; Fuller Seminary, 3; Wesleyan Theological Society, *Doctrinal Position of WTS* (1978), 1; ECC, pp. 5, 23; BC (Ashland), *A Centennial Statement* (Ashland, Ohio: Brethren Publishing Co., 1984), p. 1; AUCECB, II; CG (Cleveland, Tenn.), 1; ICFG, I. Yet these organizations also seem to endorse plenary inspiration if not also to engage in dialogue with something like the concept of biblical inerrancy; see above, pp. 113, 146, 158, 164, 166, 176-177, 185, 199, 223-224.

2. Although this affirmation does not receive much emphasis it is important for Evangelicals that they assert apostolic authorship where the biblical text testifies to its own authorship as apostolic. See LCMS, *Inspiration*, p. 9; Robert Preus, "Notes on the Inerrancy of Scripture," *Concordia Theological Monthly* 38 (June 1967): 373; Gerhard Maier, personal interview, Tübingen, April 27, 1983. Also see International Council on Biblical Inerrancy, *The Chicago Statement on Biblical Inerrancy* (1978), Exp.; Henry, *GRA*, 4:39.

3. Henry, *GRA*, 4:141ff.; Gordon Clark, *Karl Barth's Theological Method* (Nutley, N.J.: Presbyterian and Reformed Publishing Co., 1963), p. 209. Classic Fundamentalist statements of these commitments are found in A. A. Hodge and B. B. Warfield, "Inspiration," in *PT*, pp. 226-227; James M. Gray, "The Inspiration of the Bible: Definition, Extent and Proof," *The Fundamentals*, 12 vols. (Chicago: Testimony Publishing, 1910–1915), 3:13-16, 25.

4. Carl Henry, *GRA*, 3:262-264; LCMS, *Inspiration*, p. 12; Saphir Athyal, "Hermeneutics: Biblical Interpretation and Evangelism," in *LEH*, p. 1005.

5. See Rudolf Bultmann, *Theology of the New Testament*, trans. Kendrick Grobel, 2 vols. in 1 (New York: Charles Scribner's, 1970), 2:237-241; Barth, *KD*, vol. I/2, pp. 553-554, 578-579, 587-591. For an example of the criticism of these views, see Henry, *GRA*, 3:455ff. Presumably one should always regard references by Evangelicals in discerning the biblical authors' intentions as entailing commitments to discerning the authorial intention only by means of grammatical-historical exegesis of the biblical text. See *GRA*, 4:308, 315.

6. Such an argument is evident in Lindsell, *BB*, p. 31; Henry, *GRA*, 4:190ff.; LCMS, *BS*, 1; AG, *The Inerrancy of Scripture* (Springfield, Mo.: Gospel Publishing House, 1976), p. 11.

7. *Chicago Statement*, Exp. cf. AG, *The Inerrancy of Scripture*, p. 4.

8. R. Johnston (see abbreviations), p. 36; Carl Henry, *GRA*, 2:14-15.

9. For discussions of the issues at stake, see Bloesch, *FEC*, p. 60; Henry, *GRA*, 4:243-244. This approach is discussed later in this chapter. Among its proponents are Daniel Fuller, "Biblical Infallibility," *Fuller Theological Seminary Bulletin* 18 (March 1968); G. C. Berkouwer, *Holy Scripture*, trans. Jack Rogers (Grand Rapids, Mich.: Eerdmans, 1975), p. 265; Gordon R. Lewis, "What Does Biblical Infallibility Mean?" *Bulletin of the Evangelical Theological Society* 6 (1963): 18, 26.

10. See pp. 112-113, 143-147. We will note again on pp. 224-225 that a similar point has been made concerning the Holiness movement.

11. Lindsell, *BB*, p. 210; Francis Schaeffer, *No Final Conflict: The Bible Without Error in All That It Affirms* (Downers Grove, Ill.: InterVarsity Press, 1975), p. 8; Henry, *GRA*, 4:495; Falwell (see abbreviations) p. 137. Those observers making a similar point though with a more open or even critical perspective regarding

biblical inerrancy (the sacredness of Scripture) in the Evangelical movement include Günther Gassmann, in *Neue transkonfessionelle Bewegungen*, ed. G. Gassmann et al. (Frankfurt: Otto Lembeck, 1976), p. 15; Mark A. Noll, "Evangelicals and the Study of the Bible," in *EMA*, p. 118; Quebedeaux, *WE*, p. 29. Additional arguments on behalf of this point are given below on pp. 296-297, 352-354.

12. For such premodern precedents, see the earlier discussion on p. 75, especially nn. 7-8. Also see Caspar Brochmann, *Universae Theologiae Systema* (1633), 81; *Preface to The Book of Concord*. Jack Rogers and Donald K. McKim, *The Authority and Interpretation of the Bible* (San Francisco: Harper & Row, 1979), p. 182. have conceded that Orthodox theologians tended to use Scripture as a source of information about science. Even Augustine, "Letter to Jerome" (405), *Epistle*, LXXXII.3, appears to have spoken of the Bible's inerrancy, particularly in its original manuscript. Also see suggestions of a theory of verbal inspiration in Calvin, *Institutes*, IV/VIII.6,9; I/VII.4. For criticisms of the emphasis on biblical inerrancy as a kind of "modern" aberration, see Sandeen, *OF*, p. 14; Rogers and McKim, *Authority*, p. xvii; Darrell Jodock, "The Impact of Cultural Change: Princeton Theology and Scriptural Authority Today," *Dialog* 22 (Winter 1983):26.

13. Emil Brunner, *Revelation and Reason*, trans. Olive Wyon (Philadelphia: Westminster, 1946), especially pp. 12, 181; James Barr, *Fundamentalism* (London: SCM, 1977), p. 36.

14. LCMS, *GS*, p. 18; Samuel Nafzger, personal letter, April 2, 1984. A similar concern is expressed by certain members of the Holiness movement like D. Dayton, "Whither Evangelicalism?" (see Chap. 7, n. 17), p. 9.

15. Henry, *GRA*, 4:139, 257; 2:87-88; Rob L. Staples, "A Response to R. S. Jordahl, 'Authority of the Scriptures: A Lutheran Perspective.'" *The Covenant Quarterly* 41 (August 1983): 85; Bloesch, *ER*, p. 57; H. Orton Wiley, *Christian Theology*, 3 vols. (Kansas City: Nazarene Publishing House, 1940–1943), 1:141; *The Fundamentals*, 12 vols. (Chicago: Testimony Publishing, 1910–1915), 8:103.

16. Henry, *GRA*, 4:249, 447.

17. *Chicago Statement*, X, Exp.

18. "Other Southern Methodist Beliefs," in *What, Why, How?* (Orangeburg, S.C.: Foundry Press, 1981), pp. 16-17; "Statement of Faith," *The Southwide Baptist Fellowship* (pamphlet; Lauren, S.C., 1966). One of the leaders in the formation of the Fundamentalist movement, William B. Riley, *The Menace of Modernism* (New York: Christian Alliance, 1917), p. 9, claimed that the King James Version was itself inerrant.

19. Henry, *GRA*, 4:354-355; Maier, *EhkM*, p. 70; *The Fundamentals*, 9:15. For Princeton theology's use of this point, see B. B. Warfield, "The Inerrancy of the Original Autographs," in *PT*, p. 272.

20. Henry, *GRA*, 4:231. cf. *Chicago Statement*, X.

21. *Chicago Statement*, VIII; Bloesch, *ER*, p. 55; Henry, *GRA*, 3:415; Lausanne Congress Group Report, *Authority and Uniqueness of Scripture Report* (1974), in *LEH*, p. 994; LCMS, *Inspiration*, pp. 10-11, 8.

22. *The Fundamentals*, 3:14-15, 35; 4:76-77; 7:33; C. Hodge, "Inspiration," in *PT*, pp. 138-139; A. A. Hodge and B. B. Warfield, "Inspiration," pp. 224-225, 226. However, perhaps questions could be raised about the actual success of the first reference in *The Fundamentals* and the second reference in Princeton theology in avoiding divine dictation. Something like the view is apparent in Calvin, *Institutes*, IV/VIII.6; David Hollaz, *Examen Theologicum Acroamaticum* (1707), 85, 87; John Quenstedt, *Theologia Didactico-Polemica* (1685), I,72, 68.

23. International Council on Biblical Inerrancy, *The Chicago Statement on Biblical Hermeneutics* (1982), XIII; Henry, *GRA*, 4:103-104; David A. Hubbard, *What We Believe and Teach* (12-page pamphlet, reprint, 1981), p. 5.
24. Morris Inch, "An Evangelical Approach to Biblical Authority," *The Covenant Quarterly* 41 (August 1983): 91. See *The Fundamentals*, 7:54, for an example. The first part of this book illustrates in detail how biblical inerrancy served the Fundamentalists, their predecessors, and their heirs as a tool for confronting the challenge of culture.
25. Henry, *GRA*, 4:267, 23; cf. ECC, pp. 12-13.
26. In addition to references in Chap. 11, n. 7, see Bloesch, *FEC*, p. 150; Carl Henry, *GRA*, 1:156, 41ff.; *GRA*, 4:518, 603; Samuel Escobar, "Evangelism and Man's Search for Freedom, Justice and Fulfillment," in *LEH*, p. 314; Tim LaHaye, *Battle for the Mind* (Old Tappan, N.J.: Revell, 1980), p. 9; Schaeffer, *SER*, pp. 46ff.; Graham, "Why Lausanne?" in *LEH*, p. 24; Marie de Védrines, "Les Eglises Réformées Evangéliques Indépendantes," *Unité des Chrétiens*, July 1984, p. 20; Han Chul-Ha, "An Asian Critique of Western Theology," *Evangelical Review of Theology* 7 (1983): 39. Most references to the breakdown of society come from North American Evangelicals. Could this cultural pessimism account for the militancy of North Americans with regard to biblical inerrancy? At least in Europe, the Konferenz Bekennender Gemeinschaften is perhaps the most critical of the social situation and is in turn among the most militant of European Evangelical organizations.

For parallel assessments of the present social situation offered by prominent social critics, see Christopher Lasch, *Culture of Narcissism* (New York: W. W. Norton, 1979), pp. 28-43, 102, 396; Philip Rieff, *The Triumph of the Therapeutic* (New York: Harper & Row, 1968), pp. 2-3, 251-252; Robert N. Bellah, et al., *Habits of the Heart* (Berkeley, Calif.: University of California Press, 1985), especially pp. 75-81, 139-141, 152.
27. Schaeffer, *SER*, p. 82; Dean Kelley, *Why Conservative Churches Are Growing* (New York: Harper & Row, 1972), pp. 36-55. For a parallel analysis of factors in the success of Evangelicalism in face of present narcissist trends, see Leonard I. Sweet, "The 1960's: The Crises of Liberal Christianity and the Public Emergence of Evangelicalism," in *EMA*, pp. 31-32, 37ff. Although the cultural context in Asia and Africa is not the same as the sense of cultural breakdown and relativism one finds in the West, the Third World's concern with nation building and its encounter with Western cultural dynamics entails that citizens of these nations are encountering a kind of cultural chaos no less than those in the West. Thus, the Evangelical movement's success in these nations, because it offers a firm structure of meaning and discipline, is to be expected, just as it answers these needs in the West. Hollenweger, *EC*, pp. 104-105, describes this dynamic in Brazil.
28. *Chicago Statement*, IV; Henry, *GRA*, 1:193-194, 229; Schaeffer, *SER*, p. 89; LCMS, *GS*, p. 12; Henri Blocher, "The Nature of Biblical Unity," in *LEH*, p. 385; Berkouwer, *Holy Scripture*, p. 314; Eui Whan Kim, "The Authority of the Bible and the Lordship of Christ," in *LEH*, p. 987; Henry, *GRA*, 3:455, lists a number of Evangelicals who insist on the propositional character of revelation.

The predominance in modern theology of the model of grounding Christian faith in religious experience has been noted by George A. Lindbeck, *The Nature of Doctrine* (Philadelphia: Westminster, 1984), p. 19. Specific examples of this tendency in some important modern theologians are cited and discussed in Chap. 27.
29. This observation by Henry, *GRA*, 3:455.

30. Carl Henry, *GRA*, 5:397; David Cook, "Significant Trends in Christology in Western Scholarly Debate," in *Jesus in the Two Thirds World*, ed. Vinay Samuel and Chris Sudgen (Bangalore: Partnership in Mission—Asia, 1983), pp. 393-394.

31. For examples of Evangelicals insisting on the universal accessibility of Christian propositions, that they have only one meaning, see ICBI, *The Chicago Statement on Biblical Hermeneutics*, VII, IX; Henry, *GRA*, 1:198; *GRA*, 3:369, 359; Schaeffer, interview; LCMS, *GS*, p. 13; Walter C. Kaiser, "Legitimate Hermeneutics," *A Guide to Contemporary Hermeneutics*, ed. Donald K. McKim (Grand Rapids, Mich.: Eerdmans, 1986), pp. 112-113, 116, 132; Lausanne Congress Group Report, *Authority and Uniqueness of Scripture Report*, in *LEH*, p. 996. Although his pietist commitments tend to prevent him from executing his intentions fully, the desire to affirm the nonperspectival meaning of biblical texts seems to be expounded by Peter Beyerhaus, *Bibel ohne Heiligen Geist?* (Bad Liebenzell: Verlag der Liebenzeller Mission, 1970), p. 20. That the commitment to ascertaining the single, fixed meaning of Scripture is rooted in the Evangelical movement's Fundamentalist heritage, in Princeton theology, is evident in C. Hodge, *Systematic Theology*, 3 vols. (New York: Scribner's, 1872–1873), 1:188, whose indebtedness to Scottish common sense realist philosophy is apparent at this point.

32. This critique is acknowledged by Henry, *GRA*, 4:256; cf. Rogers and McKim, *Authority and Interpretation*, pp. 196-197.

33. For examples of such a criticism of mainline theology by Evangelicals, see Henry, *GRA*, 1:218, 229; Francis Schaeffer, as quoted in Falwell (see abbreviations) p. 168; John Warwick Montgomery, "An Exhortation to Exhorters," *Christianity Today*, March 16, 1973, p. 606. These criticisms are more fully developed in Chap. 27.

34. Schaeffer, *SER*, pp. 25, 91; Henry, *GRA*, 1:164, 239; Clark Pinnock, *Biblical Revelation: The Foundation of Christian Theology* (Chicago: Moody Press, 1971), p. 128; Donald Dayton, private interview, Strasbourg, France, September 3, 1985.

35. AG, *The Inerrancy of Scripture*, pp. 9-10; Henry, *GRA*, 4:171, 200, 361; R. Johnston, p. 25; Preus, "Notes on Inerrancy," p. 368.

36. Lindsell, *BB*, pp. 210, 201. References to Evangelicals in n. 11 are also pertinent.

37. Schaeffer, *SER*, pp. 50-51; Henry, *GRA*, 1:255.

38. William Ames, *The Marrow of Theology*, ed. John D. Eusden (Boston, 1968), p. 188. For an earlier discussion with reference to relevant texts concerning common sense realism and its impact on American culture, see above, pp. 56-57, especially n. 16 of that section. Also noteworthy as a brief sketch of the impact this philosophical orientation had and has had on Evangelical views of Scripture is Marsden, *BA*, pp. 81ff.

39. Pertinent primary sources for summarizing the common sense commitments are texts by the movement's founder, Thomas Reid, *Essays on the Intellectual Powers of Man*, ed. A. D. Woozley (London: Macmillan, 1941), pp. 21, 79, 149, 289, 331, 347, 366-367, 380-382, 398ff.; Thomas Reid, *Essays on the Active Powers of Man*, in *The Works of Thomas Reid*, compiled by William Hamilton, vol. 2, 7th ed. (Edinburgh: Maclachlan and Stewart, 1872), pp. 580, 582, 589, 662, 679.

40. Timothy Weber, "The Two-Edged Sword," in *The Bible in America*, ed. N. Hatch and M. Noll (New York: Oxford University Press, 1982), pp. 115-116.

41. F. Burton Nelson, "An Evangelical Approach to Biblical Authority," *The Covenant Quarterly* 41 (1983): 94.

42. Beyerhaus, *BHG*, pp. 21, 18, 11, despite his apparent intentions to affirm the possibility of a single, descriptive meaning, claims that the Bible is rightly understood only in faith. The Konferenz Bekennender Gemeinschaften, *Orientierungshilfe*, 3, 4, also takes this position. John Howard Yoder, "The Use of the Bible

in Theology," in *The Use of the Bible in Theology: Evangelical Options*, ed. Robert K. Johnston (Atlanta: John Knox, 1985), p. 105, and Maier, *EhkM*, p. 91, show an openness to acknowledging a variety of possible perspectives on what constitutes the Bible's center. In *EhkM*, p. 54, Maier even insists that all theology must have a subjective component. This is reflected in his argument (ibid., pp. 47, 56) that the theologian must remain "open" to the sovereignty of God, the superiority of the Bible's truth as operating presuppositions. Whether this represents a kind of method of presuppositionalism, which we shall soon describe, or an indebtedness to the more subjectivist philosophical hermeneutics of Hans-Georg Gadamer, *Wahrheit und Methode*, 2nd ed. (Tübingen: J. C. B. Mohr, 1965), pp. 288, 355, 356 (English translation: *Truth and Method*), is an open question (see n. 51). Other Evangelicals who at least appear to reflect such an indebtedness insofar as they speak of understanding as a "fusion of horizons" are C. René Padilla, "Biblical Foundations: A Latin American Study," *Evangelical Review of Theology* 7 (April 1983): 80, 85-86; Anthony C. Thiselton, "Speaking and Hearing," lecture delivered at the Billy Graham Center, Wheaton, Ill., March 20-22, 1985, pp. 2, 4-5; Donald Bloesch, "A Christological Hermeneutic: Crisis and Conflict in Hermeneutics," in *UB*, pp. 83-84.

43. Orlando Costas, *The Church and Its Mission* (Wheaton, Ill.: Tyndale, 1975), pp. 245, 252; Wilson W. Chow, "Biblical Foundations: An East Asian Study," *Evangelical Review of Theology* 7 (April 1983): 102; George Cummings, "Who Do You Say that I Am? A North American Minority Answer to the Christological Question," in *JTTW*, pp. 320, 334-335. See also the relevant references in the preceding note. For other expressions of the need to do contextual theology, while avoiding any kind of method of correlation, see Chap. 27, n. 80.

44. C. Hodge, *Systematic Theology*, 1:573-574.

45. See Abraham Kuyper, *Principles of Sacred Theology*, trans. J. Hendrik DeVries (Grand Rapids, Mich.: Baker, 1980), pp. 248-256.

46. I am indebted to Gerstner, in *E*, pp. 39-52, for this typology. A good example of a theologian embodying all of these methods is John Stott, *Basic Christianity*, 2nd ed. (Downers Grove, Ill.: InterVarsity, 1971), pp. 8, 13, 22ff., 39-40, and idem, *Understanding the Bible* (Glendale, Calif.: Regal Books, 1972), p. 202.

47. Norman Geisler, *Philosophy of Religion* (Grand Rapids, Mich.: Zondervan, 1974). Although he does engage in endeavors to prove the biblical miracles, his prior step is to appeal to God's existence; see Norman Geisler, *Miracles and Modern Thought* (Grand Rapids, Mich.: Zondervan, 1982), p. 75. Cf. Thomas Aquinas, *Summa Theologica* (1265–1273), I, Q.2, Art.3.

Stott, *BC*, p. 13; B. B. Warfield, *The Inspiration and Authority of the Bible* (reprint; Philadelphia: Presbyterian and Reformed Publishing, 1970), p. 75; Archibald Alexander, "The Bible and the Natural World," in *PT*, pp. 94, 95.

48. John Warwick Montgomery, *The Shape of the Past: A Christian Response to Secular Philosophies of History* (Minneapolis: Bethany Fellowship, 1976), especially pp. 143, 293-295; LCMS, *Inspiration*, p. 10, while not primarily founding biblical inerrancy on empirical evidence, is open to this manner of confirming the Bible's inerrancy.

49. A. Alexander, "Inaugural Address," in *PT*, pp. 75, 77-78. For Warfield's earlier and later positions, in addition to pertinent references in Chap. 3, n. 9, see B. B. Warfield, "Herman Bavinck," in *PT*, p. 305, for his use of an evidentialist approach, and Warfield, *The Inspiration and Authority of the Bible*, p. 212, for an additional example of his deductive, "presuppositionalist" approach.

Another Evangelical employing this approach is Josh McDowell, *Evidence that*

Demands a Verdict: Historical Evidence for the Christian Faith (San Bernadino, Calif.: Campus Crusade, 1972).

50. John H. Gerstner, *A Bible Inerrancy Primer* (Grand Rapids, Mich.: Baker, 1965); Stott, *Understanding the Bible*, p. 202; E. J. Carnell, *The Case for Orthodox Theology* (Philadelphia: Westminster, 1959), p. 35 (however, see his use of evidentialist apologetics as discussed in C. Brown, *Miracles and the Critical Mind* [Grand Rapids: Eerdmans, 1984] pp. 203ff.); Gottfried Osei-Mensah, "The Authoritative Word," *IFES Review 1979*, 1; AG, *The Inerrancy of Scripture*, p. 7. Others employing this approach include Warfield, "Inspiration," in *PT*, p. 283, and the International Council on Biblical Inerrancy, *The Chicago Statement on Biblical Hermeneutics*, Commentary I.

51. Henry, *GRA*, 1:215; 3:247, 428; 4:27, 41; Cornelius Van Til, *Defense of the Faith* (Philadelphia: Presbyterian and Reformed, 1955), pp. 179-259; Abraham Kuyper, *Encyclopedia of Sacred Theology* (New York: Scribner's, 1898). Although there is currently some debate about whether Schaeffer was a presuppositionalist, and it is likely that he may have employed a variety of approaches, see his use of this method in Francis Schaeffer, *The God Who Is There* (Downers Grove, Ill.: InterVarsity Press, 1968), especially pp. 87ff. The position of the OPC is evident in John P. Galbraith, *Why the Orthodox Presbyterian Church?* (Philadelphia: The Orthodox Presbyterian Church, n.d.), p. 3. Among others apparently employing this approach are the Evangelical Congregational Church, *The Inspiration and Authority of the Bible* (pamphlet; Myerstown, Pa., n.d.), pp. 5-6; Falwell (see abbreviations), p. 8; G. W. Bromiley, "The Church Doctrine of Inspiration," in *Revelation and the Bible*, ed. Carl Henry (Grand Rapids, Mich.: Baker, 1958), p. 213; Preus, "Notes on Inerrancy," pp. 365, 374-375; Hans-Lutz Poetsch, "Hermeneutische Grundsätze, aufgezeigt am Himmelfahrtsbericht Christi," in *Die Bibel verstehen*, ed. Gerhart Grüninger, Hans-Lutz Poetsch, and Theodore Reuter (Gross Oesingen: Heinrich Harms, 1985), p. 18.

On the question of Maier's method, see the discussion in n. 42. At some points in his career Warfield employed a kind of presuppositionalism (see n. 49). That such an approach may have earlier precedents in Princeton theology, see C. Hodge, "Inspiration," pp. 136-137. It should also be noted that despite its reliance on presuppositionalism the *Chicago Statement*, Exp., also employs an appeal to Christ's attitude toward the Scripture.

The questionable status of Maier in relation to presuppositionalism also pertains to the kind of method actually employed by the CRC, Kuyper, the LCMS, and other conservative Lutherans. For, like Maier and unlike Henry, their presuppositions are not some theological principle, but faith. Thus one is tempted to press the similarities between this group and the neoorthodox notion that the Bible is known only in faith (cf. Barth, *KD*, vol. I/1, p. 343). The difference may be in that unlike their neoorthodox colleagues these conservatives insist on the plenary inspiration of Scripture.

52. Henry, *GRA*, 1:225, 258, 260; 2:272ff., 311ff.; 3:148.; Poetsch, "Hermeneutische Grundsätze," p. 22. This sort of argumentation from a presuppositionalist perspective may be employed by Marsden, "Evangelicals, History, and Modernity," in *EMA*, pp. 100ff.; C. Brown, *Miracles*, pp. 285ff., and Ronald Sider, "Miracles, Historical Methodology and Modern Western Christianity," in *JTTW*, pp. 358, 364, though it is uncertain whether they have in fact ultimately employed an "evidentialist" approach like Montgomery.

53. Henry, *GRA*, 1:241; Van Til, *DF*, pp. 179-259. Theologically conservative Lutherans are not so inclined to appeal to the bar of reason but rather to faith in order to authorize their presuppositions.
54. Henry, *GRA*, 1:85, 256; 2:78, 322; *Chicago Statement*, XIII; CRC, pp. 36, 55-56; Hans-Lutz Poetsch, "The Question of Biblical Authority vis-à-vis Rome: Luther and Lutherans Today" (lecture delivered at Concordia Seminary, Fort Wayne, Ind., 1984), p. 4; Preus, "Notes on Inerrancy," p. 374.
55. "New Dispute Looms over 'Errors' in Scripture," *Christianity Today*, April 26, 1963, p. 29; James Davison Hunter, *Evangelicalism: The Coming Generation* (Chicago: University of Chicago Press, 1987), pp. 31, 27.
56. C. Hodge, *Systematic Theology*, 1:171; Falwell, quoted in Erling Jorstad, *The Politics of Moralism* (Minneapolis: Augsburg, 1981), p. 49; Henry, *GRA*, 1:162-163; Lindsell, *BB*, pp. 34-35, 40-71, 162, 171; *Chicago Statement*, Pref., XII; LCMS, *BS*, 1; GARB, I,V; BBF, I,V. Although there are doubtless proponents of this position outside North America my failure to identify any without ambiguity may be significant.
57. Proponents of these respective approaches are cited in nn. 48-51. For more proponents of each, see the analysis of Bloesch, *FEC*, pp. 25-26.
58. Lindsell, *BB*, pp. 175, 168. Henry, *GRA*, 4:206, applauds some efforts at harmonization. For a detailed defense of the practice, see Craig L. Blomberg, "The Legitimacy and Limits of Harmonization," in *HAC*, pp. 139-174.
59. Noll, in *EMA*, pp. 103-104, 109, 116ff; Noll, in *BFC*, especially 27-36, 56-90. For the impact of common sense philosophy on Evangelical attitudes, see Mark Ellingsen, "Common Sense Realism: The Cutting Edge of Evangelical Identity," *Dialog* 24 (1985): 200-201.
60. Maier, *EhkM*, pp. 48, 56; Deutsche-Skandinavische Theologentagung, *Die Sittenser Erklärung* (1968), 3, in *Weg und Zeugnis*, ed. Rudolf Bäumer, Peter Beyerhaus, and Fritz Grünzweig, 2nd ed. (Bad Liebenzell: Verlag der Liebenzeller Mission, 1981), p. 113; George Eldon Ladd, "The Search for Perspective," *Interpretation* 25 (1971): 57ff.; Sider, in *JTTW*, pp. 364, 368-369; Henry, *GRA*, 2:292-293; Robert Preus, "May the Lutheran Church Legitimately Use the Historical-Critical Method?" *Affirm* (Spring, 1973), 35; CRC, pp. 30-31, 55-56.
61. See n. 52 for references. This approach goes back to the time of *The Fundamentals*, 9:33ff.; 3:102-103.
62. This supposition was particularly prominent in Princeton theology; see A. A. Hodge and B. B. Warfield, "Inspiration," p. 232. The supposition continues to operate for Henry, *GRA*, 4:336.
63. Clark Pinnock, "The Inerrancy Debate Among the Evangelicals," *Theology, News and Notes* (1976), 12; Maier, *EhkM*, p. 71, seems to have a similar view in speaking of the Bible's infallibility, but not its "anthropological inerrancy."

    Letha Scanzoni and Nancy Hardesty, *All We're Meant to Be* (Waco, Tex.: Word, 1974), especially pp. 18-19; Virginia Mollenkott, *Women, Men and the Bible* (Nashville: Abingdon, 1977); cf. Paul King Jewett, *Man as Male and Female* (Grand Rapids, Mich.: Eerdmans, 1975), especially pp. 112-113, 134-135.
64. Henry, *GRA*, 1:232; Moisés Silva, "The Place of Historical Reconstruction in New Testament Criticism," in *HAC*, pp. 109, 383. Cf. Berkouwer, *Holy Scripture*, pp. 180, 252; Bo Giertz, *Gott spricht zu Dir* (Wuppertal: Aussaat Verlag, 1976), p. 146; CRC, p. 53; AG, *Inerrancy of Scripture*, p. 10; *The Fundamentals*, 4:100-101; 5:16-17; 7:61. For information concerning the impact of the critical mindset, see Quebedeaux, *WE*, p. 15.

65. Information on the international character of this controversy is provided by Henry Morris, *History of Modern Creationism* (San Diego, Calif.: Master Book, 1984), pp. 293ff. This information confirmed locally by Peter Beyerhaus, personal letter, May 9, 1985; Tokunboh Adeyemo, "Evangelical Christian Affirmations" (unpublished lecture, n.d.), p. 5; David Parker, "The Evangelical Heritage of Australian Protestantism," *The Evangelical Quarterly* 57 (1985): 54.

66. Henry Morris, personal letter, June 24, 1985. The Doctrinal Statements of the Institute and the Creation Research Society, provided in Morris, *History of Modern Creationism*, pp. 358, 339, indicate the more conservative orientation of the former. For similar hard-line views, see BBF, V; GARB, V.

67. Francis Schaeffer, *Genesis in Space and Time* (Downers Grove, Ill.: InterVarsity, 1973), pp. 57-133; Henry, *GRA*, 6:146, 205.

68. Ronald L. Numbers, "The Dilemma of Evangelical Scientists," in *EMA*, p. 159. A crucial contribution to the theistic evolution view was made by Bernard Ramm, *The Christian View of Science and Scripture* (Grand Rapids, Mich.: Eerdmans, 1954), especially p. 9.

69. Numbers, "Dilemma," p. 151, describes this sort of "gap theory," which is espoused by the dispensationalist *Scofield Reference Bible*. C. Hodge, *What Is Darwinism?* p. 173; Warfield, "Calvin's Doctrine of Creation," in *PT*, pp. 297-298. For reference to Bryan, see Chap. 4, n. 10.

70. Dewey Beegle, *The Inspiration of Scripture* (Philadelphia: Westminster, 1963). For his subsequent views on inspiration, see Dewey Beegle, *Scripture, Tradition, and Infallibility* (Grand Rapids, Mich.: Eerdmans, 1973), pp. 206, 258, 262, 309. Jewett's book, *Man as Male and Female*, as well as J. Rogers and D. McKim, *Authority and Interpretation*, set off similar far-flung controversies. Still more recent controversies were ignited by several Conservative Evangelical publications in this decade which took controversial positions concerning Scripture. Texts which sparked such debate include Robert Gundry, *Matthew: A Commentary on His Literary and Theological Art* (Grand Rapids, Mich.: Eerdmans, 1981); J. Ramsey Michaels, *Servant and Son: Jesus in Parable and Gospel* (Atlanta: John Knox, 1981); James D. G. Dunn, "The Authority of Scripture According to Scripture," *Churchman* 96 (1982): 104-122, 201-225.

71. Henry, *GRA*, 4:201, 202; Preus, "Notes on Inerrancy," pp. 368-369; Maier, *EhkM*, p. 71.

72. Henry, *GRA*, 5:406-407; ICBI, *The Chicago Statement on Biblical Hermeneutics*, Append.; *Chicago Statement*, 12; Pinnock, "Inerrancy Debate," p. 12; B. B. Warfield, "The Antiquity and Unity of the Human Race," in *PT*, pp. 290-291.

73. R. Johnston (see abbreviations), p. 45. Paul Jewett, "A Response from Dr. Jewett," *Theology, News and Notes* (1976), 22; Henry, *GRA*, 5:402; CRC, pp. 21, 25-26; *Chicago Statement*, Exp.

74. Hubbard, *What We Believe and Teach*, p. 6; references in n. 9. For Evangelical institutions outside North America reflecting this position, see above, pp. 111-112. Among North American institutions maintaining a position which could be consistent with the idea of limited inerrancy, as they speak only of the Bible's "trustworthiness" or inspiration, or its infallibility only "for faith and life," see CN, IV; WC, V; Evangelical Congregational Church, *Discipline*, 7th ed. (Myerstown, Pa., 1983), 104 (hereafter, unless another text is cited explicitly, an Arabic numeral appearing in conjunction with a reference to this church designates the appropriate paragraph of this particular document); MBC, II; BC (Ashland), 2; ECC, pp. 5, 23; IVCF, I; WEF. For Pentecostal churches, see those discussed in Chap. 8.

75. See n. 63 above for the reference to Pinnock. For his most recent statement, see Clark Pinnock, *The Scripture Principle* (San Francisco: Harper & Row, 1984), especially pp. 78, 117.

76. Nicholas Wolterstorff, "How God Speaks," *Reformed Journal* (September 1969), 17-18. Marsden, "Evangelicals, History, and Modernity," p. 101, claims that Abraham Kuyper regarded the biblical writers as kinds of "impressionistic painters," not factual reporters. See Abraham Kuyper, *Principles of Sacred Theology*, trans. J. Hendrik DeVries (Grand Rapids, Mich.: Eerdmans, 1954), p. 549.

77. The propositional character of revelation has been criticized in part by the characterization of revelation by Bernard Ramm, *Special Revelation and the Word of God* (Grand Rapids, Mich.: Eerdmans, 1961), pp. 154-160, as "conceptual" in character. This propositional character is further criticized by Bloesch, *ER*, p. 21, when he insists that the Word cannot be identified with the biblical text. And the concept is further undermined by efforts to identify religious language as an expression of a particular context as do Wayan Mastra, "Christology in the Context of the Life and Religion of the Balinese," in *JTTW*, p. 231; Cummings, in *JTTW*, p. 320; and Dunn, "Authority," pp. 207, 210, 215-222. The inadequacy of human language to portray God is maintained by Donald Bloesch, *Essentials of Evangelical Theology*, 2 vols. (San Francisco: Harper & Row, 1978–1979), 1:26.

78. Gundry, *Matthew*, pp. 623ff.; Michaels, *Servant and Son*, pp. 33-34, 64.

79. The early impact of Cullmann, particularly on Fuller Seminary, has been noted by David Hubbard, personal correspondence, January 27, 1987 and Sheppard, *BH*, pp. 89-90. Barth's impact also has been noted by Sheppard and by Quebedeaux, *WE*, p. 152. Gerhard Sauter, "Einführung in die deutsche Ausgabe," in James Barr, *Fundamentalismus* (Munich: Chr. Kaiser, 1981), p. 19, observes the similar influence of Barth among German Evangelicals.

80. Barth, *KD*, vol. I/2, pp. 520-521, 588-589; vol. I/1 (7th ed.), pp. 111-113, 342ff.; vol. IV/1 (2nd ed.), pp. 368-372. Barth's position on the compatibility of biblical/ salvation and critical history is stated in *KD*, vol. I/2, p. 548. Some interpreters also see a shift in Barth away from perspectivalism and a phenomenological view of language where meaning is a function of appropriation. A more descriptive view of language, which posits the accessibility of a text's meaning for all interpreters, is given in *KD*, vol. I/2, p. 815.

81. Costas, *The Church and Its Mission*, p. 252.

82. Berkouwer, *Holy Scripture*, p. 275; Billy Graham, *How to Be Born Again* (Waco: Word, 1977), pp. 39-40; Staples, "A Response," p. 85.

83. Billy Graham, *Angels: God's Secret Agents* (Garden City, N.Y.: Doubleday, 1975), p. 15; Graham, in *LEH*, p. 28.

84. George E. Ladd, "The Resurrection of Jesus Christ," in *Christian Faith and Modern Theology*, ed. Carl Henry (Grand Rapids, Mich.: Baker, 1971), pp. 273-274, 278ff.; Bloesch, *FEC*, pp. 85, 173, 181; cf. Bloesch, *ER*, pp. 93-94; Bloesch, in *UB*, pp. 86, 101. The impact of neoorthodox and other mainline theological models on the Evangelical movement is further indicated by references in nn. 42-43. It was significant also to learn from my interview with him on March 14, 1985, that the eminent British Evangelical G. W. Bromiley considers himself to be at one with Barth's hermeneutic.

85. See Chap. 6, n. 14.

86. Beyerhaus, *BHG*, p. 19, has rejected the Protestant Orthodox concept of the inspiration of Scripture. In my interview with Maier he stressed that it was sufficient for Evangelicals to stress the Bible's "entire trustworthiness." For a similar orientation, see Blocher, in *LEH*, pp. 388-389. For additional references concerning

European Evangelical disclinations about the concept of inerrancy, see pp. 112-113, and Chap. 8, nn. 8, 9.

87. See references to pertinent contemporary Holiness theologians cited in Chap. 2, n. 31. In assessing their contention the data presented in Chap. 2, n. 42 must be kept in mind also. Likewise it should be noted that the Evangelical Congregational Church, while not affirming biblical inerrancy in its *Discipline*, does affirm it in its official brochure, *The Inspiration and Authority of the Bible*, p. 5. Also the large number of Holiness churches officially affirming or at least in dialogue with the concept of inerrancy or infallibility should be noted. See CN, IV; WC, V; FMC, V; CMA, 4.

88. See n. 45 for reference. Cf. Barth, *KD*, vol. I/1, p. 343.

89. See Chap. 10, n. 29 for references to Robertson. When assessing information in Chap. 8 about the Pentecostal churches one should also keep in mind the counterevidence provided in n. 21 of that chapter concerning historic Pentecostal views of Scripture.

90. See n. 11. This point was also made to me by Roger Nicole and David Wells in a private interview, South Hamilton, Mass., March 11, 1985.

91. Bloesch, *FEC*, pp. 13, 11.

92. Quebedeaux, *WE*, p. 29; Sheppard, *BH*, pp. 84, 90, 92.

93. This is even the case with respect to the Holiness and Pentecostal theologians presently criticizing the Evangelical movement. Their preoccupation with the problems posed by the characteristic Evangelical view of Scripture indicates their ongoing dialogue with the concept of inerrancy. The position of those Evangelicals outside North America who do not engage in a dialogue with the concept is discussed more fully on pp. 223, 112-113.

94. Henry, *GRA*, 4:589-590; Bloesch, *FEC*, p. vii; Marsden, in *EMA*, p. xvi; Francis A. Schaeffer, interview, November 12, 1983.

95. A recent text dealing with this question is Bernard Ramm, *After Fundamentalism* (San Francisco: Harper & Row, 1983).

96. Gerhard Rost, "Die Selbständige Evangelisch-Lutherische Kirche," in *Weg und Zeugnis*, ed. Rudolf Bäumer, Peter Beyerhaus, and Fritz Grünzweig, 2nd ed. (Bad Liebenzell: Verlag der Liebenzeller Mission, 1981), p. 89; David Valleskey, "Evangelical Lutheranism and Today's Evangelicals and Fundamentalists," *Wisconsin Lutheran Quarterly* 80 (1983), especially pp. 204, 206; cf. LCMS, *A Lutheran Stance toward Ecumenism* (St. Louis: Concordia, 1974), p. 10. One way of summarizing conservative Lutheran reservations to the Evangelical movement might be to say that these Lutherans are rejecting the relative openness of Evangelicals to recognizing a common apostolic faith in different Confessional traditions (see Internationale Konferenz Bekennender Gemeinschaften, 2[c]).

97. Relevant references are in Chap. 8, n. 68.

98. Henry, *GRA*, 2:13; Beyerhaus, in *LEH*, p. 293; Klaas Runia, "The Trinitarian Nature of God as Creator and Man's Authentic Relationship with Him: The Christian World View," in *LEH*, pp. 1013, 1016.

99. This observation concerning the relative importance of the issue has been made by Elmer Towns, "Independent Fundamental Baptists Looking toward 2000 A.D.," in *Roots and Origins of Baptist Fundamentalism*, ed. James O. Combs (n.p.: John the Baptist Press, 1984), p. 129. The openness to diversity is evident in the references below. It is endorsed by Blocher, in *LEH*, p. 388. Such toleration has its roots in *The Fundamentals*, 11:98.

100. For a few examples of the numerous affirmations of premillennialism, see Dallas Theological Seminary, *Catalog for 1976–77*, p. 9; New Tribes Mission, *Doctrinal*

Statement, 3; LM, 5; IFCA, 15; AG, 14; COGIC, p. 63; GARB, XIX; AUCECB, X; Det Norske Misjonsforbund (as per "Dette laerer Misjonsforbundet," *Vårt Land* [Oslo], June 20, 1984, p. 8); Beyerhaus, in *LEH,* p. 292. Postmillennialist perspectives are suggested by John Jefferson Davis, *Christ's Victorious Kingdom* (Grand Rapids, Mich.: Baker, 1987). Prime voices also seem to be certain modern proponents of the Wesleyan-revivalist heritage as well as the so-called Christian reconstructionist movement led by Rousas Rushdoony; cf. *Frankfurter Erklärung zur Grundlagenkrise der Mission* [*Frankfurt Declaration*] (1970), 38; McGavran, in *LEH,* p. 107. Quebedeaux, *WE,* p. 153, also suggests that this is the view of Richard Mouw. The amillennialist perspective seems embodied in organizations taking no official stand on the millennium or in those like the ECC, p. 23, or the CCCC (noted by Clifford R. Christensen, personal letter, December 26, 1984) espousing the validity of diverse positions. See Anthony A. Hoekema, *Created in God's Image* (Grand Rapids, Mich.: Eerdmans, 1986), pp. 30-31, 91-95, 201-202, 218-222, 243.

101. Bloesch, *ER,* p. 75; Henry, *GRA,* 4:468; Maier, interview; The Evangelical Alliance [of Great Britain] (see abbreviations). Also recall that this affirmation is usually regarded as the fifth of Fundamentalism's five points.

102. Kenneth S. Kantzer, "Unity and Diversity in Evangelical Faith," in *E,* pp. 58-59. Also see pertinent references in the previous note. It is true that in a recent survey by *Christianity Today,* reported in its issue of February 6, 1987, p. 9-I, the premillennialist position continued to be endorsed as the favored position of most of the magazine's readers.

103. This assessment by Bloesch, *FEC,* pp. 31, 57. See also the relevant citations in n. 100.

104. IFCA, 15; WC, XVIII; OMF, 8; Slavic Gospel Association, *SGA Doctrinal Statement* (n.d.) 7; George Dollar, *A History of Fundamentalism in America* (Greenville, S.C.: Bob Jones University Press, 1973), p. 265. Even Schaeffer, *SER,* pp. 78-79, hinted at an imminent end. The Fundamentalist, American Baptist Association, *1984 Yearbook* (Texarkana: Bogard Press, 1984), p. [9], states that all future meetings "are contingent upon the second coming of Christ." Also see Chap. 20, n. 3.

   For a characterization of the millennialist views of the televangelists, see Hadden and Swann, *Prime Time Preachers,* pp. 94-95. Billy Graham's views on an imminent end of the world are quoted in Martin Marty, *Righteous Empire: The Protestant Experience in America* (New York: Dial Press, 1970), pp. 256-257.

105. On the debate, see Bloesch, *FEC,* p. 57.

106. One should recall that Lutheranism has not been divided by the millennial speculations engaged in by its pietists. See Chap. 2, n. 21 for references. This appropriately "Lutheran millennialism" seems acceptable even to arch Fundamentalists like Dollar, *A History,* pp. 38-39.

107. N. 33 provides two examples of this critique.

Chapter 14: Traditional Creedal Affirmations

1. Virtually all the churches and organizations discussed in Part II affirm these creedal formulations. In that connection it is also interesting to note that Evangelical members of LCED also affirmed the doctrine of Christ's two natures.

   The degree to which the Evangelical movement, despite its self-image, really avoids a creedal orientation must be called into question on the basis of the actual practice of its organizations. All of the churches here considered, except the Plymouth Brethren and the Churches of Christ, insist on a kind of creedal subscription to their statements of faith. Henry's comments were made in my interview with him on July 8, 1986. See also Chap. 12, n. 2 for additional references.

2. Henry, *GRA*, 5:213; Timothy Smith, "The Doctrine of the Sanctifying Spirit: Charles G. Finney's Synthesis of Wesleyan and Covenant Theology," *Wesleyan Theological Journal* 13 (Spring 1978): 107-108; cf. Blocher, *LEH*, p. 382.

3. Prof. and Mrs. Peter Beyerhaus, private interview, Tübingen, April 15, 1983.

4. Henry, *GRA*, 5:45, 113.

5. Ibid., pp. 221, 235ff.; J. Gresham Machen, *My Idea of God*, ed. Joseph Newton (Boston: Little, Brown, 1926–1927), pp. 46, 48; SBC, II; *The Westminster Confession of Faith*, II; FMC, I; MBC, I; FEEBF, I; NAE. For an indication of the roots of this sort of language in Protestant Orthodoxy, see John Gerhard, *Loci Theologici* (1621), III,85.

6. Nicholas Wolterstorff, "God Everlasting," in *God and the Good*, ed. Clifton J. Orlebeke and Lewis B. Smedes (Grand Rapids, Mich.: Eerdmans, 1975), pp. 182, 187; Tite Tienou, "Biblical Foundations: An African Study," *Evangelical Review of Theology* 7 (April 1983): 95; Michael Nazir Ali, "Christology in an Islamic Context," in *JTTW*, p. 210.

7. Henry, *GRA*, 2:181; 4:166, 356; 5:12, 62, 65, 254, 272, 286; 6:456. In *GRA*, 5:313-314, it is also claimed that Gordon Clark and Cornelius Van Til held such positions. Henry Morris, personal letter, June 24, 1985; Han Chul-Ha, "An Asian Critique," *Evangelical Review of Theology* 7 (1983): 36; Runia, in *LEH*, p. 1015.

8. Donald Bloesch, *Essentials of Evangelical Theology*, 2 vols. (San Francisco: Harper & Row, 1978-1979), 1:28; Henry, *GRA*, 5:119, 292, 304.

9. Henry, *GRA*, 5:41, 134; C. Hodge, *Systematic Theology*, 3 vols. (New York: Scribner's, 1872–1873), 1:369ff.

10. Henry, *GRA*, 2:59-60; 5:325, 139, 136, 59; 6:37, 321, 328, 481; Bloesch, *FEC*, p. 18; Rodrigo Tano, "Toward an Evangelical Asian Theology," *Evangelical Review of Theology* 7 (April 1983): 160; C. Stacey Woods, *Some Ways of God* (2nd printing, Downers Grove, Ill.: InterVarsity Press, 1975), p. 24; Blocher, in *LEH*, pp. 384, 391; Runia, in *LEH*, p. 1016; Cook, in *JTTW*, pp. 393-394; SBC, II; *The Westminster Confession of Faith*, II; *The Fundamentals*, 12 vols. (Chicago: Testimony Publishing, 1910–1915), 8:56, 11:24. For these themes in Calvin, see *Institutes*, I/V.5; IV/XVII.24.

Correspondingly Evangelicals, at least Henry in *GRA*, 6:290-291, are led to deny the *communicatio idiomatum* (the communication of the attributes of Christ's two natures). Also see G. C. Berkouwer, *The Triumph of Grace in the Theology of Karl Barth* (Grand Rapids, Mich.: Eerdmans, 1956), p. 303.

11. Henry, *GRA*, 4:139.

12. *Formula of Concord* (1577), Ep. VII.33; SD VII.120. Also see Chap. 21, n. 13.

13. Thus the CN, VI, and the WC, IX, speak of "innocent" children not accountable for their sins. Others insisting on a complete Fall include Schaeffer, *SER*, pp. 24, 19; Bloesch, *FEC*, p. 20; OMF, 4; LM, 3; CMA, 5; ICFG, *Creedal Statements* (n.d.), 6; GARB, 6.

14. Schaeffer, *SER*, p. 88; Henry, *GRA*, 1:405, 333-334; 397-398, 4:553; 6:454, 512.

15. Henry, *GRA*, 1:279, 386; 2:87, 130; 5:380. In *GRA*, 5:346, 354-355, Henry lists a number of Evangelical theologians who he says share the logic of his thought on this point. These include Abraham Kuyper, Charles Hodge, and A. H. Strong. The widespread character in the Evangelical movement of this series of logical interconnections has been noted by Kantzer, in *E*, pp. 42-43.

16. See Chap. 13, nn. 47, 52. Additional instances of the second, more presuppositionalist approach include Schaeffer, *SER*, pp. 83, 11; Runia, in *LEH*, pp. 1008-1009. The approach even seems to have been employed in *The Fundamentals*, 6:35-36. The continuity between the empirical apologists for God and the tradition's common sense realism are evident in the use of cosmological arguments by the founder of the Scottish philosophy, Thomas Reid, *Essays on the Active Powers of Man*, in *The Works of Thomas Reid*, vol. 2, compiled by Sir William Hamilton, 2 vols. (Edinburgh: Maclachlan and Stewart, 1872), p. 522.

17. T. B. Barratt, *Femti korte prekener* (Oslo, 1941), p. 11. It is common to indict the Pentecostal tradition for a weak doctrine of sin; see Nils Bloch-Hoell, *The Pentecostal Movement* (Oslo: Universitetsforlaget, 1964), p. 115. But strong affirmations of sin are made by AG, 4; ICFG, III; *Bekenntnis der "Schweizerischen Pfingstmission"* (n.d.), 3.

18. These good intentions are evident in the strong Evangelical statements on sin cited in nn. 13, 17 and on p. 233. In addition one also can identify affirmations in Evangelical literature which portray the status of the Christian as *simul iustus et peccator*. Among these are Stott, *BC*, p. 100; Henry, *GRA*, 3:24; CN, V; IFCA, 8; *The Westminster Confession*, VI; *The Fundamentals*, 5:55; 6:125. But it must be noted that several of these texts, notably Stott, Henry, CN, and the IFCA, use language which suggests that the Christian is only *partially* sinner, *partially* righteous ("on the way" to the purging of sin). But the usual Lutheran conception of the matter is to regard the Christian as simultaneously *totally* sinful and *totally* righteous, see Martin Luther, *Lectures on Galatians* (1535), WA 40^1, 368f., 26ff./ LW 26:232-233; Martin Luther, *Die dritte Disputation gegen die Antinomer* (1538–1539), WA 39^1, 564, 3ff.; Martin Luther, *Against Latomus* (1521), WA 8, 57-90/ LW 32:157-204.

19. See J. D. Hunter, *American Evangelicalism* (New Brunswick: Rutgers University Press, 1983), pp. 88-89. He points out Graham's propensity to avoid preaching with much force on the topics of sin and hell. And the same reflects in Bright's presentations of the "Four Spiritual Laws."

20. Gordon Clark, quoted in Henry, *GRA*, 5:390-391. Also see *GRA*, 6:511; 2:35; COGIC, pp. 53, 62; PAC, VIII.1; *The Westminster Confession*, XXXII; II; IFCA, 16; Evangelical Congregational Church [see abbreviations], 114; *The Fundamentals*, 3:92; 8:68, 72; David Wells, "An American Evangelical Theology: The Painful Transition from Theoria to Praxis," in *EMA*, p. 84, notes that the use of such a Greek, dualistic view of persons typifies the Evangelical movement.

21. In the view of Roger Lundin, "Offspring of an Odd Union: Evangelical Attitudes towards the Arts," in *EMA*, p. 144, this sort of dualism is characteristic of typical Evangelical thought patterns; cf. Bloesch, *FEC*, p. 39. The special early Pentecostal preoccupation with demons is noted by Bloch-Hoell, *Pentecostal Movement*, p. 47. Jeffrey K. Hadden and Charles E. Swann, *Prime Time Preachers* (Reading, Mass.: Addison-Wesley, 1981), p. 94, note how this theme influences the ministry of Oral Roberts. Other Evangelicals emphasizing a dualist warfare between God and Satan include Beyerhaus, in *LEH*, p. 289; GARB, IV; BBF, IV. The latter two Fundamentalist churches also view Satan as a god of the world. There are biblical precedents (2 Cor. 4:4; John 12:31) for the idea of Satan as god of the world.

22. Francis A. Schaeffer, private interview, November 12, 1983.

23. International Congress on World Evangelization Working Group Report, *An Answer to Lausanne* (1974), 23.

24. Schaeffer, SER, p. 28; Henry, *GRA*, 4:506, 605; George E. Ladd, "The Resurrection of Jesus Christ," in *Christian Faith and Modern Theology*, ed. Carl Henry (Grand Rapids: Baker, 1971), p. 267; Padilla, in *LEH*, p. 133; Runia, in *LEH*, p. 1011.
25. This pessimistic assessment was offered by Eric Gritsch, *Born Againism* (Philadelphia: Fortress, 1982), p. 53.
26. *FC*, Ep.I.2; *The Scots Confession* (1560), Art. XVII; *The Heidelberg Catechism*, Q.57; *The Second Helvetic Confession* (1566), Chap. XXVI; Council of Trent, *Decree Concerning Purgatory*, 25th Session, 1563. Despite its similarities to Evangelical views which we have examined, the Lutheran Confessional position differs markedly in its insistence that sin is regarded as rendering the image of God totally lacking (see *FC*, SD I.10ff.).

Chapter 15: The Work of Christ

1. A good number of the churches and organizations cited in the second part describe the atonement in this way. Among the more prominent proponents of this view are *Frankfurt Declaration*, 21; Bloesch, *ER*, pp. 60-61; Falwell (see abbreviations), pp. 7, 10; FMC, XI; ICFG, *CS*, 7; IFCA, 3b; CBAA; BBF, VIII; MBC, IV; EFC, 3; OMF, 3: UFM, 4: IVCF, 3; DEA.
2. Also see *The Fundamentals*, 12 vols. (Chicago: Testimony Publishing, 1910–1915), 6:50,122.
3. Leonard Hutter, *Loci Communes Theologici* (1619), 408, 430; David Hollaz, *Examen Theologicum Acroamaticum* (1707), 736; *The Westminster Confession*, VII, XI.
4. Henry, *GRA*, 6:335, makes this observation.
5. *GRA*, 6:331, 328 and Falwell, p. 106, evidence this criticsm. This tendency to subordinate divine wrath to divine love is apparent in Albrecht Ritschl, *Der christliche lehre von der Rechtfertigung und Versöhnung* (Bonn, 1889), pp. 218ff.; Paul Tillich, *Systematic Theology*, three volumes in one (Chicago: University of Chicago Press, 1967), 1:279-281; Barth, *KD*, vol. II/1 (4th ed.), pp. 429-430. But some Evangelicals, like R. Johnston, p. 103, do correlate divine justice and love in a similar manner.
6. Henry, *GRA*, 6:404, and R. Johnston, p. 103, simply illustrate what is common in much popular Evangelical piety.
7. Henry, *GRA*, 6:356, provides a clear articulation of this commitment. For the criticism of this view of the atonement, see Gustaf Aulén, *Christus Victor*, trans. A. G. Hebert (New York: Macmillan, 1972), p. 90.
8. Such criticisms by Eric Gritsch, *Born Againism* (Philadelphia: Fortress, 1982), pp. 98, 105, and LCUSA Division for Theological Studies, *The Born-Again Movement: A Response* (1983), among others. For Luther's views on the righteousness of God, see his *Lectures on Romans* (1515–1516), WA 56, 172, 3/LW25, 151.
9. *The Westminster Confession*, VIII,XI; *The Heidelberg Catechism*, Q.37; Anglicanism, *The Thirty-Nine Articles* (1571), II; *The* [Methodist] *Articles of Religion* (1783–1784), 2.20; [Baptist] *Second London Confession* (1689), VIII.5; XI.3; *The* [Mennonite] *Waterland Confession* (1580), XII; Council of Trent, *Decree concerning the Sacrifice of the Mass*, 22nd Session (1562), Chap. 1.
10. A. M. Hills, *Fundamental Christian Theology*, 2 vols. (Pasadena: Kinne, 1931), 2:44ff., 88ff.; Paul Peter Waldenström, *The Reconciliation*, trans. J. G. Princell (Chicago: John Martenson, 1888), especially pp. 18, 100-101. Also see some affinities to this view in an early Holiness theologian, H. Orton Wiley, *Christian*

Theology, 3 vols. (Kansas City, Mo.: Nazarene Publishing House/Kingshighway Press, 1940–1943), 2:252ff., 275.

11. Henry, *GRA*, 3:23, 68, 69; 4:507, 542, 611; 6:437-438, 478, 502; Graham, in *LEH*, p. 35; Bloesch, *ER*, pp. 60-6l; R. Johnston, p. 73; Beyerhaus, in *LEH*, p. 289; Stott, *BC*, pp. 47ff. The use of classic view language is rooted in *The Fundamentals*, 1:43; 5:56; 10:57, and, as Joel Carpenter, "From Fundamentalism to the New Evangelical Coalition," in *EMA*, p. 9, has shown, the idea of Christ's warfare with Satan was a major theme of the Prophetic movement.

12. Norberto Saracco, "The Liberating Options of Jesus," in *JTTW*, p. 60; Orlando E. Costas, "Proclaiming Christ in the Two Thirds World," in *JTTW*, p. 4. For the actual use of the classic view by an Evangelical theologian in dialogue with liberation themes, see Padilla, in *LEH*, pp. 119-120, 122-123.

13. The concern to affirm the personal character of the devil in face of mainline theology's neglect is voiced by Henry, *GRA*, 6:239. Also see GARB, IV; ICFG, *CS*, 5; IFCA, 14; *The Fundamentals*, 10:115, 121. The critique of mainline theology's relative neglect of divine righteousness and wrath is evident in Henry, *GRA*, 6:354; Falwell, p. 106; *The Fundamentals*, 6:43-44, 57. Also see Roger Nicole, "The Nature of Redemption," in *Christian Faith and Modern Theology*, ed. Carl Henry (Grand Rapids: Baker, 1971), pp. 220-221.

14. *Frankfurt Declaration*, 23; *The Lausanne Covenant*, 3; *Keele Congress Statement* (1967), 11; NAE, *Saving the Seventies* (1970); AG, *Constitution and Bylaws*, (1981), Bylaws, Art. VIII, Sec. 3.a; Padilla, in *LEH*, p. 118; John Stott, "The Biblical Basis of Evangelism," in *LEH*, p. 76. Cf. implicit denials of universalism by WC, XIX, XXI; FMC, XXII; GARB, XX; FEEBF, XI; OMF, 9; UFM, 9; Fuller, 10.

15. Henry, *GRA*, 4:597; 6:92-93, 511. But Quebedeaux, *WE*, p. 21, notes that Clark Pinnock has expressed an openness to this view. ERCD, 3(4), concedes that some Evangelicals remain open to the possibility of the salvation of those who have never heard of Christ.

16. T. B. Barratt, quoted in Nils Bloch-Hoell, *The Pentecostal Movement* (Oslo: Universitetsforlaget, 1964), p. 114. B. B. Warfield, *Two Studies in the History of Doctrine* (New York: The Christian Literature Co., 1897), p. 230; C. Hodge, *Systematic Theology*, (New York: Scribner's, 1872–1873), 1:26-27. For information on the CRC, see Chap. 8, n. 7. The logic of this position has been extended a bit further by Neal Punt, *Unconditional Good News* (Grand Rapids: Eerdmans, 1980); he argues that all are elect except those who reject Christ.

17. These affirmations are held by Evangelical churches of the Reformed tradition subscribing to *The Westminster Confession*, III, VIII, and *The Articles of the Synod of Dort* (1618–1619), trans. Thomas Scott (Philadelphia: Presbyterian Board of Publication, 1841), pp. 261ff. BBF, X, and FEEBF, VI, refer to election but probably not double predestination. See subsequent discussion of Amyraldianism.

Explicit Evangelical rejections of the idea of limited atonement are voiced by Bloesch, *ER*, p. 87, and G. C. Berkouwer, "Vragen Ronden de Relijdenis," *Gerefoormeerd Theologisch Tydschrift* 63 (1963): 1-41. The insistence that salvation is offered to all is evident in Holiness churches like the WC, IX, and CN, VII, as well as in the EMF, the LCMS, BS, 11ff., and the *Frankfurt Declaration*, 31.

18. The Evangelical commitment to the importance of personal faith is well illustrated by the references in n. 22. A handful of the literally thousands of indications of the Evangelical commitment to the centrality of evangelism and foreign missions follows: *Keele Statement*, 22ff.; *Frankfurt Declaration*, 26,41; NAE, *Resolutions*

(1974), p. 4; Evangelical Congregational Church, 125; IFCA, 10; ICFG, *CS*, 16; SBC, XI; BBF, XIX; Underground Evangelism, *Statement of Faith* (n.d.); IVCF, *Purpose* (n.d.), 3; Graham, in *LEH*, p. 30; Timothy L. Smith, "An Historical Perspective on Evangelicalism and Ecumenism," *Mid-Stream* 22 (July/October 1983): 310; Falwell, pp. 7, 55-56; Gerhard Maier, private interview, April 27, 1983; Quebedeaux, *WE*, pp. 7, 53; Henry, *GRA*, 3:21. References in n. 21 below are pertinent also.

19. Bloesch, *ER*, p. 38; Quebedeaux, *WE*, pp. 20-21; Arthur M. Climenhaga, "Mission—and Neo-Universalism," in *The Church's Worldwide Mission: Proceedings of the Congress on the Church's Worldwide Mission 9-16 April* [1966] *at Wheaton College, Wheaton, Ill.* (Waco, Tex.: Word, 1966), pp. 96-110. The presence of such universalism in the Roman Catholic tradition is suggested in the Second Vatican Council's *Lumen Gentium* (1964), 16.

20. Dean Kelley, *Why Conservative Churches Are Growing* (New York: Harper & Row, 1972).

21. The issues at stake are nicely summarized by Rodger C. Bassham, *Mission Theology: 1948–1975* (Pasadena: Wm. Carey Library, 1979), esp. pp. 344-351, 167-169. A good example of the ecumenical establishment's identification of evangelism and social action is evident in the WCC Vancouver Assembly Issue Group Report, *Witnessing in a Divided World* (1983), 34, 35, 40, 41. For a few of the numerous Conservative Evangelical references to the priority or at least the distinctiveness of evangelism in relation to social action, see Graham, in *LEH*, pp. 31, 34; McGavran, in *LEH*, pp. 94, 101; Henry, *GRA*, 4:495, 570; Falwell, p. 184; John Howard Yoder, as quoted by Escobar, in *LEH*, p. 320; Ronald J. Sider, "Rich Christians in an Age of Hunger," *Evangelical Review of Theology* 4 (April 1980): 82; Costas, in *JTTW*, p. 4; AG, *A Statement of Social Concern* (1968); *Frankfurt Declaration*, 41ff.

22. Good News Movement, *The Junaluska Affirmation* (1975); Henry, *GRA*, 1:152-153; 2:8, 31, 3:42, 64; 4:61, 553; 5:17; 6:501; Stott, in *LEH*, pp. 70, 76; *Frankfurt Declaration*, 22; AG, *Homosexuality* (1979), pp. 10, 8; BGC, 6; CN, IX.

    Other texts where it is stated or connoted that the Christian has a "duty" to respond to grace (often by becoming regenerate) include *Chicago Declaration of Evangelicals to Social Concern* (1973), 5; BBF, X, IX; GARB, X; ICFG, *CS*, 13, 9; CCCC, 4; ECC, pp. 9, 13-14; EFC, 5-6, FEEBF, V, VI; Fédération Evangélique de France; *Keele Statement*, 11, 10; NAE, 4, 5.

23. B. B. Warfield, *Selected Shorter Writings of Benjamin Warfield*, ed. John E. Meeker, 2 vols. (Nutley, N.J.: Presbyterian and Reformed Publishing, 1970-1973), 2:115; G. Millon, "Fondement Biblique des Eglises de Professants," in S. Bénétreau and G. Millon, *Les Eglises de Professants* (Paris: S.P.B., 1957), p. 48; WC, VIIIff.; FMC, VIIIff.; CN, VII, IX; Evangelical Congregational Church, 106-109, 111; EMF (as noted by Francis Guiton, "La Doctrine et l'Esprit du Méthodisme," *L'Evangeliste*, October-December 1956, p. 260); PHC, *The Pentecostal Holiness Church Manual 1981* (Franklin Springs, Ga.: Advocate Press, n.d.), Sec. III.2 (refers to faith as an "act," "the result of divine persuasion"). Some other Holiness-related churches and organizations, notably CMA, 5-7, LM, 3, and OMF, 4-6, do not reflect as much synergist tendencies, as they tend to restrict discussion of divine-human cooperation to the image of "empowerment" and not speak about the human response of faith as a duty. Their focus is not so much on the character of faith as a human act. (The ICFG, V-VIII, holds a kind of middle ground, maintaining Keswick influence but using images suggesting a kind of Roman Catholic version of synergism by "preparation for grace.") No doubt these tendencies may be a function of the influence of the

Keswick movement on them. But as Marsden, *FAC*, pp. 98ff., has pointed out the Keswick theme of "Let go and let God" seems to make God wait on an act of faith. Thus at worst we have a spiritual dictatorship of the human will, at best surely a kind of synergism. Its concept of "empowerment," "enablement," as we saw in the NAE statement still seems to reflect an Arminian orientation.

Other notable Evangelical persons and institutions reflecting a kind of Arminian synergist perspective at some points include Gottfried Osei-Mensah, "The Holy Spirit in World Evangelization," in *LEH*, p. 259, who claims that Christians need divine "help" [presumably in the sense of cooperation], the AUCECB, IV, which claims that the Spirit works only with our consent, and Francis Schaeffer, who states in *The Church before the Watching World* (Downers Grove, Ill.: InterVarsity, 1971), p. 92, that in conversion "man is not simply a zero." Nor should the Fuller Sem. statement (6) that the Spirit only "persuades" Christians be overlooked as a synergistic statement within the Evangelical movement.

24. Here and hereafter, references to the doctrinal positions of the National Association of Free Will Baptists refer to the Association's *Treatise Revision of the Treatise and Practices of the Free Will Baptists* (1948), and the accompanying Roman numeral refers to the corresponding chapter of the treatise. Here, in the preceding two paragraphs, and in nn. 22-23 all citations to texts have also included reference to those segments of the texts which indicate the primary function they have ascribed to grace in bringing about redemption.

25. FC, SD II.90; *The Westminster Confession*, IX, XVI (speaks only of the Spirit's "enabling" others); Council of Trent, *Decree Concerning Justification*, Sixth Session, 1547, Chaps. IVff. Other texts are noted on p. 322.

26. For references to the affirmation of double predestination by Evangelicals, see the Reformed churches noted in Chap. 8 which subscribe to historic Reformation Confessional documents. See n. 17 for references to these documents and to those taking alternative positions. Diversity within the movement among those embracing double predestination is evident in the CRC's apparently infralapsarian position (see A. C. Piepkorn, *Profiles in Belief*, 4 vols. [New York: Harper & Row, 1977-1979], 2:338), and the OPC's supralapsarianism (see John P. Galbraith, *Why The Orthodox Presbyterian Church?* [Philadelphia: The Orthodox Presbyterian Church, n.d.], pp. 7, 8).

27. Henry, *GRA*, 6:88-89.

28. *FC*, SD XI. See also n. 16 above.

Chapter 16: Justification and the Christian Life

1. International Congress on World Evangelization Working Group Report, *An Answer to Lausanne* (1974), 10.

2. Henry, *GRA*, 3:65; cf. 4:65, 444; 3:53; 2:64; 1:329.

3. See the reference in Chap. 10, n. 30.

4. Among the numerous possible references one notes such an affirmation in the following representatives of each type of Evangelical organization cited in Part 2: The Reformed churches cited in virtue of their subscription to *The Westminster Confession*, XI, or *The Heidelberg Catechism*, Q.62-63; CN, IX; AD, 4; COGIC, pp. 56-57; IFCA, 6; MBC, 4; AUCECB, IV; BBF, XI,X; CBAA; BC (Ashland), 3/5; ECC, p. 7; EFC, 6; SBC, IV; Church of England Evangelical Council, *Keele Congress Statement*, 10; Good News Movement, *The Junaluska Affirmation* (1975); LM, 3; CC, 8; DEA; AEAM, 4; Association d'Eglises de Professants des Pays Francophones; *Base Doctrinale* (1972); WEF.

5. See pertinent references in n. 17 of the preceding chapter.
6. Henry, *GRA*, 3:176; 4:491; *Scofield Reference Bible* (New York, 1917), pp. 95, 1115; C. I. Scofield, "The Grace of God," in *The Fundamentals*, 12 vols. (Chicago: Testimony Publishing, 1910–1915), 11:45ff.; Konferenz Bekennender Gemeinschaften, *Orientierungshilfe*, 5; Bo Giertz, *Evangelisch Glauben: Hilfen zum Verstehen* (Erlangen: Martin Luther Verlag, 1981), p. 38. For references to some affirmation of *simul iustus et peccator* by Evangelicals, see Chap. 14, n. 18.
7. Merrill Tenney, gen. ed., *The Zondervan Pictorial Encyclopedia of the Bible*, 5 vols. (Grand Rapids, Mich.: Zondervan, 1977), 3:769. Something like this commitment is also affirmed by Bernard Ramm, *The Evangelical Heritage* (Waco: Word, 1973), p. 13; WEF, CEPRC, VII. For references to this commitment in Lutheranism, see *Apology of the Augsburg Confession* (1531), Art.IV.2; FC, SD III.6; Martin Luther, *Die Promotionsdisputation von Palladius und Tilemann* (1527), WA 39¹, 205, 1.
8. Bill Bright, personal letter, August 15, 1986.
9. See Chap. 15, n. 23 for references.
10. Evangelical Alliance [of Great Britain] (see abbreviations), DEA; ERCD, 4(1); SBC, IV; WC, XI; BBF, III, IX, XII; Graham, in *LEH*, p. 35; Henry, *GRA*, 4:494-495; 6:392; Rolando Gutierrez Cortes, "Christology and Pastoral Action in Latin America," in *JTTW*, p. 92; S. Bénétreau, "Qu'est-ce qu'une Eglise de Professants?" in *Les Eglises de Professants*, ed. S. Bénétreau and G. Millon (Paris: S.P.B., 1957), pp. 18-19.
11. Henry, *GRA*, 4:445-446; CRC, p. 58; Maier, *EhkM*, pp. 10-11, 22ff., 58; LCMS, *GS*, p. 10.
12. Henry, *GRA*, 2:334; 3:116.
13. See *GRA*, 6:356; Schaeffer, *CM*, pp. 28-29; *The Westminster Confession*, XI, XIX; GARB, VIII, XIV; BBF, VIII, XIII; *SBC*, II.2, XIII. A few of the countless examples of the movement's reliance on a satisfaction/substitutionary view are cited in Chap. 15, n. 1.
14. Bloesch, *FEC*, p. 65; Norman L. Geisler, *Options in Contemporary Christian Ethics* (Grand Rapids, Mich.: Baker, 1981), p. 32; Osei-Mensah, in *LEH*, p. 263.
15. References to the French churches on p. 241 and Chap. 15, n. 22. Other examples of Evangelicals making repentance a necessary condition for salvation include AG, *Homosexuality* (1979), p. 9; Evangelical Congregational Church, 108; NAE, *Spiritual Renewal* (1970); Stott, *BC*, pp. 16, 18. For an indication of the theme of "preparation for grace" in classical Pietism, see P. J. Spener, *Theologische Bedenken*, ed. F.A.C. Hennicke (Halle: Gebauersche Buchhandlung, 1838), p. 21. References in n. 30 of Chap. 6 are pertinent.
16. Council of Trent, *Decree Concerning Justification*, Sixth Session, 1547, Chaps. IVff.; Thomas Aquinas, *Summa Theologica*, I-II, Q.114, Art.2.
17. Henry, *GRA*, 4:498; Council of Trent, *Decree Concerning Justification*, Chap. X. In Daniel R. Fuller, *Gospel and Law* (Grand Rapids: Eerdmans, 1980), pp. 112ff., 144, and *The Fundamentals*, 5:68-69, there is sufficient disclarity concerning whether references to the ongoing transformation of the Christian pertain to justification or sanctification as to suggest that justification might be construed by their readers as an ongoing process.
18. For a third use of the law in the various mainline churches, see p. 257. Also see Spener, *PD*, pp. 44, 57ff. A few instances where such a concern for specifically designating the character of Christian life as a central theological priority explicitly acknowledged by Evangelicals include ECC, pp. 8, 13; AG, 5b; Stott, *BC*, p. 115; Bénétreau, in *Les Eglises*, p. 20; Padilla, in *LEH*, p. 135.

19. For EFC reference, see *What Is The Evangelical Free Church?* (unpaginated booklet, Minneapolis, n.d.) [p. 5]. On the whole the theme of Christian freedom is relatively neglected among Evangelicals. In *The Fundamentals*, 11:50, Scofield did reject the use of the law in the Christian life; see "The Grace of God," in *The Fundamentals*. Also see *The Fundamentals*, 3:92; 10:61-63; Fuller Seminary, 7; *Keele Statement*, 13; Paul A. Mickey, *Essentials of Wesleyan Theology* (Grand Rapids, Mich.: Zondervan, 1980), p. 159; *SBC*, XII; Bénétreau, in *Les Eglises*, p. 21. It should be noted that at least in the last two cases references to the Christian's freedom are still made with significant stipulations of the Law.

20. *Berlin Declaration on Ecumenism* (Full Version) (1974), 6b; *Constitution and Rules of Procedure of the Anglican Evangelical Assembly* (n.d.), 2.1.1.2; *An Answer to Lausanne*, 11; Wheaton, '83, *Letter to the Churches* (1983), I (subsequent references in the text to Wheaton '83, accompanied by Roman numerals, denote this document); EMF; AG, 5(b); Henry, *GRA*, 6:398-399; G. Millon, "Fondement Biblique des Eglises de Professants," in S. Bénétreau and G. Millon, *Les Eglises de Professants* (Paris: S. P. B., 1957), p. 49. Also see references in the following notes, particularly as this tendency manifests itself in the life-style standards of various organizations. Pertinent at this point and quite typical is the rejection of "situational ethics" by Evangelicals like Klaus Bochmühl, "The Ten Commandments: are they still valid?" *Ministry*, 67 (March 1985): 4; *Keele Statement*, 13.

21. For the function of Scripture or the Word as a rule of constraint, see "Church of God [Cleveland, Tenn.] Teachings," in *Introducing the Church of God* (unpaginated booklet; Cleveland, Tenn., n.d.); C. Emilio Nunez, "Towards an Evangelical Latin American Theology," *Evangelical Review of Theology*, (April 1983): 129; Bénétreau, *Les Eglises*, p. 16; *Chicago Statement*, Pref., Exp. For references to the imitation of Christ or the call to believers to function as examples, see Reformed Ecumenical Synod, *Statements on the Social Calling of the Church* (1980), 7; MBC, XV; Evangelical Congregational Church, 131; Escobar, in *LEH*, p. 320; Jim Wallis, "What Does Washington Have to Say to Grand Rapids?" *Sojourners*, July 1977, p. 4; Henry, *GRA*, 4:531, 533; 6:337; John Howard Yoder, *The Politics of Jesus* (reprint; Grand Rapids: Eerdmans, 1983), pp. 12, 122, 190, 241; Sider, *RCAH*, p. 77.

22. See the discussion on life-style standards (Membership/Practical Commitments) for the Holiness and most Pentecostal churches in Chap. 8. For strictures on slang and swimming with the opposite sex, see *Congregational Holiness Church Inc. Discipline* (Griffin, Ga., n.d.), p. 3, and CG (Cleveland), "Church of God Teachings," 31. Various Scandinavian Pentecostals reject the eating of blood foods (see Nils Bloch-Hoell, *The Pentecostal Movement* [Oslo: Universitetsforlaget, 1964], p. 219). The biblical rubrics on covering women's heads during worship (1 Cor. 7:5) are affirmed by the Brethren in Christ Church, *Decorum in Worship* (unpaginated pamphlet; Nappanee, Ind.: Evangel Press, 1972). Likewise, the mandate that women wear long hair (1 Cor. 11:14, 15) and be moderate in the use of cosmetics is a rubric of CG (Cleveland), "Church of God Teachings," 27, 28. It should also be noted that some Holiness churches forbid profit-making commercialism ventures in the name of the church. See *FMC*, Chap. VIII, 804; *WC*, Chap. V, 197.

Strictures against certain kinds of behavior regarded as normal in the broader society are part of the Evangelical movement's pre-Fundamentalist heritage. Thus, playing cards, attending the theater, and dancing were rejected by Abraham Kuyper, *Lectures on Calvinism* (Grand Rapids, Mich.: Eerdmans, 1931), pp. 73ff.

Likewise, dancing and attendance at the theater were forbidden by the early Puritans (see Stoeffler, *REP*, pp. 140-141).

23. David Valleskey, "Evangelical Lutheranism and Today's Evangelicals and Fundamentalists," *Wisconsin Lutheran Quarterly* 80 (1983): 208-209.

24. References are given on p. 257.

25. This assessment by Quebedeaux, *WE*, p. 93, D. Dayton, "Holiness and Pentecostal Churches," *The Christian Century*, August 15–22, 1979, p. 719, and Bloch-Hoell, *Pentecostal Movement*, pp. 116-117.

26. Churches which affirm healing as a viable possibility include AG, 12; ICFG, XIV; PAC, V.5; CG, 11; COGIC, pp. 73-74; Congregação Cristã do Brasil, *Articles of Faith* (1946), 12; PHC, 12; CN, XV; CMA, 8. The last three Pentecostal churches as well as CMA, 8, and BC (Ashland), 3/9, combine this commitment with the practice of anointing the sick with oil.

27. Henry, *GRA*, 4:503-504, 507.

28. New Tribes Mission, *Doctrinal Statement*, 6; *The Westminster Confession*, XVII; IFCA, 7; GARB, XIII; BBF, XV; SBC, V. Those clearly opting only for the need for perseverence or holiness as basis for assurance include EMF (as per S. Samouélian, *Le Réveil Méthodiste* [Nimes, 1974], pp. 88ff.); AG, 5(b); Bloesch, *ER*, p. 70; Stott, *BC*, p. 134; *The Fundamentals*, 10:76.

29. BC (Ashland) holds this position, as its failure to affirm "eternal security" caused the schism of the "Grace Brethren"; AG, *Constitution and Bylaws* (1981), Bylaws, Art. VIII/B, Sec.1; WC, XIII; FMC, XIV.

30. A. C. Piepkorn, *Profiles in Belief*, 4 vols. (New York: Harper & Row, 1977–1979), 3:16, observes a shift in the FMC away from a belief that one can be purged from all evil thoughts. Of course today the possibility of cleansing from all inward sin is still affirmed. In addition to the Holiness churches mentioned, see CN, X; EMF (as per Samouélian, *Le Réveil*, pp. 86, 82); PHC, 10. Keswick modifications of perfectionist teaching are most evident in CMA, 7, and to some extent perhaps in John Stott, *BC*, pp. 100-101, 137. The important Norwegian pentecostal T. B. Barratt, *Femti korte prekener* (Oslo, 1941), pp. 48, 128, seems to have held a similar view.

   For Wesley's views on the "process character" of perfection, what he calls the need to "perfect holiness," see his *A Plain Account of Christian Perfection* (1741), pp. 271, 257. For this interpretation I am indebted to Albert Outler, "Introduction," *John Wesley* (New York: Oxford, 1964), p. 31.

31. IFCA, 8; Marlin E. Miller, "The Church in the World: A Mennonite Perspective," *The Covenant Quarterly* 41 (August 1983): 47; Yoder, *PJ*, p. 120; Henry, *GRA*, 6:337.

32. This is the position of most Holiness churches: WC, XI, XIV; FMC, XIII; CN, X; EMF (see Samouélian, *Le Réveil*, p. 86). Others distinguishing justification from sanctification almost to the point of dividing them include Bloesch, *ER*, p. 69; Henry, *GRA*, 4:501; BBF, X-XII; LCMS, *BS*, 17, 9; *The Westminster Confession*, XI.

   This position correlates with the concept of "forensic justification" (see p. 314, where other relevant references are cited). For a full discussion of the implications of this characteristic Evangelical orientation see Richard Jensen, "Justification: Where Faith and Experience Meet," *The Covenant Quarterly* 41 (August 1983): 31-37.

33. Bo Giertz, "Taufe, Wiedergeburt, Bekehrung in Rahmen des Ordo Salutis," in *TWB*, pp. 57, 60-61, 65. Also see Yoder, *PJ*, p. 226. It should be noted that for the first group listed in the preceding note, at least for WC, XIV, it is maintained

that sanctification begins in justification (so in that sense most Evangelicals do relate the two). However, it is never made clear how justification entails *actual, concrete holiness* for believers, whether there is any sense in which the gift of sanctification as something more than a mere possibility is actually given in justification. In the case of Holiness churches *entire sanctification* is temporally distinct from justification.

34. John Baier, *Compendium Theologiae Positivae* (1685), 577, 574; David Hollaz, *Examen Theologicum Acroamaticum* (1707), 928; *FC,* SD III.32; *The Westminster Confession,* XI.

35. In *Thoughts on Christian Perfection* (1760), in *John Wesley,* ed. Albert C. Outler (New York: Oxford University Press, 1964), p. 293, Wesley clearly indicates the temporal priority of justification to complete sanctification. Yet, in *The Scripture Way to Salvation,* in ibid., p. 274, and in *On God's Vineyard (1788),* in ibid., p. 108, he clearly states that sanctification properly begins in justification. In Holiness church statements alluded to in n. 33, this phrasing is reflected.

36. In addition to those cited in the text, see PHC, 10-11; Congregational Holiness Church, *Articles of Faith* (1921), 5.

37. It is interesting to note that a number of Lutheran charismatics, particularly Theodore Jungkuntz, *A Lutheran Charismatic Catechism,* 2nd ed. (published by the author, 1982), pp. 8-9, appear to embrace something like this orientation, albeit with an insistence that ecstasy is not a work of grace distinct from justification. Sanctification and ecstasy are said to provide nothing intrinsically new (no "second work of grace"). They represent nothing more than what is given in baptism/justification. See Carter Lindberg, *The Third Reformation?* (Macon, Ga.: Mercer University Press, 1983), pp. 224-229, for an evaluation of this view as held by Larry Christenson and Arnold Bittlinger. Especially, see Larry Christenson, ed., *Welcome, Holy Spirit* (Minneapolis: Augsburg, 1987), pp. 111, 196, for a similar statement by an international consultation of Lutheran charismatics.

38. See also texts noted below on pp. 314-315. On the sense in which Holiness churches do and do not posit such a simultaneity, see n. 32 above.

39. Bloesch, *ER,* pp. 37, 69, 107; Francis Schaeffer, personal interview, November 12, 1983; Henry, *GRA,* 3: 134, 121. See also George Marsden, "The Evangelical Denomination," in *EMA,* p. x; Donald W. Dayton, "Whither Evangelicalism? The Holiness Heritage between Calvinism and Wesleyanism" (lecture presented at the Sixth Oxford Institute Methodist Theological Studies Conference, n.d.), p. 8; David Forrester, "Anglican Evangelicalism," *The Clergy Review* 60 (1975): 778; Larry Christenson, "Hermeneutics in the Charismatic Renewal" (lecture presented at the 16th International Ecumenical Seminar, Strasbourg, June 19, 1982), p. 19. For the views of other Lutheran charismatics, see Chap. 7, n. 19.

40. EFC, *What Is The Evangelical Free Church?* p. 12. Also see Francis Guiton, "La Doctrine et l'Esprit du Méthodisme," *L'Evangéliste,* October-December 1956, p. 260; Svenska kyrkans fria Synod (Free Synod in the Church of Sweden), *Vad är Svenska Kyrkan?* (1986), 9; *Fundamental Principles of Evangelical [Dissident] Christians and Baptists [in USSR]* (n.d.), 3.

41. Additional Evangelical texts insisting on the necessity of regeneration are referred to in Chap. 15, n. 22.

42. Such a view has precedence in *The Fundamentals,* 5: 68-69.

43. See Chap. 6, n. 24 for references.

44. For references to these commitments, see especially nn. 40, 41, and Chap. 15, n. 18.

45. *Berlin Declaration on Ecumenism* (Full Version), 1. cf. Henry, *GRA*, 1: 390; ibid., 3: 278.
46. See Chap. 13, n. 26 for references.
47. Bloch-Hoell, *Pentecostal Movement*, pp. 99ff. Sweet, in *EMA*, p. 43, has offered a similar account of the success of the Evangelical movement as a whole, one quite compatible with Kelley's.
48. This sort of characterization of Roman Catholic concerns for holiness or sanctification has been offered by the Methodist-Roman Catholic Conversations, *Denver Report* (1971), 7; *Salvation and the Church: An Agreed Statement by the Second Anglican–Roman Catholic International Commission, ARCIC* II (1987), 14; Lutheran–Roman Catholic Dialogue (U.S.A.), *Justification by Faith* (Common Statement) (1983), §101, §103 (stresses that the Catholic emphasis is on the doxological response of faith); Bernard Lonergan, *Method in Theology* (New York: Seabury, 1972), p. 241. Among the many historians characterizing the medieval period as a time of chaos and showing the church's role in providing social cohesion, see Steven Ozment, *The Age of Reform 1250–1550* (New Haven/London: Yale University Press, 1980), pp. 1-5, 20-22. Such characterizations seem confirmed by statements of the Council of Trent, *Bull of Convocation* (1542); *Decree Concerning the Opening*, First Session, 1545; *Decree Concerning Justification*, X, XI, which speak of the council's primary concern to bring about moral-spiritual reform in the church.
49. For more detailed discussions and documentation of the concerns of these traditions, see pp. 117-119, 124-125.

Chapter 17: Church and Ministry

1. Henry, *GRA*, 4: 229; "Editorial," *Wheaton '83 Newsletter*, No. 8, p. 1. A similar observation on the practice of de-emphasizing ecclesiology for the sake of soul-winning or other Evangelical priorities is evident in Arthur Johnston, *The Battle for World Evangelism* (Wheaton, Ill.: Tyndale, 1978), pp. 71-72; Blocher, in *LEH*, pp. 388-389; Bloesch, *FEC*, p. 127.
2. Among the numerous examples which may be cited are MBC, VI, XV; BGC, 7; AUCECB, V; CMA, 9; EFC, 8; ECC, p. 16; ICFG, XVI; CC, 12; LM, 4; Henry, *GRA*, 4: 438, 568; ibid., 3:43-44; S. Bénétreau, "Qu'est-ce qu'une Eglise de Professants?" in *Les Eglises de Professants*, ed. S. Bénétreau and G. Millon (Paris: S. P. B., 1957), pp. 23-24; *Lausanne Covenant*, 6. Evangelical and Fundamentalist Presbyterians could also be included as holding this view depending on how one reads *The Westminster Confession*, XXV. The issue in a statement like this as well as in others like Fuller Sem., 9, and WC, XVI, which connect the Church with God's Word and sacraments/ordinances is whether these acts of God call the Church into being or whether they merely flow from the fellowship of believers.
3. Evangelical disinclinations pertaining to creedal formulations for describing the Church are evident in the failure to appeal to these images in most of the Statements of Faith we have considered. Exceptions to this are evident in Wheaton '83 (see abbreviations), I, and Webber, *CR*, pp. 55-71.
    References for the views of these mainline traditions are provided below, on p. 325.
4. Assessments akin to this are offered by Bloesch, *FEC*, p. 148; Marsden, in *E*, pp. 136-137.
5. Among numerous examples are WC, Const., Art. III; COGIC, pp. 83-84; MBC, VI; BGC, 7; Association Evangélique d'Eglises Baptistes de Langue Française,

II.1; EMF (as per S. Samouélian, *Le Réveil Méthodiste* [Nimes, 1974], p. 101). Also see Bénétreau, in *Les Eglises*, p. 25; Marlin E. Miller, "The Church in the World: A Mennonite Perspective," *The Covenant Quarterly* 41 (1983): 49; Harold O. J. Brown, "The Role of Discipline in the Church," *The Covenant Quarterly* 41 (August 1983): 51; *The Fundamentals*, 12 vols. (Chicago: Testimony Publishing, 1910–1915), 9:8.

One of the most striking instances of the enforcement of discipline is evident in the EREI, *Statuts Obligatoires des Eglises* (n.d.), Art. 3, where members are directed to raise their children in the "Protestant religion" (a kind of counterpromise to the pledge enforced on many Roman Catholic parents).

6. This tendency is most apparent in the exposition by Bénétreau, in *Les Eglises*, pp. 20, 28, concerning the position of the Eglises de Professants in France, all of which are Free Churches (and identify with the Free Churches in the rest of Europe). For a few references to separatism in Fundamentalist organizations, see p. 155; Chap. 4, n. 15; Chap. 8, n. 53.

7. Others taking this position include MBC, VII; AG, 10; Bloesch, *FEC*, p. 127; Howard Snyder, "The Church as God's Agent in Evangelism," in *LEH*, pp. 327, 344.

8. Evangelical Alliance [of Great Britain] (see abbreviations); DEA; RC-P, II, 84; ERCD, Int. (1); SBC, *Report of Committee on Baptist Faith and Message;* USSR Dis. Bapt., 6; ECC, p. 7; PB (as per Davis Duggins, in personal letters); LM, 4. Pietism's emphasis on the universal priesthood is evident in Spener, *PD*, p. 92.

9. Vatican II, *Lumen Gentium*, (1964), 6; Council of Trent, *Canons on the Sacrament of Order*, 23rd Session, 1563, Canon 6. The PAC's position is elaborated further above, p. 269. Explicit articulations of a low view of the ministry by Evangelicals are evident in ECC, pp. 18-19; FEEBF, "The Church," III; Association Evangélique d'Eglises Baptistes de Langue Française, II.2; *The Fundamentals*, 9:6. It is perhaps significant that relatively few statements of faith of Conservative Evangelical churches have an article on the ministry.

10. For the Anglican position, see Packer, in *TCU*, p. 54; *Keele Congress Statement*, 64, 69. Also see FEEBF, VII; Henry, *GRA*, 2:22. For the ministry described in terms of Word and sacrament, see Bloesch, *FEC*, p. 72; Evangelical Congregational Church, 120; Fuller Sem., 9.

11. Information from G. Dollar, *A History of Fundamentalism in America* (Greenville: Bob Jones University Press, 1973), p. 245, and Quebedeaux, *WE*, p. 54.

12. National Association of Free Will Baptists, XVII; Association Evangélique d'Eglises Baptistes de Langue Française, II.2; AG, *Constitution and Bylaws* (1981), Bylaws VII.1; RC-P, II, 91.

13. David S. Schuller, Merton P. Strommen, and Milo L. Brekke, eds., *Ministry in America* (San Francisco: Harper & Row, 1980), p. 389.

14. AG, *Constitution and Bylaws*, Art.VII, Sec. 2. Information on other churches from D. Dayton, "The Holiness and Pentecostal Churches," *The Christian Century*, August 15-22, 1979, p. 790.

15. This observation also made by Hatch, in *EMA*, p. 193, among others.

16. Henry, *GRA*, 4:224; Webber, *CR*, pp. 127-128; Clark Pinnock, *Biblical Revelation: The Foundation of Christian Theology* (Chicago: Moody Press, 1971), p. 105. See also the similar views of numerous Lutheran charismatics in Larry Christenson, ed., *Welcome, Holy Spirit* (Minneapolis: Augsburg, 1987), pp. 72-73.

17. Konferenz Bekennender Gemeinschaften, *Orientierungshilfe des Theologischen Konvents für Schriftauslegung* (n.d.), 8; Noll, *BFC*, p. 154.

18. See Vatican II, *Lumen Gentium*, 25; Anglican–Orthodox Conversations, *Moscow Statement* (1976), 17.
19. Henry, *GRA*, 2:15; 4:95, 448; Packer, in *TCU*, pp. 51-53; Eui Whan Kim, "The Authority of the Bible and the Lordship of Christ," in *LEH*, p. 986; A. Alexander, "Inaugural Address," in *PT*, p. 79; *The Fundamentals*, 11:102-103, 117-118; *Chicago Statement*, I. For an example of this Fundamentalist position, see Falwell, pp. 27ff., 53, 57. Other pertinent references in Chap. 4, n. 2.
20. See WEF, CEPRC, IV.
21. This point has been suggested by Bloesch, *FEC*, p. 38. Concerning Conservative Evangelical Lutherans, see the discussion below, p. 327.
22. Similar appeals to tradition to authorize certain interpretations of Scripture are evident in Princeton theology; see A. A. Hodge and B. B. Warfield, "Inspiration," in *PT*, pp. 229, 231; C. Hodge, "The Theology of the Intellect and That of the Feelings," in *PT*, p. 194.
23. Other examples of this same sort of appeal to the Church's teaching authority are R. Johnston (see abbreviations), p. 74; Blocher, in *LEH*, p. 388; Maier, *EhkM*, pp. 54-56; Donald C. Frisk, *Covenant Affirmations: This We Believe* (Chicago: Covenant Press, 1981), p. 29; Henry, *GRA*, 4:224; *CRC*, p. 57.
24. These points became obvious when in interviews with them (see Introduction, nn. 4, 38) both defined Evangelical without reference to the sacraments. Others confirming my observation include Eric Gritsch, *Born Againism* (Philadelphia: Fortress, 1982), p. 92; David Forrester, "Anglican Evangelicalism," *The Clergy Review* 60 (1975): 776; Bloesch, *FEC*, p. 59.
25. A. C. Piepkorn, *Profiles in Belief*, 4 vols. (New York: Harper & Row, 1977–1979), 4:42, provides this information.
26. For the prioritization of the pulpit in American Protestantism, see Richard Quebedeaux, *By What Authority* (San Francisco: Harper & Row, 1982), p. 19. For documentation concerning C. Hodge's critique of Calvin, see Bloesch, *FEC*, pp. 59, 166.
27. Bloesch, *FEC*, p. 59, makes this observation. For a few examples, see EFC, 7; CMA, 9; COGIC, p. 75; BC (Ashland), 3/9; BGC, 8; CBAA; IFCA, 12; CC, 13. The position of a Holiness church like WC, XVII, is somewhat ambiguous. It still refers to Baptism and the Lord's Supper as sacraments but their principal purpose seems to be for believers to "profess" their faith.
28. See Ernst Wilhelm Erdlenbruch and Heinz-Adolf Ritter, *Freie evangelische Gemeinden* (Witten: Bundes-Verlag, 1985), pp. 40-41. Examples of other Evangelical organizations practicing exclusively or at least encouraging believer's baptism include EMF (as per Samouélian, *Le Réveil*, p. 92); EFC (as per Thomas A. McDill, personal letter, May 13, 1985); MBC, IX; Brethren in Christ Church, *The Brethren in Christ and Believer's Baptism* (6-page pamphlet, n.d.); AG, 6; UFM, *Policies and Practice;* all the Baptist churches are discussed in Chap. 8 (e.g., the BGC, 9; GARB).
29. AG, 6, 7; ICFG, *CS*, 12, 14; CN, X, XIII; Blocher, in *LEH*, pp. 390, 396.
30. For Zwingli's position, see his *Von dem touff* (1525), in *Huldreich Zwinglis Sämtliche Werke*, ed. Emil Egli, Walther Köhler, et al. (Leipzig: Verlag von M. Heinsius Nachfolger, 1927), 4:225-226, 240-242. Sattler's position is sketched in Tilman J. van Braght, *Martyr's Mirror* (1660), in George H. Williams, ed., *Spiritual and Anabaptist Writers*, Library of Christian Classics 25 (London: SCM, 1957), p. 140. Arguments in favor of a direct indebtedness to these Reformers are sketched in Chap. 6, n. 7. Points to the contrary are apparent in that the modern Baptist movement originated in the British Isles, and that its propagation on the European continent was accomplished largely in the person of Oncken who was himself

originally sent back to his homeland as a British missionary. For these assessments, see W. L. Lumpkin, "Backgrounds of the Baptist Movement," *Baptist Confessions of Faith*, ed. W. L. Lumpkin (4th printing: Valley Forge, Pa.: Judson, 1980), pp. 1lff.; G. Keith Parker, ed., *Baptists in Europe: History & Confessions of Faith* (Nashville: Broadman, 1982), pp. 53ff.

31. CA, IX, X; FC, SD VII.35; *The Westminster Confession*, XXVIII, XXIX; *The Heidelberg Catechism*, Q.76, 78-79; Walter Künneth, "Thesen über Wiedergeburt—Taufe—Bekehrung," in *TWB*, pp. 106-107. Giertz, in *TWB*, pp. 68-69; though apparently hesitant about baptismal regeneration (according to its president, Paul E. Larsen, personal letter, October 22, 1986), ECC, p. 17, uses language akin to Lutheranism to describe the sacraments and believes Christ is present in them; FMC, XVII, uses language akin to Calvin to describe the sacraments; WC, Const., Art. V, and will baptize infants even though the overall drift of its views moves in the direction of a purely symbolic view.

32. Among Lutherans this tendency has been made evident by my interview with Prof. and Mrs. Peter Beyerhaus, Tübingen, April 15,1983, and by Helmut Burkhardt, *Die biblische Lehre von der Bekehrung* (Giessen and Basel: Brunnen Verlag, 1978), pp. 66-69.

33. See pertinent references in Chap. 13, n. 96.

34. Forrester, "Anglican Evangelicalism," p. 776; Falwell, (see abbreviations) p. 57; *The Evangelical Methodist Church Discipline*, rev. ed. (Altoona, Pa., 1962), pp. 53, 118ff.

35. Also see COGIC, p. 77. For other references to anointing the sick, see Chap. 16, n. 26.

36. According to Brethren in Christ Church publications officer Glen Pierce, personal contact, November 23, 1985, various Brethren congregations celebrate the rite in the context of a full meal.

37. See n. 28 of the Introduction, above.

38. For references, see relevant texts in nn. 3, 9.

39. Relevant references are found in Chap. 6, nn. 31, 24.

40. See n. 19 for sample Evangelical criticisms of the role of tradition. But also see nn. 16, 21-23.

41. Pierard, in *EMA*, p. 168. On the earlier "nativist" orientation, see ibid., pp. 162-163; Ahlstrom, *RHAP*, pp. 855, 555ff.

42. Also see Snyder, in *LEH*, p. 352. But see the problem raised in n. 2 concerning such texts.

43. See p. 325, below.

44. See p. 335-336, below, for references.

45. See n. 10; also National Association of Free Will Baptists, XVII. For references concerning the mainline traditions, see p. 325 below. In addition, the compatibility of this definition with the Anglican tradition, *The Thirty-Nine Articles*, XXIII, should be noted.

46. Quebedeaux, BWA, pp. 21-22, is helpful in showing that the tendency to focus on the preacher's personality is rooted in American revivalism. That Evangelicals or at least Pentecostals are preoccupied with this dimension is confirmed by Falwell, p. 181, William W. Menzies, *Anointed to Serve* (Springfield, Mo.: Gospel Publishing House, 1971), pp. 336-337, and n. 13. See n. 12 for references in Evangelical literature to a preoccupation with the pastor's spirituality.

47. Council of Trent, *The True Catholic Doctrine Concerning the Sacrament of Order*, 23rd Session, 1563, Chap. IV.

48. Henry, *GRA*, 4:160, 161, 167, 374; Packer, *TCU*, p. 58.

49. James Tull, *The Atoning Gospel* (Macon, Ga.: Mercer University Press, 1982), pp. 190-192; Bund Evangelisch-Freikirchlicher Gemeinden in der DDR, *Rechenschaft vom Glauben* (Berlin: Union Verlages, 1980), II/I.3.

50. On Anglican Evangelicals, see Paul A. Welsby, *A History of the Church of England 1945-1980* (New York: Oxford University Press, 1984), p. 212; *Keele Statement,* 76. On the impact of Lewis, see Robert E. Webber, "Are Evangelicals Becoming Sacramental?" *Ecumenical Trends,* March 1985, p. 36.

51. This observation is made by David Hubbard and Clinton McLemore, "Evangelical Churches," in *Ministry in America,* ed. D. Schuller, M. Strommen, and M. Brekke (San Francisco: Harper & Row, 1980), p. 370.

52. In addition to relevant sections of n. 31, see *GK, IV.*27, 52, 53, 79.

53. Carl McIntire, private interview, Frankfurt, West Germany, February 23, 1984.

54. See Chap. 13, n. 96, for references to the importance of these issues to conservative Lutherans. In a personal letter of June 4, 1985, Robert Webber, a leader of the "Catholic [Ecumenical] Evangelicals," expressed optimism that his group will remain open to the "low church" majority.

55. European Lutheran–Reformed Dialogue, *Leuenberg Concord* (1973), 15-20; Lutheran–Reformed Dialogue (USA), *Joint Statement on the Lord's Supper* (1983).

Chapter 18: Social Ethics

1. *1970 Discipline of The Southern Methodist Church,* 55; *1978 Discipline of The Southern Methodist Church,* 55. Also noteworthy is the claim of LCMS, *BS,* 34, that the Church's only recourse in the affairs of the state is to preach the Word of God. Gert Wendelborn, *Gottes Wort und die Gesellschaft* (Berlin: Union Verlag, 1979), pp. 77-78, represents an example of a European commentator unaware of developments in this area in American Evangelicalism.

2. For earlier discussions of these factors, with appropriate references, see above, pp. 56, 63-69, 92-93, 126-127. The argument for the inability of common sense realism adequately to account for the self's relationship to institutions has been made by Mark Noll, "Common Sense Traditions and American Evangelical Thought," *American Quarterly* 37 (Summer 1985): 226. He sees this as a function of certain mind-matter, self-mind dualisms in the Scottish philosophy.

   One must not conclude that the individualistic drift in the thought-patterns of Pietism, in the sense that individual believers and their experience are the ultimate judge of doctrine (see Spener, *PD,* p. 106), totally eradicated social consciousness. Yet classical Pietism does not seem to have had a true social ethic, not an ethic for reform of the social order, just an ethic for the individual Christian's social involvement.

3. This observation by Wendelborn, *Gottes Wort,* pp. 68-69.

4. See pp. 253-254, above, for references. For some references to Conservative Evangelical prioritization of evangelism over social action, see Chap. 15, n. 21.

5. *Lausanne Covenant,* 5; *Chicago Declaration of Evangelicals to Social Concern* (1973), 3.

6. Carl F. H. Henry, *The Uneasy Conscience of Modern Fundamentalism* (Grand Rapids, Mich.: Eerdmans, 1947). This assessment of its impact made by R. Johnston (see abbreviations), pp. 78-79. Another influential text has been T. Smith, *Revivalism and Social Reform* (Nashville: Abingdon, 1957).

7. Statistics from a 1978–1979 survey conducted by Princeton Religious Research Center, reported on and analyzed by James Davison Hunter, *American Evangelicalism* (New Brunswick: Rutgers University Press, 1983), p. 116.

8. WV policy is described in Chap. 10. The priority it gives to evangelism in relation to social action has been articulated by Mooneyham, *MHB*, p. 2. This emphasis on interpersonal social involvement is also reflected in Kenneth S. Kantzer, "Summing Up: An Evangelical View of Church and State," in *Christian Thought and Action* (Carol Stream, Ill.: Christianity Today, 1985), p. 28; Beyerhaus, in *LEH*, p. 287.

9. See Chap. 15, n. 21. Some, like Yoder, *PJ*, pp. 157, 247-248, and as quoted by Escobar, in *LEH*, p. 320, suggest that priority should be given to the building of Christian community. Examples of Evangelicals' critique of the ecumenical movement on grounds of its improper prioritizations have been offered by John Alexander, private interview, Philadelphia, December 1, 1983; *Berlin Declaration on Ecumenism* (Full Version) (1974), 10-11; Hatch, in *EMA*, p. 193; J. I. Packer, "How to Recognize a Christian Citizen," in *CTA*, p. 5.

10. Lausanne Congress Group Report, *In-Depth Evangelization Programs Report*, in *LEH*, p. 696; Mooneyham, *MHB*, p. 2. This is also reported to be the position of John Stott (see Carl Henry, *Confessions of a Theologian* [Waco, Tex.: Word, 1986], p. 350). Opposition to this position is implicitly given by Fundamentalists like George Dollar, *A History of Fundamentalism in America* (Greenville, S.C.: Bob Jones University Press, 1973), pp. 287-288, and by charismatic Larry Christenson, as quoted in Carter Lindberg, *The Third Reformation?* (Macon, Ga.: Mercer University Press, 1983), p. 248.

11. For this characterization, particularly of *Christianity Today* during its earliest years, see R. Johnston (see abbreviations), p. 85; Robert Booth Fowler, *A New Engagement: Evangelical Political Thought, 1966–1976* (Grand Rapids: Eerdmans, 1982), pp. 36-37. The same tendency to avoid delineating specific actions seems to characterize Billy Graham's approach (see Fowler, p. 47).

   For background on Bob Jones' critique of Falwell, see Jeffrey K. Hadden and Charles E. Swann, *Prime Time Preachers* (Reading, Mass.: Addison-Wesley, 1981), p. 155.

12. This observation by Hadden and Swann, *Prime Time Preachers*, pp. 95-96. The relationship between conservative Evangelical anticommunism and the American way of life is discussed above on p. 94. For selected references to this anticommunism, see Carl McIntire, *A Critique of the WCC* (pamphlet, 1983), p. 11; Falwell, "Future-Word," pp. 213, 214-215; Henry, *GRA*, 4:547, 570-571; 6:260, 474; Klaus Bockmühl, *Herausforderung des Marxismus* (Giessen: Brunnen Verlag, 1977); Beyerhaus, *LEH*, pp. 286-287; Konferenz Bekennender Gemeinschaften, "Offener Brief an den Kultusministerien der deutschen Bundesländer" (1977), in *Weg und Zeugnis*, ed. Rudolf Bäumer, Peter Beyerhaus, and Fritz Grünzweig, 2nd ed. (Bad Liebenzell: Verlag der Liebenzeller Mission, 1981), p. 313; NAE, *The Communist Threat* (1967).

13. For a defense of free-market capitalism, see Harold Lindsell, *Free Enterprise: Judeo-Christian Defense* (Wheaton, Ill.: Tyndale House, 1982). Likewise, note the editorial position of *Christianity Today*, as sketched by R. Johnston (see abbreviations), pp. 86-87. The support of Reagan programs by the Moral Majority and the Roundtable (led by James Robison) is common knowledge. (See Hadden and Swann, *Prime Time Preachers*, pp. 125-144, and Erling Jorstad, *The Politics of Moralism* [Minneapolis: Augsburg, 1981], especially pp. 81-104.)

   For a few examples of: (1) anti-abortion, see Schaeffer, *CM*, p. 69; Falwell, "Future-Word," pp. 195ff.; AG, *Abortion;* "Editorial: What Price Abortion?" *Christianity Today*, March 2, 1973, p. 39; Konferenz Bekennender Gemeinschaften, "Rettet das Leben!" (1979), in *Weg und Zeugnis*, especially p. 339; (2)

antipornography, see Falwell, "Future-Word," pp. 201-203; NAE, *Control of Obscenity* (1965), pp. 2-3 (also Anita Bryant's crusade against homosexuality); (3) opposition to secular humanism in the schools, see Falwell, "Future-Word," pp. 199-200; cf. Konferenz Bekennender Gemeinschaften, "Offener Brief zu die Kultusministerien," in *Weg und Zeugnis*, pp. 312 ff.; (4) antifeminism, see Billy Graham, "Jesus and the Liberated Woman," *Ladies Home Journal*, December 1970, p. 42; Harold Lindsell, *The World, the Flesh, and the Devil* (Washington: Canon Press, 1973), especially pp. 149-151; the opposition of the Kyrklig Förnyelse in Sweden to women's ordination seems pertinent to this point; and (5) opposition to the peace movement in favor of a strong national defense, see McIntire, *A Critique of the WCC*, p. 7; Falwell, "Future-Word," pp. 212-213.

14. "Tidings" (announcement of fourth conference of the Internationale Konferenz Bekennender Gemeinschaften) (unpaginated pamphlet, 1982).

15. SBC, *A Statement of Social Principles*, in C. Brownlow Hastings, *Introducing Southern Baptists: Their Faith & Their Life* (New York: Paulist, 1981), p. 141; Oscar Sakrausky, "The Spiritual Foundation of Europe," lecture presented at the 4th Conference of the Internationale Konferenz Bekennender Gemeinschaften, Strasbourg, France, September 30, 1982; cf. Falwell, "Future-Word," p. 212.

16. Falwell, "Future-Word," p. 206. Information about *Christianity Today* is provided by Fowler, *A New Engagement*, p. 171. IVCF was an early leader in the recent struggle against racism, banning segregation as an official policy as early as 1948. See Pete Lowman, *The Day of His Power* (Leicester, England: Inter-Varsity, 1983), p. 301.

17. "Graham's Mission to Moscow," *Christianity Today*, December 1, 1978, p. 52; Falwell, "Future-Word," pp. 190, 212, 213. For Schaeffer's views, see Bloesch, *FEC*, p. 62.

18. NAE, *Environment and Ecology* (1971), p. 3; Sakrausky (see n. 15).

19. See R. Johnston, pp. 86-87.

20. Henry, *GRA*, 6:474; John Warwick Montgomery, "God's Country," *Christianity Today*, January 30, 1970, p. 40; Nicholas Wolterstorff, "Reflections on Patriotism," *The Reformed Journal*, July-August 1976, pp. 10-13; Mark Hatfield, *Conflict and Conscience* (Waco, Tex.: Word, 1971), pp. 65, 67-68, 161.

21. Henry, *GRA*, 4:552; 5:163; 6:407ff.

22. Ibid., 6:451. Cf. Fowler, *A New Engagement*, p. 81. Similar openness to the responsibility to challenge unjust laws is expressed by Mark Hatfield, *Conflict and Conscience*, p. 167; Mark Hatfield, *Between a Rock and a Hard Place* (Waco, Tex.: Word, 1976), pp. 72-73.

23. Carl F. H. Henry, personal letter, January 4, 1987. Similar reservations stated by Stanley Mooneyham of WV are also cited in Hadden and Swann, *Prime Time Preachers*, pp. 154-155.

24. AG, *Abortion*, NAE, *Abortion* (1971), p. 4; Bloesch, *FEC*, p. 135.

25. Brethren in Christ Church views are articulated by C. N. Hostetter Jr., *The Christian and War* (unpaginated pamphlet; Elizabethtown, Pa., n.d.). This topic is discussed again and other "peace churches" are noted on p. 280.

26. R. Johnston, pp. 88-90, provides examples of these positions in *The Reformed Journal*. For Hatfield, see his *Conflict and Conscience*, pp. 20, 36, 54, and *Between a Rock and a Hard Place*, pp. 37, 208. The WV viewpoint has been articulated by Stanley Mooneyham, *What Do You Say to a Hungry World?* (Waco, Tex.: Word, 1975), pp. 210-211.

The WV development scheme is sketched in *World Vision International* (12-page brochure, n.d.), pp. 2, 7-8. A good example of the appearance of such a view, emphasizing indigenous self-development, in WCC statements is evident in its Nairobi Assembly Section Report, *Human Development: Ambiguities of Power, Technology, and Quality of Life* (1975), 5-7, 11-13, 17. For reference to NAE spokesmen raising questions about the advisability of school prayer, see *Time,* September 10, 1984, p. 30.

27. See n. 20 for references.

28. For an example of this orientation, see Jim Wallis, *Agenda for Biblical People* (New York: Harper & Row, 1976), p. 137. Henry, *GRA,* 6:436-437, notes how widely these questions are raised in Evangelical circles.

29. This trend is suggested by Fowler, *A New Engagement,* p. 96, and is made evident by the present leadership of ESA.

30. Fowler, *A New Engagement,* p. 130, cites a number of radicals calling for this kind of revolution. In the earlier stages of the "radical Christian" movement an important influence was exerted by Church of the Brethren leaders Art Gish and Dale Brown (see Quebedeaux, *WE,* p. 147). Fowler, p. 124, notes the radicals' prior concern with the plight of the poor. See Jim Wallis, "A View from the Evangelical Left," in *CTA,* p. 27. Skepticism about the ecology movement has been voiced by John Alexander, "What Matters?" *The Other Side,* July-August 1974, p. 4.

For a few examples of this group's positions on: (1) resource distribution, see *Chicago Declaration of Evangelicals to Social Concern,* 6; Sider, *RCAH,* especially p. 82; R. Johnston, pp. 98-100; (2) simple life-style, see Sider, *RCAH,* p. 82; Clark H. Pinnock, "The Secular Prophets and the Christian Faith," in *Quest for Reality: Christianity and the Counter-Culture,* ed. Carl Henry et al. (Downers Grove, Ill.: InterVarsity, 1973), pp. 133-135; cf. Wheaton '83, (see abbreviations), III; (3) disarmament, see Jim Wallis, "Nuclear War by 1999?" *Sojourners,* February 1977, p. 4; *The Seoul Declaration, toward an Evangelical Theology for the Third World* (1982) 4; and (4) feminism, see Chap. 13, note 63, and Fowler, *A History,* pp. 199ff. Evangelical homosexuality has even been given a kind of support by Letha Scanzoni and Virginia Mollenkott, *Is the Homosexual My Neighbor?* (New York: Harper & Row, 1978), p. 122.

31. Orlando Costas, *The Church and Its Mission* (Wheaton, Ill.: Tyndale, 1975), pp. 221, 223; *Thailand Statement* (1980), quoted by Costas in *JTTW,* p. 4; Norberto Saracco, "The Liberating Options of Jesus," in *JTTW,* pp. 59-60.

32. Richard G. Hutcheson Jr., *Mainline Churches and the Evangelicals* (Atlanta: John Knox, 1981), p. 170, notes Costas' influence. American Evangelicals relying on these commitments include Sider, in *JTTW,* pp. 352, 369, and *Sojourners* magazine (see Quebedeaux, *WE,* p. 150).

33. This characterization by Fowler, *A New Engagement,* p. 139. Such an "approach-avoidance" pattern with regard to Marxism and liberation theology is evident in David Ho Sang and Roger Ringenberg, "Towards an Evangelical Caribbean Theology," *Evangelical Review of Theology* 7 (1983): 144-145; Escobar et al, in *LEH,* pp. 60-61; Sider, in *JTTW,* p. 369; Costas, *The Church and Its Mission,* pp. 221, 251.

34. Jim Wallis, "The Vehicle for the Vision," *Sojourners,* January 1977, p. 3; Clark Pinnock, "The Christian as a Revolutionary Man," *The Post-American,* I, No. 4 (1972). Cf. Yoder, *PJ,* p. 151; Fowler, *A New Engagement,* pp. 118-122.

35. This assessment by Fowler, *A New Engagement,* p. 125. See for example Sider, *RCAH,* pp. 82-83.

36. Fowler, *A New Engagement,* p. 127, notes the impact of this view. See Yoder, *PJ,* pp. 150ff.

37. Yoder, *PJ*, pp. 150-152, 205, 207, 240, 242-248. Cf. *The Waterland Confession* (1580), XXXVI-XXXVII.
38. See p. 278 for two other Conservative Evangelical churches still maintaining this position. Like COGIC, the Brethren in Christ Church, *The Christian View of Race* (pamphlet; Nappanee, Ind.: Evangel Press, n.d.), and *Ecology* (6-page brochure, n.d.), exhibit a social ethical orientation at least akin to the progressive centrists, if not the radicals. Other peace churches, like the MBC, exhibit nowhere near the social concern that these churches do. (See *We Recommend . . .* [Fresno, Cal.: MBC, 1978].) At earlier stages in their history, the AG (see William W. Menzies, *Anointed to Serve* [Springfield, Mo.: Gospel Publishing House, 1971], pp. 326-328), and the Russian Baptists as well as the All-Union Council of Evangelical Christians-Baptists [in the USSR], largely under the influence of Mennonites, practiced pacifism in the early stages of their development. (See Walter Sawatsky, *Soviet Evangelicals since World War II* [Kitchener, Ont., and Scottdale, Pa.: Herald Press, 1981], pp. 37, 115ff.)
39. Yoder, *PJ*, pp. 151-153, 247-250; Jim Wallis, "The Move to Washington, D.C.," *Post-American* 4 (August-September 1975): 4. Cf. Fowler, *A New Engagement*, pp. 127-128.
40. Richard J. Mouw, *Politics and the Biblical Drama* (Grand Rapids, Mich.: Eerdmans, 1976), pp. 112-113, 98ff., 137-138.
41. Francis Schaeffer, as quoted in Falwell (see abbreviations), pp. 167-168; Henry, *GRA*, 4:586-588. Fowler, *A New Engagement*, p. 78, notes how even Henry has received criticism for his trail-blazing efforts in social ethics.
42. Examples of radicals not so inclined fervently to affirm detailed inerrancy include John Alexander, "Some Inerrant Thoughts on Scripture," *The Other Side*, May-June 1976, p. 9; Jim Wallis, "Revolt on Evangelical Frontiers: A Response," *Christianity Today*, June 21, 1974, p. 20; Donald Dayton, personal letter, January 24, 1985.
43. Examples of such criticisms include Wallis, *Agenda for Biblical People*, p. 1; John Alexander, "The Making of a Young Evangelical," *The Other Side*, March-April 1975, pp. 2-4, 60, 62.
   For references to radical Evangelicals who in arguing for women's rights make their points by criticizing the authority of certain biblical authors, see Chap. 13, n. 63.
44. John Alexander, private interview, Philadelphia, December 1, 1983. Quebedeaux, *WE*, p. 166, suggests that there are a number of left-wing Evangelicals in North America who have reached this point.
45. See R. Johnston (see abbreviations), pp. 76, 79-80.
46. Hatfield, *Conflict and Conscience*, p. 36. A few of the countless examples of this orientation follow: *Chicago Declaration of Evangelicals to Social Concern*, 11; International Congress on World Evangelization (Lausanne Congress) Working Group Report, *An Answer to Lausanne*, 7; NAE, *Saving the Seventies* (1970); Henry, *GRA*, 3:122, 125; 4:525, 576; Yoder, *PJ*, pp. 12ff., 122; Padilla, in *LEH*, p. 145; Jim Wallis, "What Does Washington Have to Say to Grand Rapids?" *Sojourners*, July 1977, p. 4; Ronald Sider, "Jesus' Resurrection and the Search for Peace and Justice," *The Christian Century*, November 3, 1982, p. 1106; Vorstand des Arbeitskreis für evangelikale Theologie, Vorstand meeting, Frankfurt, November 15, 1985; MBC, *Peace and Nonresistance* (1969); SBC, XV; *The Westminster Confession*, XXIII.
47. Schaeffer, *CM*, pp. 32, 116, 121. For information on the Christian reconstructionists, see Rodney Clapp, "Democracy as Heresy," *Christianity Today*, February

20, 1987, pp. 17-23. For this sort of interpretation of Bright's and Robertson's views, see Henry, *GRA*, 6:440.

48. See Chap. 7, n. 3. The position of the Radical Reformation is well articulated in *The Waterland Confession*, XXXVII, insofar as it shows how Christology authorizes the social ethic of its Anabaptist subscribers.

49. USSR Dis. Bapt., 7; SBC, XVII; CBAA; Falwell, "Future-Word," pp. 189, 192-193; Kantzer, "Summing Up," pp. 28-29. The separation of church and state among European Evangelicals is also implied insofar as they largely belong to Free Churches not associated with (separate from) state sponsorship.

50. Falwell, "Future-Word," p. 191.

51. Henry, *GRA*, 4:512, 535, 546; 6:406, 414, 450, 454; Rodrigo Tano, "Toward an Evangelical Asian Theology," *Evangelical Review of Theology* 7 (April 1983): 164-165; Stott, *BC*, p. 142 (speaks explicitly of the two kingdoms). The appeal by Jerry Falwell, "Future-Word," pp. 188, 189, to common values shared by Christians and non-Christians suggests an appeal to the creation doctrine as warrant for ethics. Also see Evangelical Congregational Church, *Discipline*, 143.1.2.5; FMC, *The Book of Discipline 1979*, §330; COGIC, pp. 129-130; AG, *Homosexuality*, p. 4; NAE, *Environment and Ecology* (1971), p. 3.

In addition to these instances one may identify occasions in Conservative Evangelical documents where both creation and Christology (or the gospel) are simultaneously appealed to as warrants. For example, see The Latin American Theological Fraternity, *From Obedience to Proclamation: The Declaration of Jarabacoa* (1983), in *Transformation* 2 (January/March 1985): 24, 26; Henry, *GRA*, 3:69ff. *The Lausanne Covenant*, 5, also combines its appeal to the doctrine of creation with an appeal to reconciliation and the gospel as ethical warrant. An appeal to the doctrine of creation as warrant is evident even in the Evangelical movement's pre-Fundamentalist forebears. See *The Fundamentals*, 12 vols. (Chicago: Testimony Publishing, 1910–1915), 6:39; Charles G. Finney's rationale for civil disobedience as cited in D. Dayton, *DEH*, p. 47.

52. Martin Luther, *Temporal Authority: To What Extent It Should Be Obeyed* (1523), WA 11, 245-280/LW 45, 81-129; Abraham Kuyper, *Lectures on Calvinism* (Grand Rapids, Mich.: Eerdmans, 1931), 78-109. For the impact of such a view on the CRC, see *Acta Synodi 1924*, pp. 113-139, 141-150. Also see Chap. 7, n. 3 for a reference to something like this view in Calvin. Cf. R. Johnston, p. 109.

Chapter 19: The Ecumenical Movement

1. See especially Chap. 13, n. 26; Chap. 11, n. 7, for references.

2. Christopher Lasch, *Culture of Narcissism* (New York: W. W. Norton, 1979), especially 28, 29, 40-41, 103, 325, 374ff.; Robert N. Bellah, et al., *Habits of the Heart* (Berkeley, Calif.: University of California Press, 1985), pp. 75-81, 139-141, 152. The analysis of Peter Berger, especially in his *The Sacred Canopy* (New York: Doubleday, 1969), applies to the impact of modernity in breaking down the norms of the religious community.

3. These reflections concerning the suitability of Evangelical theological themes for our Western cultural context do not entail a conscious neglect of the situation in Asia, Africa, and Latin America. The question of the appropriateness of these themes for these regions is noted in the next chapter. Focusing on their appropriateness for the West simply underlines that the logic of Evangelical theology is more dictated by Western (perhaps American) concerns, such that its appropriateness for other regions tends more to be a fortuitous accident.

4. See n. 24 of the Introduction, above, for examples.
5. *Berlin Declaration on Ecumenism* (Full Version), 1-2.
6. Henry, *GRA*, 6:32; AG, *Rejection of the World Council of Churches*, (1955), 1, in Hollenweger, *EC*, p. 588.
7. Gerhard Rost and Gerhard Maier, "Einführung," in *TWB*, p. 7; John P. Galbraith, *Why The Orthodox Presbyterian Church?* (Philadelphia: The Orthodox Presbyterian Church, n.d.), pp. 4-5.
8. Henry, *GRA*, 4:17, 538; 6:267, 363; Packer, "How to Recognize a Christian Citizen," in *CTA*, p. 5; Bloesch, *FEC*, p. 80; Susumu Uda, "Biblical Authority and Evangelism," in *LEH*, p. 87; Internationale Konferenz Bekennender Gemeinschaften, *Für die unverfälschte Fortsetzung von Lausanne* (1974), 4; *Berlin Declaration on Ecumenism* (Full Version), 6. Also see Rodger C. Bassham, *Mission Theology: 1948–1975* (Pasadena: Wm. Carey Library, 1979), p. 225, for a similar assessment by Billy Graham. For general Evangelical critiques of liberation theology, see n. 26 of Introduction.
9. Letter, Bekenntnisbewegung to EKD, p. 262; Kurt Heimbucher, "Evangelische Allianz und Weltkirchenrat," *Evangelischer Allianzbrief*, December 1984, p. 3; Robert Dubarry, "Brève Histoire de l'Association," in *Association Evangélique d'Eglises Baptistes de Langue Française 1921–1971* (published pamphlet, n.d.), p. 47; Jerry Falwell, "Future-Word," in *The Fundamentalist Phenomenon*, ed. Falwell et al. (Garden City, N.Y.: Doubleday, 1981), p. 218.

    Purported hierarchical tendencies in the WCC are charged by W. Dayton Roberts, *Strachan of Costa Rica. Missionary Insights and Strategies* (Grand Rapids, Mich.: Eerdmans, 1971), p. 68; Henry, *GRA*, 4:590.
10. Carl McIntire, *A Critique of the World Council of Churches by the International Council of Christian Churches* (published pamphlet, 1983), pp. 7ff.
11. Kirchliche Sammlung um Bibel und Bekenntnis, *Ratzeburger Thesen zur Leuenberger Konkordie* (1972), in *Weg und Zeugnis*, ed. Rudolf Bäumer et al., 2nd ed. (Bad Liebenzell: Verlag der Liebenzeller Mission, 1981), pp. 188-193; *Wheaton Declaration* (1966), 72; Bloesch, *FEC*, pp. 101-102; Henry, *GRA*, 3:381. This does seem to be the approach of the *Leuenberg Concord*, 1.17, 29ff.

    Among other Evangelicals accusing the ecumenical movement of perverting the gospel are CMA, *Manual*, p. 208; IFCA, Art. IV, Sec. 2(a); UFM, *Policies and Practice* (unpaginated brochure, Bala-Cynwyd, Pa., n.d.).
12. Henry, *GRA*, 1:406; Peter Beyerhaus, "The Ecclesiological-Ecumenical Situation Before Vancouver 1983" (lecture presented at the 4th Conference of the Internationale Konferenz Bekennender Gemeinschaften, Strasbourg, France, October 2, 1982); Carl F. H. Henry and W. Stanley Mooneyham, eds., *One Race, One Gospel, One Task. World Congress on Evangelism, Berlin 1966*, 2 vols. (Minneapolis: World Wide Publications, 1967), 1:16; *Wheaton Declaration*, 72; AG, *Rejection of the World Council of Churches*, 7, in Hollenweger, *EC*, p. 589; Timothy L. Smith, "An Historical Perspective on Evangelicalism and Ecumenism," *Mid-Stream* 22 (July/October 1983): 321.
13. Henry, *GRA*, 4:273.
14. Heimbucher, "Evangelische Allianz," p. 3; Gert Wendelborn, *Gottes Wort und die Gesellschaft* (Berlin: Union Verlag, 1979), p. 94; *Erklärung des Theologischen Konventes zum Arnoldshainer Anti-Rassismus-Beschluss* (1970), in *Weg und Zeugnis*, p. 226.
15. Günther Gassmann, in *Neue transkonfessionelle Bewegungen*, ed. G. Gassmann et al. (Frankfurt: Otto Lembeck, 1976), pp. 16-17.
16. See nn. 31-33 of the preceding chapter.

17. Henry, *GRA*, 3:121.
18. This characterization is by Richard G. Hutcheson Jr., *Mainline Churches and the Evangelicals: A Challenging Crisis?* (Atlanta: John Knox, 1981), pp. 169-170. For the Latin American situation, particularly in Costa Rica, where Evangelicals have been divided over the inroads of liberation theology and the failure to prioritize evangelism, see *Lutheran World Information, 8/85*, p. 14. But Bassham, *Mission Theology*, pp. 262-263, claims that at least as recently as 1969 Latin American Evangelicals were still prioritizing evangelism.
19. This priority is suggested insofar as, at least in the planning process, the Faith and Order Commission's first post-Lima study devoted to social implications of church unity still was concerned to address questions concerning church unity, how the impact of distinct cultures on creedal formulations may challenge church unity. (See *Notes for a Study, Lima*, in *Towards Visible Unity* [Geneva: WCC, 1982], p. 229.)
20. Peter Beyerhaus, private interview, April 15, 1983, and other European Evangelical theologians have reacted with some appreciation of BEM. (See *Stellungnahme des Hauptvorstands der Deutschen Evangelischen Allianz zum "LIMA-PAPIER"* [1984]; Heimbucher, "Evangelische Allianz," p. 3.) But the Ludwig-Hofacker-Vereinigung raises questions concerning the adequacy of BEM's Christology (see Heimbucher, p. 3). And, most significantly, the Deutsche Evangelische Allianz statement notes an undue emphasis in BEM on the need to achieve common understanding on the sacraments and the ordained ministry as the chief means of unity. This is done at the cost of appropriate emphasis on the believer's appropriation of the gospel through conversion and regeneration. In short, BEM's priorities are deemed incorrect by these Evangelicals.
21. For examples of this kind of hermeneutic in WCC statements, see *Towards Visible Unity*, pp. 136, 185; WCC Vancouver Assembly Issue Group Report, *Learning in Community* (1983), 21, 27; WCC Conference on Faith, Science and the Future Section Report, in *The Nature of Science and the Nature of Faith* (Cambridge, Mass., 1979), 2, 1. Criticisms of the ecumenical movement for its views on biblical authority have been leveled by Evangelicals like Henry (*GRA*, 4:17, 234).
22. *The Lausanne Covenant*, 7; *Berlin Declaration on Ecumenism* (Full Version), 7(g); EFC, *What Is The Evangelical Free Church?* p. 7; Heimbucher, "Evangelische Allianz," p. 3.
23. This observation by Bassham, *Mission Theology*, p. 246.
24. Among those maintaining that Christians already possess a "spiritual unity" are NAE, 7; WEF; *Constitution of the International Council of Christian Churches*, II(j); EPA, *Doctrinal Statement* (n.d.), g; CCCC, 7; Blocher, in *LEH*, pp. 380-382; Gerstner, in *E*, pp. 32-33.
25. This aim has been explicitly articulated by Campus Crusade–Europe Director, Kalevi Lehtinen, private interview, March 23, 1984; Pete Lowman, *The Day of His Power* (Leicester, England: InterVarsity, 1983), pp. 336-337.
26. Lehtinen, interview; for the grounding of this orientation in classical Pietism, see Spener, *PD*, p. 99.
27. Beyerhaus, "The Ecclesiological-Ecumenical Situation Before Vancouver 1983"; McIntire, *A Critique of the WCC*, p. 1. cf. Bloesch, *FEC*, pp. 5-6.
28. EFC, *What Is The Evangelical Free Church?* pp. 4-5; cf. *The Lausanne Covenant*, 7; Bloesch, *FEC*, pp. 130-131; Webber, *CR*, pp. 55ff.
29. David Hubbard and Clinton McLemore, "Evangelical Churches," in *Ministry in America*, ed. D. Schuller, M. Strommen, and M. Brekke (San Francisco: Harper & Row, 1980), p. 392.

30. Günther Gassmann and Harding Meyer, *The Unity of the Church, LWF Report* 15 (Geneva, 1983), pp. 9, 12-15, 30-32.
31. Bassham, *Mission Theology,* pp. 230, 241, contends that the Evangelical movement has not yet been able explicitly to articulate its model for church unity. But something like the model of reconciled diversity has been advocated by G. W. Bromiley, *The Unity and Disunity of the Church* (Grand Rapids, Mich.: Eerdmans, 1958), p. 90; Bloesch, *FEC,* p. 133; Blocher, in *LEH,* pp. 382, 391, 394-395, who would ground the idea of unity in the midst of diversity in the pattern of the Trinity. Also see Timothy Smith's views, discussed above, p. 230.
32. LCMS, *The Nature and Implications of the Concept of Fellowship* (1981), pp. 24-27.
33. Sandeen, *OF,* pp. 4-5, describes the logic of this Zionism implicit in dispensationalist thought. George Dollar, *A History of Fundamentalism* (Greenville, S.C.: Bob Jones University Press, 1973), pp. 60-62, documents the appearance of these themes in the pre-Fundamentalist Prophetic Conferences. Cf. David A. Rausch, *Zionism within Early American Fundamentalism, 1878-1918: A Convergence of Two Traditions* (New York, 1979).

Evangelicals maintaining such a position in the present include Falwell's "Future-Word," pp. 190, 215; Henry, *GRA,* 6:488-489; 5:193; 3:26, 119, 143; Francis Schaeffer, *Joshua and the Flow of Biblical History* (Downers Grove, Ill.: InterVarsity Press, 1975), pp. 56-65, 113; Beyerhaus, in *LEH,* pp. 292-293; GARB, XVIII.
34. The ecumenical movement is rejected on these grounds by Harold Lindsell, as quoted by Bassham, *Mission Theology,* p. 213; Dollar, *A History,* p. 253; AG, *General Council Minutes, 1963,* p. 41.

Chapter 20: The Essence of Conservative Evangelicalism

1. Polemics mark the corpus of Francis Schaeffer's work and occupy many pages of Henry's *GRA*. For example, see Schaeffer, *SER,* pp. 50ff.; Henry, *GRA,* 4:196-200, 470-475, 555-592. Among those maintaining that the movement is held together by polemics are H. Bolleter, "Wer sind die Evangelikalen?" lecture broadcast on Swiss radio, Btrg. III/1; "An Interview with Donald Dayton," *Faith and Thought* 1 (Spring 1983): 26; John H. Yoder, "A Critique of North American Evangelical Ethics," *Transformation* 2 (January/March 1985): 29, 31. Also maintaining the continuing influence of the [Fundamentalist] separatist influence on the Evangelical movement are John H. Yoder, private interview held during the Lutheran World Federation Assembly, Budapest, July 30, 1984, and Timothy L. Smith, "An Historical Perspective on Evangelicalism and Ecumenism," *MidStream* 22 (1983): 320-321.

Earlier discussion has shown that the Evangelical movement is also held together by a common theological logic, including an emphasis on sanctification or the regenerate life-style. Some, like Blocher, in *LEH,* p. 380, suggest that the Church/Evangelicalism is held together by a common commitment to evangelism.
2. This point's qualification, that Evangelicals at least remain *in dialogue with* these concepts, permits our description of Evangelicalism to take account of Evangelicals on the left wing of the movement. For further elaboration, see pp. 296-297.
3. I did not feel authorized to add these features to the description in view of the fact that they were not unanimously mentioned by my numerous Evangelical contacts as essential features of Conservative Evangelical identity. However, it should be noted that strong arguments have been made on behalf of the expectation

of Christ's imminent return as an essential feature of this identity. We have already noted that some Pentecostals deem eschatology to be a governing commitment in Pentecostalism (Chap. 7, n. 26). And it has been identified as the spur to evangelism by *The Lausanne Covenant* (1974), 15, and Beyerhaus, in *LEH*, p. 294. Among those Evangelicals insisting that belief in an imminent second coming is an essential feature of Evangelicalism are those listed in Chap. 13, n. 104, and also Prof. and Mrs. Peter Beyerhaus, interview, April 15, 1983; Gerhard Maier, interview, April 27, 1983; DEA; Evangelical Alliance [of Great Britain] (see abbreviations); Henry, *GRA*, 3:20, 73-74; 4:474; FMC, XIX; WC, XVIII; ICFG, XV.

4. These commitments are quite clearly illustrated by Schaeffer, *SER*, p. 24, and Howard Loewen, as discussed by Henry, *GRA*, 4:267. See my earlier discussion on pp. 209-210 for further elucidation of and documentation for these points.

5. Robert Webber, personal letter, June 4, 1985.

6. See earlier discussion and references above on pp. 113-114, 142, 143, 225, and Chap. 13, n. 90. Also see Henry, *GRA*, 4:179. Likewise David A. Hubbard, *What We Believe and Teach* (pamphlet, reprinted 1981), p. 5, and in his March 13, 1985 interview with me, implies that the affirmation of plenary inspiration is what gives the Evangelical movement its distinct identity. Also recall that even in the case of European Evangelicals, heavily influenced by Pietism, and Third World Evangelicals, these parties are still in dialogue with these concepts, either affirming infallibility in a qualified sense or at least (in the case of European conservatives) affirming divine inspiration.

7. See earlier discussions, above, on pp. 121, 123-124, 128, 132-134, 253-257; also see Chap. 16, n. 39; Chap. 2, n. 38. The last note speaks to those who would have hesitations about our contention concerning the centrality of sanctification as a commitment which unifies all Evangelicals.

8. See Chap. 15, n. 18 for a few references to the priority Conservative Evangelicals place on evangelism and foreign missions. James Davison Hunter, *American Evangelicalism* (New Brunswick: Rutgers University Press, 1983), pp. 67-68, shows how this priority reflects strongly in the attitudes of American Evangelicals.

9. See Yoder, "A Critique," and T. Smith, "An Historical Perspective" (cited in n. 1); Bernard Ramm, *The Evangelical Heritage* (Waco: Word, 1973), pp. 91-92; Chap. 17, n. 5. The Fundamentalist churches and organizations discussed in Part II maintain a separatist position. Also see Chap. 4, n. 15.

10. See Chap. 13, n. 26, for references to this characteristic Evangelical assessment of the contemporary social context. Also see my earlier discussion on p. 255. These observations concerning the generative context of Conservative Evangelicalism confirm an earlier study by the Institute for Ecumenical Research. See Günther Gassmann, et al., eds., *Neue transkonfessionelle Bewegungen* (Frankfurt: Verlag Otto Lembeck, 1976), p. 12.

11. Bloesch, *FEC*, p. 56. Also see Chap. 14, nn. 23, 24, for other pertinent references.

Chapter 21: The Proclamation of the Gospel in Contemporary Society

1. By "mainline churches" I refer to the large historic churches which largely control the religious establishment and exercise the most visible Christian influence on the cultures of their nations. These churches usually are comprised of a membership reflecting marked diversity. However, as we have noted, at least in recent decades the leadership in these churches generally has been more liberal and ecumenically inclined. Richard G. Hutcheson Jr., *Mainline Churches and the Evangelicals: A Challenging Crisis?* (Atlanta: John Knox, 1981), pp. 39, 36-37.

2. See pp. 118-119, 128, 256-257 and corresponding notes for discussion and references concerning these other traditions' overriding concerns. For the Lutheran emphasis, see n. 7 below.

3. See Heiko A. Oberman, "The Shape of Late Medieval Thought: The Birthpangs of the Modern Era," *Archiv für Reformationsgeschichte* 64 (1973): 13-33; Lewis S. Spitz, *The Renaissance and Reformation Movements* (Chicago: Rand McNally, 1971), p. 325.

4. *The Smalcald Articles* (1537), III/II.2-4.

5. Martin Luther, *Lectures on Romans* (1515–1516), WA 56, 172, 3/LW 25, 151.

6. *SA,* III/III.24ff.

7. *Apology,* IV.2; *FC,* SD III.6.

8. Relevant references and pertinent earlier discussion of characteristic Conservative Evangelical assessments of our social context and the fit between these and its theological emphases are given on pp. 208-209, 254-256, 296-299, and in Chap. 13, n. 26.

9. *CA,* I.1-4; III.1-2; *Apology,* I;1; III.1; *The Second Helvetic Confession,* II,XI; *The Thirty-Nine Articles,* I,II; *The* [Methodist] *Articles of Religion,* 1,2; [Baptist] *Second London Confession* (1677), I,VIII; *The* [Mennonite] *Waterland Confession,* I-III, VIII.

10. Martin Luther, *Lectures on Genesis* (1535–1536), WA 42, 44, 8/LW 1, 58-59; Martin Luther, *Predigten des Jahres 1533,* WA 37, 41, 14. See Paul Althaus, *The Theology of Martin Luther,* trans. Robert Schultz (Philadelphia: Fortress, 1970), pp. 199-200.

11. *FC,* SD VIII.20, 31, 36, 4; Martin Luther, *Die Disputation de divinitate et humanitate Christi* (1540), WA 39ᴵᴵ, 93, 4ff.

12. For the Reformers' purpose, see *FC,* SD, VII.4,2; cf. Cyril of Alexandria, *De incarnatione unigeniti,* in *Sources chrétiennes* (Paris, 1940—), 97:292; *The Westminster Confession,* VIII.7; [Baptist] *Second London Confession,* VIII.7.

13. Martin Luther, *Gospel for the Main Christmas Service* (1522), WA 10ᴵ/ᴵ, 188, 6/ LW 52, 46; Martin Luther, *Sermons on the Gospel of St. John* (1540), WA 47, 210, 11/LW 22, 504. Cf. references in Chap. 14, n. 12.

14. Henry, *GRA,* 2:59-60, explicitly affirms the *finitum non capax infiniti.* But the positions of Evangelicals cited in Chap. 14, n. 10 also imply a rejection of the *finitum capax infiniti.*

15. Martin Luther, *On the Councils and the Church* (1539), WA 50, 589, 21/LW 41, 103. Cf. Martin Luther, *Works on the First Twenty-two Psalms* (1519–1521), WA 5,50,9/LW 14,316; *FC,* SD VIII.31-38, 44-45.

16. See Chap. 14, nn. 7, 9, for selected references.

17. See pp. 232-233, above.

Chapter 22: Justification and the Christian Life

1. *Apology,* IV.2; *FC,* SD III.6; *SA,* II/I.1, does designate Christology rather than justification as the "first and chief article." But these loci are deemed compatible/ identical.

2. *FC,* SD III.6; Martin Luther, *Die Promotionsdisputation von Palladius und Tilemann* (1527), WA 39ᴵ, 205,1.

3. See Chap. 16, especially pp. 245-246.

4. See pp. 244-247, above.

5. *FC,* Ep. III.8-11; *FC* SD III; 18-24. cf. *The Westminster Confession,* XI; Angli-canism, *The Thirty-Nine Articles,* XI,XII; *The* [Methodist] *Articles of Religion,* 9, 10; relevant mainline documents are cited on p. 314.
6. *SA* III/XIII.1; Martin Luther, *The Freedom of a Christian* (1520), WA 7, 25, 34/ LW 31, 351-352; cf. relevant documents cited on p. 315.
7. This analogy was framed by Martin Luther, *Treatise on Good Works* (1520), WA 6, 207, 15/LW 44, 26-27.
8. Examples of how Evangelicals understand Lutherans in this way are apparent in Bloesch, *FEC,* p. 114; Marlin E. Miller, "The Church in the World: A Mennonite Perspective," *The Covenant Quarterly* 41 (1983): 46. For the prominence of a purely forensic understanding of justification in Lutheranism, see David Hollaz, *Examen Theologicum Acroamaticum* (1707), 928; LCMS, *BS,* 1 7. Gerhard Forde, "Forensic Justification and Law in Lutheran Theology," in *Justification by Faith, Lutherans and Catholics in Dialogue VII,* ed. H. George Anderson et al. (Min-neapolis: Augsburg, 1985), p. 291, notes the continuing impact of the forensic view on Lutheranism.
9. For references to the element of struggle in the Christian life, see *SA,* III/III.40; Martin Luther, *Defense and Explanation of All the Articles* (1521), WA 7, 344, 6/LW 32,28; Martin Luther, *Commentary on Psalm 51* (1538), WA 40^{II}, 322, 6-11/LW 12, 307. For references to this theme in other mainline Protestant traditions, see *The Westminster Confession,* XVI.6; *The Second Helvetic Confession,* XVI; Anglicanism, *The Thirty-Nine Articles,* XV; [Baptist] *Second London Confession,* XVI.6. By implication these references suggest the concept of *simul iustus et peccator,* the believer as *totally* righteous and *totally* sinful. For references in the Lutheran tradition to a more explicit affirmation of the concept, see *GK,* II.54, and the texts cited in Chap. 14, n. 18.

As Chap. 4, n. 18, indicates, this way of understanding the *simul* differs from its characteristic treatment by the Evangelical movement (as it usually deems the Christian *partly* sinful and *partly* righteous). Yet this difference need not divide Lutherans and Conservative Evangelicals. For at times the Lutheran tradition has also conceptualized the *simul* in terms of a *partim-partim.* (See Martin Luther, *Lectures on Romans* [1515–1516], WA 56, 442, 12ff./LW 25,434; Martin Luther, *D. Martin Lutheri tertia disputatio [de loco Rom 3, 28],* WA 39^{I}, 83,16-17.) The occasional reliance of this tradition on a Greek philosophical view of persons also opens the way to a compatibility with the partim-partim view, as on such grounds one is only partly righteous and only partly sinful. (See above, pp. 233-235, especially Chap. 14, n. 26.)

That precedents exist for not considering this issue church-dividing are evident in the U.S.A.'s Lutheran–Roman Catholic dialogue. For the Roman Catholic tra-dition like the Evangelical movement apparently rejects conceptualizing the *simul* in terms of a *totus-totus* (Council of Trent, *Canons Concerning Justification,* Sixth Session, 1547, Canon 25,7), though it does seem somewhat open to a *partim-partim* view (Council of Trent, *Decree Concerning Original Sin,* Fifth Session 1546; *Decree Concerning Justification,* Chap. XI). Yet members of the dialogue do not deem this issue as necessarily dividing Lutherans and Roman Catholics (H. George Anderson et al., eds., *Justification by Faith* [Minneapolis: Augsburg, 1985], §§102-104). Why should the same issue divide the Evangelical movement and Lutheranism?

10. See the earlier discussion on pp. 250-252 and its associated notes for pertinent references. See especially Chap. 16, n. 33 for a fuller discussion of the sense in

which even those related to Holiness teaching who claim that sanctification begins in justification/regeneration actually do not relate these two realities.

11. William Ames, *Fides est acquiescentia cordis in Deo. Medulla* (1627 ed.), pp. 184ff.; Spener, *PD*, pp. 119, 117. The predominance of this image in Pietism has been argued by Martin Schmidt, "Spener and Luther," *Luther-Jahrbuch* 24 (1957), 102-129. It is even present in Calvin, *Institutes,* IV/XV.6. Conservative Evangelicals employing this image include Bloesch, *ER*, p. 38; Henry, *GRA*, 4:496, 524; 6:501-502; Paul A. Mickey, *Essentials of Wesleyan Theology* (Grand Rapids: Zondervan, 1980), p. 159; Padilla, in *LEH*, p. 142; Yoder, *PJ*, pp. 226, 213; Rudy Budiman, "The Theology of the Cross and the Resurrection in our Unique Salvation," in *LEH*, pp. 1052-1054, 1056-1057. Such a view of justification is even articulated by Pat Robertson's colleague, Ben Kinchlow (see Maynard Good Stoddard, "CBN's Remarkable Ben Kinchlow," *The Saturday Evening Post*, April 1983.)

12. Henry, *GRA*, 3:130; 4:498; 6:337; Bloesch, *FEC*, p. 131. Also see Yoder, *PJ*, pp. 95, 116, 215, 230-232. It is not clear what Henry means in *GRA*, 6:337, by his description of Christian life as "continuing conformity" to Christ.

13. This commitment has been articulated by Henry, *GRA*, 4:366; Bloesch, *FEC*, p. 15.

14. *FC*, Ep. VI.1.

15. LCMS embraces a third use in *GS*, pp. 8-9.

16. Werner Elert, *Law and Gospel*, trans. Edward Schroeder (Philadelphia: Fortress, 1967), pp. 40-43; Forde, "Forensic Justification," p. 302. A more or less mediating position, rejecting a third use of the law but with an openness to receiving guidance from biblical commandments *(Gebote)* which may guide the Christian, has been proposed by Wilfried Joest, *Gesetz und Freiheit*, 3rd ed. (Göttingen: Vandenhoeck & Ruprecht, 1961), especially p. 198; Paul Althaus, *The Theology of Martin Luther*, trans. Robert Schultz (Philadelphia: Fortress, 1970), p. 271. Hans Schwarz, "The Word," in *Christian Dogmatics*, ed. Carl Braaten and Robert Jenson, 2 vols. (Philadelphia: Fortress, 1984), 2:275-276, also seems open to something like a third use of the law.

17. For references to the law-gospel distinction, see Martin Luther, *Lectures on Galatians* (1535), WA 40^1, 510, 16/LW 26, 330; ibid., WA 40^1, 207, 17ff./LW 26, 115; *FC*, SD V. 1, 27. For references to the Christian's freedom from the law, see Martin Luther, *Preface to the Epistle of St. Paul to the Romans* (1546), WADB 7, 21, 1/LW 35, 376; *CA* XXVIII. 51.

18. For references to the law-gospel distinction among Evangelicals, see Chap. 16, n. 6. The commitment to presenting justification apart from any mixture of works has been affirmed by a number of nondispensationalist Evangelicals including members of the Evangelical–Roman Catholic Dialogue (1977–1984), Int. (1); Stott, *BC*, p. 96; AUCECB, IV; GARB, XI; BBF, XI; ECC, p. 15. Recent survey results noted by David Hubbard and Clinton McLemore, "Evangelical Churches," in *Ministry in America*, ed. D. Schuller, M. Strommen, and M. Brekke (San Francisco: Harper & Row, 1980), p. 392, show that the piety of American Evangelicals is not excessively legalistic.

19. Martin Luther, *Kirchenpostille* (1522), WA 10^{1,1}, 456,8ff. For a discussion of this passage and the dispute about its meaning, see Gerhard Ebeling, *Word and Faith*, trans. James W. Leitch (Philadelphia: Fortress, 1963), pp. 62-65. Forceful critiques of the claims that a third use appears in Luther have been mounted by Werner Elert, *Zwischen Gnade und Ungnade* (München: Evangelischer Pressverband, 1948), especially pp. 161-162; Forde, "Forensic Justification," p. 301.

20. Luther, *Lectures on Galatians* (1535), WA 40¹, 240, 17/LW 26, 137.
21. Ibid., WA 40¹, 253,18/LW 26, 145.
22. Ibid., WA 40¹, 570, 18/LW 26,373. Cf. Martin Luther, *First Lectures on the Psalms* (1513–1516), WA 3, 463, 30/LW 10, 405.
23. Martin Luther, *Die dritte Disputation gegen die Antinomer* (1538–1539), WA 39¹, 513,4. Also see Martin Luther, *Theses Concerning Faith and Law* (1535), WA 39¹, 47, 37/LW 34, 113, as he insists that because of sin it is necessary to adhere to certain commands.
24. Such a hermeneutic and functional treatment of the concepts of law and gospel seems in the background of the positions of Joest, *Gesetz und Freiheit*, especially pp. 198, 195, Althaus, *Theology of Martin Luther*, p. 271, and Forde, "Forensic Justification," pp. 293-294, 301-302. For a description of this neoorthodox functionalist view of Scripture, see pp. 222-223, above.
25. A "functional" distinction seems to be reflected in Luther, *Lectures on Romans* (1515–1516), WA 56, 408, 18/LW 25, 398. Their distinction on the basis of content as well as functions is evident in *FC*, SD V.17-21.
26. Spener, *PD*, p. 47. This characterization of Pietism in general has been offered by Gustaf Aulén, *Christus Victor*, trans. A. G. Hebert (New York: Macmillan, 1972), pp. 133-134. The context for the Lutheran Confessions' affirmation of a third use of the law is evident in *FC*, Ep. VI.8. The context for Calvin's affirmation is evident in his *Institutes*, Pref.; II/VIII.13.
27. *CA*, XII.8; *FC*, SD XII.33. For references to the perfectionist view held by Evangelicals, see pp. 250-251 and its associated notes.
28. Spener, *PD*, pp. 80-81. For references to the Methodist view, see Chap. 16, n. 30. Also the coincidence of the advocacy by some Evangelicals of the concept of eternal security of the believer (see Chap. 16, n. 28 for references) and the condemnation of it by the *CA*, XII.7, need not constitute a church-dividing issue. At least it has not been considered such in contemporary Lutheran–Reformed dialogues. Thus why should the same issue divide Lutherans and Conservative Evangelicals?
29. For references, see pp. 246-247, 250, and associated notes.
30. *The Westminster Confession*, XVI, XVIII; Calvin, *Institutes*, III/XIV.20; [Baptist] *Second London Confession*, XVI.2; Anglicanism, *The Thirty-Nine Articles*, XII; *The* [Methodist] *Articles of Religion*, 10. For the concept of "preparation for grace" or at least the idea of prayer as such a preparation in two of these traditions, see p. 247, above.
31. Thomas Aquinas, *Commentary on Saint Paul's Epistle to the Ephesians*, trans. Matthew L. Lamb (Albany, N.Y.: Magi Books, 1966), p. 96; Aquinas, *Summa Theologica*, I-II, Q.109, 112, 114; Council of Trent, *Decree Concerning Justification*, Chs. V-VII.
32. Philip Melanchthon, *Loci Communes* (1535 ed.), in *Corpus Reformatorum*, ed. Henricus Bindseil (New York: Johnson Reprint, 1963), 21:376, 658. Cf. Council of Trent, *Decree Concerning Justification*, Chap. VII.
33. See Chap. 16, n. 48 for references.
34. Chap. 16 largely showed that the theology of the Evangelical movement is generally not Pelagian, and that to a great extent its particular conceptualizations are conditioned by the overriding Conservative Evangelical concern with sanctification and regeneration.

Chapter 23: Church and Ministry

1. Martin Luther, *Treatise on the Power and Primacy of the Pope* (1537), 69-70; Martin Luther, *The Babylonian Captivity of the Church* (1520), WA 6, 564, 12/

LW 36 113; *The Faith and Practise of Thirty [Baptist] Congregations Gathered According to the Primitive Pattern* (1651), 58. Insofar as Calvin, *Institutes,* IV/ III.10,13-15, advocates the election of ministers, perhaps one could say that the Reformed tradition also maintains a view of the ordained ministry as an office only functionally distinct from the priesthood of all believers. But in fact it is surprising to learn that the concept of the universal priesthood does not play as prominent a role in Calvin and the Reformed Confessions as it does in the Lutheran tradition. Indeed, one finds in the Reformed heritage more explicit reference to, or a priority given to, a higher view of the ministry as divinely instituted; see below.

2. The *CA,* V.1, and its notion of the divine institution of the office of ministry suggests a high view of the ministry. A willingness to acknowledge episcopal authority is not just an accidental development in Lutheranism but part of its Confessional heritage. See *CA* XXVIII, 21-22,55; *Apology,* XIV.1; *SA,* III/X.1. Also see Martin Luther, *Infiltrating and Clandestine Preachers* (1532), WA 30ᴵᴵᴵ, 525, 10/LW40, 391-392; Luther, *On the Councils and the Church* (1539), WA 50, 632-633, 35ff./LW 41, 154. For an indication of Lutheranism's historic openness to a reformed papacy, see Philip Melanchthon's subscription to *SA;* Luther, *Lectures on Galatians* (1535), WA 40ᴵ, 181, 1-10/LW 26, 99.

   For indications of a high view of the ministry in these other traditions (in the case of Mennonites at least insofar as they distinguish clergy from laity on the basis of the former's superior spirituality), see *The Second Helvetic Confession,* XVIII; Calvin, *Institutes,* IV/III.1, 10; Anglicanism, *The Thirty-Nine Articles,* XXXVI; Methodism, *General Rules* (1739), 8; *The* [Mennonite] *Dordrecht Confession,* IX. One Baptist Confession, *Short Confession of Faith in XX Articles by John Smyth* (1609), 16, refers to the role of bishops in the Church and to the episcopal function of ministers.

3. *CA,* IX,X; *Apology,* II.36,IX,X; *SA,* III/VI; *GK,* V.8-9; *FC,* Ep. VII.2; *FC,* SD II.15. For the Lutheran insistence that ordinarily God uses external means, see *SA,* III/VIII.3; *FC,* SD XI.76. For a classic statement of the Reformed view, see Calvin, *Institutes,* I/IX.1-3; IV/XIV.15; IV/XV.14,20; IV/XVII.3, 10,11,18,31. Cf. Anglicanism, *The Thirty-Nine Articles,* XXV, XXVII, XXVIII; *The* [Methodist] *Articles of Religion* (1783–1784), 16-18.

4. *FC,* SD VII.35. Also see *GK,* V. 8-9; *SA,* III/VI.1.

5. *FC,* SD VII.35-37.

6. *GK,* IV.10,35,52-55; V. 16-19. Cf. Calvin, *Institutes,* IV/XVII.33.34. But *The Westminster Confession* XXIX, and *The Second Helvetic Confession,* XXI, appear to suggest like Lutheranism that Christ is present (at least in a detrimental way) even to unbelievers.

7. *Apology,* II.35,36; *FC,* SD II.15; *The Small Catechism* (1529), IV.10; Anglicanism, *The Thirty-Nine Articles* IX,XXVII; Council of Trent, "Canons on the Sacraments in General," *Decree Concerning the Sacraments,* Seventh Session, 1547, Cans. 6-9; Council of Trent, *Decree Concerning Original Sin,* Fifth Session, 1546, 5. It might be possible to construe *The* [Methodist] *Articles of Religion,* 17, and *The Westminster Confession,* XXVII, as open to the idea of baptismal regeneration. In virtually all these documents, though not necessarily in the articles cited above, one can identify these traditions' authorization of infant baptism.

8. Luther made a similar argument in *Concerning Rebaptism* (1528), WA 26, 167-168, 36ff./LW 40, 256.

9. See Chap. 17, n. 18 for references. Luther even affirmed the universal Church's infallibility in *Theses Concerning Faith and Law* (1535), WA 39¹, 48, 5/LW 34, 113.

10. For a full discussion with references to this and other ways in which segments of the Evangelical movement function with appeals to the Church's teaching authority, see pp. 261-263.

11. For other references and the ambiguity surrounding some of these texts, see Chap. 17, nn. 42, 2.

12. See Chap. 17, nn. 5-6 for references.

13. See pp. 271-272 for earlier discussion and pertinent references.

14. The condemnation of Anabaptists by *FC*, SD XII.11, for their alleged denial of infant sin would seem not to pertain to those Evangelicals who practice only believer's baptism but still have a service of infant blessing as a sign of the need of children for redeeming grace. For an exposition of this practice in several Baptist churches, see *Lutheran–Baptist Dialogue [USA]: Three Common Statements* (1981), "Baptism and the Theology of the Child," 3. Cf. WC, Const., Art. V.

15. For references, see pp. 260-261, 269, 325-326, and associated notes.

16. For references, see pp. 260, 269-270, 325-326, and associated notes.

17. For a fuller discussion with references, see pp. 241-242, 246-247, 256, and associated notes.

18. Such a view may be implied by Henri de Lubac, *Catholicisme* (Paris: Cerf, 1965), pp. 47ff.; J. M. Tillard, "Eglise et salut: Sur la sacramentalité d'Eglise," *Nouvelle Revue de Théologie* 106 (1984): 665,668; *ERCD* 3(3), sharply states the Evangelical case for the priority of the gospel over the Church.

19. *Salvation and the Church: ARCIC II,* (see Chap. 16, n. 48), 25-32. The insistence that outside the Church there is no salvation has been articulated in the Reformed tradition by *The Second Helvetic Confession*, XVII. The concept of the Church as Christ's bride in *The Westminster Confession*, XXV could suggest an affirmation of the Church's nurturing, maternal function. *ERCD*, 3(3), could be understood to imply Evangelical recognition of the Roman Catholic insistence on the Church's role as an instrument of salvation.

20. Bloesch, *ER*, p. 77; Webber, *CR*, pp. 64-65. For more information on the "Catholic [Ecumenical] Evangelicals," see Chap. 17, above.

21. Henry, *GRA*, 4:160,161,167; R. Johnston (see abbreviations), p. 74. Cf. Council of Trent, *Decree Concerning the Canonical Scriptures*, Fourth Session, 1546; Vatican I, *Dei Filius*, Third Session, April 24, 1870, Chap. II; Vatican II, *Dei verbum* (1965), 11.

22. See R. Johnston, p. 55. A reappropriation of Mariology and the cult of saints has been advocated by Bloesch, *FEC*, p. 134. Key Yuasa, "The Image of Christ in Latin American Indian Popular Religiosity," in *JTTW*, p. 83; RC-P, II,63.

23. *The Eucharist: A Lutheran–Roman Catholic Statement* [USA] (1967), II; *The Eucharist. Final Report of the Joint Roman Catholic–Lutheran Commission* (1978), 14-19, 49-51; Anglican–Roman Catholic Conversations, *Windsor Statement* (1971), 6-12; Anglican–Roman Catholic Conversations, *Elucidation* (1979), 6.

24. Renewed sacramental appreciation by these traditions is suggested by their official representatives' affirmation of the real presence in the sacraments in the following dialogues: Methodist–Roman Catholic Conversations, *Denver Report*, 83; Methodist–Roman Catholic Conversations, *Dublin Report* (1976), 54-60; Lutheran–Reformed Dialogue, *Leuenberg Concord*, 15-20.

25. In addition to the bilateral dialogue document subsequently cited in this paragraph, see *The Eucharist: Final Report of the Joint Roman Catholic–Lutheran Commission*, 61.

26. Thomas Aquinas, *Summa Theologica*, III. Q.83, Art. 1; Council of Trent, *Canons on the Sacrifice of the Mass*, 22nd Session 1562, Canon 4.

   For the traditional Protestant understandings of this Roman Catholic teaching, see *CA*, XXIV.21-22; *Apology*, XXIV.9,14; *The Heidelberg Catechism*, Q.80.

27. Other Evangelicals employing language compatible with the concept of Eucharistic sacrifice include New Tribes Mission, *Doctrinal Statement*, 10; Costas, in *LEH*, p. 686; *Keele Congress Statement*, 68.

28. Also see Chap. 16, n. 26.

29. See pp. 263, 265, above.

30. *The Report of Hedio*, in *The Marburg Colloquy* (1529), WA 30^{III},142,15/LW 38,34.

31. In his *On the Blessed Sacrament of the Body of Christ and the Brotherhoods* (1517), WA 2, 742-758/LW 35,49-73, it is particularly noteworthy how Luther at one point will insist that the sacraments' sign not be identified with the elements but with the entire liturgical action of eating and drinking (ibid., WA 2,742,17/LW 35,49). Christ's body and blood play no important role, for the sacrament is said to signify not Christ but incorporation with him and the saints (ibid., WA 2,743,20-23/LW 35,51). But something like the real presence of Christ in the sacrament is affirmed in ibid., WA 2,749,10/LW 35,59, precisely in order to convey the theme of conformity to Christ as an outcome of the sacrament. This downplaying of the real bodily presence of Christ is even more evident in *The Babylonian Captivity of the Church* (1520) WA 6,533,14-17/LW 36,66-67, as he claims that the sacraments do not "contain in their being a power efficacious for justification" and so are not effective "signs" unless faith is present. Is this not a position akin to what Calvin later developed, that Christ is present only through faith? It is interesting to note that this statement emerges from a context in which Luther was concerned to urge the exercise of faith by Christians (a concern not unlike that which conditions the characteristic Conservative Evangelical treatment of the sacraments/ordinances).

   A recent argument on behalf of this sort of position on the sacraments, at least in Luther, has been provided by Ralph W. Quere, "Changes and Constants: Structure in Luther's Understandings of the Real Presence in the 1520's," *The Sixteenth Century Journal* 16 (Spring 1985): 45-78. In part his argument is that this alternative strand in Luther's thinking on the sacraments represents the Reformer's early indebtedness to Augustine. Certainly, one finds in Augustine a tendency to minimize the real presence in contexts where, like Luther and Conservative Evangelicals, he was concerned to encourage the practice of the Christian life or where he combatted unbridled rationalism. See, for example, his *Homilies on the Gospel of St. John* (406-407, 419-424), Trac. XXVI, par. 18; Trac. XXVII, par. 1; *Expositions on the Book of Psalms* (n.d.), III.1,3; XCIX.8. Yet, when the concerns shift as in his *On the Trinity* (399-422), III.10.21, there Augustine could affirm something like the real presence.

32. *GK*, IV.65,71-86; Luther, *The Babylonian Captivity of the Church* (1520), WA 6, 528,10/LW 36,59; Calvin, *Institutes*, IV/XV.3-6.

Chapter 24: The Work of Christ

1. A few of the innumerable examples in the Lutheran tradition are *GK*, II.31; III.115-116; Martin Luther, *Lectures on Galatians* (1535), WA 40^{I}, 440, 15/LW 26,281-282; *Lectures on Genesis* (1535–1536), WA 42,140,3ff./LW 1,188; ibid. (1541–1542), WA 43,432,5/LW 5,5. Cf. Gustaf Aulén, *Christus Victor*, trans. A. G.

Hebert (New York: Macmillan, 1972), pp. 119ff. Examples of the classic view in other traditions are given below, p. 339.

2. *CA*, III.3-5; *SA*, III/III.38-39; Luther, *Lectures on Galatians* (1535), WA 40¹,297, 32/LW 26,177. For a few references to the satisfaction theory in these traditions, see Chap. 15, n. 9.

3. See pp. 238-240, and associated notes for examples.

4. See Chap. 15, n. 13, for references.

5. For samples of these denials, see Chap. 15, n. 14.

6. Harold Lindsell, "Universalism," in *LEH*, pp. 12-13. See also Neal Punt's view (described in Chap. 15, n. 16).

7. Additional examples of proponents of this view are given in Chap. 13, n. 100.

8. Some relevant references in Chap. 14, n. 26.

9. Barth, *KD*, vol. III/2, pp. 21, 81, 188-189, 293-297,391; ibid., vol.IV/1, p.548.

10. *Apology*, II.18, 15; FC,SD I.10, states that the image of God is lost in sin. cf. *FC*, Ep.II.20-21. Also see *The Heidelberg Catechism*, Q.6. It might be possible to read Anglicanism's *The Thirty-Nine Articles*, IX, and Methodism's *The Articles of Religion*, 7, in this way.

11. See pp. 234-235, and corresponding notes.

12. International Congress on World Evangelization (Lausanne Congress) Working Group Report, *An Answer to Lausanne*, 23.

Chapter 25: Social Ethics

1. For the classic Lutheran presentation of the two-kingdom ethic, see Luther, *Temporal Authority* (1523), WA 11,251,1ff./LW 45,90-91; ibid., WA 11,249,24/LW 45,88. References to the social ethical models of several other mainline churches appear above in Chap. 18, n. 48, and below in n. 9 of this chapter. Among other Western churches there is some ambiguity about the actual theological orientation for social ethics of the Anglican community, though its history includes some attention to a distinction between the civil and spiritual realms (*The Thirty-Nine Articles*, XXXVII) and the reliance on appeal to the natural law as an authorization for ethics. (See James M. Gustafson, *Protestant and Roman Catholic Ethics* [London: SCM, 1979], pp. 60, 12, 3, 2.) Similar ambiguity pertains in Methodism, though one can discern a certain Christocentric tendency in one of its German-American branches, the Evangelical United Brethren, *The Confession of Faith*, XVI. At least since the time of Vatican II the Roman Catholic heritage, which always has and still continues to authorize its social ethical positions by appeal to the natural law in combination with insights of the Augustinian distinction of the two kingdoms (see Vatican II, *Gaudium et Spes* [1965], 76, 43), now often subordinates these themes to redemption (see ibid., 22), so that all distinction between the two kingdoms could be regarded as obliterated by a Christocentrism.

2. That government is to be structured according to principles of the law is perhaps most clearly articulated by Martin Luther, *Predigten über das 2. Buch Mose* (1524–1527), WA 16,353,26. Also see *Apology*, XVI.3-8.

3. The gospel's role in inspiring good works is perhaps no more clearly and authoritatively stated than in *SA*, III/XIII. Cf. Luther, *Temporal Authority*, WA 11,255,12/ LW 45,96.

4. Among contemporary Lutheran theologians this point is made by Gerhard Forde, "Christian Life," in *Christian Dogmatics*, ed. Carl Braaten and Robert Jenson, 2 vols. (Philadelphia: Fortress, 1984), 2:455-456. Luther himself made a similar critique in *Temporal Authority*, WA 11, 251,22/LW 45,91; In ibid., WA 11,253,17/

LW 45,93-94, he sketches how Christians should be motivated by the gospel but have their political actions structured by the law.

For references to the characteristic Reformed view, see Calvin, *Institutes*, IV/ XX.9,2; *The Second Helvetic Confession*, XXX.

5. See pp. 283-284 and Chap. 18, n. 51 for references.
6. See Chap. 18, n. 49 for a few examples.
7. See Chap. 18, nn. 31-33 for references.
8. Examples of such a reductionism are evident in the liberation theology of Rubem Alves, *A Theology of Human Hope* (St. Meinard, Ind.: Abbey Press, 1974), pp. 98-99; as he reduces God to nothing more than a symbol for "what it takes to make and keep life human," a description of events that serve this purpose.
9. See Chap. 15, n. 21 for some references to this concern on the part of Conservative Evangelicals.
10. WCC Nairobi Assembly Section Report, *Confessing Christ Today* (1975), 18-19. It was acknowledged at the Assembly that the report, most likely its expressed regret over the reduction of Christian faith by some to political-philosophical conceptualities, was influenced by the Lausanne Congress. (See *Breaking Barriers: Nairobi 1975*, ed. David M. Paton [London: SPCK, 1976], pp. 41-42.)
11. For a few examples, see Chap. 18, nn. 46-48.
12. See *Leuenberg Concord*, 39. A soon-to-be completed study of the Institute for Ecumenical Research on the social ethical teachings of the churches is in the process of confirming that this is not a church-dividing difference.

Chapter 26: A Theology for the Born Again

1. One might also claim that the Wesleyan churches represent a special problematic for ecumenical conversations, particularly those influenced by the Pentecostal emphasis on baptism with the Holy Spirit. However, inasmuch as even their most distinct theological commitment, the concept of entire sanctification/perfection (FMC, p. 363; CN, Pre.), is embedded in Wesley (see p. 121 above), it seems to follow that many of the issues raised by Holiness churches could be dealt with in the context of dialogues with the Methodist heritage.
2. The argument for this point was summarized in some detail on pp. 225-227, 296-297, above. Also see Chap. 20, n. 6. Jack B. Rogers, in an interview, March 13, 1985, claimed that if not hermeneutics, then theological methodology (particularly the question of the role of human experience in relation to divine revelation) may be the crucial issue dividing Conservative Evangelicals and the mainline. The possibility that "church practice" is the real issue for Evangelicals in their relation with the mainline was suggested by G. W. Bromiley in his interview with me on March 14, 1985.
3. Campus Crusade–Europe director, Kalevi Lehtinen, private interview, March 23, 1984, was the only Evangelical I have encountered who took such a position. In his interview with me he unambiguously expressed his sympathies with Pietism.
4. The divisive character of some of these themes has been made clear to me by LCMS, *GS*, pp. 8-9, and in my meeting with the Vorstand des Arbeitskreis für evangelikale Theologie, November 15, 1985.

Chapter 27: Scripture and Theological Method

1. This assessment concerning the impact of neoorthodoxy also by Richard G. Hutcheson Jr., *Mainline Churches and the Evangelicals: A Challenging Crisis?* (Atlanta: John Knox, 1981), pp. 22, 39-40, 168-169. Cf. Bloesch, *ER*, p. 44.

2. Among the countless critiques are Georg Huntemann, "Karl Barth: Legacy or Wrong Way?" (seminar paper presented at the 4th Conference of the Internationale Konferenz Bekennender Gemeinschaften, Strasbourg, France, October 1, 1982); Cornelius Van Til, *The New Modernism: An Appraisal of the Theology of Barth and Brunner*, rev. ed. (Philadelphia: Presbyterian and Reformed, 1972), especially p. 304; Schaeffer, *SER*, pp. 50-51; Henry, *GRA*, 1:191-192; IFCA, Art. IV, Sec. 2(c). Additional criticisms of contemporary theology by the Evangelical movement, cited below, also bear on this point.

3. Rudolf Bultmann, *Jesus Christ and Mythology* (New York: Scribner's, 1958), especially pp. 16, 18. Barth's chagrin about these developments was expressed in his "Rudolf Bultmann: An Attempt to Understand Him," in *Kerygma and Dogma*, vol. 2, ed. Hans Bartsch (London: S.P.C.K., 1962), pp. 83-132.

4. Langdon Gilkey, *Naming the Whirlwind* (Indianapolis: Bobbs-Merrill, 1969), p. 77.

5. Thomas Altizer, *Toward a New Christianity* (1967), p. 123. Such an assessment has also been made by Henry, *GRA*, 1:192; 3:199.

Gert Wendelborn, *Gottes Wort und die Gesellschaft* (Berlin: Union Verlag, 1979), pp. 96-97, observes the usual critique made by the Bekenntnisbewegung of contemporary theology. The latter is regarded as having become a "Theology of 'Isms'" *(Theologien der Genitive)*.

6. Paul Tillich, *Systematic Theology*, 3 vols. in one (Chicago: University of Chicago Press, 1967), 2:115; ibid., 1:159; Rudolf Bultmann, *Theology of the New Testament*, trans. K. Grobel, 2 vols. (New York: Scribner's, 1951, 1955), 1:191.

For examples of this critique by Evangelicals of mainline theology for purportedly grounding its claims in human experience, see Chap. 13, n. 33. A similar critique is framed by Evangelicals outside of North America, as is evident in Beyerhaus, *BHG*, pp. 12, 13-14. A few references to the Evangelical insistence on propositional revelation are provided in Chap. 13, n. 28.

7. Rubem Alves, *A Theology of Human Hope* (St. Meinard, Ind.: Abbey Press, 1974), pp. 165-166; Jürgen Moltmann, *Theology of Hope* (New York: Harper & Row, 1967), pp. 190-191.

8. David Tracy, *Blessed Rage for Order* (New York: Seabury, 1978), pp. 134, 46.

9. Karl Barth, *Epistle to the Romans*, trans. E. C. Hoskyns (New York: Oxford University Press, 1933), pp. 8, 10, 18; Barth, *KD*, vol. I/1, pp. 111-113; ibid., vol. I/2, pp. 519, 557-558, 561-562, 572-573, 578-579, 586-595, especially pp. 591, 592. For information about the development of an alternative view in Barth wherein he seems open to the universal accessibility of Scripture's meaning, see Chap. 13, n. 80.

10. Among theologians already considered, Barth, *Epistle to the Romans*, pp. 8, 10, 18, Bultmann, *Theology of the New Testament*, 2:237-238, Alves, *Theology of Human Hope*, pp. 107-108, 179, and Tillich, *Systematic Theology*, 1:35, use some notion of the Word of God as a principle for criticizing Scripture. This characterization of mainline theology has been offered by Henry, *GRA*, 4:50-51, 281, 302; 3:434, 467; Bloesch, *ER*, pp. 92-93; David A. Hubbard, *What We Believe and Teach* (12-page pamphlet, reprinted 1981), p. 5. Subsequently in his career Barth may have shifted grounds and designated the canonical text rather than the biblical authors' intentions as authoritative; see his *KD*, vol. I/2, pp. 560-561.

For an example of a rejection by a so-called revisionist theologian of the biblical authors' intention as criterion for determining the Word of God, see Paul Ricoeur, *Interpretation Theory* (Fort Worth, Tex.: TCU Press, 1976), pp. 87-88, 92-93.

For a similar orientation, see Hans-Georg Gadamer, *Warheit und Methode*, 2nd ed. (Tübingen: J. C. B. Mohr, 1965), p. 276 (Eng.: *Truth and Method*).

11. Such a functionalism is evident in the theology of Barth, *KD*, vol. I/1, pp. 111-113; Bultmann, *Theology of the New Testament*, 2:238; Gerhard Ebeling, *Word and Faith* (Philadelphia: Fortress, 1963), pp. 331-332.

12. In a study on behalf of world Lutheranism conducted by the Institute for Ecumenical Research this interpretive supposition seems to have even been identified as characteristic of the essence of Lutheran identity. See its *Lutheran Identity* (1977), pp. 27, 29-30. This view is also maintained by Carl Braaten, "Prolegomena to Christian Dogmatics," in *Christian Dogmatics*, ed. Carl Braaten and Robert Jenson, 2 vols. (Philadelphia: Fortress, 1984), 1:63-65, significantly enough, in a volume designed to function as a textbook in American Lutheran seminaries.

13. Martin Luther, *Table Talk* (1542), WATR 5,157,17/LW 54,424-425; Martin Luther, *Preface to the New Testament* (1522), WADB 6,10,33/LW 35,362.

14. See the earlier discussion of this issue, above, p. 318; for references. See notes cited there.

15. Bultmann, *Jesus Christ and Mythology*, pp. 16,18; Tillich, *Systematic Theology*, 1:239, 240; 2:100; Barth, *KD* vol.I/1, pp. 342ff.; ibid., vol.I/2, pp. 520-521; Oscar Cullmann, *Christ and Time*, trans. Floyd V. Filson (London: SCM, 1951), p. 99.

16. See Wolfhart Pannenberg, *Jesus—God and Man*, trans. Lewis Wilkins and Duane Priebe (Philadelphia Westminster, 1968), pp. 97-98; Ebeling, *Word and Faith*, pp. 294-297; Peter Stuhlmacher, *Schriftauslegung auf dem Wege zur biblischen Theologie* (Göttingen: Vandenhoeck & Ruprecht, 1975), pp. 120ff. Most of those relying on such an approach are more or less indebted to the suppositions concerning hermeneutics and historical research articulated by Gadamer, *Wahrheit und Methode*, especially pp. 286-290, 499, 505-506.

17. Henry, *GRA*, 2:288-289; 5:37-38; John Warwick Montgomery, *Crisis in Lutheran Theology* (Grand Rapids, Mich.: Baker, 1967), pp. 29-30; Han Chul-Ha, "An Asian Critique of Western Theology," *Evangelical Review of Theology* 7 (1983): 41-42; Schaeffer, *SER*, pp. 20-21. Cf. Maier, *EhkM*, p. 44; John H. Gerstner, "The Nature of Revelation," in *Christian Faith and Modern Theology*, ed. Carl Henry (Grand Rapids: Baker, 1971), p. 100, and pertinent observations by Evangelicals cited in n. 10 for other criticisms of the mainline advocacy of a distinction between Word and Scripture for the sake of criticizing the biblical text.

18. Evangelical criticisms of such a viewpoint with reference to its inevitable subjectivistic outcomes include those offered by the *Chicago Statement*, III; Henry, *GRA*, 5:14,71,93-94,142; 6:471; 4:57, 58, 560; Montgomery, *Crisis in Lutheran Theology*, pp. 101-102; Beyerhaus, *BHG*, p. 5.

19. Henry, *GRA*, 3:295, 430-432; 1:388ff.; Marsden, *FAC*, pp. 114, 215, regards such a theory of knowledge as a main point of division between Fundamentalism and its opponents. For Kant's view, see his *Kritik der reinen Vernunft* (Leipzig, 1877), pp. 17-18, 156-157, 231ff.

20. For indications of the adoption of these presuppositions by the WCC, see Chap. 19, n. 21.

21. This criticism is raised by Henry, *GRA*, 5:145, 229, 353.

22. *GRA*, 2:66; 3:216; 6:31, 71, 400; 5:226-227, 376, indicates that Feuerbach is very much a conversation partner for Evangelicals in assessing their views in relation to mainline theology. For Feuerbach's views, see his *The Essence of Christianity*, ed. E. Graham Waring and F. W. Strothmann (New York: Frederick Ungar, 1957), pp. 10, 12.

23. Maier, *EhkM*, p. 44; ma Djongwé Daïdanso, "An African Critique of African Theology," *Evangelical Review of Theology* 7 (April 1983): 71; Henry, *GRA*, 1:191, 218, 248; 5:98, 122, 184; John Warwick Montgomery, *Where Is History Going?* (Grand Rapids, Mich.: Zondervan, 1969), p. 191; IFCA, Art. IV, Sec. 2(c). Cf. Blocher, in LEH, p. 391.

24. Henry, *GRA*, 2:65-66, suggests this connection to Western culture's narcissism at several points.

25. This observation concerning the outcome of a critical hermeneutic is offered by R. Johnston (see abbreviations), p. 25. Cf. *The Seoul Declaration*, 2; *Diakrisis*, 4/1983, 7, as cited in Erich Geldbach, "Evangelikalismus: Versuch einer historischen Theologie," *Die Kirchen und ihre Konservativen*, ed. Reinhard Frieling (Göttingen: Vandenhoeck & Ruprecht, 1984), p. 76.

26. See pp. 208-210, and its associated notes for a fuller discussion and references to Evangelicals making a parallel argument on behalf of their ability to maintain divine transcendence.

27. This characterization by Henry, *GRA*, 4:236.

28. See Chap. 13, n. 60 for references to a rejection by some Evangelicals of certain principles of the historical-critical method. The characteristic Evangelical solution of assuming the veracity of the biblical accounts until disproven has precedents in Princeton theology; see A. A. Hodge, *Outlines of Theology*, in *PT*, p. 214; A. A. Hodge and B. B. Warfield, "Inspiration," in *PT*, p. 232. It is evident also at points in Henry, *GRA*, 2:314-317, 322-323; 4:397, interview, July 9, 1986 and perhaps others using the method of presuppositionalism (see pp. 214-215 and Chap. 13, nn. 51-52 for references).

29. For references to Evangelicals who may be employing this approach, see Chap. 13, nn. 42, 52. In an interview, March 13, 1985, Ray Anderson has explicitly acknowledged his indebtedness to Gadamer's alternative view of history.

   For references to a few mainline theologians who endeavor to redefine the principles of historical research in order to make faith a viable supposition, see n. 16.

30. These three principles were first enunciated by Ernst Troeltsch, *Gesammelte Schriften*, vol. 2 (Tübingen, J.C.B. Mohr, 1913), pp. 729-753; Ernst Troeltsch, "Historiography," in *Encyclopedia of Religion and Ethics*, vol. 6, ed. James Hastings (New York: Scribner's, 1914), pp. 716-723. Virtually all mainline theology is in some dialogue with these principles. Even in the few instances where they are rejected by theologians influenced by Gadamer these three principles are very much in view.

31. See Chap. 13, n. 84, for a few Evangelicals who have been influenced in this way.

32. See pp. 27-28, 225, for earlier discussions of these dynamics. Also see Quebedeaux, *WE*, p. 84, for confirmation of the minority status of the Evangelical left within the Evangelical movement.

33. For further discussion of the variety of narrative and canonical approaches to hermeneutics, see pp. 369-370 below; Gabriel Fackre, "Narrative Theology: An Overview," *Interpretation* 37 (1983): 340-352; Brevard S. Childs, "Childs versus Barr," review of *Holy Scripture: Canon, Authority, Criticism,* by James Barr, in *Interpretation* 38 (1984): pp. 66-67. My remarks reflect the basic suppositions of the family of approaches indebted to the work of Hans Frei and Brevard Childs.

   One should not overlook the differences between the particular kind of narrative approach which I shall describe and the canonical hermeneutics of Childs (see subsequent discussion on pp. 366, 369-370), though subsequent discussion will show their compatibility. Also it must be recognized that proponents of these approaches are sometimes uncomfortable being identified as "narrative theologians" or "canonical exegetes." Thus I simply use these terms as a shorthand designation to refer to the fundamental interpretive suppositions of Frei, Childs, and those who share these suppositions, not with the pretension that these terms adequately describe what these suppositions and their adherents are about. With this focus on the interpretive suppositions and their logical outcome, not on the thought and person of Frei and Childs as such, it goes without saying that any reflections concerning possible compatibility between their views on hermeneutics and those of the Evangelical movement would not necessarily be embraced by either man. My interest is simply to indicate the degree to which the interpretive suppositions with which they operate logically accommodate the concerns of Conservative Evangelicals.

34. ICBI, *The Chicago Statement on Biblical Hermeneutics* (1982), XVI; LCMS, *Study Edition of a Statement of Scriptural and Confessional Principles* (1972), p. 29; Yoder, *PJ*, pp. 14, 15, 24, 26, 57. These commitments also seem evident in the appeal to a "grammatical-historical" interpretation of Scripture by Henry, *GRA*, 4:104, 392; 2:272, 197; and Lindsell, *BB*, p. 37.

   Compare these commitments with Hans Frei, *The Eclipse of Biblical Narrative* (New Haven, Conn.: Yale University Press, 1974), pp. 1ff., especially p. 11; Brevard S. Childs, *Introduction to the Old Testament as Scripture* (Philadelphia: Fortress, 1979), pp. 72-83, 485-486; Brevard S. Childs, *The New Testament as Canon: An Introduction* (Philadelphia: Fortress, 1985), pp. 37ff., especially p. 48.

35. Childs, *NTC*, pp. 545, 228-229; Childs, *OTS*, pp. 16, 298-299, 426. Cf. Frei, *Eclipse*, especially pp. 11-12; Hans W. Frei, "Theology and the Interpretation of Narrative: Some Hermeneutical Considerations" (lecture presented at Haverford College, Haverford, Penn., 1982), p. 7.

36. Henry, *GRA*, 2:307-308, 310, 319; Carl Henry, "Narrative Theology: An Evangelical Appraisal" (lecture delivered at Yale Divinity School, New Haven, November 1985), pp. 12, 10; Larry Christenson, *The Charismatic Renewal among Lutherans* (Minneapolis: Bethany Fellowship, 1976), p. 101; Larry Christenson, ed., *Welcome, Holy Spirit* (Minneapolis: Augsburg, 1987), pp. 43-48, 150-155; LCMS, *Inspiration*, pp. 10, 11-12; Robert Preus, "Notes on the Inerrancy of Scripture," *Concordia Theological Monthly* 38 (1967): 372, 374, 365; Robert Preus, personal letters, April 9, 1984; February 20, 1984; Hans-Lutz Poetsch, "Zu den Begriffen 'Verbalinspiration' und 'Irrtumslosigkeit' der Heiligen Schrift," in *Die Bibel—Gottes Wort*, ed. Heinrich Dierks (Gross Oesingen: Verlag der Lutherischen Buchhandlung Heinrich Harms, 1982), pp. 17-18, 12, 22-23; Moises Silva, "The Place of Historical Reconstruction in New Testament Criticism," in *HAC*, pp. 110-111; C. Hodge, *Systematic Theology*, 3 vols. (New York: Scribner's, 1872), 1:573-574; *The Fundamentals*, 12 vols. (Chicago: Testimony Publishing, 1910-1915), 10:97; 7:76, 81. Cf. *Chicago Statement*, XIII, XV, Exp.; references on p. 215 and in Chap. 13, n. 51. Henry, *GRA*, 3:384, even appeals explicitly to the philosophical models of Ludwig Wittgenstein in arguing that Christian faith has its own methods of verification proper to it. For references to those associated with the Dutch Reformed heritage, see Alvin Plantinga and Nicholas Wolterstorff, eds., *Faith and Rationality* (Notre Dame, Ind.: University of Notre Dame, 1983), especially pp. 4, 77, 90-91, 163, 170-177, 248-257. See also George Marsden, "Evangelicals, History, and Modernity," in *EMA*, p. 100.

37. ICBI, *The Chicago Statement on Biblical Hermeneutics*, III; Stott, BC, p. 138; Konferenz Bekennender Gemeinschaften, *Orientierungshilfe*, 5; *The Fundamentals*, 6:98; 7:59; Bo Giertz, *Evangelisch Glauben*, p. 36; Kim, in *LEH*, p. 988. Compare these commitments with Frei, TIN, pp. 21-22; Childs, *OTS*, p. 671.

38. Frei, *Eclipse*, pp. 10-11, 12-16. To the degree that it is clear that the "narratives" in question are established by the Church's formation of the canon, it might be possible to regard this proposal as consistent with Childs' canonical hermeneutics. But Childs does have reservations about the usefulness of designating the whole canon as "narrative." See his *NTC*, p. 545; *OTS*, p. 299.

The Evangelical concern to maintain the unity of Scripture is evident in Henry, *GRA*, 2:196; 4:468; 5:250-251, 402. R. Johnston (see abbreviations), p. 72; Poetsch, "Verbalinspiration und Irrtumslosigkeit," p. 13; Maier, *EhkM*, p. 53; Blocher, in *LEH*, p. 385; Athyal, in *LEH*, p. 1004; Lausanne Congress Group Report, *The Report of the Study Group on the Role of Hermeneutics in the Theology of Evangelization Report* (1974), in *LEH*, p. 1006; *The Fundamentals*, 3:19-20; 9:39; COGIC, p. 40; LCMS, *Inspiration*, pp. 12-14; CRC, p. 58; Albrecht-Bengel-Haus, 2. In fact, at least one Evangelical, Yoder, in *UB*, p. 111, is even willing to speak of the entire canon as "narrative in its framework."

39. Hans Frei, *The Identity of Jesus Christ* (Philadelphia: Fortress, 1975), pp. xv, xvii; Frei, *Eclipse*, pp. 320, 323; Hans Frei, "Remarks in Connection with a Theological Proposal" (lecture delivered at Harvard University, Cambridge, Mass., December 7, 1969), p. 9; George A. Lindbeck, *The Nature of Doctrine* (Philadelphia: Westminster, 1984), pp. 119, 101-102. For a few examples of this commitment by members of the Evangelical movement, see Chap. 13, n. 31. Also see LCMS, GS, p. 13.

40. Frei, *Eclipse*, p. 323.

41. References in Chap. 13, nn. 42-43, 45.

42. Ricoeur, *Interpretation Theory*, pp. 17, 55, 79; Gabriel Fackre, *The Christian Story* (rev. ed.; Grand Rapids, Mich.: Eerdmans, 1984), pp. 4-10, 14-16, 26-30; Edgar McKnight, *Meaning in Texts* (Philadelphia: Fortress, 1978), especially pp. 250-251.

43. Childs, *OTS*, pp. 77, 72-74; Childs, *NTC*, pp. 38-39. Perhaps Childs' claim in his *Old Testament Theology in a Canonical Context* (Philadelphia: Fortress, 1986), pp. 12-13, 28, that Old Testament theology is done in faith by the theologian is governed by these assumptions, but it is not clear. See also Childs, *NTC*, p. 292. He does speak of such a theology as descriptive in *OTT*, p. 12, but also claims that it has constructive features.

44. Childs, *NTC*, pp. 24, 546.

45. Childs, *CVB*, p. 69; Childs, *OTS*, p. 371.

46. Childs, *CVB*, p. 69. Cf. Childs, *NTC*, pp. 53, 156, 163, 165, 197-198; Childs, *OTS*, pp. 72-73.

47. Frei, TIN, p. 26; Frei, *Identity*, p. xv. ICBI, *The Chicago Statement on Biblical Hermeneutics*, VII. Barth, *KD*, vol. I/2, pp. 810-830, once embraced such a scheme.

48. Frei, *Eclipse*, pp. 15-16, 319-320; Childs, *NTC*, p. 545. Evangelicals reflecting this exegetical sensitivity include Henry, *GRA*, 4:103, 104, 109; 3:480, 456-457; R. Johnston, p. 70; Athyal, in *LEH*, p. 1003. Such sensitivity is strongly reflected in the ICBI *Chicago Statement*, Exp., perhaps more so than in its *The Chicago Statement on Biblical Hermeneutics*, XIII, XIV.

49. See William Wimsatt, *The Verbal Icon* (London: Methuen, 1954), pp. 249, 250, xvi-xvii, 3ff.; I. A. Richards, *Principles of Literary Criticism* (New York: Harcourt, Brace and World, 1925), pp. 224, 251.

50. *Assertio omnium articulorum M. Lutheri per bullam Leonis X* (1520), WA 7,98f.,40; *SA*, III/VIII.3.

51. David Hollaz, *Examen Theologicum Acroamaticum* (1707), III 2,1,qu.4; John Quenstedt, *Theologia Didactico-Polemica* (1685), I,cap.2,qu.16. For a fuller discussion of the two different hermeneutical suppositions in Luther, each one employed in different pastoral contexts, see Mark Ellingsen, "Luther as Narrative Exegete," *Journal of Religion* 63 (October 1983): 394-413. Compatible conclusions have been reached by David Lotz, "Sola Scriptura: Luther on Biblical Authority," *Interpretation* 35 (July 1981): 263, 268-269, who goes so far as to claim that in Luther there is no functionalist understanding of a fallible Scripture becoming Word of God.

52. Frei, TIN, pp. 11-12, 21; Childs, *NTC*, p. 53; Childs, *OTS*, pp. 80-82.

53. A. Alexander, "Nature and Evidence of Truth," in *PT*, pp. 69-71. For this supposition in common sense realism, see Thomas Reid, *Essays on the Intellectual Powers of Man*, ed. A. D. Woozley (London: Macmillan, 1941), pp. 28, 369. For references to the other Evangelicals mentioned in the text, as well as to others making a kind of de facto appeal to tradition, see pp. 261-263, Chap. 17, nn. 22-23 there. For the statement from Vaux-sur-Seine, see Chap. 6, n. 12.

54. Frei, TIN, p. 18; Childs, *OTS*, p. 76. Something like the plenary authority of Scripture, if not its plenary inspiration, is affirmed somewhat explicitly by Childs, *NTC*, pp. 30, 42.

55. Martin Luther, *In XV Psalmes graduum* (1532/1533 [1540]), WA 40[III], 254, 23. Cf. Martin Luther, *Bibel-und Buchzeichnungen Luthers* (1541), WA 48, 31,4.

56. Calvin, *Institutes*, I/VI.3; I/VII.4; IV.VIII.6.

57. See again, Council of Trent, *Decree Concerning the Canonical Scriptures*, 4th Session, 1546, where verbal inspiration with divine dictation is affirmed. Vatican I, *Dei Filius*, 3rd Session, April 24, 1870, Chap. II, also affirmed biblical inerrancy.

58. Erich Auerbach, *Mimesis*, trans. Willard Trask (Princeton, N.J.: Princeton University Press, 1953), pp. 14-15.

59. See relevant references in Chap. 8, n. 68.

60. Herman Bavinck, *Gereformeerde Dogmatiek* (Kampen: J. H. Kok, 1928-1930), 1:414.

61. See Chap. 3, n. 11, for references.

62. Henry, *GRA*, 4:16; 5:19; D. Dayton, "Whither Evangelicalism?" (lecture presented at the Sixth Oxford Institute Methodist Theological Studies Conference, n.d.), p. 9; "Discussion with Kwame Bediako," in *JTTW*, pp. 163, 166; Gnadauer Verband, *Von der Autorität der Heiligen Schrift* (1961), 4-5, in *Weg und Zeugnis*, ed. Rudolf Bäumer, et al., 2nd ed. (Bad Liebenzell: Verlag der Liebenzeller Mission, 1981), p. 137. Gerald Sheppard, "Scripture in the Pentecostal Tradition: Part Two," *Agora*, II, No. 1, pp. 14, 19, claims that the entire Pentecostal tradition was shaped by a kind of figural interpretation of Scripture which deemed the biblical narrative normative for religious experience. Frei is also invoked in the discussion.

The argument that the Evangelical insistence on propositional revelation does not preclude revelation's personal, experiential character has been made by D. A. Carson, "Recent Developments in the Doctrine of Scripture," in *HAC*, pp. 25-26.

63. This assessment is by Richard Mouw, "The Bible in Twentieth Century Protestantism: A Preliminary Taxonomy," in *BA*, p. 151.

64. Reid, *Essays on the Intellectual Powers of Man*, p. 196.

65. Childs, *OTS*, pp. 59, 81. Compatible understandings of the formation of the canon have been articulated by Henry, *GRA*, 4:448; Poetsch, "Verbalinspiration und Irrtumslosigkeit," pp. 23-24; LCMS, *Inspiration*, pp. 17-18.

   In *NTC*, p. 44, Childs may not state the case for the inherent authority of the biblical canon quite as strongly. (Could he even be denying its infallibility?) Yet even at this point he insists that the canon is not "created by the Church." As for his claim that the canon's authority derives from its unique witness to Christ, is this any more than a claim akin to the conservative Lutheran argument that the gospel's truth does not derive from Scripture, that the gospel is the true material principle of theology? (See LCMS, *GS*, pp. 14-15, 18.)

66. Henry, "Narrative Theology," pp. 12, 22-23; Henry, *GRA*, 6:137; 4:92; 3:449, 451; 1:209; Schaeffer, *SER*, pp. 50-51; CRC, pp. 56-57.

67. For an acknowledgment by an Evangelical that the concern to verify the Bible's claims empirically is a post-Enlightenment agenda, see Henry, *GRA*, 1:78-79; 2:282-283. One might respond to Evangelical concerns that a narrative hermeneutic posits a "double truth" theory by noting that this approach's bracketing of scientific and historical questions in order to concentrate on the biblical text is no forfeiture of a concern for truth but is precisely the kind of challenge to the modern critical-empirical mindset which has been called for by Evangelicals like Henry, *GRA*, 2:292. Narrative and canonical approaches, then, do not forfeit a concern for truth but ground truth in Scripture, not making it depend upon historical-empirical verifiability.

68. Childs, *NTC*, p. 545; Childs, *OTT*, p. 6, 16-17.

69. See Frei, *Identity*, pp. 135ff., 6-7.

70. Ibid., pp. 150-151.

71. See Frei, TIN, pp. 10-11. Presumably, historical evidence which disconfirmed these other accounts would not necessarily undermine the credibility of the Christian faith as it would in the case of Jesus' resurrection (1 Cor. 15:14, 17).

72. See the relevant references in n. 36, above.

73. See p. 220; Chap. 13, nn. 71, 72.

74. Among those referring only to the Bible's infallibility in matters of salvation/faith and ethics are: WEF; EREI; EMF; CN, IV; ECC, *Covenant Constitution;* USSR Dis. Bapt., 1; Underground Evangelism, *Statement of Faith*.

75. See p. 220, above, and Chap. 13, n. 72 for references.

76. Ralph A. Bohlmann, "Lutherans and inerrancy," *The Lutheran Witness*, March 1983, p. 34. Cf. Montgomery, *Crisis in Lutheran Theology*, p. 43; Carson, in *HAC*, p. 31.

77. Henry, *GRA*, 3:384-385. Such philosophical commitments are also implied by those Evangelicals, particularly those employing the method of presuppositionalism, who distinguish Christian truth-claims from science and history so that the former cannot be disconfirmed by the presuppositions of the latter. See *GRA*, 1:85,256; 2:78, 322; 3:351; 6:27, 108, 241; LCMS, *Inspiration*, pp. 10, 11-12; *Chicago Statement*, XII-XIII. Also see Yoder, in *UB*, pp. 116-117. Cf. Warfield, "The Antiquity and Unity of the Human Race," in *PT*, pp. 290, 291.

78. Henry, *GRA*, 1:258, 261.

79. Childs, *NTC*, pp. 442-443.

80. Henry, *GRA*, 5:402; 6:267-268, 447-448; Blocher, in *LEH*, pp. 387ff.; Yoder, *UB*, p. 111; R. Johnston (see abbreviations), pp. 45, 66; Larry Christenson, "Hermeneutics in the Charismatic Renewal," lecture presented at the 16th International Ecumenical Seminar, Strasbourg, June 19, 1982, p. 15; Mastra, in *JTTW*, p. 247; ICBI, *The Chicago Statement on Biblical Hermeneutics*, Appnd. See Mark 10:1-12 for biblical precedent for this kind of "contextualization."

81. Henry, *GRA*, 2:197; 3:399; 4:457-458; Gerald T. Sheppard, "Canon Criticism: The Proposal of Brevard Childs and an Assessment for Evangelical Hermeneutics," *Studia Biblica et Theologica* (1976): 3-17; Fackre, *The Christian Story;* Frank W. Spina, "Canonical Criticism: Childs versus Sanders," in *Interpreting God's Word for Today*, ed. Wayne McCown and James Massey (Anderson, Ind.: Warner, 1982), pp. 188-189; cf. Peter W. Macky, "Living in the Great Story," *Theology, News and Notes*, December 1981, pp. 22ff.

82. Henry, "Narrative Theology," pp. 12ff.: E. B. Smick, "Old Testament Theology: The Historico-genetic Method," *Journal of the Evangelical Theological Society* 26 (1983): 146ff.; Carson, in *HAC*, p. 32; Kevin J. Vanhoozer, "The Semantics of Biblical Literature: Truth and Scripture's Diverse Literary Forms," in *HAC*, pp. 54-56, 72, 85. Also see Chap. 2 of an otherwise sympathetic Evangelical evaluation of literary approaches, Tremper Longmann III, *Literary Approaches to Biblical Interpretation* (Grand Rapids: Zondervan, 1987).

83. This is the assessment of Henry, *GRA*, 2:292.

84. Sider, in *JTTW*, pp. 361-362.

85. Henry, *GRA*, 4:179; Vorstand des Arbeitskreis für Evangelikale Theologie, November 15, 1985. This assessment is suggested also by David A. Hubbard, private interview, March 13, 1985; DEA; Paul A. Mickey, *Essentials of Wesleyan Theology* (Grand Rapids: Zondervan, 1980), pp. 107, 120-121; Russell P. Spittler, "Scripture and the Theological Enterprise: View from a Big Canoe," in *UB*, p. 73. Cf. Richard J. Coleman, *Issues of Theological Conflict*, 2nd ed. (Grand Rapids: Eerdmans, 1980), pp. 168-169, 180-181.

86. The possible convergence between narrative approaches to theology and the Evangelical movement indicates that narrative hermeneutics' views on the possibility of identifying the normative, descriptive meaning of certain segments of Scripture are compatible with Scottish common sense realism. In view of the impact of this philosophy on American society, narrative and canonical hermeneutics would seem to have the potential to help develop a truly "indigenous American theology." The development of such a theology could be one of the important results of a mainline church–Conservative Evangelical dialogue in the United States.

87. For references to others who deem the characteristic Conservative Evangelical view of Scripture as the cutting edge of the movement, see p. 225, above.

88. For examples of this emerging convergence, see Methodist–Roman Catholic Conversations, *Denver Report*, 6-10; Methodist–Roman Catholic Conversations, *Dublin Report*, 25-26, 54ff.; Methodist–Roman Catholic Conversations, *Honolulu Report* (1981), 6ff.; Lutheran–Methodist Conversations (1984); European Lutheran–Reformed Dialogue, *Leuenberg Concord*, 29ff.; Reformed–Roman Catholic Conversations, *The Presence of Christ in Church and World* (1977), 91.

89. For assessments by Evangelicals concerning the influence of neoorthodoxy on contemporary ecumenical dialogue results, see Chap. 19, n. 11. In addition to the *Leuenberg Concord* cited in the preceding note, this assessment may also be confirmed in the international Lutheran–Roman Catholic Conversations, *Malta Report* (1972), 24, 18. For references to the impact of "contextual theology" on the ecumenical movement, see Chap. 19, n. 21.

90. Henry, *GRA*, 1:187-188, 390; 3:422; 4:33. Cf. Noll, *BFC*, p. 146.

Conclusion

1. For the admission by an Evangelical that narrative hermeneutics might function as a legitimate means of grace, see Carl F. H. Henry, "Narrative Theology: An Evangelical Appraisal" (lecture, Yale Divinity School, November 1985), p. 22.
2. See pp. 244-245, above.
3. See p. 253 and corresponding notes.
4. See pp. 117-119, 127-128, 256-257, and corresponding notes.
5. A similar, more fully developed proposal with reference to the resources in Pietism for facilitating a Lutheran–Conservative Evangelical dialogue has been offered by Paul Kuenning, "Pietism: A Lutheran Resource for Dialogue with Evangelical-ism," *Dialog* 24 (Fall 1985): 285-292.
6. For example, see Albrecht Ritschl, *Geschichte des Pietismus*, 3 vols. (Bonn: Marcus, 1880–1886); Martin Schmidt, *Wiedergeburt und Neuer Mensch: Gesammelte Studien zur Geschichte des Pietismus* (Witten: Luther Verlag, 1969), p. 153.

Bibliographical Index

In lieu of a bibliography, italicized numbers in index entries signify the page and note in which full bibliographical data for a publication by that person or organization can be located. Under certain index entries, usually names or technical terms, a number that refers to a page in the text itself is italicized. This indicates the place where readers can obtain a definition of the term or an identification of the person in question. Due to considerations of space, references to endnotes are limited to those that supply bibliographical data.

Index of Names

Index of Institutions

Index of Subjects